PUBLISHED BY

Practical PowerShell Press
Naperville, IL 60565

Library of Congress Control Number: 2019951123
ISBN: 978-1-7340889-0-8

First Print Edition - Printed and bound in the United States of America

Technical Reviewer: Dave Stork, Tom Lilly
Indexing: Indexmatic2 by Indiscripts
CopyEditor: Deb Scoles

Cover: Damian Scoles * Mt. Rainer (2018)

AUTHOR

DAMIAN SCOLES

Damian Scoles has been a Microsoft MVP for the past seven years, specifically for Office Apps and Services and now Cloud and Datacenter Management. He is currently based out of the Chicago area and started out managing Exchange 5.5 and Windows NT. He has worked with Office 365 since BPOS and has experience with Azure AD, the Security and Compliance Center, and Exchange Online. Contributions to the community include helping on TechNet forums, creating PowerShell scripts that are located in the TechNet Gallery, writing detailed PowerShell / Office365 / Exchange blog articles (https://justaucguy.wordpress.com/), tweets (https://twitter.com/PPowerShell) and creating PowerShell videos on YouTube (https://www.youtube.com/channel/UClxHtLF0c_VAkjw5rzsV1Vg). As a third time author, Damian has poured his knowledge of the Security and Compliance Center as well as PowerShell into this book. He hopes you will enjoy reading it as much as he did writing it.

Technical Reviewer

DAVE STORK

Dave Stork is an Exchange/Office Apps and Services MVP since 2014. But long ago he started his Exchange career with Exchange 2003 and that version got him hooked. He is currently a Senior Technical Specialist and consultant at OGD ict-diensten, specialized in Exchange and Office 365.

He blogs (https://dirteam.com/dave) and tweets (https://twitter.com/dm-stork) about Exchange and other relevant topics for several years now and in time has expanded this community work with contributing to podcasts, speaking at several events and user group meetings in and outside his native Netherlands. He poured most of his knowledge and experience into the Practical PowerShell Exchange Server 2016 book and reviewed the Practical PowerShell Exchange Online book.

TOM LILLY

Tom Lilly began his career in IT as a helpdesk technician in 2010, where he was first exposed to Exchange 2003 and other technologies. His experience has grown since then to focus on Microsoft cloud technologies such as Azure and Office 365. One facet of that has been Microsoft security solutions, such as the Security and Compliance Center. He has had many speaking engagements in front of user groups and larger organizations. He has a newly-relaunched blog at https://justanitblog.com and tweets under @TheTomLilly.

If you are reading a book on a subject as specialized as the use of PowerShell in the Security and Compliance Center (SCC), my assumption would be that you are sufficiently proficient in PowerShell and need no detailed introduction on its history and usefulness. Thus, I will not spend any time trying to "sell" you on PowerShell. In case this isn't true, the previous books by the author should be able to get you started on the path of becoming a PowerShell guru.

While one might be familiar with PowerShell, getting to use it with a new product can often be challenging. If you've had the pleasure of working with the Exchange (or Exchange Online) PowerShell cmdlets, you've probably come to appreciate the simplicity, robustness and versatility of a management system fully built on PowerShell from the get-go. Sadly, this doesn't hold true for many (any?) other Microsoft products. We can debate on the "why", but the simple truth is that most of the other PowerShell modules and implementations pale in comparison to Exchange's. And what's even more frustrating, you might run into consistency issues, as every different team at Microsoft seems to have their own understanding on how best to implement PowerShell support.

This is one of the reasons why a book on PowerShell focused on the SCC might be helpful to you – it can point out all those little differences and annoyances. Another reason is the change in learning practices brought forth by the cloud. While previously we had numerous courses, labs and books to help you get started or master a given product, things in the cloud change so frequently, that often times the effort put in preparing such content is considered unjustified. In turn, a person looking to develop his skills on a given subject is often forced to gain knowledge from raw documentation articles or to scour the web for blogs and code samples. Having a resource that puts it all together in a package such as the current book, and combines it with the insights of a well-versed and field-tested author is becoming the exception. By supporting the book and the author and keeping this "tradition" alive, you are not only helping yourself, but others as well.

But let's talk some more about the role of PowerShell for the SCC. While the Office 365 Security and Compliance Center has its roots in a modified version of the Exchange Admin Center, and thus inherits some of the PowerShell brilliance that powers the Exchange Admin Console (EAC), there's a lot missing. Starting with the very limited RBAC controls, the implementation of PowerShell cmdlets for the SCC is lacking on several fronts, which in turn makes the life of any IT Pro working with it a bit harder. This doesn't mean that you should only focus on the UI though, as many valuable functionalities, such as the content search permissions filters or information barriers are only configurable via PowerShell. On the other hand, as the SCC has grown over the years, features that have no corresponding PowerShell cmdlets have been introduced. Some of those can be managed via Graph API calls, which can easily be adapted for use with PowerShell, but others have no support for the Graph or use some internal APIs and can only be managed via the UI.

In effect, simply knowing which tasks can be performed via PowerShell can save you time, and the book can be used as a quick reference. Its value goes well beyond that though, as it will not just list the different cmdlets, but will explain how they relate to each other and which corresponding UI bits are powered by them. Take for example eDiscovery – just using the Get-ComplianceCase cmdlet will barely give you any useful information. The book however goes to explain the different building blocks and the role they play, along with providing you with numerous examples. The same holds true throughout the different chapters, each giving you clear, concise and tested examples, used to solve real-life issues, as well as sharing best practices.

Of course, PowerShell remains the tool of choice for performing bulk operations, automating simple or complex tasks, and thanks to its extensibility, for integrating solutions across the different Office 365 PowerShell modules and products. You can expect to learn a thing or two on that front too!

Vasil Michev

Microsoft MVP | Office Apps and Services

Exchange Server 2016 - Second Edition

This book is in its second edition of my first book, with MVP Dave Stork. It has been updated to reflect changes in Exchange 2016 over the past six months as well as an additional 100+ pages of new material covering Public Folders, security and more. Dave and I literally spent hundred of hours researching, testing and writing the material that is in this book. With the additional topics we have covered the breadth and width of Exchange 2016. With this book you will be able to confidentially manage your Exchange server with PowerShell. **Already for sale here:**

www.PracticalPowerShell.com

Office 365: Exchange Online

If you support mailboxes in Office 365, then this book is for you. Whether using hybrid or just Azure AD, Exchange Online gives you email without the server administration. However, even with that freedom comes the need for management. This means configuring users, security, routing and more. PowerShell provides a back door to this configuration and allows for a much more robust back-end for your users and your enterprise. Remember that this book takes a practical approach to PowerShell and strives to use real world examples and scripting to help you learn to manage your Exchange Online tenant. **Already for sale here:**

www.PracticalPowerShell.com

COMING SOON!

Exchange Server 2019

Exchange Server 2019 was released earlier this year. This book was written to help those that manage Exchange Server to get a handle on the most useful tool in your arsenal for Exchange management - PowerShell! Also included is a section on Windows Core, which is a supported OS for Exchange Server now. Included will be tips, tricks, best practices and real world PowerShell examples for you to use and learn from.

The book itself is still under development. Any updates on this title **will be placed on the publishers website here:**

www.PracticalPowerShell.com

Office 365 - Microsoft Teams

With the sunsetting of Skype Online, an new emphasis has been placed on Microsoft Teams. As such, those who manage their Office 365 tenant will need to learn more about PowerShell and Teams. In this book we cover PowerShell extensively for those coming from Skype (Online) and to those running Teams already. The book itself is still under development. Any updates on this title **will be placed on the publishers website here**:

www.PracticalPowerShell.com

Acknowledgments

About this book

As PowerShell is a crucial tool in administrating cloud services, it's an important and valuable skill to possess. Unfortunately learning it by yourself can be a daunting task. That is why this book was written, to help the average IT Pro/Administrator learn the fundamentals (and perhaps a little beyond that) of PowerShell. Believing that a practical approach will help the reader understand and learn these useful skills and help him or her to become proficient in Exchange PowerShell for all of their work and become a more productive and valuable employee almost immediately after reading this book.

Damian Scoles

I would like to thank my kids for their support and understanding while I worked on this book. The writing of this book was a bit easier and harder at the same time. However, now that it is completed, I can spend more time with them. I especially want to thank my wife who put in a lot of time correcting my mistakes and lack of consistency. Without her help I would not have been able to produce such a high quality book.

I would also like to acknowledge and thank other IT professionals/MVPs who have helped me in various ways with advice, feedback, etc. to achieve this end product. Those include: Tony Redmond, Paul Cunningham, Bhargav Shukla and many others.

Errata

In writing this book, a lot of effort was put into making the information as accurate as possible. Any errors that are reported will be recorded here:

http://www.practicalpowershell.com/errata

Expect this document to be updated if any issues are found. If, for some reason, you want to report something that is not there go ahead and report it on that page.

Additional support can be found by emailing *input@practicalpowershell.com*.

Table of Contents

Preface

Chapter Layout and Conventions xiv
    Chapter Layout. xiv
    Conventions xiv
Author's Notes and Findings xv

Introduction

The Security and Compliance Center (SCC) and PowerShell. 1
Why PowerShell and Not the Security and Compliance Center. 1
Security and Compliance Center PowerShell 2
Command Structure 2
    Cmdlet Examples. 2
Piping 3
Protecting Yourself and What If 4
Command Discovery Techniques 5
PowerShell Modules 6
Getting Help!?! 6
Cloud-Only vs Synced Environments 8
    Non-Synced Accounts (Cloud-Only) 8
    Synced Accounts 9

1. PowerShell Basics

Security and Compliance Center PowerShell: Where to Begin 10
Variables 10
Arrays 11
Hash Tables 12
CSV Files. 12
Operators 13
Loops. 14
    Foreach-Object. 14
    Do { } While () 15
    Export-CSV 16
    How to Use these Cmdlets 17
Functions 17
PowerShell Tools 18
    PowerShell ISE 18

PowerShell Repositories 21
Alternatives to ISE 21
ISE Plug-ins and More 22
PSharp Plug-in for PowerShell 23

2. Beyond the Basics

Formatting 24
    Capitalization 24
    Commenting 25
    Mind Your Brackets! 28
Command Output 29
    Cmdlet Output Formatting 29
    Filtering 31
    Splitting 32
Scripting in Color 35
    Color Coding Examples 35
Miscellaneous 38
    Quotes 38
    Code Signing 39

3. Connecting With PowerShell

Introduction 43
Connecting to the Security and Compliance Center 44
        Security and Compliance Center PowerShell Cmdlets 45
Multi-Factor Authentication (MFA) 46
Closing and Removing Connections 47
        Revealing PowerShell Sessions 48

4. Identity Management

Introduction 50
Directory Synchronization (DirSync) 51
    History 51
Preparing Your AD - IdFix 52
    Option 1 – Express Installation 56
    Option 2 – Customize 57
PowerShell and Directory Synchronization 61
What Needs to be Performed Where? 62
    Active Directory 62
    Azure Active Directory Connect 66
    Azure AD Connect – Connectors 68
Licensing 71
Azure AD Recycle Bin 79

5. Security

Layered Security 82
Role Groups 83
   PowerShell 83
   Management Roles per Role Groups. 86
Assigning Role Group Membership 88
   Mail Flow Administrator Role 88
   Reviewer Role. 90
   Records Management 91
   Security Administrator 92
   Organization Management. 93
   Supervisory Review. 94
   Compliance Administrator 95
   Security Reader 95
   eDiscovery Manager/Administrator 96
   Service Assurance User. 98
   Compliance Data Administrator. 99
   Security Operator 99
   Data Investigator 100
   Global Reader. 100
Removing User(s) From Role Groups 101
Management Roles 107
Audit in Security and Compliance Center. 109
   Searching the Admin Audit Log 110

6. Data Loss Prevention

Introduction. 113
Sensitive Information Types. 114
Custom Sensitive Information Types 116
Fingerprints 123
Keyword Dictionaries 126
Exact Data Match (EDM). 129
   Requirements 130
   PowerShell 130
DLP Compliance 136
Other DLP Cmdlets 140

7. Compliance

Introduction. 141
Compliance Cases 142
Compliance Searches 145
   What is a Compliance Search? 145

PowerShell 145
Set-ComplianceSearch 150
Set-ComplianceSearchAction 151
Get-CaseHold Cmdlets. 151
Retention Compliance 157
PowerShell 157
Teams Retention Compliance Policies and Rules 162

8. Supervision

Introduction. 166
Getting Started. 167
Remove Cmdlets 171
Set Cmdlets. 171
Supervision Reporting 172
Viewing Supervised Emails 173
Security and Compliance Center. 173
Outlook Configuration 174

9. Alerting

Introduction 176
Activity Alerts 177
Alerts Polices 182
Beyond the New. 185

10. Information Barriers

Introduction 187
Information Barriers. 188
What are Information Barriers? 188
Getting Started with Information Barriers. 188
Permissions required. 188
Restrictions in Teams 189
Prerequisites 190
Administrative Consent 190
PowerShell 192
Real World Experience 197
Caveats to Blocking 197
Documenting Settings (Script) 198
PowerShell 198

11. Threats & Mail Flow

Introduction 205
Threat Management 206

Dashboard. 206
Investigations 206
Explorer. 207
Submissions 208
Attack Simulator 208
Review 210
Policy. 210
Threat Tracker 211
Mail Flow 211

12. Device Management

Introduction. 215
Security and Compliance Center PowerShell 218
Tenant Policy and Rule 219
Device Conditional Access. 221
Device Configuration 224

13. Labels and File Plans

Introduction. 228
Labels. 229
Creating Labels. 230
Conditions 231
Encryption 238
Content Marking 243
Endpoint Protection 246
Additional Cmdlets 246
Label Policies 247
File Plans. 250
How To Use File Plan Properties? 256

14. Building Scripts

How to Begin 258
Documentation of SCC 259
PowerShell and Change 265
Coding the Script. 266
Script Building Summary 270

A. Best Practices

What is a Best Practice? 271
Summary of Best Practices. 271
PowerShell Best Practices 272
Commenting 272

Useful Comments 272
Variable Naming 273
Variable Block 273
Matching Variables to Parameters 274
Preference Variables 274
Naming Conventions, this time for Functions and Scripts 275
Singular Task Functions 275
Signing Your Code 276
Filter vs. Where 276
Error Handling 276
Write-Output / Write-Verbose 276
'#Requires' 278
Set-StrictMode -Version Latest 280
Capitalization 282
Using full command names 282
Cmdlet Binding 283
Script Structure 284
Quotes 285
Running Applications 285
Conclusion and Further Help 285

B. Miscellaneous

Introduction 287
Menus 288
Aliases 292
New-Alias 293
Set-Alias 294
Removing an Alias 294
Foreach-Object (%) 295
PowerShell Interface Customization 299

C. Microsoft Secure Score

Introduction 304
Score Analyzer 307
Removed Tasks in 2018 308
PowerShell and Microsoft Secure Score 308
Detailed Analysis 309

Preface

Chapter Layout and Conventions

Before you begin reading the book, I wanted to provide some background information on the structure and layout of the book.

Chapter Layout

The book is laid out in a way in which the reader can progress from beginning knowledge of PowerShell to immersion in the Security and Compliance Center PowerShell and end up in reference material for future follow-up and further reading. The book has been laid out like so:

Introduction: Brief introduction into the book and PowerShell

Chapters 1 to 3: Introduction to PowerShell using PowerShell cmdlets and examples from the Security and Compliance Center.

Chapters 4 to 14: Each chapter covers a different topic for the Security and Compliance Center (SCC) from DLP Holds to Information Barriers, Labels, Security and more. Extensive PowerShell examples and code are provided to assist in your learning of PowerShell for the SCC.

Appendices: Additional helpful PowerShell tips as well as further reading

Conventions

Throughout the book, the author uses some consistent tools to help you, the reader, learn about PowerShell for the Security and Compliance Center. These conventions come in many forms, from screenshots of actual script / cmdlet results, to PowerShell code that is indented and a different font, as well as providing '**Note**' notes along the way to help provide further information for the reader.

Additionally, sources or reference materials are all click-able links (digital edition) for future reading and exploration of ideas brought up in this book.

As an added bonus, any real world issues or problems found are included in this book. This is done because the author wants to provide the best experience for the reader and to help them understand that sometimes there are issues with PowerShell in the Security and Compliance Center. Thus a raw, unbiased view is provided.

Author's Notes and Findings

WARNING

*** The below section contains observations and opinions related to issues found when making this book. These errors and issues may be fixed by the time you read this, so be aware of that. ***

While writing this book, the author ran into a few issues and oddities along the way. Some of the features discussed in this book (at least at the time of publication) were either just reaching General Availability (GA) or the feature was in Preview. For example, for EDM, the DLP EDM cmdlets were being added and removed from the SCC PowerShell module for testing purposes. Below is a list of items that the author thought was important enough to place at the beginning of the book to inform the reader of the bumpy road ahead when using PowerShell with the SCC

(1) Some features are ONLY available in the Security and Compliance Center itself, with no PowerShell cmdlets to utilize:

- Threat Management
- MailFlow
- Cloud App Security

(2) Some features are ONLY available in PowerShell for the Security and Compliance Center:

Information Barriers

(3) Some features have just been released or are in preview and as such, there isn't a lot of information on these sections of the SCC:

- Information Barriers
- Exact Data Match (EDM)

(4) Help in the Security and Compliance Center is inconsistent at the moment - some observations:

- Missing examples in Get-Help for numerous cmdlets
- Missing synopsis for multiple cmdlets
- Parameters are not always indicative of what the cmdlet accepts (misspelling on at least one parameter)
- Help in Microsoft Docs is missing for some cmdlets as well. If the Get-Help information for a cmdlet is lacking, then this will make it even worse for finding relevant examples. Some cmdlets are new, so this is understandable, but others were released very recently.

(5) Errors when running cmdlets

Permissions to run a cmdlet are not discoverable:

- Watson errors will occur when querying permissions on cmdlets.

```
PS C:\> Get-ManagementRole -Cmdlet Add-RoleGroupMember
WARNING: An unexpected error has occurred and a Watson dump is being generated: The QueryFilter '(WildcardString
IgnoreCase(InternalDownlevelRoleEntries)=c,Add-RoleGroupMember,*)' is not supported, only ComparisonFilter and
CompositeFilter are supported.
The QueryFilter '(WildcardString IgnoreCase(InternalDownlevelRoleEntries)=c,Add-RoleGroupMember,*)' is not supported,
only ComparisonFilter and CompositeFilter are supported.
    + CategoryInfo          : NotSpecified: (:) [Get-ManagementRole], NotSupportedException
    + FullyQualifiedErrorId : System.NotSupportedException,Microsoft.Exchange.Management.RbacTasks.GetManagementRole
    + PSComputerName        : nam05b.ps.compliance.protection.outlook.com
```

- Watson errors also register on other cmdlets

DLP Keyword Dictionaries generates errors about:

- Limits to uploading content (100Kb limit on file and 1MB on connection limit)

```
PS C:\> New-DlpKeywordDictionary -Name 'Medical Terms' -Description 'Medical Lexicon' -FileData $file
Data
Sending data to a remote command failed with the following error message: The current deserialized object size of the
data received from the remote client computer exceeded the allowed maximum object size. The current deserialized
object size is 10572800. The allowed maximum object size is 10485760. For more information, see the
about_Remote_Troubleshooting Help topic.
    + CategoryInfo          : OperationStopped: (nam05b.ps.compl...ion.outlook.com:String) [], PSRemotingTransportExce
   ption
    + FullyQualifiedErrorId : JobFailure
    + PSComputerName        : nam05b.ps.compliance.protection.outlook.com

PS C:\> New-DlpKeywordDictionary -Name 'Medical Terms' -Description 'Medical Lexicon' -FileData $fileData
The keword dictionary file size exceeds the maximum file size of 100 KB..
    + CategoryInfo          : NotSpecified: (:) [New-DlpKeywordDictionary], ErrorKeywordDic...nvalidException
    + FullyQualifiedErrorId : [Server=BY2NAM05WS013,RequestId=044ac57b-8ea9-4524-bcff-f0e9f33c5642,TimeStamp=8/3/2019
   6:53:48 PM] [FailureCategory=Cmdlet-ErrorKeywordDictionaryFileSizeInvalidException] 8E208330,Microsoft.Office.Comp
   liancePolicy.Tasks.NewDlpKeywordDictionary
    + PSComputerName        : nam05b.ps.compliance.protection.outlook.com
```

** **Note** ** A lot of these items have been raised for awareness or have bug reports with Microsoft already and they could be fixed by the time you read this book. No guarantees on what will be fixed, broken or otherwise because Microsoft owns and maintains the PowerShell module for the Security and Compliance Center as you would expect.

(6) New-AdminAuditLogSearch

```
PS C:\> New-AdminAuditLogSearch -StartDate 8/1/19 -EndDate 8/20/19 -StatusMailRecipients Damian@sccbook2.onmicrosoft.com

WARNING: An unexpected error has occurred and a Watson dump is being generated: Failed to locate the system arbitration
 mailbox for organization "FFO.extest.microsoft.com/Microsoft Exchange Hosted Organizations/sccbook2.onmicrosoft.com -
FFO.extest.microsoft.com/Microsoft Exchange Hosted Organizations/sccbook2.onmicrosoft.com/Configuration".
Failed to locate the system arbitration mailbox for organization "FFO.extest.microsoft.com/Microsoft Exchange Hosted
Organizations/sccbook2.onmicrosoft.com - FFO.extest.microsoft.com/Microsoft Exchange Hosted
Organizations/sccbook2.onmicrosoft.com/Configuration".
    + CategoryInfo          : NotSpecified: (:) [New-AdminAuditLogSearch], AuditLogSearchA...tFoundException
    + FullyQualifiedErrorId : Microsoft.Exchange.Management.AuditLogSearchArbitrationMailboxNotFoundException,Microsof
   t.Exchange.Management.SystemConfigurationTasks.NewAdminAuditLogSearch
    + PSComputerName        : nam01b.ps.compliance.protection.outlook.com
```

(7) Protection Alerts in PowerShell - unable to add multiple Operations:

```
New-ProtectionAlert -Name 'User Change Alert' -Descript
ivity -Operation AddedUser,DeletedUser,ChangedUserLicense,SetLicenseProperties -N
Multiple operations provided . Please provide a logical operation name
    + CategoryInfo          : NotSpecified: (:) [New-ProtectionAlert], MissingLog
    + FullyQualifiedErrorId : [Server=BY2NAM05WS011,RequestId=4dabe40c-5b81-4e4f-
   Microsoft.Office.CompliancePolicy.Tasks.NewProtectionAlert
    + PSComputerName        : nam05b.ps.compliance.protection.outlook.com
```

However, notice that if we use the Set-ProtectionAlert to change the Operation value to any other value that was included in the multiple actions, They are added or changed without issue:

```
PS C:\> Set-ProtectionAlert -Identity 'User Change Alert' -Operation AddedUser,DeletingUser
Multiple operations provided . Please provide a logical operation name
    + CategoryInfo          : NotSpecified: (:) [Set-ProtectionAlert], MissingLogicalOperationNameException
    + FullyQualifiedErrorId : [Server=BY2NAM05WS011,RequestId=0bb5814c-cf2d-4126-aba7-e5709af28c1e,TimeStamp
   Microsoft.Office.CompliancePolicy.Tasks.SetProtectionAlert
    + PSComputerName        : nam05b.ps.compliance.protection.outlook.com

PS C:\> Set-ProtectionAlert -Identity 'User Change Alert' -Operation ChangeUserLicense
PS C:\> Set-ProtectionAlert -Identity 'User Change Alert' -Operation AddedUser,ChangeUserLicense
Multiple operations provided . Please provide a logical operation name
    + CategoryInfo          : NotSpecified: (:) [Set-ProtectionAlert], MissingLogicalOperationNameException
    + FullyQualifiedErrorId : [Server=BY2NAM05WS011,RequestId=782717f6-7d73-400b-a036-2ad295737981,TimeStamp
   Microsoft.Office.CompliancePolicy.Tasks.SetProtectionAlert
    + PSComputerName        : nam05b.ps.compliance.protection.outlook.com

PS C:\> Set-ProtectionAlert -Identity 'User Change Alert' -Operation AddUser,ChangeUserLicense
Multiple operations provided . Please provide a logical operation name
    + CategoryInfo          : NotSpecified: (:) [Set-ProtectionAlert], MissingLogicalOperationNameException
    + FullyQualifiedErrorId : [Server=BY2NAM05WS011,RequestId=07a650f2-6ee2-4cf3-a932-61adfc9c6623,TimeStamp
   Microsoft.Office.CompliancePolicy.Tasks.SetProtectionAlert
    + PSComputerName        : nam05b.ps.compliance.protection.outlook.com

PS C:\> Set-ProtectionAlert -Identity 'User Change Alert' -Operation DeletedUser
PS C:\> Set-ProtectionAlert -Identity 'User Change Alert' -Operation AddedUser
PS C:\> Set-ProtectionAlert -Identity 'User Change Alert' -Operation ChangeUserLicense
```

(8) Cmdlet issues:

Get-InformationBarrierReportDetails

```
PS C:\> Get-InformationBarrierReportDetails
We cannot currently process your request, please wait a few minutes and try again.
    + CategoryInfo          : InvalidOperation: (:) [Get-InformationBarrierReportDetails], FfoReportingException
    + FullyQualifiedErrorId : [Server=BY2NAM05WS006,RequestId=380f03eb-8a65-46cd-8823-1dbb6ec4bf85,TimeStamp=8/9/2019
   1:18:47 AM] [FailureCategory=Cmdlet-FfoReportingException] D9590C71,Microsoft.Exchange.Management.FfoReporting.Get
   InformationBarrierReportDetails
    + PSComputerName        : nam05b.ps.compliance.protection.outlook.com
```

Get-InformationBarrierReportSummary

```
PS C:\> Get-InformationBarrierReportSummary
We cannot currently process your request, please wait a few minutes and try again.
    + CategoryInfo          : InvalidOperation: (:) [Get-InformationBarrierReportSummary], FfoReportingException
    + FullyQualifiedErrorId : [Server=BY2NAM05WS006,RequestId=cbd997c7-9b4c-4229-afb2-8f2debd88876,TimeStamp=8/9/2019
   1:18:55 AM] [FailureCategory=Cmdlet-FfoReportingException] D9590C71,Microsoft.Exchange.Management.FfoReporting.Get
   InformationBarrierReportSummary
    + PSComputerName        : nam05b.ps.compliance.protection.outlook.com
```

New-SupervisoryReviewPolicy2

```
PS C:\> New-SupervisoryReviewPolicyV2 -Name 'Legal Mail Review Policy' -Reviewers damian@practicalpowe
rshell.com,brian@practicalpowershell.com -Comment 'Review email from Legal department'
WARNING: An unexpected error has occurred and a Watson dump is being generated: Failed to load binding information,
jobRunId: 1393a28c-e3fa-458f-8039-2d2f4c68f6af, missingBindings: [PublicFolderBinding,SharePointBinding].
Failed to load binding information, jobRunId: 1393a28c-e3fa-458f-8039-2d2f4c68f6af, missingBindings:
[PublicFolderBinding,SharePointBinding]
    + CategoryInfo          : NotSpecified: (:) [New-SupervisoryReviewPolicyV2], FailedToLoadBindingsException
    + FullyQualifiedErrorId : Microsoft.Exchange.Compliance.TaskDistributionCommon.FailedToLoadBindingsException,Micro
   soft.Office.CompliancePolicy.Tasks.NewSupervisoryReviewPolicy
    + PSComputerName        : nam05b.ps.compliance.protection.outlook.com
```

Get-SupervisoryReviewActivity

```
PS C:\> Get-SupervisoryReviewActivity -PolicyId '90ce5bb1-e6ea-4b2b-ae9f-ee87fb5ddb71' -StartDate 8/1/19 -EndDate 8/4/19
   | Sort-Object Timestamp -Descending | fl
WARNING: An unexpected error has occurred and a Watson dump is being generated: Remote powershell invocation failed
with error: The term 'Get-SupervisoryReviewActivity' is not recognized as the name of a cmdlet, function, script file,
or operable program. Check the spelling of the name, or if a path was included, verify that the path is correct and try
 again..
Remote powershell invocation failed with error: The term 'Get-SupervisoryReviewActivity' is not recognized as the name
of a cmdlet, function, script file, or operable program. Check the spelling of the name, or if a path was included,
verify that the path is correct and try again..
    + CategoryInfo          : NotSpecified: (:) [Get-SupervisoryReviewActivity], RpsInvocationFailedException
    + FullyQualifiedErrorId : Microsoft.Exchange.Management.Transport.RpsInvocationFailedException,Microsoft.Office.Co
   mpliancePolicy.Tasks.GetSupervisoryReviewActivity
    + PSComputerName        : nam05b.ps.compliance.protection.outlook.com
```

New-DLPKeywordDictionary --> File has 97000 lines

```
PS C:\> New-DlpKeywordDictionary -Name 'Medical Terms' -Description 'Medical Lexicon' -FileData $file
Data
Sending data to a remote command failed with the following error message: The current deserialized object size of the
data received from the remote client computer exceeded the allowed maximum object size. The current deserialized
object size is 10572800. The allowed maximum object size is 10485760. For more information, see the
about_Remote_Troubleshooting Help topic.
    + CategoryInfo          : OperationStopped: (nam05b.ps.compl...ion.outlook.com:String) [], PSRemotingTransportExce
   ption
    + FullyQualifiedErrorId : JobFailure
    + PSComputerName        : nam05b.ps.compliance.protection.outlook.com
```

Reduce the number of lines, we eventually get this message:

```
PS C:\> New-DlpKeywordDictionary -Name 'Medical Terms' -Description 'Medical Lexicon' -FileData $file
Data
The keword dictionary file size exceeds the maximum file size of 100 KB..
    + CategoryInfo          : NotSpecified: (:) [New-DlpKeywordDictionary], ErrorKeywordDic...nvalidException
    + FullyQualifiedErrorId : [Server=BY2NAM05WS013,RequestId=044ac57b-8ea9-4524-bcff-f0e9f33c5642,TimeStamp=8/3/2019
   6:53:48 PM] [FailureCategory=Cmdlet-ErrorKeywordDictionaryFileSizeInvalidException] 8E208330,Microsoft.Office.Comp
   liancePolicy.Tasks.NewDlpKeywordDictionary
    + PSComputerName        : nam05b.ps.compliance.protection.outlook.com
```

Introduction

The Security and Compliance Center (SCC) and PowerShell

Beginning with Exchange Server 2007, Microsoft introduced PowerShell to enhance the Exchange Server product. PowerShell was a radical change at the time when Microsoft was known for its GUI interfaces. Yes, Microsoft had some command line access to its OS's (think DOS), but by adding a command line interface, Microsoft had suddenly put the gauntlet down and announced to the world that it was serious about it products and providing an enhancement that would appeal to those who would look down on Microsoft because of the GUI-based approach.

While Exchange Server 2007 ran what was then known as PowerShell 1.0, and while it was a good addition to existing Exchange Server management it was not perfect. It was not as flexible as it is today and was sorely in need of enhancement. Over the years Microsoft has produced PowerShell versions 1.0 to the current 6.1. There are PowerShell modules for Active Directory, Exchange and SharePoint. Now with the age of cloud systems like Office 365 there are PowerShell modules for Exchange Online, Teams, Azure AD and also the focus of this book the Security and Compliance Center (SCC).

Over time Microsoft has increased the functionality of these various modules. With the Security and Compliance Center in particular, additional components have been added with their respective PowerShell cmdlets like Labels and Fingerprints. Expect these cmdlets to keep changing as Microsoft continues to add additional functionality.

Why PowerShell and Not the Security and Compliance Center

There are many reasons to use PowerShell to manage and manipulate the Security and Compliance Center. Some of the reasons are obvious while others may require some explanation. Below is a list of reasons of why you should learn about PowerShell in the SCC:

- PowerShell allows the use of standard Windows commands that you would run in the Command Prompt.
- PowerShell brings powerful commands to the table to enable you to work with a complex environment.
- PowerShell is integrated with almost all of Microsoft's on-premises and cloud applications and third-party vendors are creating modules for PowerShell to manage their products.
- PowerShell allows for heavy automation. While this would seem to be geared to larger environments, smaller shops can utilize scheduling for common tasks – reporting, maintenance, bulk maintenance, etc. – to reduce the time needed and human errors in managing their Office 365 Tenants.
- Some things just cannot be done in the GUI. This is important. This is not advertised or spelled out by Microsoft. There are many options or configurations that can ONLY be performed with PowerShell. To make this clear, PowerShell is not limited in its management of Exchange as the GUI is. So it is important to learn it when learning about the Security and Compliance Center.
- PowerShell works with objects. These objects can enable you to do powerful tasks in the SCC.
- PowerShell can get a task done in fewer lines than say VBScript. Some will find this to be an advantage as it can take less time to accomplish a task by writing it in PowerShell.
- PowerShell works with many technologies – XML, WMI, CIM, .NET, COM and Active Directory. The last one is important as you will see later, we can tie scripts together between multiple modules if necessary.
- PowerShell provides a powerful help and search function. When working with new PowerShell command, Get-Help is extremely useful as it can provide working examples of code. Searching for commands is easy as well and if you know what you want to manipulate (e.g. policies), just searching for commands with a keyword of 'policy' can help direct your Get-Help query to find the relevant command.

Security and Compliance Center PowerShell

Simply put, the SCC Shell is the original Windows PowerShell with a module loaded specifically with SCC-oriented cmdlets.

Cmdlet (definition) - is a single PowerShell command like Get-Label. Pronunciation: 'commandlet'.

Module (definition) - is a collection of additional PowerShell cmdlets that are grouped together for one purpose or function. Example modules are SCC, Exchange Online and Teams. There are many more, but these examples are relevant to this book.

Command Structure

PowerShell cmdlets come in two basic groupings - safe exploratory cmdlets (ones starting with 'GET' for example) and others that can configure or modify the SCC configuration (SET, REMOVE, etc.) which are not as safe and can be dangerous to a production SCC environment).

Anatomy of a PowerShell Cmdlet:

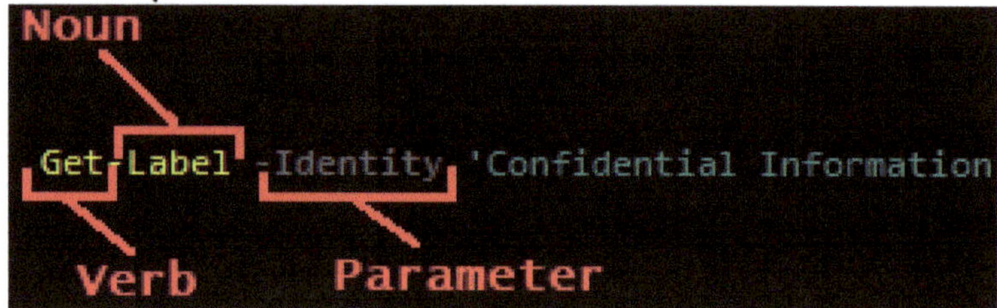

Verb - The action part of the cmdlet. Whether this is Get, Remove, List, Set or Add and more that are less common. These words are the first word of the cmdlet and to the left of the dash of the cmdlet name.
Noun - The word or words to the right of the dash of the PowerShell cmdlet name. These words help describe what is being affected in he Security and Compliance Center. Examples include - ComplianceTag, DLPComplianceRule, RoleGroup and more.
Parameter(s) - These are the options which are selected and upon which the PowerShell cmdlet will act. To get an idea of what parameters are present for each cmdlet you will need to do run a Get-Help <cmdlet> -full. We will review that later in this chapter.
Switch - Options that can be toggled for a cmdlet that don't need additional information (-WhatIf for example).

Cmdlet Examples

Add-RoleGroupMember
Adds a user in Azure AD to one of the many role groups in the SCC.

Get-HoldComplianceRule
Lists all of the Hold Compliance Rules in the SCC.

When exploring PowerShell for the SCC for the first time, it is advisable to start with the Get cmdlets as these cmdlets will provide the beginner to PowerShell the following items:

- A view into Compliance Cases that exists
- List role holders in the SCC
- Non-destructive PowerShell practice
- A means to generating reports or the SCC

Get cmdlets are benign in the sense that the current environment is not being changed or re-configured. This provides for safe learning or exploration not only for PowerShell but your SCC configuration as well. It is highly recommended that you review some basic cmdlets like the following as a good starting point for your venture into SCC PowerShell:

Get-AuditConfig	Get-DevicePolicy	Get-DLPKeywordDictionary
Get-CaseGoldRule	Get-RoleGroup	Get-Group
Get-Label	Get-ActivityAlert	Get-ManagementRole

** **Note** ** We can list all Get cmdlets with one command 'Get-Command Get-*'

Piping

Single cmdlets are the core part of PowerShell. However you can combine the results gathered by one cmdlet and feed this to another cmdlet in PowerShell which then processes results from the previous cmdlet. This process is known as piping. By combining two cmdlets together like this we now have a very powerful tool to construct one-liners. Caution should be used as not all cmdlets can be piped into another or vice versa.

One-liner (definition) – In PowerShell a one-liner literally is either a single command that performs a function or it is comprised of a set of cmdlets that are paired together with a pipe symbol '|'.

For an example of piping we are passing information from Get-Label to Remove-Label to remove all existing labels. If we did not use the pipelining feature, you would have to perform the Remove-Label for each label instead of using the pipeline method, which will run this for all labels in one cmdlet. The pipe allows us to do that in bulk, which saves time and produces a single table of results.

Get-Label | Remove-Label

** **Note** ** Some cmdlets may return too many results and are often restricted to a set limit. A way around this limit is to use '-ResultSize' and specifying a larger number, like 2,000, or using 'Unlimited' which will provide as many results it can find without restrictions.

Sample output:

```
PS C:\> get-label | Remove-Label

Confirm
Are you sure you want to perform this action?
Removing Compliance Rule            onmicrosoft.com\Confidential Information'.
[Y] Yes  [A] Yes to All  [N] No  [L] No to All  [?] Help (default is "Y"):
```

An alternative to piping would require quite a bit more effort, and some techniques we have not covered yet. The code would involve basically gathering all the labels and storing their identities in a variable and the reading through the variable and running Get-Label for each label stored in that variable:

```
$Labels = Get-Label
Foreach ($Label in $Labels) {
   Remove-Label -Name $_.Name
}
```

The results are the same, while the complexity has gone up substantially. Some combined cmdlets can save server resources in terms of CPU and memory usage. As these cmdlets are run in the cloud on Microsoft's own servers, if we were to run too many cmdlets or cmdlets that involve large amounts of users, throttling is introduced in an effort to control resources on Microsoft's side:

```
WARNING: Micro delay applied. Actual delayed: 23494 msecs, Enf
CN=[BL2PR19MB0884]-B2BUpgrade-2017-01-04T06:20:58.7025615Z,CN=
Settings,CN=Configuration,CN=                              ,CN
Sid^S-1-5-21-3051500314-1587441862-2330332534-14823787^PowerSh
BudgetType: PowerShell
ActiveRunspaces: 0/20
Balance: -1288082/2160000/-3000000
PowerShellCmdletsLeft: 400/400
ExchangeCmdletsLeft: 200/200
CmdletTimePeriod: 5
DestructiveCmdletsLeft: 120/120
DestructiveCmdletTimePeriod: 60
QueueDepth: 100
MaxRunspacesTimePeriod: 60
RunSpacesRemaining: 20/20
LastTimeFrameUpdate: 5/20/2018 5:18:35 AM
LastTimeFrameUpdateDestructiveCmdlets: 5/20/2018 5:18:35 AM
LastTimeFrameUpdateMaxRunspaces: 5/20/2018 5:18:35 AM
Locked: False
LockRemaining: 00:00:00
```

Protecting Yourself and What If

PowerShell is powerful. PowerShell can thus cause some havoc in your Security and Compliance Center. How can you protect your infrastructure from your missteps?

- Run Get cmdlets first to get a general familiarity of PowerShell in the SCC
- Use the WhatIf switch when running cmdlets: this will show what would have occurred if a cmdlet was run.

An example of the WhatIf switch would be what would happen if you were to get Compliance Cases in the and remove the Compliance Cases:

```
Get-ComplianceCase | Remove-ComplianceCase -WhatIf
```

Whatif: Deleting the compliance case "Hold for some mailboxes" will also remove all searches and search actions associated with this case. Do you want to continue?
Whatif: Deleting the compliance case "Case # 4302-1" will also remove all searches and search actions associated with this case. Do you want to continue?

Notice the WhatIf statement in front of each result. If this command was run in production, all cases would be deleted. However, because we ran the same command with the WhatIf switch only a simulation was run, no Compliance Cases were removed.

Command Discovery Techniques

A certain amount of discovery involves understanding the SCC. With this knowledge, finding commands that are necessary to perform actions becomes easier. For example querying role permissions to look for rogue administrators in the SCC. Circling back to labels. We need to manipulate some information or create a report on labels in our Security and Compliance Center. If you don't know what commands that can be run, we rely on a specific cmdlet called 'Get-Command'. With this we can find cmdlets we need:

```
Get-Command *label*
```

Running this will look for any PowerShell cmdlet that has the word 'label' in it. The wildcard '*' that is located in front and behind the word 'label' just means that we are searching for any command that may or may not have additional letters before or after the word "label". A small portion of the results are listed below:

```
PS C:\> Get-Command *label*

CommandType     Name                   Version     Source
-----------     ----                   -------     ------
Function        Get-Label              1.0         tmp_ayq4err3.bg1
Function        Get-LabelPolicy        1.0         tmp_ayq4err3.bg1
Function        Get-LabelPolicyRule    1.0         tmp_ayq4err3.bg1
Function        New-Label              1.0         tmp_ayq4err3.bg1
Function        New-LabelPolicy        1.0         tmp_ayq4err3.bg1
Function        Remove-Label           1.0         tmp_ayq4err3.bg1
Function        Remove-LabelPolicy     1.0         tmp_ayq4err3.bg1
Function        Remove-RecordLabel     1.0         tmp_ayq4err3.bg1
Function        Set-LabelPolicy        1.0         tmp_ayq4err3.bg1
```

Now, let's say we actually need to look at Sensitive Information Types in the environment:

```
Get-Command *SensitiveInfo*
```

```
PS C:\> Get-Command *sensitiveInfo*

CommandType     Name                                              Version     Source
-----------     ----                                              -------     ------
Function        Get-DlpSensitiveInformationType                   1.0         tmp_ayq4err3.bg1
Function        Get-DlpSensitiveInformationTypeRulePackage        1.0         tmp_ayq4err3.bg1
Function        New-DlpSensitiveInformationType                   1.0         tmp_ayq4err3.bg1
Function        New-DlpSensitiveInformationTypeRulePackage        1.0         tmp_ayq4err3.bg1
Function        Remove-DlpSensitiveInformationType                1.0         tmp_ayq4err3.bg1
Function        Remove-DlpSensitiveInformationTypeRulePackage     1.0         tmp_ayq4err3.bg1
Function        Set-DlpSensitiveInformationType                   1.0         tmp_ayq4err3.bg1
Function        Set-DlpSensitiveInformationTypeRulePackage        1.0         tmp_ayq4err3.bg1
```

As you can see, the Get-Command is useful for finding cmdlets in PowerShell that you can use in the SCC. We can also start with a noun, like Get and use the wildcard to discover all Get cmdlets in a module:

```
Get-Command Get-*
```

Small sample:

```
CommandType     Name                          Version     Source
-----------     ----                          -------     ------
Function        Get-ActivityAlert             1.0         tmp_lakiiynf.c2m
Function        Get-AdminAuditLogConfig       1.0         tmp_lakiiynf.c2m
Function        Get-AuditConfig               1.0         tmp_lakiiynf.c2m
Function        Get-AuditConfigurationPolicy  1.0         tmp_lakiiynf.c2m
```

PowerShell Modules

When working with the SCC and because of its dependency on Azure Active Directory we may need other cmdlets in order to perform certain actions. When working in the default SCC Shell, PowerShell cmdlets for Azure Active Directory are not preloaded. In order to load these cmdlets, we may need to install the module. With PowerShell 5.0 we can download modules of all sorts using the 'Install-Module' cmdlet like so:

Install-Module -Name AzureAD

** **Note** ** If this is the first time the Install-Module cmdlet has been run, you may receive a message about a 'NuGet Provider'. This provider is what allows the interaction between PowerShell and the NuGet repository where the modules are stored. Make sure to answer yes as to whether to install it.

```
PS C:\> Install-Module  -Name  AzureAD

NuGet provider is required to continue
PowerShellGet requires NuGet provider version '2.8.5.201' or newer to interact with NuGet-based repositories. The NuGet
 provider must be available in 'C:\Program Files\PackageManagement\ProviderAssemblies' or
'C:\Users\administrator \AppData\Local\PackageManagement\ProviderAssemblies'. You can also install the NuGet
provider by running 'Install-PackageProvider -Name NuGet -MinimumVersion 2.8.5.201 -Force'. Do you want PowerShellGet
to install and import the NuGet provider now?
[Y] Yes  [N] No  [S] Suspend  [?] Help (default is "Y"): y
```

Once the NuGet module has installed, we can now install the AzureAD module via the NuGet provider:

```
Untrusted repository
You are installing the modules from an untrusted repository. If you trust this repository, change its
InstallationPolicy value by running the Set-PSRepository cmdlet. Are you sure you want to install the modules
'PSGallery'?
[Y] Yes  [A] Yes to All  [N] No  [L] No to All  [S] Suspend  [?] Help (default is "N"): y
```

** **Note** ** As we can see from the above screenshot, this repository is initially untrusted by default. This is to be expected. We can set this repository as a trusted repository with this one-liner:

Set-PSRepository -Name PSGallery -InstallationPolicy Trusted

Once the module is installed we can now connect to AzureAD to work with this part of an Office 365 tenant:

Connect-AzureAD

After the PowerShell module has loaded, additional cmdlets are available.

Getting Help!?!

Along with Get-Command, Get-Help will assist you in exploring PowerShell for the SCC.

When faced with running a new cmdlet in PowerShell or just figuring out what other options are available for a PowerShell cmdlet, the Get-Help and Get-Command cmdlets are extremely helpful. If you've used Linux or Unix they are like the man pages of old where a description of what the command can do, where it can be run, various examples of how the command can be used and more. When using the Get-Help and Get-Command, just like other PowerShell commands, there are switches that you can use to help enhance the basic cmdlet. For example, take this cmdlet:

Get-Help New-RetentionCompliancePolicy

The above command returns some information on the New-RetentionCompliancePolicy cmdlet:

```
NAME
    New-RetentionCompliancePolicy

SYNOPSIS
    This cmdlet is available only in the Office 365 Security & Compliance Center. For more information, see Office 365
    Security & Compliance Center PowerShell (https://technet.microsoft.com/library/mt587091.aspx).

    Use the New-RetentionCompliancePolicy cmdlet to create new retention policies in the Security & Compliance Center.

    For information about the parameter sets in the Syntax section below, see Exchange cmdlet syntax
    (https://technet.microsoft.com/library/bb123552.aspx).


SYNTAX
    New-RetentionCompliancePolicy -Name <String> [-Comment <String>] [-Confirm <SwitchParameter>] [-Enabled <$true |
    $false>] [-ExchangeLocation <MultiValuedProperty>] [-ExchangeLocationException <MultiValuedProperty>] [-Force
    <SwitchParameter>] [-ModernGroupLocation <MultiValuedProperty>] [-ModernGroupLocationException
    <MultiValuedProperty>] [-OneDriveLocation <MultiValuedProperty>] [-OneDriveLocationException
    <MultiValuedProperty>] [-PublicFolderLocation <MultiValuedProperty>] [-RestrictiveRetention <$true | $false>]
    [-SharePointLocation <MultiValuedProperty>] [-SharePointLocationException <MultiValuedProperty>] [-SkypeLocation
    <MultiValuedProperty>] [-SkypeLocationException <MultiValuedProperty>] [-WhatIf <SwitchParameter>]
    [<CommonParameters>]


DESCRIPTION
    New policies are not valid and will not be applied until a retention rule is added to the policy.

    You need to be assigned permissions in the Office 365 Security & Compliance Center before you can use this cmdlet.
    For more information, see Permissions in Office 365 Security & Compliance Center
    (https://go.microsoft.com/fwlink/p/?LinkId=511920).


RELATED LINKS
    Online Version http://technet.microsoft.com/EN-US/library/2711442f-22bb-4a35-9938-575d24608e43(EXCHG.160).aspx

REMARKS
    To see the examples, type: "get-help New-RetentionCompliancePolicy -examples".
    For more information, type: "get-help New-RetentionCompliancePolicy -detailed".
    For technical information, type: "get-help New-RetentionCompliancePolicy -full".
    For online help, type: "get-help New-RetentionCompliancePolicy -online"
```

Notice the main sections: Name, Synopsis, Syntax, Description, Related Links and Remarks. The command we ran provided us with a nice summary of what this command can do and the Related Link section points you to the online documentation for this cmdlet. However, what is missing is the switches or options that are available for the cmdlet as well as some examples on how to use the cmdlet as well. To get these, run the following:

```
Get-Help Get-RetentionPolicy -Full
```

The same first section appear: Name, Synopsis, Syntax and Description. However, a few additional sections appear now - Parameters:

```
PARAMETERS
    -Name <String>
        The Name parameter specifies the unique name of the retention policy. If the value contains spaces, enclose
        the value in quotation marks.

        Required?                    true
        Position?                    1
        Default value
        Accept pipeline input?       False
        Accept wildcard characters?  false


    -Comment <String>
        The Comment parameter specifies an optional comment. If you specify a value that contains spaces, enclose the
```

When you work with a command that you are unfamiliar with, it would be advisable to start with the -Full switch to get all information on the cmdlet as well as some examples on how to use the command. The major weakness of the help command as well as the Online help is that some commands are very complex and have so many options that they don't feel as complete as they might. This means that even after finding the right parameters, it may take some time to get the right results. If you find yourself in this situation, you can turn to your favorite Internet search engine to find the right syntax OR possibly get a close enough example that a bit of tweaking will make the cmdlet run the way you expect.

Inputs, Outputs and Examples:

```
INPUTS

        To see the input types that this cmdlet accepts, see Cmdlet Input and Output Types
        (http://go.microsoft.com/fwlink/p/?linkId=616387). If the Input Type field for a cmdlet is blank, the cmdlet
        doesn't accept input data.


OUTPUTS

        To see the return types, which are also known as output types, that this cmdlet accepts, see Cmdlet Input and
        Output Types (http://go.microsoft.com/fwlink/p/?linkId=616387). If the Output Type field is blank, the cmdlet
        doesn't return data.


    -------------------------- Example 1 --------------------------

    New-RetentionCompliancePolicy -Name "Regulation 123 Compliance" -ExchangeLocation "Kitty Petersen", "Scott
    Nakamura" -SharePointLocation "http://contoso.sharepoint.com/sites/teams/finance"

    This example creates a retention policy named "Regulation 123 Compliance" for the mailboxes of Kitty Petersen and
    Scott Nakamura, and the finance SharePoint Online site.
```

Cloud-Only vs Synced Environments

For anyone who manages Office 365, knowing what PowerShell cmdlets will work with their environment is a crucial piece of information. In that spirit we want to make sure that these differences are clearly delineated in the rest of the book and when we are working with PowerShell. The important thing to remember is that if your accounts and other objects are not synced to the cloud you will need to make your changes in Office 365 directly and not to anything on-premises like Active Directory. This is simply because Office 365 is in this scenario your source of truth and it is the master copy of these objects. If, however, you have Active Directory and you are syncing these objects to the cloud your on-premises Active Directory is the source of truth or Start of Authority. Those synced objects need to be changed in your on-premises Active Directory, to be more precise those synced attributes are actual only read-only in the cloud.

Non-Synced Accounts (Cloud-Only)

For those who do not want any infrastructure for their email services, this is a common setup. In this configuration, all your objects exist in Office 365 only. All management tools and scripts will run against these cloud-only objects. The Admin Console for your tenant should show all of these objects as 'cloud-only' and this only manageable from Office 365's connections.

Synced Accounts

It is common, but not entirely true of all of these environments, that a synced environment will have AD on-premises as a source of authority for all user and group objects in Office 365.

What's Next?

In this introduction we have just scratched the surface of what is available in PowerShell for the Security and Compliance Center. Let's go ahead and get in deep with PowerShell in Chapter 1.

<table><tr><td>1</td><td>

PowerShell Basics

</td></tr></table>

In This Chapter

- Variables
- Arrays
- Hash Tables
- CSV Files
- Operators
- Loops
- Functions
- PowerShell Tools
  - ISE
  - ISE Plug-Ins and More

Security and Compliance Center PowerShell: Where to Begin

This book is not a beginner's guide to PowerShell and while we assume that you, the reader, know at least something about PowerShell, we will quickly cover some basic PowerShell topics. What is covered in this chapter is necessary in order to form our building blocks for the more advanced chapters later in this book. Those building blocks will provide practical knowledge for using PowerShell with the Security and Compliance Center (SCC). Theory can be useful, but for production environments, practical tips and tricks (and scripts!) are far more useful for working in your environment.

In the Introduction, we covered one-liners, cmdlets and getting help in the PowerShell interface. We are now going to turn our attention to building PowerShell parts that make up these elements in PowerShell. Remember that a PowerShell cmdlet consists of a verb and a noun. Remember that PowerShell cmdlets provide various parameters as we saw with the Get-Help in the Introduction to this book.

In the next few pages we will introduce you to some important concepts that are key to building your scripts for the Security and Compliance Center. These concepts include variables, arrays, loops and more. Learning these will provide you with the building blocks for your scripts. There will be some basic topics which will introduce you to these elements. These topics will give you the tools to begin building scripts in future chapters of this book.

Variables

When scripting, a variable is a place for storing data. A variable can store data for different lengths of time, but most importantly, the data stored in the variable can be retrieved or referenced by cmdlets later in a script for performing a task. The data stored in variables is of a certain type, such as strings, integers, arrays and more. Variables are essential in PowerShell scripting, and it should become apparent how useful they are when working with the Security and Compliance Center.

Example - Variables

Variable	Variable Type
$Value = 1	Integer
$FirstName = "Damian"	String

Variables are not restricted to static content or a single object or value, and they can store complex, nested structures as well. For example, if we use a variable to store information on all labels:

$AllLabels = Get-Label

The $AllLabels variable stores information on each Label as a single object and can contain as many objects as there are labels in the SCC environment. This content is unlikely to change as the script using that information will likely be stored for repeated use in a script. However, a variable containing the current value of a property of a label or policy might change repeatedly in a script loop, replacing the variable content on each pass. For example, while looping through an array (example on page 4), the label name could be stored in a temporary variable (e.g. $Name) and with each pass of in the loop, the contents of $name would change to the label name in the current line of an array. Thus, the contents of a variable is not necessarily static and can be changed during the processing of a script.

Arrays

Arrays are used to store a collection of objects. This collection of data is more complex than what would be stored in a normal variable (above).

Example

$Values = 1,2,3,4,5
$Names = "Dave","Matt","John","Michael"

As you can see from the above example, the array contains a row of values which can be used by a script for queries or manipulation. To retrieve on value, we can use a bracket '[]' after the array name and pick a value. Values positions numbering starts at '0':

$Values[0]   Would be '1'
$Names[3]   Would be 'Michael'

Even more complex than arrays are multi-dimensional arrays. The $AllLabels variable example above is an example of this type of variable. This type is used to store more complex, structured information.

Example of Arrays (Multi-dimensional)

If we were to store all the information about all the Labels in an array of arrays, there would be a 'list' of arrays. Each line is essentially its own array of values. Visually, this is how the data is stored in the array [the top line contains the column headers for the underlying values]:

"DisplayName","Workload","Disabled","Mode"
"Confidential Information","Exchange, SharePoint","False","Enforce"
"Reserved","Exchange, SharePoint","False","Enforce"

Hash Tables

Hash tables are similar in form and function to arrays, but with a twist in that they consist of key:value pairs instead of individual data points. To initialize a hash table, the command is similar to an array:

$Hash = @ { }

Notice the use of the '{' brackets and not '('. Once initialized we can populate the data like so:

Example

In the below data sample, the name of each label matched up with the status of the label. As can be seen by the data set, the data is stored in pairs:

$LabelStatus= @{Confidential='True' ; Reserved='False'; HR='True'}

To display the contents of the hash table, simply run '$LabelStatus':

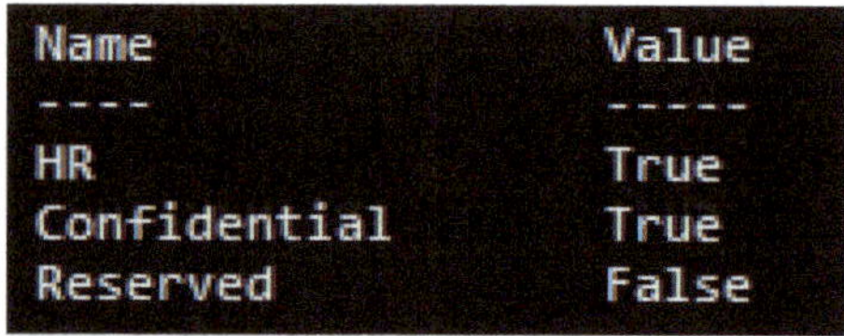

In most scenarios, an array is the way to go for data storage and manipulation. However, hash tables provide for more complex data storage and indexing with its data pairs.

CSV Files

Comma-Separated Values (CSV) files are files used to store static data, outside of using variables. This data can be pre-created and then used by a script post creation or a CSV file can be generated by a script either as an end result or an intermediary step to be used at a later point. CSV files can be considered an alternative option to using arrays. They can be used to contain data in a way similar to how an array would store data. One of the differences is that CSVs are files and arrays are stored in memory (RAM), which means that arrays only exist while a script is running and CSV files can be used to store information which should be kept, like for input or output purposes. They can also be looped through, like an array. CSV files can be manually created in a program like Excel for total control or created by a running script with an Export-CSV cmdlet to export the data.

Arrays are preferable for storing data within a script because no file is created and left behind to cleanup at a later date. The exception would be if I have an external program or process that generates a CSV file which contains lists of values that need to be imported or used for a process involving a PowerShell script.

The format of the CSV file looks something like this:

```
Name,CreatedBy,Workload,Comment,Tooltip,Settings,DisplayName
Confidential Information,Damian Scoles,"Exchange, SharePoint",This label looks for confident
Confidential Information - New!,Damian Scoles,"Exchange, SharePoint",This label looks for co
```

PowerShell scripts that use CSV files commonly read CSV files and store the contents in a variable to be used by the script. Import-CSV is the command to perform this task.

Example
$CSVFileData = Import-CSV "C:\Data\SensitiveInformationTypes.csv"

In the section on Loops, we will review what can be done with data stored in the variable, after it has been imported from a CSV file.

Operators

Operators are used in PowerShell to compare two objects or values. This can be particularly useful for when "If.. Then" or "Where-Object" is used.

Operators can include the following:

-eq	Equal	-and	TRUE when both are TRUE
-lt	Less than		e.g. (3 -eq 3) -and (1 -lt 3)
-gt	Greater than		TRUE
-ne	Not equal	-or	TRUE when either is TRUE
-ge	Greater than or equal		e.g. (3 -lt 3) -or (2 -eq 2)
-le	Less than or equal		TRUE
-like	Like Good for single wildcards e.g. "*mailbox"	-xor	TRUE when only one is TRUE e.g. (1 -eq 1) -xor (2 -eq 2) FALSE
-match	Matches criteria (non-case sensitive) Also can use double wildcards e.g. "*mailbox*"	-not / !	When a condition is not TRUE e.g. -not (1 -eq 1) FALSE
-cmatch	Match criteria (case-sensitive) e.g. "*Mailbox*"		
-contains	Exact match in a collection		

Example

$SensitiveInformationTypes = Get-DlpSensitiveInformationType
Foreach ($SensitiveInformationType in $SensitiveInformationTypes) {
    If ($SensitiveInformationType.Publisher -eq "Damian Scoles") {
        $SensitiveInformationType
    }
}

The previous example will list any Sensitive Information Type registered by "Damian Scoles"

Another example would be if we wanted to count how many were published by Microsoft:

```
$Count = 0
$SensitiveInformationTypes = Get-DlpSensitiveInformationType
Foreach ($SensitiveInformationType in $SensitiveInformationTypes) {
   If ($SensitiveInformationType.Publisher -eq "Microsoft Corporation") {
      $Count++
   }
}
Write-host "$Count sensitive information types are published by Microsoft."
```

Operators will work with strings and numbers types. Less than and greater than operators will work against text:

```
If ("Mouse" -lt "Wolf) {
   Write-Host "The Wolf eats the Mouse!"
}
```

The output from this comparison would result in:

```
The Wolf eats the Mouse!
```

The operators, with strings, work off the numerical values of each letter in the words added together and compared.

Loops

Loops can be used to process or generate a series of data, perhaps an array (or an array of arrays) of data stored in variables (like our $CSVFileData variable in the previous section). A loop can also use a counter for a series of values as well. Here are a few different ways to create loops in PowerShell:

Types

```
Foreach { }
Do { } While ()
```


Foreach-Object

Foreach-Object (Foreach) loops can be used to process each element of an array either stored in a variable or a CSV file. The array can have a single or multiple elements. The Foreach loop will stop when there are no more lines to read or process, although the more lines there are, the longer it will take to complete.

Example

Let's take our $CSVFileData variable that has stored the data we pre-created in a CSV file. The variable now contains two 'rows' of usable data. We can use the data to document what was found in the SCC.

** **Note** ** In the below code, with each loop, the variable $line, will be filled with a row from the CSV variable. You can then do something with that data in $line. After the loop is finished, Foreach will read the next line in $CSVFileData and enter it in $line. And so forth until all rows have been read.

A simple example of a Foreach loop would look like this: (Complete code):

```
$CSVFileData = Import-CSV "C:\Data\SensitiveInformationTypes.csv"
Foreach ($Line in $CSVFileData) {
    $Workload = $Line.Workload
    $DisplayName = $Line.DisplayName
    Write-Host "The Label $DisplayName affects the $Workload workloads."
}
```

The output would look like this:

```
The Label Confidential Information affects the Exchange,SharePoint workloads.
The Label Confidential Information - Imported affects the Exchange,SharePoint workloads.
```

In this example, the loop created a simple visual representation of the data, but the representation was repeated in a standard manner using a loop and a write-host cmdlet.

Do { } While ()

Do While and While loops allow a loop to continuously run until a condition has been met. The key difference between the two is that a While loop will evaluate a condition prior to any code executing (the code between the brackets of a While loop may not even run once) whereas a Do...While loop will execute code first (guaranteeing at least one time execution of code) and then checking for a particular condition. Whether this conditional exit is an incremental counter, waiting for a query result or a certain key to be pressed, the Do...While loop provides some interesting functionality that can be used in PowerShell and with the Security and Compliance Center.

When looping code with a While loop, an example of conditional exit is the counter variable. Simply put, the counter variable keeps track of the number of times a loop has run. Each time the below loop runs, the counter value increases by 1 ($Counter++). When the $Counter variable reaches 1,000, the script block will stop processing and PowerShell will move on to the next section of code.

Example – While Loop

```
$Counter = 1
While ($Counter -lt 1000) {
    Write-Host "This is pass # $Counter for this loop."
    $Counter++
}
```

** **Note** ** The $Counter++ near the end of the loop is shorthand for $Counter = $Counter +1. Also some properties being exported may actually contain multiple values or special characteristics that could complicate an export.

Also notice that the 'While' statement is at the top of the loop unlike the Do...While loop that follows.

Example – Do While Loop

```
$Counter = 1
Do {
    Write-Host "This is pass # $Counter for this loop."
    $Counter++
} While ($Counter -ne 1000)
```

In the above sample, we use a counter variable ($Counter) which is incremented by 1's using $Counter++. On each pass the script writes a line to the screen (write-host "This is pass # $Counter for this loop."). The resulting output from the code loops something like this:

```
This is pass # 4 for this loop.
This is pass # 5 for this loop.
This is pass # 6 for this loop.
This is pass # 7 for this loop.
This is pass # 8 for this loop.
This is pass # 994 for this loop.
This is pass # 995 for this loop.
This is pass # 996 for this loop.
```

Once the variable ($Counter) gets to 1,000, the script will exit.

```
This is pass # 994 for this loop.
This is pass # 995 for this loop.
This is pass # 996 for this loop.
This is pass # 997 for this loop.
This is pass # 998 for this loop.
This is pass # 999 for this loop.
```

Notice that a result with 1,000 is not shown above and this is because the counter is increased after the write-host statement and the $Counter variable is increased from 999 to 1,000 and exits. In order to show a result with 1,000 the $Counter variable needs to be moved:

Example

```
$Counter = 0
Do {
    $Counter++
    Write-Host "This is pass # $Counter for this loop."
} While ($Counter -ne 1000)
```

Export-CSV

Export-CSV – This cmdlet can create a CSV file to be used by another script or another section of code in the same script.

When exporting to a CSV file, make sure to use the –NoTypeInformation (-NoType) option in order to remove the extraneous line that gets inserted into the exported CSV. This extra line can affect the use of the CSV file later. See below for an example of what happens when exporting a complete list of Compliance Cases to a CSV file:

** **Note** ** In order to use the CSV later in the script, the –NoType option should be used.

Export-CSV -NoType

```
ComplianceCases1.csv - Notepad
File   Edit   Format   View   Help
"Name","Description","CaseType","Status","LastModifiedBy"
"Hold for some mailboxes","","eDiscovery","Active","Damian Scoles"
"Case # 4302-1","Legal Case ? R&D ? 10-2018","eDiscovery","Active","Damian Scoles"
```

Export-CSV

```
ComplianceCases2.csv - Notepad
File   Edit   Format   View   Help
#TYPE Selected.System.Management.Automation.PSCustomObject
"Name","Description","CaseType","Status","LastModifiedBy"
"Hold for some mailboxes","","eDiscovery","Active","Damian Scoles"
"Case # 4302-1","Legal Case ? R&D ? 10-2018","eDiscovery","Active","Damian Scoles"
```

How to Use these Cmdlets

These cmdlets are most useful for pulling in information from an external source or exporting the information for a later script or for reporting purposes. When importing the contents of a CSV file, we can use a variable to store the contents to be pulled out later by a loop or some other method.

Functions

Functions are blocks of code that can be called upon within the same script. This block of code becomes a reusable operation that can be called on multiple times in a script. Functions can also re-utilized in other scripts, saving time. The function, since it is comprised of reusable code, helps to save time in coding by removing duplicate coding efforts as well as reducing the size of the script removing duplicate code. Which, depending on how much code is involved and how often it is called, can improve the performance and efficiency of a PowerShell script, as well as make it more maintainable.

Example

```
#Label Doc
Function DocumentLabels {
   Get-Label | Export-Csv $LabelsDestination -NoTypeInformation
   $Labels = Get-Label
   Foreach ($Label in $Labels) {
      $Name = $Label.Name
      $File = "L-"+$Name+".txt"
      $LabelDestination = $Path+"\"+$File
      $Label.settings > $LabelDestination
   }
} #End of the DocumentLabels function

DocumentLabels
```

In the above example, the function is begun with the word 'Function' and enclosed in { } brackets. The function is then called by the very last line where the 'DocumentLabels' matches the name of the function, which executes the code contained within the brackets.

The previous code sample checks for Labels configured in the Security and Compliance Center. The last line of the script above calls the function (with the code contained within the '{' and '}' brackets) and the code in the brackets executes. A PowerShell function by itself will not do anything unless it is called upon.

PowerShell Tools

PowerShell ISE

PowerShell ISE [*Integrated Scripting Environment*] is one tools you should get familiar with when working with PowerShell. The tool comes installed by default with Windows 2012, 2012 R2 and 2016. If you are still using an older version of Windows (2008R2 and before) ISE is not pre-installed and it will be necessary to download the installation and install it on the server.

The ISE has many useful features such as color coding of PowerShell cmdlet types as well as the indicators that are provided for loops (Foreach, If Else, etc.), to aid in checking matching brackets for example. ISE's built-in spell checker makes this tool very useful. ISE is also PowerShell-aware which means you can quickly find the relevant cmdlet or recently defined variable after only typing a few characters.

PowerShell ISE Graphical Interface

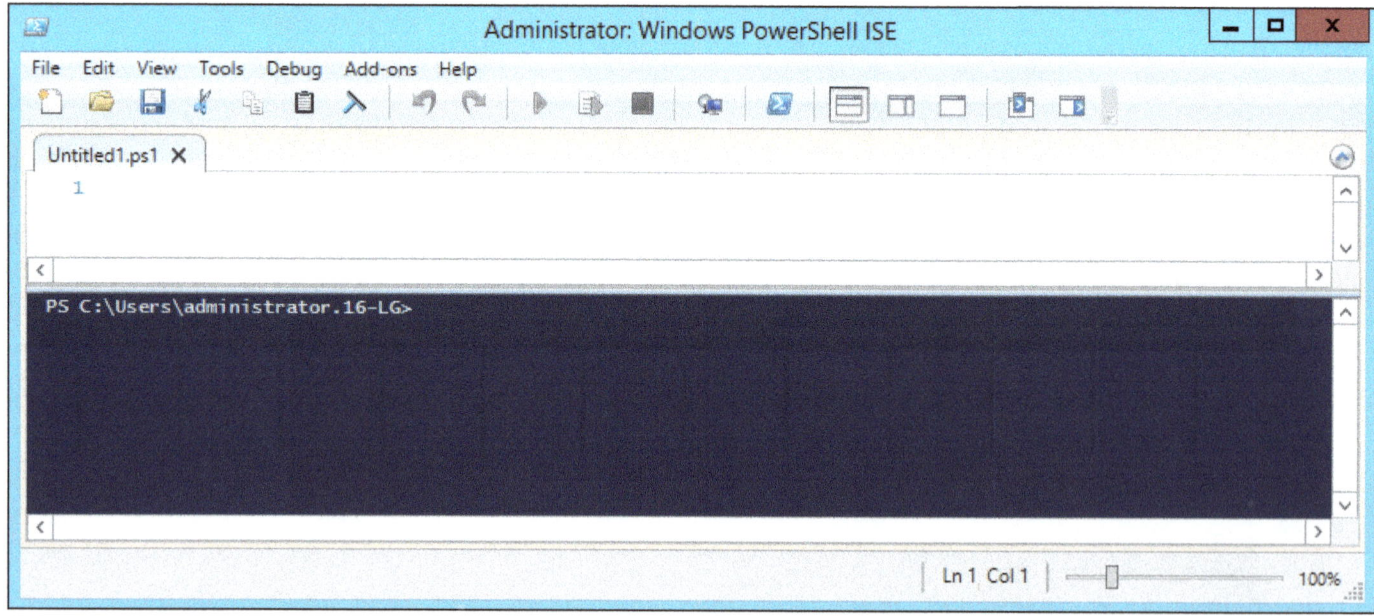

The ISE tool is a great way to help visualize a script (indentation, color, etc), while not necessary or required to assist the coder visually in writing PowerShell scripts. ISE can also be used to interactively debug scripts, stepping through the code as it is executed, allowing you to inspect variables for example.

Logical groupings are denoted by the '-' symbol on the left of the screen:

```
Licensing.ps1 X
 1 ⊖Foreach ($Line in $Users) {
 2      # Configure variables
 3      $Upn = $Line.upn
 4      $Location = (Get-MsolUser -UserPrincipalName $Upn).UsageLocation
 5      $Licensed = (Get-MsolUser -UserPrincipalName $Upn).IsLicensed
 6 ⊖    If ($Locaton -eq $Null) {
 7          Set-msoluser -UserPrincipalName $Upn -UsageLocation "US"
 8      }
 9 ⊖    If ($Licensesd -eq $False) {
10          Set-MsolUserLicense -UserPrincipalName $Upn -AddLicenses "<tenant>:ENTERPRISEPACK"
11      }
12      $LicenseOptions = New-MsolLicenseOptions -AccountSkuId "<tenant>:ENTERPRISEPACK" -DisabledPlans $Disabledoptions
13      Set-MsolUserLicense -User $upn -LicenseOptions $LicenseOptions
14      $Status = (Get-MsolUser -User $Upn).Licenses[0].ServiceStatus
15  }
16
```

Different components of the PowerShell scripts are shown in different colors. Comments are green, variables are red and cmdlets are color coded blue:

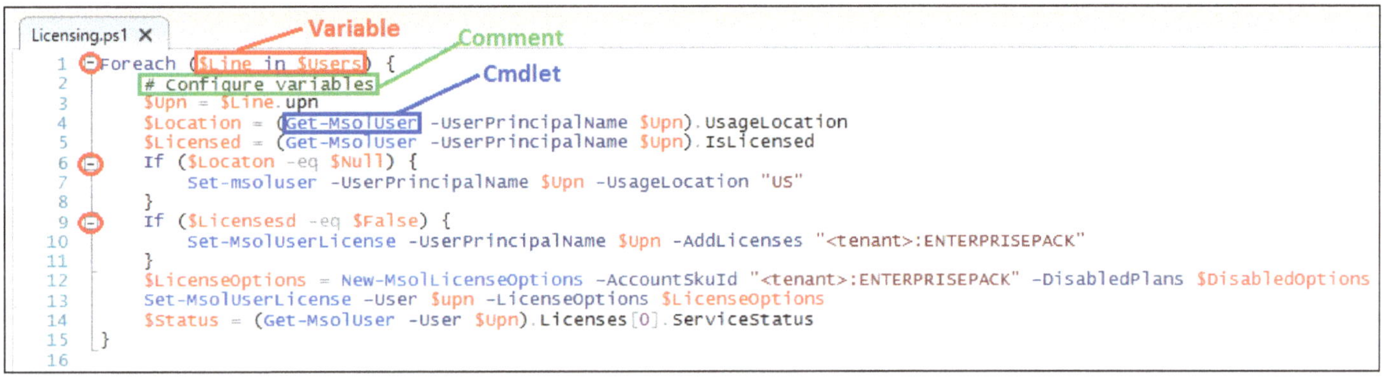

```
Licensing.ps1 X          ┌─ Variable        Comment
 1 ⊖Foreach ($Line in $Users) {
 2      # Configure variables          Cmdlet
 3      $Upn = $Line.upn
 4      $Location = (Get-MsolUser -UserPrincipalName $Upn).UsageLocation
 5      $Licensed = (Get-MsolUser -UserPrincipalName $Upn).IsLicensed
 6 ⊖    If ($Locaton -eq $Null) {
 7          Set-msoluser -UserPrincipalName $Upn -UsageLocation "US"
 8      }
 9 ⊖    If ($Licensesd -eq $False) {
10          Set-MsolUserLicense -UserPrincipalName $Upn -AddLicenses "<tenant>:ENTERPRISEPACK"
11      }
12      $LicenseOptions = New-MsolLicenseOptions -AccountSkuId "<tenant>:ENTERPRISEPACK" -DisabledPlans $Disabledoptions
13      Set-MsolUserLicense -User $upn -LicenseOptions $LicenseOptions
14      $Status = (Get-MsolUser -User $Upn).Licenses[0].ServiceStatus
15  }
16
```

Loops can be verified by clicking at / near bracket to see where the closing bracket is [paired brackets highlighted]:

```
66 ⊖    if ($success -ne $false) {
67          write-verbose "Test passed for server $name."
68 ⊖    } else {
69          write-verbose "Test failed for server $name."
70      }
```

If we click on the '-' sign on the left side, it will collapse A section of code is enclosed by a bracket pair:

```
66 ⊞    if ($success -ne $false) {...} else {
69          write-verbose "Test failed for server $name."
70      }
```

Some of the formatting is NOT done by the ISE tool. Indentation is up to you to do. I recommend the use of indenting each loop. Following is an example of this. This technique is used for readability and is not required for the code to run properly:

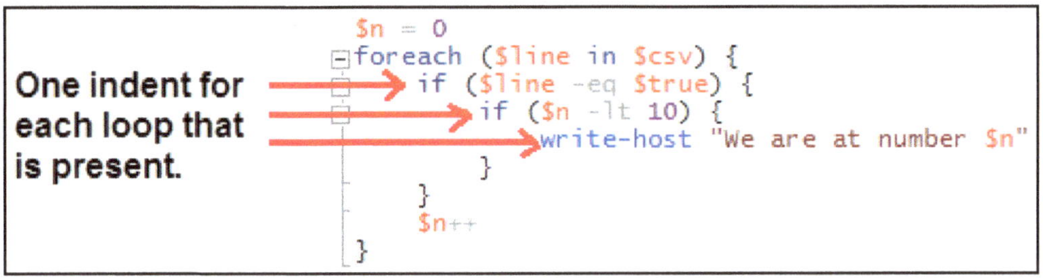

```
                 $n = 0
                 ⊖foreach ($line in $csv) {
One indent for   →    if ($line -eq $true) {
each loop that   →        if ($n -lt 10) {
is present.      →            write-host "We are at number $n"
                         }
                     }
                     $n++
                 }
```

** **Note** ** Each indent is created by using the TAB key.

In the next example of indentation, s not using indentation at all, the script would be hard to read and understand where the different loops or groupings start / end:

```
2    if( $tryWMI ) {
3    ## WMI depends on RPC. CIM depends on WinRM, but C
4    try {$Page_Managed = Get-WMIObject -computer $name
5    } catch {Write-Verbose "$($TestID): Was not able t
6    $nulldata = $true
7    }
8    }
```

Now notice the red brackets highlight the bracketing to show the way cmdlets are grouped.

```
if( $tryWMI ) {
    ## WMI depends on RPC. CIM depends on WinRM
    try {
        $Page_Managed = Get-WMIObject -computer
    } catch {
        Write-Verbose "$($TestID): Was not able
        $nulldata = $true
    }
}
```

Indentation falls into the same category as comments, which we will cover on Page 27. While not required to be used, they make the script much easier to use, understand and troubleshoot in case of problems or errors. Creating a script is one of many uses for the tool, as the ISE tool also allows for running the script. In the lower portion of the tool is a PowerShell interface used for script execution.

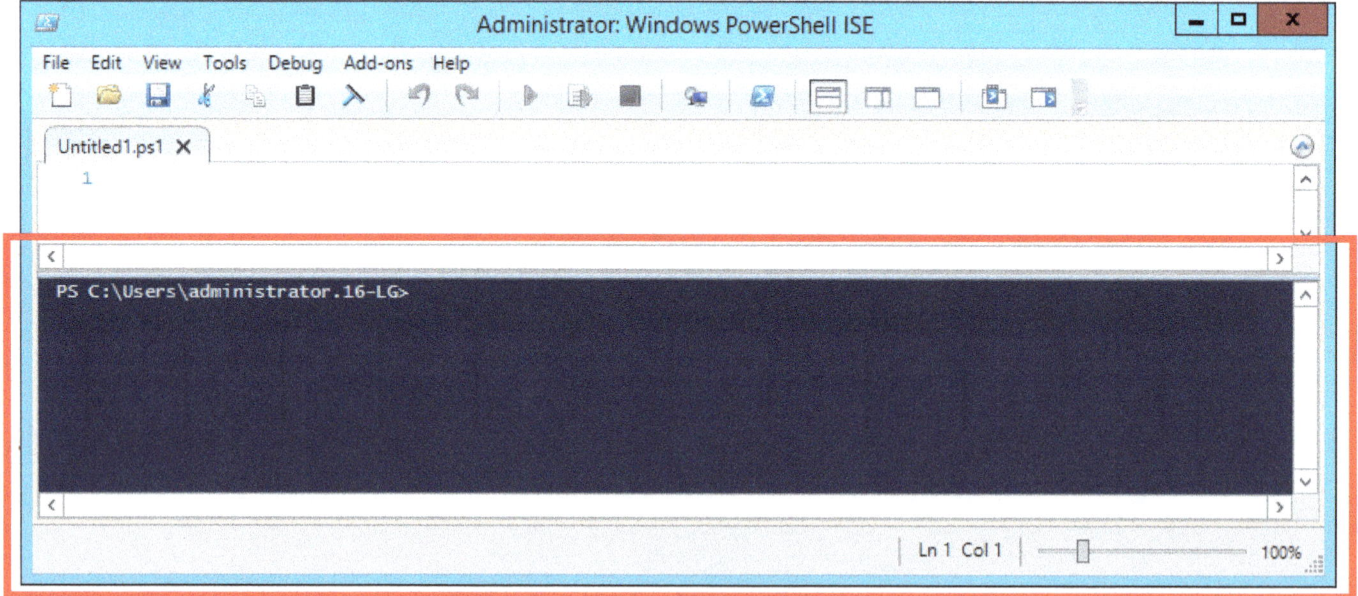

PowerShell modules can be imported in order to expand its capabilities. For Active Directory this module can be loaded with this one-liner.

Active Directory

```
import-module activedirectory
```

After the module is loaded, AD cmdlets such as Get-AdUser and Get-ADDomain Controller can now be run.

Modules can also be pre-loaded into a PowerShell profile to make this even easier. Read up more on this here:

https://blogs.technet.microsoft.com/heyscriptingguy/2012/05/24/use-a-module-to-simplify-your-powershell-profile/

PowerShell Repositories

Another great resource for scripting are PowerShell Repositories. PowerShell repositories contain pre-written code and also allow you to create your own repositories for sharing code internally or with the Public, depending on the scope of the project. Below are three examples of PowerShell repositories:

DevOps: https://devblogs.microsoft.com/powershell/using-powershellget-with-azure-artifacts/
GitHub: https://www.github.com
GitLab: https://about.gitlab.com/

Alternatives to ISE

Notepad and Notepad++. Notepad is a very basic way to edit a PowerShell script. It is best used for quickly copying and pasting scripts or scripts that require very little work. Notepad++ is program similar to the PowerShell ISE in that it can handle multiple languages, however the ISE is much more versatile. Auto-Completion of PowerShell cmdlets and variable names are incredibly useful while coding longer scripts.

Visual Studio Code is also now the recommended tool for Microsoft over PowerShell ISE. The product is a noteworthy take on PowerShell script editing and is worth a look at here - https://4sysops.com/archives/visual-studio-code-vscode-as-powershell-script-editor/. Visually it has a more modern take on script editing:

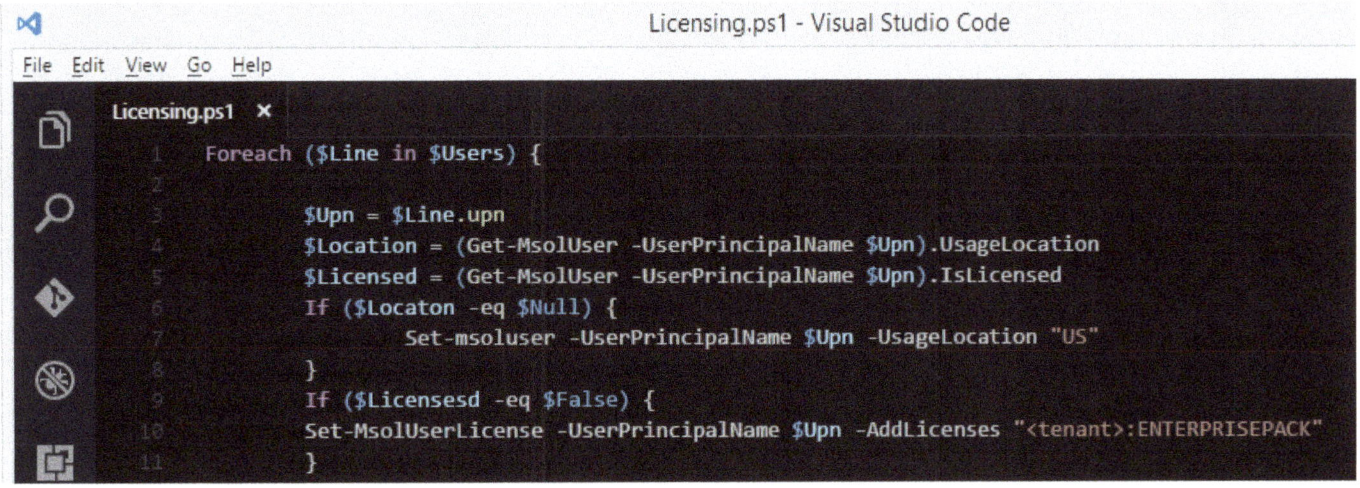
Licensing.ps1 - Visual Studio Code
File Edit View Go Help
Licensing.ps1
Foreach ($Line in $Users) {
$Upn = $Line.upn
$Location = (Get-MsolUser -UserPrincipalName $Upn).UsageLocation
$Licensed = (Get-MsolUser -UserPrincipalName $Upn).IsLicensed
If ($Locaton -eq $Null) {
Set-msoluser -UserPrincipalName $Upn -UsageLocation "US"
}
If ($Licensesd -eq $False) {
Set-MsolUserLicense -UserPrincipalName $Upn -AddLicenses "<tenant>:ENTERPRISEPACK"
}

It has visual identifiers for comments, variables, text strings and has even more advanced features for identifying correct brackets keywords and more.

ISE Plug-ins and More

Plug-ins for ISE provide even more functionality for those coding in PowerShell.   Additional functionality and features can be added to PowerShell ISE with plug-ins created by third party authors. Here are some sample plug-ins for the PowerShell ISE program:

ISE Steroids - http://www.powertheshell.com/isesteroids/

ISE Steroids makes coding within the ISE more interactive. The plug-in provides assistance with your coding, making sure that the correct syntax is used.

For example, the right use of quotes ' or " is shown below:

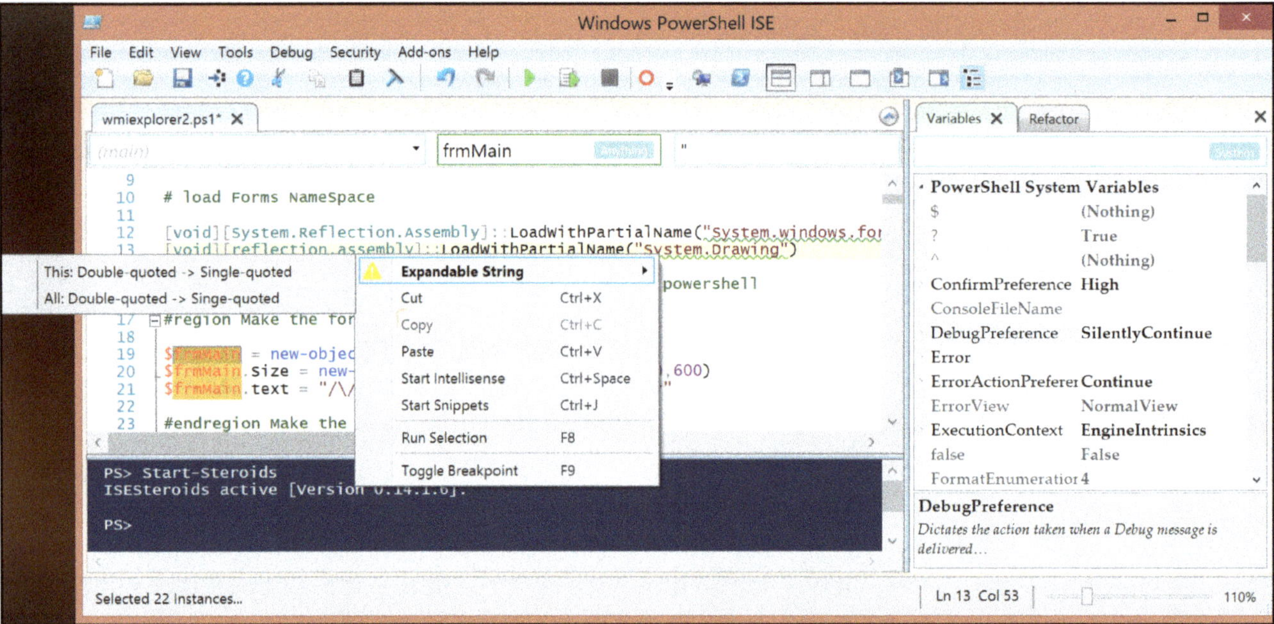

The plug-in also provides help on PowerShell cmdlets:

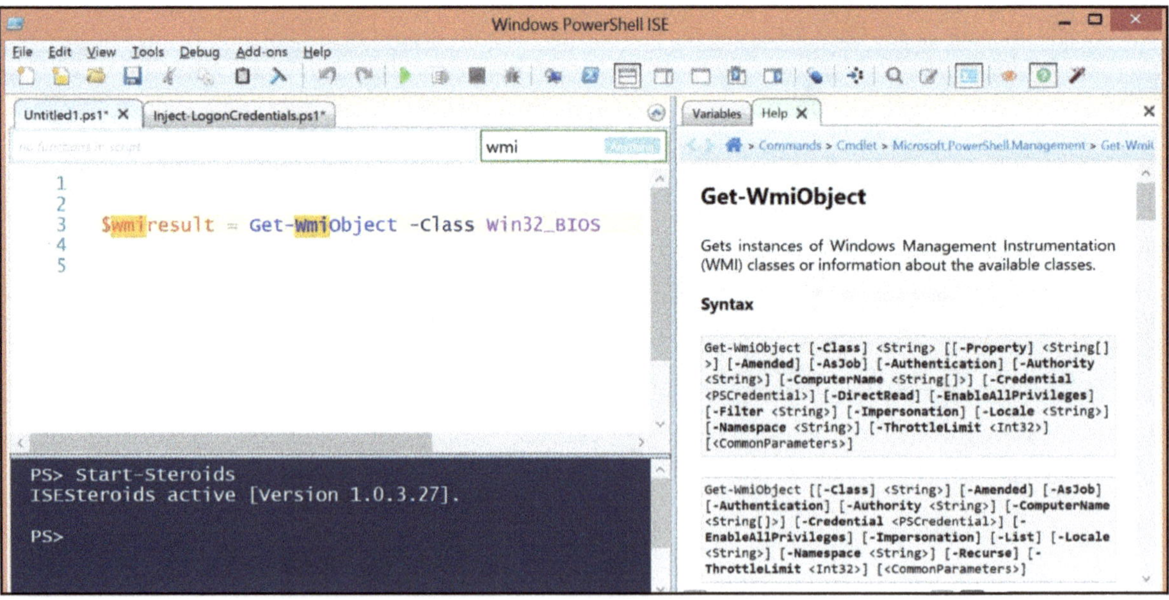

PSharp Plug-in for PowerShell

The PSharp ISE plug-in, created by PowerShell MVP Doug Finke, was designed to make PowerShell ISE more powerful than it already is. The plug-in allows for identifying variables, commands and functions with a single keystroke. Like any other, it is worth evaluating to see if it meets your needs.

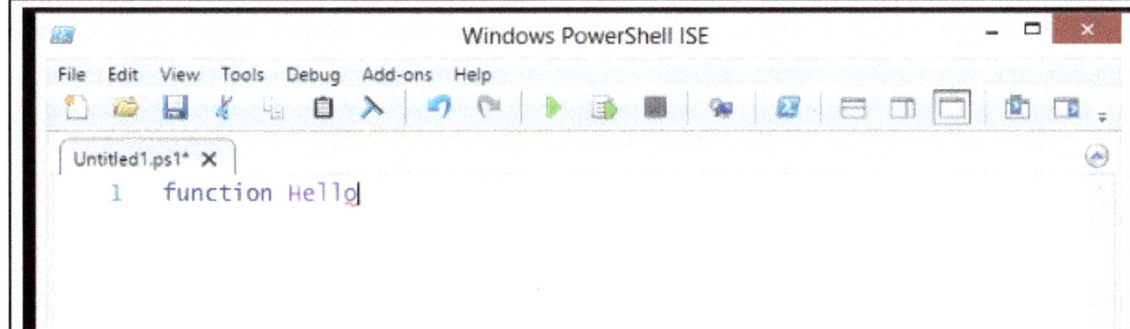

http://www.powershellmagazine.com/2013/08/18/psharp-makes-powershell-ise-better/

Sample of PSharp used with two open scripts. Note the variables and commands and where these are located in the script:

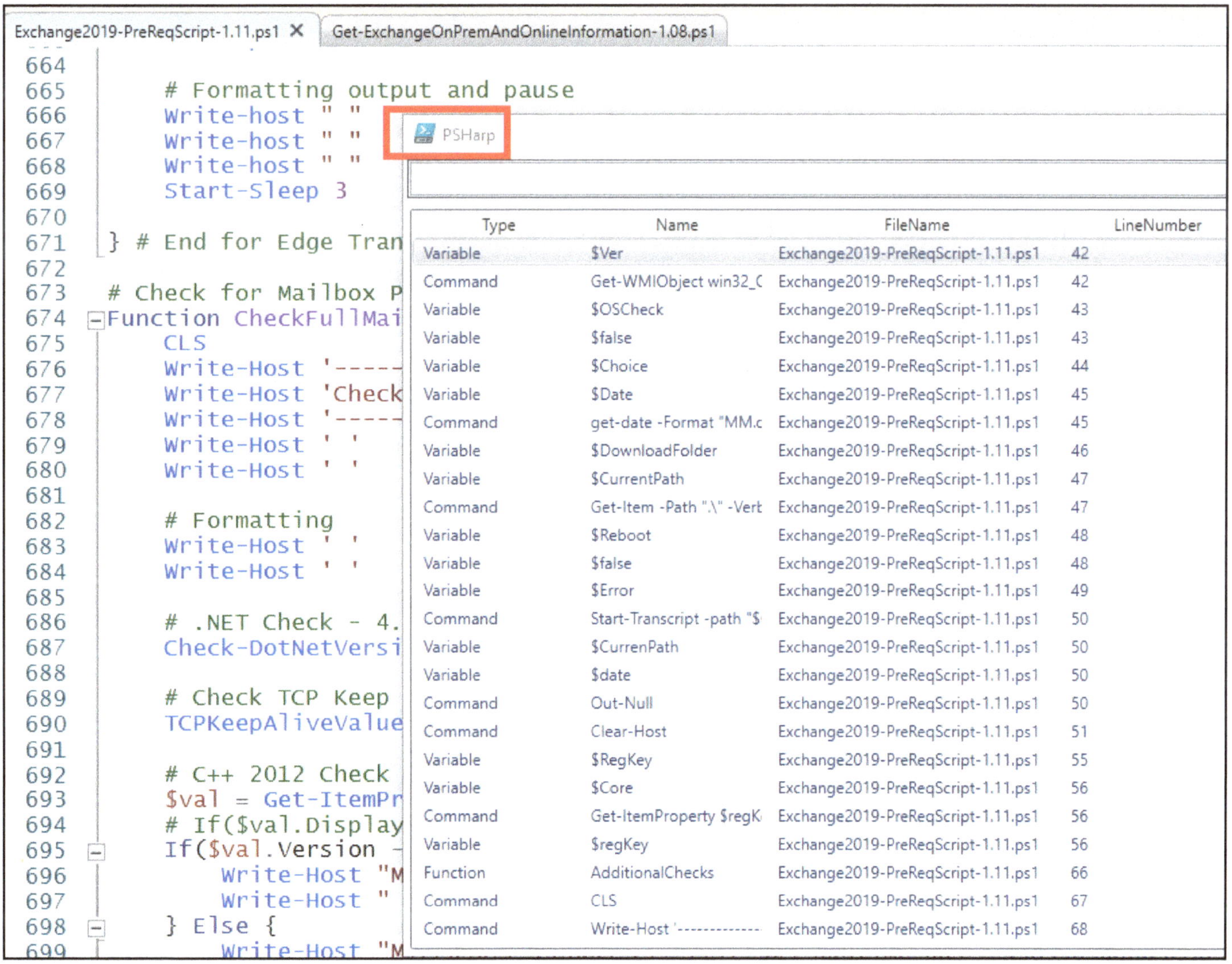

```
664
665         # Formatting output and pause
666         Write-host " "
667         Write-host " "
668         Write-host " "
669         Start-Sleep 3
670
671    } # End for Edge Tran
672
673      # Check for Mailbox P
674    Function CheckFullMai
675         CLS
676         Write-Host '-----
677         Write-Host 'Check
678         Write-Host '-----
679         Write-Host ' '
680         Write-Host ' '
681
682         # Formatting
683         Write-Host ' '
684         Write-Host ' '
685
686         # .NET Check - 4.
687         Check-DotNetVersi
688
689         # Check TCP Keep
690         TCPKeepAliveValue
691
692         # C++ 2012 Check
693         $val = Get-ItemPr
694         # If($val.Display
695         If($val.Version -
696             Write-Host "M
697             Write-Host "
698         } Else {
699             Write-Host "M
```

Type	Name	FileName	LineNumber
Variable	$Ver	Exchange2019-PreReqScript-1.11.ps1	42
Command	Get-WMIObject win32_C	Exchange2019-PreReqScript-1.11.ps1	42
Variable	$OSCheck	Exchange2019-PreReqScript-1.11.ps1	43
Variable	$false	Exchange2019-PreReqScript-1.11.ps1	43
Variable	$Choice	Exchange2019-PreReqScript-1.11.ps1	44
Variable	$Date	Exchange2019-PreReqScript-1.11.ps1	45
Command	get-date -Format "MM.c	Exchange2019-PreReqScript-1.11.ps1	45
Variable	$DownloadFolder	Exchange2019-PreReqScript-1.11.ps1	46
Variable	$CurrentPath	Exchange2019-PreReqScript-1.11.ps1	47
Command	Get-Item -Path ".\" -Verb	Exchange2019-PreReqScript-1.11.ps1	47
Variable	$Reboot	Exchange2019-PreReqScript-1.11.ps1	48
Variable	$false	Exchange2019-PreReqScript-1.11.ps1	48
Variable	$Error	Exchange2019-PreReqScript-1.11.ps1	49
Command	Start-Transcript -path "$	Exchange2019-PreReqScript-1.11.ps1	50
Variable	$CurrenPath	Exchange2019-PreReqScript-1.11.ps1	50
Variable	$date	Exchange2019-PreReqScript-1.11.ps1	50
Command	Out-Null	Exchange2019-PreReqScript-1.11.ps1	50
Command	Clear-Host	Exchange2019-PreReqScript-1.11.ps1	51
Variable	$RegKey	Exchange2019-PreReqScript-1.11.ps1	55
Variable	$Core	Exchange2019-PreReqScript-1.11.ps1	56
Command	Get-ItemProperty $regK	Exchange2019-PreReqScript-1.11.ps1	56
Variable	$regKey	Exchange2019-PreReqScript-1.11.ps1	56
Function	AdditionalChecks	Exchange2019-PreReqScript-1.11.ps1	66
Command	CLS	Exchange2019-PreReqScript-1.11.ps1	67
Command	Write-Host '-------------	Exchange2019-PreReqScript-1.11.ps1	68

2 Beyond the Basics

In This Chapter

Formatting
- Capitalization
- Commenting
- Mind Your Brackets

Command Output
- Cmdlet Output Formatting
- Filtering
- Splitting
- Scripting in Color

Miscellaneous
- Quotes
- Code Signing

Formatting

A working PowerShell script can be written quickly and without any formal formatting or standards. The script will probably function and perform the tasks it was coded for. However, a useful well-coded script should have more. A script should be easily read by another person or when you revisit an old script later, there should be a description of the script at the top and plenty of commenting in the script to provide information about its workings.

In this section, we will cover topics like capitalization, comments and bracketing. The use of these techniques will make your PowerShell scripts more usable and readily accessible to those who may use your scripts.

Capitalization

We must note that even though capitalization can be used throughout our scripts, PowerShell is NOT case sensitive. One use case scenario for capitalization is to help make PowerShell cmdlets and their arguments more readable:

PowerShell Cmdlet Example:

No capitalization
new-supervisoryreviewpolicyv2

Each word is capitalized
New-SupervisoryReviewPolicyV2

Visually the second cmdlet example would make the scripts more readable. We can see the individual words in the cmdlet and possibly allow us to decipher what the cmdlet is used for. While the non-capitalized one seems flat, with the words seemingly running together.

Capitalization can vastly improve the readability of the script by providing visual clues for each new word in a variable where words are mashed together:

Variable Example:

No capitalization
$caseholdrules

Each word is capitalized
$CaseHoldRules

This capitalization is analogous to syllable emphasis in pronouncing words. The capital letters emphasize the important parts and give the reader a visual cue as to what is being run. While this convention is not required by PowerShell as it is case-insensitive. Another example would be function names:

Function Example:

No capitalization
function exportlabelpolicies {
}

Each word is capitalized
Function ExportLabelPolicies {
}

In summary, while these changes will not increase the speed of your script, nor make the script run cleaner, it will make it easier for troubleshooting and understanding how a script is structured.

Commenting

Comments. Do we really need these? Comments in PowerShell are not required, however they are extremely useful. If you have a team that shares scripts, then comments can be quiet beneficial to all. Not only can scripting logic be explained, or versioning be tracked, but each section of the script can be described and documented for yourself or others who will run the script.

PowerShell 1.0 (Historical)

If you write a script that needs to run on all versions of PowerShell, PowerShell 1.0 does not like certain commenting syntax. The '#' is the only accepted way of making a block of comments. The '#' needs to be in front of each line that needs to be treated as a comment versus executable content. Sample of this:

```
# *********************
# *   Export Labels   *
# *********************
```

Modern PowerShell - v2 to v6

The more 'modern' versions of PowerShell have more options in formatting comments that are put into scripts. The below example shows the starting of a comment block with a '<#' and ending the same comment block with '>#'.

```
<#
    .Synopsis
        Document your Security and Compliance Center environment

    .Description
        Exports all settings from the Security and Compliance Center to files to k
        used for documentation or recreation.

    .Example
        .\DocumentSCC-1.3.ps1

    .Inputs
        None.   You cannot pipe objects to this script.
#>
```

Comments can also use the format of '#' in front of each line just like we have in PowerShell 1.0. The example under PowerShell 1.0 (Historical) can also be used in PowerShell 5.x and 6.x. Comments can be single lines as well:

```
# Get-ComplianceCase $ComplianceCasesName | Export-CSV -Notype $Destination
```

The example above is an instance where I wanted to comment out a line for troubleshooting other code around this one line. Another example is inline commenting, however that is not recommended as is makes reading more challenging:

```
Get-RoleGroupMember -Identity $RoleGroupName # List Role Group Members for a group
```

Uses

What are the main drivers for comment utilization in scripts?

- Providing a detailed description of the purpose of the script as well as how to use the script
- Breaking the script into sections
- Providing a quick description of a section
- To block out a line of code for future use
- To block out a line of code that did not work

Take time to provide at least a very basic framework for other script users to get the gist of your script. Adding comments will provide an additional benefit to your scripts. It allows you, the coder, to go back to an old script and quickly figure out what the script was for and allow for possible modification of one or more sections, as needed. Reusable code will also save time down the line when coding new scripts for new purposes.

With script writing, you might find it easier to comment as the script is built, if nothing else it provides a helpful reminder to yourself of which parts are performing certain functions in the script. For example, while building a script for checking Pagefile settings, making sure to comment on what step you're on in the process: (the code below is a sample and not a complete script):

```powershell
# Set the ideal PageFile size
$Page_Ideal = $RAMinMB + 10

# Retrieve the Minimum PageFile size
try {$Page_min = (Get-CIMInstance -ComputerName $name -ClassName win32_pagefilesetting -Property * -ErrorAction Stop).initialsize
}catch {$WMI=$true;write-host "The server $name is inaccessible by CIM, trying WMI." -foregroundcolor yellow}
if( $WMI ) {
    ## WMI depends on RPC. CIM depends on WinRM, but CIM failed, so we try WMI before we give up.
    try {$Page_min = (Get-WMIObject -Computer $name -Class win32_pagefilesetting -Property * -ErrorAction Stop).initialsize
    } catch {$up=$false;write-host " The server $name is inaccessible by WMI, this is not good." -foregroundcolor red}
}

# Retrieve the Maximum PageFile size
try {$Page_max = (Get-CIMInstance -ComputerName $name -ClassName win32_pagefilesetting -Property * -ErrorAction Stop).maximumsize
}catch {$WMI=$true;write-host "The server $name is inaccessible by CIM, trying WMI." -foregroundcolor yellow}
if( $WMI ) {
    ## WMI depends on RPC. CIM depends on WinRM, but CIM failed, so we try WMI before we give up.
    try {$Page_max = (Get-WMIObject -Computer $name -Class win32_pagefilesetting -Property * -ErrorAction Stop).maximumsize
    } catch {$up=$false;write-host " The server $name is inaccessible by WMI, this is not good." -foregroundcolor red}
}
```

Note the comments lines that are enclosed in red rectangles. Each comment block describes a logical section of the script, almost like a script block. I did this so I could describe each section of my script with a single concise line of text.

The symbol for commenting (#) can also be used to remove a line in the script from executing. Using the '#' in front of a one-liner in a script would essentially turn the cmdlet into a comment and no longer be executable in PowerShell. This technique is commonly used in order to duplicate a line of code, allowing for the original line to be saved while new versions of the line are concocted:

Example – Troubleshooting Code

Original line (which fails and needs more options for output)
Get-DlpSensitiveInformationType | where {$_Publisher -eq 'Microsoft Corporation'}

Comment the line, duplicate and modify
Get-DlpSensitiveInformationType | where {$_Publisher -eq 'Microsoft Corporation'}
Get-DlpSensitiveInformationType | where {$_.Publisher -eq 'Microsoft Corporation'}

Notice the original line above and the new corrected line below. I did this because the first command failed The variable listed in the line ' $_Publisher' was missing a '.' in between the '_' and the 'P'.

Another reason to comment out a line is PowerShell is to either remove old code or remove troubleshooting code.

Example – Removing Old Code
$ComplianceTag = Get-ComplianceTag $Name
Write-host "Compliance tag name is $ComplianceTag."

Becomes….
$ComplianceTag = Get-ComplianceTag $Name
Write-host "Compliance tag name is $ComplianceTag."

Note on this, that after a script has tested out and verified as performing its function, these sorts of lines should be cleaned up to get rid of code no longer needed.

Mind Your Brackets!

One of the more important aspects of writing loops and code sections in PowerShell is making sure your brackets are all correct and in the right place. Take a look at the code section below. Red arrows are drawn below to show which bracket goes with which set of code: 

```
 6 $files = get-childitem $location
 7
 8 # Loop for each file to get IP Addresses
 9 foreach ($file in $files) {
10     $name = $file.name
11     $csv = import-csv $location"\"$name
12     foreach ($line in $csv) {
13         if ($line -like "#") { }
14         else {
15
16 # Get the Client IP
17             $info = $line.cip
18             if ($info -ne "cip") {
19                 foreach ($value in $info) {
20                     if ($value -ne $null) {
21
22 # Client IP also contains the port number which we will remove here
23                         $ID = $value.Split([char]0x003A)
24                         $CIP = $ID[0]
25                         $cipresults += $cip
26                     }
27                 }
28             }
29         }
30     }
31 }
32
32 # Optional - Remove Duplicates
```

Why are brackets important? If each section of code is not closed properly, it could execute incorrectly or not execute at all. If you are using Windows PowerShell ISE, any issues with brackets should be obvious:

```
        Missing Bracket                 All Brackets Present

   foreach ($line in $var) {       foreach ($line in $var) {
       if ($line -eq "20") {           if ($line -eq "20") {
                                        }
   }                               }
```

As PowerShell ISE will show related brackets with gray marking the other bracket in a pair.

Notice the underlined bracket in the red rectangle in the left code sample as well as the missing '-' in the blue rectangle as well. These are two visual clues that the PowerShell ISE can provide for us while coding in PowerShell. These clues let us know that our brackets are not correct and that something is amiss. The only weakness with this visual clue is that sometimes the red squiggly does not mean that the exact same kind of bracket is missing:

Example – Different Bracket Missing

```
foreach ($line in $csv) {

    if ($that -eq $that {

    }

}
```

The correct code block looks like this:

```
foreach ($line in $csv) {
    if ($that -eq $that) {
    }
}
```

Notice that the if () block on the top code block was missing the right bracket. Notice that the '{' bracket actually had the red squiggly under it, even though a ')' was missing. In the same vein, a missing quote can also cause a bracket to get a red squiggly placed under it:

```
write-host "B... Bl... Bla... Blah!"
foreach ($line in $csv) {
    write-host "
}
```

One missing quote causes all of this. Corrected:

```
write-host "B... Bl... Bla... Blah!"
foreach ($line in $csv) {
    write-host "That was the quote we needed."
}
```

No more issues.

Command Output

The default results that are provided by PowerShell cmdlets are lackluster and in some cases not useful at all. The output needs to be tweaked. This section will cover ways to improve PowerShell cmdlet output, from filtering out unwanted results, to tweaking values stored in variables, to formatting tables and even adding a bit of color to PowerShell output.

Cmdlet Output Formatting

Formatting. Boring. Do we really need to format our output? Who's going to care?

Any PowerShell script author should. By default the formatting for PowerShell leaves much to be desired. Property values on objects could be truncated, values you need may not be the defaults and more. Formatting will help you create better output, more usable output and allow you to get more out of the SCC via PowerShell.

How do we do this? Let's cover some of the basics. At the end of a PowerShell cmdlet we can add some more characters to change the format of the output. The characters are:

Switch	Name	Purpose
| FL	Format-List	All object properties are displayed in a list format
| FT	Format-Table	Object properties displayed in a table format
| FT -AutoSize	Format-Table + Auto	Object properties displayed in a table format extra spaces removed
| FT -wrap	Format-Table + Wrap	Object properties displayed in multi-line fashion

Get-RoleGroup cmdlet using FL which will display 'all' an objects properties in list format:

```
PS C:\> Get-RoleGroup | fl

RunspaceId                    : 84ceacd1-98c7-4302-933e-296f4d594738
ManagedBy                     : {}
RoleAssignments               : {FFO.extest.microsoft.com/Microsoft Exchange Hosted Organizations/SCCBook.onmicrosoft.com/Review-Reviewer}
Roles                         : {FFO.extest.microsoft.com/Microsoft Exchange Hosted Organizations/SCCBook.onmicrosoft.com/Review}
DisplayName                   : Reviewer
ExternalDirectoryObjectId     :
Members                       : {}
SamAccountName                :
Description                   : Use a limited set of the analysis features in Office 365 Advanced eDiscovery. Members of this group can see
RoleGroupType                 : Standard
```

Get-RoleGroup cmdlet using FT which will display a select number of attributes in a table format:

```
PS C:\> Get-RoleGroup | ft

Name                       AssignedRoles
----                       -------------
Reviewer                   {FFO.extest.microsoft.com/Microsoft Exchange Hosted Organizations/SCCBook.onmicrosoft.com/Review}
TenantAdmins               {}
OrganizationManagement     {FFO.extest.microsoft.com/Microsoft Exchange Hosted Organizations/SCCBook.onmicrosoft.com/View-Only Retention Manag
                           FFO.extest.microsoft.com/Microsoft Exchange Hosted Organizations/SCCBook.onmicrosoft.com/Reset Password, FFO.extes
SecurityAdministrator      {FFO.extest.microsoft.com/Microsoft Exchange Hosted Organizations/SCCBook.onmicrosoft.com/Manage Alerts, FFO.extes
                           FFO.extest.microsoft.com/Microsoft Exchange Hosted Organizations/SCCBook.onmicrosoft.com/View-Only Device Managemen
RecordsManagement          {FFO.extest.microsoft.com/Microsoft Exchange Hosted Organizations/SCCBook.onmicrosoft.com/RecordManagement, FFO.ex
                           Exchange Hosted Organizations/SCCBook.onmicrosoft.com/Transport Rules, FFO.extest.microsoft.com/Microsoft Exchange
SupervisoryReview          {FFO.extest.microsoft.com/Microsoft Exchange Hosted Organizations/SCCBook.onmicrosoft.com/Supervisory Review Admin
MailFlowAdministrator      {FFO.extest.microsoft.com/Microsoft Exchange Hosted Organizations/SCCBook.onmicrosoft.com/View-Only Recipients}
ComplianceAdministrator    {FFO.extest.microsoft.com/Microsoft Exchange Hosted Organizations/SCCBook.onmicrosoft.com/View-Only Retention Manag
                           FFO.extest.microsoft.com/Microsoft Exchange Hosted Organizations/SCCBook.onmicrosoft.com/View-Only Manage Alerts,
ServiceAssuranceUser       {FFO.extest.microsoft.com/Microsoft Exchange Hosted Organizations/SCCBook.onmicrosoft.com/Service Assurance View}
SecurityReader             {FFO.extest.microsoft.com/Microsoft Exchange Hosted Organizations/SCCBook.onmicrosoft.com/View-Only Manage Alerts,
                           FFO.extest.microsoft.com/Microsoft Exchange Hosted Organizations/SCCBook.onmicrosoft.com/View-Only DLP Compliance
eDiscoveryManager          {FFO.extest.microsoft.com/Microsoft Exchange Hosted Organizations/SCCBook.onmicrosoft.com/Export, FFO.extest.micro
                           Hosted Organizations/SCCBook.onmicrosoft.com/Review, FFO.extest.microsoft.com/Microsoft Exchange Hosted Organizatio
```

Why would we want to use FT or FL? FT allows us to create a usable table, good for quick reference. Whereas FL will show all properties of an object and may reveal properties we did not know existed. The list of attributes could then be used to create a better or more concise list of properties in table format:

```
PS C:\> Get-RoleGroup Reviewer | fl role*


RoleAssignments : {FFO.extest.microsoft.com/Microsoft Exchange Hosted Organizations/SCCBook.onmicrosoft.com/Review-Reviewer}
Roles           : {FFO.extest.microsoft.com/Microsoft Exchange Hosted Organizations/SCCBook.onmicrosoft.com/Review}
RoleGroupType   : Standard
```

Using the property list from the above FL we can now select relevant properties to put in a table format. Also notice the use of an asterisk ('*') which is used as a wildcard character representing any number of characters on its side of the string. Let's pick all values with 'content' for the Get-CaseHoldRule cmdlet. We can now run this in a table format:

```
PS C:\> Get-CaseHoldRule | ft content*

ContentDateFrom ContentDateTo ContentMatchQuery
--------------- ------------- -----------------
                              Bob Smith(c:c)(date=2018-01-01T06:00:00Z..2018-02-28T20:09:42.691Z)
                              Bob Smith
```

What if we pick too many attributes and the values could become truncated as is evidenced above with the '...' displayed.

```
PS C:\> Get-CaseHoldRule | ft Name,HolddurationDisplay*,HoldContent,Priority,Workload,Mode,Policy

Name                HoldDurationDisplayHint HoldContent Priority Workload              Mode    Policy
----                ----------------------- ----------- -------- --------              ----    ------
Teacher Lawsuit Days                                  0        0 Exchange, SharePoint Enforce 0c70eac9-adfb-4574-b66f-c4...
Hold 2              Days                               0        0 Exchange, SharePoint Enforce f02f65bd-1cd0-401b-90cc-c8...
```

To fix this, first we need to widen the PowerShell Windows to a number greater that the normal 80. You may need some trial and error on exact size numbers. After that, we can run the same cmdlet with the | FT, but now followed by an '-auto' switch. The '-auto' switch will take all of the results and create a 'neat table' that makes all property values fit on the screen. The downside to the switch is that it will hold the results from being displayed as PowerShell is calculating how the properties will all fit on the screen properly.

```
PS C:\> Get-CaseHoldRule | ft Name,HoldDurationDisplay*,HoldContent,Priority,Workload,Mode,Policy -auto

Name                  HoldDurationDisplayHint HoldContent Priority Workload              Mode    Policy
----                  ----------------------- ----------- -------- --------              ----    ------
Teacher Lawsuit Days                                    0        0 Exchange, SharePoint Enforce 0c70eac9-adfb-4574-b66f-c41ff4df80a8
Hold 2          Days                                    0        0 Exchange, SharePoint Enforce f02f65bd-1cd0-401b-90cc-c86f866b8c5e
```

This creates a readable output and displays the values properly in one table, auto adjusted (-auto) to condense the information displayed. FT and FL will become important tools for building reports or figuring out what properties to select from objects in the Security and Compliance Center.

Filtering

In addition to formatting output with FL and FT we can also filter the output. Filtering with PowerShell involves selecting or limiting the reported set of properties on an object to a meaningful subset of properties of an object that can be used or manipulated. One use case for filtering is creating reports on items in the Security and Compliance Center like Labels, Hold and Compliance Cases. For example, the default output of 'Get-ComplianceTag' only displays the default properties RunspaceId, RetentionAction, RetentionType, IsRecordLabel, HasRetentionAction, ReviewerEmail, EventTypeId and Notes. While these values are relevant to the object, it's hard to create a great report off this.

Tweaking Our PowerShell Results

First we need to figure out what we want to filter or focus on. Do we want to find all Compliance Tags in the Security and Compliance Center with a particular phrase in the name? Without a filter, the Get-ComplianceTag command will display all Compliance Tags:

```
Get-ComplianceTag
```

Results look like this:

```
PS C:\> get-compliancetag | ft

RunspaceId                               RetentionAction RetentionType    IsRecordLabel HasRetentionAction ReviewerEmail EventTypeId Notes
----------                               --------------- -------------    ------------- ------------------ ------------- ----------- -----
fa39d5da-bbf5-44d6-acc1-10340bb237b4 Delete              TaggedAgeInDays          False              False
fa39d5da-bbf5-44d6-acc1-10340bb237b4 Delete              TaggedAgeInDays          False              False
fa39d5da-bbf5-44d6-acc1-10340bb237b4 Delete              TaggedAgeInDays          False              False                                       This is
```

In order to filter results based off a certain result, 'Where-Object ' (Where) can be used as a trigger for PowerShell cmdlets. Below are two examples. Filter for Tags whose Comment property is not empty (notice the -ne operator):

```
Get-ComplianceTag | Where {$_.Comment -ne ''} | Ft
```

```
RunspaceId                               RetentionAction RetentionType    IsRecordLabel HasRetentionAction ReviewerEmail EventTypeId Notes
----------                               --------------- -------------    ------------- ------------------ ------------- ----------- -----
fa39d5da-bbf5-44d6-acc1-10340bb237b4 Delete              TaggedAgeInDays          False              False
fa39d5da-bbf5-44d6-acc1-10340bb237b4 Delete              TaggedAgeInDays          False              False                                       This is
```

** Note ** in the above code, there are two individual (') characters and not a single quote (")

Filter for all Compliance Tags whose 'Name' property equals 'Test Label 1' (notice the -eq operator):

```
Get-ComplianceTag | Where {$_.Name -eq 'Test Label 1'} | Ft
```

```
RetentionAction RetentionType    IsRecordLabel HasRetentionAction ReviewerEmail EventTypeId Notes

--------------- -------------    ------------- ------------------ ------------- ----------- -----
Delete          TaggedAgeInDays          False              False                                      This is
```

** **Note** ** $_. is the equivalent of current object and 'Name' is a property of that object.

The filters noticeably reduce the number of Compliance Tags that are reported by the PowerShell command. Contained inside the '{ }' is the criteria for the filter to work. The '$_.Name' part allows us to specifically pick the Name property on a Compliance Tag. Then using an operator to decide the criteria to match a particular value in the property. In the above example we are filtering the results to display only Compliance Tags that have a name that matches 'Test Label 1'. The below sample operators are all case insensitive.

Sample operators:

-eq	Equal To
-lt	Less Than
-gt	Greater Than
-ne	Not Equal To

Filtering allows a search for common criteria on a bulk basis. This is useful for limiting results to only Compliance Tags we need. We can also use the '-Filter' parameter on some cmdlets in order to refine search results:

```
Get-User -Filter {Name -eq 'Damian Scoles'}
```

```
Name          RecipientType

----          -------------
Damian Scoles User
```

Splitting

Scenario #1

Call it parsing, call it whatever. Sometimes the values stored in a CSV or variable have unwanted characters or need to be separated in order to be used for the rest of the script. Let's walk through a couple of scenarios that will better explain the usefulness of the technique.

For this example we have a script that is searching a text file for a chunk of text or a phrase. When this phrase is found, it is stored in such a way that the phrase itself is stuck with other information that is not needed, for example:

```
$Search = "Online Version http://technet.microsoft.com/EN-US/library/5573a9b9-bc97-4460-818a-b35fc3523eaa(EXCHG.160).aspx"
```

If we want to display just the URL for the TechNet, we need to find a way to split out the other information from the URL. Taking a look at the line, we see that the other data in the variable is separated by spaces. If we can split the value up by spaces and then select the last item, this will accomplish our task. We need to deploy different techniques to accomplish this task.

First we will split up the entire line using a delimiter of a space. This will result in several values stored in a variable for us to pick apart.

```
$Array = ($Search.Line).split(' ')
```

Once this is run, we can then see what the $Array variable has stored in order for us to pull apart the data:

```
PS C:\> $Array
Online
Version
http://technet.microsoft.com/EN-US/library/5573a9b9-bc97-4460-818a-b35fc3523eaa(EXCHG.160).aspx
```

Notice that we created some blank lines that precede our expected URL line. Now that we have the data separated into separate values, we need to be able to select the last value. For an array (the way our current data is stored), we simply need to get a count of the objects in the array and then call just the last object -which is equal to the total number of objects in the array minus 1 as arrays start on a zero value, not one.

```
$Count = $Array.Count - 1
```

** Note ** the '.Count' after $Array, is a property of the $Array which relates to how many items are in $Array

Then we can feed that value into the array and store the URL into a variable called $URL:

```
$URL = $Array[$Count]
```

** **Note** ** To pull the last value in an array, we can use an index number if '-1' like so: $Array[-1]

If we then type in $URL, we'll see that we indeed have captured only the URL:

```
PS C:\> $Count = $Array.count - 1
PS C:\> $URL = $Array[$Count]
PS C:\> $URL
http://technet.microsoft.com/EN-US/library/5573a9b9-bc97-4460-818a-b35fc3523eaa(EXCHG.160).aspx
```

Scenario #2

Using the same 'Split' cmdlet in PowerShell, let's explore another real scenario. Translating an acquisition's employees display names into aliases in Active Directory, this could be used for adding users to AD, sync to Azure AD and then references in the Security and Compliance Center. In this scenario we know that Active Directory aliases are a combination of first and last names.

Alias	First Name	Last Name
JohnSmith	John	Smith
MichaelLarraday	Michael	Larraday

In some cases some of the names use the middle initials in their name. We would have something like this:

```
John M. Smith
Michael G Larraday
```

Notice that John has a middle initial with a period and Michael does not. We need to be able to account for both types of middle initials. First, let's split the name up into its three parts:

$Name = $SourceName.Split(' ')

The variable $name would look something like this for each name:

$Name = John, M., Smith
$Name = Michael, G, Larraday

Remember the data is stored like this:

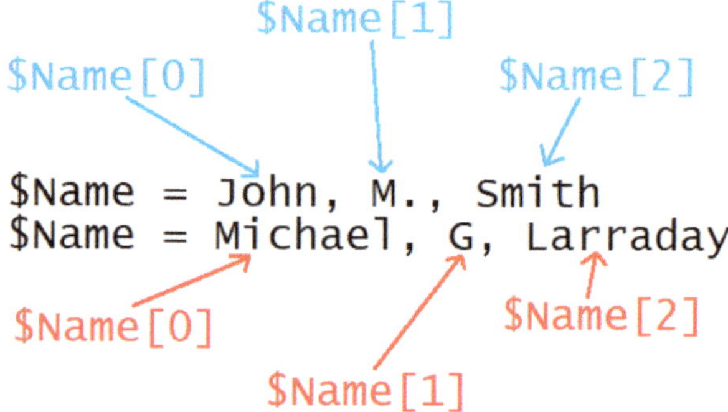

In order to get the alias, we need to add the last name to the first name and store it in the $alias variable.

$Alias = $Name[0]+$Name[2]

This effectively ignores the middle initial which would be $name[1]:

$Alias = JohnSmith
$Alias = MichaelLarraday

Possible Complication

Like a lot of technology used in production, nothing is ever that simple. There is always some wrench thrown into the mix. In the second scenario we assume that the user will have a middle name and we will have to ignore that to create the alias. What if the user has no middle name listed in the source? What would happen?

Bob Delol

If we parsed it, we would get $Name[0] = "Bob" and $Name[1] = "Delol". There would be no $Name[2]. Now we follow the same formula before:

$Alias = $Name[0]+$Name[2]

Our results would be less than ideal:

$Alias = "Bob"

To resolve this we would need some sort of logic to handle that:

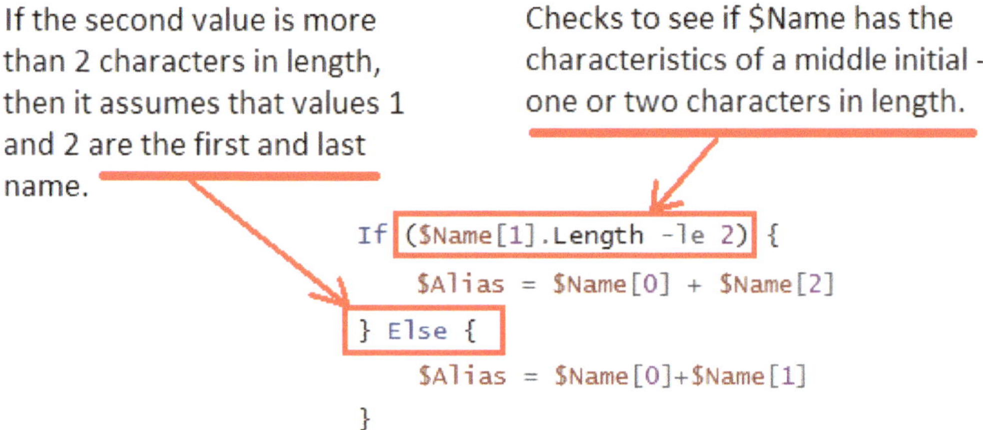


```
If ($Name[1].Length -le 2) {
    $Alias = $Name[0] + $Name[2]
} Else {
    $Alias = $Name[0]+$Name[1]
}
```

So Bob Smith would end up as "BobSmith". The rest would have their middle initial ignore as well and put together. The point of this exercise is that in real life scenarios, sometimes adjustments need to be made in order to get the results required.

Scripting in Color

Why is color important in PowerShell?

Normally, while using PowerShell, we see black and white or blue and white. PowerShell provides extra colors in its output for a more visual indication of the type of information presented on the console:

Examples

- Report failures in red
- Reporting success in blue or white
- Warnings reporting in yellow
- Make different code sections
- Menus can be color coded

Color Coding Examples

Reporting that a test failed: (This sample code verifies that a certain Data Loss Prevention (DLP) Sensitive Information Type Rule Package is created):

```
$FileTypes = (Get-ChildItem C:\temp\scc\xml\* -Include *.xml).Name

Foreach ($FileType in $FileTypes) {
  $Name = $FileType.Name
  Try {
     $Newdlp = New-DlpSensitiveInformationTypeRulePackage -FileData (Get-Content -Path "C:\temp\scc\xml\$Name" -Encoding Byte) -ErrorAction STOP
```

```
    } Catch {
        Write-host "The new DLP Sensitive Information Type Rule Package was " -ForegroundColor White
-NoNewline
        Write-Host "not created!" -ForegroundColor Red
    }
}
```

```
The new DLP Sensitive Information Type Rule Package was not created!
```

Notice the contrast of the red with the white in the results of the commands. Also note that -NoNewLine was used as well to compress the result to one line in the output. The '-NoNewLine' option allows for us to consolidate many lines of 'Write-Host' into one. If we were to remove this switch from the above code and use this code sample:

```
Write-host "The new DLP Sensitive Information Type Rule Package was " -ForegroundColor White
Write-Host "not created!" -ForegroundColor Red
```

The results would look vastly different:

```
The new DLP Sensitive Information Type Rule Package was
not created!
```

Use care with –NoNewLine because too many lines can cause the formatting to look just as bad.

Code Sample

```
$FileTypes = (Get-ChildItem C:\temp\scc\xml\* -Include *.xml).Name

Foreach ($FileType in $FileTypes) {
    $Name = $FileType
    Try {
        $Newdlp = New-DlpSensitiveInformationTypeRulePackage -FileData (Get-Content -Path "C:\temp\scc\
xml\$Name" -Encoding Byte) -ErrorAction STOP
    } Catch {
        Write-host "The new DLP Sensitive Information Type Rule Package was " -ForegroundColor White
-NoNewLine
        Write-Host "not created!" -ForegroundColor Red -NoNewLine
    }
}
```

Results:

```
PS C:\> .\DLPImport.ps1
The new DLP Sensitive Information Type Rule Package was not created!The new DLP Sensitive Information Type Rul
e Package was not created!The new DLP Sensitive Information Type Rule Package was not created!
```

As you can see, too many can cause the output to be unusable and it even carries over to the PowerShell prompt being dragged into the mess.   Another example is to create a colorful menu:

While the above code sample is a bit overboard, it illustrates the technique of coloring PowerShell output:

```
$ColorMenu = {
    Write-Host "*********************************************" -ForegroundColor Cyan
    Write-Host "* Export Security and Compliance Center Config *" -ForegroundColor Cyan
    Write-Host "*********************************************" -ForegroundColor Cyan
    Write-Host " "
```

```powershell
    Write-Host "** Document SCC Settings ** " -ForegroundColor White
    Write-Host " "
    Write-Host "    1) Document Labels" -ForegroundColor Yellow
    Write-Host "    2) Document Compliance Tags" -ForegroundColor Yellow
    Write-Host "    3) Document Compliance Case" -ForegroundColor Yellow
    Write-Host "    4) Document DLP Keyword Dictionary" -ForegroundColor Yellow
    Write-Host " "
    Write-Host "    10) Create New Labels" -ForegroundColor Magenta
    Write-Host "    11) Create New Compliance Tags" -ForegroundColor Magenta
    Write-Host "    12) Create Compliance Case" -ForegroundColor Magenta
    Write-Host "    13) Create DLP Keyword Dictionary" -ForegroundColor Magenta
    Write-Host " "
    Write-Host "    99) EXIT" -ForegroundColor Red
    Write-Host " "
    Write-Host "    Select an Option [1..99]?" -ForegroundColor Green
}
```

The key to making this work is the Invoke-Command used to display the $Menu variable as this colorful menu:

```powershell
Invoke-Command -ScriptBlock $ColorMenu
```

```
***************************************************
* Export Security and Compliance Center Config *
***************************************************

** Document SCC Settings **

    1) Document Labels
    2) Document Compliance Tags
    3) Document Compliance Case
    4) Document DLP Keyword Dictionary

** Document SCC Settings **

    10) Create New Labels
    11) Create New Compliance Tags
    12) Create Compliance Case
    13) Create DLP Keyword Dictionary

    99) EXIT

    Select an Option [1..99]?
```

The ScriptBlock parameter specifies that code stored in the $ColorMenu variable will execute, which is a colorful menu.

Lastly, an example of coloring would be HTML formatting. HTML color can be used, for example, in creating reports with cells of a particular mean. Red could be used to indicate an Error, yellow used to indicate a Warning and green to indicate Success. This would provide for a quick visual read of the data and allow for the recipient of the report to quickly determine what to concentrate efforts on or to troubleshoot as needed.

Miscellaneous

In this section we'll cover a variety of topics that are important to PowerShell in general and the Security and Compliance Center PowerShell specifically.

Quotes

Quotes are rather important when it comes to a PowerShell script. Missing quotes can throw off your script and cause it not to run. The wrong kind of quote can prevent a PowerShell script from functioning properly. The question is what quotes are good for what.

Quotes would seem to be an innocuous part of coding PowerShell. However, they are quite important. Microsoft has a set of rules to handle quotes and should be required reading for coding in PowerShell:

https://technet.microsoft.com/en-us/library/hh847740.aspx

Single Quote (')

The single quote is the default quote to use for most, if not all quotes in PowerShell. The single quote is a literal interpretation of whatever exists between them. For example, if we take the code sample below, using a Write-Host command to display the contents of a quote, the information is shown in a one to one fashion and all variables are ignored:

Example Code

```
$Score = 300
Write-Host 'My top score in bowling is $score.'
```

Results are:

```
My top score in bowling is $score.
```

As you can see, the variable was ignored with the single quote.

Double Quote (")

Double quotes will not allow a literal interpretation and will display values that are store in variables even when between the quotes.

Example Code

```
$Score = 300
Write-Host "My top score in bowling is $score."
```

Results are:

```
My top score in bowling is 300.
```

Notice the difference between the single and double quotes.

Quotes within Quotes (' " " ')

There are two ways to handle a set of quotes within quotes and prove to be quite useful in a script. One use, shown in the example below, would be to display a book title in a sentence. Without this option, the title of the book would not be displayed in double quotes:

Example 1

Write-Host 'The title of this book is "Practical PowerShell: Security Compliance and Center".'

Results are:

```
The title of this book is "Practical PowerShell: Security Compliance and Center".
```

Example 2

Write-Host "The title of this book is ""Practical PowerShell: Security Compliance and Center""."

Results are the same as can be seen here:

```
The title of this book is "Practical PowerShell: Security Compliance and Center".
```

Example 3

Write-Host 'The title of this book is 'Practical PowerShell: Security Compliance and Center'.'

Results:

```
The title of this book is  Practical PowerShell: Security Compliance and Center.
```

Notice the complete lack of quotes in the resulting output. So if quotes are needed, the quotes need to be correctly ordered.

As a rule of thumb, start with single quotes, unless a variable or a non-literal display of information is needed then use double quotes if needed. If a variable is in between quotes, use double quotes.

Code Signing

What is it?

When a PowerShell script is signed, the code block only validates if a script has not been modified by anyone other than the original author. Code signing does not validate that the script is functional or certified. The intention of code signing is solely to make sure that the code written by the author is not modified by another scripter and passed along as the author's work, or worse, malicious code may have been added.

Why Use It?

By default, PowerShell execution is restricted to Remote Signed scripts:

Remote Signed: Requires that all scripts and configuration files downloaded from the Internet be signed by a trusted publisher.

When a script is not digitally signed, the script will not run. If a script is signed, but cannot be validated, it cannot be run. Verification at this level is just one level of protection against running rogue PowerShell scripts. However, it should not be the only level of protection. Ideally, a Dev or QA environment should be used for PowerShell script testing to validate both the code signing and functionality of the script.

How to Use It

There are a few configuration options to use when configuring digital signing options in Windows PowerShell. The PowerShell cmdlet used to configure this is Set-ExecutionPolicy.

- **Restricted:** Does not load configuration files or run scripts. "Restricted" is the default execution policy.
- **AllSigned:** Requires that all scripts and configuration files be signed by a trusted publisher, including scripts that you write on the local computer.
- **RemoteSigned:** Requires that all scripts and configuration files downloaded from the Internet be signed by a trusted publisher.
- **Unrestricted**: Loads all configuration files and runs all scripts. If you run an unsigned script that was downloaded from the Internet, you are prompted for permission before it runs.
- **Bypass:** Nothing is blocked and there are no warnings or prompts.
- **Undefined:** Removes the currently assigned execution policy from the current scope. This parameter will not remove an execution policy that is set in a Group Policy scope.

In order to run a script that has not been digitally signed, you must set the Execution Policy for PowerShell scripts to Unrestricted:

```
Set-ExecutionPolicy –ExecutionPolicy Unrestricted
```

In some organizations, PowerShell is restricted and locked down to prevent unauthorized scripts from running. The Execution Policy for PowerShell would be set to 'Restricted' in this case. If an unsigned script with this execution policy set, you will receive an error like so:

```
PS C:\> .\prereq1.ps1
.\prereq1.4.ps1 : File C:\prereq1.ps1 cannot be loaded because running scripts is disabled on this system.
For more information, see about_Execution_Policies at http://go.microsoft.com/fwlink/?LinkID=135170.
At line:1 char:1
+ .\prereq1.4.ps1
+ ~~~~~~~~~~~~~~~
    + CategoryInfo          : SecurityError: (:) [], PSSecurityException
    + FullyQualifiedErrorId : UnauthorizedAccess
PS C:\>
```

The policy for PowerShell execution restrictions can be implemented with a GPO in the following GPO location:

```
Computer Configuration -- Policies -- Administrative Templates: Policy Definitions (ADMX) -- Windows
Components -- Windows PowerShell
```

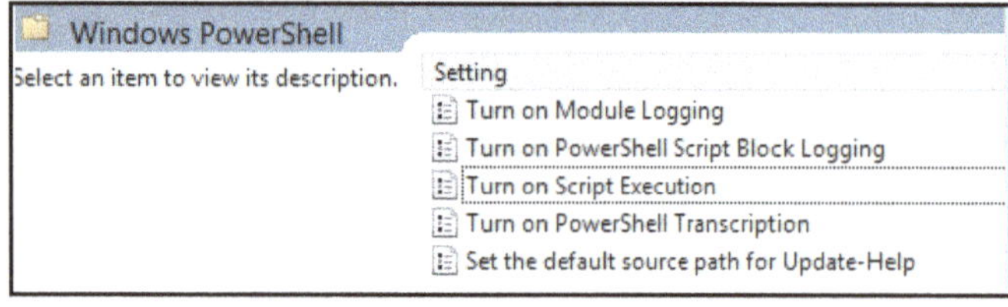

By default, this setting is not configured for the GPO:

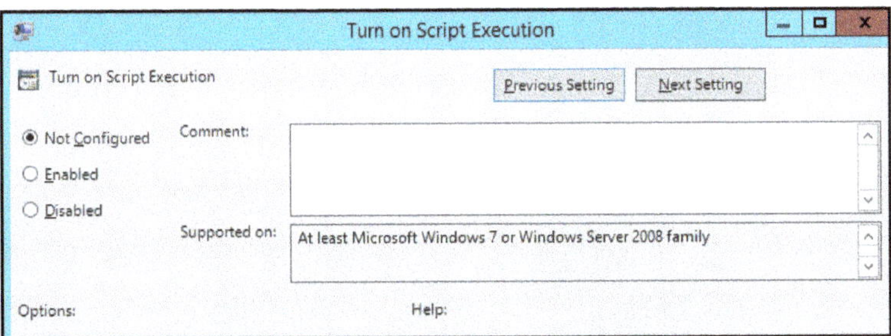

To restrict PowerShell code execution in the GPO, the setting needs to be enabled and a setting chosen.

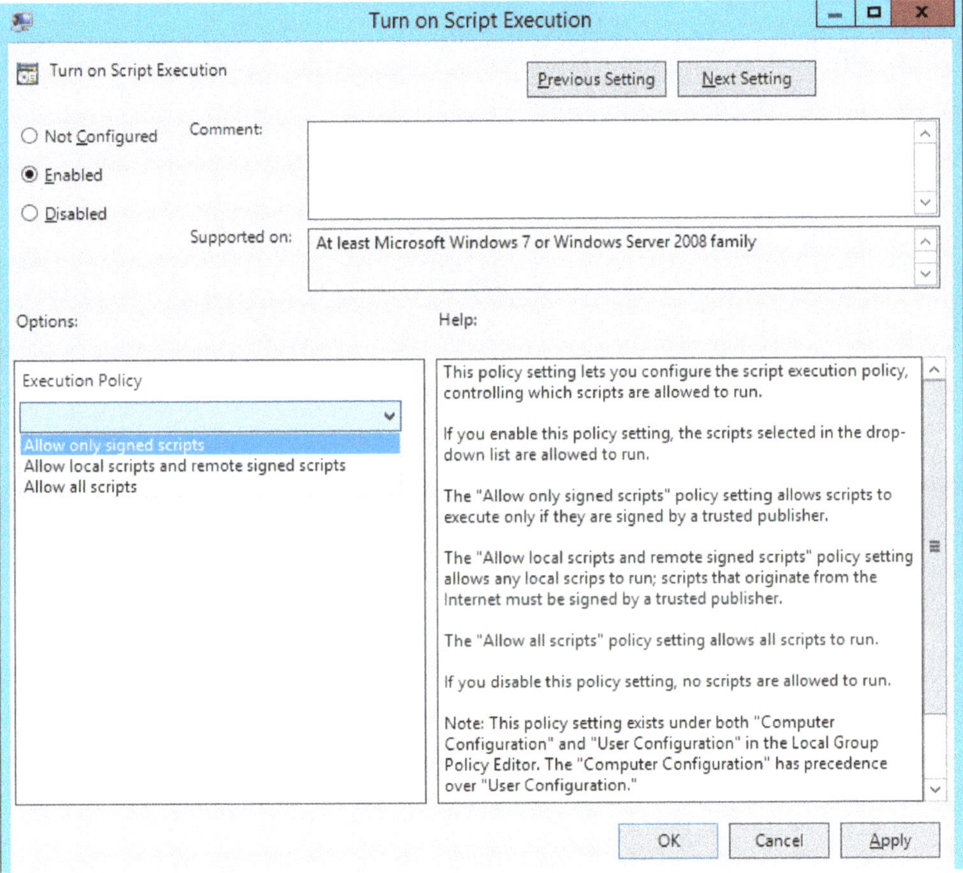

Signing Your Code

So how do you sign your scripts and what are the requirements?

Requirements – your script and a certificate to sign it with.

To sign it, the Set-AuthenticodeSignature cmdlet needs to be used. First acquire a signing certificate either from a third party or internally. Then bring up a PowerShell session in order to sign the script. One method, which was spelled out by the Scripting Guy! From Microsoft is to store the certificate in a variable and then run the Set-AuthenticodeSignature cmdlet to sign the script:

```
$Cert=(dir cert:currentuser\my\ -CodeSigningCert)
```

Set-AuthenticodeSignature .\MyScript.ps1 $Cert –TimeStampServer "http://timestamp.globalsign.com/scripts/timstamp.dll"

Using the TimeStampServer option is recommended which will prevent the script from failing if the certificate expires:

```
-TimestampServer <String>
    Uses the specified time stamp server to add a time stamp to the signature. Type the URL of the time stamp server
    as a string.

    The time stamp represents the exact time that the certificate was added to the file. A time stamp prevents the
    script from failing if the certificate expires because users and programs can verify that the certificate was
    valid at the time of signing.
```

What is added to the script once it is signed?

When a script is signed, a code block is added to the end of a PowerShell script.

```
AntispamCommon.ps1 - Notepad
File  Edit  Format  View  Help

filter topN
{
  param (
    $top = 10)

  if ($script:count -lt $top)
  {
    write-output ($_)
    $script:count = $script:count + 1
  }
}

# SIG # Begin signature block
# MIIavQYJKoZIhvcNAQcCoIIarjCCGqoCAQExCzAJBgUrDgMCGgUAMGkGCisGAQQB
# gjCCAQSgwZBZMDQGCisGAQQBgjCCAR4wJgIDAQAABBAfzDtgwUsITrckOsYpfvNR
# AgEAAgEAAgEAAgEAAgEAMCEwCQYFKw4DAhoFAAQUKOzFl7KMitsRe2naqD/c+ump
# KAmgghWCMIIEwzCCA6ugAwIBAgITMwAAAG9lLVhtBxFGKAAAAAAAbzANBgkqhkiG
# 9w0BAQUFADB3MQswCQYDVQQGEwJVUZETMBEGA1UECBMKV2FzaGluZ3RvbjEQMA4G
# A1UEBxMHUmVkbW9uZDEeMBwGA1UEChMVTWljcm9zb2Z0IENvcnBvcmF0aw9uMSEw
# HwYDVQQDExhNaWNyb3NvZnQqVGltZS1TdGFtcCBQQ0EwHhcNMTUwMzIwMTczMjAy

# BgNVBAoTFU1pY3Jvc29mdCBDb3Jwb3JhdGlvbjEhMB8GA1UEAxMYTWljcm9zb2Z0
# IFRpbWUtU3RhbXAgUENBAhMzAAAAb2UtWG0HEUYoAAAAAABvMAkGBSsOAwIaBQCg
# XTAYBgkqhkiG9w0BCQMxCwYJKoZIhvcNAQcBMBwGCSqGSIb3DQEJBTEPFw0xNTA3
# MTAwMDIZMTRaMCMGCSqGSIb3DQEJBDEWBBSO+72hib43aVD/cYMaY9DgkEixWjAN
# BgkqhkiG9w0BAQUFAASCAQCneZqiNluOlBo1S419v5kkIU0l5XBCt3jkQashnmTs
# xBFuShKfl60kq1QqzNP5k94rPX2hKFP9c7NVWB/1rXp+g4ExvCH0FhgK8/S8C5NI
# CE4Q1fgVlo4BstrUAcyvdfPerHrxeTVRfZEh1B3SCZixObTYirwJ76kzLI7P5HkZ
# 63peq8yZE+hd3c2FEYMuknrYFezosmvlnDKi8XFdwf/xlX3cbLEkviNXzItprsP1
# Z5DIJONQRkCqckzxTOnhIKJ8vQQqsLPbCCzdRDZcQ8UzFANunXFuGGWPQpn3bqj2
# beNm5c1+6i1kXwS6AJ591RmwtlikLFLtlnD2P6KjpbkI
# SIG # End signature block
```

Notice that the code signature is commented out to prevent any execution issues within the script.

For internal only scripts, a self-signed certificate can be sufficient. If the script is going to be used outside of your environment, a third party certificate must be used. The key is to use the correct kind of certificate – Class III or code-signing certificate – to generate the signature block.

    ** **Note** ** Remember that you will need to purchase a certificate in order to sign a script. There are various third-part Certificate Authorities to purchase certificates from.

<table><tr><td>3</td><td># Connecting With PowerShell</td></tr></table>

In this Chapter

Introduction
Connecting to the Security and Compliance Center
- Security and Compliance Center PowerShell Cmdlets
Multi-Factor Authentication (MFA)
Closing and Removing Connections
- Revealing PowerShell Sessions
- Removing PowerShell Sessions

Introduction

The Security and Compliance Center (https://protection.office.com) has two management interfaces that we can use to manage settings, objects and more. We have PowerShell and the Admin Center in Office 365. Each has its merits as well as items that can only be configured in them. As such, you should be familiar with both of these when administrating the Security and Compliance Center for your tenant. For the purposes of this book, we will concentrate most of our time and energy on the PowerShell interface when logged in as an Administrator. But for illustrative purposes, we should also briefly review the web interface for the Security and Compliance Center:

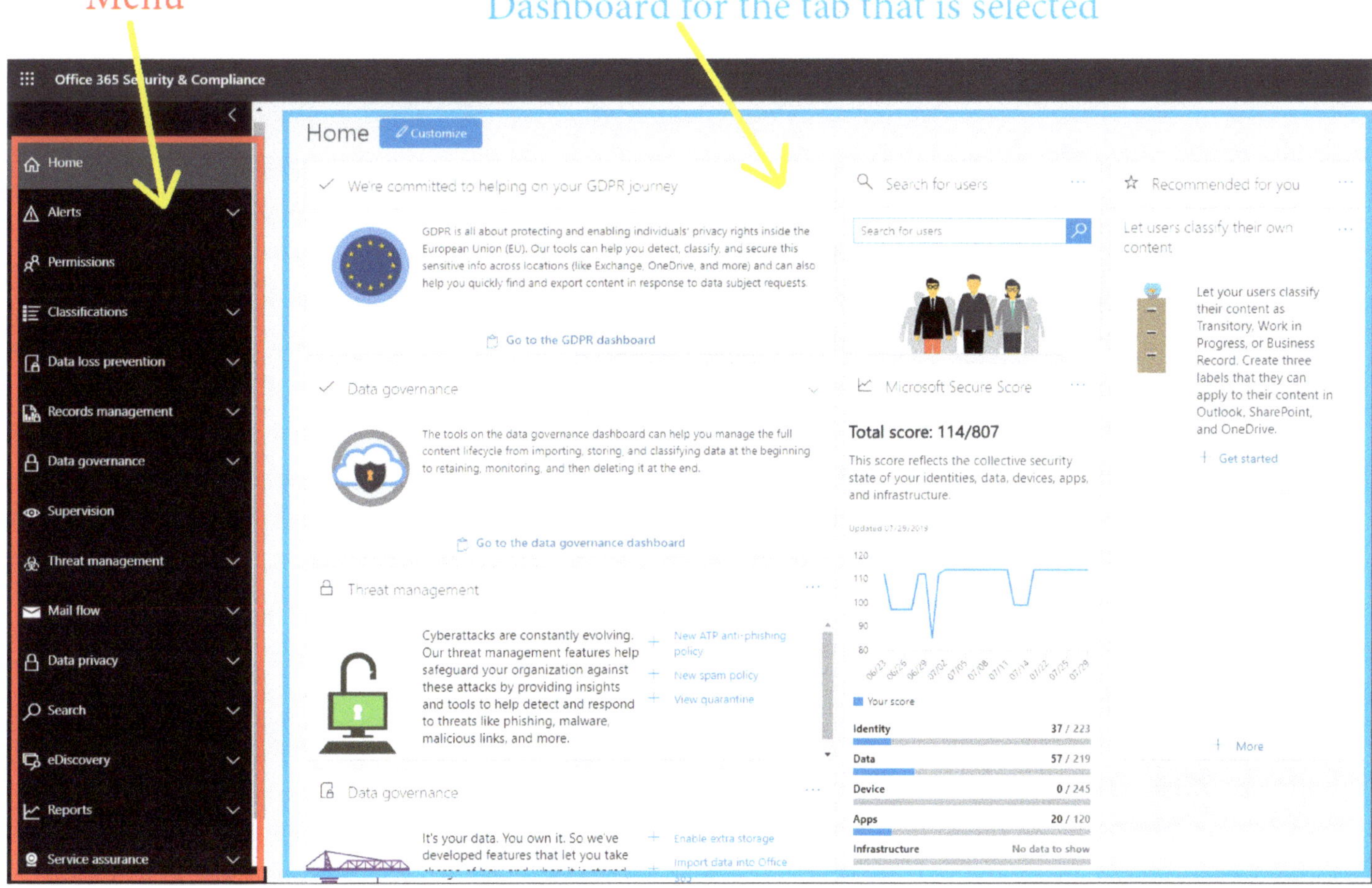

When working in the SCC, the menu should be your guide as to where to go for configuring items:

Alerts: Managing alerts in the SCC - view, create and manage alerting
Permissions: Grant, remove and view permissions for users in your tenant, with respect to the SCC
Classifications: Manage Labels, Label Policies and Sensitive Information types
Data Loss Prevention: Manage DLP policies, App permissions and Device Management settings
Records Management: Manage the new File Plan feature in the SCC
Supervision: Manage Supervision settings for mail flow
Threat Management: Manage threats to your tenant, perform attacks, review quarantines and more
Mail Flow: Provides insight into mail flowing into your tenant and perform message traces
Data Privacy: Contains the GDPR dashboard and allows you to manage data privacy requests
Search: Search content in your tenant, search audit logs and perform app discovery
eDiscovery: Perform eDiscovery and Advanced eDiscovery tasks in your tenant
Reports: Manage reports, download reports and schedule reports
Service Assurance: Microsoft's assurance on how they run their service for you, their customer

Now that we've reviewed the web interface for the SCC, let's dive into utilizing PowerShell to connect and manage the SCC.

** **Note** ** The menu displayed is dependent on licensing (E3/E5) and role assigned.\

Connecting to the Security and Compliance Center

To connect to PowerShell for the Security and Compliance Center, we need to open up a regular Windows Power-Shell window. Once we have that window, we can first enter credentials and store them in a variable to be used by the session that we will open to our tenant. We can do that like so:

```
$LiveCred = Get-Credential
```

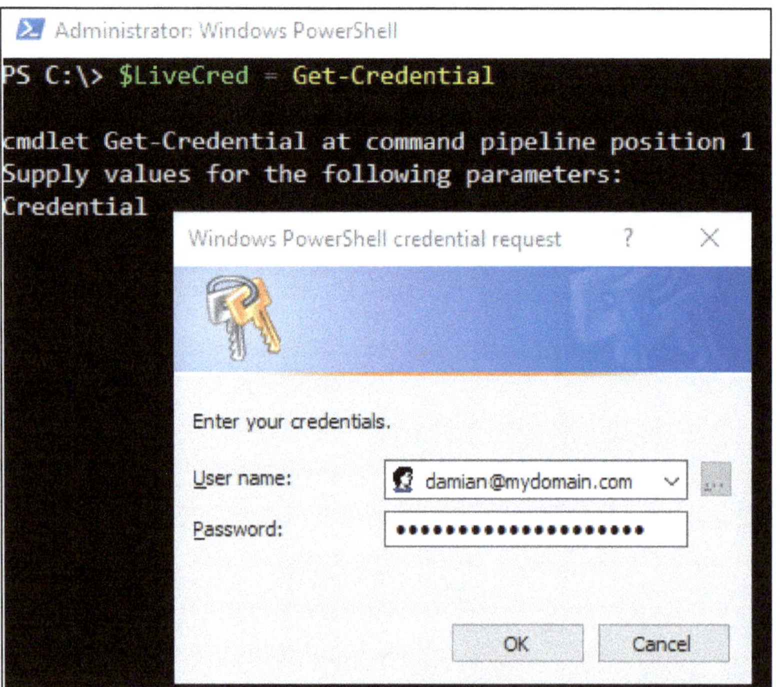

Now that we've entered our credentials we need to create a session with those credentials and the SCC Endpoint:

```
$Session = New-PSSession -ConfigurationName Microsoft.Exchange -ConnectionUri https://ps.
compliance.protection.outlook.com/powershell-liveid/ -Credential $LiveCred -Authentication Basic
-AllowRedirection
```

```
PS C:\> $Session = New-PSSession -ConfigurationName Microsoft.Exchange -ConnectionUri https://ps.compliance.protection.o
utlook.com/powershell-liveid/ -Credential $LiveCred -Authentication Basic -AllowRedirection
WARNING: Your connection has been redirected to the following URI:
"https://nam05b.ps.compliance.protection.outlook.com/powershell-liveid?PSVersion=5.1.17763.592 "
```

Notice two items in the above one-liner:

Authentication: Basic - This is not a typo, nor is it a security concern. The overall connection is made over a secure **HTTPS link** - see the ConnectionURI value. Thus the connection is secure and the password can be sent clear text (basic authentication) between your computer and Office 365.

Redirection - This allows the connection to be redirected to the current endpoint servicing the SCC.

Once we have the session criteria in place, we can establish the connection with the below one-liner:

```
Import-PSSession $Session
```

```
PS C:\> Import-PSSession $Session
WARNING: The names of some imported commands from the module 'tmp_zknhpvnj.hoc' include unapproved verbs that might
make them less discoverable. To find the commands with unapproved verbs, run the Import-Module command again with the
Verbose parameter. For a list of approved verbs, type Get-Verb.

ModuleType Version    Name                            ExportedCommands
---------- -------    ----                            ----------------
Script     1.0        tmp_zknhpvnj.hoc                {Add-ComplianceCaseMember, Add-eDiscoveryCaseAdmin, Add-Ro...
```

Security and Compliance Center PowerShell Cmdlets

Now that a connection has been established, we need to figure out what cmdlets are available in the tenant. In a PowerShell session for an on-premises server, a group of cmdlets can be filtered based off the server name. For an Office 365 tenant, there is no 'server' to filter for. However, there is a name revealed after the Import-PSSession is established, in this example 'tmp_zknhpvnj.hoc', that can be used to filter cmdlets available. This Name string will change with every new PowerShell session to the Security and Compliance Center:

```
ModuleType Version    Name                            ExportedCommands
---------- -------    ----                            ----------------
Script     1.0        tmp_zknhpvnj.hoc                {Add-ComplianceCaseMember, Add-eDiscoveryCaseAdmin, Add-Ro...
```

Cmdlets can now be found with either of these two one-liners:

```
Get-Command -Module 'tmp_zknhpvnj.hoc'
Get-Command | Where {$_.Source -eq 'tmp_zknhpvnj.hoc'}
```

```
PS C:\> Get-Command | Where {$_.Source -eq 'tmp_zknhpvnj.hoc'}
CommandType     Name                                               Version     Source
-----------     ----                                               -------     ------
Function        Add-ComplianceCaseMember                           1.0         tmp_zknhpvnj.hoc
Function        Add-eDiscoveryCaseAdmin                            1.0         tmp_zknhpvnj.hoc
Function        Add-RoleGroupMember                                1.0         tmp_zknhpvnj.hoc
Function        Enable-ComplianceTagStorage                        1.0         tmp_zknhpvnj.hoc
Function        Execute-UnifiedPolicyCmdletBatch                   1.0         tmp_zknhpvnj.hoc
Function        Export-FilePlanProperty                            1.0         tmp_zknhpvnj.hoc
```

Multi-Factor Authentication (MFA)

Multi-Factor Authentication (MFA) is an additional layer of security that can be provided for your PowerShell sessions. Most if not all workloads for Office 365 now have an option to deploy this for anyone connecting via PowerShell. It is highly recommended and a Microsoft Best Practice to enforce MFA for PowerShell connections to any workload. For this book we will look at how we can make a MFA connection to the Security and Compliance Center.

    ** **Note** ** It's highly recommended that Administrators use MFA as it prevents 99.5% of attacks.

Now, establishing a connection to the SCC via PowerShell and MFA takes a few steps. First, we need to connect to either an Exchange Servers Admin Center page (EAC) or to Exchange Online, both through a browser. Once connected, proceed to the Hybrid tab and click on the Configure button for Exchange Online PowerShell:

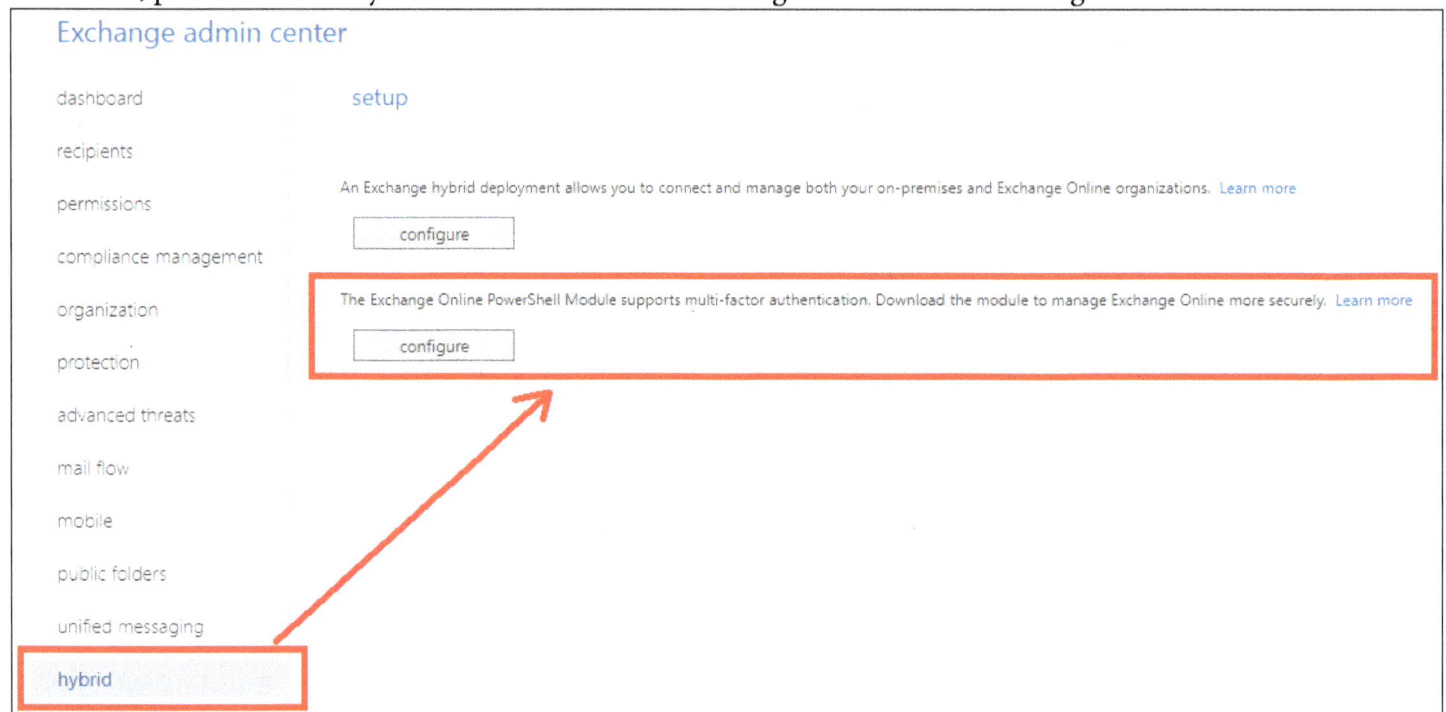

Clicking on this option will initiate a download of the MFA module. Make sure your security settings on your browser allow for this download. Click 'Install' and wait for the module install to complete:

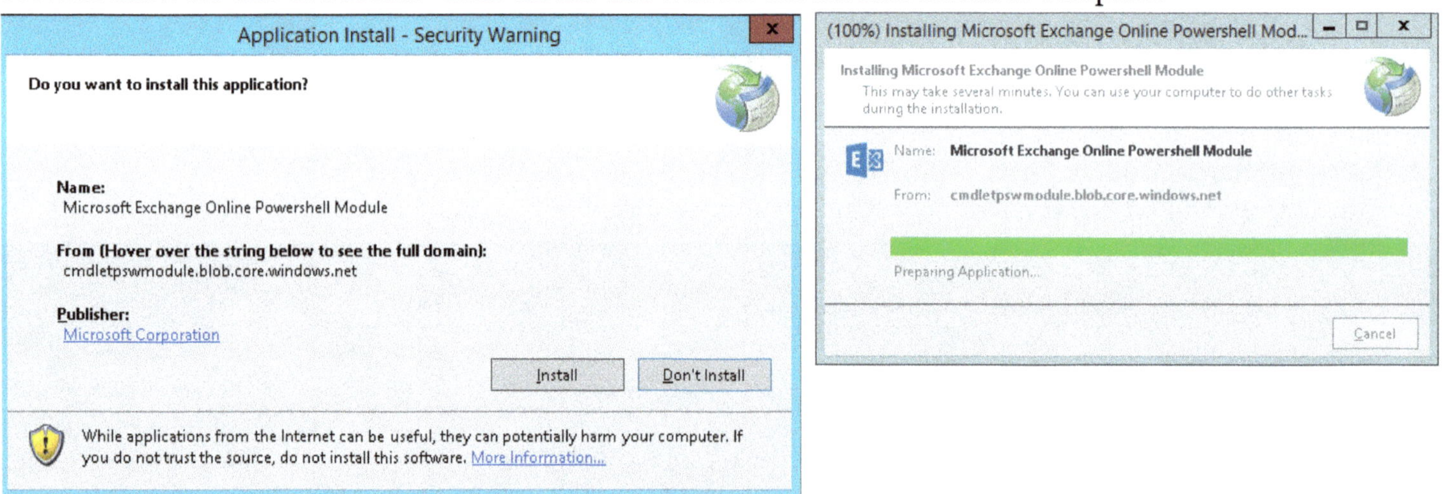

    ** **Note** ** This is supported in Edge/IE as the default browser.

Once the module is done downloading and installing we now have a new PowerShell console. Note that this can be used for the Security and Compliance Center as well as Exchange Online:

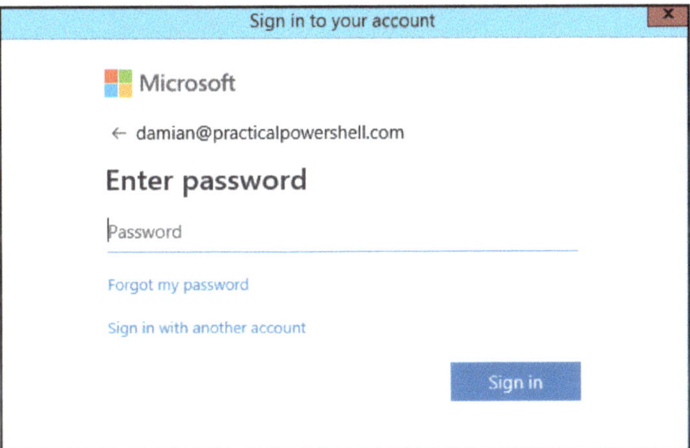

We can now open a MFA session using this one-liner:

Connect-IPPSSession -UserPrincipalName damian@practicalpowershell.com

This brings up an authentication prompt:

After authenticating, we now have an open PowerShell session to the Security and Compliance Center:

** **Note** ** You experience may vary, depending on browser, Azure AD Join and other configurations outside the scope of this book.

Closing and Removing Connections

Over time, PowerShell sessions tend to break or stop working. Broken connections can cause issues in scripts and with general work when connected to Office 365. Office 365 also has a limit on the number of connections per user. All of these factors lead to one place - we should close unused connections. The process is relatively straight forward.

Revealing PowerShell Sessions

First, let's take a look at how we can see what connections we have open and depending on your session(s), you may have one or more session connected to one or more endpoints in Office 365. What PowerShell cmdlets are available to us:

```
Get-Command *-PSSession
```

This provides us with quite a few cmdlets:

```
Connect-PSSession
Disconnect-PSSession
Enter-PSSession
Exit-PSSession
Export-PSSession
Get-PSSession
Import-PSSession
New-PSSession
Receive-PSSession
Remove-PSSession
```

To reveal current sessions on the local machine, we will use 'Get-PSSession' which seems to be the obvious choice:

```
PS C:\> Get-PSSession

 Id Name          ComputerName    ComputerType    State      ConfigurationName      Availability
 -- ----          ------------    ------------    -----      -----------------      ------------
  2 WinRM2         nam05b.ps.co... RemoteMachine   Opened     Microsoft.Exchange        Available
```

If we have multiple sessions, we can see the different endpoints, which is shows as 'ComputerName':

```
PS C:\> Get-PSSession | ft -auto

 Id Name   ComputerName                                   ComputerType  State  ConfigurationName  Availability
 -- ----   ------------                                   ------------  -----  -----------------  ------------
  2 WinRM2 nam05b.ps.compliance.protection.outlook.com    RemoteMachine Opened Microsoft.Exchange    Available
  3 WinRM3 outlook.office365.com                          RemoteMachine Opened Microsoft.Exchange    Available
```

If we look at a detailed view of the connections we can also see the two connections use what appears to be different versions of WinRM. Most other settings are the same:

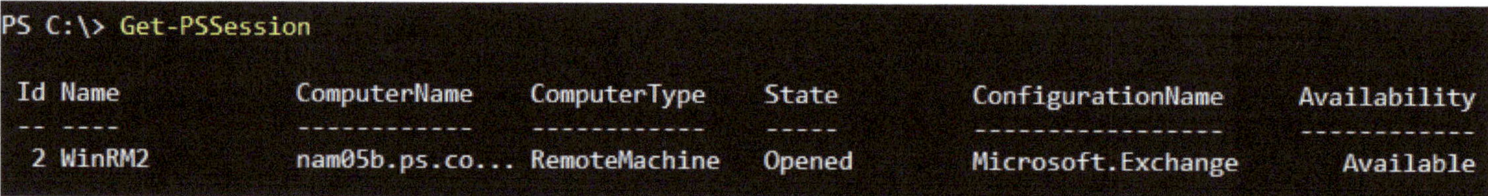

Removing PowerShell Sessions

Okay. So we see we have multiple sessions, how do we close one or the other session, or even both sessions? We use the Remove-PSSession cmdlet:

Examples from the Remove-PSSession cmdlet:

```
Example 1: Remove sessions by using IDs

PS C:\>Remove-PSSession -Id 1, 2

This command removes the PSSessions that have IDs 1 and 2.
Example 2: Remove all the sessions in the current session

PS C:\>Get-PSSession | Remove-PSSession

- or -

PS C:\> Remove-PSSession -Session (Get-PSSession)

- or -

PS C:\> $s = Get-PSSession
PS C:\> Remove-PSSession -Session $s
```

So, for removing one session, we can use the ID, which in our case is either 2 or 3.

```
Remove-PSSession -Id 2
```

Or

```
Remove-PSSession -Id 3
```

If we want to remove all sessions, the easiest way is:

```
Get-PSSession | Remove-PSSession
```

None of these one-liners elicits any response and simply removes the specified session.

Expired Session

PowerShell sessions do expire over time, either due to timeouts on the connected resource or due to issues in the session (bug, network, etc.). It is possible for a session to Office 365 to time out. Make sure to remove the session and then restart a new session.

4   # Identity Management

In this Chapter

Introduction
Directory Synchronization
Preparing Your AD - IdFix
Install of Azure AD Connect
PowerShell and Directory Synchronization
What Needs to be Performed Where?
Licensing
Azure AD Recycle Bin

Introduction

When investing in a cloud provider like Office 365, identity management becomes a clearly important component. For this book we will cover identity management with respect to Office 365 (Azure Active Directory), Active Directory and PowerShell. There are a few ways to handle identities in Office 365 – separate directories, hybrid and cloud only directory. Each of these has its advantages and disadvantages and these should be considered before engaging in any cloud services with Office 365.

- **Separate Directories** – Internal Active Directory and Azure Active Directory are completely separate. In this environment a user maintains two different identities and possibly two different passwords.
- **Hybrid** – Internal Active Directory users and group objects are synced to Azure Active Directory. Users have one identity and possibly a shared password.
- **Cloud Only** – No on-premises Active Directory. Company is using only cloud identities for their application authentication.
- ** **Note** ** Okta, Ping and other products can also provide the same functionality.

For this chapter and the majority of the book, we will work with hybrid environments as this arrangement is the most commonly used. This does not mean that the concepts in this book won't translate to the other two scenarios, but there will be different ways to handle examples and scripts in this book for those scenarios. With a hybrid environment, a company can have on-premises services and services while maintaining cloud services and share a single identity source. This is certainly the biggest strength of a hybrid environment. As such its configuration should be planned and setup. The two major considerations are components that Microsoft supplies for identity management:

- **Active Directory Federation Services (ADFS)** – Can provide a login portal for Office 365 services. Allows for proxied authentication to an on-premises Active Directory. Can also be leveraged for additional application authentication beyond Office 365 as well as complicated claims rules for additional login and resource access control.
- **Directory Synchronization** – Synchronizes objects from an on-premises Active Directory to Azure Active Directory (Office 365). Can provide additional functionality, including password synchronization, password write-back, Exchange Hybrid and more. The product has also changed names many times over the years.

While ADFS can be beneficial to a company using Office 365 services we will not be discussing it for this book. Instead we will turn to directory synchronization and PowerShell when used for identity management in Office 365.

Directory Synchronization (DirSync)

What is it?

Dirsync is the synchronization of on-premises Active Directory objects to Azure Active Directory and thus Office 365. It essentially mirrors your AD in the cloud and keeps it constantly updated. The synchronized objects in O365 can now for instance be users and groups. You choose the objects you want to synchronize. In some cases information or even objects can be synced from the cloud to on-premises, depending on what options are chosen for the Azure AD Connect configuration. Objects anchored in AD, should be managed in AD. There are protections in place that block changes to these objects in Azure AD. A good, technical deep dive can be found here:

https://dirteam.com/dave/2015/03/30/azure-active-directory-synchronization-an-introduction-part-1/

Commonly deployed with Office 365 services, directory synchronization now provides enterprises with a compelling set of features and functionality that precludes the use of ADFS. Additionally with the new Conditional Access feature, the case for using ADFS solely for Office 365 is even less compelling. However, it should be known that the feature set is continually changing over time. Microsoft provides this synchronization product that has changed from relying on ADFS to supplanting it for most configuration of Office 365.

History

Here is a brief history of the directory synchronization product and its changes over the years:

Current revision history of Directory Synchronization
https://docs.microsoft.com/en-us/azure/active-directory/connect/active-directory-aadconnect-version-history#115610

Directory Sync – First sync client for connecting your on-premises AD to BPOS. BPOS was replaced by Office 365 and DirSync continually added features with each revision. DirSync also initially started out as a 32-bit program and shifted to 64-bit prior to its replacement came into being. This product is currently out of support as of April of 2017.

Azure AD Synchronization – This was the first major revision of the directory synchronization product by Microsoft. The last version of this product was 1.0.494.0501 released in May of 2015. Its initial release was 1.0.419.0911 released in September of 2014. With such a short time line, the product did however, add some features along the way – password sync with multiple Active Directories to Office 365, OAuth2 support and password sync. This product is currently out of support as of April of 2017.

Azure AD Connect – This is the latest iteration of the directory synchronization product. According to Microsoft, this is a product rename of the product. This renamed directory synchronization product added quite a lot of new features with its release. The current revision, at the time of the writing of this book was 1.3.21.0 (August 1, 2019). The initial release was version 1.0.8641.0 and this was released in June of 2015. Additional features provided by the product – Express installation option, configuring ADFS, Upgrade from DirSync, staging mode, reduced sync interval from three hours to 30 min, Domain and OU filtering, scheduling of sync, PowerShell enhancements and much more. Potential authentication methods include Pass-Through Authentication (PTA) and Password Hash Synch (PHS)

As we can see, the directory synchronization product has changed greatly over the years.

Preparing Your AD - IdFix

For Hybrid environments with an on-premises Active Directory and Azure AD, one of the key component of a user's identity are the User Principal Names (UPNs) for all users. The UPN is important for accessing resources in a Hybrid environment. Microsoft recommends that the UPN and the Primary SMTP address match (and SIP for those who use Skype/Microsoft Teams). This recommendation is so that the end user does not experience pop-ups and is able to connect to resources without issue.

Prior to enabling directory synchronization Microsoft recommends running a tool called IdFix. This utility will analyze the various attributes in Active Directory and determine if there are any potential issues with connecting to an Office 365 tenant. The tool can be downloaded from here as of the writing of this book:

https://www.microsoft.com/en-us/download/details.aspx?id=36832

Any errors that are found by this tool should be remediated prior to a directory sync tool being installed and syncing data to Office 365 – Azure AD Connect for example. Once the tool is downloaded, it can be run just by double-clicking on the executable:

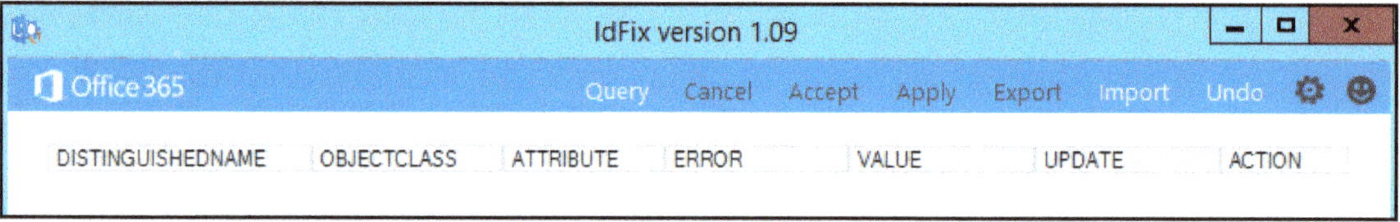

Click Query to see if there are any issues that need to be resolved:

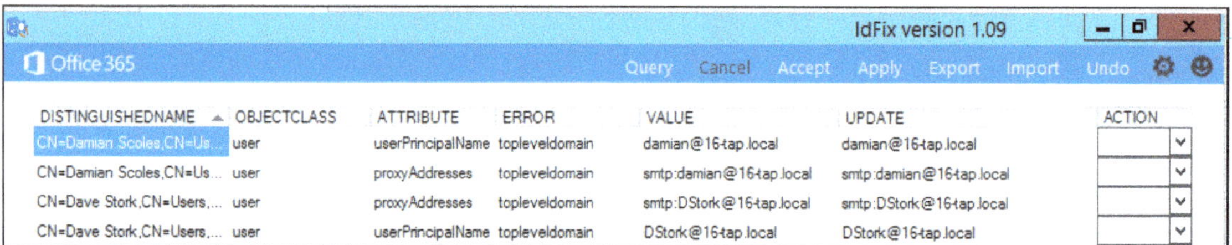

Although IdFix can fix a lot of things by itself, for this example we will export these results as a CSV. Simply click 'Export' and select a location to export the results to a CSV file. Since IdFix can export the results in a CSV format, the CSV file can be used with PowerShell later. The CSV file can be used as a data source for correcting user issues with PowerShell.

> ** **Note** ** The CSV used here is for educational purposes and production environments mat encounter more complex issues.

Let's take the IdFix CSV file and use it to correct any user objects with an invalid User Principal Name. The script needs to read in the CSV file, run a loop to process all the entries and correct only those invalid entries matching that criteria. The CSV file contains the following fields:

```
IDFix.csv - Notepad
File  Edit  Format  View  Help
DISTINGUISHEDNAME,OBJECTCLASS,ATTRIBUTE,ERROR,VALUE,UPDATE,ACTION
"CN=ADRMS,CN=Users,DC=16-TAP,DC=Local",user,userPrincipalName,topleveldomain,adrms@16-TAP.Local,adrms@16-TAP.Local,
"CN=Damian Scoles,CN=Users,DC=16-TAP,DC=Local",user,userPrincipalName,topleveldomain,damian@16-tap.Local,damian@16-TAP.Local
"CN=Damian Scoles,CN=Users,DC=16-TAP,DC=Local",user,proxyAddresses,topleveldomain,SMTP:damian@16-tap.local,SMTP:damian@16-ta
"CN=Damian Scoles,CN=Users,DC=16-TAP,DC=Local",user,mail,topleveldomain,damian@16-tap.local,damian@16-tap.local,
"CN=Dave Stork,CN=Users,DC=16-TAP,DC=Local",user,proxyAddresses,topleveldomain,SMTP:DStork@16-tap.local,SMTP:DStork@16-tap.1
"CN=Dave Stork,CN=Users,DC=16-TAP,DC=Local",user,userPrincipalName,topleveldomain,dstork@16-TAP.Local,dstork@16-TAP.Local,
"CN=Dave Stork,CN=Users,DC=16-TAP,DC=Local",user,mail,topleveldomain,DStork@16-tap.local,DStork@16-tap.local,
```

DISTINGUISHEDNAME VALUE	OBJECTCLASS UPDATE	ATTRIBUTE ACTION	ERROR

For the below example, the UserPrincipalName (UPN) needs to be updated to match the primary SMTP address. One thing to remember is that while most organizations may use the SAMAccountName for authentication in Active Directory as well as for applications, some applications will rely on the UPN so care needs to be taken:

Example Script – Fix UserPrincipalName

This code section will start an error log file and populate header information of the file:

```
# Get date for the file name
$Date = Get-Date -Format "MM.dd.yyyy-hh.mm-tt"
# Create a file for errors
$ErrorFileName = "C:\Downloads\IdFix\$date-Errors.txt"
$ScriptErrors = "This is the error file for problems creating or modifying users on $date.`r
`n-------------------------------------------------------------------- `r`n" | Out-File -FilePath $ErrorFileName
```

The CSV file is imported for the loop below:

```
# Import the CSV File
$Csv = Import-Csv "c:\downloads\IdFix\IdFix.csv"
Foreach ($Line in $Csv) {
```

First, only lines with the ObjectClass of 'User' to proceed:

```
If ($Line.ObjectClass-eq "User") {
```

Then, examining the same line, the script looks for an 'Attribute' value of UserPrincipalName and allows it to proceed:

```
If ($Line.Attribute -eq "UserPrincipalName") {
```

This section verifies the identity of the user, so that the correct mailbox can be modified:

```
$User = $Line.DistinguishedName
Try {
    $Address = (Get-Mailbox $user -ErrorAction STOP).PrimarySmtpAddress
} Catch {
    $ScriptErrors = "User $User mailbox was not found." | Out-File -FilePath $ErrorFileName
}
```

Sets the Primary SMTP address to be applied to the user to correct the error:

```
$PrimarySMTPAddress = $Address.Address
```

This code section sets the user properties correctly to fix the issues found in the IdFix report:

```
Try {
    Set-ADUser -Identity $User -UserPrincipalName $PrimarySmtpAddress
} Catch {
    $ScriptErrors = "Unable to change the UPN for the user $user" | Out-File -FilePath $ErrorFileName
}
```

Post script run, an IdFix query is run again:

DISTINGUISHEDNAME ▲	OBJECTCLASS	ATTRIBUTE	ERROR	VALUE	UPDATE
CN=Damian Scoles,CN=Us...	user	proxyAddresses	topleveldomain	smtp:damian@16-tap.local	smtp:damian@16-tap.local
CN=Dave Stork,CN=Users,...	user	proxyAddresses	topleveldomain	smtp:DStork@16-tap.local	smtp:DStork@16-tap.local

For the next error on the list, there is an issue with one of the defined proxy addresses that are on all accounts in Active Directory. To change this, the default address policy may need to be removed and then the offending proxy address can be removed.

Example Script – Remove Bad SMTP Addresses

The purpose of the script is to query only users that have ProxyAddress issues (as found in the CSV file from IdFix). After those values are filtered, the script will attempt to remove the offending SMTP address from the ProxyAddresses on a user account. Any errors encountered will be appended to a log file for later review. The script code is below.

In the first section, the current date is stored in the value with a particular format in the $Date variable:

```
$Date = Get-Date -Format "MM.dd.yyyy-hh.mm-tt"
```

A logging file gets created, with a unique name and is populated with a header for reference:

```
$ErrorFileName = "C:\Downloads\IdFix\$date-ProxyErrors.txt"
$ScriptErrors = "This is the error file for problems creating or modifying users on $Date.`r
`n-------------------------------------------------------------- `r`n" | Out-File -FilePath $ErrorFileName
```

Then the IdFix CSV file is imported into the $CSV variable:

```
# Import the CSV File
$Csv = Import-Csv "c:\downloads\IdFix\IdFix.csv"
```

This loop has some complicated steps and each will be reviewed and split for clarity. First the $CSV file is used for a Foreach loop, with each line in the CSV loaded into the $Line variable:

```
Foreach ($Line in $Csv) {
```

Since the script is for user objects only, the first IF…THEN loop is started to filter for only user objects:

```
If ($Line.OBJECTCLASS -eq "User") {
```

Since the script then looks for the ProxyAddresses issues, another IF…THEN loop is started to filter for this:

```
If ($Line.Attribute -eq "ProxyAddresses") {
```

Variables are set for the loop, two are pulled from the $CSV and one is $Null for each loop. The $BadSMTP address variable will store the value that needs to be removed. The reset of these variables is to make sure no data is retained for each loop:

```
$Fail = $Null
$User = $Line.DISTINGUISHEDNAME
$BadSMTP = $Line.Value
```

In order to remove an address, the EmailAddressPolicyEnabled value needs to be $False.

```
Try {
    $PolicyApplied = (Get-Mailbox $User -ErrorAction STOP).EmailAddressPolicyEnabled
} Catch {
    $ScriptErrors = "User $user mailbox was not found." | Out-File -FilePath $ErrorFileName
}
```

If the Policy is enabled, this loop will set the 'EmailAddressPolicyEnabled' value to $False, in preparation for removing the bad SMTP Address:

```
If ($PolicyApplied) {
    Try {
        Set-Mailbox $User -EmailAddressPolicyEnabled $False -ErrorAction STOP
    } Catch {
        $ScriptErrors = "The EmailAddressPolicyEnabled property for $user cannot be changed." | Out-File
        -FilePath $ErrorFileName
        $Fail = $True
    }
}
```

The next IF…ELSE code section looks to see if the policy change failed. If it did not, then the address can be removed. To remove the value, first a Get-ADUser cmdlet needs to be used with the –identity and –property parameters. The results of this cmdlet are piped ('|') to a Set-ADUser cmdlet. Notice that there is a –Remove parameter. This allows PowerShell to remove a particular value from a property on an AD Object.

```
If ($Fail -ne $True) {
    Try {
        Get-ADUser -identity $User -property * | Set-ADUser -remove @{'ProxyAddresses' = $BadSMTP}
    } Catch {
        $ScriptErrors = "Cannot remove $BadSMTP from the mailbox of $User." | Out-File -FilePath
        $ErrorFileName
    }
}
```

The purpose of this code section is to make the change if the EmailAddressPolicy is NOT enabled by default. The code is separate because there are no blockers to removing a bad Proxy Address:

```
} Else {
    Try {
        Get-ADUser -identity $User -property * | Set-ADUser -Remove @{'ProxyAddresses' = $BadSMTP}
    } Catch {
        $ScriptErrors = "Cannot remove $BadSMTP from the mailbox of $User." | Out-File -FilePath
        $ErrorFileName
    }
}
```

Note in the Try..Catch code, there's code to export an error message to a logging file. No output should be seen if the script runs successfully. If IdFix is run again, the proxy address errors should be gone. If they are not, check the logging file for details.

New IdFix Query – very clean, error count is low after these two scripts were run:

DISTINGUISHEDNAME ▲	OBJECTCLASS	ATTRIBUTE	ERROR	VALUE	UPDATE
CN=Migration.8f3e7716-20...	user	userPrincipalName	topleveldomain	Migration.8f3e7716-2011-43e4-96b1-aba62d229136@16-TAP.Local	Migration.8f3e7716-2011-43e4-9

Install of Azure AD Connect

You can download the latest version of Azure AD Connect from Microsoft here:

https://www.microsoft.com/en-us/download/details.aspx?id=47594

Once downloaded, the installation process can take us in two different directions – Express or Custom. Let's explore our options with the installation process:

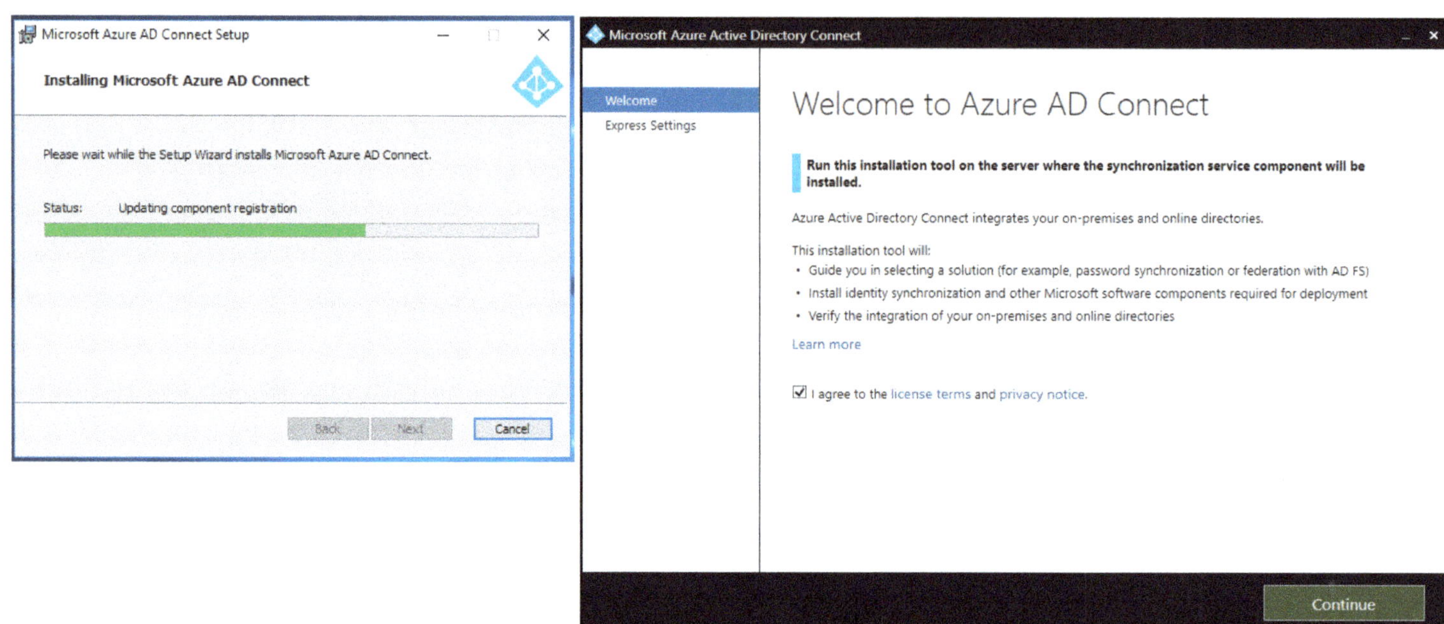

** **Note** ** Azure AD Connect will change over time as will the screens shown here.

Option 1 – Express Installation

This method allows for a quick install of the directory synchronization product and allow the quickest and easiest setup. This option is great if advanced features are not required or the environment is not complex.

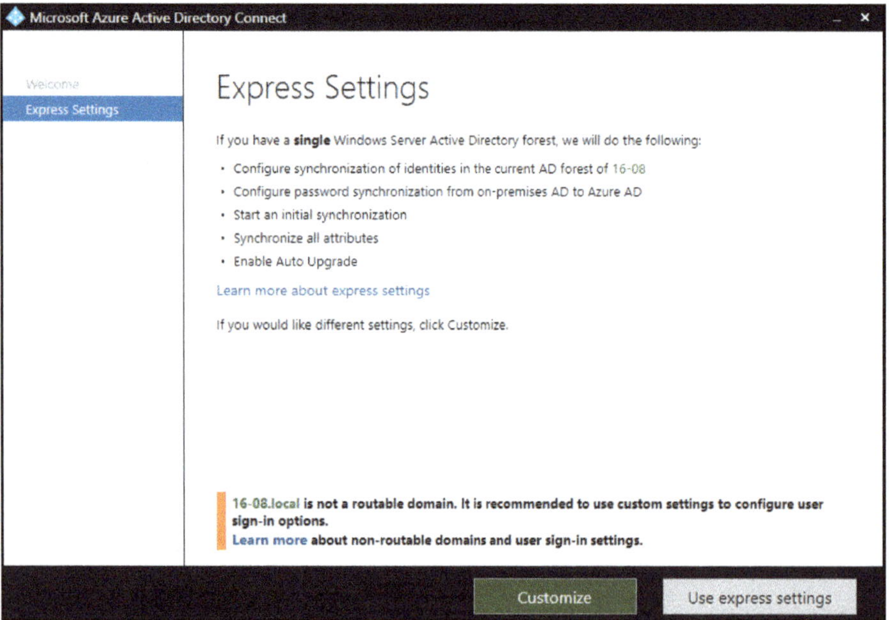

Option 2 – Customize

This installation option allows for a more complex installation process and the availability to choose (or not to choose) some of the more advanced options available with the directory synchronization.

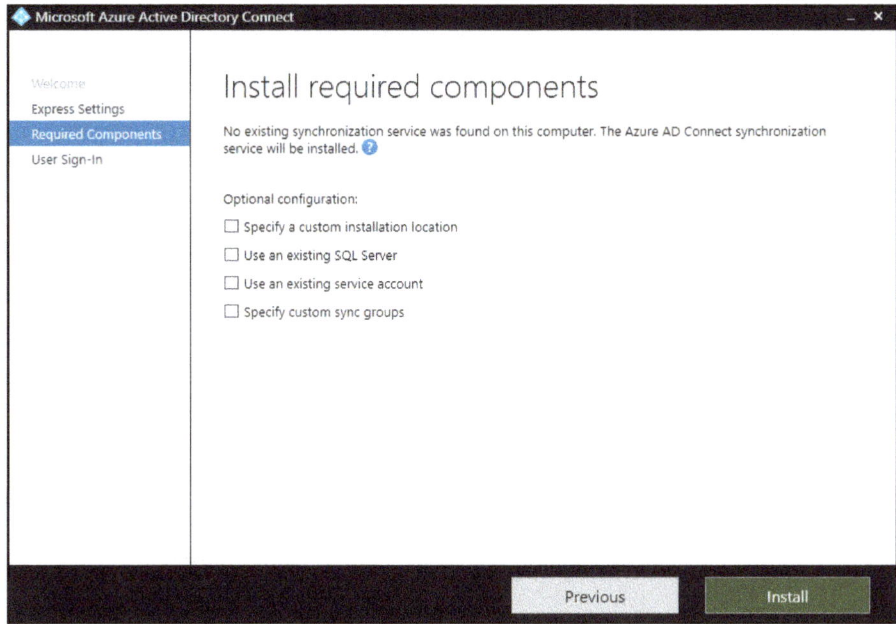

If you are unsure what these options mean, click on the blue question mark at the top, which will bring up a web link with an explanation of the options which goes to this website - http://go.microsoft.com/fwlink/?LinkID=530302. It is obvious that we can change the plain vanilla settings by changing:

- **Custom Installation location** - Where Azure AD Connect is installed (maybe we want it on the D drive).
- **SQL** - Use a SQL server instead of using the Windows Database (recommended for larger installations).
- **Service Account** - Use a pre-created service account instead of the service account the wizard will create for you. Make sure to check the requirements for this account before selecting it as an option.
- **Sync Group** - Specify your own group names instead of using the four that are created by the Azure AD Connect wizard.

For this installation example, we'll leave the settings at default for this stage.

Wait for the installation to complete:

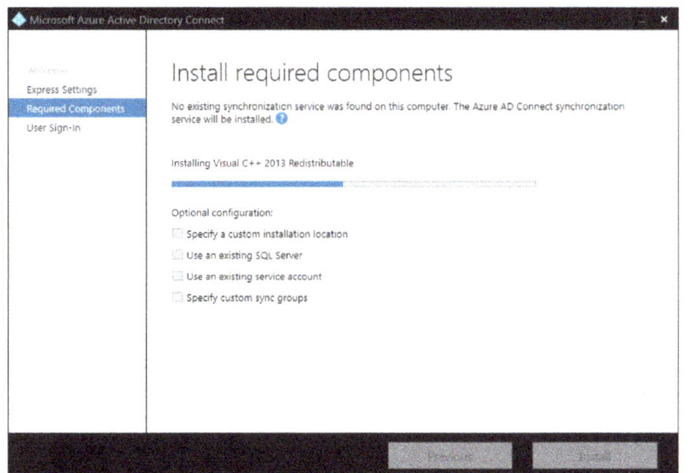

We are then provided a list of sign-in choices:

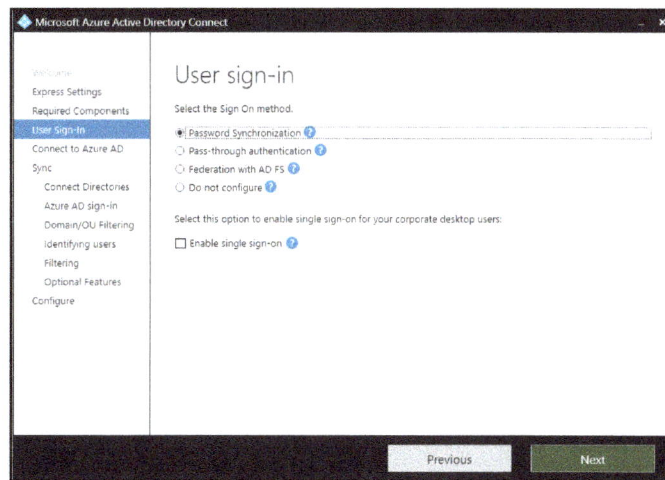

Each method of authentication is different and the option chosen would depend on your environment:

- **Password Synchronization** - Default option. User password synced to Office 365. User authenticates with the same password they use on-premises.
- **Pass-Through Authentication** - Azure AD uses your internal Active Directory to authenticate users.
- **Federation with ADFS** - Allows for a federated sign-in where corporate users do not need to re-enter their password.
- **Single Sign-On** - Users connect to their cloud services using SSO while on a corporate network.
- **Do Not Configure** - You control the federated authentication system (i.e. third party federation).

For our example, we will use Password Synchronization, but Pass-Through Authentication would work as well. After choosing that, we'll need to connect to our Office 365 Tenant:

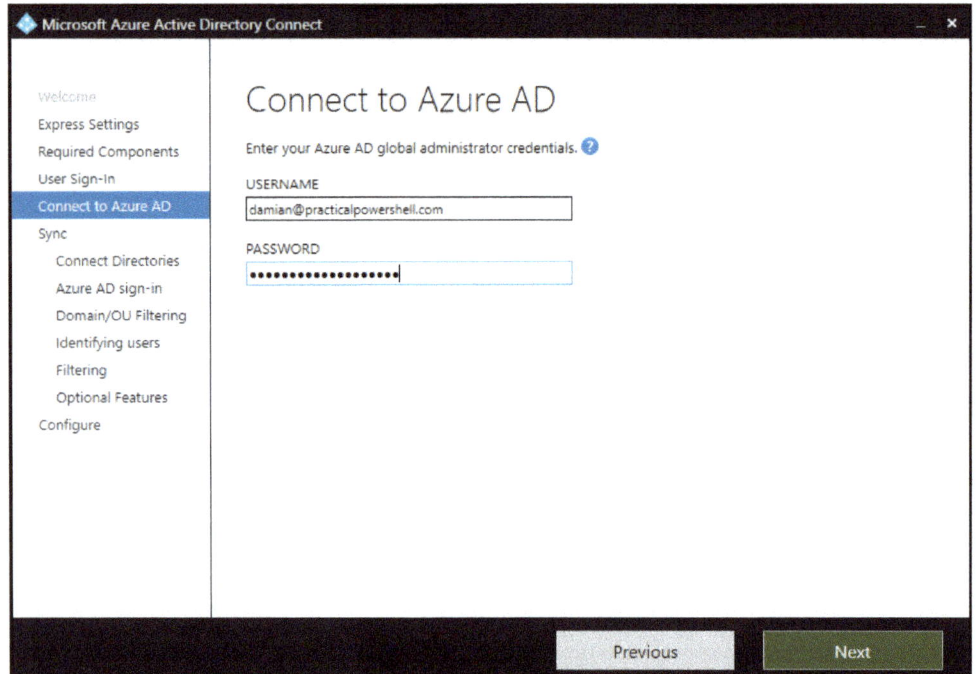

** **Note**** In order to make the connection above, the account needs to be a Global Administrator

Then we'll need connect to Active Directory as our source directory:

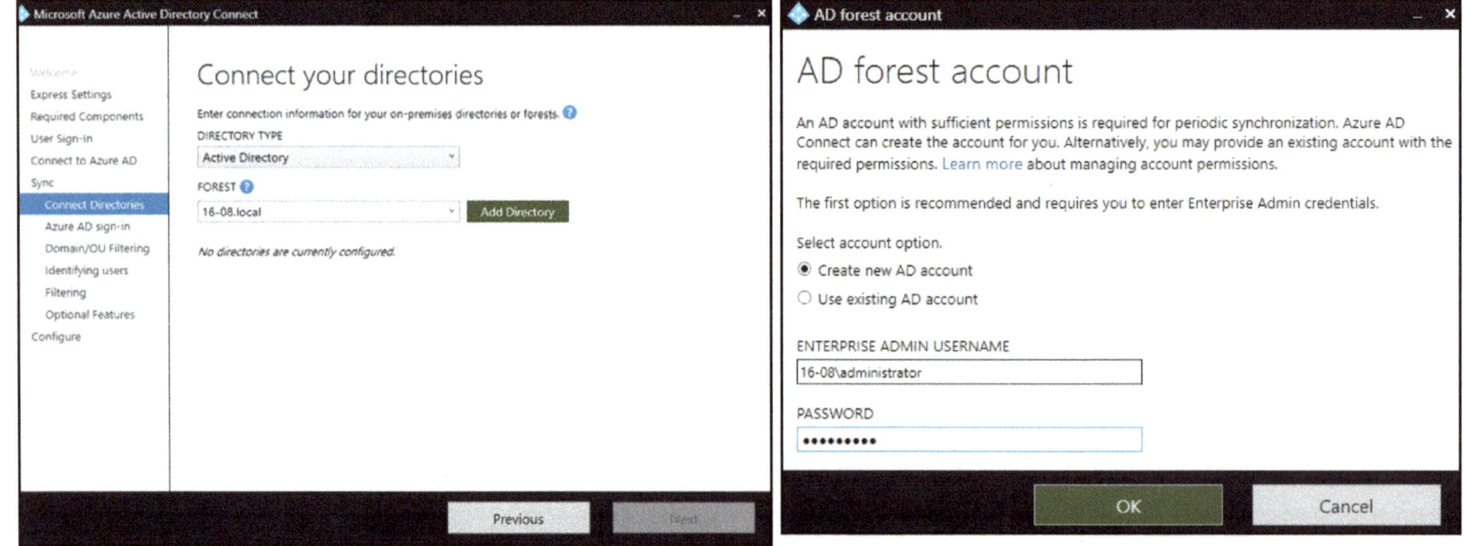

When entering the Forest Name, there are some considerations that need to be made. For flat directories, with no Root and Child domains to worry about, the default domain that is populated will suffice for the configuration of this page. However, if you have a more complex environment (Cross-Forest), you will need to choose the correct configuration for your environment. Azure AD Connect will connect to the Root Domain if it exists when setting up. If there are objects in the Root that do not need to be synchronized, these can be filtered out by choosing which partitions to synchronize.

Clicking OK and then Next will add the source directory. We need to choose an attribute for the user name and a user's User Principal Name (UPN) is typically used:

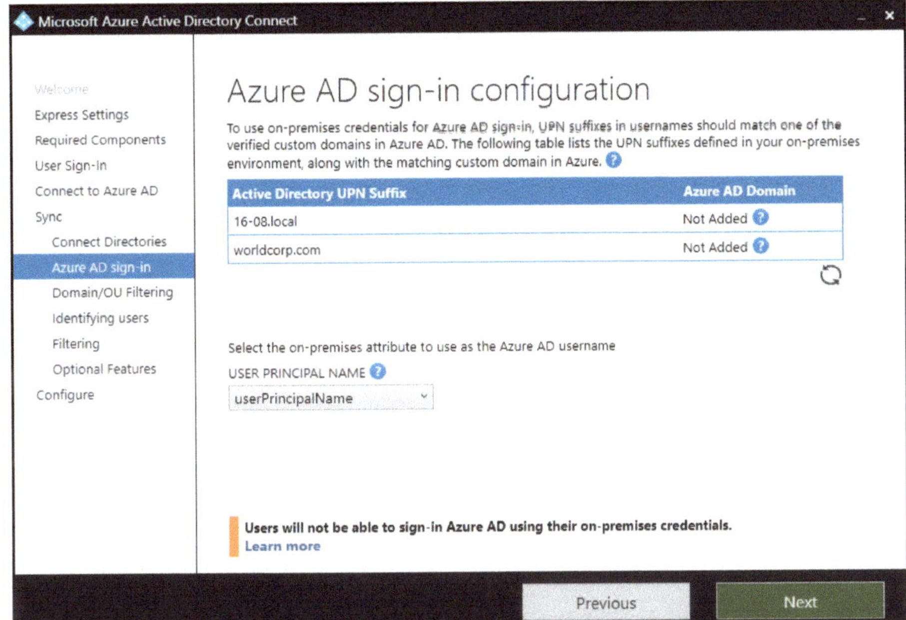

Then we can choose what OU's to sync. On the left we sync all OUs, on the right we have only some OUs selected:

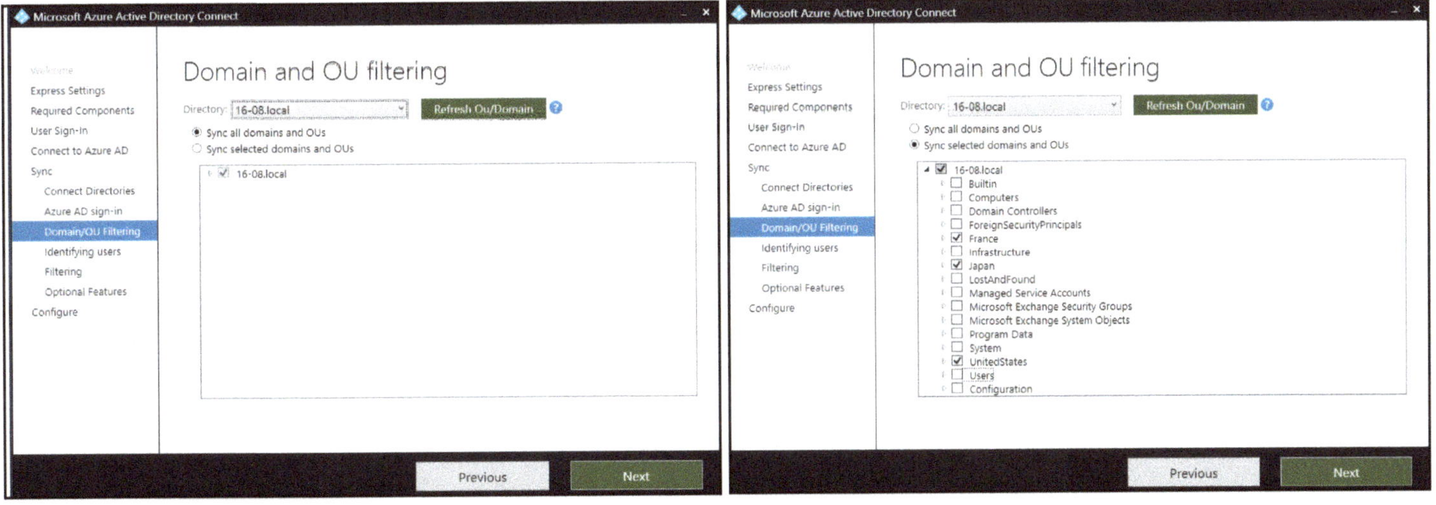

Choose your unique identifier (defaults shown):

Keep defaults for production or change for testing only:

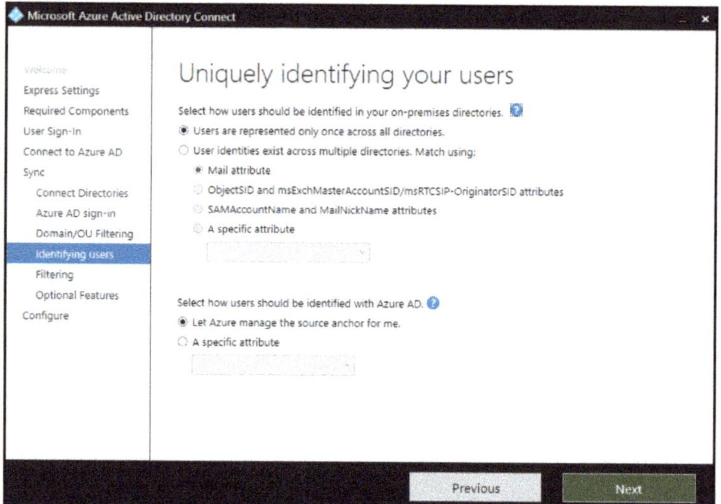

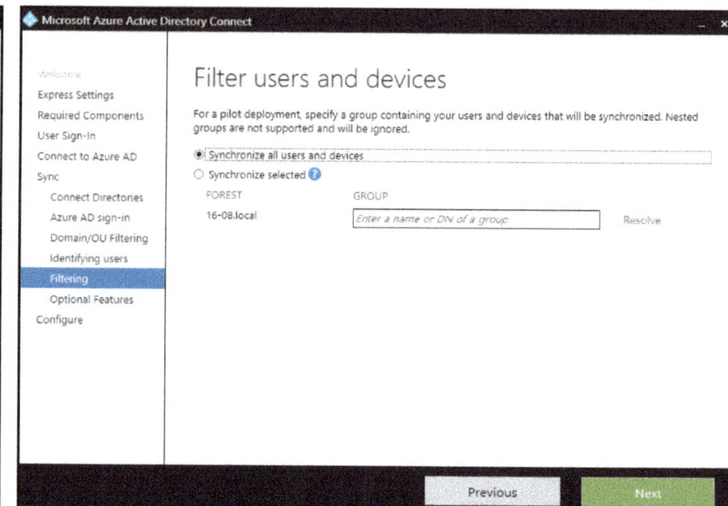

Lastly, a long list of optional features for Office 365 can be chosen. Be careful to read the list as some are in preview and may not work as expected or may be removed or modified:

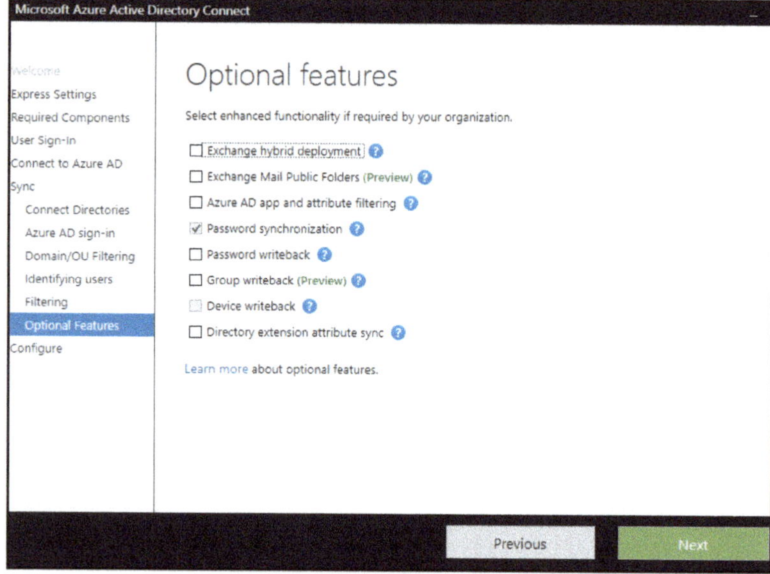

Brief explanation of the options:

- **Exchange hybrid deployment** - Allows for coexistence of Exchange and Exchange Online as well as synchronizing relevant Exchange attributes to Azure Active Directory (AD).
- **Exchange Mail Public Folders (Preview)** - Enables the synchronization of relevant attributes for Mail Enabled Public Folders to Exchange Online.
- **Azure AD app and attribute filtering** - Allows for custom attribute synchronization.
- **Password synchronization** - Synchronizes passwords from Active Directory (AD) to Azure AD.
- **Password writeback** - Enables password changes that are made in Azure AD will synchronize to an on-premises AD.
- **Group writeback (Preview)** - Office 365 groups that are created will be synchronized with AD.
- **Device writeback** - Devices that are registered in Azure AD will be written back to AD.
- **Directory extension attribute sync** - Custom attributes that are on objects synced to the cloud can sync.

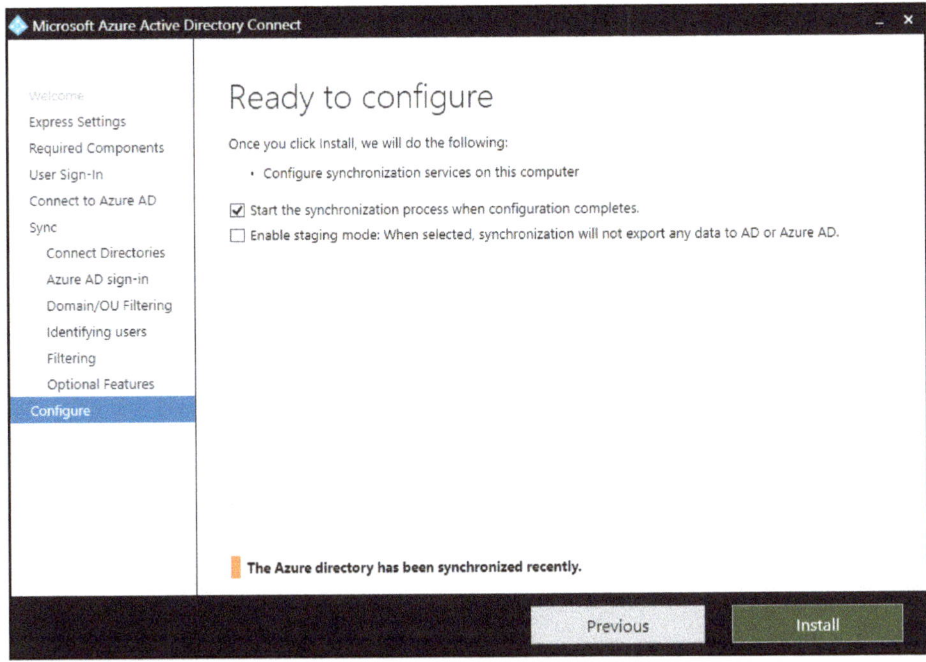

PowerShell and Directory Synchronization

Now that we've reviewed the basics of directory synchronization, let's cover the part that matters, specifically for this book, PowerShell. So what can we do with PowerShell with respect to Identity Management, Office 365 and in the end the Security and Compliance Center. Simply put, a lot:

- Change AD attributes that are synced to Office 365 and revealed in Azure AD
- Modify the synchronization schedule
- Initial a full or delta sync process
- Modify cloud attributes
- Document current ADSync settings
- Add/Remove objects to be synced to the cloud

What complicates things from here from a PowerShell perspective and general management perspective for Identities and Office 365 is that we can run PowerShell for these tasks in three different places. These 'management spaces' are Active Directory, Azure AD Connect and Azure Active Directory:

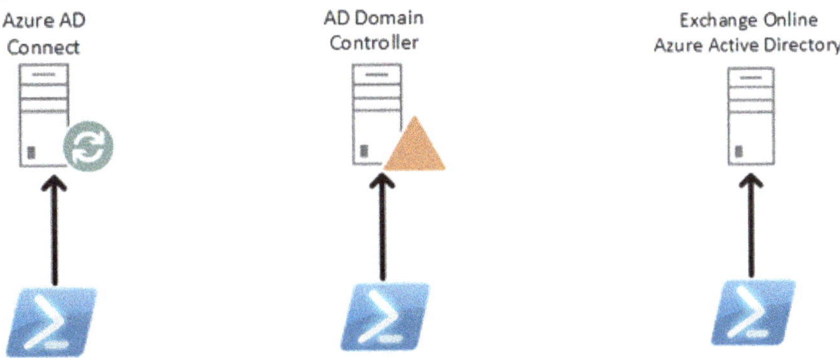

But aren't all of these aligned, synced and in the end, one and the same? The short answer is yes, and no. Each of these spaces has its specific purpose and places and this should be thought of as such.

What Needs to be Performed Where?

Active Directory

Active Directory is a good place to start because it is known as the Source of Authority in a synced environment. This means that all identities and objects originate in Active Directory. Users, Groups and more sync from Active Directory to your Azure AD Tenant (Office 365). Be sure to realize that not all attributes will sync with Office 365. Check out the Microsoft documentation on this here:

https://docs.microsoft.com/en-us/azure/active-directory/connect/active-directory-aadconnectsync-attributes-synchronized

Key attributes we can sync and manipulate in Active Directory are the User Principal Name, email addresses, password, and more. Let's see how we can make those changes. After we make the changes we will switch modes to the Azure AD Connect server processes and use PowerShell to sync the changes to Office 365.

Unlike most PowerShell cmdlets, this one produces a list of information instead of reporting the data in a table format:

```
PS C:\> Get-ADSyncConnector


ConnectorTypeName                : Extensible2
Identifier                       : b891884f-051e-4a83-95af-2544101c9083
Version                          : 18
InternalVersion                  : 1
FormatVersion                    : 1
Name                             : scoles.onmicrosoft.com - AAD
Description                      :
CreationTime                     : 10/13/2016 5:20:38 PM
LastModificationTime             : 7/25/2017 7:22:06 PM
Partitions                       : {default}
RunProfiles                      : {Full Import, Full Synchronization, Delta Import, Delta Synchroniz
ComponentProvisioningMappings    : {}
PasswordManagementSettings       : Microsoft.IdentityManagement.PowerShell.ObjectModel.ConnectorPassw
Schema                           : Microsoft.IdentityManagement.PowerShell.ObjectModel.Schema
AllParameterDefinitions          : {UserName, Password}
ConnectivityParameters           : {UserName, Password}
GlobalParameters                 : {}
CapabilityParameters             : {}
SchemaParameters                 : {}
ObjectInclusionList              : {contact, device, group, user}
AttributeInclusionList           : {accountEnabled, alias, alternativeSecurityId, altRecipient...}
AnchorConstructionSettings       : {Microsoft.IdentityManagement.PowerShell.ObjectModel.ConnectorAnch
                                   Microsoft.IdentityManagement.PowerShell.ObjectModel.ConnectorAncho
```

To get a table view, we would have to add a '| Ft' to the cmdlet, like so:

```
PS C:\> Get-ADSyncConnector | ft

ConnectorTypeNam Identifier                Version  InternalVersion   FormatVersion Name
e
---------------- ----------                -------  ---------------   ------------- ----
Extensible2      b891884f-051e...              18                 1               1 scoles.onmicr...
AD               beb5059c-4203...           34708                 0               1 MEDIEVAL.LOCAL
```

New Object Creation

Creating objects can be performed with either AD Users and Computers (ADUC) or with PowerShell. If you are creating users in bulk then PowerShell will be the most efficient method. Singular user creation is often better left to ADUC, the exception being if you have a script that reads in a list of user attributes, perhaps from a CSV file or HR System, and can create objects from the data it contains. First, let's see how we can create local AD user accounts:

```
Get-Help New-ADUser -Examples

----------------------- EXAMPLE 1 ------------------------

C:\PS>New-ADUser GlenJohn -Certificate (new-object System.Security.Cryptography.X509Certificates.X509Certificate
-ArgumentList "export.cer")

----------------------- EXAMPLE 2 ------------------------

C:\PS>New-ADUser GlenJohn -OtherAttributes @{title="director";mail="glenjohn@fabrikam.com"}

----------------------- EXAMPLE 3 ------------------------

C:\PS>New-ADUser GlenJohn -Type iNetOrgPerson -Path "DC=AppNC" -server lds.Fabrikam.com:50000
```

The examples provided are rather basic. Most organizations would like their users to have good display names, aliases, base passwords, maybe address information, phone number and more. We can do all of this via Power-Shell.

Example

A good example of this is a company that uses a third party HR application that keeps track of all of their employees. The same application exports a list of new employees on a weekly basis so that IT can create the accounts before new employees start working there. The export has a known list of fields and IT has a PowerShell script. In the CSV file there are a series of fields included - Display Name, Alias, First Name, Last Name, Office, Department, Title, Street Address, City, State, Zip Code and Office Number. The password is stored in a secure file that can be referenced by PowerShell.

We can store the password and CSV files in variables for later use:

```
$Password = Cat C:\SecureString.Txt | ConvertTo-SecureString
$CSV = Import-CSV \\FS-01\HR\NewEmployees.csv
```

Once those are stored, we can use a Foreach loop that will then insert the new employees information onto a new AD User account:

```
New-ADUser -Name $Displayname -SamAccountName $UserID -GivenName $FirstName -surname
$lastname -DisplayName $Displayname -Office $Office -Department $Department -Title $Title
-StreetAddress $StreetAddress -City $City -State $State -PostalCode $ZipCode -AccountPassword
$Password -path $OrgUnit -OfficePhone $WorkNumber
```

Once the user is created the object will be synchronized to Azure AD when the Azure AD Synchronization process runs. If the object needs to be synced immediately, a manual process via PowerShell may be run.

```
PS C:\> Start-ADSyncSyncCycle Delta

                                    Result
                                    ------
                                    Success
```

Modify

For modifying AD objects we use the Set-ADUser cmdlet. AD user objects have dozens of attributes we need to make sure that what we are modifying will make it to MSOnline.

Get-Help Set-ADUser -Examples

```
----------------------- EXAMPLE 1 -----------------------
C:\PS>Set-ADUser AntonioA1 -HomePage 'http://fabrikam.com/employees/AntonioA1' -LogonWorkstations
'AntonioA1-DSKTOP,AntonioA1-LPTOP'

----------------------- EXAMPLE 2 -----------------------
C:\PS>Get-ADUser -Filter 'Name -like "*"' -SearchBase 'OU=HumanResources,OU=UserAccounts,DC=FABRIKAM,DC=COM'
-Properties DisplayName | % {Set-ADUser $_ -DisplayName ($_.Surname + ' ' + $_.GivenName)}
----------------------- EXAMPLE 3 -----------------------
C:\PS>Set-ADUser GlenJohn -Replace @{title="director";mail="glenjohn@fabrikam.com"}
```

Let's explore what we can do with manipulating user object properties.

Example

Let's change the offices for a couple of users. One of them works in Chicago, Illinois and the other works in Barneveld, Netherlands.

    Set-ADUser Damian -Office 'Chicago'
    Set-ADUser Dave -Office 'Barneveld'

We can then verify these changes with a Get-ADUser and perhaps using the 'Filter' parameter to look for specific offices:

Get-ADUser -Filter {Office -eq 'Chicago'}

```
DistinguishedName : CN=Damian Scoles,CN=Users,DC=AAD,DC=LOCAL
Enabled           : True
GivenName         : Damian
Name              : Damian Scoles
ObjectClass       : user
ObjectGUID        : 90ba0b4d-15bc-43e6-9b74-1bc051743bb7
SamAccountName    : damian
SID               : S-1-5-21-1816188163-520225533-903613565-1107
Surname           : Scoles
UserPrincipalName : damian@PracticalPowerShell.Com
```

Get-ADUser -Filter {Office -eq 'Barneveld'}

```
DistinguishedName : CN=Dave Stork,CN=Users,DC=AAD,DC=LOCAL
Enabled           : True
GivenName         : Dave
Name              : Dave Stork
ObjectClass       : user
ObjectGUID        : e1591617-3f62-4eb2-884c-6af0e9b77a7b
SamAccountName    : Dave
SID               : S-1-5-21-1816188163-520225533-903613565-1108
Surname           : Stork
UserPrincipalName : Dave@PracticalPowerShell.Com
```

Again, do not forget that for user objects that are synced to Azure AD, not all properties that we can manipulate are actually synced to the cloud. These attributes will in the end be very important as they can be referenced in Information Barriers and other portions of the Security and Compliance Center.

Another common attribute to modify on-premises is the users' User Principal Name. The UPN is potentially a very important attribute for your users connecting to Office 365 resources. This attribute is typically used as the login for accessing those resources, which should match the users' Primary SMTP address. If you have any users with login issues, this is one attribute to check for first as well as the users logon name in Azure AD.

Removing Objects

A directory is only as good as the objects that are present in it. If there are objects that are no longer needed or reference users that no longer work for an organization, then we can remove them with PowerShell. Again this can be singular or en masse, preferably with a CSV file.

PowerShell

In order to remove user objects we can use the Remove-ADUser cmdlet. Remember that if this account is removed from Active Directory it will no longer be in sync with the corresponding object in Office 365. The object will be placed in the Azure AD Recycle Bin (See pg. 79 for more information). If the object is restored, then the matching object in Azure AD will also be restored (within 30 days). Now let's remove some objects:

Remove-ADUser

```
------------------------- EXAMPLE 1 -------------------------
C:\PS>Remove-ADUser -Identity GlenJohn
------------------------- EXAMPLE 2 -------------------------
C:\PS>Search-ADAccount -AccountDisabled | where {$_.ObjectClass -eq 'user'} | Remove-ADUser
------------------------- EXAMPLE 3 -------------------------
C:\PS>Remove-ADUser -Identity "CN=Glen John,OU=Finance,OU=UserAccounts,DC=FABRIKAM,DC=COM"
```

Example

If we have some users who have left an organization:

```
$Users = Import-CSV \\FS-01\HR\EmployeeRemoval.CSV
Foreach ($User in $Users) {
   $Exist = $True
   $Identity = $Users.Identity
   Remove-ADUser -Identity $Identity
   Try {
      $Exist = Get-ADUser -Identity $Identity -ErrorAction STOP
   } Catch {
      $Exist = $False
   }
   If ($exist -eq $False) {
      Write-Host "User $Identity has been successfully removed."
   } Else {
      Write-Host "The user has not been removed." -ForegroundColor Yellow
   }
}
```

Azure Active Directory Connect

After Active Directory, the next service to work with is the Azure AD Connect server we installed earlier in the chapter. In this section we will deal with PowerShell and the directory synchronization cmdlets available on the server where Azure AD Connect is installed.

In order to begin, we will need to open up Windows PowerShell. After opening it, we need to verify the module is loaded.

```
Get-Module
```

```
PS C:\> Get-Module

ModuleType  Name                              Exported(
----------  ----                              ---------
Manifest    Microsoft.PowerShell.Management    {Add-Com|
Manifest    MSOnline                           {Add-Mso|
```

We do not see ADSync listed, then we make sure to run 'Import-Module ADSync'. This cmdlet will load the PowerShell cmdlets for Azure AD Connect. Notice the changes below:

```
PS C:\> Get-Module

ModuleType  Name                              Exported|
----------  ----                              ---------
Binary      ADSync                             {Add-ADS|
Manifest    Microsoft.PowerShell.Management    {Add-Com|
Manifest    MSOnline                           {Add-Mso|
```

What cmdlets are available to us once this PowerShell module is loaded? We can find these with this one-liner:

```
Get-Command | Where {$_.ModuleName -eq 'AdSync'}
```

Total cmdlets available:

```
(Get-Command | where {$_.ModuleName -eq 'AdSync'}).Count
```

The above one-liner provides output that we have 92 cmdlets available.

Sync Schedule Adjustment

First, let's work with the basics of the AD Sync Scheduler. We can find the initial settings with the Get-ADSyncScheduler:

```
PS C:\> Get-ADSyncScheduler

AllowedSyncCycleInterval            : 00:30:00
CurrentlyEffectiveSyncCycleInterval : 00:30:00
CustomizedSyncCycleInterval         :
NextSyncCyclePolicyType             : Delta
NextSyncCycleStartTimeInUTC         : 10/10/2017 6:03:41 AM
PurgeRunHistoryInterval             : 7.00:00:00
SyncCycleEnabled                    : True
MaintenanceEnabled                  : True
StagingModeEnabled                  : False
SchedulerSuspended                  : False
SyncCycleInProgress                 : False
```

Notice the default sync cycle is indeed 30 minutes as per Microsoft's change from the original three hours in a previous version of the tool. Also notice that the Staging Mode is not configured, no sync is in progress nor is the scheduler paused. There are some settings that we can configure for the sync scheduler itself. Consider these requirements:

- The updates need to occur on a less frequent basis and increased from 30 minutes to 45 minutes.
- The run history needs to be kept for 30 days instead of the typical 7 days.

Unfortunately the PowerShell cmdlet needed to configure these settings has no usable examples:

```
Get-Help Set-ADSyncScheduler –Examples
```

```
NAME
    Set-ADSyncScheduler

ALIASES
    None


REMARKS
    None
```

To adjust the schedule, we can use a one-liner like the following, which adjusts the purge interval from 7 days to 30 days and Sync Cycle interval up to 45 minutes, from 30 minutes:

```
Set-ADSyncScheduler -PurgeRunHistoryInterval 30.00:00:00 -CustomizedSyncCycleInterval 00:45:00
```

```
Set-ADSyncScheduler -PurgeRunHistoryInterval 30.00:00:00 -CustomizedSyncCycleInterval 00:45:00
 The sync interval you provided will only become effective after a sync cycle. You can choose to wait for the
c sync cycle to happen in next 30.00 minutes, or you can manually start a sync cyle by running Start-ADSyncSyn
```

We can then verify the changes with 'Get-ADSyncScheduler:'

```
AllowedSyncCycleInterval              : 00:30:00
CurrentlyEffectiveSyncCycleInterval   : 00:30:00
CustomizedSyncCycleInterval           : 00:45:00
NextSyncCyclePolicyType               : Delta
NextSyncCycleStartTimeInUTC           : 8/21/2019 4:12:44 AM
PurgeRunHistoryInterval               : 30.00:00:00
SyncCycleEnabled                      : True
MaintenanceEnabled                    : True
StagingModeEnabled                    : False
SchedulerSuspended                    : False
SyncCycleInProgress                   : False
```

After 30 minutes, these changes will then go into effect and your synchronizations will be 45 minutes apart instead of 30 minutes.

Modifying the scheduler for the directory synchronization is just one part of the scheduler. We can also kick off full syncs and delta syncs with PowerShell as well. This is a common task for migrations when changes are made to user's information, new users are created in Active Directory or possible an additional distribution group needs to sync for the Office 365 tenant. In this case, we'll need to manually initiate the sync process using a single PowerShell cmdlet:

```
Start-ADSyncSyncCycle
```

What examples do we have for this cmdlet? None. However, if we review the full Get-Help of the cmdlet, we see this near the top:

```
NAME
    Start-ADSyncSyncCycle

SYNTAX
    Start-ADSyncSyncCycle [[-PolicyType] <SynchronizationPolicyType> {Unspecified |
    Delta | Initial}] [[-InteractiveMode] <bool>] [<CommonParameters>]
```

When it comes to PowerShell cmdlets, this one has one of the fewest if not the fewest configurable options. If we would like to start a sync based on just recent changes, we can use a policy type of 'delta':

Start-ADSyncSyncCycle –PolicyType Delta

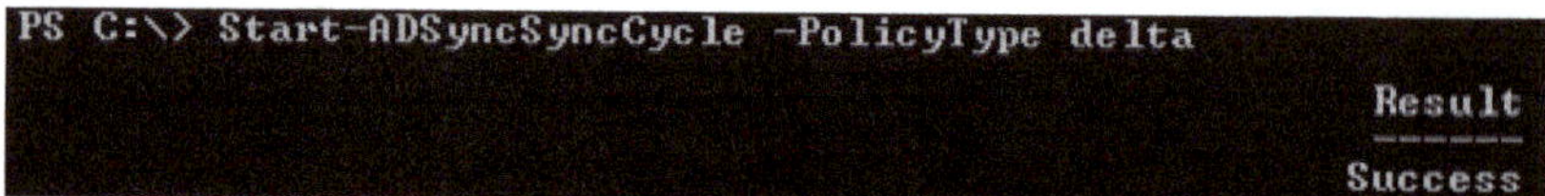

And Azure AD Connect will show the connections being made:

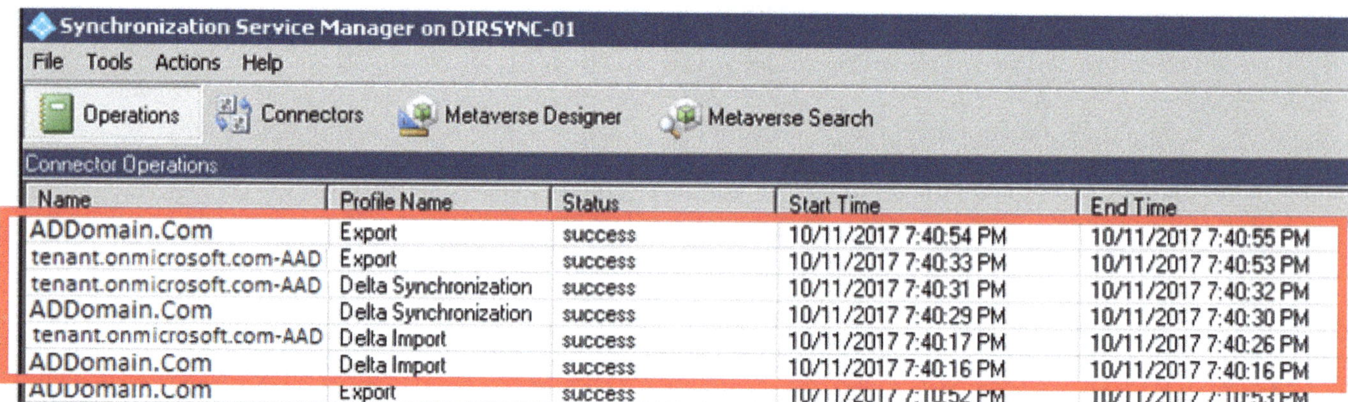

Name	Profile Name	Status	Start Time	End Time
ADDomain.Com	Export	success	10/11/2017 7:40:54 PM	10/11/2017 7:40:55 PM
tenant.onmicrosoft.com-AAD	Export	success	10/11/2017 7:40:33 PM	10/11/2017 7:40:53 PM
tenant.onmicrosoft.com-AAD	Delta Synchronization	success	10/11/2017 7:40:31 PM	10/11/2017 7:40:32 PM
ADDomain.Com	Delta Synchronization	success	10/11/2017 7:40:29 PM	10/11/2017 7:40:30 PM
tenant.onmicrosoft.com-AAD	Delta Import	success	10/11/2017 7:40:17 PM	10/11/2017 7:40:26 PM
ADDomain.Com	Delta Import	success	10/11/2017 7:40:16 PM	10/11/2017 7:40:16 PM
ADDomain.Com	Export	success	10/11/2017 7:10:52 PM	10/11/2017 7:10:53 PM

** **Note** ** The 'ADDomain.Com' refers to the FQDN used in your on-premises AD while the 'tenant.onmicrosoft.com' refers to your Office 365 default domain.

However, if we need to perform a full sync, for example if there is a problem with a delta sync or there is a need to force a fuller sync, we can use the 'Initial' Policy Type:

Start-ADSyncSyncCycle –PolicyType Initial

If it is successful, the PowerShell window should show this:

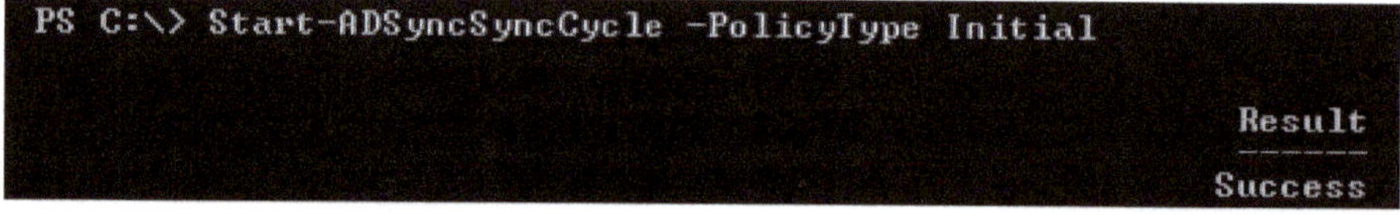

Azure AD Connect – Connectors

Connectors are what allows objects and attributes to sync between the two environments. One syncs objects from your on-premises Active Directory to Azure AD Connector and the other syncs Azure AD Connector to and from AzureAD. Installing Azure AD Connect should create both of these connectors. If you have more than one source Active Directory forest one connector is created per forest.

PowerShell

Let's start with the Get-*Connector* cmdlets with the thought of exploring what is available to modify before adding or changing existing connectors. This will allow for a non-destructive examination of the environment.

```
Get-Command Get*connector* | Where {$_.ModuleName -eq 'ADSync'}
```

```
CommandType   Name                                                ModuleName
-----------   ----                                                ----------
Cmdlet        Get-ADSyncConnector                                 ADSync
Cmdlet        Get-ADSyncConnectorHierarchyProvisioningDNComponent ADSync
Cmdlet        Get-ADSyncConnectorHierarchyProvisioningMapping     ADSync
Cmdlet        Get-ADSyncConnectorHierarchyProvisioningObjectClass ADSync
Cmdlet        Get-ADSyncConnectorParameter                        ADSync
Cmdlet        Get-ADSyncConnectorPartition                        ADSync
Cmdlet        Get-ADSyncConnectorPartitionHierarchy               ADSync
Cmdlet        Get-ADSyncConnectorRunStatus                        ADSync
Cmdlet        Get-ADSyncConnectorStatistics                       ADSync
Cmdlet        Get-ADSyncConnectorTypes                            ADSync
Cmdlet        Get-ADSyncSchedulerConnectorOverride                ADSync
```

The first cmdlet will display information on the two connectors involved in the Azure AD Connector process of directory synchronization:

```
Get-ADSyncConnector | ft
```

```
ConnectorTypeName Identifier                            Version InternalVersion FormatVersion Name
----------------- ----------                            ------- --------------- ------------- ----
Extensible2       b891884f-051e-4a83-95af-2544101c9083        1               1             1 OnlineExchangeBook.onmi...
AD                720faf5e-2407-464e-a43a-c9aff1967a5b        8               0             1 AAD.LOCAL
```

Notice that the top one is for our Azure AD tenant and AAD.LOCAL is for our on-premises AD. Now we can also review the configuration of several items when it comes to our Azure AD Connect server. Some examples are - connector details, rules and server configuration.

The first is the easiest and is a variation of the last PowerShell cmdlet we ran. First, we will look at the connector for our local Active Directory to Office 365:

```
Get-ADSyncConnector -Name AAD.LOCAL
```

```
ConnectorTypeName              : AD
Identifier                     : 720faf5e-2407-464e-a43a-c9aff1967a5b
Version                        : 8
InternalVersion                : 0
FormatVersion                  : 1
Name                           : AAD.LOCAL
Description                    :
CreationTime                   : 12/16/2017 5:56:40 AM
LastModificationTime           : 12/16/2017 5:57:00 AM
Partitions                     : {AAD.LOCAL}
RunProfiles                    : {Full Import, Full Synchronization, Delta Import, Delta Synchronization...}
ComponentProvisioningMappings  : {}
Schema                         : Microsoft.IdentityManagement.PowerShell.ObjectModel.Schema
AllParameterDefinitions        : {}
ConnectivityParameters         : {forest-login-domain, forest-login-user, password, forest-name...}
GlobalParameters               : {Connector.GroupFilteringGroupDn}
CapabilityParameters           : {}
SchemaParameters               : {}
ObjectInclusionList            : {computer, contact, container, domainDNS...}
AttributeInclusionList         : {adminDescription, assistant, c, cn...}
AnchorConstructionSettings     : {}
ListName                       :
CompanyName                    :
Type                           : AD
Subtype                        :
ExtensionConfiguration         : Microsoft.IdentityManagement.PowerShell.ObjectModel.ConnectorExtensionConfiguration
PasswordHashConfiguration      : <password-hash-sync-config><enabled>1</enabled><target>{B891884F-051E-4A83-95AF-2544101
                                 C9083}</target></password-hash-sync-config>
AADPasswordResetConfiguration  :
```

Notice the detail in the connector. There are a couple of properties above that can be expanded. The way we can tell is that we something like *'Microsoft.IdentityManagement,PowerShell.ObjectModel....'*. This means that there are more details that can be expanded, like so:

```
(Get-ADSyncConnector -Name AAD.LOCAL).Schema
```

```
Identifier          : 00000000-0000-0000-0000-000000000000
ObjectTypes         : {msDFSR-Content, device, msWMI-IntRangeParam, samServer...}
AttributeTypes      : {Name:attributeSecurityGUID Type:Binary MultiValued:False, Name:msDS-FilterContainers
                      Type:String MultiValued:True, Name:legacyExchangeDN Type:String MultiValued:False,
                      Name:cOMProgID Type:String MultiValued:True...}
IsConnectorSchema   : True
IntrinsicAttributes : {Name:dn Type:String MultiValued:False, Name:msIdm-ObjectCustomData Type:String
                      MultiValued:False}
AllDNComponents     : {}
```

We can also dig into the server configuration and dump a series of files using the ' Get-ADSyncServerConfiguration' cmdlet (note this cannot be used to restore an Azure AD Connect Server):

```
Get-ADSyncServerConfiguration -path c:\Download\Export
```

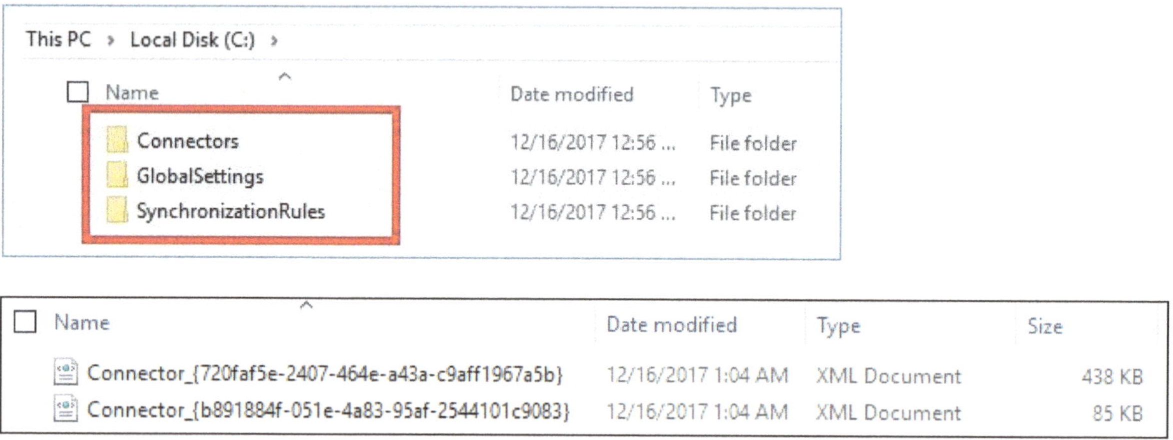

Lastly, we can export or review our rules as well with Get-ADSyncRule. The rules contain a lot of information and
we can create a basic table of these rules like this:

```
Get-ADSyncRule |Ft
```

```
Identifier                             InternalId                             Name
----------                             ----------                             ----
d3f9498a-bfeb-4752-a137-dc0185f30ebf   d3f9498a-bfeb-4752-a137-dc0185f30ebf   In from AAD - User Join
b5b2f5c4-0562-499f-b8ac-159a71e5d7d4   b5b2f5c4-0562-499f-b8ac-159a71e5d7d4   Out to AAD - User ExchangeOnline
953e6c8e-6f5b-4a09-8642-73ef8346d45a   953e6c8e-6f5b-4a09-8642-73ef8346d45a   Out to AAD - User LyncOnline
1215f7cd-9b83-4286-8961-e7a4e9d0176d   1215f7cd-9b83-4286-8961-e7a4e9d0176d   Out to AAD - User SharePointOnline
8a708140-dd80-45f6-8875-b8581a1148fa   8a708140-dd80-45f6-8875-b8581a1148fa   Out to AAD - Contact ExchangeOnline
3ef9f7c7-6c9f-44cc-9029-67ba4cd87107   3ef9f7c7-6c9f-44cc-9029-67ba4cd87107   Out to AAD - Contact SharePointOnline
a19533b6-187c-4838-be75-0b063bf3c635   a19533b6-187c-4838-be75-0b063bf3c635   Out to AAD - Group Join
c994d0b3-4d85-41ba-8921-638a7ba62e6f   c994d0b3-4d85-41ba-8921-638a7ba62e6f   Out to AAD - Group ExchangeOnline
5b51f5ac-eb9a-4fd3-807a-a8f2b0c098c1   5b51f5ac-eb9a-4fd3-807a-a8f2b0c098c1   Out to AAD - Group SharePointOnline
65e35432-0554-4bff-9b3a-c6a0075f8afb   65e35432-0554-4bff-9b3a-c6a0075f8afb   In from AAD - Contact Join
df2afd59-cba1-4457-b761-34218738b70b   df2afd59-cba1-4457-b761-34218738b70b   In from AAD - Group Join
83fb9ec2-a62a-4ae0-9985-d24740d2a534   83fb9ec2-a62a-4ae0-9985-d24740d2a534   In from AAD - User NGCKey
06d37554-d537-4512-9c84-1e103d895a7c   06d37554-d537-4512-9c84-1e103d895a7c   Out to AAD - User AzureRMS
5982c026-314f-4f28-a27b-a175c08a0216   5982c026-314f-4f28-a27b-a175c08a0216   Out to AAD - User Join
7073f0e6-f5f2-4138-b9a5-71d39c2ed172   7073f0e6-f5f2-4138-b9a5-71d39c2ed172   Out to AAD - User Identity
b4992e49-d422-4ce6-b64c-8f974ea91c60   b4992e49-d422-4ce6-b64c-8f974ea91c60   Out to AAD - User DynamicsCRM
2df63f43-b635-4099-9949-d6465b4279c7   2df63f43-b635-4099-9949-d6465b4279c7   Out to AAD - User Intune
c6fcfd30-a2d3-45bd-bb21-5615ab3a89d1   c6fcfd30-a2d3-45bd-bb21-5615ab3a89d1   Out to AAD - Contact Join
7231d454-9b01-4353-a3d6-777e4bca77de   7231d454-9b01-4353-a3d6-777e4bca77de   Out to AAD - Contact Identity
f93886e1-d3d3-4072-bbd6-fc71339c907c   f93886e1-d3d3-4072-bbd6-fc71339c907c   Out to AAD - Contact DynamicsCRM
3d6b34fe-389c-4e22-8b06-9a34f46e1dc8   3d6b34fe-389c-4e22-8b06-9a34f46e1dc8   Out to AAD - Contact Intune
71b73c46-399a-4e72-af54-968043594649   71b73c46-399a-4e72-af54-968043594649   Out to AAD - Contact LyncOnline
524e1a9b-f6b7-49f0-b409-2a028b779bf1   524e1a9b-f6b7-49f0-b409-2a028b779bf1   Out to AAD - Contact AzureRMS
01fe57d3-ecf5-4f92-ab3e-8e5b4ef89829   01fe57d3-ecf5-4f92-ab3e-8e5b4ef89829   Out to AAD - Group Identity
a32f3f1e-8fce-4d97-ad15-d808ac4c3d92   a32f3f1e-8fce-4d97-ad15-d808ac4c3d92   Out to AAD - Group DynamicsCRM
65a52197-6431-4786-beea-e555db6eba88   65a52197-6431-4786-beea-e555db6eba88   Out to AAD - Group Intune
f72da3c0-d7c6-4f6e-86e9-ef5995a8ff74   f72da3c0-d7c6-4f6e-86e9-ef5995a8ff74   Out to AAD - Group LyncOnline
04e0bc86-62a6-46be-abdf-fc5ba891b6f5   04e0bc86-62a6-46be-abdf-fc5ba891b6f5   Out to AAD - Group AzureRMS
ce1a39f6-8687-40fa-8669-4f8039a211cf   ce1a39f6-8687-40fa-8669-4f8039a211cf   Out to AAD - User OfficeProPlus
0944998d-0fd7-4e3b-898b-0abafccea6a8   0944998d-0fd7-4e3b-898b-0abafccea6a8   In from AAD - Device Common
f24495d3-e42e-4dba-a532-fd43ecbc58fa   f24495d3-e42e-4dba-a532-fd43ecbc58fa   Out to AAD - Device Join SOAInAD
c0d06dbc-b809-4b23-a260-4a83f2ca7c0b   c0d06dbc-b809-4b23-a260-4a83f2ca7c0b   In from AD - User Join
f9f9d40d-675b-4d4d-973f-86b94677b5fe   f9f9d40d-675b-4d4d-973f-86b94677b5fe   In from AD - InetOrgPerson Join
eda3d821-dfdd-4e6f-be6a-8ef4d8e34f6b   eda3d821-dfdd-4e6f-be6a-8ef4d8e34f6b   In from AD - User AccountEnabled
fd49d788-4cdd-4a25-a12c-78bea21a5d66   fd49d788-4cdd-4a25-a12c-78bea21a5d66   In from AD - InetOrgPerson AccountEnabled
5dfce29d-2dc3-4722-b279-272477a8c0b0   5dfce29d-2dc3-4722-b279-272477a8c0b0   In from AD - User Common
11835c40-0c62-4935-87a0-65ac5ef1f2b0   11835c40-0c62-4935-87a0-65ac5ef1f2b0   In from AD - InetOrgPerson Common
```

It is important to note that the previous rule list contains the default rules created by the Azure AD Connect installation process. Custom rules can be added and existing rules can be modified. However, because of the nature of the default rules, this is not recommended as you could do some damage to your Office 365 tenant.

Further reading on modifying these rules:

https://social.msdn.microsoft.com/Forums/SqlServer/en-US/c5189e16-a219-445e-9a17-d02937bda27f/azure-ad-connect-staging?forum=WindowsAzureAD

A more detailed version of the rule can be displayed with a one-liner like this:

Get-ADSyncRule -Identifier d3f9498a-bfeb-4752-a137-dc0185f30ebf | Fl

```
Identifier                : d3f9498a-bfeb-4752-a137-dc0185f30ebf
InternalId                : d3f9498a-bfeb-4752-a137-dc0185f30ebf
Name                      : In from AAD - User Join
Version                   : 1
Description               :
ImmutableTag              : Microsoft.IdentityManagement.PowerShell.ObjectModel.ImmutableTag
Connector                 : b891884f-051e-4a83-95af-2544101c9083
Direction                 : Inbound
Disabled                  : False
SourceObjectType          : user
TargetObjectType          : person
Precedence                : 111
PrecedenceAfter           : 00000000-0000-0000-0000-000000000000
PrecedenceBefore          : 00000000-0000-0000-0000-000000000000
LinkType                  : Join
EnablePasswordSync        : False
JoinFilter                : {Microsoft.IdentityManagement.PowerShell.ObjectModel.JoinConditionGroup}
ScopeFilter               : {Microsoft.IdentityManagement.PowerShell.ObjectModel.ScopeConditionGroup}
AttributeFlowMappings     : {Destination:accountEnabled FlowType:Direct Expression:  ValueMergeType: Update,
                            Destination:cloudAnchor FlowType:Direct Expression:  ValueMergeType: Update,
                            Destination:cloudSourceAnchor FlowType:Expression Expression: ImportedValue("sourceAnchor")
                            ValueMergeType: Update, Destination:countryCode FlowType:Direct Expression:
                            ValueMergeType: Update...}
SoftDeleteExpiryInterval  : 00:00:00
SourceNamespaceId         : b891884f-051e-4a83-95af-2544101c9083
TargetNamespaceId         : cc31d470-9786-447f-8594-40abe13f9f78
VersionAgnosticTag        : Microsoft.InfromAADUserJoin.
TagVersion                : 5
IsStandardRule            : True
IsLegacyCustomRule        : False
JoinHash                  : [sourceAnchor=sourceAnchor CS=True]
```

As we can see, these can dig in and get some good detail on our sync rules for Azure AD Connect with PowerShell.

Licensing

Another case for using PowerShell in managing your Office 365 tenant is mass licensing manipulation. While the Portal for your tenant will allow for mass changes, the manipulation that it is capable is also limited. Only 100 accounts can be modified at any one time. If there is a need to adjust more at one time, then PowerShell is required to make the changes successful. PowerShell is especially useful if more complex changes are required – licensing determined by groups or granular licensing is needed.

** **Note** ** There is one more method to license users in bulk. This method is called Group Based Licensing. Basically using the Azure AD Console you can add and remove licenses for a group of users based on their group membership. The below code on the next page shows how licenses can be applied to users in an individual manner.

First and foremost, what PowerShell cmdlets are available for these changes? Make sure a connection is opened up via the Windows PowerShell Azure Module – connect to the tenant and then the MSOL Service.

```
Get-Command *license*
```

```
CommandType          Name
----------           ----
Function             Get-LicenseVsUsageSummaryReport
Cmdlet               New-MsolLicenseOptions
Cmdlet               New-MsolLicenseOptions
Cmdlet               Set-MsolUserLicense
Cmdlet               Set-MsolUserLicense
```

Starting with the first cmdlet can provide some information about license usage:

```
Get-LicenseVsUsageSummaryReport | ft -Auto
```

```
Date                   TenantGuid          Workload NonTrialEntitlements TrialEntitlements ActiveUsers
----                   ----------          -------- -------------------- ----------------- -----------
9/7/2016 12:00:00 AM                       EXO      395                  0                 0
9/7/2016 12:00:00 AM                       LYO      375                  0                 0
9/7/2016 12:00:00 AM                       SPO      375                  0                 3
9/7/2016 12:00:00 AM                       Yammer   375                  0                 1
```

Where would licensing be stored? Maybe the information is stored in the properties of a user account in Azure AD. To get all the properties from a user account in Azure AD, the Get-MSOLUser cmdlet can be used for this:

```
Get-MsolUser -UserPrincipalName damian@domain.com | fl
```

Deep in the properties for this user we can see that there is an Enterprise License installed for the tenant this user account is in:

```
LastName                            : Scoles
LicenseReconciliationNeeded         : False
Licenses                            : {Domain:ENTERPRISEPACK}
```

However, the licenses assigned are not granular and we need to find out what options can be set via PowerShell. Cutting to the chase, the cmdlet needed is not as obvious:

```
Get-MsolAccountSku
```

The cmdlet only has one parameter "TenantID" and one example, which is just the base cmdlet. What information will this provide us?

```
ExtensionData       : System.Runtime.Serialization.ExtensionDataObject
AccountName         : Domain
AccountObjectId     : a59a9dcf-a1c7-4dfa-b98c-d9b0fc4a8fd2
AccountSkuId        : Domain:ENTERPRISEPACK
ActiveUnits         : 375
ConsumedUnits       : 63
LockedOutUnits      : 0
ServiceStatus       : {Microsoft.Online.Administration.ServiceStatus, Microsoft.Online.Administration.ServiceStatus,
                       Microsoft.Online.Administration.ServiceStatus, Microsoft.Online.Administration.ServiceStatus...}
SkuId               : 6fd2c87f-b296-42f0-b197-1e91e994b900
SkuPartNumber       : ENTERPRISEPACK
```

Notice the information in the red rectangle, the information is repeating and not detailed. PowerShell has a tendency to oversimplify values when it cannot display them properly. That is the same case here. We will use PowerShell on the ServiceStatus value to reveal all of its contents. Also note the 'AccountSkuId' property listed above. This value will provide us a way to dig into what license types are available to us in PowerShell.

First, capture the field in a variable:

```
$ServiceStatus = (Get-MsolAccountSku | Where {$_.SkuPartNumber -eq "ENTERPRISEPACK"}).
ServiceStatus
```

Then display the variable in a table format:

```
$ServiceStatus | ft
```

```
ServicePlan                          ProvisioningStatus
--------------------------           -------------------
PROJECTWORKMANAGEMENT                 Success
SWAY                                  Success
INTUNE_O365                           PendingInput
YAMMER_ENTERPRISE                     Success
RMS_S_ENTERPRISE                      Success
OFFICESUBSCRIPTION                    Success
MCOSTANDARD                           Success
SHAREPOINTWAC                         Success
SHAREPOINTENTERPRISE                  Success
EXCHANGE_S_ENTERPRISE                 Success
```

The same information can be displayed for a single user:

```
$Upn = "damian@domain.com"
(Get-MsolUser -User $Upn).Licenses[0].ServiceStatus
```

The above PowerShell is handy to validate any individual changes.

From the above Service Plans, a determination of what can be licensed is shown below:

Service Plan	What License Does this Apply to?
PROJECTWORKMANAGEMENT	Office 365 Planner Preview
SWAY	Sway
INTUNE_O365	Intune
YAMMER_ENTERPRISE	Yammer
RMS_S_ENTERPRISE	Rights Management Service
OFFICESUBSCRIPTION	Office ProPlus
MCOSTANDARD	Lync Online (Plan 2)
SHAREPOINTWAC	Office Online
SHAREPOINTENTERPRISE	SharePoint Online (Plan 2)
EXCHANGE_S_ENTERPRISE	Exchange Online

The above chart can be found at the below Microsoft link. The Service Plans on the left are the ones that would be referenced in with PowerShell scripts - https://blogs.technet.microsoft.com/treycarlee/2014/12/09/powershell-licensing-skus-in-office-365.

Now that we have the license options for this particular license SKU, how can these options be turned on and off for the users in Office 365? The most common method is to create what is called a 'Disabled Plan' which is essentially a set of options above that need to be unlicensed from a user account. Instead of enabling what is needed, PowerShell will need to disable what is unneeded. The reason for this will be apparent in the below script and available parameters.

Sample Script - Disable Licenses

```
# Read Users from CSV list
$Users = Import-Csv "c:\Scripting\UserList.csv"
```

In the array $DisabledOptions, disabled Service Plans are stored like so:

```
#Set disabled options
```

```
$DisabledOptions = @()
$DisabledOptions += "SHAREPOINTENTERPRISE"
$DisabledOptions += "MCOSTANDARD"
$DisabledOptions += "OFFICESUBSCRIPTION"
$DisabledOptions += "SHAREPOINTWAC"
$DisabledOptions += "PROJECTWORKMANAGEMENT"
$DisabledOptions += "SWAY "
$DisabledOptions += "INTUNE_O365"
$DisabledOptions += "RMS_S_ENTERPRISE"
```

Then a loop is used to process each user in the CSV file:

```
# Loop each account to set location and license options.
Foreach ($Line in $Users) {
```

Then PowerShell checks for the user's location and if the same account is licensed:

```
$Upn = $Line.Upn
$Location = (Get-MsolUser -UserPrincipalName $Upn).UsageLocation
$Licensed = (Get-MsolUser -UserPrincipalName $Upn).IsLicensed
```

For this section, if the location is not set, a location of 'US' will be configured:

```
If ($Location -eq $Null) {
    Set-MsolUser -UserPrincipalName $Upn -UsageLocation "US"
}
```

** **Note** ** Valid country codes can be found here - https://www.iso.org/obp/ui/#search

Next, if the user is not licensed, this block will add a valid license to the user:

```
If ($Licensed -eq $False) {
    Set-MsolUserLicense -UserPrincipalName $Upn -AddLicenses "<tenantname>:ENTERPRISEPACK"
}
```

Note: "<tenantname>" should be replaced with the Office 365 tenant name.   This can be obtained using Login-AzureRmAccount, which will prompt for credentials and then reveal the tenant information:

```
Environment          : AzureCloud
Account              : Damian@domain.onmicrosoft.com
TenantId             : ########-####-####-####-############
SubscriptionId       :
SubscriptionName     :
CurrentStorageAccount :
```

The tenant name in the above screenshot is the 'Domain' part of the Account property.

A valid set of license options is stored in the $LicenseOptions variable:

```
$LicenseOptions = New-MsolLicenseOptions –AccountSkuId "<tenantname>:ENTERPRISEPACK" –
DisabledPlans $DisabledOptions
```

The license options are then applied to the user account:

```
Set-MsolUserLicense –User $Upn –LicenseOptions $LicenseOptions
$Status = (Get-MsolUser -User $Upn).Licenses[0].ServiceStatus
```

After the script completes, the current licensing options for the user account can be verified with PowerShell first:

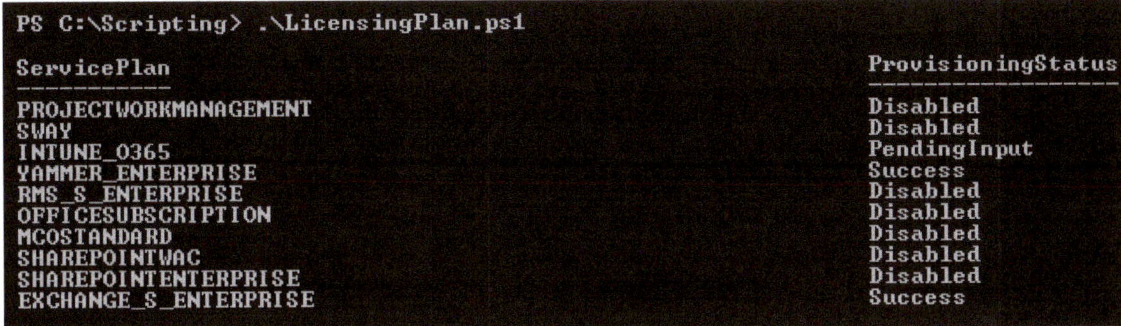

The results can also be verified in the Office 365 console:

Before

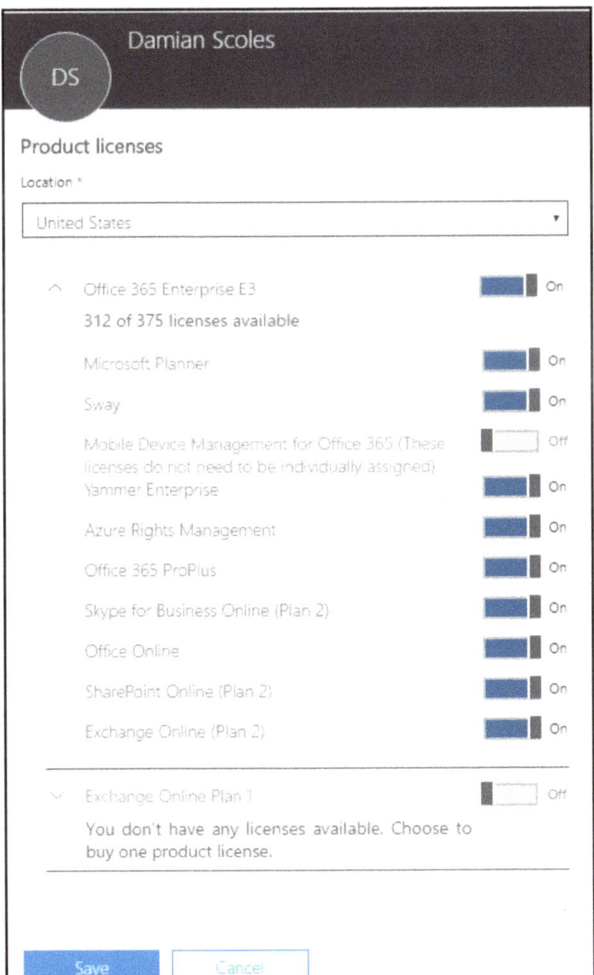

After

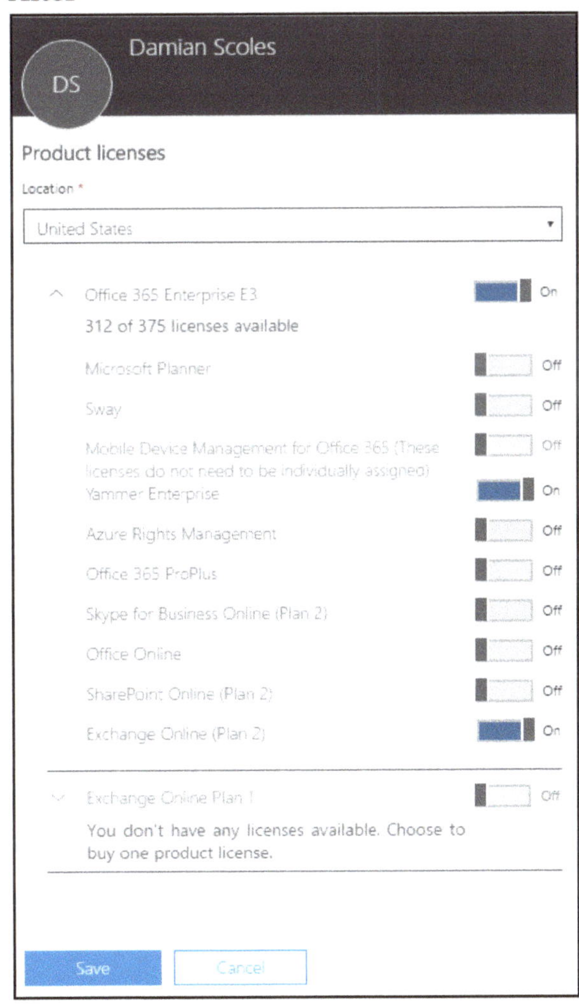

Why is this the solution? Unfortunately the licensing for Office 365 does not work in a cumulative manner or allow the option to choose which options to enable. For Office 365, Microsoft requires the licensing to be applied in a subtractive manner. For example with an E3 license (previous page) there are essentially 10 sub-licenses. By default, assigning an E3 license will enable all of these sub-licenses. However, if there are users that are only required to have Exchange Online, the other nine need to be disabled and instead of just enabling the Exchange Online license.

** **Note** ** The screen shots above are illustrative only and not indicative of current license options.

The option to select and unselect license options is important as need changes, user roles change, and organizational apps needs change and so on. Being able to add or remove individual licenses are important for maintaining strict access to applications that may only be necessary for a particular user's job function.

It should also be noted that the above methodology is aimed at limiting access of end users to services that an enterprise may not want to roll out to every user. The code could then be used to add services once a user population has been properly trained in how to use a particular service like Sway or Planner for some examples.

Sample Script 2

Take the same scenario where licenses need to be adjusted. IT management has decided that there will be licensing tiers to make sure that users only have access to applications that are required for them to do their jobs. The list of requirements is divided into four different licensing groups. Here are the requirements (by group):

Warehouse	Marketing	InfoWorkers	IT
EXCHANGE_S_ENTERPRISE	SWAY	INTUNE_O365	PROJECTWORKMANAGEMENT
SHAREPOINTWAC	YAMMER_ENTERPRISE	YAMMER_ENTERPRISE	SWAY
	RMS_S_ENTERPRISE	RMS_S_ENTERPRISE	INTUNE_O365
	OFFICESUBSCRIPTION	OFFICESUBSCRIPTION	YAMMER_ENTERPRISE
	MCOSTANDARD	MCOSTANDARD	RMS_S_ENTERPRISE
	SHAREPOINTWAC	SHAREPOINTWAC	OFFICESUBSCRIPTION
	SHAREPOINTENTERPRISE	SHAREPOINTENTERPRISE	MCOSTANDARD
	EXCHANGE_S_ENTERPRISE	EXCHANGE_S_ENTERPRISE	SHAREPOINTWAC
			SHAREPOINTENTERPRISE
			EXCHANGE_S_ENTERPRISE

In order to make this work properly, Active Directory Groups need to be assigned and then the licensing can be applied in a per group manner. First, the group assignment needs to occur in order to prepare for assigning licenses on a per group basis.

Sample Source CSV File

```
SamAccountNameGroup
Administrator,IT
Guest,Warehouse
Krbtgt,Marketing
Damian,IT
```

Sample Script Code

```powershell
# Read Users from CSV list
$Users = Import-Csv "c:\Scripting\GroupsToUsers.csv"

Foreach ($Line in $Users) {
    # 'normalize' variables
    $Member = $Line.SamAccountName
    $Group = $Line.Group

    # Add user to the group listed in the CSV file
    Try {
        Add-ADGroupMember -Identity $Group -Member $Member -ErrorAction STOP
        Write-Host "Successfully added $Member to the group $Group." -ForegroundColor Cyan
    } Catch {
        Write-Host "Could not add $Member to the group $Group." -ForegroundColor Yellow
    }
}
```

When run, the users are added to their respective groups:

```
PS C:\Scripting> .\UsersToGroups.ps1
Successfully added Administrator to the group IT.
Successfully added Guest to the group warehouse.
Successfully added krbtgt to the group Marketing.
Successfully added damian to the group IT.
Successfully added dstork to the group IT.
Successfully added tuser01 to the group Marketing.
Successfully added tuser02 to the group warehouse.
Successfully added adrms to the group IT.
Successfully added jton to the group Marketing.
Successfully added jforth to the group Marketing.
Successfully added jwithers to the group Marketing.
Successfully added GlenJohn to the group IT.
Successfully added wtell to the group Marketing.
Successfully added bfranklin to the group warehouse.
```

Now the groups have been populated, the disabled plans can be created – one per AD group:

```powershell
# Disabled Options for Warehouse workers
$DisabledOptionsWH = @()
$DisabledOptionsWH += "SWAY"
$DisabledOptionsWH += "YAMMER_ENTERPRISE"
$DisabledOptionsWH += "RMS_S_ENTERPRISE"
$DisabledOptionsWH += "OFFICESUBSCRIPTION"
$DisabledOptionsWH += "MCOSTANDARD"
$DisabledOptionsWH += "SHAREPOINTENTERPRISE"
$DisabledOptionsWH += "EXCHANGE_S_ENTERPRISE"
$DisabledOptionsWH += "SHAREPOINTENTERPRISE"
$DisabledOptionsWH += "PROJECTWORKMANAGEMENT"
```

```
# Disabled Options for Marketing
$DisabledOptionsMKT = @()
$DisabledOptionsMKT += "PROJECTWORKMANAGEMENT"

# Disabled Options for Information Workers
$DisabledOptionsIW = @()
$DisabledOptionsIW += "PROJECTWORKMANAGEMENT"
$DisabledOptionsIW += "SWAY"

# Disabled Options for Information Technology
# None - all active at this time
```

After the licensing options are configured, the user lists need to be created so that licenses can be assigned by group membership:

```
# Store group members into variables
$IW = Get-ADGroup "IT" | Get-AdGroupMember
$Marketing = Get-ADGroup "Marketing" | Get-AdGroupMember
$Warehouse = Get-ADGroup "Warehouse" | Get-AdGroupMember
```

Next the connection to Office 365 needs to be established:

```
# Connect to the Security and Compliance Center
Write-Host "Enter the password for Office 365 administrative rights." -ForegroundColor Cyan
Read-Host -SecureString | ConvertFrom-SecureString | Out-File "c:\scripting\securestring.txt"
$Password = cat "c:\scripting\securestring.txt" | ConvertTo-SecureString
$UserName = "<UPN of Global Admin>"
$O365Cred = New-Object -TypeName System.Management.Automation.PSCredential -ArgumentList $Username, $Password
$Session = New-PSSession -ConfigurationName Microsoft.SCC -ConnectionUri https://ps.compliance.protection.outlook.com/powershell-liveid/ -Credential $LiveCred -Authentication Basic -AllowRedirection
Import-PSSession $Session
```

Then a connection to the Microsoft Azure Active Directory tenant needs to be established:

```
# Connect to MSOL Service
Connect-MsolService -Credential $O365Cred
```

After all the connections are made (Office 365 and MSOL Service) and the variables are populated with the users to be configured for proper licensing, a licensing code block will be run for each group (a repeat of previous code):

```
# Set licensing for Information Workers
Foreach ($Line in $IW) {

    # Set variables
    $Upn = $Line.UserPrincipalName
    $Location = (Get-MsolUser -UserPrincipalName $Upn).UsageLocation
    $Licensed = (Get-MsolUser -UserPrincipalName $Upn).IsLicensed

    # Set location to United States
```

```
If ($Location -eq $Null) {
    Set-MsolUser -UserPrincipalName $Upn -UsageLocation "US"
}

# Assign full license to start with
If ($Licensed -eq $False) {
    Set-MsolUserLicense -UserPrincipalName $Upn -AddLicenses "<tenantname>:ENTERPRISEPACK"
}

# Remove 'excess' license options
$LicenseOptions = New-MsolLicenseOptions –AccountSkuId "<tenantname>:ENTERPRISEPACK" –
DisabledPlans $DisabledOptions
Set-MsolUserLicense –User $Upn –LicenseOptions $LicenseOptions
}
```

Repeat the same code above, simply switching out this one line for each group to be configured:

```
Foreach ($Line in $IW) {
```

Which becomes:

```
Foreach ($Line in $Marketing) {
```

And:

```
Foreach ($Line in $Warehouse) {
```

Now all users have their licensing configured per IT Management. Again, this code is for assigning licenses manually with PowerShell and does not rely on Azure AD Group Based Licensing.

Azure AD Recycle Bin

Azure AD has a Recycle Bin (similar to on-premises Active Directory) for objects that are removed from the tenant. These objects stay in the Recycle Bin for 30 days and then the objects are removed permanently. There are no direct PowerShell cmdlets (like Get-RecycleBin) for the Recycle Bin in Office 365. In order to find objects, the Get-MSOLUser cmdlet has a switch for this:

```
-ReturnDeletedUsers [<SwitchParameter>]
    If set, only users in the recycling bin will be deleted.

    Required?                      false
    Position?                      named
    Default value
    Accept pipeline input?         false
    Accept wildcard characters?    false
```

The 'ReturnDeletedUsers' will provide a list of users that were removed and are now awaiting for permanent deletion:

```
UserPrincipalName          DisplayName          isLicensed
-----------------          -----------          ----------
jdoe@domain.com            John Doe             False
hcastille@domain.com       Harold Castille      True
bhope@domain.com           Bob Hope             False
thill@domain.com           Thomas Hill          False
```

These same users can be removed with the Remove-MSOLUsers. Let's go through the process for an Office 365 tenant. Users that were recently deleted can be found in the Deleted Users tab under Users in the Office 365 interface:

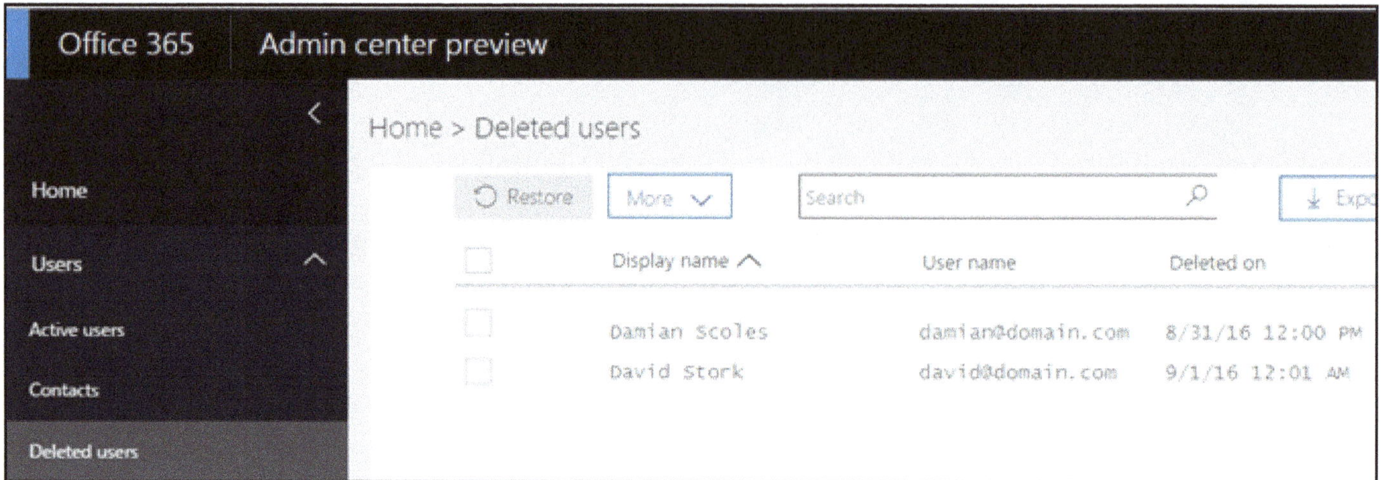

In order to properly remove users from the Recycle Bin, we first need the UPN and ObjectID. The UPN is needed to verify which user will be deleted while the ObjectID is actually used by PowerShell to remove the users [Don't forget to run Connect-MSOLService first]:

Get-MsolUser -ReturnDeletedUsers | Select UserPrincipalName, ObjectId

```
UserPrincipalName          Objectid
-----------------          --------
jdoe@domain.com            105856af-663a-49a8-bdad-efe8947ef70a
hcastille@domain.com       1b0ed587-4cf4-4e46-b5c5-5efab200007c
bhope@domain.com           866e6c23-629d-4239-aed9-c731173811dc
thill@domain.com           98fab817-b97b-436e-8854-47638b1af079
```

Example 1

Removing only one user from the Recycle Bin can be done with a one-liner. The only criteria needed as mentioned above, is the ObjectID from the list of objects in the Recycle Bin.

Remove-MsolUser -RemoveFromRecycleBin -ObjectId 98fab817-b97b-436e-8854-47638b1af079

```
PS C:\> Remove-MsolUser -RemoveFromRecycleBin -ObjectId 98fab817-b97b-436e-8854-47638b1af0

Confirm
Continue with this operation?
[Y] Yes  [N] No  [S] Suspend  [?] Help (default is "Y"): y
```

Then verify that the user is removed:

Get-MsolUser -ReturnDeletedUsers | select UserPrincipalName, ObjectId

```
UserPrincipalName          Objectid
-----------------          --------
jdoe@domain.com            105856af-663a-49a8-bdad-efe8947ef70a
hcastille@domain.com       1b0ed587-4cf4-4e46-b5c5-5efab200007c
bhope@domain.com           866e6c23-629d-4239-aed9-c731173811dc
```

Example 2

Removing all users in the Recycle Bin requires a query to get the objects stored in the Recycle Bin and then a cm-dlet to remove these objects. Is this example the ObjectID does not need to be specified as we are removing all items.

```
Get-MsolUser -ReturnDeletedUsers | Remove-MsolUser -RemoveFromRecycleBin
```

```
PS C:\> Get-MsolUser -ReturnDeletedUsers | Remove-MsolUser -RemoveFromRecycleBin

Confirm
Continue with this operation?
[Y] Yes   [N] No   [S] Suspend   [?] Help (default is "Y"): y

Confirm
Continue with this operation?
[Y] Yes   [N] No   [S] Suspend   [?] Help (default is "Y"): y

Confirm
Continue with this operation?
[Y] Yes   [N] No   [S] Suspend   [?] Help (default is "Y"): y
```

Then verify that the user is removed:

```
Get-MsolUser -ReturnDeletedUsers | select UserPrincipalName, ObjectId
```

```
PS C:\> Get-MsolUser -ReturnDeletedUsers | select UserPrincipalName, ObjectId
PS C:\> _
```

End Result – empty Recycle Bin.

Further Reading

Restoring objects from the Azure AD Recycle Bin - https://social.technet.microsoft.com/wiki/contents/articles/35910.azure-ad-recycle-bin-how-to-restore-objects.aspx

5   Security

In This Chapter
- Layered Security
- Role Groups
- Assigning Role Group Membership
- Removing User(s) From Role Groups
- Management Roles
- Audit in Security and Compliance Center

Layered Security

Ingrained in the coding of the Security and Compliance Center are layers of security that are used to prevent unauthorized access to various areas of this Office 365 workload like mailbox data, Data Loss Prevention (DLP) configuration and more. The ecosystem of security consists of multiple layers that enable a complex setup with administrators given access to all, some or none of this Office 365 interface. Typically the security layers concern is more on the administration side of the Security and Compliance Center, however, some conditions can also be applied to user access as well.

Role Groups are a special type of Security Group that contains Security Groups, other Role Groups and users which are also known as Role Group members. Group members can be added and removed to fit the needs of an organization. Management Roles are assigned to the groups. Management Role Scopes are also assigned to control what rights a Role Group member can exercise within Exchange.

Management Roles are groups of responsibilities that are grouped logically to help an administrator perform a certain task. These roles are assigned to Role Groups as part of this arrangement.

Auditing is the process of keeping track of changes. In the case of the Security and Compliance Center we have auditing for Admin changes PowerShell or EAC as well as auditing for mailbox access. Auditing can be monitored and reports generated for compliance and security requirements for an organization. Admin Audit logging and mailbox auditing is on by default as of the writing of this book, however additional auditing can be configured.. Check your region privacy settings before enabling any additional auditing features.

In this chapter we will cover these topics in-depth and as they relate to PowerShell.

Role Groups

Like any of the other workloads in Office 365, there are Role Groups and Management Roles that control access to various features and functions. Roles Groups are vehicles to be used to assign certain permissions to users in your organization.

PowerShell

Let's take a look at how we can reveal and work with these Role Groups in the SCC PowerShell.

```
Get-Command *RoleGroup*
```

We see we have a series of cmdlets that can be used to work with the Role Groups as well as the members of those same groups:

Add-RoleGroupMember	Remove-RoleGroup
Get-RoleGroup	Remove-RoleGroupMember
Get-RoleGroupMember	Set-RoleGroup
New-RoleGroup	Update-RoleGroupMember

First, let's review what Role Groups are available. We can use the second cmdlet in the list above 'Get-RoleGroup' to show what Role Groups are available:

```
Name                    AssignedRoles
----                    -------------
Reviewer                {FFO.extest.microsoft.com/Microsoft Exchange Hosted Organizations/______.onmicrosoft.com/Review}
RecordsManagement       {FFO.extest.microsoft.com/Microsoft Exchange Hosted Organizations/______.onmicrosoft.com/RecordManagement}
SecurityAdministrator   {FFO.extest.microsoft.com/Microsoft Exchange Hosted Organizations,______.onmicrosoft.com/Manage Alerts,
                        FFO.extest.microsoft.com/Microsoft Exchange Hosted Organizations______ onmicrosoft.com/View-Only Manage
                        Alerts, FFO.extest.microsoft.com/Microsoft Exchange Hosted Organizations,______.onmicrosoft.com/View-Only
                        Device Management, FFO.extest.microsoft.com/Microsoft Exchange Hosted
                        Organizations/______ onmicrosoft.com/DLP Compliance Management...}
OrganizationManagement  {FFO.extest.microsoft.com/Microsoft Exchange Hosted Organizations/______.onmicrosoft.com/View-Only
                        Retention Management, FFO.extest.microsoft.com/Microsoft Exchange Hosted
                        Organizations/______.onmicrosoft.com/Manage Alerts, FFO.extest.microsoft.com/Microsoft Exchange Hosted
                        Organizations/______ onmicrosoft.com/Role Management, FFO.extest.microsoft.com/Microsoft Exchange Hosted
                        Organizations______ onmicrosoft.com/View-Only Manage Alerts...}
SupervisoryReview       {FFO.extest.microsoft.com/Microsoft Exchange Hosted Organizations______.onmicrosoft.com/Supervisory
                        Review Administrator}
ComplianceAdministrator {FFO.extest.microsoft.com/Microsoft Exchange Hosted Organizations,______.onmicrosoft.com/View-Only
                        Retention Management, FFO.extest.microsoft.com/Microsoft Exchange Hosted
                        Organizations/______ onmicrosoft.com/Manage Alerts, FFO.extest.microsoft.com/Microsoft Exchange Hosted
                        Organizations______ onmicrosoft.com/View-Only Manage Alerts, FFO.extest.microsoft.com/Microsoft Exchange
                        Hosted Organizations,______.onmicrosoft.com/View-Only Device Management...}
SecurityReader          {FFO.extest.microsoft.com/Microsoft Exchange Hosted Organizations______ onmicrosoft.com/View-Only Manage
                        Alerts, FFO.extest.microsoft.com/Microsoft Exchange Hosted Organizations,______ onmicrosoft.com/View-Only
                        Device Management, FFO.extest.microsoft.com/Microsoft Exchange Hosted
                        Organizations/scoles.onmicrosoft.com/View-Only DLP Compliance Management,
                        FFO.extest.microsoft.com/Microsoft Exchange Hosted Organizations,______ onmicrosoft.com/Security Reader}
eDiscoveryManager       {FFO.extest.microsoft.com/Microsoft Exchange Hosted Organizations______.onmicrosoft.com/Export,
                        FFO.extest.microsoft.com/Microsoft Exchange Hosted Organizations/______ onmicrosoft.com/RMS Decrypt,
                        FFO.extest.microsoft.com/Microsoft Exchange Hosted Organizations,______ onmicrosoft.com/Review,
                        FFO.extest.microsoft.com/Microsoft Exchange Hosted Organizations______ onmicrosoft.com/Preview...}
TenantAdmins            {}
ServiceAssuranceUser    {FFO.extest.microsoft.com/Microsoft Exchange Hosted Organizations______ onmicrosoft.com/Service Assurance
                        View}
MailFlowAdministrator   {FFO.extest.microsoft.com/Microsoft Exchange Hosted Organizations______ onmicrosoft.com/View-Only
                        Recipients}
HelpdeskAdmins          {}
```

There are sixteen different Role Groups with many roles assigned to them. These roles will help you decide how to split out responsibilities. Each Role Group as a set of Assigned Roles that determine what that group can do. These Assigned Roles are known as Management Roles. These roles can also be reviewed in PowerShell in detail to see what they allow a Role Group member to do.

Let's take a sample Role Group to see what we can find out about the Role Groups:

Get-RoleGroup Reviewer | Fl

```
PS C:\> Get-RoleGroup Reviewer | fl

RunspaceId                 : d6a9246b-5f6e-40cb-903c-44cf5f9ebcf8
ManagedBy                  : {}
RoleAssignments            : {FFO.extest.microsoft.com/Microsoft Exchange Hosted
                             Organizations/________.onmicrosoft.com/Review-Reviewer}
Roles                      : {FFO.extest.microsoft.com/Microsoft Exchange Hosted Organizations/________.onmicrosoft.com/Review}
DisplayName                : Reviewer
ExternalDirectoryObjectId  :
Members                    : {FFO.extest.microsoft.com/Microsoft Exchange Hosted
                             Organizations/________.onmicrosoft.com/5fc8abf1-2178-4043-b601-4802e0a703cd,
                             FFO.extest.microsoft.com/Microsoft Exchange Hosted
                             Organizations/________.onmicrosoft.com/77893d3e-0064-40fd-ad52-fa86e3c2226d}
SamAccountName             :
Description                : Use a limited set of the analysis features in Office 365 Advanced eDiscovery. Members of this group
                             can see only the documents that are assigned to them.
RoleGroupType              : Standard
LinkedGroup                :
Capabilities               : {}
```

In red we have the Management Role that is assigned to the group and in blue is a detailed description of purpose of the Role Group. To see what all Role Groups are capable of, we can get the name and description like so:

Get-RoleGroup | Fl DisplayName,Description

```
DisplayName : Reviewer
Description : Use a limited set of the analysis features in Office 365 Advanced eDiscovery. Members of this group can
              see only the documents that are assigned to them.

DisplayName : Records Management
Description : Members of this management role group have permissions to manage and dispose record content.

DisplayName : Organization Management
Description : Members of this management role group have permissions to manage Exchange objects and their properties
              in the Exchange organization. Members can also delegate role groups and management roles in the
              organization. This role group shouldn't be deleted.

DisplayName : Security Administrator
Description :

DisplayName : Compliance Data Administrator
Description : Manage settings for device management, data protection, data loss prevention, reports, and preservation.

DisplayName : Security Operator
Description : Manage security alerts, and also view reports and settings of security features.

DisplayName : Company Administrator
Description : Membership in this role group is synchronized across services and managed centrally. This role group is
              not manageable through Microsoft Exchange. Members of this role group may include cross-service
              administrators, as well as external partner groups and Microsoft Support. By default, this group may not
              be assigned any roles. However, it will be a member of the Organization Management role group and will
              inherit the capabilities of that role group.

DisplayName : Security Reader
Description :
```

```
DisplayName : Compliance Administrator
Description : Manage settings for device management, data loss prevention, reports, and preservation.

DisplayName : Supervisory Review
Description : Control policies and permissions for reviewing employee communications.

DisplayName : eDiscovery Manager
Description : Perform searches and place holds on mailboxes, SharePoint Online sites, and OneDrive for Business
              locations.

DisplayName : Service Assurance User
Description : Access the Service Assurance section in the Security & Compliance Center. Members of this role group can
              use this section to review documents related to security, privacy, and compliance in Office 365 to
              perform risk and assurance reviews for their own organization.

DisplayName : MailFlow Administrator
Description :

DisplayName : Data Investigator
Description : Perform searches on mailboxes, SharePoint Online sites, and OneDrive for Business locations.

DisplayName : Helpdesk Administrator
Description : Membership in this role group is synchronized across services and managed centrally. This role group is
              not manageable through Microsoft Exchange. Members of this role group may include cross-service helpdesk
              or password administrators, as well as external partner groups and Microsoft Support. By default, this
              group is not assigned any roles. However, it will be a member of the View-Only Organization Management
              role group and will inherit the rights of that group.

DisplayName : Global Reader
Description : View reports, alerts, and settings of security and compliance features.
```

Notice that there are gaps in the information available. In order to get a better understanding of these roles, we need to go to Microsoft's documentation Online. Easiest way to find this is with a search query with your favorite search engine:

Search Terms: MailFlow Administrator

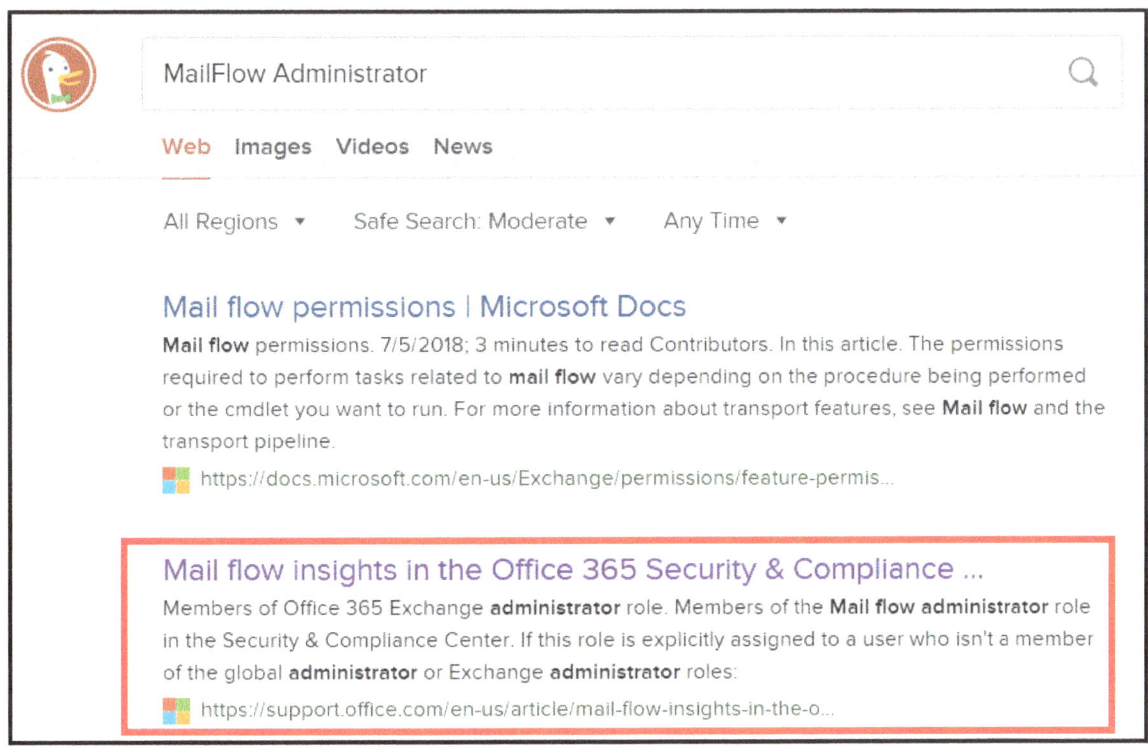

We click on the search result above and are provided with a description of the Mail Flow Administrator:

- The user may log in to the Security and Compliance Center directly at https://protection.office.com.
- The user will only have read-only permission to the mail flow dashboard.
- The user won't have access to the Office 365 admin portal.

Additionally, more Role Group descriptions can be found here:

https://docs.microsoft.com/en-us/office365/securitycompliance/permissions-in-the-security-and-compliance-center#relationship-of-members-roles-and-role-groups

Security Reviewer

"Members have read-only access to a number of security features of Identity Protection Center, Privileged Identity Management, Monitor Office 365 Service Health, and Office 365 Security & Compliance Center. Membership in this role group is synchronized across services and managed centrally. This role group is not manageable through the administrator portals. Members of this role group may include cross-service administrators, as well as external partner groups and Microsoft Support. By default, this group may not be assigned any roles. However, it will be a member of the Security Reader role groups and will inherit the capabilities of that role group. "

Security Administrator

"Membership in this role group is synchronized across services and managed centrally. This role group is not manageable through the administrator portals. Members of this role group may include cross-service administrators, as well as external partner groups and Microsoft Support. By default, this group may not be assigned any roles. However, it will be a member of the Security Administrators role groups and will inherit the capabilities of that role group. All of the read-only permissions of the Security reader role, plus a number of additional administrative permissions for the same services: Azure Information Protection, Identity Protection Center, Privileged Identity Management, Monitor Office 365 Service Health, and Office 365 Security & Compliance Center. "

Management Roles per Role Groups

In order to get a list of the Management Roles in each Role Group, we need to tinker a bit with PowerShell to get a list that visually makes sense. The limitation to overcome is that the amount of Management Roles can be large for some of the Role Groups, which leads to incomplete listings like this:

```
Name                        RoleAssignments
----                        ---------------
Reviewer                    {Review-Reviewer}
RecordsManagement           {RecordManagement-Records Management}
OrganizationManagement      {Search And Purge-Organization Management, DLP
                            Management...}
ComplianceAdministrator     {View-Only Retention Management-Compliance Adm
                            Recipients-Compliance Administrator...}
SupervisoryReview           {Supervisory Review Administrator-Supervisory
SecurityAdministrator       {Audit Logs-Security Administrator, Device Man
                            Management-Security Administrator...}
TenantAdmins                {}
HelpdeskAdmins              {}
SecurityReader              {Security Reader-Security Reader, View-Only Ma
                            Reader}
eDiscoveryManager           {Export-eDiscovery Manager, Case Management-eD
```

We'll have to use a loop and some special formatting in order to get a good display. Using the code below, we can do this:

```
$Output = Get-RoleGroup
Foreach ($Line in $Output) {
   $Name = $Line.Name
   Write-Host "$Name" -ForegroundColor Cyan
   Write-host "----------------------------" -ForegroundColor Cyan
   $Roles = $Line.RoleAssignments
   Foreach ($Role in $Roles) {
      Write-host " $Role" -ForegroundColor White
   }
}
```

The output from the above script looks something like this (truncated):

```
ComplianceAdministrator
---------------------------
 View-Only Retention Management-Compliance Administrator
 Case Management-Compliance Administrator
 DLP Compliance Management-Compliance Administrator
 View-Only Recipients-Compliance Administrator
 View-Only Audit Logs-Compliance Administrator
 Organization Configuration-Compliance Administrator
 RecordManagement-Compliance Administrator
 Hold-Compliance Administrator
 View-Only Device Management-Compliance Administrator
 Device Management-Compliance Administrator
 Retention Management-Compliance Administrator
 View-Only Record Management-Compliance Administrator
 View-Only Manage Alerts-Compliance Administrator
 Compliance Search-Compliance Administrator
 View-Only DLP Compliance Management-Compliance Administrator
 Compliance Administrator-Compliance Administrator
 Manage Alerts-Compliance Administrator
 Disposition Management-Compliance Administrator

SupervisoryReview
---------------------------
 Supervisory Review Administrator-Supervisory Review

SecurityAdministrator
---------------------------
 Audit Logs-Security Administrator
 Device Management-Security Administrator
 DLP Compliance Management-Security Administrator
 View-Only DLP Compliance Management-Security Administrator
 View-Only Manage Alerts-Security Administrator
 View-Only Device Management-Security Administrator
 Manage Alerts-Security Administrator
 Security Administrator-Security Administrator
 View-Only Audit Logs-Security Administrator
```

... and so on until all Role Assignments are listed additionally for Tenant Admins, HelpDesk Admins, Security Reader, eDiscovery Manager, Service Assurance User and Mail Flow Administrator.

Assigning Role Group Membership

Now that we've covered the Role Groups and what they are responsible for, we can cover how to add and remove users from these groups. First, adding a member to a group. In the set of cmdlets for managing Role Groups, there is a cmdlet called 'Add-RoleGroupMember' that is used to add users that exist in Azure AD to the various Role Groups present in the SCC.

PowerShell

Some practical examples are provided below. First example shows the user 'Colleen' being added to the Mail Flow Administrators group:

    Add-RoleGroupMember -Identity MailFlowAdministrator -Member Colleen

In this next example, we are adding a user Ed Wright (alias is 'EWright') to the Reviewer Role Group:

    Add-RoleGroupMember -Identity Reviewer -Member EWright

Now that we've seen how users can be added to groups, let's do a deeper dive into the effects on a user who now has access to the SCC. We will see the PowerShell cmdlets they are allowed to use as well as how the SCC GUI itself changes from Role Group to Role Group.

Mail Flow Administrator Role

A Mail Flow Administrator has only one assigned role in the SCC and that is 'View-Only Recipients':

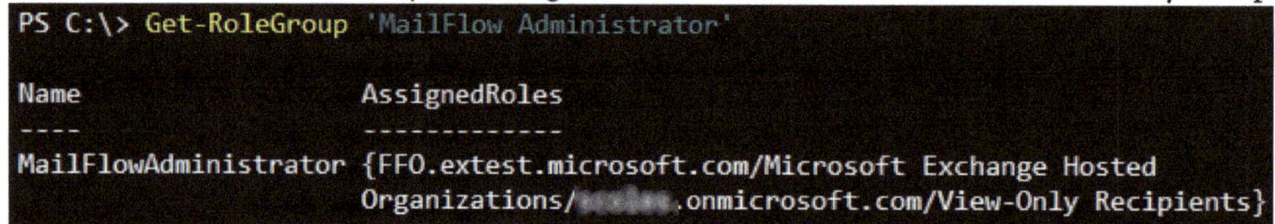

The Security and Compliance Center looks like this when the Mail Flow Administrator role is assigned:

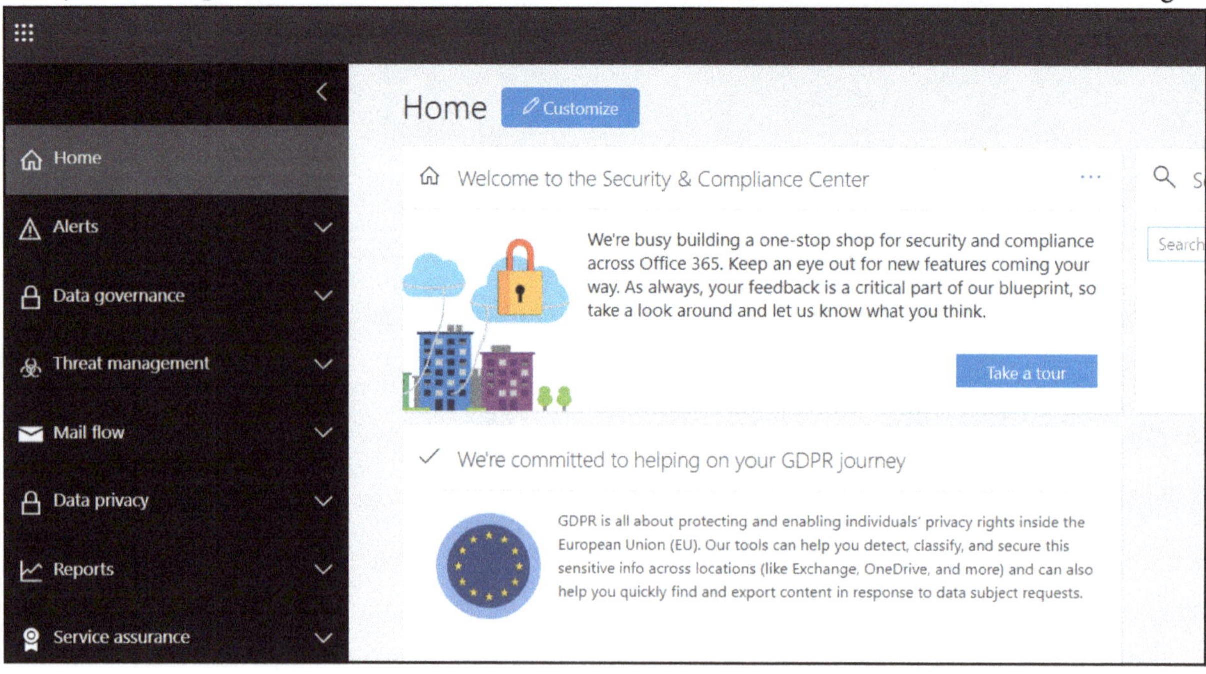

If we specifically look at Mail Flow in the menu, we see that we only have the dashboard revealed:

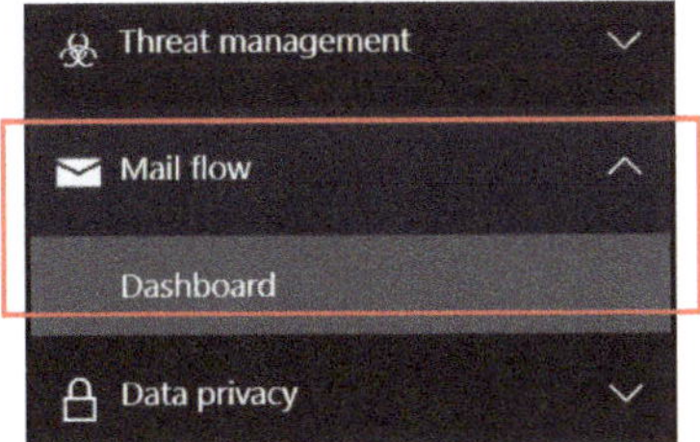

Clicking on the dashboard under Mail Flow also reveals that some features and functions have been removed for this role:

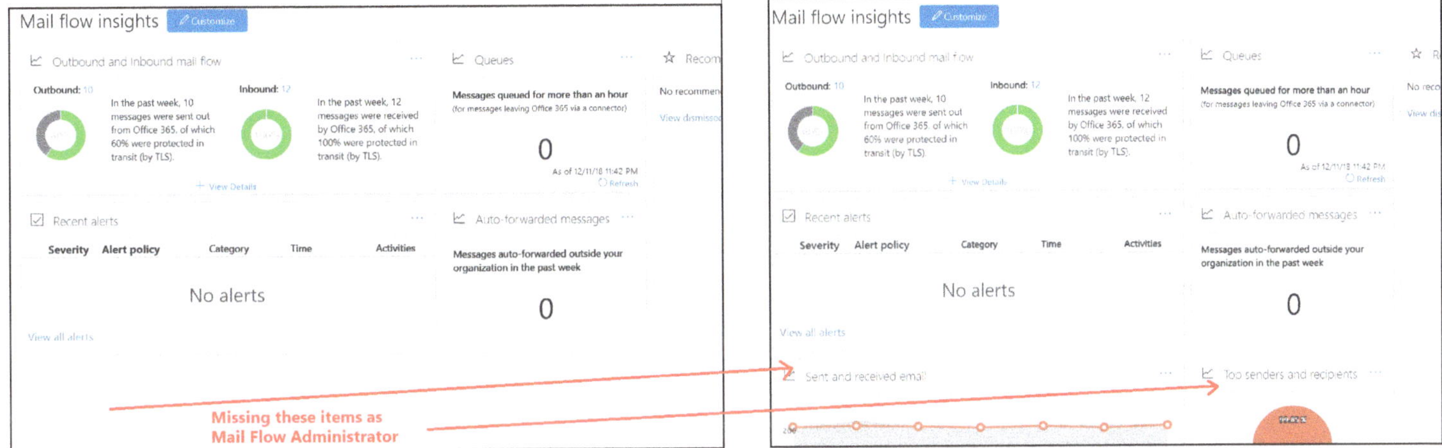

PowerShell as a Mail Flow Administrator

If an account only has the above role and then logs into the Security and Compliance Center via PowerShell, a limited set of PowerShell cmdlets for the Security and Compliance center are made available. These can be revealed with a little bit of PowerShell. In the below code, the section - where {$_.Source -Like 'tmp*'} - will reveal only SCC cmdlets:

```
Get-Command | Where {$_.Source -Like 'tmp*'}
```

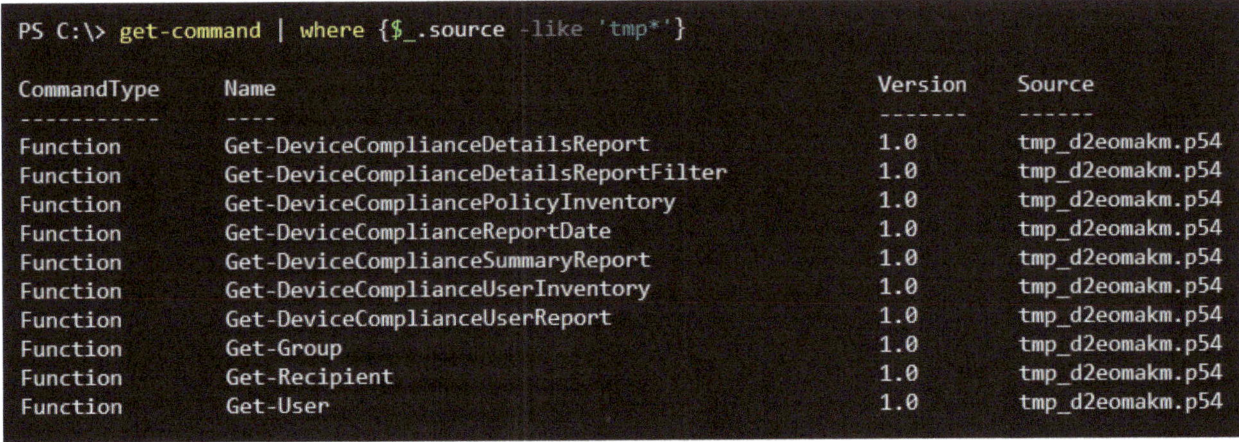

Notice that the cmdlets are, like the role is configured, Read Only cmdlets. This means that this role is allowed to check in on some functions, specifically around Device Compliance. We are provided with ten cmdlets with this Role Group.

Reviewer Role

A reviewer in the Security and Compliance Center is also a limited role. This role has only one role assigned to it leaving it with limited responsibilities as well:

```
RoleAssignments               : {FFO.extest.microsoft.com/Microsoft Exchange Hosted
                                Organizations/        .onmicrosoft.com/Review-Reviewer}
```

PowerShell as a Reviewer

After logging in as a user with this new role, we can also review what PowerShell cmdlets are available:

Get-Command | Where {$_.Source -Like 'tmp*'}

```
PS C:\> get-command | where {$_.Source -like "tmp*"}

CommandType     Name                                    Version     Source
-----------     ----                                    -------     ------
Function        Get-CaseHoldPolicy                      1.0         tmp_wvfdhqk0.3bd
Function        Get-CaseHoldRule                        1.0         tmp_wvfdhqk0.3bd
Function        Get-ComplianceCase                      1.0         tmp_wvfdhqk0.3bd
Function        Get-ComplianceCaseMember                1.0         tmp_wvfdhqk0.3bd
Function        Get-ComplianceCaseMemberCandidate       1.0         tmp_wvfdhqk0.3bd
Function        Get-ComplianceCustodian                 1.0         tmp_wvfdhqk0.3bd
Function        Get-ComplianceEmailSetting              1.0         tmp_wvfdhqk0.3bd
Function        Get-ComplianceNotice                    1.0         tmp_wvfdhqk0.3bd
Function        Get-ComplianceSearch                    1.0         tmp_wvfdhqk0.3bd
Function        Get-ComplianceSearchAction              1.0         tmp_wvfdhqk0.3bd
```

Again, it's a smaller role and the amount of PowerShell cmdlets that are available is small - ten in total.

The Security and Compliance Center is again altered for this role:. Search and Investigation replaces Reports from the previous view:

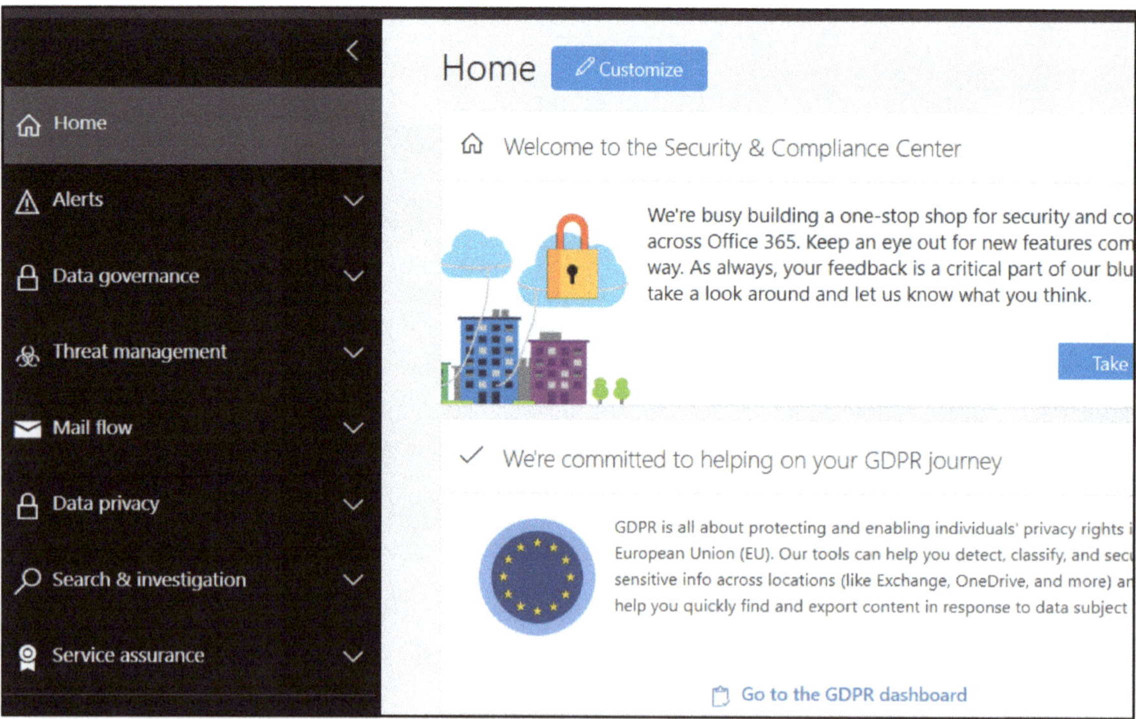

The real focus of this role is in the Search and Investigation part of the Security and Compliance Center:

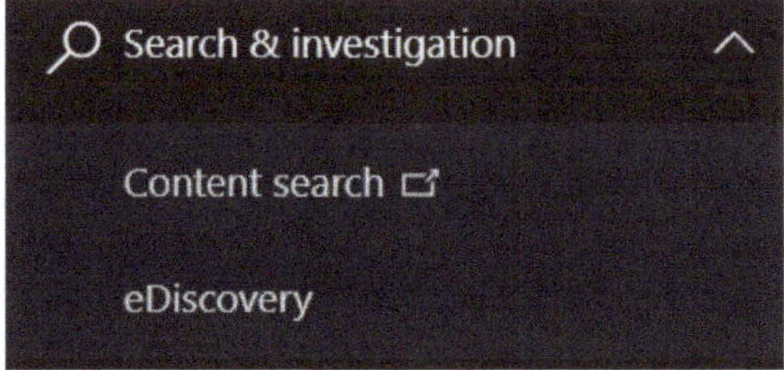

Records Management

Records Management also has one role assigned to it in the SCC and that is 'Record Management':

"Allow viewing and editing configuration and reports for the Record Management feature".

```
RoleAssignments : {FFO.extest.microsoft.com/Microsoft Exchange Hosted
                  Organizations/          .onmicrosoft.com/RecordManagement-Records Management}
```

Very little in the way of interaction or options are now provided to the user with this role.

```
PS C:\> get-command | Where {$_.Source -like "tmp*"}

CommandType     Name                                              Version   Source
-----------     ----                                              -------   ------
Function        Get-DataRetentionReport                           1.0       tmp_cfeowtqu.kye
Function        Remove-RecordLabel                                1.0       tmp_cfeowtqu.kye
```

We can see that the Get-DataRetentionReport has potential from a PowerShell perspective:

```
PS C:\> Get-DataRetentionReport

Organization        Date                       Action           DataSource MessageCount
------------        ----                       ------           ---------- ------------
      .onmicrosoft.com 11/30/2018 12:00:00 AM RetentionDeletion Exchange   0
      .onmicrosoft.com 12/1/2018 12:00:00 AM  RetentionDeletion Exchange   0
      .onmicrosoft.com 12/2/2018 12:00:00 AM  RetentionDeletion Exchange   0
      .onmicrosoft.com 12/3/2018 12:00:00 AM  RetentionDeletion Exchange   0
      .onmicrosoft.com 12/4/2018 12:00:00 AM  RetentionDeletion Exchange   0
      .onmicrosoft.com 12/5/2018 12:00:00 AM  RetentionDeletion Exchange   0
      .onmicrosoft.com 12/6/2018 12:00:00 AM  RetentionDeletion Exchange   0
      .onmicrosoft.com 12/7/2018 12:00:00 AM  RetentionDeletion Exchange   0
      .onmicrosoft.com 12/8/2018 12:00:00 AM  RetentionDeletion Exchange   0
      .onmicrosoft.com 12/9/2018 12:00:00 AM  RetentionDeletion Exchange   0
      .onmicrosoft.com 12/10/2018 12:00:00 AM RetentionDeletion Exchange   0
```

In addition to the restricted cmdlets available for the Records Management role, we also see that when we log into the Security and Compliance Center as a user with the Records Management role.

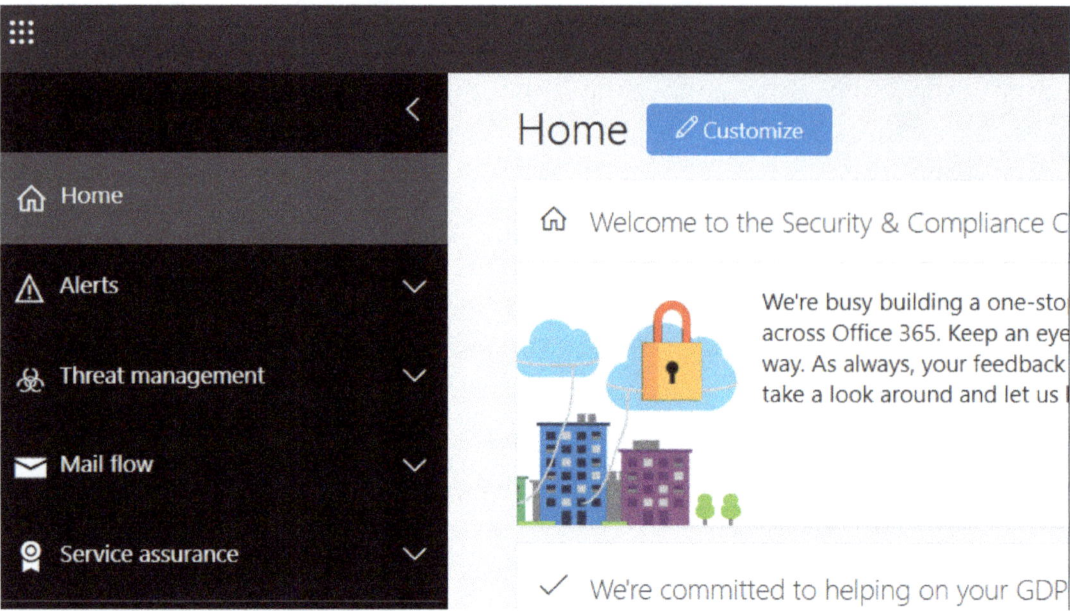

Security Administrator

This role entails a lot more responsibility and thus quite a few more PowerShell cmdlets. This role has access to around 100 cmdlets in the Security and Compliance Center:

Get-ActivityAlert	Migrate-DlpFingerprint	Remove-DlpSensitiveInformationType
Get-AdminAuditLogConfig	New-ActivityAlert	Remove-DlpSensitiveInformationTypeRulePackage
Get-ContentIndexingProcess	New-AdminAuditLogSearch	Remove-InformationBarrierPolicy
Get-DeviceComplianceDetailsReport	New-DeviceConditionalAccessPolicy	Remove-ProtectionAlert
Get-DeviceComplianceDetailsReportFilter	New-DeviceConditionalAccessRule	Remove-ThreatResponsePolicy
Get-DeviceCompliancePolicyInventory	New-DeviceConfigurationPolicy	Remove-ThreatResponseRule
Get-DeviceComplianceReportDate	New-DeviceConfigurationRule	Search-AdminAuditLog
Get-DeviceComplianceSummaryReport	New-DeviceTenantPolicy	Set-ActivityAlert
Get-DeviceComplianceUserInventory	New-DeviceTenantRule	Set-AuditConfig
Get-DeviceComplianceUserReport	New-DlpCompliancePolicy	Set-DeviceConditionalAccessPolicy
Get-DeviceConditionalAccessPolicy	New-DlpComplianceRule	Set-DeviceConditionalAccessRule
Get-DeviceConditionalAccessRule	New-DlpComplianceRuleV2	Set-DeviceConfigurationPolicy
Get-DeviceConfigurationPolicy	New-DlpEdmSchema	Set-DeviceConfigurationRule
Get-DeviceConfigurationRule	New-DlpFingerprint	Set-DeviceTenantPolicy
Get-DevicePolicy	New-DlpKeywordDictionary	Set-DeviceTenantRule
Get-DeviceTenantPolicy	New-DlpSensitiveInformationType	Set-DlpCompliancePolicy
Get-DeviceTenantRule	New-DlpSensitiveInformationTypeRulePackage	Set-DlpComplianceRule
Get-DlpCompliancePolicy	New-InformationBarrierPolicy	Set-DlpComplianceRuleV2
Get-DlpComplianceRule	New-ProtectionAlert	Set-DlpEdmSchema
Get-DlpComplianceRuleV2	New-ThreatResponsePolicy	Set-DlpKeywordDictionary
Get-DlpDetectionsReport	New-ThreatResponseRule	Set-DlpSensitiveInformationType
Get-DlpEdmSchema	Remove-ActivityAlert	Set-DlpSensitiveInformationTypeConfig
Get-DlpKeywordDictionary	Remove-DeviceConditionalAccessPolicy	Set-DlpSensitiveInformationTypeRulePackage
Get-DlpSensitiveInformationType	Remove-DeviceConditionalAccessRule	Set-InformationBarrierPolicy
Get-DlpSensitiveInformationTypeConfig	Remove-DeviceConfigurationPolicy	Set-PolicyConfig
Get-DlpSensitiveInformationTypeRulePackage	Remove-DeviceConfigurationRule	Set-ProtectionAlert
Get-InformationBarrierPoliciesApplicationStatus	Remove-DeviceTenantPolicy	Set-ThreatResponsePolicy
Get-InformationBarrierPolicy	Remove-DeviceTenantRule	Set-ThreatResponseRule
Get-InformationBarrierRecipientStatus	Remove-DlpCompliancePolicy	Start-ContentIndexingProcess
Get-PolicyConfig	Remove-DlpComplianceRule	Start-InformationBarrierPoliciesApplication
Get-ProtectionAlert	Remove-DlpComplianceRuleV2	Stop-InformationBarrierPoliciesApplication
Get-ThreatResponsePolicy	Remove-DlpEdmSchema	Test-DataClassification
Get-ThreatResponseRule	Remove-DlpKeywordDictionary	Test-InformationBarrierPolicy
Import-ExchangeDlpPolicy		

Also, unlike the few roles we've examined so far, this Management Role has access to PowerShell cmdlets with more than just Get cmdlets. We see Import, New, Remove, Search, Set, Start, Stop and Test verbs available. We also see that this role has quite a few Role Assignments to it:

```
(Get-RoleGroup SecurityAdministrator).RoleAssignments
```

```
ations,______.onmicrosoft.com/Audit Logs-Security Administrator
ations,______.onmicrosoft.com/Device Management-Security Administrator
ations,______.onmicrosoft.com/DLP Compliance Management-Security Administrator
ations,______.onmicrosoft.com/View-Only DLP Compliance Management-Security Administrator
ations,______.onmicrosoft.com/View-Only Manage Alerts-Security Administrator
ations,______.onmicrosoft.com/View-Only Device Management-Security Administrator
ations,______.onmicrosoft.com/Manage Alerts-Security Administrator
ations,______.onmicrosoft.com/Security Administrator-Security Administrator
ations,______.onmicrosoft.com/View-Only Audit Logs-Security Administrator
ations,______.onmicrosoft.com/Sensitivity Label Administrator-Security Administrator
ations,______.onmicrosoft.com/IB Compliance Management-Security Administrator
ations,______.onmicrosoft.com/View-Only IB Compliance Management-Security Administrator
```

This role could also include some cross-service administrators. As we can see above, it has access to roles relevant to Information Barriers, Audit Logs, Device Management, and some view only roles like DLP, Alerts, etc.

Organization Management

This Role Group has even more responsibility than the previous role with up to 278 PowerShell cmdlets available. Below is a very small chunk from the list:

```
PS C:\> Get-Command | Where {$_.Source -like 'tmp*'}

CommandType     Name                              Version    Source
-----------     ----                              -------    ------
Function        Add-ComplianceCaseMember          1.0        tmp_jjabn4mp.gwt
Function        Add-eDiscoveryCaseAdmin           1.0        tmp_jjabn4mp.gwt
Function        Add-RoleGroupMember               1.0        tmp_jjabn4mp.gwt
Function        Create-FilePlanFirstRunLabels     1.0        tmp_jjabn4mp.gwt
Function        Enable-ComplianceBoundaryStorage  1.0        tmp_jjabn4mp.gwt
Function        Enable-ComplianceFeature          1.0        tmp_jjabn4mp.gwt
Function        Enable-ComplianceTagStorage       1.0        tmp_jjabn4mp.gwt
Function        Export-FilePlanProperty           1.0        tmp_jjabn4mp.gwt
Function        Get-ActivityAlert                 1.0        tmp_jjabn4mp.gwt
Function        Get-AdminAuditLogConfig           1.0        tmp_jjabn4mp.gwt
Function        Get-AuditConfig                   1.0        tmp_jjabn4mp.gwt
```

This role has full access to the tenant as well as what is in the Security and Compliance Center. The interface used at https://protection.office.com is not restricted either. This user with this role would bear great responsibility and be tasked with a higher level of access in an Office 365 tenant. In terms of least permissions, very few users should have this role assigned.

We can also see there are even more Roles assigned than the Security Administrator role group:

```
ions/████.onmicrosoft.com/Search And Purge-Organization Management
ions/████.onmicrosoft.com/DLP Compliance Management-Organization Management
ions/████.onmicrosoft.com/Case Management-Organization Management
ions/████.onmicrosoft.com/Manage Alerts-Organization Management
ions/████.onmicrosoft.com/Compliance Administrator-Organization Management
ions/████.onmicrosoft.com/View-Only Manage Alerts-Organization Management
ions/████.onmicrosoft.com/Security Administrator-Organization Management
ions/████.onmicrosoft.com/View-Only DLP Compliance Management-Organization Management
ions/████.onmicrosoft.com/View-Only Device Management-Organization Management
ions/████.onmicrosoft.com/Audit Logs-Organization Management
ions/████.onmicrosoft.com/RecordManagement-Organization Management
ions/████.onmicrosoft.com/Retention Management-Organization Management
ions/████.onmicrosoft.com/Security Reader-Organization Management
ions/████.onmicrosoft.com/Role Management-Organization Management
ions/████.onmicrosoft.com/Organization Configuration-Organization Management
ions/████.onmicrosoft.com/View-Only Retention Management-Organization Management
ions/████.onmicrosoft.com/View-Only Recipients-Organization Management
ions/████.onmicrosoft.com/Hold-Organization Management
ions/████.onmicrosoft.com/View-Only Record Management-Organization Management
ions/████.onmicrosoft.com/Device Management-Organization Management
ions/████.onmicrosoft.com/Compliance Search-Organization Management
ions/████.onmicrosoft.com/Service Assurance View-Organization Management
ions/████.onmicrosoft.com/View-Only Audit Logs-Organization Management
ions/████.onmicrosoft.com/Disposition Management-Organization Management
ions/████.onmicrosoft.com/Sensitivity Label Administrator-Organization Management
ions/████.onmicrosoft.com/IB Compliance Management-Organization Management
ions/████.onmicrosoft.com/View-Only IB Compliance Management-Organization Management
```

Supervisory Review

The Supervisory Review Role is a relatively new role that allows the holder to review emails from user's that are under Supervision. The role grants these users access to Supervisory mailboxes for users they are assigned to monitor. Emails being monitored can be viewed in the SCC by the user with this role or via an exposed mailbox (see Chapter 8 Supervision for more information). As we can see below, we have a limited set of cmdlets that are exposed to this Role and they are contain the Supervisory noun in them:

```
PS C:\> Get-Command | where {$_.Source -like "tmp*"}

CommandType     Name                                      Version     Source
-----------     ----                                      -------     ------
Function        Get-Recipient                             1.0         tmp_defcjij3.jtz
Function        Get-SupervisoryReviewActivity             1.0         tmp_defcjij3.jtz
Function        Get-SupervisoryReviewOverallProgressReport 1.0        tmp_defcjij3.jtz
Function        Get-SupervisoryReviewPolicy               1.0         tmp_defcjij3.jtz
Function        Get-SupervisoryReviewPolicyReport         1.0         tmp_defcjij3.jtz
Function        Get-SupervisoryReviewPolicyV2             1.0         tmp_defcjij3.jtz
Function        Get-SupervisoryReviewReport               1.0         tmp_defcjij3.jtz
Function        Get-SupervisoryReviewRule                 1.0         tmp_defcjij3.jtz
Function        Get-SupervisoryReviewTopCasesReport       1.0         tmp_defcjij3.jtz
Function        New-SupervisoryReviewPolicy               1.0         tmp_defcjij3.jtz
Function        New-SupervisoryReviewPolicyV2             1.0         tmp_defcjij3.jtz
Function        New-SupervisoryReviewRule                 1.0         tmp_defcjij3.jtz
Function        Remove-SupervisoryReviewPolicy            1.0         tmp_defcjij3.jtz
Function        Remove-SupervisoryReviewPolicyV2          1.0         tmp_defcjij3.jtz
Function        Set-SupervisoryReviewPolicy               1.0         tmp_defcjij3.jtz
Function        Set-SupervisoryReviewPolicyV2             1.0         tmp_defcjij3.jtz
Function        Set-SupervisoryReviewRule                 1.0         tmp_defcjij3.jtz
```

Compliance Administrator

The Compliance Administrator has nearly as many PowerShell cmdlets as does the Organization Management role. The total number of cmdlets is 222 in the Security and Compliance Center. These cmdlets are exposed because the Compliance Administrator has quite a few assigned roles:

```
ons/      .onmicrosoft.com/View-Only Retention Management-Compliance Administrator
ons/      .onmicrosoft.com/Case Management-Compliance Administrator
ons/      .onmicrosoft.com/DLP Compliance Management-Compliance Administrator
ons/      .onmicrosoft.com/View-Only Recipients-Compliance Administrator
ons/      .onmicrosoft.com/View-Only Audit Logs-Compliance Administrator
ons/      .onmicrosoft.com/Organization Configuration-Compliance Administrator
ons/      .onmicrosoft.com/RecordManagement-Compliance Administrator
ons/      .onmicrosoft.com/Hold-Compliance Administrator
ons/      .onmicrosoft.com/View-Only Device Management-Compliance Administrator
ons/      .onmicrosoft.com/Device Management-Compliance Administrator
ons/      .onmicrosoft.com/Retention Management-Compliance Administrator
ons/      .onmicrosoft.com/View-Only Record Management-Compliance Administrator
ons/      .onmicrosoft.com/View-Only Manage Alerts-Compliance Administrator
ons/      .onmicrosoft.com/Compliance Search-Compliance Administrator
ons/      .onmicrosoft.com/View-Only DLP Compliance Management-Compliance Administrator
ons/      .onmicrosoft.com/Compliance Administrator-Compliance Administrator
ons/      .onmicrosoft.com/Manage Alerts-Compliance Administrator
ons/      .onmicrosoft.com/Disposition Management-Compliance Administrator
ons/      .onmicrosoft.com/IB Compliance Management-Compliance Administrator
ons/      .onmicrosoft.com/View-Only IB Compliance Management-Compliance Administrator
ons/      .onmicrosoft.com/Data Investigation Management-Compliance Administrator
```

The Compliance Administrator has quite a few View-Only assigned roles in the Security and Compliance Center. From the list of assigned roles and the plethora of PowerShell cmdlets available we can assume this is also a higher profile role in the SCC. This role has access to Information Barrier info, View-Only on DLP Compliance, Recipients Audit Logs, Records, Alerts and Device Management.

If an organization already has a Compliance Administrator, this would obviously match well. These individuals will need to have access to compliance cases, review Records and be able to pull various bits of information from the SCC.

Security Reader

The Security Reader group is also a cross workload security group, so members might be pulled from other sources. This role is a limited role in the Security and Compliance Center. There are five assigned roles which are all a variety of View-Only for items in the SCC:

```
ations/      .onmicrosoft.com/Security Reader-Security Reader
ations/      .onmicrosoft.com/View-Only Manage Alerts-Security Reader
ations/      .onmicrosoft.com/View-Only DLP Compliance Management-Security Reader
ations/      .onmicrosoft.com/View-Only Device Management-Security Reader
ations/      .onmicrosoft.com/View-Only IB Compliance Management-Security Reader
```

As such, it also has a limited set of 22 PowerShell cmdlets to use:

```
Get-ActivityAlert                             Get-DeviceComplianceDetailsReport
Get-DeviceComplianceDetailsReportFilter       Get-DeviceCompliancePolicyInventory
Get-DeviceComplianceReportDate                Get-DeviceComplianceSummaryReport
Get-DeviceComplianceUserInventory             Get-DeviceComplianceUserReport
Get-DeviceConditionalAccessPolicy             Get-DeviceConditionalAccessRule
Get-DeviceConfigurationPolicy                 Get-DeviceConfigurationRule
Get-DevicePolicy                              Get-DeviceTenantPolicy
Get-DeviceTenantRule                          Get-DlpCompliancePolicy
Get-DlpComplianceRule                         Get-DlpDetectionsReport
Get-DlpEdmSchema                              Get-DlpKeywordDictionary
Get-DlpSensitiveInformationType               Get-DlpSensitiveInformationTypeRulePackage
Get-InformationBarrierPoliciesApplicationStatus  Get-InformationBarrierPolicy
Get-InformationBarrierRecipientStatus         Get-InformationBarrierReportDetails
Get-InformationBarrierReportSummary           Get-OrganizationSegment
Get-ProtectionAlert                           New-DlpEdmSchema
Remove-OrganizationSegment                    Set-DlpEdmSchema
Set-InformationBarrierPolicy                  Set-OrganizationSegment
Start-InformationBarrierPoliciesApplication   Stop-InformationBarrierPoliciesApplication
Test-InformationBarrierPolicy
```

The above cmdlets, while restrictive, do cover the wide variety of components - Device Compliance, Exact Data Match (EDM), Information Barriers, and some DLP.

eDiscovery Manager/Administrator

The eDiscovery Manager role is an interesting security option in the Security and Compliance Center. The role is actually one of two roles - eDiscovery Manager and the eDiscovery Administrator - and we see this in the GUI and in PowerShell for the SCC:

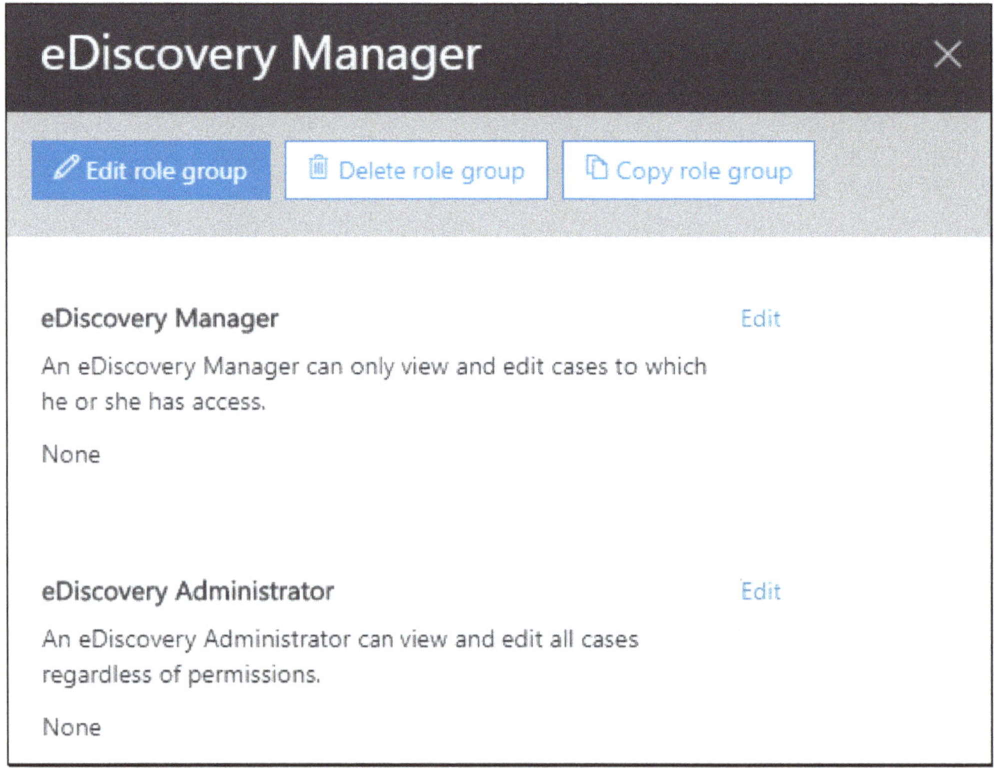

In PowerShell, we see there are special cmdlets to handle the eDiscovery Administrator:

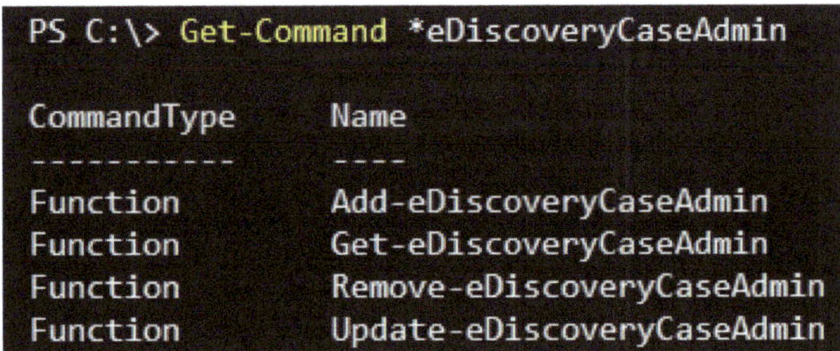

```
PS C:\> Get-Command *eDiscoveryCaseAdmin

CommandType        Name
-----------        ----
Function           Add-eDiscoveryCaseAdmin
Function           Get-eDiscoveryCaseAdmin
Function           Remove-eDiscoveryCaseAdmin
Function           Update-eDiscoveryCaseAdmin
```

We need these cmdlets because the eDiscovery Administrator is NOT listed in the list of all Role Groups:

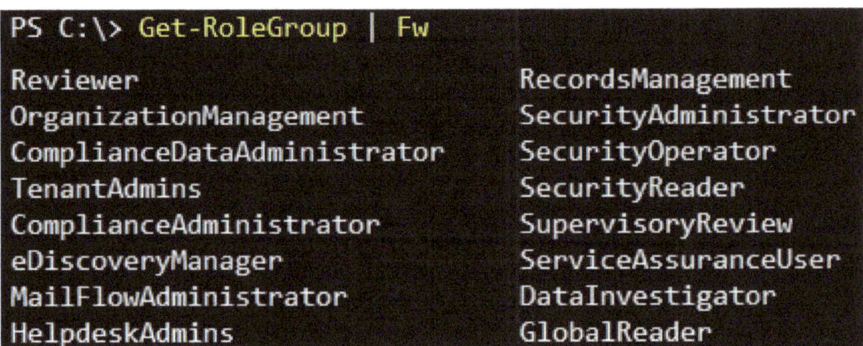

```
PS C:\> Get-RoleGroup | Fw

Reviewer                        RecordsManagement
OrganizationManagement          SecurityAdministrator
ComplianceDataAdministrator     SecurityOperator
TenantAdmins                    SecurityReader
ComplianceAdministrator         SupervisoryReview
eDiscoveryManager               ServiceAssuranceUser
MailFlowAdministrator           DataInvestigator
HelpdeskAdmins                  GlobalReader
```

Of the two, the Administrator Role has greater responsibilities. How do we know this? They both have the same assigned roles according to the GUI of the SCC:

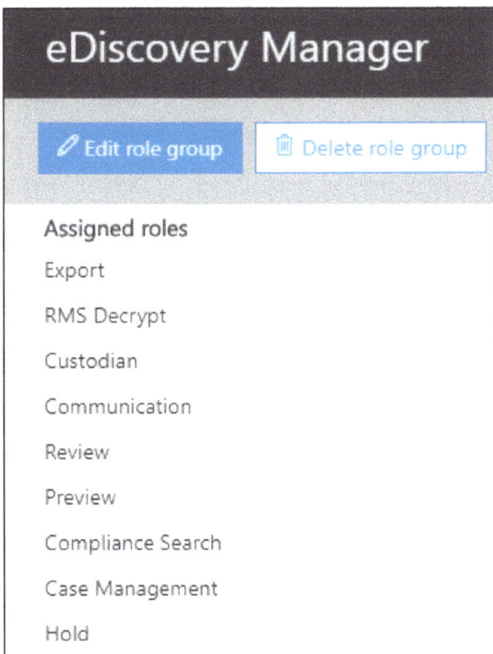

However, on the same screen we see the vital difference between the two roles. The eDiscovery Administrator's permissions apply to all users, whereas the eDiscovery Manager has to be granted access:

eDiscovery Manager	eDiscovery Administrator
An eDiscovery Manager can only view and edit cases to which he or she has access.	An eDiscovery Administrator can view and edit all cases regardless of permissions.

The eDiscovery Manager role has access to 68 PowerShell cmdlets as does the eDiscovery Administrator. As such, the Administrator role only really needs to be applied to a person who needs access to all cases in the SCC and should be treated like a Global Admin with a limited or small number of people having access. From a discovery perspective, the Admin rights would enable the assigned user rights to see all of the cases that were listed in the SCC and gather details for reporting purposes.

Service Assurance User

The Service Assurance User role is probably one of, if the most restrictive role present that can be assigned to a user in the SCC. While it does have one assigned role, like others discussed previously:

```
Organizations/████.onmicrosoft.com/Service Assurance View-Service Assurance User
```

The 'Service Assurance View' role only has access to one cmdlet - 'Get-User'. Outside of PowerShell, this role has this description:

> *"Access the Service Assurance section in the Security & Compliance Center. Members of this role group can use this section to review documents related to security, privacy, and compliance in Office 365 to perform risk and assurance reviews for their own organization."*

The primary interface for this use is logging into the Security and Compliance Center and click on Software Assurance:

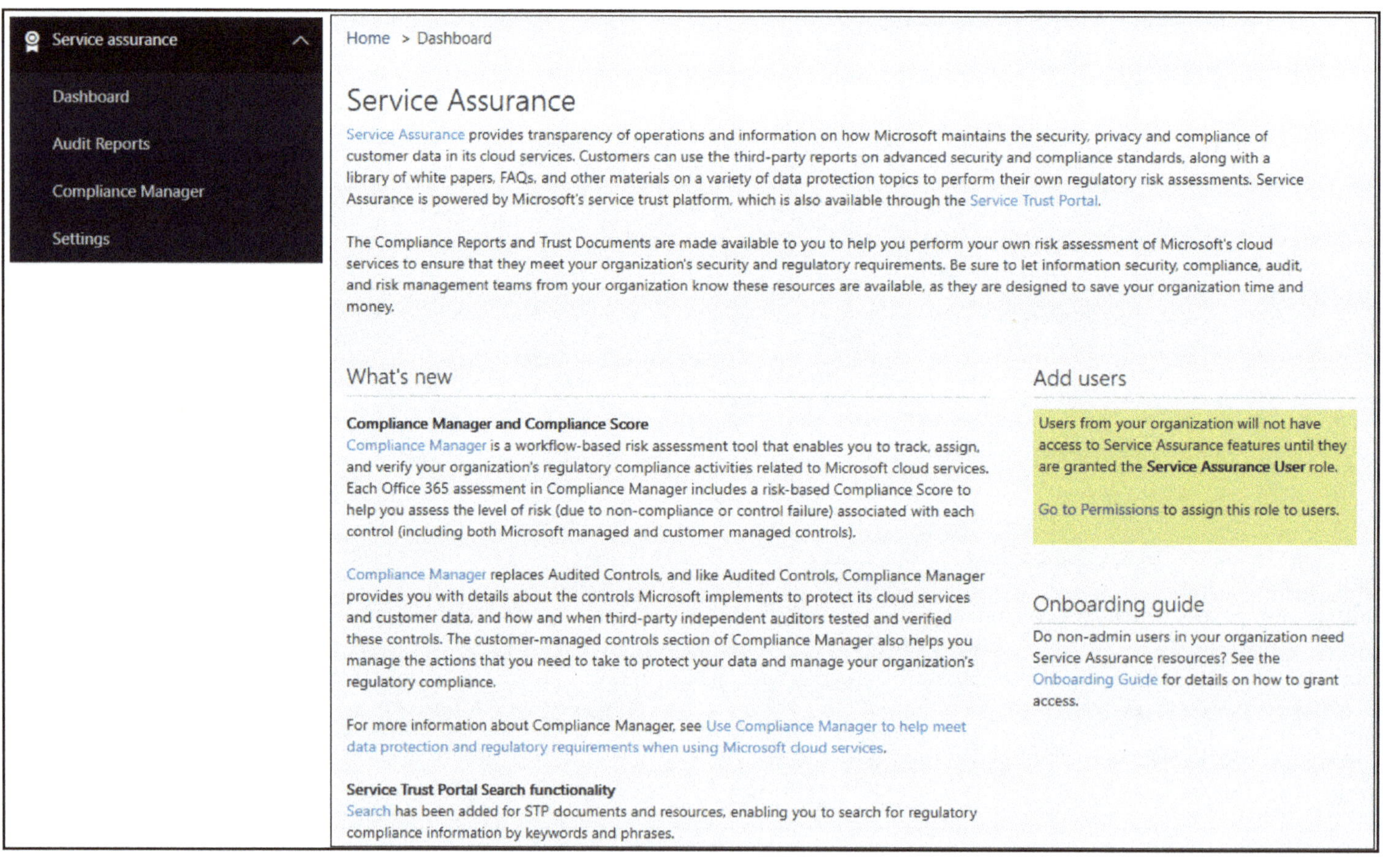

Compliance Data Administrator

Compliance Data Administrators are focused on settings for data protection, reports, device management and DLP. It has 17 assigned roles to it with half of them View-Only:

```
ınizations/████ onmicrosoft.com/Organization Configuration-Compliance Data Administrator
ınizations/████ onmicrosoft.com/View-Only Device Management-Compliance Data Administrator
ınizations/████ onmicrosoft.com/RecordManagement-Compliance Data Administrator
ınizations/████ onmicrosoft.com/Disposition Management-Compliance Data Administrator
ınizations/████ onmicrosoft.com/View-Only Audit Logs-Compliance Data Administrator
ınizations/████ onmicrosoft.com/View-Only Retention Management-Compliance Data Administrator
ınizations/████ onmicrosoft.com/Compliance Search-Compliance Data Administrator
ınizations/████ onmicrosoft.com/Manage Alerts-Compliance Data Administrator
ınizations/████ onmicrosoft.com/Compliance Administrator-Compliance Data Administrator
ınizations/████ onmicrosoft.com/View-Only DLP Compliance Management-Compliance Data Administrator
ınizations/████ onmicrosoft.com/View-Only Record Management-Compliance Data Administrator
ınizations/████ onmicrosoft.com/View-Only Manage Alerts-Compliance Data Administrator
ınizations/████ onmicrosoft.com/Retention Management-Compliance Data Administrator
ınizations/████ onmicrosoft.com/View-Only Recipients-Compliance Data Administrator
ınizations/████ onmicrosoft.com/Device Management-Compliance Data Administrator
ınizations/████ onmicrosoft.com/Sensitivity Label Administrator-Compliance Data Administrator
ınizations/████ onmicrosoft.com/IB Compliance Management-Compliance Data Administrator
```

With the amount of assigned roles, it isn't surprising the Compliance Data Administrator has access to 210 PowerShell cmdlets. The cmdlets comprise of File Plan Management, Supervisor, Compliance, Device Compliance, Alerting and DLP Sensitive Information Types. With the wide range of responsibilities, this role should also be restrictive in its membership.

Security Operator

A Security Operator is a role design for reviewing Audit Logs, Information Barrier Settings, DLP Compliance Management, Device Management, and Alert Logs. This role group has the following assigned roles:

```
anizations/████.onmicrosoft.com/View-Only Manage Alerts-Security Operator
anizations/████.onmicrosoft.com/View-Only Device Management-Security Operator
anizations/████.onmicrosoft.com/Compliance Search-Security Operator
anizations/████.onmicrosoft.com/Manage Alerts-Security Operator
anizations/████.onmicrosoft.com/View-Only Audit Logs-Security Operator
anizations/████.onmicrosoft.com/View-Only DLP Compliance Management-Security Operator
anizations/████.onmicrosoft.com/Security Reader-Security Operator
anizations/████.onmicrosoft.com/View-Only IB Compliance Management-Security Operator
```

These associated roles have a combined total of 57 cmdlets available to them with about half of the cmdlets of the 'Get' variety. The reset of the cmdlets allow for work with Alerts, logs, Compliance Searches, Information Barrier review and more.

Data Investigator

A Data Investigator can perform searches in Exchange Online (mailboxes), SharePoint sites and in OneDrive accounts. The role group has nine assigned roles which are as follows:

```
anizations/█████.onmicrosoft.com/RMS Decrypt-Data Investigator
anizations/█████.onmicrosoft.com/Custodian-Data Investigator
anizations/█████.onmicrosoft.com/Compliance Search-Data Investigator
anizations/█████.onmicrosoft.com/Export-Data Investigator
anizations/█████.onmicrosoft.com/Preview-Data Investigator
anizations/█████.onmicrosoft.com/Data Investigation Management-Data Investigator
anizations/█████.onmicrosoft.com/Communication-Data Investigator
anizations/█████.onmicrosoft.com/Review-Data Investigator
anizations/█████.onmicrosoft.com/Search And Purge-Data Investigator
```

With these assigned roles, a limited set of PowerShell cmdlets are available for use. The cmdlets are concentrated on a set of Compliance Search cmdlets (Get, New, Remove and Set):

```
Get-CaseHoldPolicy          Get-CaseHoldRule
Get-ComplianceCase          Get-ComplianceCaseMember
Get-ComplianceSearch        Get-ComplianceSearchAction
Get-Recipient               Invoke-ComplianceSearchActionStep
New-ComplianceSearch        New-ComplianceSearchAction
Remove-ComplianceSearch     Remove-ComplianceSearchAction
Set-ComplianceSearch        Set-ComplianceSearchAction
Start-ComplianceSearch      Stop-ComplianceSearch
```

Global Reader

For the last role group, we will look at Global Reader. The Global Reader role is entirely oriented to View-Only roles. The roles cover Alerts, Auditing, Record Management, Retention, Device Management, DLP and Information Barriers.

```
anizations/█████.onmicrosoft.com/Security Reader-Global Reader
anizations/█████.onmicrosoft.com/View-Only Manage Alerts-Global Reader
anizations/█████.onmicrosoft.com/View-Only Audit Logs-Global Reader
anizations/█████.onmicrosoft.com/View-Only Record Management-Global Reader
anizations/█████.onmicrosoft.com/View-Only Retention Management-Global Reader
anizations/█████.onmicrosoft.com/Service Assurance View-Global Reader
anizations/█████.onmicrosoft.com/View-Only Device Management-Global Reader
anizations/█████.onmicrosoft.com/View-Only DLP Compliance Management-Global Reader
anizations/█████.onmicrosoft.com/View-Only IB Compliance Management-Global Reader
```

It is interesting to note that even with a lot of View-Only roles, this role group has access to 62 PowerShell cmdlets. A few non View-Only cmdlets are provided as well, like Remove-OrganizationSegment, Set-OrganizationSegment, and Set-DLPEdmSchema.

** **Note** ** It should be noted that any of these built-in role groups cannot be modified in terms of assigned roles. If you try, you will receive an error like this:

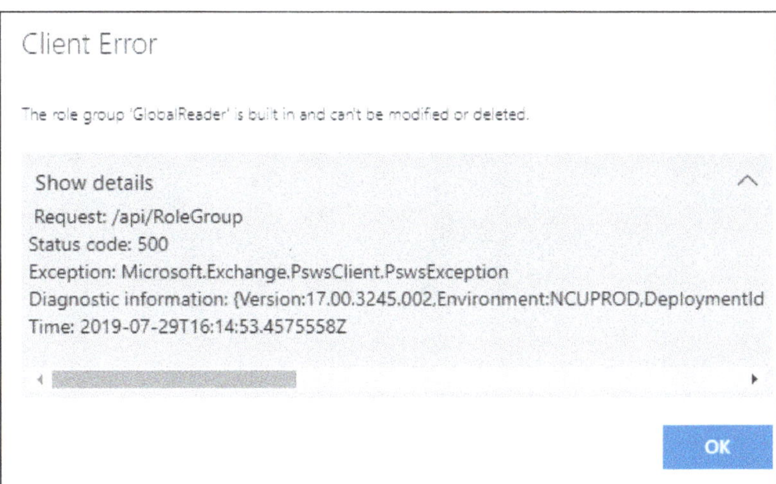

Removing User(s) From Role Groups

Removing a user from a Role Group is an easy task to perform. If we remember back when we listed all of the cmdlets for working with Role Groups, there was a cmdlet called 'Remove-RoleGroupMember'. Before removing a user from the Role Group we can also verify that they are still in the Role Group:

Get-RoleGroupMember -Identity mailflowadministrator

Now that we confirmed the user is in the group, we can move forward with removing the user from the intended Role Group.

Remove-RoleGroupMember -Identity mailflowadministrator -Member Colleen

```
PS C:\> Remove-RoleGroupMember -Identity mailflowadministrator -Member colleen

Confirm
Are you sure you want to perform this action?
Removing the member "colleen" from the role group "mailflowadministrator".
[Y] Yes  [A] Yes to All  [N] No  [L] No to All  [?] Help (default is "Y"): y
PS C:\>
```

After removing permissions, it would be advisable for the affected user to log out of the Security and Compliance Center, close any open PowerShell sessions and exit PowerShell completely. Doing so will eliminate any potential access errors when in PowerShell or the GUI interface for the Security and Compliance Center.

If we hadn't confirmed the user first, we would have seen an error like this:

```
PS C:\> remove-RoleGroupMember -Identity eDiscoveryManager -Member EWright

Confirm
Are you sure you want to perform this action?
Removing the member "EWright" from the role group "eDiscoveryManager".
[Y] Yes  [A] Yes to All  [N] No  [L] No to All  [?] Help (default is "Y"): a
The recipient "EWright" isn't a member of the group "FFO.extest.microsoft.com/Microsoft Exchange Hosted
Organizations/        .onmicrosoft.com/Configuration/eDiscoveryManager".
    + CategoryInfo          : InvalidData: (EWright:SecurityPrincipalIdParameter) [Remove-RoleGroupMember], MemberNotF
   oundException
    + FullyQualifiedErrorId : [Server=BY2NAM05WS011,RequestId=d8b6ffff-1f10-439a-959d-635a91492fb9,TimeStamp=12/14/201
   8 9:32:18 PM] [FailureCategory=Cmdlet-MemberNotFoundException] 7FCA8A7A,Microsoft.Exchange.Management.RbacTasks.Re
   moveRoleGroupMember
    + PSComputerName        : nam05b.ps.compliance.protection.outlook.com
```

What about multiple users or Role Groups?

We have a user that is in multiple groups. This same user has been reassigned and no longer needs these rights in the Security and Compliance Center. How can we remove them? We can use a combination of the script we used before to identity all members in all groups with the above Remove-RoleGroupMember cmdlet. First issue will be to identify the user and then once identified as a group member, remove that member.

One User in Multiple Groups

For this scripting example we'll run through some typical errors and problems that can often occur when drafting your own script. Remember that your script will likely have issues upon drafting, so knowing how to troubleshoot can come in handy.

First Code iteration:

```
$UserToRemove = "Ed Wright"
$RoleGroupNames = (Get-RoleGroup).Name
Foreach ($RoleGroupName in $RoleGroupNames) {
    Write-Host "Examining Role Group - " -ForegroundColor White -NoNewline
    Write-host "$RoleGroupName ....." -ForegroundColor Yellow
    $RoleGroupMembers = (Get-RoleGroupMember -Identity $RoleGroupName).Name
    Foreach ($RoleGroupMember in $RoleGroupMemebers) {
      If ($RoleGroupMember -eq $UserToRemove) {
      #Remove-RoleGroupMember -Identity $RoleGroupName -Member $UserToRemove -Confirm:$False
        Write-Host "Testing - FOUND - in the $RoleGroupName Role Group!" -ForegroundColor White
      }
    }
}
```

Problem One - Script not matching the user to remove.

First troubleshooting mechanism we can place in the script is a pair of lines that displayed the Role Group being examined:

```
    Write-Host "Examining Role Group - " -ForegroundColor White -NoNewline
    Write-host "$RoleGroupName ....." -ForegroundColor Yellow
```

Result:

```
PS C:\> .\FindUserToRemove.ps1
Exmamining Role Group - Reviewer .....
Exmamining Role Group - RecordsManagement .....
Exmamining Role Group - OrganizationManagement .....
Exmamining Role Group - ComplianceAdministrator .....
Exmamining Role Group - SupervisoryReview .....
Exmamining Role Group - SecurityAdministrator .....
Exmamining Role Group - TenantAdmins .....
Exmamining Role Group - HelpdeskAdmins .....
Exmamining Role Group - SecurityReader .....
Exmamining Role Group - eDiscoveryManager .....
Exmamining Role Group - ServiceAssuranceUser .....
Exmamining Role Group - MailFlowAdministrator .....
```

Now we can see that each group is listed correctly. Secondly, we can add a code section to remove the user. However, some lines are commented out we need to validate that the script was finding the correct members. We can add some 'Write-Host' lines to display results to again validate the script was working:

```
# Remove-RoleGroupMember -Identity $RoleGroupName -Member $UserToRemove
Write-Host "Testing - FOUND - in the $RoleGroupName Role Group!" -ForegroundColor White
```

Ran the script again, however no members were matching: (essentially a repeat of the first run):

```
PS C:\> .\FindUserToRemove.ps1
Exmamining Role Group - Reviewer .....
Exmamining Role Group - RecordsManagement .....
Exmamining Role Group - OrganizationManagement .....
Exmamining Role Group - ComplianceAdministrator .....
Exmamining Role Group - SupervisoryReview .....
Exmamining Role Group - SecurityAdministrator .....
Exmamining Role Group - TenantAdmins .....
Exmamining Role Group - HelpdeskAdmins .....
Exmamining Role Group - SecurityReader .....
Exmamining Role Group - eDiscoveryManager .....
Exmamining Role Group - ServiceAssuranceUser .....
Exmamining Role Group - MailFlowAdministrator .....
```

The third section added was to list each member of the group, to make sure that we were pulling members. This was done because no users were showing a match even though we knew the name was correct.

```
$RoleGroupMembers = (Get-RoleGroupMember -Identity $RoleGroupName).Name
$RoleGroupMembers
```

As we can see below, the script does identify all users in a Role Group. However is it not matching our one user:

```
PS C:\> .\FindUserToRemove.ps1
Examining Role Group - Reviewer .....
Damian Scoles
Examining Role Group - RecordsManagement .....
Ed Wright
Examining Role Group - OrganizationManagement .....
Damian Scoles
Examining Role Group - ComplianceAdministrator .....
Ed Wright
Examining Role Group - SupervisoryReview .....
Examining Role Group - SecurityAdministrator .....
Examining Role Group - TenantAdmins .....
Damian Scoles
Examining Role Group - HelpdeskAdmins .....
Examining Role Group - SecurityReader .....
Ed Wright
Examining Role Group - eDiscoveryManager .....
Ed Wright
Examining Role Group - ServiceAssuranceUser .....
Examining Role Group - MailFlowAdministrator .....
Colleen
```

Then, adding the $RoleGroupMember variable on a separate line after "Foreach ($RoleGroupMember in $RoleGroupMemebers) {" in order to see if the individual members would be listed. We can remove the $RoleGroupMembers variable to keep the results clean. Running the script again, we are left with no results:

```
PS C:\> .\FindUserToRemove.ps1
Exmamining Role Group - Reviewer .....
Exmamining Role Group - RecordsManagement .....
Exmamining Role Group - OrganizationManagement .....
Exmamining Role Group - ComplianceAdministrator .....
Exmamining Role Group - SupervisoryReview .....
Exmamining Role Group - SecurityAdministrator .....
Exmamining Role Group - TenantAdmins .....
Exmamining Role Group - HelpdeskAdmins .....
Exmamining Role Group - SecurityReader .....
Exmamining Role Group - eDiscoveryManager .....
Exmamining Role Group - ServiceAssuranceUser .....
Exmamining Role Group - MailFlowAdministrator .....
```

This means that there is an issue with the code between those two variables. Examining one line we see there is a tyop (!) and once this was corrected, we are able to identify which groups the user is in.

Tyop (!)

```
$RoleGroupMembers = (Get-RoleGroupMember -Identity $RoleGroupName).Name
$RoleGroupMembers
Foreach ($RoleGroupMember in $RoleGroupMemebers) {
    $RoleGroupMember
    IF ($RoleGroupMember -eq $UserToRemove) {
```

Easy error to fix:

```
Foreach ($RoleGroupMember in $RoleGroupMembers) {
```

Once corrected, we can remove extra variables and here is the final code:

```
$UserToRemove = "Ed Wright"
$RoleGroupNames = (Get-RoleGroup).Name
Foreach ($RoleGroupName in $RoleGroupNames) {
   Write-Host "Examining Role Group - " -ForegroundColor White -NoNewline
   Write-host "$RoleGroupName ....." -ForegroundColor Yellow
   $RoleGroupMembers = (Get-RoleGroupMember -Identity $RoleGroupName).Name
   Foreach ($RoleGroupMember in $RoleGroupMembers) {
     IF ($RoleGroupMember -eq $UserToRemove) {
    # Remove-RoleGroupMember -Identity $RoleGroupName -Member $UserToRemove -Confirm:$False
       Write-Host "Testing - " -ForegroundColor White -NoNewline
       Write-Host "FOUND - " -ForegroundColor Green -NoNewline
       Write-Host "in the $RoleGroupName Role Group!" -ForegroundColor White
   }
  }
}
```

Results:

```
PS C:\> .\FindUserToRemove.ps1
Examining Role Group - Reviewer .....
Examining Role Group - RecordsManagement .....
Testing - FOUND - in the RecordsManagement Role Group!
Examining Role Group - OrganizationManagement .....
Examining Role Group - ComplianceAdministrator .....
Testing - FOUND - in the ComplianceAdministrator Role Group!
Examining Role Group - SupervisoryReview .....
Examining Role Group - SecurityAdministrator .....
Examining Role Group - TenantAdmins .....
Examining Role Group - HelpdeskAdmins .....
Examining Role Group - SecurityReader .....
Testing - FOUND - in the SecurityReader Role Group!
Examining Role Group - eDiscoveryManager .....
Testing - FOUND - in the eDiscoveryManager Role Group!
Examining Role Group - ServiceAssuranceUser .....
Examining Role Group - MailFlowAdministrator .....
```

Now that the code is correct, we can uncomment the removal line:

```
# Remove-RoleGroupMember -Identity $RoleGroupName -Member $UserToRemove  -Confirm:$False
```

Becomes:

```
Remove-RoleGroupMember -Identity $RoleGroupName -Member $UserToRemove  -Confirm:$False
```

Error Correction:

If we want to put some error checking in we can add a Try {} Catch set of code around the removal. This would be good in case you do not have the correct rights to add / remove users from Role Groups because it would provide a visual to the effect that the user was not removed:

```
Try {
    Remove-RoleGroupMember -Identity $RoleGroupName -Member $UserToRemove -Confirm:$False
    -ErrorAction STOP
} Catch {
    Write-host "The User $UserToRemove was not removed from the Role Group - $RoleGroupName.
    Please review this change" -ForegroundColor Red
}
```

If there was an error, you would see an error like this:

```
The User Ed Wright was not removed from the Role Group - SecurityReader.  Please review this change.
```

Validation

The easiest way to validate membership is to run the previous script we used to get all users in each group. With the removal of 'Ed' we see the groups are cleaner now:

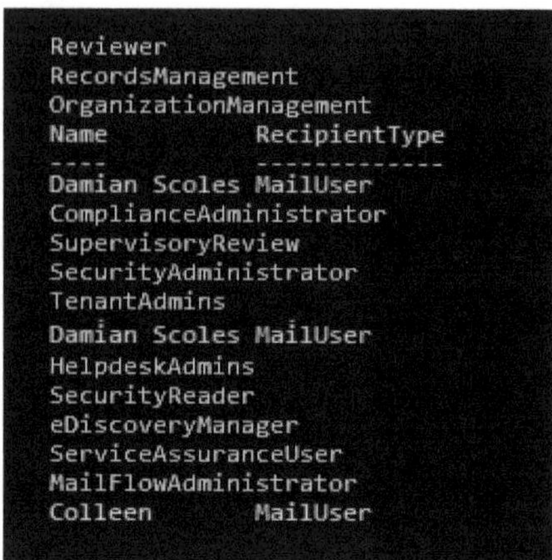

Removing multiple users from one group

In this example we have one group that needs to be cleaned up so we need a script that will remove a set of users from the Role Group.   For this scenario we have a list of users that need to be removed from one of the Role Groups. The names are stored in a CSV file.

Known Items

```
Role Group - Reviewer
List of users - UsersToRemove.CSV
```

PowerShell

```
$CSV = Import-CSV UsersToRemove.CSV
$RoleGroupName = 'Reviewer'

Foreach ($Line in $CSV) {
  $Name = $Line.Name
  Remove-RoleGroupMember -Identity $RoleGroupName -Member $Name -Confirm:$False
}
```

Once complete, the script will not provide any feedback because we have '-Confirm:$False'. If we would like to confirm each removal, we would remove this. A re-run of the script would then prompt us for each users removal from the Reviewers Role Group.

Management Roles

Permissions for managing the Security and Compliance Center are broken down into a concept called Management Roles. Each of these roles can be assigned to a user in order to allow that person to configure those portions of Exchange. Role Groups are security groups within the SCC to which the Management Roles are assigned to so that a member of this Role Group has the rights granted to it. Role Groups in Exchange vary from a View-Only Recipients all the way up to Organization Management. Let's explore these Management Roles and then Role Groups in order to get a better idea of how security is layered in the SCC.

PowerShell

Let's explore what cmdlets are available for Management Role management in PowerShell:

    Get-Command *ManagementRole*

This only provides us with this one cmdlet:

    Get-ManagementRole

We are restricted because RBAC security customization in Office 365 in general is very limited. We have to work within the framework provided by Microsoft's hosted services. A quick review of these Management Roles can be found here:

```
PS C:\> Get-ManagementRole

Name                                   RoleType
----                                   --------
View-Only Retention Management         ViewOnlyRetentionManagement
Export                                 Export
RMS Decrypt                            RmsDecrypt
Manage Alerts                          ManageAlerts
Role Management                        RoleManagement
View-Only Manage Alerts                ViewOnlyManageAlerts
Supervisory Review Administrator       SupervisoryReviewAdmin
View-Only Device Management            ViewOnlyDeviceManagement
Organization Configuration             OrganizationConfiguration
DLP Compliance Management              DLPComplianceManagement
Review                                 Review
Disposition Management                 DispositionManagement
View-Only DLP Compliance Management    ViewOnlyDLPComplianceManagement
RecordManagement                       RecordManagement
Audit Logs                             AuditLogs
Security Reader                        SecurityReader
Security Administrator                 SecurityAdmin
Preview                                Preview
Service Assurance View                 ServiceAssuranceView
Search And Purge                       SearchAndPurge
View-Only Audit Logs                   ViewOnlyAuditLogs
Compliance Administrator               ComplianceAdmin
Device Management                      DeviceManagement
Compliance Search                      ComplianceSearch
Case Management                        CaseManagement
Retention Management                   RetentionManagement
View-Only Record Management            ViewOnlyRecordManagement
View-Only Recipients                   ViewOnlyRecipients
Hold                                   Hold
```

Get-ManagementRole

With the same cmdlet we can also get a brief description of each role:

```
Name                                  Description
----                                  -----------
View-Only Retention Management        Allow viewing configuration and reports for the Retention Management feature.
Export                                Lets people export the mailbox and site content that was returned from a search.
RMS Decrypt                           Lets people decrypt RMS-protected content when exporting search results.
Manage Alerts                         Lets people view and edit the settings and reports for alerts.
Role Management                       Lets people manage role group membership and create or delete custom role groups.
View-Only Manage Alerts               Allow viewing configuration and reports for the Manage Alerts feature.
Supervisory Review Administrator      Lets people manage supervisory review policies, including which communications to
                                      review and who should perform the review.
View-Only Device Management           Allow viewing configuration and reports for the Device Management feature.
Organization Configuration            Lets people run, view, and export audit reports and manage compliance policies for
                                      DLP, devices, and preservation.
DLP Compliance Management             Lets people view and edit settings and reports for data loss prevention (DLP)
                                      policies.
Review                                Lets people use Office 365 Advanced eDiscovery to track, tag, analyze, and test
                                      documents that are assigned to them.
Disposition Management                Control permissions for accessing Manual Disposition in the Security & Compliance
                                      Center.
View-Only DLP Compliance Management   Lets people view the settings and reports for data loss prevention (DLP) policies.
RecordManagement                      Allow viewing and editing configuration and reports for the Record Management
                                      feature.
Audit Logs                            Lets people turn on and configure auditing for their Office 365 organization. This
                                      role also lets people view the organization's audit reports, and then export these
                                      reports to a file.
Security Reader                       Allows viewing configuration and reports for Security features.
Security Administrator                Allows viewing and editing configuration and reports for Security features.
Preview                               Lets people view a list of items that were returned from a content search. They'll
                                      also be able to open each item from the list to view its contents.
Service Assurance View                Lets people download the documents available on the Service Assurance section.
                                      Content includes independent auditing and compliance documentation and
                                      trust-related guidance for using Office 365 features to manage regulatory
                                      compliance and security risks.
Search And Purge                      Lets people bulk-remove data that matches the criteria of a content search.
View-Only Audit Logs                  Lets people view and export their organization's audit reports. Because these
                                      reports might contain sensitive information, this role should only be assigned to
                                      those with an explicit need to view this information.
Compliance Administrator              Lets people view and edit settings and reports for compliance features.
Device Management                     Lets people view and edit settings and reports for device management features.
Compliance Search                     Lets people perform searches across mailboxes and get an estimate of the results.
Case Management                       Lets people create, edit, delete, and control access to eDiscovery cases.
Retention Management                  Lets people manage retention policies.
View-Only Record Management           Allow viewing configuration and reports for the Record Management feature.
View-Only Recipients                  Lets people view information about users and groups.
Hold                                  Lets people place content in mailboxes, sites, and public folders on hold. When on
                                      hold, a copy of the content is stored in a secure location. Content owners will
                                      still be able to modify or delete the original content.
```

Typically we would be able to dig into the Management Roles and PowerShell cmdlets to see what it takes to run particular cmdlets. However, at the time of the writing of this book, this functionality is broken:

```
PS C:\> Get-ManagementRole -Cmdlet Add-RoleGroupMember
WARNING: An unexpected error has occurred and a Watson dump is being generated: The QueryFilter '(WildcardString
IgnoreCase(InternalDownlevelRoleEntries)=c,Add-RoleGroupMember,*)' is not supported, only ComparisonFilter and
CompositeFilter are supported.
The QueryFilter '(WildcardString IgnoreCase(InternalDownlevelRoleEntries)=c,Add-RoleGroupMember,*)' is not supported,
only ComparisonFilter and CompositeFilter are supported.
    + CategoryInfo          : NotSpecified: (:) [Get-ManagementRole], NotSupportedException
    + FullyQualifiedErrorId : System.NotSupportedException,Microsoft.Exchange.Management.RbacTasks.GetManagementRole
    + PSComputerName        : nam05b.ps.compliance.protection.outlook.com
```

Audit in Security and Compliance Center

It seems like a lifetime ago, but there was once a time when there wasn't an express need to audit the system administrator. They were the trusted IT support people who handled the thankless job of maintaining the servers in corporate datacenters. With the advent of multiple compliance-based standards, the auditing of the actions of an administrator have become important. Microsoft recognized this in Exchange 2010 with the advent of Admin Audit Logging and has continued this forward by enabling this logging capability in Office 365.

Admin Audit Logging is in a way self-explanatory. Basically the actions of an Administrator in Office 365 are being tracked in a way that can be audited and searched for possible misdeeds. This includes unauthorized access or even a bad configuration. The log can be dumped for examination by a third party, examined in the Security and Compliance Center or even just simply displayed to the screen.

PowerShell

What PowerShell cmdlets are available for this part of the Security and Compliance Center's security mechanisms? Well, let's find out:

```
Get-Command *AdminAudit*
```

This provides a short list of cmdlets:

Let's start off with reviewing what the Admin Audit Log is configured for:

```
Get-AdminAuditLogConfig
```

```
RunspaceId                          : 4a5271fd-0459-467d-809f-c1ddf4a1efaa
AdminAuditLogEnabled                : True
LogLevel                            : Verbose
TestCmdletLoggingEnabled            : False
AdminAuditLogCmdlets                : {*}
AdminAuditLogParameters             : {*}
AdminAuditLogExcludedCmdlets        : {}
AdminAuditLogAgeLimit               : 90.00:00:00
LoadBalancerCount                   : 3
RefreshInterval                     : 10
PartitionInfo                       : {}
UnifiedAuditLogIngestionEnabled     : False
UnifiedAuditLogFirstOptInDate       :
AdminDisplayName                    :
ExchangeVersion                     : 0.10 (14.0.100.0)
Name                                : Default
DistinguishedName                   : CN=Default,CN=Configuration,CN████████.onmicrosoft.com,OU=Microsoft Exchange Hosted
                                      Organizations,DC=FFO,DC=extest,DC=microsoft,DC=com
Identity                            : FFO.extest.microsoft.com/Microsoft Exchange Hosted
                                      Organizations,████████.onmicrosoft.com/Configuration/Default
ObjectCategory                      :
ObjectClass                         : {msExchAdminAuditLogConfig}
WhenChanged                         :
WhenCreated                         :
WhenChangedUTC                      :
WhenCreatedUTC                      :
ExchangeObjectId                    : 08075a1f-b49e-4769-983d-be2587651f3b
OrganizationId                      : FFO.extest.microsoft.com/Microsoft Exchange Hosted
                                      Organizations,████████.onmicrosoft.com - FFO.extest.microsoft.com/Microsoft Exchange
                                      Hosted Organizations,████████.onmicrosoft.com/Configuration
Id                                  : FFO.extest.microsoft.com/Microsoft Exchange Hosted
                                      Organizations/████████.onmicrosoft.com/Configuration/Default
Guid                                : 08075a1f-b49e-4769-983d-be2587651f3b
```

Notice that the log age limit is 90 days, plenty of time to generate reports from and get history from as well. Two other parameters are important - AdminAuditLogCmdlets and AdminAuditLogParameters which refer to all cmdlets and all parameters. The parameter 'AdminAuditLogExcludedCmdlets' is also blank which means no cmdlets are being blocked from the log either. The default level of logging ('Log Level') is set to 'Verbose' in Office 365, which is a marked contrast to Exchange Server (where it originated) which the 'Log Level' is 'None'. The Verbose LogLevel setting also adds two additional bits of information:

    ModifiedProperties (old and new)
    ModifiedObjectResolvedName properties

What has changed with the Admin Audit Log over the past versions is the addition of the UnifiedAuditLog parameters. These two parameters link Exchange On-Premises and Exchange Online. Only one can be configured. The UnifiedAuditLogIngestionEnabled parameter can be set to True or False. The default is False, which only audits and allows searches of Exchange On-Premises servers. If the setting is configured for True, the Admin Audit Logs for Office 365 are recorded in Office 365 and searches will be allowed after the fact. Other configurable parameters for the Admin Audit Log are:

    AdminAuditLogCmdlets
    AdminAuditLogParameters
    AdminAuditLogExcludedCmdlets

The auditable cmdlets and parameters can be fine-tuned if that is desired, but to get a true sense of what an admin is doing the default configuration is the way to go. The third parameter 'AdminAuditLogExcludedCmdlets' allows for exclusions from the entirety of what is defined in the first two cmdlets. For example, if all cmdlets are chosen '*' to be audited, one could exclude certain cmdlets that may not be important like running Get-MessageTrackingLog or any Get cmdlets as well. This would allow for a more fine-tuned set of Admin Audit Logs.

Lastly, the amount of time included in the logs can also be adjusted from the default of 90 days. If the value is set for 0, all the logs are purged. Setting a number less than the default will truncate what is available in the Admin Audit Log as well.

    Get-Help Search-AdminAuditLog -Full
    Get-Help New-AdminAuditLogSearch -Full

Searching the Admin Audit Log

You will notice that there are two cmdlets for handling searches of the Admin Audit Log:

    New-AdminAuditLogSearch
    Search-AdminAuditLog

So which of these cmdlets are we supposed to use for searching the logs? Let's review some examples from these two cmdlets to compare the two:

    New-AdminAuditLogSearch

```
------------------------------ Example 1 ------------------------------
New-AdminAuditLogSearch -Name "Mailbox Quota Change Audit" -Cmdlets Set-Mailbox -Parameters
UseDatabaseQuotaDefaults, ProhibitSendReceiveQuota, ProhibitSendQuota -StartDate 01/24/2015 -EndDate 02/12/2015
-StatusMailRecipients david@contoso.com, chris@contoso.com

------------------------------ Example 2 ------------------------------
New-AdminAuditLogSearch -ExternalAccess $true -StartDate 07/25/2015 -EndDate 10/24/2015 -StatusMailRecipients
admin@contoso.com,pilarp@contoso.com -Name "Datacenter admin audit log"
```

Search-AdminAuditLog

```
------------------------ Example 1 ------------------------
Search-AdminAuditLog -Cmdlets Set-Mailbox -Parameters UseDatabaseQuotaDefaults, ProhibitSendReceiveQuota,
ProhibitSendQuota -StartDate 01/24/2015 -EndDate 02/12/2015 -IsSuccess $true

------------------------ Example 2 ------------------------
Search-AdminAuditLog -Cmdlets New-RoleGroup, New-ManagementRoleAssignment

------------------------ Example 3 ------------------------
Search-AdminAuditLog -ExternalAccess $true -StartDate 09/17/2015 -EndDate 10/02/2015
```

Reviewing the two cmdlets, the help reveals a small difference between the two cmdlets. The first one, New-AdminAuditLogSearch cmdlet examples both include the 'StatusMailRecipients' parameter and the parameter is required for the cmdlet. Thus the only way to get the results is via an email. This email is generated and delivered within a period of 15 minutes. If the results need to be displayed on the screen, then the cmdlet to use is Search-AdminAuditLog. An example of this would be:

Search-AdminAuditLog -Cmdlets Set-InformationBarrierPolicy -StartDate 6/1/19 -EndDate 7/28/19

Which, in a sample tenant, would produce results like this:

```
RunspaceId          : 5eee8af4-fe89-40a5-8d7d-3b039ebc4153
ObjectModified      : FFO.extest.microsoft.com/Microsoft Exchange Hosted Organizations/
CmdletName          : Set-InformationBarrierPolicy
CmdletParameters    : {Identity, State}
ModifiedProperties  : {PolicyBlob, IBPolicyState}
Caller              : damian@practicalpowershell.com
ExternalAccess      :
Succeeded           : True
Error               : None
RunDate             : 7/25/2019 5:47:13 AM
OriginatingServer   : BY2NAM05WS005 (15.20.2115.005)
ClientIP            :
SessionId           :
AppId               :
ClientAppId         :
Identity            : 316605e2-1fc6-4323-7eee-08d710c38b06
IsValid             : True
ObjectState         : New

RunspaceId          : 5eee8af4-fe89-40a5-8d7d-3b039ebc4153
ObjectModified      : FFO.extest.microsoft.com/Microsoft Exchange Hosted Organizations/
CmdletName          : Set-InformationBarrierPolicy
CmdletParameters    : {Identity, State}
ModifiedProperties  : {PolicyBlob, IBPolicyState}
Caller              : damian@practicalpowershell.com
ExternalAccess      :
Succeeded           : True
Error               : None
RunDate             : 7/25/2019 5:47:28 AM
OriginatingServer   : BY2NAM05WS005 (15.20.2115.005)
ClientIP            :
SessionId           :
AppId               :
ClientAppId         :
Identity            : 11c0722f-9f33-43a4-888a-08d710c393f6
IsValid             : True
ObjectState         : New
```

New-AdminAuditLogSearch

As of the writing this book, this cmdlet is experiencing issues and has been reported as buggy:

```
PS C:\> New-AdminAuditLogSearch -StartDate 8/1/19 -EndDate 8/20/19 -StatusMailRecipients Damian@sccbook2.onmicrosoft.com

WARNING: An unexpected error has occurred and a Watson dump is being generated: Failed to locate the system arbitration
  mailbox for organization "FFO.extest.microsoft.com/Microsoft Exchange Hosted Organizations/sccbook2.onmicrosoft.com -
FFO.extest.microsoft.com/Microsoft Exchange Hosted Organizations/sccbook2.onmicrosoft.com/Configuration".
Failed to locate the system arbitration mailbox for organization "FFO.extest.microsoft.com/Microsoft Exchange Hosted
Organizations/sccbook2.onmicrosoft.com - FFO.extest.microsoft.com/Microsoft Exchange Hosted
Organizations/sccbook2.onmicrosoft.com/Configuration".
    + CategoryInfo          : NotSpecified: (:) [New-AdminAuditLogSearch], AuditLogSearchA...tFoundException
    + FullyQualifiedErrorId : Microsoft.Exchange.Management.AuditLogSearchArbitrationMailboxNotFoundException,Microsof
    t.Exchange.Management.SystemConfigurationTasks.NewAdminAuditLogSearch
```

Normally after the cmdlet is run, the results will be emailed to the Administrator's mailbox. The cmdlet does have some limitations:

'After the New-AdminAuditLogSearch cmdlet is run, the report is delivered to the mailboxes you specify within 15 minutes. The log is included as an XML attachment on the report email message. The maximum size of the log that can be generated is 10 megabytes (MB).'
https://technet.microsoft.com/en-us/library/ff459243(v=exchg.160).aspx

This is behavior that Exchange Online and On-premises display when the cmdlet is run.

In This Chapter

Introduction
Custom Sensitive Information Types
Fingerprints
Keyword Dictionaries
Exact Data Match (EDM)
DLP Compliance
Other DLP Cmdlets

Introduction

Data Loss Prevention (DLP) is a concept of preventing vital information from leaving an organization. This information could be leaked by email, sharing and more. An organization that depends on Office 365 for many services can leverage DLP to help maintain control of how their data is shared or not shared. We can create rules for OneDrive, SharePoint, Exchange and more and the rules can be applied to one or more workloads as needed. While DLP is just one of the many tools available to tenants, it is also a fairly complex tool.

What we also find is that while most tasks can be performed in PowerShell, there are some tasks that still cannot be performed in it. For this chapter we will concentrate on what we can do, what each part of the process requires, any limitations as well as any advantages to using PowerShell for DLP.

The PowerShell cmdlets for DLP in the Security and Compliance Center are considerably complex due to the layers that are involved. From Sensitive Information Types, to Rules to Policies and more.

Important components for DLP:

Sensitive Information Type - A pattern that can be matched to content is a document or object in Office 365 - examples include Credit Card Information, Social Security Numbers and Personally Identifiable Information (PII).
DLP Policy - Used to select what content is affected (which workload - like Exchange or Teams...).
DLP Rule - Combines the DLP Policy with a set of conditions and or Sensitive Information Type to help control content in a tenant.

For this chapter we will first start with the Sensitive Information Types - custom, fingerprint, etc. and then proceed to using these to build out DLP Policies and then DLP Rules.

Sensitive Information Types

Sensitive Information Types are specific sets of criteria to be used by DLP in the SCC that tells DLP what to look for in content. We'll need to identify what we are looking for before we can construct any sort of policies and rules. Do we need to look for particular documents (fixed format) or do we need to construct a set of keywords or an entire dictionary of keywords with which to help tag documents in Office 365. We then need to know what workload and what level of protection or action that will be taken.

For this part of the chapter we will look at the various Sensitive Information Types that we can create for our DLP Policies and Rules. We have quite a bit of PowerShell to look forward to, time to dive right in.

PowerShell

Like any other workload or feature in the SCC, there are a few PowerShell cmdlets that are available to use. Let's see what we have:

    Get-Command *Sensitive*

This provides us with these cmdlets:

    Get-DlpSensitiveInformationType
    Get-DlpSensitiveInformationTypeRulePackage
    New-DlpSensitiveInformationType
    New-DlpSensitiveInformationTypeRulePackage
    Remove-DlpSensitiveInformationType
    Remove-DlpSensitiveInformationTypeRulePackage
    Set-DlpSensitiveInformationType
    Set-DlpSensitiveInformationTypeRulePackage

Now that we have a series of cmdlets to use to work with Sensitive Information Types in the SCC, let's explore what we have by default and then see what it takes to create these for ourselves.

Get-DlpSensitiveInformationType

In a new tenant, we find that there are numerous pre-created Sensitive Information Types in our tenant. All of these were published by Microsoft. A total of 100 Sensitive Information Types are included. Here is a small sample:

```
PS C:\> Get-DlpSensitiveInformationType

Id                                      Name                                         Publisher
--                                      ----                                         ---------
fb621f20-3876-4cfc-acec-8c8e73ca32c7    Turkish National Identification number       Microsoft Corporation
50842eb7-edc8-4019-85dd-5a5c1f2bb085    Credit Card Number                           Microsoft Corporation
0e9b3178-9678-47dd-a509-37222ca96b42    EU Debit Card Number                         Microsoft Corporation
16c07343-c26f-49d2-a987-3daf717e94cc    U.K. National Insurance Number (NINO)        Microsoft Corporation
a44669fe-0d48-453d-a9b1-2cc83f2cba77    U.S. Social Security Number (SSN)            Microsoft Corporation
91da9335-1edb-45b7-a95f-5fe41a16c63c    German Driver's License Number               Microsoft Corporation
a2f29c85-ecb8-4514-a610-364790c0773e    Canada Social Insurance Number               Microsoft Corporation
```

If there are any others that are defined and we need to document just those, we need to filter out the Microsoft ones. We can do so by looking at all DLP Sensitive Information Types and filter for any that do not have Microsoft Corporation as its publisher:

Get-DlpSensitiveInformationType | where {$_.Publisher -ne 'Microsoft Corporation'}

```
Id                                    Name                     Publisher           Type
--                                    ----                     ---------           ----
1fc4e0c3-62cd-4886-8a58-ec8bbb793eec  test                     Damian Scoles       Fingerprint
aef38428-a35d-489a-8568-bc1440643ab1  Community Bank Account Number  Damian Scoles  Entity
791b1558-a0aa-49e4-bc31-e03b24d43e73  ConfidentialInformation  Damian Scoles       Entity
```

For statistics or tracking purposes, we can also get counts of both of these items (differences highlighted):

$CreatedCount** = (Get-DlpSensitiveInformationType | Where {$_.Publisher **-ne 'Microsoft Corporation'}
).Count
$MicrosoftCount** = (Get-DlpSensitiveInformationType | Where {$_.Publisher **-eq 'Microsoft Corporation'}
).Count

If we reveal the values of the variables, we will see we only have a few created ones:

```
PS C:\> $CreatedCount
6
PS C:\> $MicrosoftCount
100
PS C:\>
```

Let's go further and check percentages. Why? Because we can with PowerShell:

$TotalCount = (Get-DlpSensitiveInformationType).Count
$PercentCreated = ($CreatedCount/$TotalCount)*100
$PercentMicrosoft = ($MicrosoftCount/$TotalCount)*100
Write-Host "Created Types are $PercentCreated % of the total, while $PercentMicrosoft % are from Microsoft."

These code lines produce this output for the percentages of DLP Sensitive Information Type percentages:

```
PS C:\> Write-Host "Created Types are $PercentCreated % of the total, while $PercentMicrosoft % are from Microsof
Created Types are 5.66037735849057 % of the total, while 94.3396226415094 % are from Microsoft.
```

Well, those results need to be cleaned up. Why don't we use some rounding in the Math function of PowerShell to do this for us? Percentages are usually set to 2 decimal places for most applications and we can do that here as well. Here is a set of Math functions that round our numbers to the decimal places we desire:

[Math]::Round($VariableToRound,2)

Or

[Math]::Round(<Formula used>,2)

In our case we would do this as we are calculating something and want to keep the number of lines of code down:

$PercentCreated = [Math]::Round(($CreatedCount/$TotalCount)*100,2)
$PercentMicrosoft = [Math]::Round(($MicrosoftCount/$TotalCount)*100,2)

Write-Host "Created Types are $PercentCreated % of the total, while $PercentMicrosoft % are from Microsoft."

Now that we've done that, we can see a better looking percentage output:

```
PS C:\> $PercentCreated = [Math]::Round(($CreatedCount/$TotalCount)*100,2)
PS C:\> $PercentMicrosoft = [Math]::Round(($MicrosoftCount/$TotalCount)*100,2)
PS C:\> Write-Host "Created Types are $PercentCreated % of the total, while $PercentMicrosoft % are from Microsoft."
Created Types are 5.66 % of the total, while 94.34 % are from Microsoft.
PS C:\>
```

What if we needed to create a new Sensitive Information Type for our tenant and apply this to content? We have two options for this. We can either use the Security and Compliance Center's new feature of adding Sensitive Info Types or we can use PowerShell:

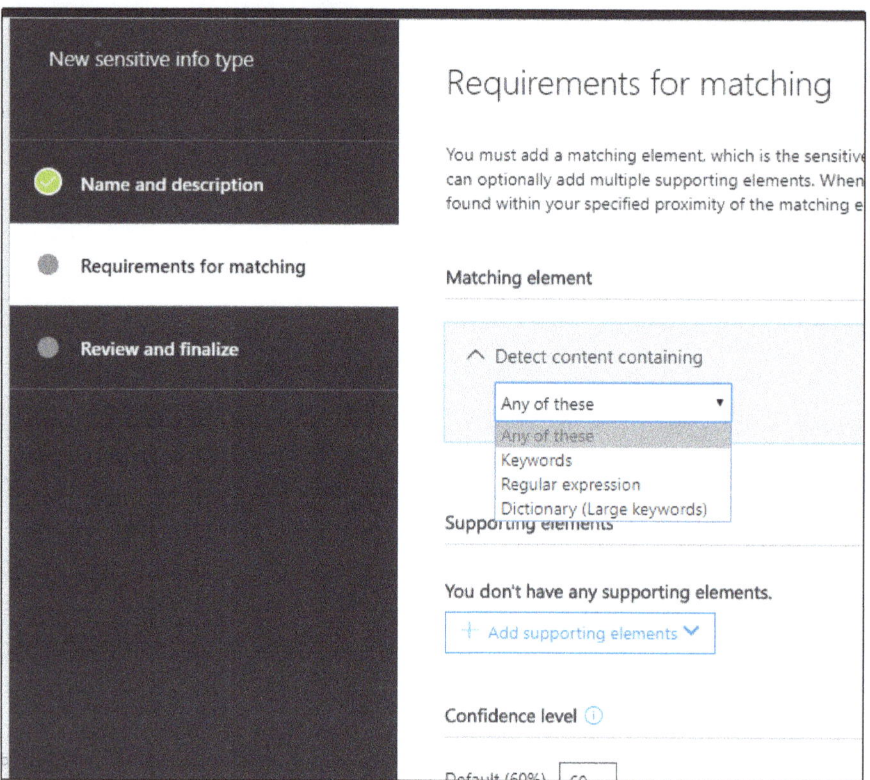

For the most control and options, using PowerShell is the best option. It requires some additional planning and understanding of all the options in order to properly create them.

Custom Sensitive Information Types

In addition to creating Sensitive Information Types, we can also create Rules Packages that are not based on a particular fingerprint, but on a set of conditions that need to match in order for a DLP rule to trigger. These Rules Packages are also known as Custom Sensitive Information Types. Like Sensitive Information Types, these were once created in Exchange Online, however, they are now only created in the SCC via PowerShell or the GUI. Creating a customer XML for the Custom Sensitive Information type is a bit complex. Microsoft has a very detailed article on creating a customer XML here:

https://docs.microsoft.com/en-us/office365/securitycompliance/create-a-custom-sensitive-information-type-in-scc-powershell

The author of this book also has a custom script for creating a working XML. The script is rudimentary but usable for production XML files. If we dig deeper into Sensitive Information types, we find that there is a concept of a

Rules Packages which is how these Sensitive Information Types are stored. We can, in fact, extract these Rules Packages with PowerShell into XML files. Why would we want to do that? We can use these XML files for documentation or verification of what we have set in the service.

Powershell:

```
Get-Help  *DlpSensitiveInformationTypeRulePackage
```

This provides us with a short list of cmdlets:

```
Get-DlpSensitiveInformationTypeRulePackage
New-DlpSensitiveInformationTypeRulePackage
Remove-DlpSensitiveInformationTypeRulePackage
Set-DlpSensitiveInformationTypeRulePackage
```

We can even see Rules Packages for already created Sensitive Information types:

```
Get-DlpSensitiveInformationType | Where {$_.Publisher -ne 'Microsoft Corporation'} | Fl
```

```
Id                     : aef38428-a35d-489a-8568-bc1440643ab1
Name                   : Community Bank Account Number
Description            : Bank Account Number (PII)
RecommendedConfidence  : 60
Publisher              : Damian Scoles
Type                   : Entity
RulePackId             : 5DA58D7A-25F1-4205-93D0-BEB10054C503

Id                     : 791b1558-a0aa-49e4-bc31-e03b24d43e73
Name                   : ConfidentialInformation
Description            : Confidetial Information Keyword Check
RecommendedConfidence  : 85
Publisher              : Damian Scoles
Type                   : Entity
RulePackId             : 6B4E981B-0D62-4423-B660-86603107AF7E
```

** **NOTE** ** Get Help for New-DlpSensitiveInformationTypeRulePackage is incorrect of the writing of the book:

```
-------------------------- Example 1 --------------------------
New-ClassificationRuleCollection -FileData ([Byte[]]$(Get-Content -Path "C:\My Documents\External Sensitive Info
Type Rule Collection.xml" -Encoding Byte -ReadCount 0))

This example imports the sensitive information type rule package C:\My Documents\External Sensitive Info Type Rule
Collection.xml.
```

However, if we simply replace the bad cmdlet specified 'New-ClassificationRuleCollection' with New-DlpSensitiveInformationTypeRulePackage, the rest of the example is technically correct. Unfortunately there are inconsistencies present in Get-Help versus what should be present. Usually it's just because a cmdlet is new and so the Synopsis, Description and Examples may be lacking. Eventually these should be populated correctly. With the above example, if you were to go to the Microsoft Docs version of the Help file, the example is correct:

```
------------------------ Example 1 ------------------------

PowerShell                                                                    Copy

New-DlpSensitiveInformationTypeRulePackage -FileData ([Byte[]]$(Get-Content -Path "C:\My Documents\External Sensitive Inf

This example imports the sensitive information type rule package C:\My Documents\External Sensitive Info Type Rule Collection.xml.
```

From here we can now use the information above to export the XML files which make up the custom sensitive information types. It is also possible you may have these XML files stored somewhere, but if you do we can export them using guidance from this article:

https://docs.microsoft.com/en-us/office365/securitycompliance/customize-a-built-in-sensitive-information-type

First we can start off with our list of sensitive information types:

Id	Name	Publisher	Type
1fc4e0c3-62cd-4886-8a58-ec8bbb793eec	test	Damian Scoles	Fingerprint
aef38428-a35d-489a-8568-bc1440643ab1	Community Bank Account Number	Damian Scoles	Entity
791b1558-a0aa-49e4-bc31-e03b24d43e73	ConfidentialInformation	Damian Scoles	Entity

Using one of the ID's above as an example, we can then store the entire item in a variable like so:

```
$RuleCollections = Get-DlpSensitiveInformationTypeRulePackage aef38428-a35d-489a-8568-bc1440643ab1
```

The we can take the $RuleCollection variable and use it to extract the XML values like so:

```
$DLPRulePackIDs = (Get-DlpSensitiveInformationType | where {$_.Publisher -ne 'Microsoft Corporation'}).RulePackID
Foreach ($DLPRulePackID in $DLPRulePackIDs) {
    $Path = (Get-Item -Path ".\" -Verbose).FullName
    $File = 'DlpSensitiveInformationTypeRulePackage-'+$DLPRulePackID+'.xml'
    $Destination = $Path+"\"+$File
    $RulesPackage = Get-DlpSensitiveInformationTypeRulePackage $DLPRulePackID
    Set-Content -Path $Destination -Encoding Byte -Value $RulesPackage.SerializedClassificationRuleCollection
    $Line = "Rules Collection for - $Identity --> $Path" | Out-file $Destination -Append
}
```

If we look over the XML file it produced, we see this:

```xml
<?xml version="1.0" encoding="utf-16"?>
<RulePackage xmlns="http://schemas.microsoft.com/office/2011/mce">
    <RulePack id="6e27ba86-fc7a-45a0-8a1b-f2ed3287e5c1">
        <Version revision="0" build="0" minor="0" major="1" />
        <Publisher id="a8f2b774-2bfd-4dfb-bc64-d36da193e511" />
        <Details defaultLangCode="en-us">
            <LocalizedDetails langcode="en-us">
                <PublisherName>          </PublisherName>
                <Name>Keyword Test 1</Name>
                <Description>Test keyword search rule creation</Description>
            </LocalizedDetails>
        </Details>
    </RulePack>
    <Rules>
        <Entity id="1e9043a3-dfa6-4b87-a68a-fcfdacbb6eb9" recommendedConfidence="85" patternsProximity="300">
            <Pattern confidenceLevel="85">
                <IdMatch idRef="test" />
            </Pattern>
        </Entity>
        <Regex id="test">keyword</Regex>
        <LocalizedStrings>
            <Resource idRef="1e9043a3-dfa6-4b87-a68a-fcfdacbb6eb9">
                <Name langcode="en-us" default="true">Keyword Test 1</Name>
                <Description langcode="en-us" default="true">Test keyword search rule creation</Description>
            </Resource>
        </LocalizedStrings>
    </Rules>
</RulePackage>
```

Now we know how to expose the current Custom Sensitive Information Types / existing Rules Packages, we can create our own Custom Sensitive Information Types. First we need to create our own XML file. For creating our own we have two choices, we can use the Microsoft site which has a guide to creating XML files based off a template, or we can use PowerShell to do so. A XML creation script, written by the author of this book, is still available in the TechNet Gallery here:

https://gallery.technet.microsoft.com/Custom-DLP-XML-Generation-43846c75

This script can help assemble a XML file based on your criteria. First, a run through and then a code explanation:

```
##########################################################
#                                                        #
#    DLP Template XML File Builder                       #
#                                                        #
#    This script will help construct a basic XML file    #
#     that can be used to create a new DLP policy and    #
#     a new transport rule to control certain information #
#     type.                                              #
#                                                        #
#                              by Damian Scoles          #
#                                                        #
##########################################################


rst we'll plug in the first couple of lines and then ask
 some information for the DLP policy.

er a filename for the xml part to be stored in.  Don't worry about the extension, it will be added (i.e. SSNRule): TestRexEx
t directory will the files be stored in (i.e. c:\temp): c:\temp
er a Publisher Name (i.e. Ben Smith from That Company): Damian Scoles
er a name for the DLP rule (i.e. SSN Rule): TestRegEx
er a description for the DLP rule: Testing RegEx
you want to modify the default proximity level of 300? (y or n): n
you want to modify the default confidence value of 85?: n
er the number of RegEx expressions to be used for this rule (i.e. 1): 1
er an ID or short name for the RegEx criteria (i.e. FormattedSSN): OfficialSensitive
nge the confidence value for this rule (85 is the default): 85
er the RegEx expression to be used for this rule: (\bOfficial\b)\s+(\bSensitive\b)|(\bOfficial_Sensitive\b)

 NOTE *** This script cannot validate the RegEx expression you entered.  Please use an external website such as http://www.regexr.co
```

The script above is almost 200 lines in length, so we will not go line by line. However, first, the output from the script matches standard XML formatting:

```xml
<?xml version="1.0" encoding="UTF-8"?>
<RulePackage xmlns="http://schemas.microsoft.com/office/2011/mce">
  - <RulePack id="4b0182f6-058a-4fc0-8a62-d2f64c58b805">
      <Version major="1" minor="0" build="0" revision="0"/>
      <Publisher id="1dd44575-c240-4b02-b85d-430c202b975b"/>
      - <Details defaultLangCode="en-us">
        - <LocalizedDetails langcode="en-us">
            <PublisherName>Damian Scoles</PublisherName>
            <Name>TestRegEx</Name>
            <Description>Testing RegEx</Description>
          </LocalizedDetails>
      </Details>
  </RulePack>
  - <Rules>
    - <Entity id="1d71e6fe-5280-4906-a951-d91c5f32b888" patternsProximity="300" recommendedConfidence="85">
        - <Pattern confidenceLevel="85">
            <IdMatch idRef="OfficialSensitive"/>
          </Pattern>
      </Entity>
      <Regex id="OfficialSensitive">(\bOfficial\b)\s+(\bSensitive\b)|(\bOfficial_Sensitive\b)</Regex>
    - <LocalizedStrings>
        - <Resource idRef="1d71e6fe-5280-4906-a951-d91c5f32b888">
            <Name langcode="en-us" default="true">TestRegEx</Name>
            <Description langcode="en-us" default="true">Testing RegEx</Description>
          </Resource>
      </LocalizedStrings>
  </Rules>
</RulePackage>
```

Hardest part about assembly a file like this is that there are quotes everywhere in the XML file. This requires a bit of gymnastics with PowerShell code. Luckily there are a few sections of the XML code that are the same between each XML file and we can pre-code those sections. The method of adding quotes is to use an escape character (`) in front of the quotes. This allows PowerShell to interpret the double quotes as we want them and not the closing of a string.

One of the first items we need to create are random GUIDs. GUIDs are unique ID's used to identify the DLP rule. We need three GUIDs and can generate these like so:

```
$Guid = New-Guid
$Guid2 = New-Guid
$Guid3 = New-Guid
```

In the below section, assuming we have populated the $Directory and $Filename variables, we can then add these lines to the top of the file:

```
Add-Content $Directory"\"$Filename  "<?xml version=`"1.0`" encoding=`"UTF-8`"?>"
Add-Content $directory"\"$Filename  " <RulePackage xmlns=`"http://schemas.microsoft.com/
office/2011/mce`">"
Add-Content $Directory"\"$Filename  "<RulePack id=`"$guid`">"
Add-Content $directory"\"$Filename  "<Version revision=`"0`" build=`"0`" minor=`"0`" major=`"1`"/>"
Add-Content $Directory"\"$Filename  "<Publisher id=`"$guid2`"/>"
```

We can then add localizations if we need something other than the default 'en-us':

```
# Placeholder for future code to accept other languages
# $Language = read-host "Choose which language for the XML file.  Default is 'en-us'."
$Language = "en-us"
Add-Content $Directory"\"$Filename  " <Details defaultLangCode=`"$Language`">"
Add-Content $Directory"\"$Filename  " <LocalizedDetails langcode=`"$Language`">"
```

Here we can specify the publisher of the XML file:

```
$Publisher = read-host "Enter a Publisher Name (i.e. Ben Smith from That Company)"
Add-Content $Directory"\"$Filename  "<PublisherName>$publisher</PublisherName>"
```

Next we need to provide a name for the DLP rule, which will be inserted into the XML:

```
$Name = read-host "Enter a name for the DLP rule (i.e. SSN Rule)"
Add-Content $Directory"\"$Filename  "<Name>$name</Name>"
```

After the name, we should provide a description that will make it easier to determine what the rule is for:

```
$Description = read-host "Enter a description for the DLP rule"
Add-Content $Directory"\"$Filename  "<Description>$Description</Description>"
```

After entering the publisher, name and descriptions, we can close this section off for the XML file:

```
Add-Content $Directory"\"$Filename  "</LocalizedDetails>"
Add-Content $Directory"\"$Filename  "</Details>"
Add-Content $Directory"\"$Filename  "</RulePack>"
Add-Content $Directory"\"$Filename  " <Rules>"
```

Some default values included in XML files for sensitive information types include a proximity and confidence level.　We can choose to keep these levels or to modify them.　For this we ask questions and then set variables ($Proximity and $Confidence) to the level requested.

```
# Set custom proximity and confidence levels
$Answer = read-host "Do you want to modify the default proximity level of 300? (y or n)"
If ($Answer -eq "y") {
   $Proximity = read-host "Enter a proximity value for the rules (300 is the default)"
} Else {
   $Proximity = "300"
}
$Answer2 = read-host "Do you want to modify the default confidence value of 85?"
If ($Answer2 -eq "y") {
   $Confidence = read-host "Enter a recommended confidence value for the rules (85 is the default)"
} Else {
   $Confidence = "85"
}
Add-Content $Directory"\"$Filename "<Entity id=`"$Guid3`" recommendedConfidence=`"$confidence`"
patternsProximity=`"$Proximity`">"
```

Next we need to enter RegEx to use for the DLP rule and we can specify one or more of these expression when building out our rule. First we ask for a number of Regex rules we need:

```
$RegexNum = read-host "Enter the number of Regex expressions to be used for this rule (i.e. 1)"
```

Initialize an array for storing lines for Regex to be inserted into the XML file:

```
$RegExID2 = @()
```

Counter to keep track of progress:

```
$Counter = 1
```

Now we start a Do...While loop that will allow us to loop while the $Counter variable is less than the number of Regex rules to be create ($RegexNum):

```
Do {
   $RegExID = Read-Host "Enter an ID or short name for the RegEx criteria (i.e. FormattedSSN)"
   $Answer3 = read-host "Change the confidence value for this rule (85 is the default)"
   If ($Answer3 -eq "y") {
      $Confidence2 = read-host "Enter the confidence value for the rules (85 is the default)"
   } Else {
      $Confidence2 = "85"
   }
   Add-Content $Directory"\"$Filename " <Pattern confidenceLevel=`"$Confidence2`">"
   Add-Content $Directory"\"$Filename "<IdMatch idRef=`"$RegExID`"/>"
   Add-Content $Directory"\"$Filename "</Pattern>"
   $RegExID2 += $RegExID
   $Counter++
}
While ($Counter -le $RegexNum)
```

Now we close off the 'Entity' Section:

```
Add-Content $directory"\"$filename "</Entity>"
```

Next we can query for each actual Regex expression to be used:

```
Foreach ($Line in $RegexID2) {
   $Regex = Read-Host "Enter the Regex to be used for this rule"
   Add-Content $Directory"\"$Filename "<Regex id=`"$line`">$Regex</Regex>"
}
```

Next we close off all of the open sections of the XML file:

```
Add-Content $Directory"\"$Filename " <LocalizedStrings>"
Add-Content $Directory"\"$Filename " <Resource idRef=`"$guid3`">"
Add-Content $Directory"\"$Filename "<Name langcode=`"$language`" default=`"true`">$Name</
Name>"
Add-Content $Directory"\"$Filename "<Description langcode=`"$language`"
default=`"true`">$Description</Description>"
Add-Content $Directory"\"$Filename "</Resource>"
Add-Content $Directory"\"$Filename "</LocalizedStrings>"
Add-Content $Directory"\"$Filename "</Rules>"
Add-Content $Directory"\"$Filename "</RulePackage>"
$FullDirectory = $Directory+"\"+$Filename
$FullDirectoryxml = $Directory+"\"+$Filenamexml
```

Next we convert our txt file, where all of the above lines have gone to produce and convert it to the end product, a XML file:

```
# Convert TXT file to an UTF8 formatted file.
$File_Content = Get-Content $Fulldirectory;
$File_Content
[System.IO.File]::WriteAllLines($FullDirectoryxml, $File_Content);
```

Now that we have a XML file, either via the script or one we created via a manual method. Let's take this file and create a Custom Sensitive Information Type. Assume our file is called NewRegexDLP.xml we can run these PowerShell lines like this to import it:

```
$File = '\\FS01\IT\DLP\ NewRegexDLP.xml'
New-DlpSensitiveInformationTypeRulePackage -FileData ([Byte[]]$(Get-Content -Path $File -Encoding
Byte -ReadCount 0))
```

```
Invariant Name Localized Name Publisher       Encrypted Exportable
-------------- -------------- ---------       --------- ----------
TestRegEx      TestRegEx      Damian Scoles False       True
```

Once our new Sensitive Information Type is imported, we can verify it exists:

```
Get-DlpSensitiveInformationTypeRulePackage -Identity TestRegEx | fl
```

```
Identity              : FFO.extest.microsoft.com/Microsoft Exchange Hosted
                        Organizations         .onmicrosoft.com/Configuration/4B0182F6-058A-4FC0-8A62-D2F64C58B805
RuleCollectionName    : TestRegEx
LocalizedName         : TestRegEx
Description           : Testing RegEx
Publisher             : Damian Scoles
```

Fingerprints

In the Security and Compliance Center, a Fingerprint refers to a standard document (Invoice or HR Form) that has been converted into a Sensitive Information Type. This Sensitive Information Type can then be used with DLP policies to block potential data leaks with a particular document. For example we could use this feature with HR forms and employee records and create a DLP policy that blocks the document from being emailed or shared externally.

Now what happens with Fingerprints is a document is processed and word patterns are stored in the Fingerprint. When a document matching these word patterns are found, then the DLP action is taken. The pattern is stored in XML file to be used in the SCC. The full document is not stored in the server, but a hash of the document is.

One thing to keep in mind is that there is a supported list of documents for the Fingerprinting process. Microsoft's list can be found here:

https://docs.microsoft.com/en-us/exchange/security-and-compliance/mail-flow-rules/inspect-message-attachments#supported-file-types-for-mail-flow-rule-content-inspection

PowerShell

Now that we know what Fingerprints are and what documents are supported, we can explore what PowerShell cmdlets are available and what we can do with them. First, Fingerprint cmdlets?

```
Get-Command *fingerprint*
```

This gives us two PowerShell cmdlets:

```
Migrate-DlpFingerprint
New-DlpFingerprint
```

Notice we do not have PowerShell cmdlets with the following verbs - Get, Remove and Set. Let's start with the New-DlpFingerprint cmdlet and see what we can do:

```
------------------------------ Example 1 ------------------------------

$Patent_Template = Get-Content "C:\My Documents\Contoso Patent Template.docx" -Encoding byte; $Patent_Fingerprint
= New-DlpFingerprint -FileData $Patent_Template -Description "Contoso Patent Template"

This example creates a new document fingerprint based on the file C:\My Documents\Contoso Patent Template.docx.
You store the new fingerprint as a variable so you can use it with the New-DlpSensitiveInformationType cmdlet in
the same PowerShell session.
```

Reviewing the Get-Help as well, there are very few options to choose from. The main ones that should be used are FileData and Description. Most other options are default/built-in ones for most PowerShell cmdlets. Let's run through some scenarios when creating these Fingerprints.

Example 1

Imagine we have a set of documents for the HR department that need to be protected because they will contain

Personally Identifiable Information (PII). For a test case, we will use an Employee Data Sheet that is in Word format; Word documents are supported for Fingerprints in the SCC. Here is what the sample document looks like:

Employee Data Sheet

Employee Name: ______________ Last ___ MI _____________ First

Address: ___________________   Home Telephone: _______________

______________________   Other Telephone: _______________

DOB: _______________   Driver's License #: _______________

SSN: _______________   State Issued: _________

Emergency Contacts:

1) Name______________________   Contact #______________________

Relationship_________________   Secondary Contact #________________________

2) Name______________________   Contact #______________________

Relationship_________________   Secondary Contact #________________________

3) Name______________________   Contact #______________________

Relationship_________________   Secondary Contact #________________________

Physician: Location and/or Phone #:

Driver's License or Photo ID Copy

Hire Date: _____________

W4 Allowances:

Insurance Types: ________

____

Uniform: Yes No

The document is stored on the HR file share at \\FS01\HR\Employee\EmployeeDatasheet.docx. Following the example, we can store the document, using Get-Content, in a variable.

```
$DatasheetContent = Get-Content '\\FS01\HR\Employee\EmployeeDatasheet.docx' -Encoding Byte
$Fingerprint = New-DLPFingerprint -FileData $DatasheetContent -Description 'EmployeeDatasheet'
```

Now that we have a Fingerprint ready, we need to take it and create a new Sensitive Information Type:

```
New-DlpSensitiveInformationType -Name "Employee Datasheet" -Fingerprints $Fingerprint -Description "Employee Datasheet"
```

With a Sensitive Information type we can now apply this to documents that exist in our ecosystem.

Example 2

HR has some confidential forms that are to be used internally by the company. They've provided IT with three forms that need to be blocked from being emailed to anyone external to the organization. First, place a copy of the document on file share so that it can be imported for creating the DLP Policy. Any form or document to be 'fingerprinted' should be blank so that no information interferes with the evaluation.

For PowerShell cmdlets, start with Get-Content (used to store the file in a variable) and then use New-FingerPrint to create the Fingerprint based off the content from the Get-Content variable. Follow this by creating a new Data Classification to be used by Transport Rules later. There are three forms to be protected:

- EmployeePII-Form.docx

- Employee-Review-2016.docx
- Termination-RequestForm.docx

Next, store the document content in a variable in preparation for Transport Rules to use the content. Let's walk through the process of taking these documents and creating Transport Rules to handle them. First import each individual document into a separate variable to be used by New-Fingerprint:

```
$HRDoc1 = Get-Content "C:\Documents\HR\EmployeePII-Form.docx" -Encoding Byte
$HRDoc2 = Get-Content "C:\Documents\HR\Employee-Review-2016.docx" -Encoding Byte
$HRDoc3 = Get-Content "C:\Documents\HR\Termination-RequestForm.docx" -Encoding Byte
```

Notice that the documents are encoded as a 'byte' type document. According to the help file on the 'Get-Help' cmdlet, there are a few data types that can be used:

ASCII, BigEndianUnicode, Byte, String, Unicode, UTF7, UTF8 and Unknown.

In choosing a Word document (which is a binary file) we need to choose 'byte' for the encoding to properly ingest the hash from the file. The 'Get-Content' cmdlet does have other parameters, but for the purposes of fingerprinting itself, no others are required. Simply put in a location of the file and what encoding to use for the document for fingerprinting and store that in a variable.

Create a Fingerprint based off the document stored in each variable:

```
$HRDoc1_Fingerprint = New-DLPFingerprint -FileData $HRDoc1 -Description "Employee PII Form"
$HRDoc2_Fingerprint = New-DLPFingerprint -FileData $HRDoc2 -Description "Employee Review 2016"
$HRDoc3_Fingerprint = New-DLPFingerprint -FileData $HRDoc3 -Description "Termination Request Form"
```

** No cmdlet can query Fingerprints that were created, to see the Fingerprints raw data, you can simply 'dump' the variable contents to the PowerShell window:

```
$HRDoc1_Fingerprint | Fl
```


Description   : Employee PII Form
ShingleCount : 20
Value   : fz382n/99+z//vdfsu/9Rv/G3/7G+vZT11Pu/v/v+//F2s9v/td9//X6sxN/dtfbz6rv3v/+9fy6U9f8W/9
                919/bM+K/7//3ePvktyX/cff/3f3/H92/Preiu/+3/N//XXs/27v3vrX/ftdW390/leb//9275517ebj375
                x8f9TtX7f/9u/etv/7//b9b6//67F+7e//5/7LP9f7//3vt37/p5f+fvs1/v//GTH//rd38919/v7v/Mf/7
                vv3o/fvur/n3/+dTz67039bc1/qf/7r+v/P/TnHs0u377/3m3/9//PbM5do6/c76f+7+yu93j9/XvN3bk9w
                Pf3v////6//uyv10x00z+Xn87Nrv7vXe3fydF3/c/qrb3X9//1eP//3eu+z/9n/M17x/f8//58/T7H/+vn/
                9kP37Kn991P7U++eD//7/M7j3md970/PxueW738//e78f924y91//n897293/P3/xdrbW/1W/e5/v5NT//9
                3Nrv/v/P5uudX3/978//vf6q5s058+vn+uzPR/9DxPrde7pf996P+f3u+//ez/vX/1/9U+36//9/259/+9f
                S/99/tf8n9/rZ61919/P+u/v//6zy/Hu5fvnZ3//79//37vff/7nzcb6/e9/f/Zjf27vzrl/f04f/85/z80
                uzus/392/Wb/ulv/9ez/3jr/3pr9Uv//x97/995D7//T7P9b/z//XLOT9szr6btfj/9r/+/0c+7z7Nza/fr
                3bx/v/+T7+9/TN3b19P/7n/97fr/dv/u+//3/7Eb2/3HQ7WX0+3jzZ79e//P95L/eP2+/9//78zfevszfo+m
                vlefy+9/++9/396KrH/90//0f/z/9/9+nRvrycP572//fn/9z8rr5+h9bX/9RvW4zd77d+ZDj//fvJ/df/z
                78//Rtv/f1v/zN7e/Nov//3b7n33x3///vqj+8+eff3/Z/H8/87+9837a//uitEX785L/9/bf37/ftMzS//
                +/79/+/ut8u+3//76v//X/+///3/Pf38nv1fW/t//mf/91/77u792/175sf/3p3z/vv02sZH/fp/v/f//1/
                ffz/+Gv/8/n/9rpf9/z/zu/9fv+r/7Gzf3bN+v7+f+y9U/f3f//t+9NT+3fHb//+c+x7/Z/Jf73Z1/9mPH3
                t+/9Rv73/dv9//7//3fvut/HxN/9z5r93d7//s/+/3z/d/d70/3r79db+vf/dv92795/P+/6v/uU2/v/17x
                /Uv1/P9v/33P6Wr/783//+vn3/raz0bP/fj7/7Pb/Xab7ubLf7/3H//e/97/f37/t9x/9vvf+///R978//b
                txd/9tz/zpre3+/P/r5/P8za31t/9/038+/v/2/9/6r/9+76+t+r/33/3+rfb8f6+99/duvv3o77dx//1/z
                /opu/f/b7/f//0/n1xPU2n9/f3399k//3nt/7s//u937/X93f35z7P7a++zf+Pz/9fz/7n/+/Ufv/1//1tt
                f9y//97b/2y+f8/ae/30vlv//9////078706n9c//9//iz/8e6RG9+e+/+T+wv/v8uTX//bmXv/7t/bd/7
                t9n2zPbz/XuDyZ/Nf37vzvTaL///3v/Pa/9/zn97rX27/P/2x/uv/75f//bUvP24z8p/f/66f261n+99/fz
                /73Pnvv/1N//zF//72f//dX83fvu38/0f8zv76Ptk/zn359zxt7f7v3sfz3/P3/+f/b3/n9M//7/fn/9j+v
                37h/PWr9j9nxv95Lf///7t6us1v/f///+H39Un99dfzW3vtnff7/d50f/2zvb/9H7+/7/1v////+7//X6/9z
                dez//v9Xvv/9dn+9++99/MbH7frPyrObqn1//dT/97/7e3/+08+6d5P5//zeyu/0k937/5Le/33vf+/0z5p
                19x//P5H19+737/XS///7t/M6+/1+/n9av272Xfu9v/zzfPs/+//zv//xuPd2n/vi//r//9Xf37fn99bt5f
                ++fr5/9v/2e5+/nsq//vzvf+51f3M9be3t730/T/0+n/Zvtfa/+off7b+v/9U3v//3/9Rvt//45/f3+9P/2

```

The New-Fingerprint cmdlet has even less options than the Get-Content cmdlet and examples from the cmdlet
```

use only the two parameters chosen above – FileData and Description. FileData references the document stored in the variable. Now that the Fingerprint has been created, it can be used by the New-DlpSensitiveInformationType cmdlet to create a data classification for a Transport Rule:

```
New-DlpSensitiveInformationType -Name "HR Confidential Form 1" -Fingerprints $HRDoc1_Fingerprint
-Description "Message contains confidential employee information."

New-DlpSensitiveInformationType -Name "HR Confidential Form 2" -Fingerprints $HRDoc2_Fingerprint
-Description "Message contains confidential employee information."

New-DlpSensitiveInformationType -Name "HR Confidential Form 3" -Fingerprints $HRDoc3_Fingerprint
-Description "Message contains confidential employee information."
```

The New-DLPSensitiveInformationType cmdlet can be used to create individual classifications or it can group multiple Fingerprints together into one classification as the parameter used for this is 'Fingerprints' not 'Fingerprint'. Make sure to separate multiple Fingerprints with a comma.

** **Note** ** Document Fingerprints can also be added to existing data classifications using the Set-DataClassification cmdlet and the -Fingerprints parameter:

```
New-DlpSensitiveInformationType -Name "HR Confidential Form 3" -Fingerprints $HRDoc3_Fingerprint
```

To verify the Fingerprints were successful in being converted to an SCC Rules Package run the following(results below):

```
Get-DlpSensitiveInformationTypeRulePackage
```

```
Invariant Name                         Localized Name                         Publisher              Encrypted  Exportable
-------------                          --------------                         ---------              ---------  ----------
Microsoft Rule Package                 Microsoft Rule Package                 Microsoft Corporation  False      True
TestRegEx                              TestRegEx                              Damian Scoles          False      True
KeywordSearch-CI                       KeywordSearch-CI                       Damian Scoles          False      True
Document Fingerprint Rule Package      Document Fingerprint Rule Package      Damian Scoles          False      True
Keyword123                             Keyword123                             Damian Scoles          False      True
Microsoft.SCCManaged.CustomRulePack    Microsoft.SCCManaged.CustomRulePack    Damian Scoles          False      True
ConfidentialInformation                ConfidentialInformation                Damian Scoles          False      True
Keyword Test 1                         Keyword Test 1                         Damian Scoles          False      True
```

Keyword Dictionaries

A Keyword Dictionary is a grouping of words that can be used for DLP purposes. These Dictionaries can contain up to 100,000 keywords and are typically groups by topic, like health care related keywords, profanity or some other grouping.

Powershell

```
Get-Command *KeywordDictionary
```

We now have a list of four PowerShell cmdlets related to Keyword Dictionaries in the SCC:

```
Get-DlpKeywordDictionary
New-DlpKeywordDictionary
Remove-DlpKeywordDictionary
```

Set-DlpKeywordDictionary

By default we have no DLP Keyword Dictionaries and we can confirm that by running the Get-DLPKeywordDictionary on a new tenant. So if we wish to work with these, we need to start by creating a new one with the New-DLPKeywordDictionary cmdlet. Here are two examples from the cmdlet:

```
------------------------ Example 1 ------------------------

$Keywords = "Aarskog's syndrome, Abandonment, Abasia, Abderhalden-Kaufmann-Lignac, Abdominalgia, Abduction
contracture, Abetalipo proteinemia, Abiotrophy, Ablatio, ablation, Ablepharia, Abocclusion, Abolition, Aborter,
Abortion, Abortus, Aboulomania, Abrami's disease, Abramo"; $EncodedKeywords =
[system.Text.Encoding]::UTF8.GetBytes($Keywords); New-DlpKeywordDictionary -Name "Diseases" -Description "Names of
diseases and injuries from ICD-10-CM lexicon" -FileData $EncodedKeywords

This example creates a DLP keyword dictionary named Diseases by using the specified values.

------------------------ Example 2 ------------------------

$Terms = Get-Content "C:\My Documents\InappropriateTerms.txt"; $Keywords = $Terms -Join ", "; $EncodedKeywords =
[system.Text.Encoding]::UTF8.GetBytes($Keywords); New-DlpKeywordDictionary -Name "Inappropriate Language"
-Description "Unprofessional and inappropriate terminology" -FileData $EncodedKeywords
```

From the above examples we see that there are a couple of steps to creating the DLP Keyword Dictionary. First, we need a list of words and store those in a variable. Once we have that list stored, they need to be converted to a format that can be interpreted by the SCC. The converter is this code section '[system.Text.Encoding]::UTF8. GetBytes' as we need to convert the list into the Binary UTF8 format according to the FileData option for New-DLP-KeywordDictionary help:

```
-FileData <Byte[]>
    The FileData parameter specifies the terms that are used in the DLP keyword dictionary. This parameter
    requires a comma-separated list of values that's binary encoded in UTF8. For more information, see the
    examples in this topic.
```

Example 1

For the first example, we are provided a list of keywords we wish to build a small dictionary of. A dictionary of words will be far easier than say individual rules for words, but also provides a common set for detection and sense of relevance.

```
$PIIKeywords = 'First Name','Last Name','State','street address','city','county','zip code','Phone
numbers','Fax numbers','email address','Social Security numbers','Account number','License
number','License Plate','Serial number'
$EncodedKeywords = [system.Text.Encoding]::UTF8.GetBytes($PIIKeywords)
New-DlpKeywordDictionary -Name 'PII' -Description 'PII Terms' -FileData $EncodedKeywords
```

```
PS C:\> $PIIKeywords = 'First Name','Last Name','State','street address','city','county','zip code','Phone numbers',
'Fax numbers','email address','Social Security numbers','Account number','License number','License Plate','Serial number'
PS C:\> $EncodedKeywords = [system.Text.Encoding]::UTF8.GetBytes($PIIKeywords)
PS C:\> New-DlpKeywordDictionary -Name 'PII' -Description 'PII Terms' -FileData $EncodedKeywords

RunspaceId         : 1a3060c6-6cdd-4293-8ee0-d2b1ac4d5acb
Identity           : 2bd7d2d2-37b4-40c5-835a-6e182b092e23
Name               : PII
Description        : PII Terms
KeywordDictionary  : first name last name state street address city county zip code phone numbers fax numbers email
                     address social security numbers account number license number license plate serial number

IsValid            : True
ObjectState        : Unchanged
```

Example 2

For this example we have been provided a list of medical terms to be used for a new DLP rule for a medical firm. The list of words is stored in a txt file on one of their file servers - \\MFS01\DLP\WordList.txt. We will need to ingest this word list to create a Keyword Dictionary in the SCC. The WordList.txt file looks like this:

```
wordlist.txt - Notepad
File  Edit  Format  View  Help
11-dehydrocorticosterone
1,2:5,6-dibenzanthracene
1,25-dihydroxycholecalciferol
1,3-diphosphoglyceric
17a-hydroxyprogesterone
17-hydroxycorticosteroid
2,3-diphosphoglycerate
2,4-dichlorophenoxyacetic
25-hydroxycholecalciferol
3,4-dihydroxyphenylalanine
3tc
4-pyridoxic
5-bromodeoxyuridine
5-hydroxyindoleacetic
5-hydroxytryptamine
5-iododeoxyuridine
```

Then we take the file and store it in a variable with an Encoding type of 'Byte' using this one liner:

```
$FileData = Get-Content Wordlist.txt -Encoding Byte -ReadCount 0
```

Then we take the encoded word list and create a new DLP Keyword Dictionary:

```
New-DlpKeywordDictionary -Name 'Medical Terms' -Description 'Medical Lexicon' -FileData $FileData
```

```
PS C:\> $fileData = Get-Content Wordlist.txt -Encoding Byte -ReadCount 0
PS C:\> New-DlpKeywordDictionary -Name 'Medical Terms' -Description 'Medical Lexicon' -FileData $fileData

RunspaceId         : 1a3060c6-6cdd-4293-8ee0-d2b1ac4d5acb
Identity           : 81aa2c2a-357e-4b95-a54a-7448b220d7c5
Name               : Medical Terms A
Description        : Medical Lexicon A
KeywordDictionary  : 1,25-dihydroxycholecalciferol
                     1,2:5,6-dibenzanthracene
                     1,3-diphosphoglyceric
                     11-dehydrocorticosterone
                     17-hydroxycorticosteroid
                     17a-hydroxyprogesterone
                     2,3-diphosphoglycerate
                     2,4-dichlorophenoxyacetic
                     25-hydroxycholecalciferol
                     3,4-dihydroxyphenylalanine
                     3tc
```

Remove a DLP Keyword Dictionary

Removing an existing DLP Keyword Dictionary is as simple as knowing the name and using a one-liner like this:

```
Remove-DlpKeywordDictionary <Name>
```

From Example 2:

```
Remove-DlpKeywordDictionary 'Medical Terms'
```

Modifying an existing DLP Keyword List

For this scenario, imagine we have a terms list that is published for a particular field. This list is usually static, but every few years changes are made either with the addition of new terms or the retirement of old words. Sometimes both additions and removals are made to terms in the list. If we have a DLP Keyword Dictionary based on this we can take that Dictionary and swap out the old list. Once we receive the new list, we can follow a similar process as we did to create the initial Dictionary:

```
$FileData = Get-Content Wordlist.txt -Encoding Byte -ReadCount 0
Set-DlpKeywordDictionary -Name 'Medical Terms' -FileData $FileData
```

Now, if we want, we can also change the description at the same time, possibly noting the date of the change for future reference:

```
Set-DlpKeywordDictionary -Name 'Medical Terms' -Description 'Medical Lexicon - 2019-08-03'
```

Additionally we could add values to an existing dictionary like so:

```
$Original = (Get-DlpKeywordDictionary -Name 'Technical Docs').KeywordDictionary.split(',').Trim()
$Original += 'Robotics','Perfect Invention'
$NewKeywords = $Original  -Join ', '
$Data = [system.Text.Encoding]::UTF8.GetBytes($NewKeywords)
Set-DlpKeywordDictionary -Identity "Technical Docs" -FileData $Data
```

** **Note** ** '.Trim() will remove any spaces are the front of a line for cleanup purposes. Results of the above code lines are produced like so:

```
KeywordDictionary
-----------------
technical specifications, research grant, development methodologies, robotics, perfect inventi...
```

Exact Data Match (EDM)

While this book was being written, it was noticed that a set of four Exact Data Match EDM related PowerShell cmdlets appeared in the Security and Compliance Center. These same cmdlets would appear and disappear in an irregular basis. As of now, the cmdlets are still available, but the feature EDM is in Preview. This was confirmed by Microsoft Docs pages as well:

Create custom sensitive information types with Exact Data Match based classification (Preview)
https://docs.microsoft.com/en-us/office365/securitycompliance/create-custom-sensitive-info-type-edm

For this section of the book, we will briefly explore this function via PowerShell. However, anything written at the publication of this edition may change by the time your begin to use it in your tenant. Make sure to refer to any current documentation and PowerShell Get-Help for these cmdlets.

Requirements

Permissions:

You must be a global admin, compliance administrator, or Exchange Online administrator to perform the tasks described in this article. To learn more about DLP Permissions, see Permissions.

Licensing:

- Office 365 E5
- Microsoft 365 E5
- Microsoft 365 Information Protection and Compliance
- Office 365 Advanced Compliance

PowerShell

```
Get-Command *DLPEdm*
```

This provides us with these cmdlets:

```
Get-DlpEdmSchema
New-DlpEdmSchema
Remove-DlpEdmSchema
Set-DlpEdmSchema
```

First, it should be noted that there are not EDM Schemas pre-built at the time of Preview and running 'Get-DlpEdm-Schema' will return a blank result. According to Microsoft's work flow for EDM, we need to first create an EDM-based classification.

Sample EDM

Using a sample EDM Schema provided by Microsoft (https://docs.microsoft.com/en-us/exchange/security-and-compliance/mail-flow-rules/inspect-message-attachments#supported-file-types-for-mail-flow-rule-content-inspection), we will produce one that we can use for Employee Records for a company. The Text file would look something this (XML Style format):

```
<EdmSchema xmlns="http://schemas.microsoft.com/office/2018/edm">
  <DataStore name="EmployeeRecords" description="Schema for patient records" version="1">
    <Field name="EmployeeID" unique="true" searchable="true" />
    <Field name="FirstName" unique="false" searchable="false" />
    <Field name="LastName" unique="false" searchable="false" />
    <Field name="SSN" unique="true" searchable="true" />
    <Field name="Phone" unique="false" searchable="true" />
    <Field name="DOB" unique="false" searchable="true" />
    <Field name="Gender" unique="false" searchable="false" />
    <Field name="Address" unique="false" searchable="false" />
```

```
        </DataStore>
    </EdmSchema>
```

Once we have our Text files saved and ready we can go ahead and import this into Office 365. Connect to the PowerShell interface for the Security and Compliance Center (see Ch 3). We can then import the Text file and convert it into an EDM Schema like so:

```
$EmployeeRecordsSchema = Get-Content .\EmployeeRecordSchema1.xml -Encoding Byte -ReadCount 0
New-DlpEdmSchema -FileData $EmployeeRecordsSchema -Confirm:$true
```

```
PS C:\> New-DlpEdmSchema -FileData $EmployeeRecordsSchema -Confirm:$true
Only one unique field can be present in EDM datastore
    + CategoryInfo          : NotSpecified: (:) [New-DlpEdmSchema], EdmFieldUniqueViolationException
    + FullyQualifiedErrorId : [Server=BY2NAM05WS007,RequestId=76d7e0a1-7022-457b-a6c2-768f00b09aaf,TimeStamp=7/31/2019
   6:12:42 PM] [FailureCategory=Cmdlet-EdmFieldUniqueViolationException] 23F19A55,Microsoft.Office.CompliancePolicy.
   Tasks.NewDlpEdmSchema
    + PSComputerName        : nam05b.ps.compliance.protection.outlook.com
```

However, according to the documentation, we can choose "Fields", plural, for this option:

> • Use *unique="true"* for the fields that contain unique values (Social Security numbers, identification numbers, etc.);
> otherwise, use *unique="false"*.

So apparently, this isn't true. For our test we will assume that the SSN field is unique. After the file value has been modified, we can re-run the cmdlets, accept the import and now we have an EDM Schema available for us:

```
PS C:\> $EmployeeRecordsSchema = Get-Content .\EmployeeRecordSchema1.xml -Encoding Byte -ReadCount 0
PS C:\> New-DlpEdmSchema -FileData $EmployeeRecordsSchema -Confirm:$true

Confirm
Are you sure you want to perform this action?
New EDM Schema for the data store 'employeerecords' will be imported.
[Y] Yes  [A] Yes to All  [N] No  [L] No to All  [?] Help (default is "Y"): y

DataStore Name  Description                   Version CreatedDate            ModifiedDate
--------------  -----------                   ------- -----------            ------------
employeerecords Schema for patient records 1          7/31/2019 1:14:43 PM 7/31/2019 1:14:43 PM
```

The EDM Schema can be pretty large, as referenced by these Microsoft Specs:

```
Up to 10 million rows of sensitive data
Up to 32 columns (fields) per data source
```

Would we be able to display all of that data or would PowerShell be limited to what is available?

After we import the EDM Schema data, we can now display the results of the import here:

```
Get-DlpEdmSchema | Fl
```

What is interesting (see the red box on the previous page) is that the entire schema file we created and imported is listed here:

```
RunspaceId          : 7eb23ef0-4b27-42be-846f-10a76b7801f6
DataStoreName       : employeerecords
Description         : Schema for patient records
Version             : 1
CreatedDate         : 7/31/2019 1:14:43 PM
ModifiedDate        : 7/31/2019 1:14:43 PM
EdmSchemaXml        : <?xml version="1.0" encoding="utf-16"?><EdmSchema
                      xmlns="http://schemas.microsoft.com/office/2018/edm"><DataStore name="EmployeeRecords"
                      description="Schema for patient records" version="1"><Field name="EmployeeID" unique="false"
                      searchable="true" /><Field name="FirstName" unique="false" searchable="false" /><Field
                      name="LastName" unique="false" searchable="false" /><Field name="SSN" unique="true"
                      searchable="true" /><Field name="Phone" unique="false" searchable="true" /><Field name="DOB"
                      unique="false" searchable="true" /><Field name="Gender" unique="false" searchable="false" /><Field
                      name="Address" unique="false" searchable="false" /></DataStore></EdmSchema>
Identity            : FFO.extest.microsoft.com/Microsoft Exchange Hosted
                      Organizations/scoles.onmicrosoft.com/Configuration/employeerecords
DistinguishedName   : CN=employeerecords,CN=Configuration,CN=scoles.onmicrosoft.com,OU=Microsoft Exchange Hosted
                      Organizations,DC=FFO,DC=extest,DC=microsoft,DC=com
Guid                : 00000000-0000-0000-0000-000000000000
ImmutableId         : 00000000-0000-0000-0000-000000000000
OrganizationId      : FFO.extest.microsoft.com/Microsoft Exchange Hosted Organizations/scoles.onmicrosoft.com -
                      FFO.extest.microsoft.com/Microsoft Exchange Hosted
                      Organizations/scoles.onmicrosoft.com/Configuration
Name                : employeerecords
IsValid             : True
```

** Notes **

Field names in the EDM Schema cannot have spaces in the field names or else an error like this occurs:

```
EDM schema failed XML schema definition validation. Error details: The 'name' attribute is invalid - The value 'Unique
Field 1' is invalid according to its datatype 'String' - The Pattern constraint failed..
    + CategoryInfo          : NotSpecified: (:) [New-DlpEdmSchema], EdmSchemaInvalidDefinitionException
    + FullyQualifiedErrorId : [Server=BY2NAM05WS006,RequestId=adf63fa8-eed3-4502-b4bd-a6782c1502e5,TimeStamp=8/3/2019
    9:48:50 PM] [FailureCategory=Cmdlet-EdmSchemaInvalidDefinitionException] 614C263F,Microsoft.Office.CompliancePolic
    y.Tasks.NewDlpEdmSchema
    + PSComputerName        : nam05b.ps.compliance.protection.outlook.com
```

If we exceed 32 fields in the EDM Schema, we receive errors like these:

```
EDM schema failed XML schema definition validation. Error details: The element 'DataStore' in namespace
'http://schemas.microsoft.com/office/2018/edm' has invalid child element 'Field' in namespace
'http://schemas.microsoft.com/office/2018/edm'..
    + CategoryInfo          : NotSpecified: (:) [New-DlpEdmSchema], EdmSchemaInvalidDefinitionException
    + FullyQualifiedErrorId : [Server=BY2NAM05WS006,RequestId=4dc93e90-7364-4e6c-a2e3-87438ed2a079,TimeStamp=8/3/2019
    9:51:19 PM] [FailureCategory=Cmdlet-EdmSchemaInvalidDefinitionException] 4B5A659,Microsoft.Office.CompliancePolicy
    .Tasks.NewDlpEdmSchema
    + PSComputerName        : nam05b.ps.compliance.protection.outlook.com
```

Once we have an EDM Schema in place we need to build an XML file that can be used for as a Sensitive Information Type:

```xml
<RulePackage xmlns="http://schemas.microsoft.com/office/2018/edm">
  <RulePack id="fd098e03-1796-41a5-8ab6-198c93c62b11">
   <Version build="0" major="2" minor="0" revision="0" />
   <Publisher id="fc553734-8306-44b4-9ad5-c388ad970528" />
   <Details defaultLangCode="en-us">
    <LocalizedDetails langcode="en-us">
     <PublisherName>PII DLP</PublisherName>
     <Name>Employee EDM Rulepack</Name>
```

```
    <Description>This rule package contains the PII sensitive information types for employee data.</
Description>
   </LocalizedDetails>
  </Details>
 </RulePack>
 <Rules>
  <ExactMatch id = "F2CC861E-3FE9-4A58-82DF-4BD259EAB371" patternsProximity = "300" dataStore
="EmployeeRecords" recommendedConfidence = "65" >
   <Pattern confidenceLevel="65">
    <idMatch matches = "SSN" classification = "U.S. Social Security Number (SSN)" />
   </Pattern>
   <Pattern confidenceLevel="75">
    <idMatch matches = "SSN" classification = "U.S. Social Security Number (SSN)" />
    <Any minMatches ="3" maxMatches ="100">
     <match matches="EmployeeID" />
     <match matches="FirstName"/>
     <match matches="LastName"/>
     <match matches="SSN"/>
     <match matches="Phone"/>
     <match matches="DOB"/>
     <match matches="Gender"/>
     <match matches="Address" />
    </Any>
   </Pattern>
  </ExactMatch>
  <LocalizedStrings>
   <Resource idRef="F2CC861E-3FE9-4A58-82DF-4BD259EAB371">
    <Name default="true" langcode="en-us">Patient SSN Exact Match.</Name>
    <Description default="true" langcode="en-us">EDM Sensitive type for detecting employee SSN.</
Description>
   </Resource>
  </LocalizedStrings>
 </Rules>
</RulePackage>
```

In the above XML, we've provided details needed to identify the purpose of the XML file. Careful planning should be done in order to get the correct fields. With our XML we can now create a Sensitive Information Type:

```
$EmployeeRulepack=Get-Content .\EmployeeRulePack.xml -Encoding Byte -ReadCount 0
New-DlpSensitiveInformationTypeRulePackage -FileData $EmployeeRulePack
```

Now, in order to complete the EDM Schema import process for the Security and Compliance Center, we need to follow some additional steps.

Download EDM Upload Agent: https://go.microsoft.com/fwlink/?linkid=2088639

Next we need to install it on the computer that will be used to upload the EDM data:

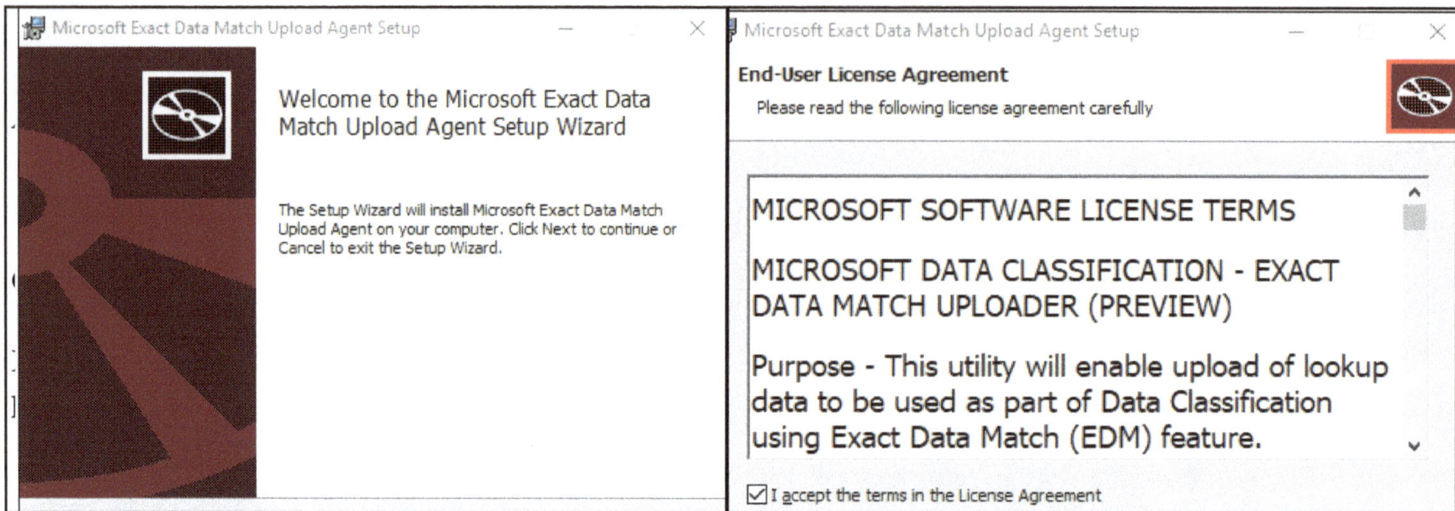

A hash file of our EDM Schema will need to be created and uploaded. When we up load the hash file we will need to specify:

Datastore Name: Provide a relevant name for the information to be stored
DataFile: CSV file with sensitive information in it
HashLocation: Location for sensitive information file's hash to be stored

We can use these values like so:

EdmUploadAgent.exe /CreateHash /DataStoreName EmployeeRecord /DataFile \\FS01\scc\EDM\ EmployeeRecords.csv /HashLocation \\FS01\scc\EDM\EmployeeRecords

If this works, you should receive a successful message:

```
Command completed successfully.
```

Otherwise a failure message should appear:

```
Command failed.
Error Type: Microsoft.DataClassification.Edm.Client.EdmServiceClientException
Error Code: InternalServerError
Response: Error: ErrorCode: SchemaNotFound
Message: Schema not found for datastore employeerecord.
Target:
InnerError: Date: 2019-08-04T03:05:42.0000000
RequestId: e863081d-3963-44b8-aeef-40bb18d91968
ErrorCode:
ClientRequestId:
DiagnosticInfo:
ActivityId:
```

This error could occur due to an error in one of the data files, or if the name of the Schema is wrong. If we check our DLP EDM Schemas in the SCC, we will see if we have the name incorrect:

```
DataStore Name    Description               Version CreatedDate            ModifiedDate
--------------    -----------               ------- -----------            ------------
employeerecords   Schema for patient records   1       7/31/2019 1:14:43 PM 7/31/2019 1:14:43 PM
```

EdmUploadAgent.exe /UploadHash /DataStoreName Employeerecords /HashFile \FS01\scc\EDM\ EmployeeRecords.EdmHash

The above cmdlet should also return a 'Completed Successfully'. As a final step, we can verify the datastore:

EdmUploadAgent.exe /GetDataStore

```
C:\Program Files\Microsoft\EdmUploadAgent>EdmUploadAgent.exe /GetDataStore
Printing list of Datastores.
Id, Name, DataLastUpdatedTime
employeerecords, employeerecords,
Command completed successfully.
```

We also need to install the EDM Upload Agent, as seen on the following pages:

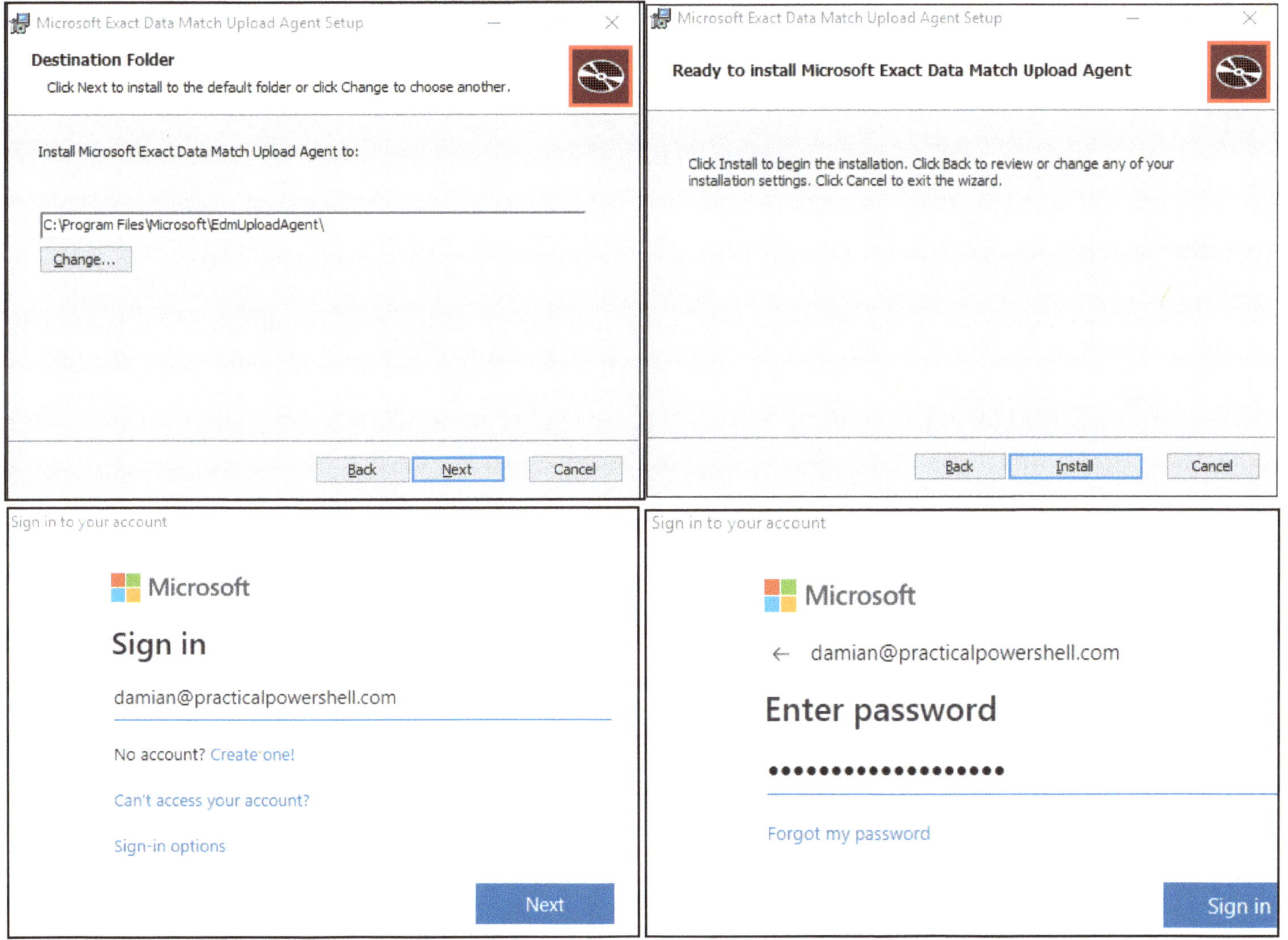

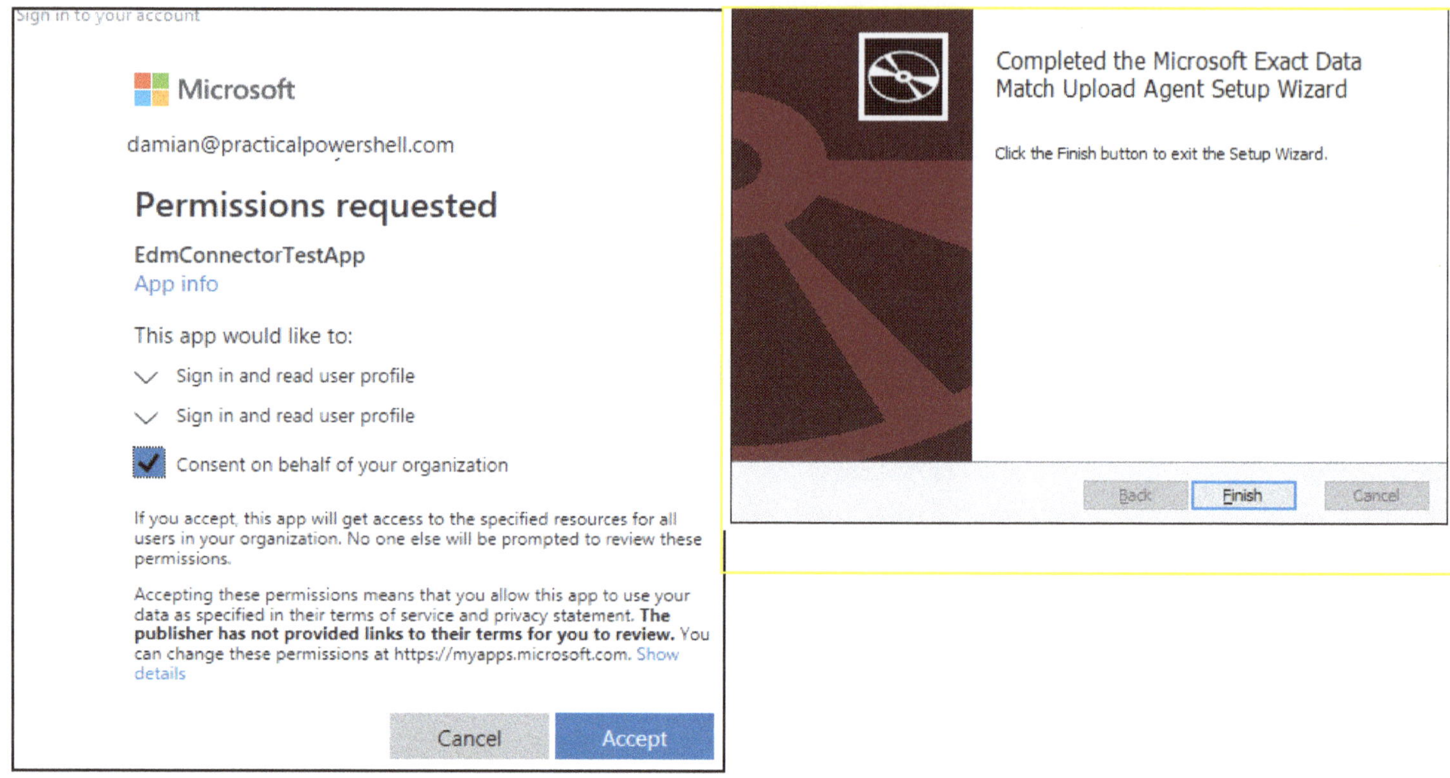

DLP Compliance

In the previous pages of this chapter we walked though how to create various Sensitive Information Types: Fingerprints and Keyword Dictionaries to Custom XML files and Exact Data Match objects. Now we need to explore what we can do with these. Using additional scenarios, help files and code samples we will explore how to configure our DLP Compliance Policies and Rules. Keep in mind the hierarchy of objects we need n order to create DLP Compliance Policies and then we create the DLP Compliance Rules. DLP Compliance Rules reference the Policies.

First step, is creating a new DLP Compliance Policy. A DLP Compliance Policy is used to determine which workloads in Office 365 will be affected. We can choose from Exchange, SharePoint, OneDrive and Teams locations as our target workloads for the policy.

PowerShell

In order to create a new DLP Compliance Policy we need the 'New-DLPCompliancePolicy' cmdlet in order to do so. The help for the New-DLPCompliancePolicy command provides us with two examples:

```
-------------------------- Example 1 --------------------------

New-DlpCompliancePolicy -Name "GlobalPolicy" -SharePointLocation All

This example creates a DLP policy named GlobalPolicy that will be enforced across all SharePoint Online locations.

-------------------------- Example 2 --------------------------

New-DlpCompliancePolicy -Name "GlobalPolicy" -Comment "Primary policy" -SharePointLocation
"https://my.url","https://my.url2" -OneDriveLocation "https://my.url3","https://my.url4" -Mode Enable

This example creates a DLP policy named GlobalPolicy for the specified SharePoint Online and OneDrive for Business
locations. The new policy has a descriptive comment and will be enabled on creation.
```

Let's take some of our previous scenarios and complete them by using a Sensitive Information Type and create some DLP Compliance Policies:

Custom Sensitive Information Type (XML Based)

For this example, we'll take the Custom Sensitive Information Type and apply it against OneDrive locations:

```
New-DLPCompliancePolicy -Name 'RegEx Document Query' -OneDriveLocation All
```

** In the next section we'll create DLP Compliance Rules with these Policies.

Fingerprints

For our previous Fingerprint examples, the documents are all stored in SharePoint. We want to be able to control how these documents are access and shared. First, we need a DLP Compliance Policy for the Fingerprints:

```
New-DLPCompliancePolicy -Name 'Employee Datasheet' -SharePointLocation All
New-DLPCompliancePolicy -Name 'HR Confidential Form 1' -SharePointLocation All
New-DLPCompliancePolicy -Name 'HR Confidential Form 2' -SharePointLocation All
New-DLPCompliancePolicy -Name 'HR Confidential Form 3' -SharePointLocation All
```

** In the next section we'll create DLP Compliance Rules with these Policies.

Keyword Dictionary

In this example, we have two Keyword Dictionaries that cover Technical Documents and PII. For these, we will want to cover any location we can (Exchange, SharePoint, OneDrive and Teams):

```
New-DLPCompliancePolicy -Name 'Technical Document Policy' -SharePointLocation All
-ExchangeLocation All -OneDriveLocation All -TeamsLocation All
New-DLPCompliancePolicy -Name 'PII' -SharePointLocation All -ExchangeLocation All -OneDriveLocation
All -TeamsLocation All
```

** In the next section we'll create DLP Compliance Rules with these Policies.

Exact Data Match (EDM)

For this example we need to set up a DLP policy for Exchange:

```
New-DLPCompliancePolicy -Name 'Employee Records' -ExchangeLocation All
```

** In the next section we'll create DLP Compliance Rules with these Policies.

New-DLPComplianceRule

After we have a DLP Compliance Policy, we need to create a DLP Compliance Rule as well. A DLP Compliance Rule is associated with a specify DLP Compliance Policy. No other settings are required. Typically a DLP Compliance Rule will be configured with other options such as Sensitive Information Types, Notifications, as well as determining access to the content affected.

```
------------------------- Example 1 -------------------------

New-DlpComplianceRule -Name "SocialSecurityRule" -Policy "USFinancialChecks" -ContentContainsSensitiveInformation
@{Name="U.S. Social Security Number (SSN)"} -BlockAccess $True

This example create a new DLP compliance rule named "SocialSecurityRule" that is assigned to the
"USFinancialChecks" policy. The rule checks for social security numbers and blocks access if it finds them.
```

Before we begin to build our new DLP Compliance Rules, let's explore some of the available options that we can use to build them:

Name: Name of the DLP Compliance Rule
Policy: Which DLP Compliance Policy is referenced by the Rule
AccessScope: We have three options for this parameter - *InOrganization* - applied to internal content only, *NotInOrganization* - applied to content accessible externally or *None* - Condition isn't used
BlockAccess: $True - only the owner, author, and site owner have access | $False - Allows access (default)
Comment: Allows us to provide a description for others to read
ContentContainsSensitiveInformation: Adds Sensitive Information Type(s) as a condition
ContentPropertyContainsWords: Condition that matches property values to content
Disabled: Allows us to disable a rule if we need to for testing or to decommission a DLP Compliance rule
GenerateAlert: Email notification sent to one or more email addresses
GenerateIncidentReport: Email notification sent to one or more email addresses
IncidentReportContent: Specifies content for incident report, can choose all or partial details
NotifyAllowOverride: Override allows when this condition met - *FalsePositive* | *WithoutJustification* | *WithJustification*
NotifyEmailCustomText: Add custom text to the notification up to 5000 characters
NotifyPolicyTipCustomText: Custom text shown to user (up to 250 characters) when conditions met
NotifyUser: Who to notify when conditions met (email address(es))
ReportSeverityLevel: *None* | *Low* | *Medium* | *High*
RuleErrorAction: If an error is encountered, what action to take - *Ignore* | *RetryThenBlock* | *Block*

Even with all of those options, it should be noted that there are quite a few options that are for Microsoft Internal use only: (not all inclusive)

```
-ExpiryDate <DateTime>
    This parameter is reserved for internal Microsoft use.

    Required?                      false
    Position?                      Named
    Default value
    Accept pipeline input?         False
    Accept wildcard characters?    false

-From <SmtpAddress[]>
    This parameter is reserved for internal Microsoft use.

    Required?                      false
    Position?                      Named
    Default value
    Accept pipeline input?         False
    Accept wildcard characters?    false
```

Below are examples for creating various DLP Compliance rules, using different Sensitive Information Types:

Custom Sensitive Information Type

> New-DLPComplianceRule -Name 'Regex Document Rule' -Policy 'Regex Document Query' -AccessScope InOrganization -ContentContainsSensitiveInformation 'TestRegEx'

For this one a block is put in place for external users.

Fingerprint

> New-DLPComplianceRule -Name 'Employee Data Sheet Fingerprint Rule' -Policy 'Employee Datasheet' -ContentContainsSensitiveInformation "Employee Datasheet" -AccessScope InOrganization -ReportSeverityLevel Medium
> New-DLPComplianceRule -Name 'HR Fingerprint Rule 1' -Policy 'HR Confidential Form 1' -ContentContainsSensitiveInformation "HR Confidential Form 1" -AccessScope InOrganization -ReportSeverityLevel High
> New-DLPComplianceRule -Name 'HR Fingerprint Rule 2' -Policy 'HR Confidential Form 2' -ContentContainsSensitiveInformation "HR Confidential Form 2" -AccessScope InOrganization -ReportSeverityLevel High
> New-DLPComplianceRule -Name 'HR Fingerprint Rule 3' -Policy 'HR Confidential Form 3' -ContentContainsSensitiveInformation "HR Confidential Form 3" -AccessScope InOrganization -ReportSeverityLevel High

For the above Rules we added the block for external users as well as setting a Report Severity Level to High for three of the four and to Medium for the Employee Datasheet.

Keyword Dictionary

> New-DLPComplianceRule -Name 'Technical Doc DLP Rule' -Policy 'Technical Document Policy' -GenerateIncidentReport 'damian@practicalpowershell.com' -IncidentReportContent All
> New-DLPComplianceRule -Name 'PII DLP Rule' -Policy 'PII'-GenerateIncidentReport 'damian@practicalpowershell.com' -IncidentReportContent All

For this rule set, we added notifications and a complete Incident report to be sent (all details).

Exact Data Match (EDM)

> New-DLPComplianceRule -Name -Policy 'Employee Records' -RuleErrorAction RetryThenBlock

For this DLP Rule we are attempting to troubleshoot some issues so we have put the Rule to try again. If it does not work, then block access to the protected content.

Other DLP Cmdlets

Get-DlpDetectionsReport

"Use the Get-DlpDetectionsReport cmdlet to list a summary of Data Loss Prevention (DLP) rule matches for SharePoint Online and OneDrive for Business in your cloud-based organization."

Get-DlpSiDetectionsReport

"Use the Get-DlpSiDetectionsReport cmdlet to view information about data loss prevention (DLP) sensitive information type detections in the Security & Compliance Center."

<table><tr><td>7</td><td># Compliance</td></tr></table>

In This Chapter

Introduction
Compliance Cases
Compliance Searches
Retention Compliance

Introduction

Compliance is a hot topic for those who have their data stored in Office 365 with concerns with GDPR and business compliance regulations. No longer are we worried about just mailbox data, we now worry about what people store in SharePoint, OneDrive, Teams and more. Because of this change in data concern, Microsoft is now working to add all of these data sources to its list of tools. In addition to this, Microsoft has also pulled some tools from Exchange Online into the Security and Compliance Center in terms of holds, retention and labeling.

Permissions and access into this data is also important to Microsoft and their tenants. Utilizing Role-Based Access Control (RBAC) to help isolate and drive secure access to data, the Role Groups that are available have increased to accommodate the increased focus on centralized data gathering and security in general.

In the realm of Compliance Microsoft uses a layered approach with Compliance Cases, Compliance Searches and Compliance Holds. This chapter will show that this allows for a more complex and also more flexible solution for creating discovery and compliance cases.

In this chapter we will explore all of these layers and decipher how these can be managed with PowerShell. We will also review the connection between PowerShell and the Security and Compliance Center website.

**** Reminder ****

When working with Compliance Cases in PowerShell, remember from Chapter 5:
- eDiscovery Manager only has access to cases that they were assigned rights.
- eDiscovery Administrator has access to all cases.

Compliance Cases

If we review the PowerShell cmdlets that are available for Compliance Cases in the Security and Compliance Center we will see this:

```
Add-ComplianceCaseMember
Get-ComplianceCase
Get-ComplianceCaseMember
Get-ComplianceCaseStatistics
New-ComplianceCase
Remove-ComplianceCase
Remove-ComplianceCaseMember
Set-ComplianceCase
Update-ComplianceCaseMember
```

By default an Office 365 tenant will not have any cases defined. However, our test tenant does and we can use this tenant to illustrate PowerShell functionality. Let's start off with the Get-ComplianceCase to see what we can reveal:

```
Get-ComplianceCase
```

```
PS C:\> Get-ComplianceCase

Name                         Status CreatedDateTime
----                         ------ ---------------
Hold for some mailboxes      Active 8/21/2017 7:09:51 PM
test                         Active 5/15/2017 8:16:50 PM
Case of the missing emails   Active 7/18/2018 3:23:45 AM
Atachment Test               Active 5/15/2017 9:03:43 PM
Case # 4302-1                Active 10/6/2018 8:25:22 PM
```

What about using '| Fl', does it reveal useful information?

```
Get-ComplianceCase "Hold for some mailboxes" | Fl
```

```
RunspaceId            : 4712a0b1-f897-467a-a37a-005726293596
TenantId              : 5d0cc54e-0082-4eb8-a300-ce17a036f3f4
Identity              : ff1efb30-95a1-4041-9f4b-1829dacb9bf1
RecentItemId          : ff1efb30-95a1-4041-9f4b-1829dacb9bf1
Name                  : Hold for some mailboxes
Description           :
SecondaryCaseType     :
ExternalId            :
Sources               :
CaseType              : eDiscovery
Status                : Active
ClosingStatus         : Unknown
CreatedDateTime       : 8/21/2017 7:09:51 PM
LastModifiedDateTime  : 8/21/2017 7:09:51 PM
ClosedDateTime        :
LastAccessTime        : 1/1/0001 12:00:00 AM
LastModifiedBy        : Damian Scoles
ClosedBy              :
IsValid               : True
ObjectState           : New
```

Well. Not really. How are we going to extract the extra information we need from these cases? Since PowerShell and the Security and Compliance Center are tied together, we need to review what is configured in the SCC to find these cases. However, the SCC interface does not specifically display a section called Compliance Cases. Where do we find these cases? With a bit of exploration of the interface we see that the Compliance Cases are actually listed under the Search & Investigation tab and then the eDiscovery option under that section:

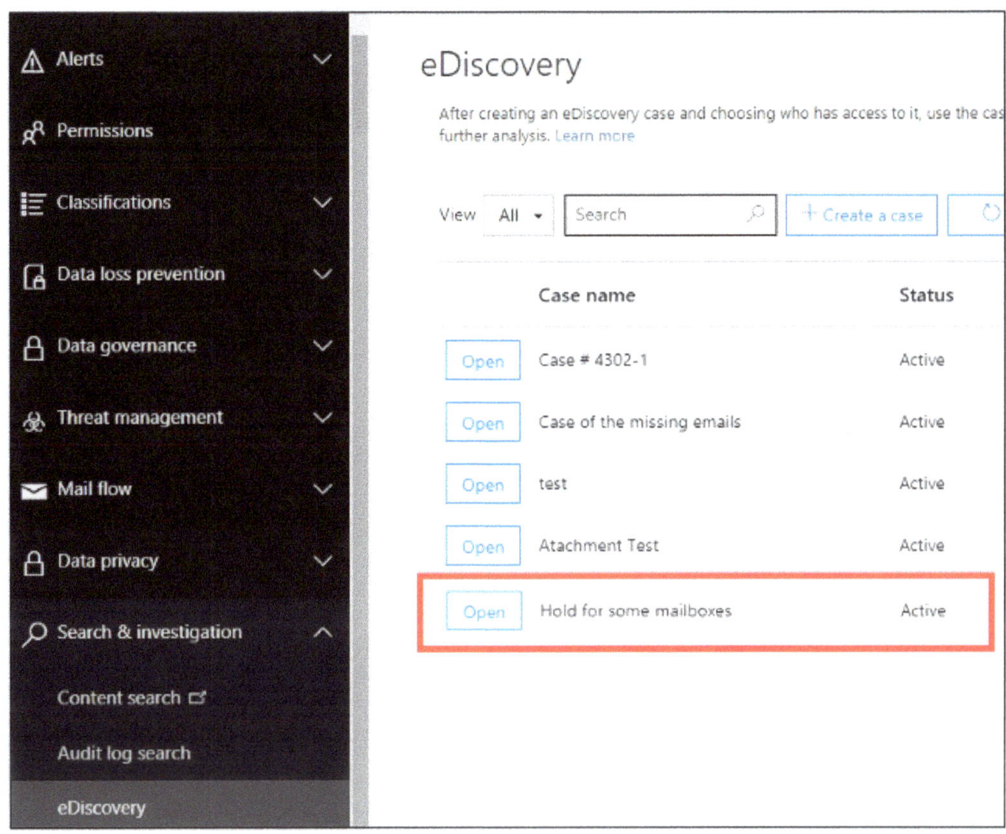

For this example, the case we are looking at is in the red rectangle above. Opening up the case we'll see that the case contains two holds and one search.

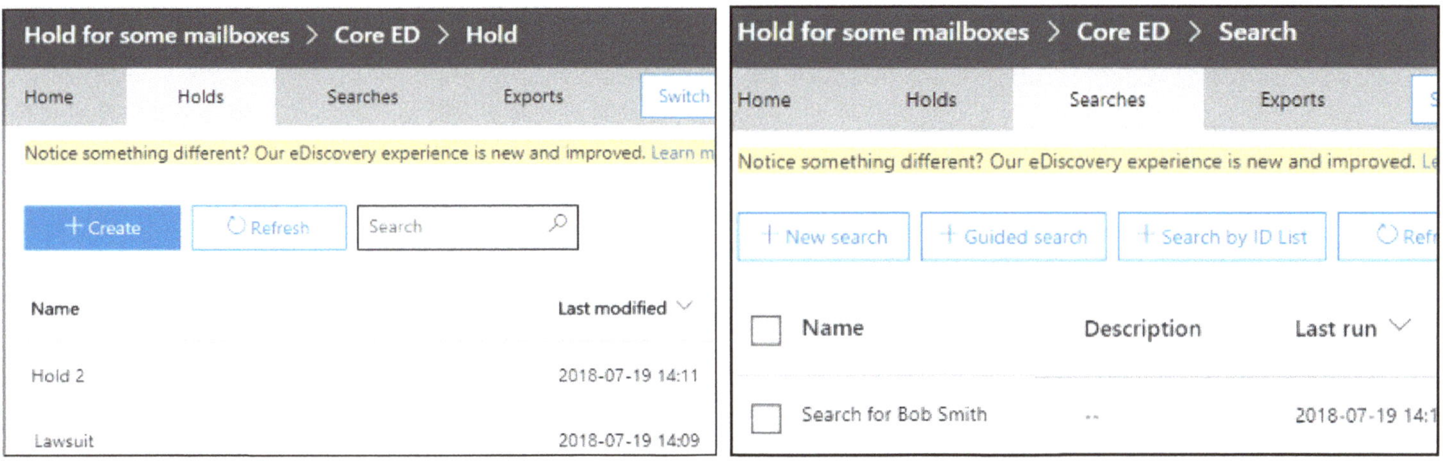

Compliance Case: A collection of Holds and/or Searches that are grouped together for a common purpose.

What if we want to create a new case in the SCC? The most obvious use is for litigation.

    New-ComplianceCase

What options do we have for creating a case?

```
-------------------------- Example 1 --------------------------

New-ComplianceCase -Name "Fabrikam Litigation"

This example creates a new eDiscovery case named Fabrikam Litigation.
```

Reviewing the Parameters that are also available, we can provide a Description as well if needed for compliance or to keep track of the purpose for the case.

    New-ComplianceCase -Name "Merger Dispute" -Description "Legal case with Shareholders (Merger)"

This would simply create a shell for us to use for this particular case. We also have Remove-ComplianceCase and Set-ComplianceCase if we need to work with the cases after they are created. The Remove cmdlet would complete-ly remove the case from the SCC as well as any holds or searches. A better option might be to use 'Set-Compli-anceCase' to close the case leaving it for historical purposes and the possibility of reopening it later on. This leaves the case present for later examination.

    Set-ComplianceCase 'Merger Dispute' -Close
    Set-ComplianceCase 'Merger Dispute' -Reopen

    ** **Note** ** neither of these commands requires you to confirm closing or reopening the case!

Once we have a case, we can manage users who will handle this case. The PowerShell cmdlets are:

    Add-ComplianceCaseMember
    Get-ComplianceCaseMember
    Remove-ComplianceCaseMember
    Update-ComplianceCaseMember

The first member of the case is the creator of the case and can be found with:

    Get-ComplianceCaseMember -Case 'Merger Dispute'

Now, if we have a legal team to handle the case, we can assign these users to the case:

    Add-ComplianceCaseMember -Case 'Merger Dispute' -Member Betsy.Smith@practicalpowershell.com

We can the verify this user has been added:

```
PS C:\> Get-ComplianceCaseMember -Case 'Merger Dispute'

Name            RecipientType
----            -------------
Damian Scoles   MailUser
Betsy Smith     MailUser
```

To further manage case members, we can use the 'Update-ComplianceCaseMember' cmdlet to completely replace all members with a new list or we can use 'Remove-ComplianceCaseMember' to remove a particular member from the case.

Compliance Searches

What is a Compliance Search?

A Compliance Search is also known as an eDiscovery Search in the SCC. This type of search is used to find data that could be used in a legal case, for general content discover and even cleanup work (Phishing emails). Compliance Searches can be limited to certain locations (Exchange or SharePoint) and even down to an individual user as well as to all Public Folders in Exchange Online. Compliance Searches are controlled by RBAC so make sure that whoever is creating the Compliance Searches has the appropriate rights to do so, as well as the people that may need access to the content at the end of the search.

PowerShell

For PowerShell, we can start off with two nouns in our search for available cmdlets - 'Compliance' and 'Search':

```
Get-Command *ComplianceSearch*
```

This provides us with a set of commands we can use to work with Compliance Searches:

```
Get-ComplianceSearch
Get-ComplianceSearchAction
New-ComplianceSearch
New-ComplianceSearchAction
Remove-ComplianceSearch
Remove-ComplianceSearchAction
Set-ComplianceSearch
Set-ComplianceSearchAction
Start-ComplianceSearch
Stop-ComplianceSearch
```

By default we should have no Compliance Searches or Compliance Search Actions.

Requirements

In order to perform a Compliance Search we need to meet the following requirements:

Security - Be a member of the Discovery Search Group or assigned the Mailbox Search Role as the Organization Management group does not have this permission by default.
Start the Search - Once a Compliance Search is created, it has to be started as well.
Apply an Action - determine what is to be done with the search results.

New-ComplianceSearch

Well, let's go ahead and start creating Compliance. Since we are new to the cmdlet, we can review Get-Help to see if we have any relevant examples to work with:

```
Get-Help New-ComplianceSearch -Examples
```

```
------------------------- Example 1 -------------------------

New-ComplianceSearch -Name "Hold Project X" -ExchangeLocation "Finance Department"

This example creates a new compliance search named Hold-Project X that searches all members of the distribution
group named Finance Department. Because the search doesn't use the ContentMatchQuery parameter, all items in the
mailboxes are searched.

------------------------- Example 2 -------------------------

New-ComplianceSearch -Name "Hold-Tailspin Toys" -ExchangeLocation "Research Department" -ContentMatchQuery
"'Patent' AND 'Project Tailspin Toys'"

This example creates a new compliance search named Hold-Tailspin Toys that searches all member of the distribution
group named Research Department. Because the search uses the ContentMatchQuery parameter, only messages that match
the query are searched.

------------------------- Example 3 -------------------------

New-ComplianceSearch -Name "AnnBeebe-InactiveMailbox" -ExchangeLocation .annb@contoso.onmicrosoft.com
-AllowNotFoundExchangeLocationsEnabled $true

This example creates a new compliance search named AnnBeebe-InactiveMailbox that searches an inactive mailbox and
returns all items in the mailbox. To search inactive mailboxes, you need to use the primary SMTP address of the
inactive mailbox, prepended with a period ("."). You also need to include the
AllowNotFoundExchangeLocationsEnabled parameter so the search doesn't try to validate the existence of the
inactive mailbox.
```

If we look at the available parameters for this cmdlet we can see we have a lot of options to choose from:

```
AllowNotFoundExchangeLocationsEnabled
Case
ContentMatchQuery
ExchangeLocation
ExchangeLocationExclusion
Force
HoldNames
IncludeOrgContent
IncludeUserAppContent
PublicFolderLocation
RefinerNames
SharePointLocation
SharePointLocationExclusion
```

With the available parameters, we can create searches in Exchange, SharePoint and more. When reviewing the full help for the cmdlet, you will note that there are quite a few parameters that are relegated to Internal Microsoft use:

```
LogLevel
OneDriveLocation
OneDriveLocationExclusion
PublicFolderLocationExclusion
```

RefinerNames
SearchNames
StatusMailRecipients
WhatIf

Now that we have that out of the way, let's work through some example Compliance Searches.

Example One - Exchange-Only Compliance Search

Your Compliance Administrator just received notice that a few people in Research and Development (RnD) are involved in a patent dispute and specifically she needs to search emails of a group of users. She hands you a list of employees in RnD that are to be searched. Keywords for the search are 'Patent' , 'US 8,965,465 B2' and 'Smart-Phone'. All of the searches need to be associated with a case called 'SmartPhone Patent Dispute'.

First, we need to read the CSV file in and store it in a variable called $CSV. The file is stored on a server called FS01 and the Compliance Administrator provides the entire path to be used:

```
$CSV = Import-CSV '\\fs01\Compliance\SmartphonePatentDispute\RnDUserList.csv'
```

The case name is also stored in a new variable called $Case:

```
$Case = 'SmartPhone Patent Dispute'
```

Then, using the criteria provided from the Compliance Administrator, we can store that in a variable to be used later as well:

```
$Criteria = "'Patent' AND 'US 8,965,465 B2' AND 'SmartPhone'"
```

We can then use a Foreach loop to process each name in the CSV, create a search for one user and associate it with an eDiscovery case:

```
Foreach ($Line in $CSV) {
   $User = $Line.User
   $Name = "$Case - $User"
   New-ComplianceSearch -Name $Name -ExchangeLocation $User -ContentMatchQuery $Criteria -Case $Case
}
```

Before we run this code, we need to make sure we create a Compliance Case:

```
New-ComplianceCase -Name $Case
```

```
PS C:\> $Case = 'SmartPhone Patent Dispute'
PS C:\> New-ComplianceCase -Name $Case


Name                          Status CreatedDateTime
----                          ------ ---------------
SmartPhone Patent Dispute     Active 7/31/2019 3:59:19 AM
```

The output from our script churns out this:

```
Name                                                           RunBy JobEndTime Status
----                                                           ----- ---------- ------
SmartPhone Patent Dispute - Rose.Will@practicalpowershell.com                  NotStarted
SmartPhone Patent Dispute - Joe.Farrow@practicalpowershell.com                 NotStarted
SmartPhone Patent Dispute - Sam.Gunn@practicalpowershell.com                   NotStarted
SmartPhone Patent Dispute - George.Frund@practicalpowershell.com              NotStarted
```

Once completed we can check our results with a couple of cmdlets:

Get-ComplianceCase 'SmartPhone Patent Dispute' | Fl

```
RunspaceId            : 8b290236-dfdc-4128-bea4-85698283cb39
TenantId              : 5d0cc54e-0082-4eb8-a300-ce17a036f3f4
Identity              : 733cabd6-a303-4e89-a7ef-672d079d84d9
RecentItemId          : 733cabd6-a303-4e89-a7ef-672d079d84d9
Name                  : SmartPhone Patent Dispute
Description           :
SecondaryCaseType     :
ExternalId            :
Sources               :
CaseType              : eDiscovery
Status                : Active
ClosingStatus         : Unknown
CreatedDateTime       : 7/31/2019 3:59:19 AM
LastModifiedDateTime  : 7/31/2019 3:59:19 AM
ClosedDateTime        :
LastAccessTime        : 1/1/0001 12:00:00 AM
LastModifiedBy        : Damian Scoles
ClosedBy              :
IsValid               : True
ObjectState           : New
```

Get-ComplianceSearch -Case $Case

```
Name                                                           RunBy JobEndTime Status
----                                                           ----- ---------- ------
SmartPhone Patent Dispute - Rose.Will@practicalpowershell.com                  NotStarted
SmartPhone Patent Dispute - Joe.Farrow@practicalpowershell.com                 NotStarted
SmartPhone Patent Dispute - Sam.Gunn@practicalpowershell.com                   NotStarted
SmartPhone Patent Dispute - George.Frund@practicalpowershell.com              NotStarted
```

Notice that all of the searches show a Status of 'NotStarted'. We can use Start-ComplianceSearch to start them.

Get-ComplianceSearch -Case $Case | Start-ComplianceSearch

```
PS C:\temp\scc\Compliance> Get-ComplianceSearch -Case $Case | Start-ComplianceSearch
PS C:\temp\scc\Compliance> Get-ComplianceSearch -Case $Case

Name                                                          RunBy         JobEndTime             Status
----                                                          -----         ----------             ------
SmartPhone Patent Dispute - Rose.Will@practicalpowershell.com  Damian Scoles 7/31/2019 4:20:22 AM Completed
SmartPhone Patent Dispute - Joe.Farrow@practicalpowershell.com Damian Scoles 7/31/2019 4:20:23 AM Completed
SmartPhone Patent Dispute - Sam.Gunn@practicalpowershell.com   Damian Scoles 7/31/2019 4:20:42 AM Completed
SmartPhone Patent Dispute - George.Frund@practicalpowershell.com Damian Scoles 7/31/2019 4:20:38 AM Completed
```

We can see our searches are all complete now as well. The next step for a Compliance Search is to assign some sort of action for the search to take. This will be assigned via the New-ComplianceSearchAction cmdlet:

New-ComplianceSearchAction

What about this cmdlet New-CompilanceSearchAction? Compliance Search Actions determine what action the search performs (Preview, Export, etc.):

```
Get-Help New-ComplianceSearchAction -Examples
```

```
------------------------- Example 1 -------------------------

New-ComplianceSearchAction -SearchName "Project X" -Preview

This example creates a preview search action for the compliance search named Project X.

------------------------- Example 2 -------------------------

New-ComplianceSearchAction -SearchName "Project X" -Export

This example creates an export search action for the compliance search named Project X.

------------------------- Example 3 -------------------------

New-ComplianceSearchAction -SearchName "Remove Phishing Message" -Purge -PurgeType SoftDelete

This example deletes the search results returned by a compliance search named Remove Phishing Message. Note that
unindexed items aren't deleted when you use the Purge parameter.
```

This cmdlet would be used after a search were created.

Example Two - Phishing Email removal

In this example your organization has received a series of Phishing emails that have been delivered to everyone's mailbox. Each mailbox has 10 copies of the same messages. We need to be able to clean up all of these messages, without any user interaction. What can we do?

First, we need to construct a Compliance Search. This search will not be connected to a Compliance Case as we don't need this feature.

```
$Name = 'Phishing Email Search'
$Criteria = "subject:'Wire Transfer Request'"
New-ComplianceSearch -Name $Name -ExchangeLocation All -ContentMatchQuery $Criteria
```

Once this is created, we can then start the search:

```
Start-ComplianceSearch -Identity $Name
```

Once the search is started, we can now create an action. Since these are Phishing emails, we need to remove them and not allow the end user any access to the emails once we complete this task. The New-ComplianceSearchAction has a couple of options we can utilize - Purge and PurgeType. The Get-Help description for the 'PurgeType' parameter is a bit deceptive as only one option is available and the other option listed is not correct as it is called 'Unknown'. This value should be 'HardDelete' according to online help for the cmdlet.

We need to run the Compliance Search Action with the same name as the Compliance Search. We will also use both purge actions:

```
New-ComplianceSearchAction -SearchName $Name -Purge -PurgeType SoftDelete
```

Make sure this is what you want to do before hitting yes to this question:

```
PS C:\> New-ComplianceSearchAction -SearchName $Name -Purge -PurgeType SoftDelete

Confirm
Are you sure you want to perform this action?
This operation will make message items meeting the criteria of the compliance search "Phishing Email Search" completely
inaccessible to users. There is no automatic method to undo the removal of these message items.

[Y] Yes  [A] Yes to All  [N] No  [L] No to All  [?] Help (default is "Y"):
```

Once this starts, any matching items will be SoftDeleted from the mailbox. Now, what if we needed to modify the search?

Set-ComplianceSearch

Once we have Compliance Searches created, we can manipulate some of their details. In order to do so, we need to utilize the 'Set-ComplianceSearch' cmdlet. Let's review what we can do with this cmdlet:

```
Get-Help Set-ComplianceSearch -Examples
```

```
-------------------------- Example 1 --------------------------

Set-ComplianceSearch -Identity "Project X" -ExchangeLocation All

This example changes the existing compliance search named Project X. The scope of the Exchange search is changed
to all mailboxes.

-------------------------- Example 2 --------------------------

Set-ComplianceSearch -Identity "Contoso Case Search 1" -HoldNames All -ExchangeLocation $null -SharePointLocation
$null

This example changes an existing compliance search that's associated with an eDiscovery case in the Office 365
Security & Compliance Center. The scope of the search is changed from searching selected mailboxes and SharePoint
sites to searching all content locations that have been placed on hold in the eDiscovery case.

-------------------------- Example 3 --------------------------

Set-ComplianceSearch -Identity "China Subsidiary Search" -Language zh-CN

This example changes the language setting for an existing compliance search to Chinese.


You might have to change the language setting if you're using non-English keywords in the search query (which is
specified in the ContentMatchQuery parameter).
```

One possible use would be changing the language of the search when it was realized that the mailboxes within scope were not native English speakers.

```
Set-ComplianceSearch -Identity $Name -Language fr-ch
```

The above would then change the search language to French (Switzerland) from US (English).

Set-ComplianceSearchAction

In addition to changing the Compliance Search, we can also manipulate the Compliance Search Action. We can do that with the 'Set-ComplianceSearchAction' cmdlet. Let's check out the 'Set-ComplianceSearchAction' cmdlet and see what we can do with it:

Get-Help Set-ComplianceSearchAction -Examples

```
-------------------------- Example 1 --------------------------

Set-ComplianceSearchAction -Identity "Project X_Export" -ChangeExportKey

This example changes the export key on the export compliance search action named Project X_Export.
```

Interesting, not much there. Let's check out the full help for the cmdlet:

```
NAME
    Set-ComplianceSearchAction

SYNOPSIS
    This cmdlet is available only in on-premises Exchange.

    Use the Set-ComplianceSearchAction cmdlet to change the export key on export compliance search actions in
    on-premises Exchange.

    For information about the parameter sets in the Syntax section below, see Exchange cmdlet syntax
    (https://technet.microsoft.com/library/bb123552.aspx).
```

Okay. So we won't be able to use this cmdlet in the Security and Compliance Center… on to the next cmdlet!

Get-CaseHold Cmdlets

These cmdlets will allow us to work with Case Holds in the SCC. Let's see what PowerShell has for us:

Get-Command *hold*

We get these commands:

Get-CaseHoldPolicy
Get-CaseHoldRule
Get-HoldCompliancePolicy
Get-HoldComplianceRule

Running Get-CaseHoldPolicy gives us an error:

```
C:\> Get-CaseHoldPolicy
 retrieve a case hold policy, please specify a policy or a case id.
    + CategoryInfo          : InvalidOperation: (:) [Get-CaseHoldPolicy], ErrorMustSpecifyCaseOrPolicyException
    + FullyQualifiedErrorId : [Server=BY2NAM05WS010,RequestId=f0a5e5a0-cb11-4f39-891f-f4c870b10f8c,TimeStamp=11/23
Exception] 1BF6472E,Microsoft.Office.CompliancePolicy.Tasks.GetCaseHoldPolicy
    + PSComputerName        : nam05b.ps.compliance.protection.outlook.com
```

It looks like we need to actually specify a Case Hold Policy in order to query it.

Okay. What about 'Get-CaseHoldRule' ?

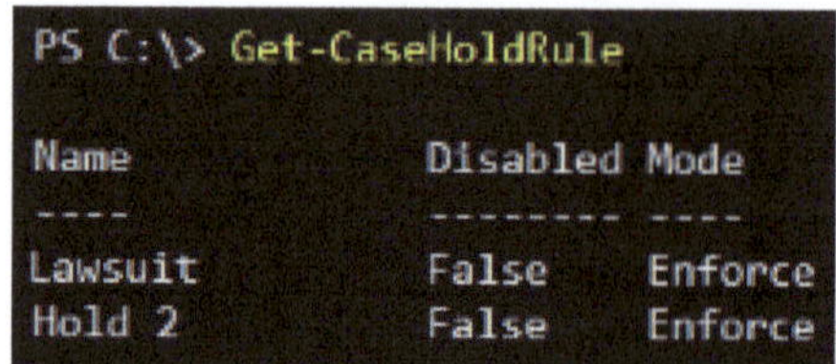

That matches what we need, so let's explore the Case Hold Rules:

```
RunspaceId               : 4712a0b1-f897-467a-a37a-005726293596
ContentDateFrom          :
ContentDateTo            :
ContentMatchQuery        : Bob Smith
HoldDurationDisplayHint  : Days
HoldContent              : 0
ReadOnly                 : False
ExternalIdentity         :
ImmutableId              : 00000000-0000-0000-0000-000000000000
Priority                 : 0
Workload                 : Exchange, SharePoint
Policy                   : f02f65bd-1cd0-401b-90cc-c86f866b8c5e
Comment                  :
Disabled                 : False
Mode                     : Enforce
ObjectVersion            : aebc1ff5-5f5b-4d7c-d1fc-08d5edab7c28
CreatedBy                : Damian Scoles
LastModifiedBy           : Damian Scoles
Guid                     : 807b2961-e907-4c21-9a59-37786f5e5e77
Identity                 : FFO.extest.microsoft.com/Microsoft Exchange Hosted Organizations/______.onmicrosoft.com/Configuration/Hold 2
Id                       : FFO.extest.microsoft.com/Microsoft Exchange Hosted Organizations/______.onmicrosoft.com/Configuration/Hold 2
IsValid                  : True
ExchangeVersion          : 0.20 (15.0.0.0)
Name                     : Hold 2
DistinguishedName        : CN=Hold 2,CN=Configuration,CN=______.onmicrosoft.com,OU=Microsoft Exchange Hosted Organizations,DC=FFO,DC=extest,DC=microso
ObjectCategory           :
ObjectClass              : {msExchUnifiedRule}
WhenChanged              : 7/19/2018 2:11:51 PM
WhenCreated              : 7/19/2018 2:11:51 PM
WhenChangedUTC           : 7/19/2018 7:11:51 PM
WhenCreatedUTC           : 7/19/2018 7:11:51 PM
ExchangeObjectId         : 807b2961-e907-4c21-9a59-37786f5e5e77
OrganizationId           : FFO.extest.microsoft.com/Microsoft Exchange Hosted Organizations/______.onmicrosoft.com - FFO.extest.microsoft.com/Microsof
                           Organizations/scoles.onmicrosoft.com/Configuration
OriginatingServer        :
ObjectState              : New
```

If we want, we can export these for later reference/documentation when building new Case Hold Rules:

    Get-CaseHoldRule | Export-CSV -Notype c:\scc\compliance\caseholdrules.csv

Now that we have the Case Hold Rules documented, we can document the search. Again, we can search for any cmdlet with 'search' in it to see what is available in the 'Get-' based cmdlets:

    Get-Command *search*

We find that there are two available to be used:

    Get-ComplianceSearch
    Get-ComplianceSearchAction

Since this is a search and not and action, we will run the first cmdlet:

```
PS C:\> Get-ComplianceSearch
PS C:\>
```

Well, that was certainly unexpected as we have a previously created search. How do we find the search then? If we look back at the previous screenshots, we have the name of the search.

Let's use that to see what we can find:

```
PS C:\> Get-ComplianceSearch "Search for Bob Smith"

Name                      RunBy          JobEndTime            Status
----                      -----          ----------            ------
Search for Bob Smith Damian Scoles 7/19/2018 7:14:01 PM Completed
```

Much better. However, this can make a more automated approach. Maybe there is a work around? Let's review the available parameters for the Get-ComplianceSearch cmdlet:

Get-ComplianceSearch[-Identity<ComplianceSearchIdParameter>][-Case<String>][-DomainController <Fqdn>] [-ResultSize <Unlimited>] [<CommonParameters>]

There is a parameter 'Case' that might be useful. Let's verify what we can do with this parameter:

```
PARAMETERS
     -Case <String>
          This parameter is reserved for internal Microsoft use.
```

That's convenient. So we have an option that could make this discovery process work, but one cmdlet gives us no results and another has useful parameters that is for Microsoft use. Let's try this parameter, just remember that Your Mileage May Vary (YMMV) on whether it works 100% of the time:

```
PS C:\> Get-ComplianceSearch -Case "Hold for some mailboxes"

Name                      RunBy          JobEndTime            Status
----                      -----          ----------            ------
Search for Bob Smith Damian Scoles 7/19/2018 7:14:01 PM Completed
```

It was successful. So this would make things a bit easier for discovery. We can get all of the searches for a particular Compliance Case and then export those details for importing in our test tenant.

Get-ComplianceSearch -Case "Hold for some mailboxes" | Export-CSV -NoTypeInformation "c:\scc\compliance\searches.csv"

```
RunspaceId                : 4712a0b1-f897-467a-a37a-005726293596
Language                  :
StatusMailRecipients      : {}
LogLevel                  : Suppressed
IncludeUnindexedItems     : True
ContentMatchQuery         : Bob Smith
SearchType                : EstimateSearch
HoldNames                 : {}
SearchNames               : {}
RefinerNames              : {}
Region                    :
Refiners                  :
Items                     : 0
Size                      : 0
UnindexedItems            : 0
UnindexedSize             : 0
SuccessResults            : {}
SearchStatistics          :
Errors                    :
ErrorTags                 : {}
NumFailedSources          : 0
JobId                     : fa776806-3d7a-4f55-6298-08d5edaba678
Name                      : Search for Bob Smith
CreatedTime               : 7/19/2018 7:13:03 PM
```

Opening the output in Notepad would look like this:

```
searches.csv - Notepad
File  Edit  Format  View  Help
"PSComputerName","RunspaceId","PSShowComputerName","Language","StatusMailRecipients","LogLevel","IncludeUninde
"nam05b.ps.compliance.protection.outlook.com","4712a0b1-f897-467a-a37a-005726293596","False","","","Suppressed
```

Now we have our holds and searches documented for our Compliance Case. The only other information that was not exported was the Exports tab, but that is not as important as those are exported results. We should not need those for the QA environment.

Putting it all together

Now that we have pulled the information in piece meal, we need a way to pull all of the cases, searches and holds and then store them in a manner that would make it easier to restore in the QA tenant. How are we going to do that?

The most difficult piece to pull together is how do we link the Case Holds to a Compliance Case so we can bundle like this:

```
Compliance Case
|-- Case Hold Rule
|-- Compliance Search
```

The problem is that when we review a Case Hold Rule we do not see a Case in the details of the hold. However, if we look closer at the resulting properties of the Case Hold Rule (Get-CaseHoldRule), we see a parameter called 'Policy' as seen below:

```
Workload                      : Exchange, SharePoint
Policy                        : 0c70eac9-adfb-4574-b66f-c41ff4df80a8
Comment                       :
```

There was another cmdlet we saw before called 'Get-CaseHoldPolicy'. Possibly this would help us track down the Case link? Let's see:

Get-CaseHoldPolicy 0c70eac9-adfb-4574-b66f-c41ff4df80a8 | Fl

```
PS C:\> Get-CaseHoldPolicy 0c70eac9-adfb-4574-b66f-c41ff4df80a8 | fl


RunspaceId          : 4712a0b1-f897-467a-a37a-005726293596
Type                : CaseHold
SharePointLocation  : {}
ExchangeLocation    : {Damian-PP}
PublicFolderLocation : {}
CaseId              : ff1efb30-95a1-4041-9f4b-1829dacb9bf1
Size                : 573828
Items               : 8
SearchLastRunTime   : 7/19/2018 7:09:24 PM
SearchStatus        : Completed
SearchError         :
Workload            : Exchange, SharePoint
Priority            : 0
```

Now we have the Case Hold Rule, linked to the Case Hold Policy which is linked to the Compliance Case. If we check that Case ID against our cases, we see it matches what we originally started with:

```
PS C:\> Get-ComplianceCase ff1efb30-95a1-4041-9f4b-1829dacb9bf1

Name                     Status CreatedDateTime
----                     ------ ---------------
Hold for some mailboxes  Active 8/21/2017 7:09:51 PM
```

The only issue becomes how we can match a Case Hold Rule to the Case if we do not have a direct link (via the Policy ID)? Well, we use PowerShell as show below with this script for Compliance Cases, Case Hold Rules and Compliance Searches:

```powershell
# Clear The Screen
CLS

$Path = (Get-Item -Path ".\" -Verbose).FullName
$ComplianceCasesNames = (Get-ComplianceCase).Name
$CaseHoldRules = Get-CaseHoldRule

Foreach ($ComplianceCasesName in $ComplianceCasesNames) {
   Write-Host "Examining Compliance Case $ComplianceCasesName" -ForegroundColor Cyan
   Write-Host "-----------------------------------------------" -ForegroundColor Cyan

   # Variables for Loop
   $Found1 = $False
   $Found2 = $True

   # Document Compliance Case
   $CurrentCaseID = (Get-ComplianceCase $ComplianceCasesName ).Identity
   $Destination = "$Path"+"\"+"$CurrentCaseID"+"-ComplianceCase.csv"
   $ComplianceCase = Get-ComplianceCase $ComplianceCasesName | Export-CSV -Notype $Destination

   # Document any Case Hold Rules
   Foreach ($CaseHoldRule in $CaseHoldRules) {
      $Policy = $CaseHoldRule.Policy
      $PolicyID = Get-CaseHoldPolicy $Policy
      $CaseID = $PolicyID.CaseID
      $ValueToCheck = (Get-ComplianceCase $CaseID).Identity
      $CaseHoldRuleName = $CaseHoldRule.Name
      # Write-host "CaseID = $CaseID / ValueToCheck = $ValueToCheck" -ForegroundColor Red
      If ($ValueToCheck -eq $CurrentCaseID) {
         $Destination2 = "$Path"+"\$CurrentCaseID-CaseHoldRule-"+"$CaseHoldRuleName"+".csv"
         $CaseHoldRule = Get-CaseHoldRule $CaseHoldRuleName | Export-CSV -Notype $Destination2
         $Found1 = $True
      }
   }
```

```
If ($Found1) {
    Write-host "Found Case Hold Rules for $ComplianceCasesName." -ForegroundColor Green
  } Else {
        Write-host "No Case Hold Rules found for Compliance Case - $ComplianceCasesName."
-ForegroundColor Yellow
  }

  # Document searches
  $Destination3 = "$Path"+"\"+"$CurrentCaseID"+"-Searches-"+"$CaseHoldRuleName"+".csv"
  $Search = Get-ComplianceSearch -Case $ComplianceCasesName

  If ($Search -eq $Null) {
    $Found2 = $False
  }

  If ($Found2) {
      Write-Host "Compliance Searches were found for Compliance Case - $ComplianceCasesName."
-ForegroundColor Green
      $Search | Export-CSV -NoTypeInformation $Destination3
  } Else {
        Write-Host "No Compliance Searches found for Compliance Case - $ComplianceCasesName."
-ForegroundColor Yellow
  }
  Write-Host ' '
}
```

The output from the script results in these files:

Name	Date modified	Type	Size
83b12434-b59e-42d3-836e-e7ee5213ef9f-ComplianceCase.csv	11/23/2018 8:30 PM	CSV File	1 KB
83b12434-b59e-42d3-836e-e7ee5213ef9f-Searches-Hold 2.csv	11/23/2018 8:30 PM	CSV File	3 KB
8725677a-e53e-4c5f-b5ee-6226055d068d-ComplianceCase.csv	11/23/2018 8:30 PM	CSV File	1 KB
8725677a-e53e-4c5f-b5ee-6226055d068d-Searches-Hold 2.csv	11/23/2018 8:30 PM	CSV File	2 KB
cbb08686-2ee5-4153-9327-6aba3f9d27f5-ComplianceCase.csv	11/23/2018 8:30 PM	CSV File	1 KB
df3de643-515d-43a0-8d20-2bc55f28af0a-ComplianceCase.csv	11/23/2018 8:29 PM	CSV File	1 KB
f3555db1-4579-4f62-ab91-b5156fd20181-ComplianceCase.csv	11/23/2018 8:30 PM	CSV File	1 KB
ff1efb30-95a1-4041-9f4b-1829dacb9bf1-CaseHoldRule-Hold 2.csv	11/23/2018 8:29 PM	CSV File	2 KB
ff1efb30-95a1-4041-9f4b-1829dacb9bf1-CaseHoldRule-Teacher Lawsuit.csv	11/23/2018 8:29 PM	CSV File	2 KB
ff1efb30-95a1-4041-9f4b-1829dacb9bf1-ComplianceCase.csv	11/23/2018 8:29 PM	CSV File	1 KB
ff1efb30-95a1-4041-9f4b-1829dacb9bf1-Searches-Hold 2.csv	11/23/2018 8:29 PM	CSV File	2 KB

When running the script, you should see something like this:

```
Windows PowerShell

Examining Compliance Case Hold for some mailboxes
------------------------------------------------
Found Case Hold Rules for Hold for some mailboxes.
Compliance Searches were found for Compliance Case - Hold for some mailboxes.

Examining Compliance Case test
------------------------------------------------
No Case Hold Rules found for Compliance Case - test.
No Compliance Searches found for Compliance Case - test.

Examining Compliance Case Case of the missing emails
------------------------------------------------
No Case Hold Rules found for Compliance Case - Case of the missing emails.
Compliance Searches were found for Compliance Case - Case of the missing emails.

Examining Compliance Case Atachment Test
------------------------------------------------
No Case Hold Rules found for Compliance Case - Atachment Test.
No Compliance Searches found for Compliance Case - Atachment Test.

Examining Compliance Case Case # 4302-1
------------------------------------------------
No Case Hold Rules found for Compliance Case - Case # 4302-1.
No Compliance Searches found for Compliance Case - Case # 4302-1.

Examining Compliance Case MMCUG Test Case 1
------------------------------------------------
No Case Hold Rules found for Compliance Case - MMCUG Test Case 1.
Compliance Searches were found for Compliance Case - MMCUG Test Case 1.
```

Retention Compliance

Previously there was a set of cmdlets dedicated to Hold Compliance Rules and Policies. However, these were replaced with Retention Compliance Policies and Rules. With this change were accommodations for Teams holds as well.

```
The Get-HoldComplianceRule cmdlet has been replaced by the Get-RetentionComplianceRule cmdlet. If you have any
scripts that use the Get-HoldComplianceRule cmdlet, update them to use the Get-RetentionComplianceRule cmdlet.
```

PowerShell

Again, we can see what cmdlets are available for Compliance Hold PowerShell cmdlets:

Get-Command *RetentionCompliance*

This provides us with eight PowerShell cmdletS:

    Get-RetentionCompliancePolicy
    Get-RetentionComplianceRule
    Get-TeamsRetentionCompliancePolicy
    Get-TeamsRetentionComplianceRule
    New-RetentionCompliancePolicy
    New-RetentionComplianceRule

```
New-TeamsRetentionCompliancePolicy
New-TeamsRetentionComplianceRule
Remove-RetentionCompliancePolicy
Remove-RetentionComplianceRule
Remove-TeamsRetentionCompliancePolicy
Remove-TeamsRetentionComplianceRule
Set-RetentionCompliancePolicy
Set-RetentionComplianceRule
Set-TeamsRetentionCompliancePolicy
Set-TeamsRetentionComplianceRule
```

We see that there is a series of cmdlets for Teams and non-Teams Compliance Rules and Policies.

> **Retention Compliance Policy** - refers to the location and content to be retained
> **Retention Compliance Rule** - refers to the created policy and determines the retention time

As we have Teams and non-Teams related cmdlets, we will start with the more generic cmdlets (without the 'Teams' noun in the cmdlet) to explore those first. Then we will explore the Teams related cmdlets at the end of this section.

Get-RetentionCompliancePolicy and Get-RetentionComplianceRule

By default, neither of these Get cmdlets should reveal anything in a new tenant as these are not pre-created items in Office 365. That being said, once we have Policies and Rules created we can list them with these two cmdlets:

```
PS C:\> Get-RetentionCompliancePolicy

Name                                      Workload                                                          Enabled Mode
----                                      --------                                                          ------- ----
Confidential Information                  Exchange, SharePoint, OneDriveForBusiness, Skype, ModernGroup     True    En...
Retain All but Voicemails                 Exchange, SharePoint, OneDriveForBusiness, Skype, ModernGroup     True    En...
First Three Test Label Policy             Exchange, SharePoint, OneDriveForBusiness, Skype, ModernGroup     True    En...
Seven Year Retention - Excluding Voicemails Exchange, SharePoint, OneDriveForBusiness, Skype, ModernGroup   True    En...
Exchange Retention Policies               Exchange, SharePoint, OneDriveForBusiness, Skype, ModernGroup     True    En...
```

```
PS C:\> Get-RetentionComplianceRule

Name                                      Policy                                      Mode     Comment
----                                      ------                                      ----     -------
ctptr-969b35e7-3d13-4063-94a8-68f4fc816503 2e2717a3-ae4f-4c77-9ed7-be564382f2c7       Enforce
ctptr-a4273d8a-93cc-4af4-92cf-2c5621a23762 2e2717a3-ae4f-4c77-9ed7-be564382f2c7       Enforce
Seven Year Retention - Excluding Voicemails dd3ef3b2-e119-43ee-9f6f-c220b80cfd6c      Enforce
lptr-153ebf59-014b-44e2-a4a5-66f97d119d15 0e76773c-c0db-4739-94ae-d0cc31586356        Enforce
lptr-e4eea698-a41d-4e51-a4be-5eb3b9fd3bbc 32e1c6a4-02e0-443a-bc82-4ef3d98da64f        Enforce
ctptr-494b890f-ca01-46a7-924d-990f742acde0 7003953b-cc52-4aab-8dbb-d2ddc76e6f6f       Enforce
lptr-66ac4c8d-31ed-4fc2-86f4-c98326790420 a8e6e7ee-a617-458c-9fb0-3995b6ba2ade        Enforce
ctptr-f96a24a9-f09b-40b1-9d42-c5875fc8feee 7003953b-cc52-4aab-8dbb-d2ddc76e6f6f       Enforce
ctptr-b1675d34-a9fc-4158-9c0f-6cc610c77ce2 2e2717a3-ae4f-4c77-9ed7-be564382f2c7       Enforce
Retain All but Voicemails                 3c9b5672-9b6d-49d0-805f-aee53e48d11c        Enforce
ctptr-8ed2da6c-552e-4820-8d6e-8e09a7edd2fc 7003953b-cc52-4aab-8dbb-d2ddc76e6f6f       Enforce
ctaptr-0f40a032-1da3-41cc-b3cd-99a2f4a8ca66 c61dd118-53ec-476d-9716-13cd071934e7      Enforce
```

Now, let's go create some Retention Compliance Policies and Rules to get a better understanding of what is possible.

New-RetentionCompliancePolicy and New-RetentionComplianceRule

In order to create a function rule we need to run both of these cmdlets in series. The first is a policy, which will define what we are retaining with options or exceptions, while the other applies that policy and enforces a time for the policy to be in place. We will run through some scenarios to help guide us in a real way to use these PowerShell cmdlets.

Scenario One

A company is moving to Office 365. Their plan is to use Exchange and OneDrive initially. All other services will be turned off (i.e. users will not have licenses for any other products on the cloud). As part of their on-premises retention policies, they are required to retain information for three years. At that point the Exchange data will be removed, but files will no longer be protected from deletion.

In order to accomplish these tasks we will have to create two sets of policies and rules for compliance. This will allow us to accommodate both options when retention ends. Let's review an example of each PowerShell cmdlet to see what we options we need to configure for these policies and rules.

New-RetentionCompliancePolicy

```
------------------------------ Example 1 ------------------------------

New-RetentionCompliancePolicy -Name "Regulation 123 Compliance" -ExchangeLocation "Kitty Petersen", "Scott
Nakamura" -SharePointLocation "http://contoso.sharepoint.com/sites/teams/finance"

This example creates a retention policy named "Regulation 123 Compliance" for the mailboxes of Kitty Petersen and
Scott Nakamura, and the finance SharePoint Online site.
```

New-RetentionComplianceRule

```
------------------------------ Example 1 ------------------------------

New-RetentionComplianceRule -Name SeptOneYear -Policy "Internal Company Policy" -RetentionDuration Unlimited

This example creates a new retention rule named SeptOneYear and adds it to the existing retention policy named
"Internal Company Policy". Content will be held indefinitely.
```

In the above examples we see we can specify Exchange locations, but the example shows individual mailboxes not all mailboxes. So how do we specify all mailboxes? We can see the syntax needed in the Get-Help for the cmdlet here:

```
-ExchangeLocation <MultiValuedProperty>
    The ExchangeLocation parameter specifies the mailboxes to include. Valid values are:

    * A mailbox
    * A distribution group or mail-enabled security group (all mailboxes that are currently members of the group).
    * The value All for all mailboxes. You can only use this value by itself.
    To specify a mailbox or distribution group, you can use any value that uniquely identifies it. For example:
```

Looks like we can specify '-ExchangeLocation All' to apply this policy to all mailboxes in Exchange Online.

If we wish this policy to be locked where no one can undo the settings, we need to use the RestrictiveRetention parameter (-RestrictiveRetention $true) as this locks out the administrator as well. Be sure this is what is required as the policy cannot be reduced, disabled or turned off.

> New-RetentionCompliancePolicy -Name '3 Year Exchange' -Comment 'Exchange three year retention policy.' -ExchangeLocation All

The same Policy could be expanded to include Modern Groups with this parameter '-ModernGroupLocation All'. While Modern Groups are not technically mailboxes, their data is stored within Exchange. It would be up to the Compliance Officer at a company to decide what needs to be covered and if Modern Groups fits the definition of what is required.

With a Retention Compliance Policy in place, we can now create a rule that will set the three year clock for items in Exchange Online. The example provided is a good starter, but not nearly enough for what we need. Yes, we can give the rule a name; yes we can provide the affected Policy ; what about duration and action? How do we specify those? We can either look at Get-Help or Microsoft Docs, whichever you're more comfortable with.

From the Help for the cmdlet, we see there are two options we need to work with - RetentionComplianceAction and RetentionDuration. With these we can specify three years and deletion of the mailbox content. Here is our new one-liner to create our Retention Compliance Rule:

> New-RetentionComplianceRule -Name 'Three Year Keep and Delete - Exchange' -Policy 'Three Year Exchange' -RetentionDuration 1095 -RetentionComplianceAction KeepAndDelete

Note that the 'RetentionDuration' parameter is listed in the number of days, which in this case is 3*365 = 1095 days. The RetentionComplianceAction is set to Keep and Delete as the items will be held and then at 1095 they will be removed from the mailbox.

Scenario Two

For this scenario, we need to place everyone in the HR and Legal departments in a seven year hold. For the data, we need to cover Exchange, OneDrive, ModernGroups and more. After the seven year period has expired the items are no longer helped for retention, but they do not need to be deleted. After seven years, no retention policy needs to apply as it is out of the legally required range for these users.

How do we get a full list of all OneDrive sites. Microsoft provides us with a site from which we can pull a list of all OneDrive URLs from this site:

> https://docs.microsoft.com/en-us/onedrive/list-onedrive-urls

Assuming we ran the script, we will use these OneDrive locations for our example:

> https://bigcompany-my.sharepoint.com/personal/nicholas_bigcompany_net
> https://bigcompany-my.sharepoint.com/personal/john_bigcompany_net
> https://bigcompany-my.sharepoint.com/personal/damian_bigcompany_net
> https://bigcompany-my.sharepoint.com/personal/sarah_bigcompany_net
> https://bigcompany-my.sharepoint.com/personal/pyra_bigcompany_net
> https://bigcompany-my.sharepoint.com/personal/max_bigcompany_net
> https://bigcompany-my.sharepoint.com/personal/sandra_bigcompany_net

Next, we will need a list of Groups that need to be covered by this policy as well. For our example, we have two Modern Groups - 'HR' and 'Legal' - that need to be covered by this policy.

```
New-RetentionCompliancePolicy -Name '7 Year Office 365 - HR and Legal' -Comment 'Legally required hold for HR and Legal departmental users.' -ModernGroupLocation HR,Legal -ExchangeLocation HR,Legal -OneDriveLocation 'https://bigcompany-my.sharepoint.com/personal/nicholas_bigcompany_net;https://bigcompany-my.sharepoint.com/personal/john_bigcompany_net;https://bigcompany-my.sharepoint.com/personal/damian_bigcompany_net;https://bigcompany-my.sharepoint.com/personal/sarah_bigcompany_net;https://bigcompany-my.sharepoint.com/personal/pyra_bigcompany_net;https://bigcompany-my.sharepoint.com/personal/max_bigcompany_net;https://bigcompany-my.sharepoint.com/personal/sandra_bigcompany_net'
```

** **Note** ** It might be worth using a variable for the OneDrive Location.

We can then use this Retention Compliance Policy and create a Retention Compliance Rule:

```
New-RetentionComplianceRule -Name 'Seven Year Keep - Office 365 - HR/Legal' -Policy 'Seven Year Office 365 - HR and Legal'' -RetentionDuration 2555 -RetentionComplianceAction Keep
```

If we look at the Advanced Options of the New-RetentionComplianceRule PowerShell cmdlet we see these options:

ApplyComplianceTag - this parameter will specify a tag that is applied to all affected content
PublishComplianceTag - specifies a label that is now visible to user apps
ContentContainsSensitiveInformation - specifies a sensitive information type as a condition for matching
ContentMatchQuery - specifies a Keyword Query Language (KQL) query for matching content **
ExcludedItemClasses - excludes certain types of messages - like *'IPM.Note.Microsoft.Voicemail.UM'*
RetentionDurationDisplayHint - changes the duration display to unit of your choice in the Security and Compliance Center console - Days, Months, or Years

** **Note** ** More information on KQL query syntax can be found here - https://go.microsoft.com/fwlink/?LinkId=269603

Now that we've created some Retention Compliance Policies and Rules, let's explore how we can manage these with Get, Remove and Set cmdlets.

Remove-RetentionCompliancePolicy and Remove-RetentionComplianceRule

In theory, since we created our Rules and Policies in a certain order, we should remove them in the same order. However, we do not have to do that. We can remove them in either order. When you remove a Policy first, we noticed that the Policy does not actually get removed at first. It hangs around:

```
PS C:\> Remove-RetentionCompliancePolicy 'C-Level Indefinite Teams Hold'

Confirm
Are you sure you want to perform this action?
Removing Compliance Policy 'C-Level Indefinite Teams Hold'.
[Y] Yes  [A] Yes to All  [N] No  [L] No to All  [?] Help (default is "Y"): y
PS C:\Scripts> Get-RetentionCompliancePolicy


Name                             Workload                                                        Enabled Mode
----                             --------                                                        ------- ----
Confidential Information         Exchange, SharePoint, OneDriveForBusiness, Skype, ModernGroup True    En
C-Level Indefinite Teams Hold    Exchange, SharePoint, OneDriveForBusiness, Skype, ModernGroup True    Pe...
Retain All but Voicemails        Exchange, SharePoint, OneDriveForBusiness, Skype, ModernGroup True    En...
```

Why did the Policy not delete? It's not because the Rule was still in place, but it is in a 'PendingDeletion' Mode:

Eventually both the Rule and Policy will be removed from the tenant after background responses are run.

Set-RetentionCompliancePolicy

After creating a Policy, we can modify quite a few settings. We can remove OneDrive locations, SharePoint locations, Exchange Locations, SkypeLocations, TeamsLocations and ModernGroupLocation as well as add additional locations for all those Office 365 workloads as well.

For a real world example, if we have a retention policy for a list of mailboxes, we can add more users as they are required by a Legal department. Or we could remove mailboxes as users leave a company or are no longer required, say for legal reasons.

Set-RetentionComplianceRule

Now, for an existing Retention Compliance Rule, we can modify the duration, excluded item classes, add sensitive information types, add tags and more. A practical example of a good usage for Set-RetentionComplianceRule is to add an ExcludedItemClass. For example, maybe we do not need to retain Voicemails, this can be changed post creation of the rule by simply running a line like this:

```
Set-RetentionComplianceRule -Name ExcludedItemClasses IPM.Note.Microsoft.Voicemail
```

** **Note** ** Items that are excluded will not be retained or protected once they are excluded.

Now they will be excluded as they were not legally required (for this scenario). MSDN has classes definitions here:

https://docs.microsoft.com/en-us/previous-versions/office/developer/office-2007/bb176446(v=office.12)

Teams Retention Compliance Policies and Rules

As was explained before, we have regular Retention Compliance Policies and Rules and Teams-centric Retention Compliance Policies and Rules. For this section we'll explore the Teams-centric ones to see what the difference is. As with the above regular cmdlets, the Teams-centric ones have the same verbs (Get, New, Remove and Set) as well as the same nouns with Retention Compliance Policies and Rules.

```
Get-TeamsRetentionCompliancePolicy
Get-TeamsRetentionComplianceRule
New-TeamsRetentionCompliancePolicy
New-TeamsRetentionComplianceRule
```

```
Remove-TeamsRetentionCompliancePolicy
Remove-TeamsRetentionComplianceRule
Set-TeamsRetentionCompliancePolicy
Set-TeamsRetentionComplianceRule
```

Just like the regular Policies and Rules, there are no Teams-centric Policies or Rules pre-created in your new Office 365 tenant. If we want to use these, we'll need to create our own. Let's explore the New-* cmdlets and their examples to see what we can do with these cmdlets. Get-Help for either cmdlet reveals no cmdlet examples:

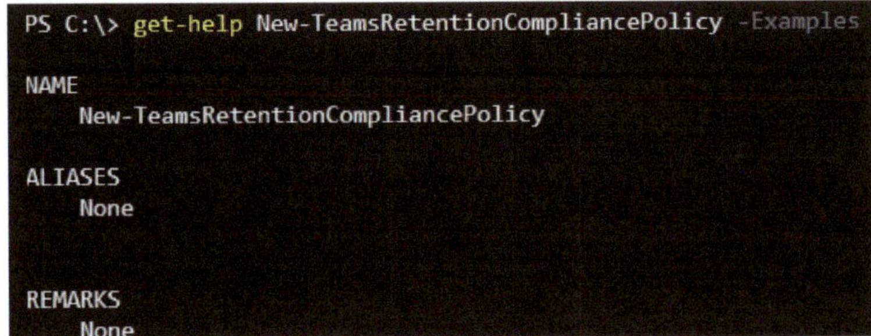

All is not lost though as Microsoft Docs contains examples for both:

New-TeamsRetentionCompliancePolicy -Name "Teams - Regulation 123 Compliance" -TeamsChannelLocation "Engineering Team", "UX Design Team" -TeamsChatLocation "Kitty Petersen", "Scott Nakamura"

and

New-TeamsRetentionComplianceRule -Name "Teams - SeptOneYear" -Policy "Teams - Internal Company Policy" -RetentionComplianceAction Keep -RetentionDuration Unlimited

We can see from the above examples that in a sense only the New-TeamsRetentionCompliancePolicy cmdlet is materially different because we have Teams specify parameters. The Retention Compliance Rule cmdlet performs the same function as it assigns a particular action and time to a particular policy that was already created. Let's work through some scenarios to see how we can apply a Retention Compliance Hold to our Teams data.

New-TeamsRetentionCompliancePolicy

First, what do we have for available options for this cmdlet? We can find these in the Get-Help or by hitting Ctrl-Space after typing in the cmdlet name. Here are ones we can use:

Name, Comment, TeamsChannelLocation, TeamsChannelLocationException, TeamsChatLocation and TeamsChatLocationException

Be aware that some parameters specified in the Get-Help are not available and are not listed as Internal Use or Microsoft Only. Let's start with two criteria that we can use to select content to be retained.

TeamsChannelLocation - We can chose individual Teams in a list or use 'All'
TeamsChatLocation - We can chose individual users in a list or select all users with 'All'

Scenario One

For this case, we have a company that needs to retain all conversations by C-Level executives in Teams for an indefinite period of time. We need to create a Policy and Rule to handle this. Remember that a Compliance Rule will need to reference an existing Compliance Policy. We have a list of users who need to be covered:

Sandy Shu, Grant Gunther and Ron West

First we will create the Retention Compliance Policy:

New-TeamsRetentionCompliancePolicy -Name 'C-Level Indefinite Teams Hold' -TeamsChannelLocation All -TeamsChatLocation 'Sandy Shu', 'Grant Gunther','Ron West'

```
Name                                Workload                                                    Enabled Mode
----                                --------                                                    ------- ----
C-Level Indefinite Teams Hold Exchange, SharePoint, OneDriveForBusiness, Skype, ModernGroup True    Enforce
```

Then we can create our Rule with an indefinite hold:

New-TeamsRetentionComplianceRule -Name 'C-Level Teams Hold Rule' -Policy 'C-Level Indefinite Teams Hold' -RetentionComplianceAction Keep -RetentionDuration Unlimited

```
Name                     Policy                                   Mode    Comment
----                     ------                                   ----    -------
C-Level Teams Hold Rule d07cead4-becf-4c27-893d-70170692d9f6 Enforce
```

To verify that we've created our Policy correctly we can get use the Get-RetentionCompliancePolicy cmdlet. Make sure to use the -DistributionDetail Switch otherwise we won't see these fields at all:

```
RunspaceId                      : 03243b97-f867-4386-946b-c62bb53b67b8
Type                            : Hold
RetentionRuleTypes              : {}
TeamsChatLocation               : {Sandy Shu,Grant Gunther,Ron West} '
TeamsChatLocationException      : {}
TeamsChannelLocation            : {All}
TeamsChannelLocationException   : {}
RestrictiveRetention            : False
Workload                        : Exchange, SharePoint, OneDriveForBusiness, Skype, ModernGroup
Priority                        : 9
ObjectVersion                   : e218711f-5551-4f80-12be-08d71605fa64
CreatedBy                       : Damian Scoles
LastModifiedBy                  : Damian Scoles
ReadOnly                        : False
ExternalIdentity                :
```

Scenario Two

We have a financial company that has a seven year retention policy for most content. Teams are now being deployed and Legal wishes to protect all teams and all chats in those Teams. The same seven year retention period needs to be applied. How can we do this in two one-liners?

New-TeamsRetentionCompliancePolicy -Name 'All Teams / Channels Retention' -TeamsChannelLocation All -TeamsChatLocation All

Now we can take the Policy, put it into a seven year Rule that does Keep and Delete for its retention action:

```
New-TeamsRetentionComplianceRule -Name 'Seven Years All Teams / Channels'  -Policy 'All Teams /
Channels Retention' -RetentionComplianceAction KeepAndDelete -RetentionDuration 2555
```

Now we've met the requirements passed down from Legal.

8   Supervision

In This Chapter

Introduction
Getting Started
- Remove Cmdlets
- Set Cmdlets
Supervision Reporting
Viewing Supervised Emails
- Security and Compliance Center
- Outlook Configuration

Introduction

Supervision is an option that Microsoft provides so that corporations can monitor an employee's activities with respect to communications platforms like Exchange Online and Teams. Some scenarios that are recognized as targets for these cmdlet are Corporate Policies, Risk Management and Regulatory Compliance. With Supervision, a user with an account in the SCC (Hybrid or O365 native user) can be monitored with this features.

Communications that trigger a Supervision Policy/Rule pair are copied to a mailbox where a supervisor can review the contents. These emails can be reviewed in OWA, Outlook and the Security and Compliance Center. One critical control is Sampling Rate which determines the percentage of emails that are pulled for supervision purposes.

Supervision in the Security and Compliance Center is comprised of these parts:

Supervision Policy - Defines the reviewer, policy name and other options.
Supervision Rule - Defines reviewers and other conditions that will trigger Supervision.
Supervised Users - Users that are being monitored by the Supervision features and who have their emails copied to reviewer mailboxes for review of their content.
Reviewers - Users who receive emails from Supervised Users and who will review email content for violations.
Groups for users - Defines a group of users to be supervised.
Sensitive Information Types - Optional, can be used for a condition to trigger Supervision.
Custom Keyword Dictionaries - Same as Sensitive Information Types, also used as a conditional trigger.
Offensive Language - Option, can be used as a condition for triggering Supervision.

PowerShell

With almost any feature in the Security and Compliance Center, we have a set of PowerShell cmdlets that will allow us to manage the said feature. Let's see what cmdlets we have for this feature:

```
Get-Command *SuperV*
```

This provides us a list of all the Supervisory cmdlets:

```
Get-SupervisoryReviewActivity
Get-SupervisoryReviewOverallProgressReport
Get-SupervisoryReviewPolicyReport
Get-SupervisoryReviewPolicyV2
Get-SupervisoryReviewReport
Get-SupervisoryReviewRule
Get-SupervisoryReviewTopCasesReport
New-SupervisoryReviewPolicyV2
New-SupervisoryReviewRule
Remove-SupervisoryReviewPolicyV2
Set-SupervisoryReviewPolicyV2
Set-SupervisoryReviewRule
```

Getting Started

First, let's make sure that our tenant has zero activity, assuming we've not configured any Supervision components yet. If we run each of the 'Get' PowerShell cmdlets from the above list, we should not return any results or activity. This is indeed the case. Now, like other components in Office 365, we need to create a Policy first and then use this in a Rule. Our first PowerShell cmdlet to use in creating Supervisory Review Policies is the New-SupervisoryReviewPolicyV2.

```
----------------------- Example 1 -----------------------

New-SupervisoryReviewPolicyV2 -Name "EU Brokers Policy" -Reviewers laura@contoso.com,julia@contoso.com -Comment
"Created by the compliance team"

This example creates a new supervisory review policy named EU Brokers Policy.
```

** **Note** ** A V2 cmdlet is simply the latest iteration of a cmdlet. Typically only one version of the cmdlet is available at any one time. If however we see a regular and V2 version of cmdlet, the advice is to use the latest version of the cmdlet because the V2 one will eventually be the one to use. However, a cautionary note should be made as well. Other cmdlets have had this occur and then the V2 cmdlet name disappears. Assuming this just means that the V2 one was renamed and the old cmdlet was removed, it could cause issues with a script. So if a script fails due to a cmdlet name not being found, check to see what the current status is of the cmdlets/naming.

With a new Supervisory Review Policy, we can set a policy's Name, Reviewers and Comments. We can set up a couple of sample Supervisory Policies - one for the Legal department and one for the HR department.

With this Supervisory Policy, we will have two reviewers:

```
New-SupervisoryReviewPolicyV2 -Name 'Legal eMail Review Policy' -Reviewers damian@
practicalpowershell.com,dave@practicalpowershell.com -Comment 'Review email from Legal
department'
```

For the HR Supervisory Policy, we will have one reviewer:

> New-SupervisoryReviewPolicyV2 -Name 'HR Mail Review Policy' -Reviewers john@practicalpowershell.com -Comment 'Review email from HR department'

After we created the two policies, we can verify they are created with the Get-SupervisoryReviewPolicyV2 cmdlet:

```
PS C:\> Get-SupervisoryReviewPolicyV2


Name                         Policy Status Last Modified By
----                         ------------- ----------------
HR Mail Review Policy        Activating    Damian Scoles
Legal Mail Review Policy Activating        Damian Scoles
```

Notice that the two policies show as Activating. We might be able to deduce that it's because we do not have a Supervisory Rule:

```
RunspaceId             : 570f2c74-4532-45e8-b5c2-37b0ed7da92b
Type                   : SupervisoryReview
ReviewMailbox          : SupervisoryReview{075e1ab4-1953-4b16-bdf2-04e247073630}@              onmicrosoft.com
Reviewers              : {}
ProvisioningStatus     : NotStarted
ProvisioningErrors     :
PolicyStatus           : Activating
IsWorkbenchPolicy      : False
Workload               : Exchange
Priority               : 0
ObjectVersion          : cfae2d72-19f1-4145-e97d-08d7192274d7
CreatedBy              : Damian Scoles
LastModifiedBy         : Damian Scoles
ReadOnly               : False
ExternalIdentity       :
Comment                : Review email from Legal department
```

Notice that there is a mailbox that was created for the review process as well:

```
ReviewMailbox          : SupervisoryReview{075e1ab4-1953-4b16-bdf2-04e247073630}@              onmicrosoft.com
```

Once we have the Supervisory Policy in place, we can create a Supervisory Rule to complete Supervision:

```
----------------------- Example 1 -----------------------

New-SupervisoryReviewRule -Name "EU Brokers Rule" -Policy "EU Brokers Policy" -SamplingRate 100 -Conditions
{(NOT(Reviewee:US Compliance)) -AND (Reviewee:EU Brokers) -AND ((trade) -OR (insider trading)) -AND (NOT(approved
by the Contoso financial team))}

This example creates a new supervisory review rule named EU Brokers Rule with the following settings:


Policy: EU Brokers Policy

Sampling rate: 100%

Conditions: Supervise inbound and outbound communications for members of the EU Brokers group that contain the
words trade or insider trading.
Exceptions: Exclude supervision for members of the EU Compliance group, or messages that contain the phrase
"approved by the Contoso financial team".
```

<u>Some sample parameters</u>
Name - Name of the Supervision Rule
Policy - Which policy is affected by this rule
Condition - What triggers the rule to copy a message to the Supervision mailbox
SamplingRate - Percent of email to review up to 100%

<u>Other parameters (no help?)</u>
ContentSources - Option that shows in the cmdlet, but no help is available
ContentContainsSensitiveInformation - No help available for this option
ContentMatchesDataModel - No help available for this option
CcsiDataModelOperator - No help available for this option

```
PS C:\> New-SupervisoryReviewRule -ContentSources
ContentSources                          WhatIf
ContentContainsSensitiveInformation     SamplingRate
Condition                               AsJob
Name                                    ErrorAction
ContentMatchesDataModel                 InformationVariable
Policy                                  Verbose
Confirm                                 InformationAction
CcsiDataModelOperator                   WarningVariable
```

Of the parameters, it appears that the Condition one is the most complicated. This is where a Rule is made, so we need to understand what is possible and if a Rule needs to be complicated:

```
-Condition <String>
    The Condition parameter specifies the conditions and exceptions for the rule. This parameter uses the
    following syntax:
    * User or group communications to supervise:((Reviewee:<emailaddress1>) -OR (Reviewee:<emailaddress2>)...).
      Exceptions use the syntax (NOT((Reviewee:<emailaddress1>) -OR (Reviewee:<emailaddress2>)...)).
    * Direction:((Direction:Inbound) -OR (Direction:Outbound) -OR (Direction:Internal)).
    * Message contains words:((<Word1orPhrase1>)-OR (<Word2orPhrase2>)...). Exceptions use the syntax
      (NOT((<Word1orPhrase1>)-OR (<Word2orPhrase2>)...)).
    * Any attachment contains words:((Attachment:<word1>)-OR (Attachment:<word2>)...). Exceptions use the syntax
      (NOT((Attachment:<word1>)-OR (Attachment:<word2>)...)).
    * Any attachment has the extension:((AttachmentName:.<extension1>)-OR (AttachmentName:.<extension2>)...).
      Exceptions use the syntax (NOT((AttachmentName:.<extension1>)-OR (AttachmentName:.<extension2>)...)).
    * Message size is larger than:(MessageSize:<size in B, KB, MB or GB>). For example (MessageSize:300KB).
      Exceptions use the syntax (NOT(MessageSize:<size in B, KB, MB or GB>))
    * Any attachment is larger than:(AttachmentSize:<size in B, KB, MB or GB>). For example (AttachmentSize:3MB).
      Exceptions use the syntax (NOT(AttachmentSize:<size in B, KB, MB or GB>))
    * Braces { } are required around the whole filter.
    * Separate multiple conditions or exception types with the -AND operator. For example,
      {(Reviewee:chris@contoso.com) -AND (AttachmentSize:3MB)}.
```

Let's try a couple of scenarios to see what it would take to create the proper conditions.

Scenario One - Legal Department

All messages from users in the Legal Department for Practical PowerShell Press that are outbound to external users, message contains the words 'Legal Document' and contains an attachment over 50Kb in size. Below are some criteria we will use:

(Reviewee:legal@practicalpowershell.com)
(Legal Document)

(AttachmentSize:50Kb)
(Direction:Outbound)

With these parameters, we can come up with a one-liner to create the respective Supervisory Rule:

New-SupervisoryReviewRule -Name 'Legal Review Rule' -Policy 'Legal Mail Review Policy' -SamplingRate 50 -Condition {(Reviewee:legal@practicalpowershell.com) -AND (Legal Document) -AND (AttachmentSize:50Kb)}

Scenario Two - HR Department

For this next scenario, we need to check for documents from HR to any other users in the organization and contains the words 'Employee Review'

(Reviewee:hr@practicalpowershell.com)
(Employee Review)
(Direction:Internal)

Again, with the right criteria we can create a rule to handle this configuration:

New-SupervisoryReviewRule -Name 'HR Review Rule' -Policy 'HR Mail Review Policy' -SamplingRate 75 -Condition {(Reviewee:hr@practicalpowershell.com) -AND (Employee Review) -AND (Direction:Internal)}

Verifying Rules and Policies

Once we have our policies in place, we can verify their creation with a Get cmdlet, like so:

Get-SupervisoryReviewPolicyV2 | Ft -Auto

```
Name                         Policy Status Last Modified By
----                         ------------- ----------------
HR Mail Review Policy        Active        Damian Scoles
Legal eMail Review Policy    Active        Damian Scoles
```

Get-SupervisoryReviewRule | Ft -Auto

```
Name               SamplingRate Condition
----               ------------ ---------
Legal Review Rule  50           (Reviewee:legal@practicalpowershell.com) -AND (Legal Document) -AND (AttachmentSize:50Kb)
HR Review Rule     75           (Reviewee:hr@practicalpowershell.com) -AND (Employee Review) -AND (Direction:Internal)
```

Remove Cmdlets

Now what if we need to remove a Rule or Policy? Well, we do NOT have a way to directly remove a Supervisory Review Rule. We would need to remove the corresponding Supervisory Review Policy. This makes some sense as the two are interlinked. Removing a Policy is as simple as specifying it's name with the Remove-SupervisoryReviewPolicyV2 cmdlet. Interesting, what is this mailboxes that is specified:

```
PS C:\> Remove-SupervisoryReviewPolicyV2 -Identity 'Legal Mail Review Policy'

Confirm
Are you sure you want to perform this action?
Removing supervisory review policy 'Legal Mail Review Policy' will also remove the corresponding mailbox
'SupervisoryReview{075e1ab4-1953-4b16-bdf2-04e247073630}        .onmicrosoft.com' and all data belonging to the mailbox
will be lost.
[Y] Yes  [A] Yes to All  [N] No  [L] No to All  [?] Help (default is "Y"): y
```

What about the mailbox listed above in the creation process or in the details of the Policy in the SCC. Would we see this mailbox with PowerShell? No. Neither Exchange nor the SCC show these mailboxes. So it must be a special hidden system mailbox. Later we will see how it can be accessed.

Now, once the Policy is removed, so is the Rule. There is no other way to remove a Rule. Trying to re-add a Policy, might error out: (Sync? Waiting for?)

```
PS C:\> New-SupervisoryReviewPolicyV2 -Name 'Legal Mail Review Policy' -Reviewers damian@practicalpowe
rshell.com,brian@practicalpowershell.com -Comment 'Review email from Legal department'
WARNING: An unexpected error has occurred and a Watson dump is being generated: Failed to load binding information,
jobRunId: 1393a28c-e3fa-458f-8039-2d2f4c68f6af, missingBindings: [PublicFolderBinding,SharePointBinding].
Failed to load binding information, jobRunId: 1393a28c-e3fa-458f-8039-2d2f4c68f6af, missingBindings:
[PublicFolderBinding,SharePointBinding].
    + CategoryInfo          : NotSpecified: (:) [New-SupervisoryReviewPolicyV2], FailedToLoadBindingsException
    + FullyQualifiedErrorId : Microsoft.Exchange.Compliance.TaskDistributionCommon.FailedToLoadBindingsException,Micro
   soft.Office.CompliancePolicy.Tasks.NewSupervisoryReviewPolicy
    + PSComputerName        : nam05b.ps.compliance.protection.outlook.com
```

Set Cmdlets

Now if we want to change any supervisory settings, for Supervisory Review, we have a couple of these available to use:

```
Set-SupervisoryReviewPolicyV2
Set-SupervisoryReviewRule
```

Now, with each of these we can see available options with Ctrl-Space or Get-Help -Full for the cmdlet. Let's start off with asking 'What can we modify for a Supervisory Review Policy?':

Add Reviewers, Replace Reviewers, how long messages are retained for review, change the comment

All of these options are quite useful.   If people leave a position or the company, using the 'AddReviewers' or 'Reviewers' parameters will allow us to swap out or add to the list as needed. Changing the retention time for these messages might match up with any current legal requirements or company Policy for review. Lastly, changing the comment may be needed in case the Rule or reviewers change.

For the Set-SupervisoryReviewRule we have fewer options to change - Conditions and SamplingRate. Each of these changes will replace the current value. So if we have a Rule that has an 80% Sampling Rate and we need to pull this back a bit to 50%, we just need the name of the Rule and we can run this:

```
Set-SupervisoryReviewRule -Identity 'Rule to be modified' -SamplingRate 50
```

If conditions need to be changed, a new set of conditions, including a required Reviewee, would need to be constructed before running the cmdlet. In the below example, we take an existing rule and remove the requirement for a pair of words and instead scan all internal emails:

```
Set-SupervisoryReviewRule -Name 'HR Review Rule'  -Condition {(Reviewee:hr@practicalpowershell.com)  -AND (Direction:Internal)}
```

No feedback, but we could check the settings with the Get-SupervisoryReviewRule cmdlet.

Supervision Reporting

After you have your tenant configured for Supervision, we have access to some PowerShell cmdlets to help with reporting activity and overall progress for Supervision emails. Below is a sample of the cmdlets as well as what they would be used for:

Get-SupervisoryReviewActivity
   Currently this cmdlet does not work and throws Dr. Watson errors.

Get-SupervisoryReviewOverallProgressReport
   This cmdlet produces this output:

```
Organization              Date                    Pending Compliant Resolved Questionable Non-Compliant
------------              ----                    ------- --------- -------- ------------ -------------
████████.onmicrosoft.com 8/2/2019 12:00:00 AM          0         0        0            0
```

Get-SupervisoryReviewPolicyReport

```
------------------------- Example 1 -------------------------

Get-SupervisoryReviewPolicyReport -StartDate 03/01/2017 -EndDate 03/31/2017

This example returns the supervisory review policy events for the month of March, 2017.

------------------------- Example 2 -------------------------

Get-SupervisoryReviewPolicyReport -Policies "EU Brokers Policy"

This example returns the supervisory review policy events for the policy named EU Brokers Policy.
```

Get-SupervisoryReviewReport

```
------------------------- Example 1 -------------------------

Get-SupervisoryReviewReport -StartDate 03/01/2017 -EndDate 03/31/2017

This example returns the supervisory review events for the month of March, 2017.

------------------------- Example 2 -------------------------

Get-SupervisoryReviewPolicyReport -Policies "US Brokers Policy"

This example returns the supervisory review events for the policy named US Brokers Policy.
```

Get-SupervisoryReviewTopCasesReport
    No examples in Get-Help for the cmdlet

Examples

Example 1

PowerShell

```
Get-SupervisoryReviewTopCasesReport | Sort-Object Policy | Format-Table Policy,Pending,Total,Date
```

Viewing Supervised Emails

After we have configured Supervisory Security, Policies and Rules and after we've tested to make sure Supervision is working as expected we have a couple of options for viewing messages that are in Supervision. First we have the Security and Compliance Center which will work for some administrators. However, there will be others that may not want to use that as part of their work flow and may feel more comfortable using Outlook instead. For both of these users, we have a way to make that happen.

Security and Compliance Center

We can now open the SCC to see any emails that may be held by the new policies:

Example 1 (HR)

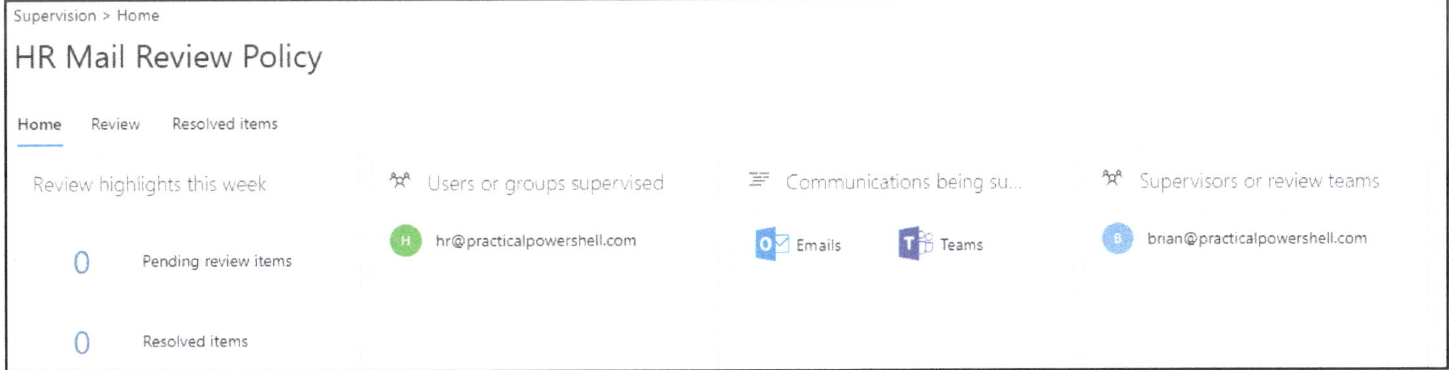

Example 2 (Legal)

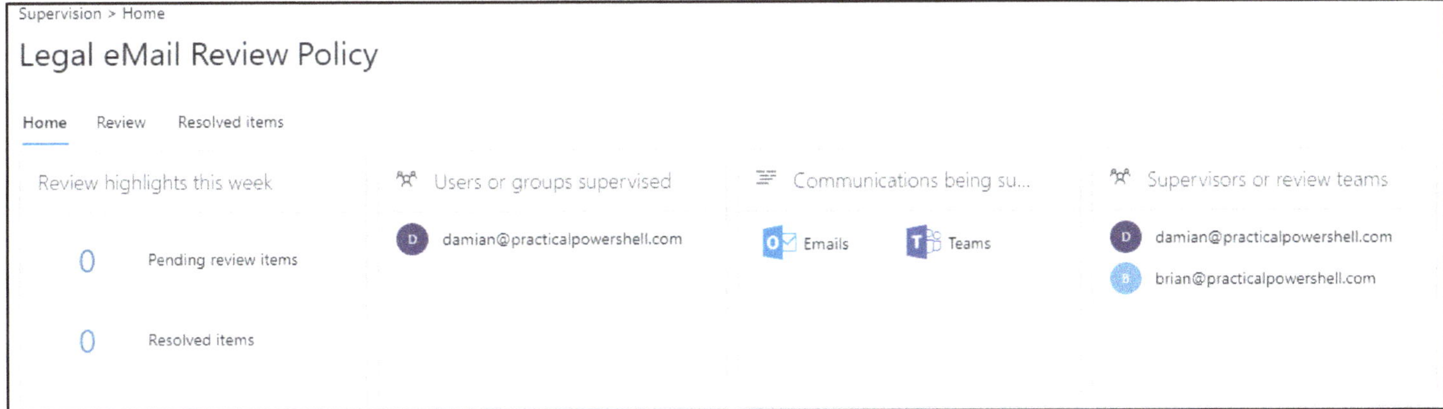

Outlook Configuration

Now, instead of using the Security and Compliance Center, we can instead use an old familiar client - Outlook. In order to configure this, we will need some prerequisite information:

(1) Email address for the Supervisory mailbox. This can be found using PowerShell or the Security and Compliance Center. Here is an example using PowerShell:

(2) Configure the Supervision Mailbox for Outlook access: (code sample below uses previous examples as reference):

> Add-MailboxPermission "SupervisoryReview{d7d59863-979b-4cc2-932d-fb2cf24e18f8}@tenant.
> onmicrosoft.com" -User damian@practicalpowershell.com -AccessRights FullAccess

> Set-Mailbox "SupervisoryReview{d7d59863-979b-4cc2-932d-fb2cf24e18f8}@tenant.onmicrosoft.
> com" -HiddenFromAddressListsEnabled: $false

(3) Open the mailbox with Outlook or OWA:

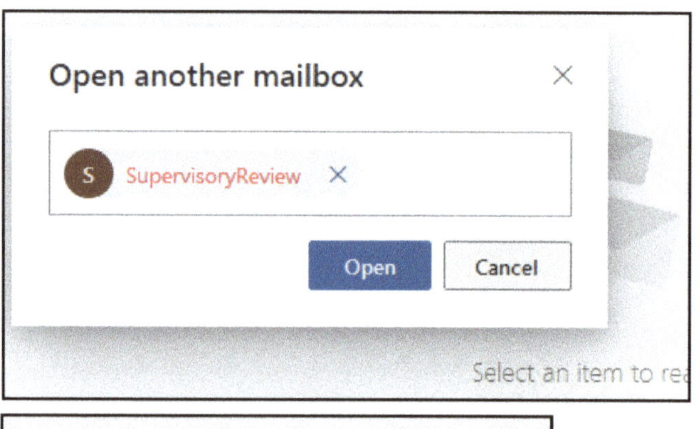

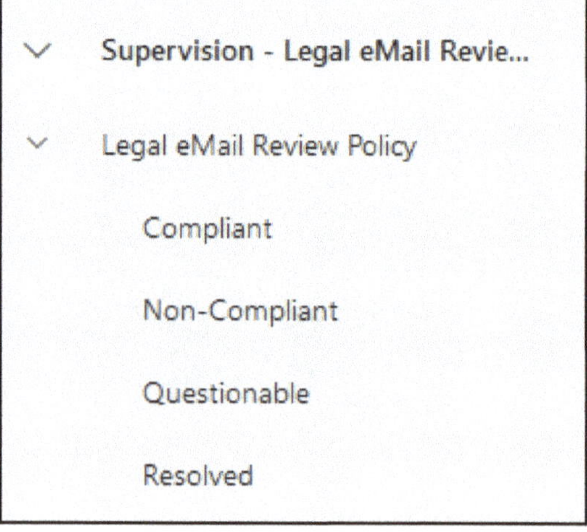

Now when emails arrive, the reviewer will be able to see emails in the above folders.

One caveat from Microsoft:

> *"Emails subject to defined policies are processed in near real-time and can be tested immediately after the policy is configured. Chats in Microsoft Teams can take up to 24 hours to fully process in a policy."*

9   Alerting

In This Chapter

Introduction
Activity Alerts
Alert Policies

Introduction

Alerts and Alert Policies are intended to help automate certain types of notifications for suspicious activity, general user activity or even possibly administrator activities. Alerts can be shown in the Alerting Dashboard or send alerts to administrators via email. Microsoft is also making changes to Alerting, so expect updates in the future and possible elimination of PowerShell cmdlets to reflect those changes.

In the Security and Compliance Center, we have two types of alerts that we can configure:

Activity Alerts: These are the original alerting objects for the Security and Compliance Center. In this chapter we will cover them for historical purposes, but would encourage the creations of the newer Alert Policies, shown below.

Alert Policies: A more advanced version of the 'Activity Alert'. Alert Polices provide some more advanced parameters in PowerShell and in the Security and Compliance Center. They are also the replacement for Activity Alerts:

Activity alerts

! We are working on a better experience for you to manage and view security and compliance alerts. Go to Alert policies

Current Alert Polices Console:

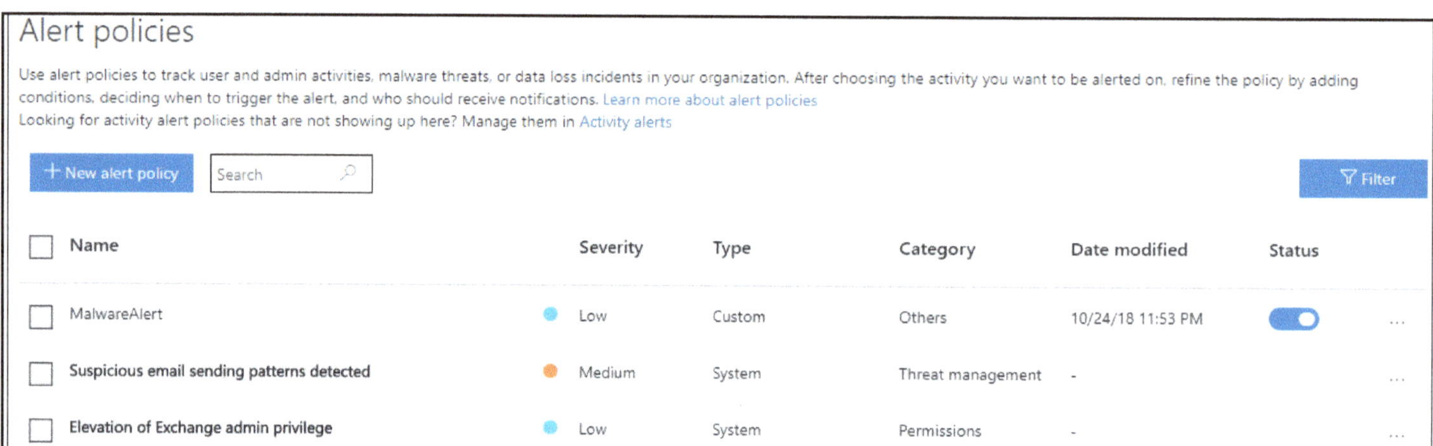

Name	Severity	Type	Category	Date modified	Status
MalwareAlert	Low	Custom	Others	10/24/18 11:53 PM	⬤
Suspicious email sending patterns detected	Medium	System	Threat management	-	
Elevation of Exchange admin privilege	Low	System	Permissions	-	

Activity Alerts

Activity Alerts are designed to notify admins of certain types of activities as they occur in your tenant. These alerts are also being phased out for a new experience with Alert Policies. We can still review the PowerShell cmdlets and effort it takes to manage Activity Alerts in the Security and Compliance Center.

PowerShell

First we need a list of PowerShell cmdlets that we can use to work with SCC Activity Alerts:

```
Get-Command *ActivityAlert
```

This provides us with a small list of cmdlets:

```
Get-ActivityAlert
New-ActivityAlert
Remove-ActivityAlert
Set-ActivityAlert
```

First, let's review what we have by default in our tenant:

```
PS C:\> Get-ActivityAlert
PS C:\>
```

None. Okay. So we have a blank slate to work with. Once we create a few of these Activity Alerts, we will revisit this cmdlet to pull some actual data and see how we can go about documenting and report on the alerts.

New-ActivityAlert

As is obvious by the cmdlet, we can use New-ActivityAlert to create new alerts in the SCC. What exactly does this mean? What alerts can we create with PowerShell and how detailed are we allowed to get. First, let's check out the examples available with the cmdlet:

```
Get-Help New-ActivityAlert -Examples
```

```
------------------------- Example 1 -------------------------

New-ActivityAlert -Name "External Sharing Alert" -Operation sharingset,sharinginvitationcreated -NotifyUser
chrisda@contoso.com,michelle@contoso.com -UserId laura@contoso.com,julia@contoso.com -Description "Notification
for external sharing events by laura@contoso.com and julia@contoso.com"

This example creates a new activity alert named External Sharing Alert that has the following properties:


Operation: sharingset and sharinginvitationcreated.


NotifyUser: chrisda@contoso.com and michelle@contoso.com.


UserId: laura@contoso.com and julia@contoso.com.
Description: Notification for external sharing events by laura@contoso.com and julia@contoso.com.
```

Reviewing the single example provided, we see that we have the following parameters: name, operation, notifyuser, UserId, and Description.   Giving the Alert a name should be easy and it should be relevant to the Alert being performed. What about Operation? Within the help for the cmdlet, there is a link to where we can find a list of the available alertable operations - https://docs.microsoft.com/en-us/office365/securitycompliance/search-the-audit-log-in-security-and-compliance. The list provided is long as it covers many operations:

File and Page Activities
Folder Activities
SharePoint list activities
Sharing and access request activities
Synchronization activities
Site permissions activities
Site administration activities
Exchange mailbox activities
Sway activities
User administration activities
Azure AD group administration activities
Application administration activities
Role administration activities
Directory administration activities
eDiscovery activities
Advanced eDiscovery activities
Power BI activities
Microsoft Teams activities
Yammer activities

As we can see, this is a pretty extensive list of general activities. Each of these activity groups has a lot of sub activities that are covered as well. Let's run through a few examples of how we can create alerts and then monitor the progress of the alerts we create.

Example 1 - eDiscovery Alerting

For this example we want to create an alert that will notify users of a group called eDiscoveryManagers. The alert will look for times when cases are create/managed, or Content Searches are performed.

```
New-ActivityAlert -Name 'eDiscovery - Cases and Search Alert' -Operation CaseAdded, CaseUpdated,
CaseAdminUpdated, CaseAdminAdded, CaseAdminRemoved -NotifyUser eDiscoveryManagers@
tenant.onmicrosoft.com -Description 'Case Management Auditing'
```

```
Description                            : Case Management Auditing
AlertScenarioAttributes                : {}
RecordType                             :
Type                                   : Custom
Operation                              : {caseadded, caseupdated, caseadminupdated, caseadminadded...}
UserId                                 : {}
AlertScenario                          : Activity
NotifyUser                             : {eDiscoveryManagers@        .onmicrosoft.com}
NotifyAllowOverride                    :
NotifyEmailCustomText                  : en-US
NotifyPolicyTipCustomText              :
NotifyPolicyTipCustomTextTranslations  : {}
EmailCulture                           : en-US
Severity                               : Low
Category                               : None
ReadOnly                               : False
ExternalIdentity                       :
```

Notice that no 'UserID' was specified like in the Example. This is because the cmdlet is not limited to a set of users, but looks for any user in the tenant that performs these actions. We also did not set a Category or Severity, but the default severity is low and the default category is none. If we would like to have either of these items used for filtered reporting (i.e. alerts by a particular category or severity level) then we would need to put a setting in.

Available Categories: None (This is the default value), DataLossPrevention, ThreatManagement, DataGovernance, AccessGovernance and Others
Available Severity Levels: None, Low, Medium or High
NotifyUser - Any notification messages that are sent, because of this Alert, will go to the specified email address.

Additional Options

Multiplier: Number of events that occur to trigger the alert
RecordType: Workload in Office 365 to be monitored. Values:
ExchangeAdmin, ExchangeItem, ExchangeItemGroup, SharePoint, SyntheticProbe, SharePointFileOperation OneDrive, AzureActiveDirectory, AzureActiveDirectoryAccountLogon, DataCenterSecurityCmdlet, ComplianceDLPSharePoint, Sway, ComplianceDLPExchange, SharePointSharingOperation, AzureActiveDirectoryStsLogon, SkypeForBusinessPSTNUsage, SkypeForBusinessUsersBlocked, SecurityComplianceCenterEOPCmdlet, ExchangeAggregatedOperation, PowerBIAudit, CRM, Yammer, SkypeForBusinessCmdlets, Discovery, MicrosoftTeams, MicrosoftTeamsAddOns, MicrosoftTeamsSettingsOperation, ThreatIntelligence
ScopeLevel: SingleUser, AllUser
Threshold: Number of events that trigger an alert, minimum of three, and works in conjunction with the TimeWindow Value
TimeWindow - specified in minutes, it represents a window of time in which the number of alerts passes the value specified in the Threshold value above. Type parameter must be *'SimpleAggregation'*
Type: Custom, ElevationOfPrivilege, SimpleAggregation, AnomalousAggregation

Example 2 - Exchange Mailbox Permissions Activity

In this example we are going to track activity for 'Exchange mailbox activities' for all users in the IT Admins group. For this we'll use the 'Multiplier' parameter and set the value to three. We are looking for a lot of activity of Admins in Exchange mailboxes.

```
New-ActivityAlert -Name 'Admin Query -Multiplier 3 - Exchange Mailbox Permissions' -Operation
AddMailboxPermissions,UpdateFolderPermissions,RemoveMailboxPermission -Notify damian@
practicalPowerShell.com
```


```
Description                            :
AlertScenarioAttributes                : {}
RecordType                             :
Type                                   : Custom
Operation                              : {swayshare, swaychangesharelevel, swayrevokeshare, swayexternalsharingoff...}
UserId                                 : {}
AlertScenario                          : Activity
NotifyUser                             : {damian@practicalPowerShell.com}
NotifyAllowOverride                    :
NotifyEmailCustomText                  : en-US
NotifyPolicyTipCustomText              :
NotifyPolicyTipCustomTextTranslations  : {}
EmailCulture                           : en-US
Severity                               : Low
Category                               : None
ReadOnly                               : False
ExternalIdentity                       :
ImmutableId                            : 00000000-0000-0000-0000-000000000000
Priority                               : 0
Workload                               : AuditAlerting
```

Example 3

For this example, we want to monitor all Sway sharing activities. We review the list of what can be audited for operations and come up with this list - SwayShare,SwayChangeShareLevel,SwayRevokeShare,SwayExternalSharingOff,SwayExternalSharingOn. The Activity Alert will be called 'Sway Share Alerts':

> New-ActivityAlert -Name 'Sway Share Alerts' -Operation SwayShare, SwayChangeShareLevel, SwayRevokeShare, SwayExternalSharingOff, SwayExternalSharingOn -Notify damian@ practicalPowerShell.com

```
Description                             :
AlertScenarioAttributes                 : {}
RecordType                              :
Type                                    : Custom
Operation                               : {addmailboxpermissions, updatefolderpermissions, removemailboxpermission}
UserId                                  : {}
AlertScenario                           : Activity
NotifyUser                              : {damian@practicalPowerShell.com}
NotifyAllowOverride                     :
NotifyEmailCustomText                   : en-US
NotifyPolicyTipCustomText               :
NotifyPolicyTipCustomTextTranslations   : {}
EmailCulture                            : en-US
Severity                                : Low
Category                                : None
ReadOnly                                : False
ExternalIdentity                        :
ImmutableId                             : 00000000-0000-0000-0000-000000000000
Priority                                : 0
Workload                                : AuditAlerting
```

Remove-ActivityAlert

This cmdlet, Remove-ActivityAlert, has very few options. We can remove one or more of these Activity Alerts with this cmdlet:

> Remove-ActivityAlert -Identity 'eDiscovery - Cases and Search Alert'

The removal process will prompt to make sure removal is OK:

```
PS C:\> Remove-ActivityAlert -Identity 'eDiscovery - Cases and Search Alert'

Confirm
Are you sure you want to perform this action?
Removing Compliance Rule 'eDiscovery - Cases and Search Alert'.
[Y] Yes  [A] Yes to All  [N] No  [L] No to All  [?] Help (default is "Y"): y
PS C:\>
```

Now, you could also remove all Activity Alerts as well:

> Get-ActivityAlert | Remove-ActivityAlert

Set-ActivityAlert

Set-ActivityAlert will allow us to modify existing Activity Alerts and change certain properties to adjust for whatever scenario you may need for the Alert. Since the default is low severity, you may want to increase it to Medium since it is an important alert to send out. Low would send the wrong impression.

Set-ActivityAlert -Identity 'eDiscovery - Cases and Search Alert' -Severity Medium

```
PS C:\> Set-activityAlert -Identity 'eDiscovery - Cases and Search Alert' -Severity Medium
PS C:\>
```

The change in severity does not register any feedback at all. However, we can verify the change like so:

(Get-ActivityAlert -Identity 'eDiscovery - Cases and Search Alert').Severity

```
PS C:\> (Get-activityAlert -Identity 'eDiscovery - Cases and Search Alert').Severity
Medium
PS C:\>
```

We can also add a Category to the Alert:

```
PS C:\> Set-activityAlert -Identity 'eDiscovery - Cases and Search Alert' -Category Others
PS C:\> (Get-activityAlert -Identity 'eDiscovery - Cases and Search Alert').Category
Others
PS C:\>
```

With the Set-ActivityAlert we can change many options for the alerts:

UserId, Operation, RecordType, Severity, Category, Threshold

What do reports look like?

After we've configured our Alerts, some with notification, we can now review any alerting in the SCC console:

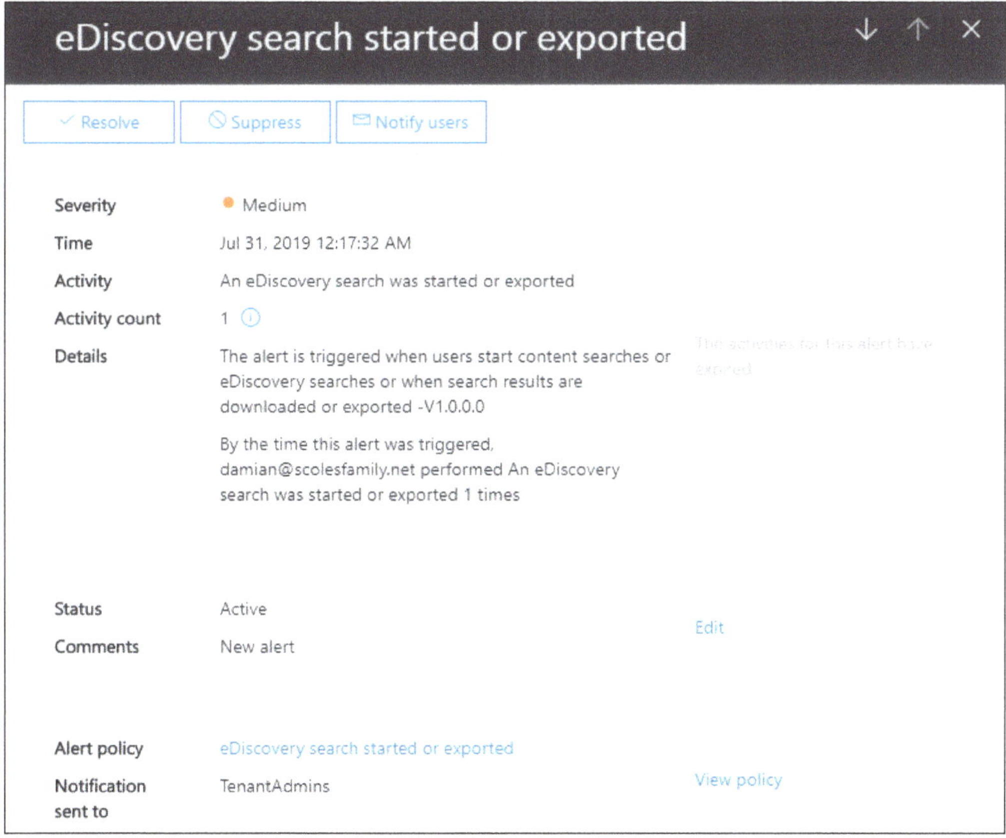

Alerts Polices

Alert Policies are here to replace the current Activity Alert. What we notice is that a lot of the parameters are the same, some are renamed and new ones have been added. We also have a similar set of PowerShell cmdlets:

PowerShell

First we need a list of PowerShell cmdlets that we can use to work with SCC Activity Alerts:

    Get-Command *ProtectionAlert

This provides us with a small list of cmdlets:

    Get-ProtectionAlert
    New-ProtectionAlert
    Remove-ProtectionAlert
    Set-ProtectionAlert

First, let's review what we may have by default in our tenant:

    Get-ProtectionAlert | Ft Name,Severity,*severity,*type,*Scenario

```
Name                                                        Severity      Severity      StreamType ThreatType        AggregationType      AlertScenario
----                                                        --------      --------      ---------- ----------        ---------------      -------------
MalwareAlert                                                Low           Low           Mail       Malware           SimpleAggregation    Protection
Suspicious email sending patterns detected                  Medium        Medium        Activity   Activity          None                 Activity
Elevation of Exchange admin privilege                       Low           Low           Activity   Activity          None                 Activity
Email messages containing malware removed after delivery    Informational Informational Mail       Malware           None                 Protection
Malware campaign detected and blocked                       Low           Low           Mail       Malware           AnomalousAggregation Protection
Email reported by user as malware or phish                  Informational Informational Activity   Activity          None                 Activity
Unusual volume of file deletion                             Medium        Medium        Activity   Activity          AnomalousAggregation Activity
Unusual external user file activity                         High          High          Activity   Activity          AnomalousAggregation Activity
eDiscovery search started or exported                       Medium        Medium        Activity   Activity          None                 Activity
Malware campaign detected in SharePoint and OneDrive        High          High          Activity   Activity          AnomalousAggregation Activity
Creation of forwarding/redirect rule                        Low           Low           Activity   Activity          None                 Activity
User restricted from sending email                          High          High          Activity   Activity          None                 Activity
Unusual increase in email reported as phish                 High          High          Activity   Activity          AnomalousAggregation Activity
Unusual volume of external file sharing                     Medium        Medium        Activity   Activity          AnomalousAggregation Activity
Email messages containing phish URLs removed after delivery Informational Informational Mail       Phish             None                 Protection
Messages have been delayed                                  High          High          None       MailFlow          CustomAggregation    MailFlow
Tenant restricted from sending email                        High          High          Activity   Activity          None                 Activity
Malware campaign detected after delivery                    High          High          Mail       Malware           AnomalousAggregation Protection
A potentially malicious URL click was detected              High          High          None       MaliciousUrlClick None                 MaliciousUrlClick
```

Now that we've seen what is available by default, lets see what we can create for Alert Policies:

Get-Help

> *No Examples*
> *Online   -   https://docs.microsoft.com/en-us/powershell/module/exchange/policy-and-compliance/New-ProtectionAlert?view=exchange-ps*

Sample code from the Online DOCs page:

    New-ProtectionAlert -Name "Content search deleted" -Category Others -NotifyUser admin@contoso.
    com -ThreatType Activity -Operation SearchRemoved -Description "Custom alert policy to track when
    content searches are deleted" -AggregationType None

> **Description** - *This example creates an alert policy that triggers an alert whenever anyone in the organization deletes a Content Search in the Office 365 Security & Compliance Center.*

So we can see that we have one example of New-ProtectionAlert work with. We can review the list of parameters of the cmdlet as well to see what we need to build a good ProtectionAlert. Remember that not all of these are required:

AggregationType: Determine how an alert is triggered with multiple occurrences. We can set this to none, SimpleAggregation or AnomalousAggregation. We can combine SimpleAggregation with the Threshold and TimeWindow parameters. AnomalousAggregation triggers alerts on highly unusual levels of activity (using baselines).

AlertBy: Specifies scope of the alerts - either based on activity or malware.

AlertFor: Reserved for Microsoft only.

Category: Adds a tag to the alert when the conditions of the alert are met. There are five available values.

Comment: Place to add extra details about the alert.

Description: Descriptive text for the alert.

Disabled: We can set this in case we need to turn an Alert Policy off.

Name: Identifies the rule for those reviewing alerts in the Alerts Dashboard.

NotificationCulture: Specify the language of alerts, using the values from the Microsoft .NET Framework CultureInfo class.

NotificationEnabled: Turns on or off notifications for the alert.

NotifyUser: Specify an email address of who to notify (internal or external address)

NotifyUserOnFilterMatch: Trigger an alert on a single match even if aggregate is specified ($True)

NotifyUserSuppressionExpiryDate: Date to which to temporarily suspend user alert notifications, after which alerts will resume.

NotifyUserThrottleThreshold: Sets a maximum number of alerts that can be sent within the NotifyUserThrottleWindow value specified.

NotifyUserThrottleWindow: Time interval used by the NotifyUserThrottleThreshold.

Operation: Like the New-ActivityAlert cmdlet, we can specify conditions to alert on. Complete list can be found here - https://go.microsoft.com/fwlink/p/?linkid=824986

Severity: Default is Low, but we can set the severity to none, low, medium or high.

ThreatType: Specify a type of activity to monitor [none, malware, phish, activity].

Threshold: Same as the New-ActivityAlert cmdlet.

TimeWindow: Same as the New-ActivityAlert cmdlet.

WhatIf: Reserved for Microsoft only.

For this next section we'll run through a couple scenarios on creating alerts and then view them in the Security and Compliance Center to get a feel for how they operate in Office 365.

Scenario One

We have a brand new tenant and we want to start alerting on the removing of users. All of the alerts will be set to Medium severity as it does not require immediate attention by IT. Notification alerts will be sent to the admin responsible for the licensing and users in Office 365 - FrankS@BigCompany.com.

```
New-ProtectionAlert -Name 'User Change Alert' -Description 'Alert when a user is added or deleted or
licensing is modified.' -Comment 'Notify Frank with alerts.' -ThreatType Activity -Operation DeletedUser
-Notifyuser 'FrankS@BigCompany.com' -Category AccessGovernance -Threshold 10 -TimeWindow 180
```

A second alert will be configured for suspicious changes, which in our case would be high volume changes of the first alert. Notification alerts will be sent to the IT groups email address (itgroup@bigcompany.com).

> New-ProtectionAlert -Name 'Mass User Change Alert' -Description 'Alert when suspicious activity occurs for adding/removing users and licensing' -Comment 'Suspicious activity alert, sent to all IT.' -ThreatType Activity -Operation DeletedUser -Notifyuser 'itgroup@bigcompany.com' -Category AccessGovernance -AggregationType AnomalousAggregation

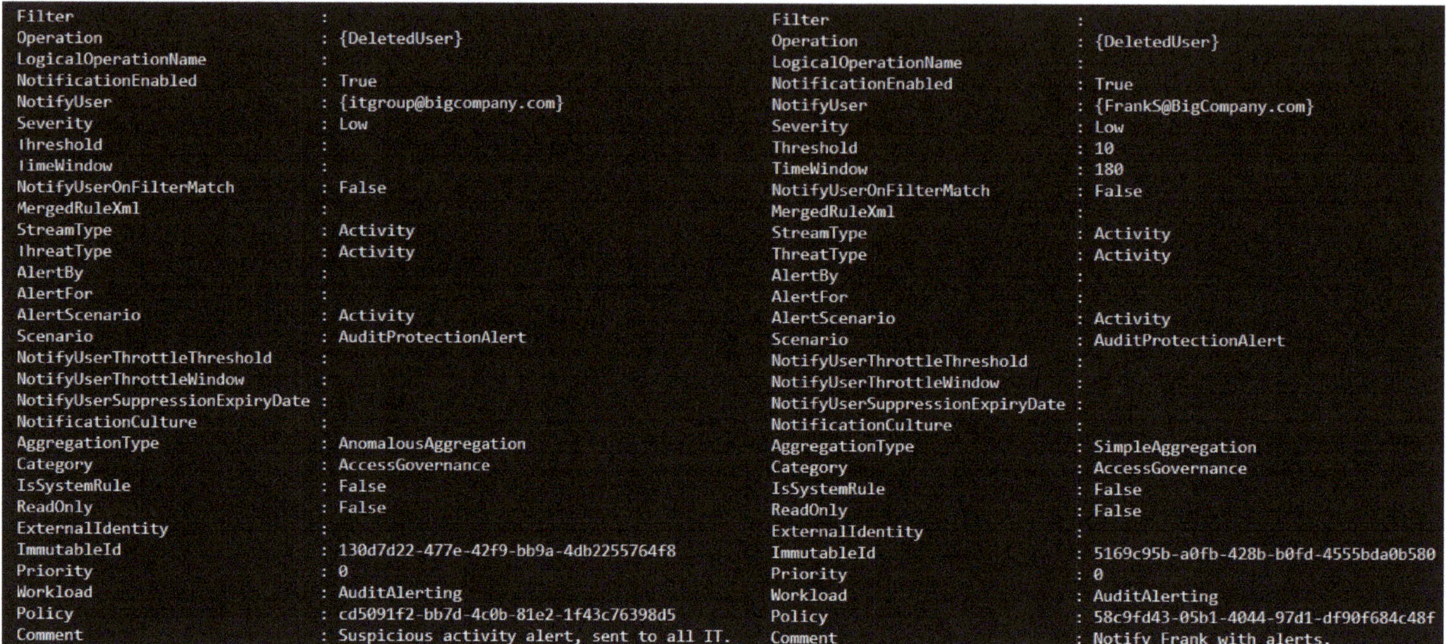

```
Filter                              :                          Filter                              :
Operation                           : {DeletedUser}            Operation                           : {DeletedUser}
LogicalOperationName                :                          LogicalOperationName                :
NotificationEnabled                 : True                     NotificationEnabled                 : True
NotifyUser                          : {itgroup@bigcompany.com} NotifyUser                          : {FrankS@BigCompany.com}
Severity                            : Low                      Severity                            : Low
Threshold                           :                          Threshold                           : 10
TimeWindow                          :                          TimeWindow                          : 180
NotifyUserOnFilterMatch             : False                    NotifyUserOnFilterMatch             : False
MergedRuleXml                       :                          MergedRuleXml                       :
StreamType                          : Activity                 StreamType                          : Activity
ThreatType                          : Activity                 ThreatType                          : Activity
AlertBy                             :                          AlertBy                             :
AlertFor                            :                          AlertFor                            :
AlertScenario                       : Activity                 AlertScenario                       : Activity
Scenario                            : AuditProtectionAlert     Scenario                            : AuditProtectionAlert
NotifyUserThrottleThreshold         :                          NotifyUserThrottleThreshold         :
NotifyUserThrottleWindow            :                          NotifyUserThrottleWindow            :
NotifyUserSuppressionExpiryDate     :                          NotifyUserSuppressionExpiryDate     :
NotificationCulture                 :                          NotificationCulture                 :
AggregationType                     : AnomalousAggregation     AggregationType                     : SimpleAggregation
Category                            : AccessGovernance         Category                            : AccessGovernance
IsSystemRule                        : False                    IsSystemRule                        : False
ReadOnly                            : False                    ReadOnly                            : False
ExternalIdentity                    :                          ExternalIdentity                    :
ImmutableId                         : 130d7d22-477e-42f9-bb9a-4db2255764f8   ImmutableId        : 5169c95b-a0fb-428b-b0fd-4555bda0b580
Priority                            : 0                        Priority                            : 0
Workload                            : AuditAlerting            Workload                            : AuditAlerting
Policy                              : cd5091f2-bb7d-4c0b-81e2-1f43c76398d5   Policy             : 58c9fd43-05b1-4044-97d1-df90f684c48f
Comment                             : Suspicious activity alert, sent to all IT.  Comment         : Notify Frank with alerts.
```

These new alerts we created will appear in the Security and Compliance Center Under Alerts --> Alert Policies:

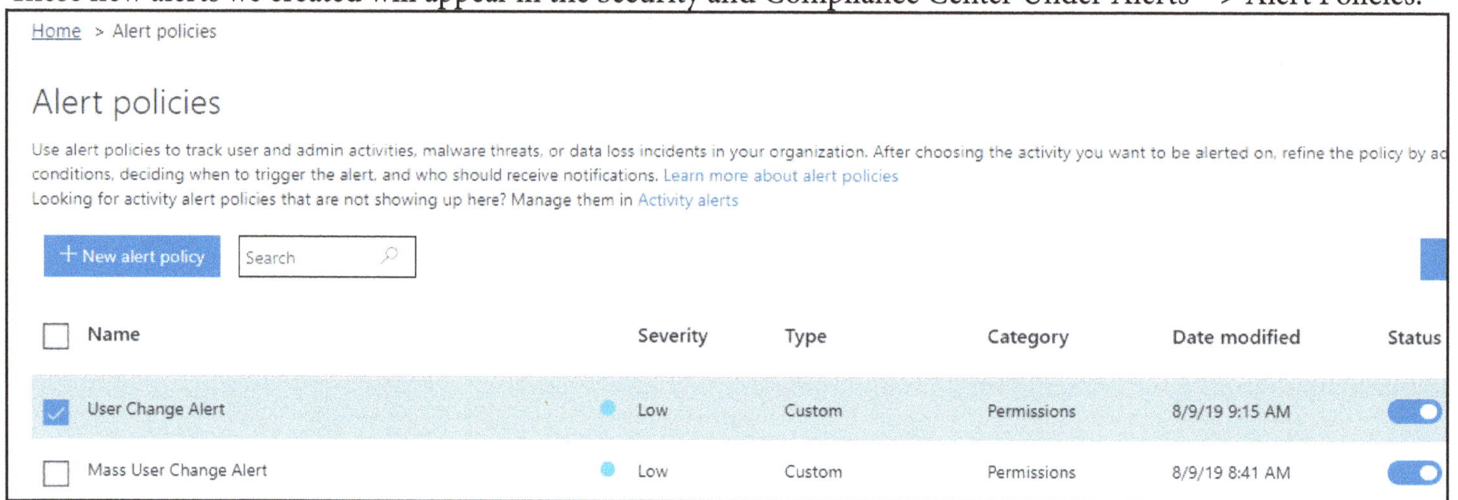

Singular alerts will now be delivered to Frank in IT immediately, whereas the other alerts, for the IT group, will need at least a week before any alerts could be delivered as background logic creates a baseline for what is to be expected in an environment. Once the baseline is ready, then any suspicious activity with User Deletions will generate alerts for the IT group.

If we need to modify this alert for new users being added or other Operations, we can simply run a one-liner to update it. Remember this will completely replace the Operation currently set:

> Set-ProtectionAlert -Identity 'User Change Alert' -Operation AddedUser

** **Note** ** We can add multiple Operations as long as the values are comma separated.

Scenario Two

A consulting firm uses Sway to create client presentations and these are all stored in their own corporate tenant. Various people have access to the presentation including other outside contractors. Problems in the past with presentations being removed without notification or permission has led to the need for some sort of alerting. For this we will create an alert to monitor the deletion of Sway data using Protection Alerts.

> New-ProtectionAlert -Name 'Sway Deletion Alert' -Description 'Alert when a user makes a Sway deletion.' -Comment 'Notify Sway Admin' -ThreatType Activity -Operation SwayDelete -Notifyuser 'SwayAdmin@BigCompany.com' -Category AccessGovernance -AggregationType None

Now we have an Alert that notifies the email address SwayAdmin@BigCompany.Com if a user deletes a Sway.

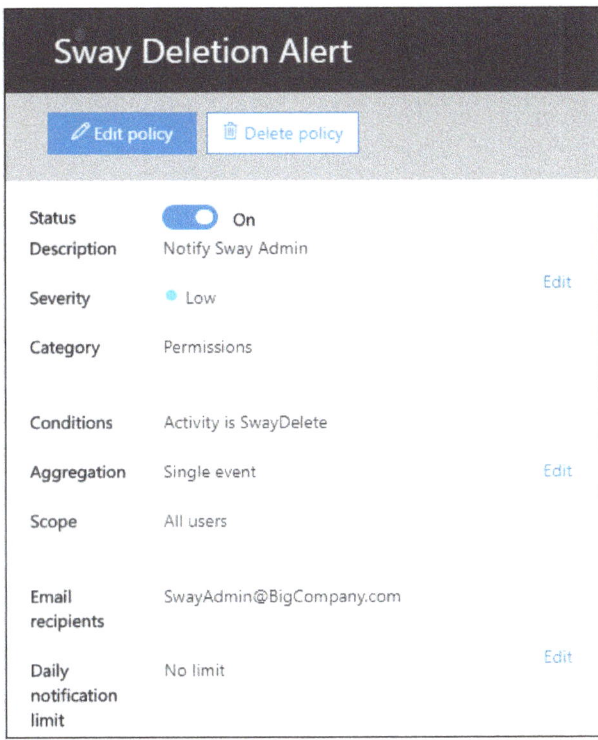

Beyond the New

Once we get beyond creating new alerts we only have three other cmdlets we can use to manage Protection Alerts. These cmdlets allow us to Get, Remove and Set. Remove is the easiest cmdlet to use as we only need an identifier for a Policy in order to remove it. However, that requires finding the Identity. We can do that with Get-Protection Alerts. However, if we run 'Get-ProtectionAlert' without any other switches or formatting, we get a blur of information that whirls by. What? It looks like Get-ProtectionAlert has Format-List as its default format. So we will simply add a Format-Table and choose two values we see in the Format-List below:

```
Guid             : a74bb32a-541b-47fb-adfd-f8c62ce3d59b
Identity         : FFO.extest.microsoft.com/Microsoft Exchange Hosted
Id               : FFO.extest.microsoft.com/Microsoft Exchange Hosted
IsValid          : True
ExchangeVersion  : 0.20 (15.0.0.0)
Name             : A potentially malicious URL click was detected
```

Get-ProtectionAlert | Ft Name

Now we have a list of all of the alerts and properties we can use with Remote and Set cmdlets:

```
Name
----
User Change Alert
Mass User Change Alert
Sway Deletion Alert
MalwareAlert
Suspicious email sending patterns detected
Elevation of Exchange admin privilege
Email messages containing malware removed after delivery
Malware campaign detected and blocked
Email reported by user as malware or phish
Unusual volume of file deletion
Unusual external user file activity
eDiscovery search started or exported
Malware campaign detected in SharePoint and OneDrive
Creation of forwarding/redirect rule
User restricted from sending email
Unusual increase in email reported as phish
Unusual volume of external file sharing
Email messages containing phish URLs removed after delivery
Messages have been delayed
Tenant restricted from sending email
Malware campaign detected after delivery
A potentially malicious URL click was detected
```

To remove an alert, we can use either the name. Examples:

Remove-ProtectionAlert -Identity 'User Change Alert'
Remove-ProtectionAlert -Identity 'Mass User Change Alert'

Now, if we have items that we need to adjust or change on an alert, we can use the name of the alerts provided above as well as the numerous options that are available. For example we can change the notified user email address:

Set-ProtectionAlert -Identity 'User Change Alert' -Notifyuser 'JennQ@BigCompany.com'

We can change the severity of the alert:

Set-ProtectionAlert -Identity 'Mass User Change Alert' -Severity High

And possibly even change the Threshold values to something higher if we are getting too many alerts:

Set-ProtectionAlert -Identity 'User Change Alert' -Threshold 10 -TimeWindow 1200

None of these changes will provide immediate feedback, but we will see the changes in the Security and Compliance Center as well as in Powershell.

In This Chapter

Introduction
Information Barriers
- Getting Started with Information Barriers
- Permissions Required
Restrictions in Teams
- Prerequisites
- Administrative Consent
PowerShell
Real World Experience
- Caveats to Blocking
Documenting Settings (Script)

Introduction

For its entire history, Office 365 did not provide technology to logically separate the people in an organization. Ideas like Ethical Firewalls did not exist in a native format. If we wanted this functionality we would need a third party product to provide the appropriate functionality. Recently Microsoft added a new concept called Information Barrier. While these cmdlets have been in the Security and Compliance Center since 2018, it's still not fully fleshed-out at the moment (this concept is limited to Teams communication) it is an important first step into this territory by Microsoft.

Not every organization will need a wall of separation like this. However, organizations like financial organizations or companies with heavy research and development teams may want to or have to (with regulations) restrict their users with whom they communicate within the company. In this chapter we will cover the requirements, prerequisites, steps for configuration and a detailed documentation script.

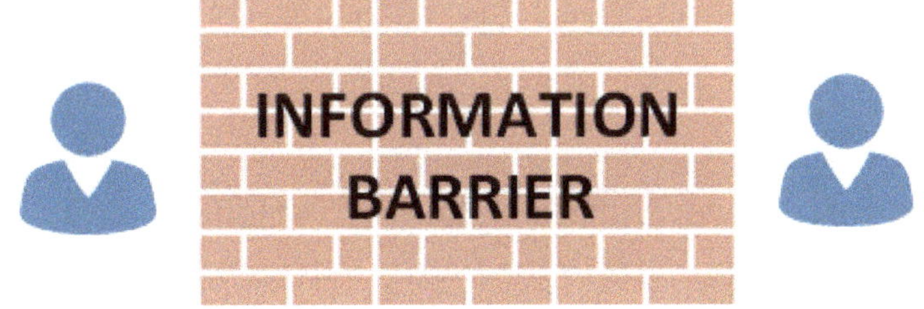

Information Barriers

https://docs.microsoft.com/en-us/office365/securitycompliance/information-barriers

What are Information Barriers?

Information Barriers are a logical construct that prevents communication between groups of people. Any of the people that are blocked from communicating need to be synced to Azure AD. The filters for users are based off of Azure AD users and the attributes that are allowed for filters. We can use one or more filters for filtering users. However, Microsoft recommends that these filters are not too complex.

Getting Started with Information Barriers

To use the Information Barrier functionality in the Security and Compliance Center, there are numerous prerequisites and caveats that you must deal with first. First, we'll start off with licensing requirements. From the official Microsoft documentation, the current licensing requirements can be found here:

https://docs.microsoft.com/en-us/office365/securitycompliance/information-barriers

Licensing Requirements

As with any feature in Office 365, Microsoft requires a license to enable the use of the feature. Information Barriers are certainly no different. When it comes to Information Barriers, you have a few choices:

- Microsoft 365 E5
- Office 365 E5
- Office 365 Advanced Compliance
- Microsoft 365 E5 Information Protection and Compliance

What you will notice is that you will need either an E5 or the Office 365 Advanced Compliance add-on license.

Office 365 Advanced Compliance - contains these features Advanced eDiscovery, Advanced Data Governance, Privileged Access Management, Customer Key and Customer Lockbox

Once we have the right licensing in place, we can proceed to the correct permissions. From Microsoft's docs, the below security groups will have access to the Information Barrier configuration settings:

Permissions required

Permission requirements for Information Barriers are (one of the following):

- Microsoft 365 global administrator
- Office 365 global administrator
- Compliance administrator

- IB Compliance Management (this is a new role!)

The reason for this is that these groups all contain the correct Management Roles. There are two roles that are assigned to the groups. We can see the new Management roles via PowerShell here:

```
PS C:\> Get-ManagementRole | where {$_.Name -like '*ib*'}

Name                                RoleType
----                                --------
View-Only IB Compliance Management  ViewOnlyIBComplianceManagement
IB Compliance Management            IBComplianceManagement
```

Take care in assigning users to any of the above Role Groups as they control communications between your end users in your tenant.

Filterable Attributes

Microsoft provides a list of user attributes that can be used in the user filters:

Co	Mail Nick Name	Proxy Address
Company	Member Of	Street Address
Department	MSExch Ext. Custom Attr. 1 to 5	Target Address
Description	Physical Delivery Office Name	Usage Location
Extension Attributes 1 to 15	Postal Code	User Principal Name
Mail		

GUI or PowerShell?

Information Barriers do not appear in the GUI part of the Security and Compliance Center and must be managed with PowerShell. While the feature may eventually appear as a tab or an option in the SCC, there are no guarantees. This using the PowerShell examples here should help guide you when implementing Information Barriers in your tenant.. Another note, we are limited at this time to this subset of restrictions in Office 365:

Restrictions in Teams

As mentioned earlier, Information Barriers provides limited functionality as of the writing of this book. At this time, the current list of what is restricted is listed below:

- Searching for a user
- Adding a member to a team
- Starting a chat session with someone
- Starting a group chat
- Inviting someone to join a meeting
- Sharing a screen
- Placing a call

Prerequisites

Before we work with any Information Barrier powershell, we need to satisfy a few requirements. Most of these requirements are easy to meet, while one may not be as easy to accomplish. Below is the official list from Microsoft on Information Barriers:

> **AD Replicated** - make sure any attribute you want to filter by is replicating correctly to your tenant
> **Scoped Directory Search** - https://docs.microsoft.com/en-us/MicrosoftTeams/teams-scoped-directory-search
> **Audit Logging On** - https://docs.microsoft.com/en-us/office365/securitycompliance/turn-audit-log-search-on-or-off
> **No Exchange Online Address Book Polices** - Remove prior to enabling Information Barriers (**)
> **PowerShell** - Security and Compliance Center and Azure PowerShell modules
> **Administrative Consent** - Follow a documented Microsoft process to enable access
>
> ** **NOTE:** This is an interesting requirement. For most organizations, the use of Address Book Policies is zero. However, in larger or complex environments, Address Book Polices are quite useful. If your organization has these in place now, planning will be needed prior to removing these to implement Information Barriers.

Administrative Consent

Administrative Consent grants certain access rights to your tenant for the Information Barrier Processor App and is applied globally to a tenant. For this task, we need to run some cmdlets in Azure (AZ PowerShell module required) in order to enable the use of Information Barriers:

Login-AzAccount

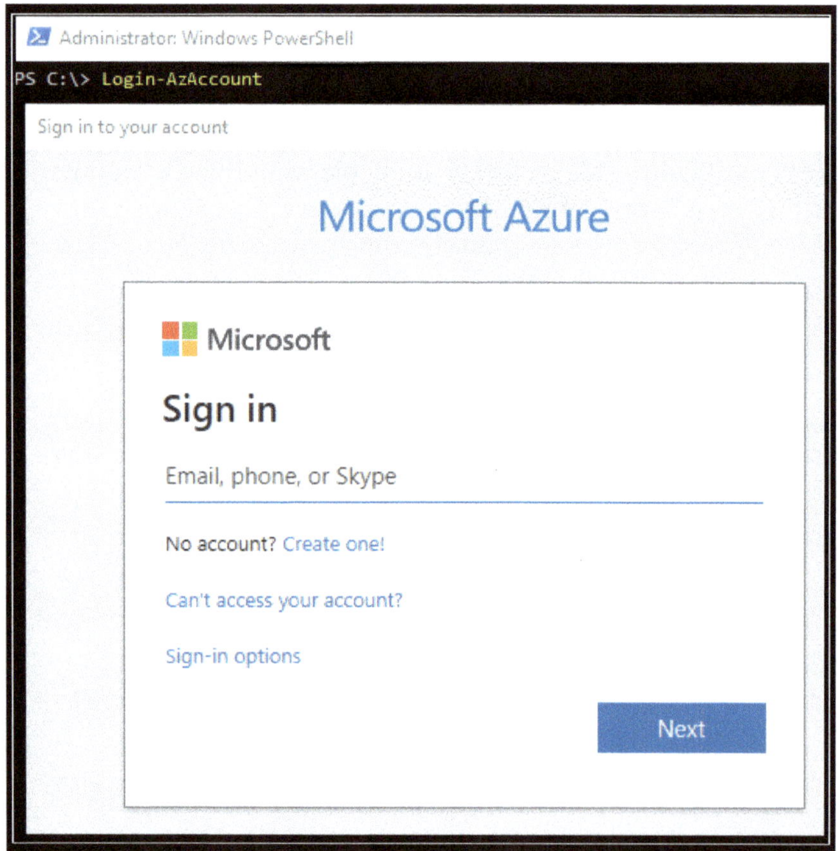

```
Account            : damian@practicalpowershell.com
SubscriptionName   : Microsoft Azure
SubscriptionId     :
TenantId           :
Environment        : AzureCloud
```

Type this into the PowerShell window (the ID represents the Information Barrier Processor App ID):

$appId = "bcf62038-e005-436d-b970-2a472f8c1982"

```
PS C:\> $appId="bcf62038-e005-436d-b970-2a472f8c1982"
```

$sp = Get-AzureRmADServicePrincipal -ServicePrincipalName $appId

```
PS C:\> $sp=Get-AzureRmADServicePrincipal -ServicePrincipalName $appId
```

if ($sp -eq $null) { New-AzureRmADServicePrincipal -ApplicationId $appId }

```
PS C:\> if ($sp -eq $null) { New-AzureRmADServicePrincipal -ApplicationId $appId }


ServicePrincipalNames : {bcf62038-e005-436d-b970-2a472f8c1982, https://policyprocessor.microsoft.com}
ApplicationId         : bcf62038-e005-436d-b970-2a472f8c1982
DisplayName           : Information Barrier Processor
Id                    : eccbb8b9-45a0-40cf-8b30-bc388c102c08
AdfsId                :
Type                  : ServicePrincipal
```

Start-Process "https://login.microsoftonline.com/common/adminconsent?client_id=$appId"

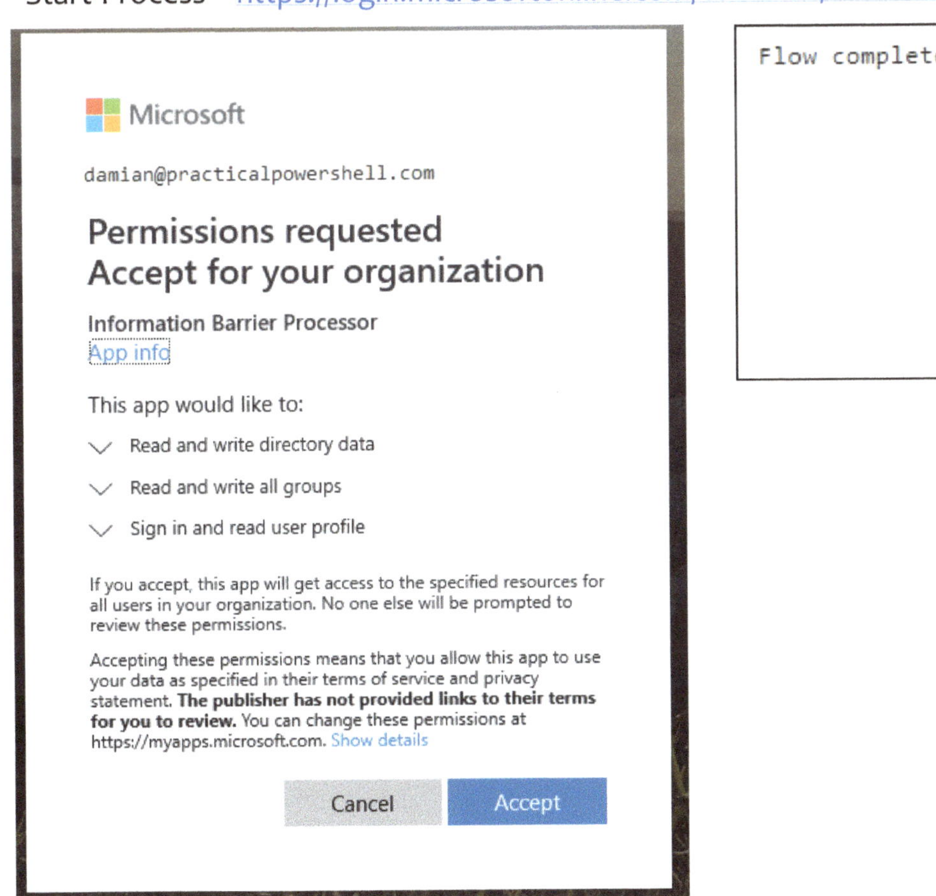

** **Note** ** You may need to re-authenticate for the Permissions request step above.

Make sure to close any open PowerShell windows, otherwise an error will be thrown when working with the Information Barrier PowerShell cmdlets:

```
PS C:\> New-InformationBarrierPolicy -Name 'Research-HR' -AssignedSegment Research -SegmentsBlocked HR
Creating a new session for implicit remoting of "New-InformationBarrierPolicy" command...
New-PSSession : [nam05b.ps.compliance.protection.outlook.com] Connecting to remote server
nam05b.ps.compliance.protection.outlook.com failed with the following error message : Access is denied. For more
information, see the about_Remote_Troubleshooting Help topic.
At C:\Users\DScoles\AppData\Local\Temp\tmp_wzt1ndzv.qbw\tmp_wzt1ndzv.qbw.psm1:137 char:17
+                 & $script:NewPSSession `
+                 ~~~~~~~~~~~~~~~~~~~~~~~
    + CategoryInfo          : OpenError: (System.Manageme....RemoteRunspace:RemoteRunspace) [New-PSSession], PSRemotin
   gTransportException
    + FullyQualifiedErrorId : AccessDenied,PSSessionOpenFailed
Exception calling "GetSteppablePipeline" with "1" argument(s): "No session has been associated with this implicit
remoting module."
At C:\Users\DScoles\AppData\Local\Temp\tmp_wzt1ndzv.qbw\tmp_wzt1ndzv.qbw.psm1:12522 char:13
+             $steppablePipeline = $scriptCmd.GetSteppablePipeline($myI ...
+             ~~~~~~~~~~~~~~~~~~~~~~~~~~~~~~~~~~~~~~~~~~~~~~~~~~~~~~~~~~~
    + CategoryInfo          : NotSpecified: (:) [], ParentContainsErrorRecordException
    + FullyQualifiedErrorId : RuntimeException
```

PowerShell

Before proceeding, close your PowerShell session to the SCC and reconnect to work with the new changes. Now that we have the basic requirements and background information on Information Barriers out of the way, let's take a look at what we can do in PowerShell. First, we need a list of cmdlets that contain the noun 'Barrier' in them. We'll run this cmdlet:

```
Get-Command *barrier*
```

This provides a list of cmdlets related to the new Information Barrier (cmdlets displayed may vary depending on permissions granted):

```
Get-InformationBarrierPoliciesApplicationStatus
Get-InformationBarrierPolicy
Get-InformationBarrierRecipientStatus
Get-InformationBarrierReportDetails
Get-InformationBarrierReportSummary
New-InformationBarrierPolicy
Remove-InformationBarrierPolicy
Set-InformationBarrierPolicy
Start-InformationBarrierPoliciesApplication
Stop-InformationBarrierPoliciesApplication
Test-InformationBarrierPolicy
```

In addition to the above cmdlets, there is another set of cmdlets that are used to create the segmentation that is used by Information Barriers to create the logical separation. These are cmdlets used to create these Organization Segments:

```
Get-Command *segment
```

Which provides us with these cmdlets:

```
Get-OrganizationSegment
```

New-OrganizationSegment
Remove-OrganizationSegment
Set-OrganizationSegment

By default there are no Information Barriers or Organization Segments in your tenant, so we should create these first. For the New-OrganizationSegment cmdlet, let's review the Get-Help and look at the examples provided for the cmdlet. What we find is that because the cmdlet is so new, there are no examples listed in the Get-Help for the cmdlet. Microsoft Docs also does not have anything online for the cmdlet. So where can we find an example of how to use the cmdlet? We can look here:

https://docs.microsoft.com/en-us/office365/securitycompliance/information-barriers-policies

Using the examples provided by this link, we can construct a one-liner to create our Organization Segments:

```
New-OrganizationSegment -Name 'Research' -UserGroupFilter "Department -eq 'Research'"
```

```
RunspaceId            : 15c6b834-4383-405c-8173-0736f130894f
Type                  : OrganizationSegment
UserGroupFilter       : Department -eq 'Research'
ExoSegmentId          : 39ee3d20-47d5-4bc7-9479-e95534f86fd3
ObjectVersion         : 349447f7-7de4-4fc5-f5a1-08d712126e74
CreatedBy             : Damian Scoles
LastModifiedBy        : Damian Scoles
Comment               :
ModificationTimeUtc   : 7/26/2019 9:44:26 PM
CreationTimeUtc       : 7/25/2019 5:18:42 AM
Identity              : FFO.extest.microsoft.com/Microsoft Exchange Hosted Organizations/       .onmicrosoft.com/Configuration/Research
Id                    : FFO.extest.microsoft.com/Microsoft Exchange Hosted Organizations/       .onmicrosoft.com/Configuration/Research
ExchangeVersion       : 0.20 (15.0.0.0)
Name                  : Research
DistinguishedName     : CN=Research,CN=Configuration,CN=       .onmicrosoft.com,OU=Microsoft Exchange Hosted Organizations,DC=FFO,DC=extest,DC=microsoft,DC=com
ObjectCategory        :
ObjectClass           : {msExchUnifiedPolicy}
WhenChanged           : 7/26/2019 4:44:26 PM
WhenCreated           : 7/25/2019 12:18:42 AM
WhenChangedUTC        : 7/26/2019 9:44:26 PM
WhenCreatedUTC        : 7/25/2019 5:18:42 AM
ExchangeObjectId      : 9eae29a4-4ce1-47c1-9eb7-031c0e46e717
OrganizationId        : FFO.extest.microsoft.com/Microsoft Exchange Hosted Organizations/       .onmicrosoft.com - FFO.extest.microsoft.com/Microsoft Exchange Hosted
                        Organizations,       .onmicrosoft.com/Configuration
Guid                  : 9eae29a4-4ce1-47c1-9eb7-031c0e46e717
OriginatingServer     :
IsValid               : True
ObjectState           : Unchanged
```

For our example, we need to create one more Organization Segment otherwise we won't be able to create any Information Barriers:

```
New-OrganizationSegment -Name 'HR' -UserGroupFilter "Department -eq 'HR'"
```

```
RunspaceId            : 15c6b834-4383-405c-8173-0736f130894f
Type                  : OrganizationSegment
UserGroupFilter       : Department -eq 'HR'
ExoSegmentId          : b2a7bd2b-9ede-4a4d-86b1-ede1ba25f962
ObjectVersion         : 81c5c9ff-61ea-4716-33ce-08d710bf7351
CreatedBy             : Damian Scoles
LastModifiedBy        : Damian Scoles
Comment               :
ModificationTimeUtc   : 7/25/2019 5:17:55 AM
CreationTimeUtc       : 7/25/2019 5:17:55 AM
Identity              : FFO.extest.microsoft.com/Microsoft Exchange Hosted Organizations/       .onmicrosoft.com/Configuration/HR
Id                    : FFO.extest.microsoft.com/Microsoft Exchange Hosted Organizations/       .onmicrosoft.com/Configuration/HR
ExchangeVersion       : 0.20 (15.0.0.0)
Name                  : HR
DistinguishedName     : CN=HR,CN=Configuration,CN=       .onmicrosoft.com,OU=Microsoft Exchange Hosted Organizations,DC=FFO,DC=extest,DC=microsoft,DC=com
ObjectCategory        :
ObjectClass           : {msExchUnifiedPolicy}
WhenChanged           : 7/25/2019 12:17:55 AM
WhenCreated           : 7/25/2019 12:17:55 AM
WhenChangedUTC        : 7/25/2019 5:17:55 AM
WhenCreatedUTC        : 7/25/2019 5:17:55 AM
ExchangeObjectId      : 52af790c-f5bb-4a63-96be-0bd6bb6d3e29
OrganizationId        : FFO.extest.microsoft.com/Microsoft Exchange Hosted Organizations       .onmicrosoft.com - FFO.extest.microsoft.com/Microsoft Exchange Hosted
                        Organizations       .onmicrosoft.com/Configuration
Guid                  : 52af790c-f5bb-4a63-96be-0bd6bb6d3e29
OriginatingServer     :
IsValid               : True
ObjectState           : New
```

Now that we have multiple organization segments to work with, we can build out some Information Barriers. The first cmdlet we need to use is 'New-InformationBarrierPolicy'. Similar to the New-OrganizationSegment, there are no examples listed in the Get-Help of the cmdlet nor is there a Microsoft Docs page for the cmdlet. We can verify no online version exists like so:

Get-Help New-InformationBarrierPolicy -Online

```
PS C:\> Get-Help New-InformationBarrierPolicy -Online
get-help : The online version of this Help topic cannot be displayed because the Internet address (URI) of the Help
topic is not specified in the command code or in the help file for the command.
At line:1 char:1
```

From the same page that listed examples for New-OrganizationSegment, we also find examples for the New-InformationBarrier cmdlet. So, following this, let's work through a sample scenario. We have two defined Organization Segments - HR and Research.

Per a corporate directive, we need to construct information barriers between these two segments. When we create the barriers, we also need to set the state to Inactive, per Microsoft best practices for Information Barrier creation. The theory on that is that we can create barriers, activate the Information Barrier app that runs in Azure and then apply them once we are sure the policies are correct in place. So for creating the base barriers, we need these parameters - Name, AssignedSegment, SegmentBlocked and State. From this we will start with blocking the HR segment from the Research segment:

New-InformationBarrierPolicy -Name 'Research-HR' -AssignedSegment Research -SegmentsBlocked HR -State InActive

```
RunspaceId              : 2e07d4cf-d7a4-4d5c-b3e5-3b2902cddc6e
Type                    : InformationBarrier
AssignedSegment         : Research
SegmentsAllowed         : {}
ExoPolicyId             : 69a9440c-4e3d-492d-8c48-d85297146576
SegmentsBlocked         : {HR}
SegmentAllowedFilter    :
BlockVisibility         : True
BlockCommunication      : True
State                   : Inactive
ObjectVersion           : 8c6df40e-e692-47cd-bfe5-08d710c2df48
CreatedBy               : Damian Scoles
LastModifiedBy          : Damian Scoles
Comment                 :
ModificationTimeUtc     : 7/25/2019 5:42:25 AM
CreationTimeUtc         : 7/25/2019 5:42:25 AM
Identity                : FFO.extest.microsoft.com/Microsoft Exchange Hosted
                          Organizations,         onmicrosoft.com/Configuration/Research-HR
Id                      : FFO.extest.microsoft.com/Microsoft Exchange Hosted
                          Organizations         onmicrosoft.com/Configuration/Research-HR
ExchangeVersion         : 0.20 (15.0.0.0)
Name                    : Research-HR
DistinguishedName       : CN=Research-HR,CN=Configuration,CN=         onmicrosoft.com,OU=Microsoft Exchange Hosted
                          Organizations,DC=FFO,DC=extest,DC=microsoft,DC=com
ObjectCategory          :
ObjectClass             : {msExchUnifiedPolicy}
WhenChanged             : 7/25/2019 12:42:25 AM
WhenCreated             : 7/25/2019 12:42:25 AM
WhenChangedUTC          : 7/25/2019 5:42:25 AM
WhenCreatedUTC          : 7/25/2019 5:42:25 AM
ExchangeObjectId        : 4809c4b8-e60d-4ffe-a7eb-d52254aa193f
OrganizationId          : FFO.extest.microsoft.com/Microsoft Exchange Hosted Organizations         onmicrosoft.com -
                          FFO.extest.microsoft.com/Microsoft Exchange Hosted
                          Organizations         onmicrosoft.com/Configuration
Guid                    : 4809c4b8-e60d-4ffe-a7eb-d52254aa193f
OriginatingServer       :
IsValid                 : True
ObjectState             : New

WARNING: Your changes will take into affect after you run Start-InformationBarrierPoliciesApplication cmdlet.
Start-InformationBarrierPoliciesApplication cmdlet only applies Active state policies.
```

We then need to create a rule where we block Research from HR:

```
New-InformationBarrierPolicy -Name 'HR-Research' -AssignedSegment HR -SegmentsBlocked Research
-State InActive
```

```
RunspaceId              : 2e07d4cf-d7a4-4d5c-b3e5-3b2902cddc6e
Type                    : InformationBarrier
AssignedSegment         : HR
SegmentsAllowed         : {}
ExoPolicyId             : 1b4679d1-3abd-4ae7-8d7d-e86731222a45
SegmentsBlocked         : {Research}
SegmentAllowedFilter    :
BlockVisibility         : True
BlockCommunication      : True
State                   : Inactive
ObjectVersion           : b44f97ea-459f-442a-e3d7-08d710c32add
CreatedBy               : Damian Scoles
LastModifiedBy          : Damian Scoles
Comment                 :
ModificationTimeUtc     : 7/25/2019 5:44:32 AM
CreationTimeUtc         : 7/25/2019 5:44:32 AM
Identity                : FFO.extest.microsoft.com/Microsoft Exchange Hosted
                          Organizations         onmicrosoft.com/Configuration/HR-Research
Id                      : FFO.extest.microsoft.com/Microsoft Exchange Hosted
                          Organizations         onmicrosoft.com/Configuration/HR-Research
ExchangeVersion         : 0.20 (15.0.0.0)
Name                    : HR-Research
DistinguishedName       : CN=HR-Research,CN=Configuration,CN=        onmicrosoft.com,OU=Microsoft Exchange Hosted
                          Organizations,DC=FFO,DC=extest,DC=microsoft,DC=com
ObjectCategory          :
ObjectClass             : {msExchUnifiedPolicy}
WhenChanged             : 7/25/2019 12:44:31 AM
WhenCreated             : 7/25/2019 12:44:31 AM
WhenChangedUTC          : 7/25/2019 5:44:31 AM
WhenCreatedUTC          : 7/25/2019 5:44:31 AM
ExchangeObjectId        : 0dae728c-72c0-4a54-926e-ef1500dcb3d9
OrganizationId          : FFO.extest.microsoft.com/Microsoft Exchange Hosted Organizations,        .onmicrosoft.com
                          FFO.extest.microsoft.com/Microsoft Exchange Hosted
                          Organizations        onmicrosoft.com/Configuration
Guid                    : 0dae728c-72c0-4a54-926e-ef1500dcb3d9
OriginatingServer       :
IsValid                 : True
ObjectState             : New
```

With those two cmdlets we now have two Information Barriers ready to be used. Let's verify that we can see these in our tenant:

```
Get-InformationBarrierPolicy | Ft Name,Guid
```

```
PS C:\> Get-InformationBarrierPolicy | ft name,guid


Name          Guid
----          ----
Research-HR   4809c4b8-e60d-4ffe-a7eb-d52254aa193f
HR-Research   0dae728c-72c0-4a54-926e-ef1500dcb3d9
```

Once we are sure that all of our settings are good and that all of the barriers we want to create are done, we can change the state of all of our policies to active like so: (Using the GUID's from above):

```
Set-InformationBarrierPolicy -Identity 4809c4b8-e60d-4ffe-a7eb-d52254aa193f -State Active
Set-InformationBarrierPolicy -Identity 0dae728c-72c0-4a54-926e-ef1500dcb3d9 -State Active
```

`** Note **` Make sure the use the GUIDs like the example above, otherwise piping Get-InformationBarrier to Set-InformationBarrier will fail.

```
PS C:\> Set-InformationBarrierPolicy -Identity 4809c4b8-e60d-4ffe-a7eb-d52254aa193f -State Active
WARNING: Your changes will take into affect after you run Start-InformationBarrierPoliciesApplication cmdlet.
Start-InformationBarrierPoliciesApplication cmdlet only applies Active state policies.
PS C:\> Set-InformationBarrierPolicy -Identity 0dae728c-72c0-4a54-926e-ef1500dcb3d9 -State Active
WARNING: Your changes will take into affect after you run Start-InformationBarrierPoliciesApplication cmdlet.
Start-InformationBarrierPoliciesApplication cmdlet only applies Active state policies.
```

To finalize the process we have one last cmdlet that needs to be run. This cmdlet will kick off the process where accounts will be segmented off:

Start-InformationBarrierPoliciesApplication

```
PS C:\> Start-InformationBarrierPoliciesApplication
WARNING: It may take several hours for the application to finish. Please check the status using
Get-InformationBarrierPoliciesApplicationStatus cmdlet. Execution of New/Set cmdlets will be prevented until start/stop
 is finished.


RunspaceId               : 2e07d4cf-d7a4-4d5c-b3e5-3b2902cddc6e
Identity                 : 5ea0bd1f-29ab-4c36-8300-7f7d0745ba55
CreatedBy                : Damian Scoles
CancelledBy              :
Type                     : ExoApplyIBPolicyJob
ApplicationCreationTime  : 07/25/2019 05:48:56
ApplicationEndTime       :
ApplicationStartTime     : 07/25/2019 05:48:56
TotalBatches             : 0
ProcessedBatches         : 0
PercentProgress          : 0
TotalRecipients          : 0
SuccessfulRecipients     : 0
FailedRecipients         : 0
FailureCategory          : None
Status                   : NotStarted
IsValid                  : True
ObjectState              : Unchanged
```

Microsoft notes that this process does take time to touch each user. The process itself takes up to 30 minutes to start and can process up to 5,000 users an hour. For larger organizations this could mean up to and past a 24 hour delay before all Information Barrier policies are applied.

If we want to validate the progress of the Application, we get use 'Get-InformationBarrierPoliciesApplicationStatus' to do so:

```
RunspaceId               : 2e07d4cf-d7a4-4d5c-b3e5-3b2902cddc6e
Identity                 : 5ea0bd1f-29ab-4c36-8300-7f7d0745ba55
CreatedBy                : Damian Scoles
CancelledBy              :
Type                     : ExoApplyIBPolicyJob
ApplicationCreationTime  : 07/25/2019 05:48:56
ApplicationEndTime       :
ApplicationStartTime     : 07/25/2019 05:48:56
TotalBatches             : 0
ProcessedBatches         : 0
PercentProgress          : 0
TotalRecipients          : 0
SuccessfulRecipients     : 0
FailedRecipients         : 0
FailureCategory          : None
Status                   : NotStarted
IsValid                  : True
ObjectState              : Unchanged
```

Real World Experience

In our scenario we walked through with PowerShell in the past few pages, we have multiple users assigned a barrier policy, two Organization Segments defined and policies that block communication between the two. How can we validate the settings work, outside of PowerShell? Well, we can have the users log into their Teams clients and see what communications are allowed or blocked.

For the first test, we have a user in one segment who is trying to IM a user in the other segment, however, we get this message from either user that tries to IM the other in their Teams client:

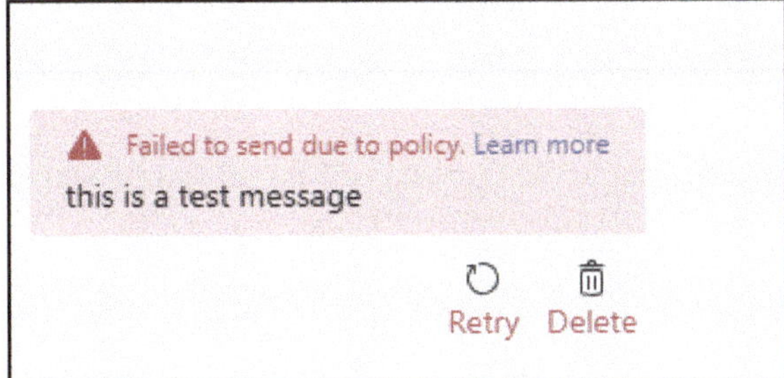

If we have an existing conversation with a user that is in the same segment, then we try to add another user in another segment, we are blocked from doing so:

Last option to try is to add a user, in a different segment, to a Team to collaborate with. However, as we should know, this will fail:

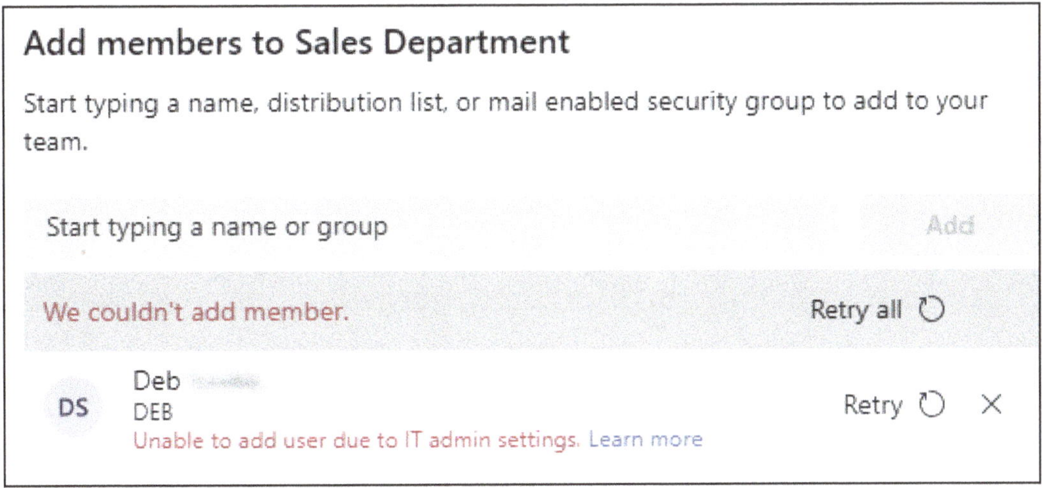

Caveats to Blocking

Information Barriers are not perfect or even complete in their attempt to block communications between teammates or co-workers. Information Barriers are restricted to Teams only and only parts of Teams. We still have Exchange Online, OneDrive, SharePoint, etc that can be shared between people. In order to handle these workloads, we could set up alerts and DLP to monitor and/or restrict sharing of information.

Documenting Settings (Script)

Now that we have our Information Barriers in place and we have users segmented in Office 365, how do we know this is working? There are a series of 'Get' PowerShell cmdlets that have to deal with Organization Segments and Information Barriers. We will utilize these for our documentation.

PowerShell

Audit logs are great for post-change monitoring and reporting for management and IT security to keep an eye on the Information Barrier changes. We can again use them for compliance reasons. Beyond auditing we may need to confirm how the Information Barrier is configured and produce this as well as the actual audit report for compliance. When it comes to documenting the settings in Information Barriers, we need to think in terms of what it takes to configure the barrier, policies, segments and apply them to users. Since we have no other interface with which to check and document these settings, we'll just use PowerShell to do this for us.

Where to start?

For an overall status check on the Information Barrier feature in the Security and Compliance Center, we should run the 'Get-InformationBarrierPoliciesApplicationStatus' cmdlet in order to validate that the Barrier Application has been started with the 'Start-InformationBarrierPoliciesApplication' cmdlet. If the 'Start-InformationBarrier-PoliciesApplication' cmdlet has not been run, we may run into errors when running this cmdlet:

```
Get-InformationBarrierPoliciesApplicationStatus
```

Typical errors when configuration has not begun:

```
PS C:\> Get-InformationBarrierPoliciesApplicationStatus
Your request failed to complete. Please retry. Error Details:
Microsoft.Exchange.Management.Tasks.IBNotEnabledForTenantException,Information Barrier feature was not enabled for the
tenant "        .onmicrosoft.com".
Status: ProtocolError
Status code: InternalServerError (500)
Status description: Internal Server Error
Response headers:
Pragma: no-cache
request-id: 5551f188-4160-4193-8c7c-64704d6c262b
X-CalculatedBETarget: mwhpr22mb0863.namprd22.prod.outlook.com
X-RUM-Validated: 1
X-UserType: Business
x-ms-appId: 00000007-0000-0ff1-ce00-000000000000
X-Psws-ErrorCode: 840001
```

Because we may get this result, we need to accommodate for this possibility. The easiest way is to use a Try and Catch {} code block. If the cmdlet fails we can stop documenting because no configuration is probably available.

Code Sample:

```
$InfoBarrier = $False
Try {
   $Test = Get-InformationBarrierPoliciesApplicationStatus -ErrorAction STOP
} Catch {
   $InfoBarrier = $False
}
```

Notice that there is a variable called $InfoBarrier which is set to true at the start of the block. This is set to true because we assume the configuration is in place. If, however, the cmdlet fails, triggering the STOP and then running the code in the Catch section, the variable is then set to False. This means no configuration is running and we can skip checking settings. If however, the $InfoBarrier variable is still true, we can proceed to the next section of code.

In order to properly document the findings, we will need some sort of output file that will be used by the script. We can define the output file in a variable block in the code like so:

```
# VARIABLES
$Path = (Get-Item -Path ".\" -Verbose).FullName
$File = "InformationBarrierDocumentation.Txt"
$Destination = $Path+"\"+$File
```

With the above lines, we tell PowerShell to get the current path, combine it with a predefined file name which together will become the destination file path for the script to export its findings to. Sample destination:

D:\Scripts\SCC\InformationBarrier\InformationBarrierDocumentation.Txt

Now that we have this we can move on to documenting. In the next block, we'll begin by writing to the documentation file with a description line (Line 1), a separator line (Line 2) and a blank line for formatting (Line 3). Following this we'll run the Get-InformationBarrierPoliciesApplicationStatus in its default format-list format. The code is here:

```
$Line = 'Information Barrier Policy Application Status' | Out-File $Destination -Append
$Line = '-------------------------------------------------' | Out-File $Destination -Append
$Line = ' ' | Out-File $Destination -Append
$Line = Get-InformationBarrierPoliciesApplicationStatus | Out-File $Destination -Append
$Line = ' ' | Out-File $Destination -Append
```

The output from these lines of code will look something like this:

```
Information Barrier Policy Application Status
-------------------------------------------------


RunspaceId              : b9aab4f8-b6de-4188-8bd5-52d7a5c9da88
Identity                : 5ea0bd1f-29ab-4c36-8300-7f7d0745ba55
CreatedBy               : Damian Scoles
CancelledBy             :
Type                    : ExoApplyIBPolicyJob
ApplicationCreationTime : 07/25/2019 05:48:56
ApplicationEndTime      : 07/25/2019 05:54:46
ApplicationStartTime    : 07/25/2019 05:48:56
TotalBatches            : 1
ProcessedBatches        : 1
PercentProgress         : 100
TotalRecipients         : 512
SuccessfulRecipients    : 512
FailedRecipients        : 0
FailureCategory         : None
Status                  : Completed
IsValid                 : True
ObjectState             : Unchanged
```

Now that we have the application documented, we can now pull information on each Information Barrier Policy. For consistency, we'll use a similar block of code, with a descriptive line, a line of '-' for separation and a blank line for formatting. Then, we'll use 'Get-InformationBarrierPolicy ' cmdlet, which by default will produce output in a list format, which may not be as useful for a summary table. For this cmdlet, we'll look at that output, pick which fields we want and then run a one-liner that will produce a table of values per policy:

```
$Line = 'Information Barrier Policies' | Out-File $Destination -Append
$Line = '-----------------------------' | Out-File $Destination -Append
$Line = ' ' | Out-File $Destination -Append
$Line = Get-InformationBarrierPolicy | ft Name, Type, AssignedSegment, SegmentsAllowed,
SegmentsBlocked, SegmentsAllowedFilter, BlockVisibility, BlockCommunication, State, CreatedBy,
CreationTimeUTC | Out-File $Destination -Append
```

The output from this code block is as follows:

```
Information Barrier Policies
----------------------------

Name        Type               AssignedSegment SegmentsAllowed SegmentsBlocked SegmentsAllowedFilter BlockVisibility BlockCommunication State  CreatedBy      CreationTimeUtc
----        ----               --------------- --------------- --------------- --------------------- --------------- ------------------ -----  ---------      ---------------
Research-HR InformationBarrier Research        {}              {HR}                                  True            True               Active Damian Scoles 7/25/2019 5:42:25 AM
HR-Research InformationBarrier HR              {}              {Research}                            True            True               Active Damian Scoles 7/25/2019 5:44:32 AM
```

The above is a concise summary table of our barrier policies. Some fields are necessarily empty because there is nothing in them. However, if the information were added later, we would have columns ready to populate. In a larger, more complex environment this would cover the cross segment filter that could occur.

Next in the list items to document are the Organization Segments. It's one of the cmdlets / sections that does not specifically mention that it is a part of Information Barriers. Similar to the other cmdlets, Get-OrganizationSegment also outputs in a list format. As such, we will pick some relevant fields and then use a table format to export the results of the cmdlet to the $Destination file. Also, same formatting before as the other two code blocks for consistency:

```
$Line = ' ' | Out-File $Destination -Append
$Line = 'Organization Segment(s)' | Out-File $Destination -Append
$Line = '-----------------------------' | Out-File $Destination -Append
$Line = Get-OrganizationSegment | Ft Name, Type, UserGroupFilter, ObjectClass, CreatedBy | Out-File
$Destination -Append
```

Output from the script looks like this:

```
Organization Segment(s)
----------------------------

Name     Type                 UserGroupFilter          ObjectClass             CreatedBy
----     ----                 ---------------          -----------             ---------
Research OrganizationSegment  Department -eq 'Research' {msExchUnifiedPolicy}   Damian Scoles
HR       OrganizationSegment  Department -eq 'HR'       {msExchUnifiedPolicy}   Damian Scoles
```

What about users in your tenant? How do we check the users to see if they are getting the policy applied? This turns out to be possible, if a bit harder when it comes to actually creating a report for the users. First, we need our description and formatting for the $Destination file, following the same format as all other sections:

```
$Line = ' ' | Out-File $Destination -Append
$Line = 'Information Barrier Recipient Status' | Out-File $Destination -Append
$Line = '------------------------------------' | Out-File $Destination -Append
```

Next, we'll need to set some variables for this section of code. The first will be a variable to store information about all of the Organization Segments. The next two of will be arrays (with the '@()') which will be used to store more complex information:

```
$OrgSegments = Get-OrganizationSegment
$AllOrgFilters = @()
$AllRecipients = @()
```

Next, we will go through each Organization Segment and store just the User Group Filter property of each Organization Segment. This will allow us to search for users with this criteria. We will use the '$UseOrgFilters' array that we defined above.

```
Foreach ($OrgSegment in $OrgSegments) {
    $OrgFilter = $OrgSegment.UserGroupFilter
    $AllOrgFilters += $OrgFilter
}
```

Next, we will add a line to our output line to help identify the columns that will present in the output that is generated from the user queries:

```
$Line = "Segment,Alias,Department,DisplayName,ExOPolicyID,IsValid" | Out-File $Destination -Append
```

Next, we will loop through each Organization Segment, which we will use to pull information from which will be used to find users:

```
Foreach ($OrgFilter in $AllOrgFilters) {
```

Simple, single attribute filter:

```
UserGroupFilter        : Department -eq 'Research'
```

The above is the easiest to deal with and the easiest to code for. However, what if there were two attributes:

```
UserGroupFilter        : Department -eq 'Research' -and PostalCode -eq '60606'
```

Harder to deal with, because now we have more than one set of criteria. If the filter gets more complete though, we would need to code some sort of logic to handle that. Now, there is a caveat to doing this work. You may not be able to cover all scenarios. The code below is a sample code, for you, the reader, to use as a base for building more complex scripts. So let's take the UserGroupFilter and see what we can do handle a more complex filter.

First, we will take the filter above with the '-and' in it. We can use this as our basis to begin building. Now when we run the script and we are working with the filter, it is stored in the $OrgFilter (from the previous Foreach loop beginning). Let's use the example where $OrgFilter = "Department -eq 'Research' -and PostalCode -eq '60606'". First, we need to split this into two values. Typically in PowerShell we would use a couple of options for this, a '-Split' parameter or we could use the '.split' function of the variable itself. So let's do that first:

```
$OrgFilterValues = $Orgfilter -split ' -and '
```

Notice the trailing and preceding spaces in the split string. We do this to remove all spaces that are not needed. Now we have these values:

```
PS C:\> $TestSplit[0]
Department -eq 'Research'

PS C:\> $TestSplit[1]
PostalCode -eq '60606'
```

Next, we need to loop through each of the Org Filters we have stored in the $OrgFilterValues variable:

```
Foreach ($OrgFilterValue in $OrgFilterValues) {
```

First, we'll remove all of the spaces that are present to prevent any mismatches later:

```
$SplitOrgFilterValues = $OrgFilterValue.Split(' ')
```

Within this loop we can now pull out the three criteria needed for finding users that are to be involved in Information Barriers. These criteria are Attribute, Operator and the Value to be found:

Attribute - what user attribute we are looking to match   *[The script defines this in the $Attribute variable]*
Operator - are we looking for an equal or not equal operator *[The script defines this in the $Operator variable]*
Value - what we are looking for in the attribute   *[The script defines this in the $Value variable]*

Then we will store the three items in separate variables:

```
$Attribute = $SplitOrgFilterValues[0]
$Operator = $SplitOrgFilterValues[1]
$Value = $SplitOrgFilterValues[2] -replace ("""","""")
```

To make this script more efficient, we will implement a function to handle each name query in the script. The reason we are using a function is that this will be a good-sized repeatable set of code. By doing so we can eliminate duplicating code sections and keep the number of code lines down making the script smaller and more efficient. Let's review what variables or values we need for the names query.

Since we are using a function, we will want to pass these variables to the function. Let's first decide on a function name. When we name it, we should name it something that is recognizable. For this exercise, let's use 'GetNames' for our function name. So in order to pass the variables, we need a line like so:

```
GetNames $Attribute $Operator $Value
```

We are passing these in order, just to make it easy on ourselves. It is NOT required for the first example, but would be for the second Function example. Now, the function will need to know how to handle it. So we have a couple of choices, both will work:

```
Function GetNames ($Attribute,$Operator,$Value) {


}
```

Alternatively, we can use a different method to perform the same task:

```
Function GetNames {

    Param(
      [parameter(position=0)]
      $Attribute,
      [parameter(position=1)]
      $Operator,
      [parameter(position=2)]
      $Value
    )


}
```

For our code sample we will use the first option as it requires fewer lines of code:

```
Function GetNames ($Attribute,$Operator,$Value ) {
```

Next we will define our variables; this one will be used for a Try and Catch later for error handling in case a query fails:

```
# Variables
$NamesQuery = $True
```

Next we search for users with the 'Get-User' cmdlet. We pull all three parameters into this. On the outside we have two If statements, one for if the $Operator is '-eq' and the other if the $Operator is '-ne'. Then inside the If statement, we perform a Try and Catch on the Get-Name filter using the $Attribute, operator and $Value parameters pulled in from the function. If the query is successful, all names are stored in the $Names variable. If it fails, the $NamesQuery variable is changed to $False.

```
# Operator Check
If ($Operator -eq '-eq') {
  Try {
    $Names = (Get-User -ErrorAction STOP | where {$_.($Attribute) -eq $Value}).DisplayName
  } Catch {
    $NamesQuery = $False
  }
}
If ($Operator -eq '-ne') {
  Try {
    $Names = (Get-User -ErrorAction STOP | where {$_.($Attribute) -ne $Value}).DisplayName
  } Catch {
    $NamesQuery = $False
  }
}
```

Now that we have a list of names we can prepare them for output to a chart. First we check the $NamesQuery variable. If it is set to $False, we skip this loop as we have no users to work with. If, however, the $NamesQuery variable is still $True, this means that we have a list of users to work with.

```
If ($NamesQuery) {
```

Assuming we were able to query names in the environment, we now need to loop through the $Names variable with a Foreach loop:

```
Foreach ($Name in $Names) {
```

First, we pull the Information Policy of the user and store it in a $RecipientStatus variable:

```
$RecipientStatus = Get-InformationBarrierRecipientStatus $Name | select Alias, $Attribute, DisplayName, ExoPolicyID, IsValid
```

Next we retrieve the ExOPolicyID value for the Policy. This requires some manipulation as the value has details we don't need. The value we need is at the end of a string of values, separated by '/' characters. We can use '.Split' to get this:

```
$ExOPolicyIDTemp = ($RecipientStatus).ExoPolicyID
$ExOPolicyID = $ExOPolicyIDTemp.split('/')[1]
```

With the ExoPolicyID, we can pull the AssignedSegment value:

```
$Segment = (Get-InformationBarrierPolicy -ExoPolicyId $ExOPolicyID).AssignedSegment
```

Now we grab information on the recipient - Alias, Department, Display Name and if it is valid:

```
$Alias = $RecipientStatus.Alias
$Department = $RecipientStatus.Department
$DisplayName = $RecipientStatus.DisplayName
$IsValid = $RecipientStatus.IsValid
```

Now we take this information, place it into one row and use 'Out-File' to export the data to a file:

```
# Export results:
$Line    =    "$Segment,$Alias,$Department,$DisplayName,$ExOPolicyID,$IsValid"    |    Out-File $Destination -Append
```

Output from this section looks like this:

```
Information Barrier Recipient Status
---------------------------------------------
Segment,Alias,Department,DisplayName,ExOPolicyID,IsValid
Research,Damian,Research,Damian Scoles,69a9440c-4e3d-492d-8c48-d85297146576,True
Research,John,Research,John Smith,69a9440c-4e3d-492d-8c48-d85297146576,True
HR,Dave,HR,Dave Stork,1b4679d1-3abd-4ae7-8d7d-e86731222a45,True
HR,Alson,HR,Alison Beck,1b4679d1-3abd-4ae7-8d7d-e86731222a45,True
```

From the above Text file, we have the basics about each user now, with the important information 'IsValid'.

11   Threats & Mail Flow

In This Chapter

Introduction
Threat Management
Mail Flow

Introduction

There are no specific PowerShell cmdlets for the Threat Management section of the Security and Compliance Center. This feature is revealed purely in the web page for the SCC. As such, we will briefly review what we can discern from the website, but we will not dive too deep as we cannot access it via PowerShell. If any cmdlets are added for the features, we'll add them to a future edition of the book.

Now, the Threat Management portion of the SCC consists of many pieces. Some of these features require an E5 and some also rely on Office 365 Advanced Threat Protection (ATP) Plan 1 or 2. So be aware that your tenant may not have these features exposed if you do not have the correct licensing.

Quick Summary of Threat Management:

Dashboard - Provides a quick overview of the Threat Management feature in the SCC.
Investigations - Brand new feature added to the SCC and is in Preview as of now. Will be an automated feature to help you with well-known threats.
Explorer - An ATP feature that allows you to investigate and respond to threats.
Submissions - Allows tenant admin to submit suspicious items (email, URL or file) for Microsoft to analyze.
Attack Simulator - Customer can simulate Phish Attacks, Brute Force and Password Spray attacks.
Review - Reporting center for Incidents, Quarantines, Restricted Users and other trends.
Policy - Configuring ATP -Phish, Safe Attachments, Safe Links, Anti-Spam/Malware and DKIM .
Threat Tracker - Let's an admin explore some well known attack campaigns as well as self-submitted ones.

Mail Flow and the Security and Compliance Center

This portion of the SCC provides a review of the current Mail Flow in your tenant as well as access to a new Message Trace tool that is in contrast to the one in Exchange Online. Similar to the Threat Management feature, Mail Flow provides a dashboard to help the administrator quickly assess some facts and findings for email flowing through their tenant. This section of the SCC has recently changed so we will go over the new look.

Threat Management

Dashboard

Our first exposure to Threat Management is the Dashboard. The Dashboard provides what you would expect from a Dashboard - a quick view of important issues relating to threats. We have information on Investigations, ATP threat prevention, Malware Trends, Global views and more. It is a good place to start and content here should be reviewed often for your Office 365 tenant. Add this page to your daily checklist for reviewing your tenant:

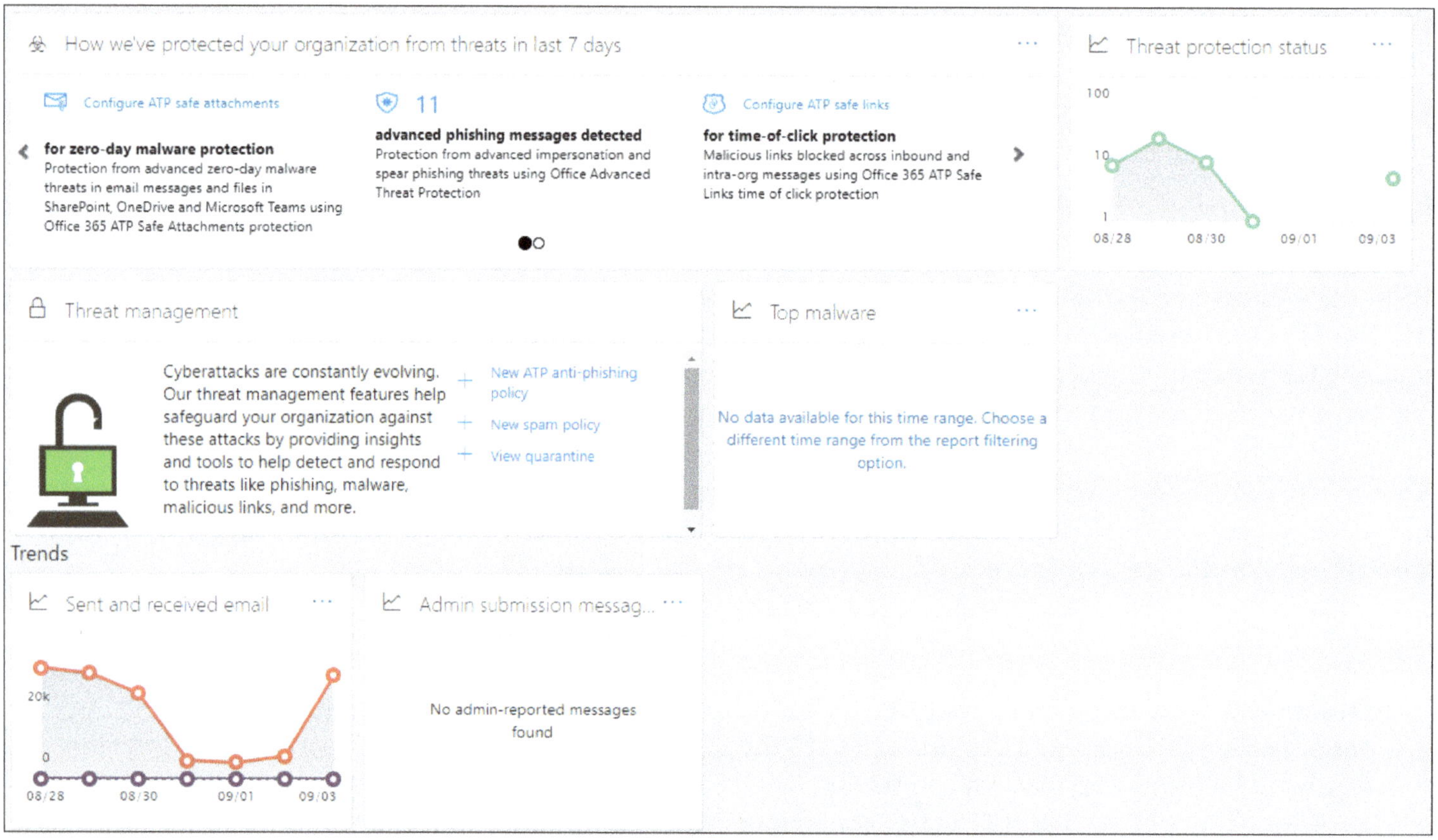

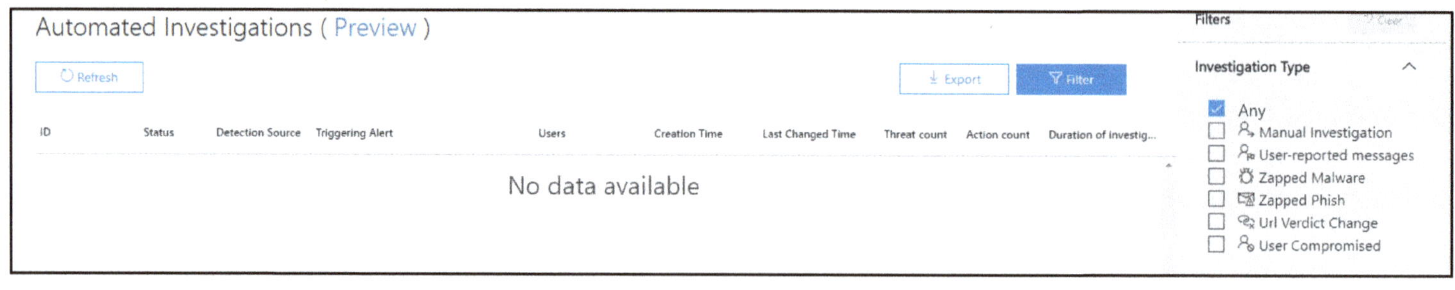

Investigations

This is a new feature that appeared recently in the SCC as of the writing of this book. The feature is in Preview and there isn't a lot of information about it on Microsoft Docs at the moment either. Look for an update in future editions of the book.

Explorer

The Explorer part of Threat Management is like a mini-dashboard where an administrator can explore items that relate to email - Malware, Phishing, self-submitted Items, all email issues as well as Malware Content (outside of email). There are options to make new Submissions for Microsoft to review as well as exporting any of the reports to CSV files.

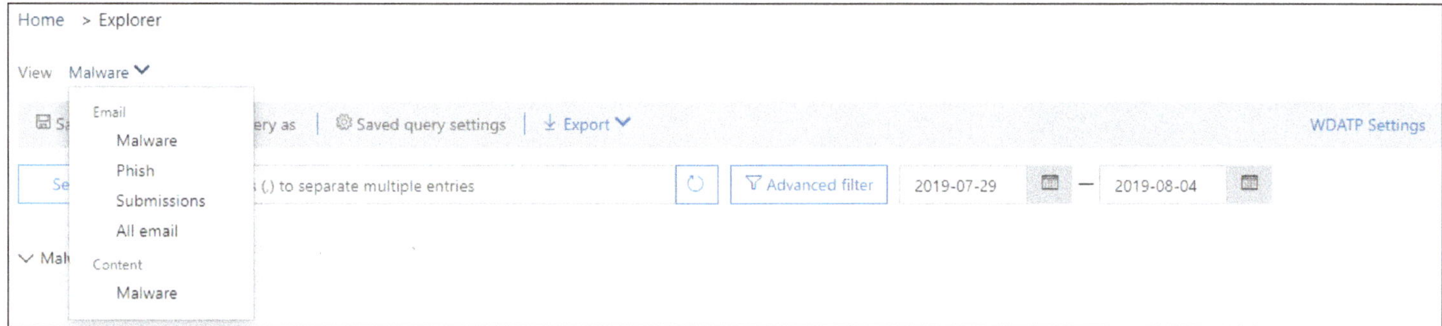

There are a plethora of filtering options as well to help an admin narrow down the source or target of these email/content issues. We also have configuration settings for Windows Defender ATP Connections settings:

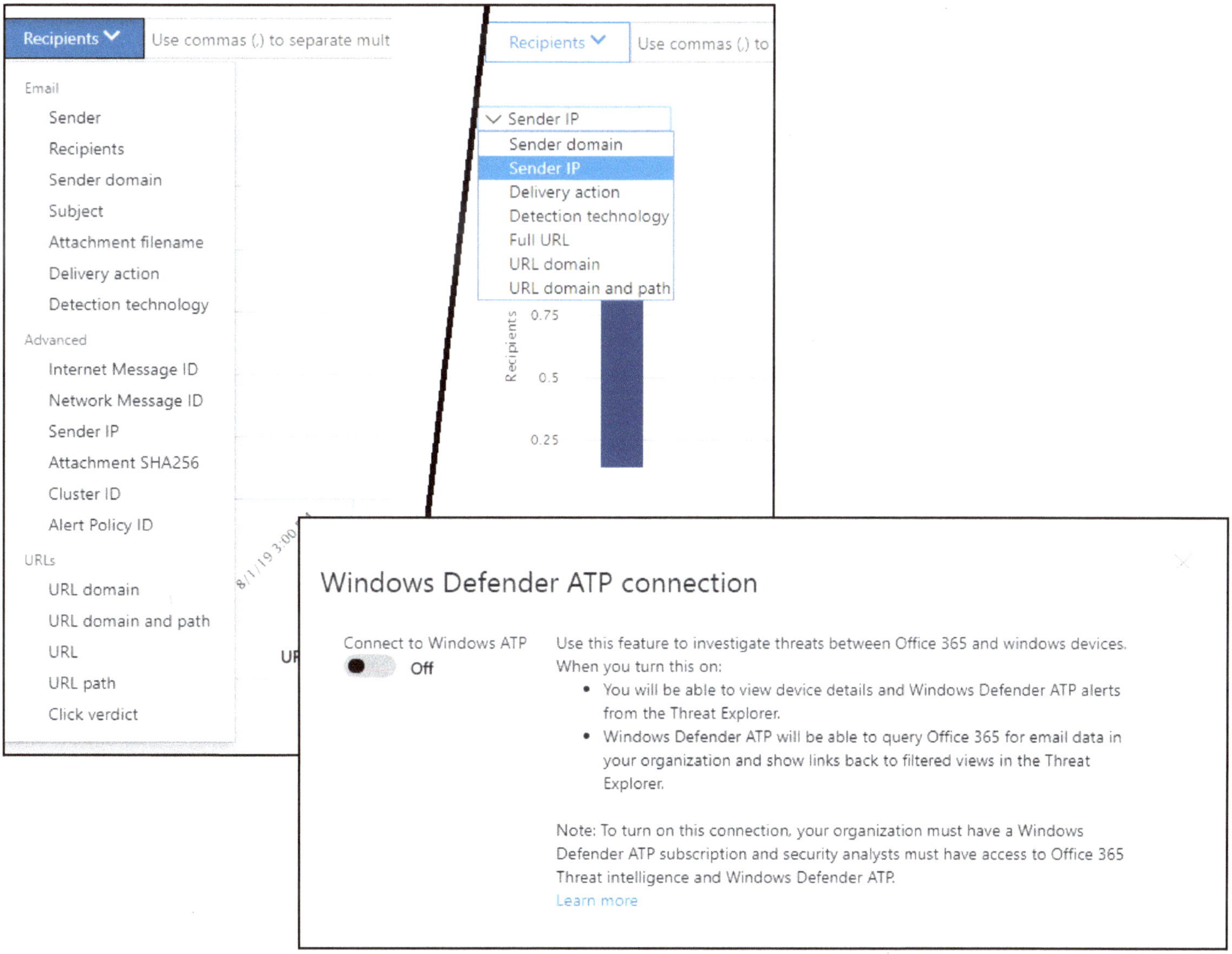

Submissions

Submissions is intended for admins to report issues they have found or are experiencing in order to help Microsoft keep up with any email, URL or content related issues they are experiencing. We can see this new interface is an option under Threat Management as well:

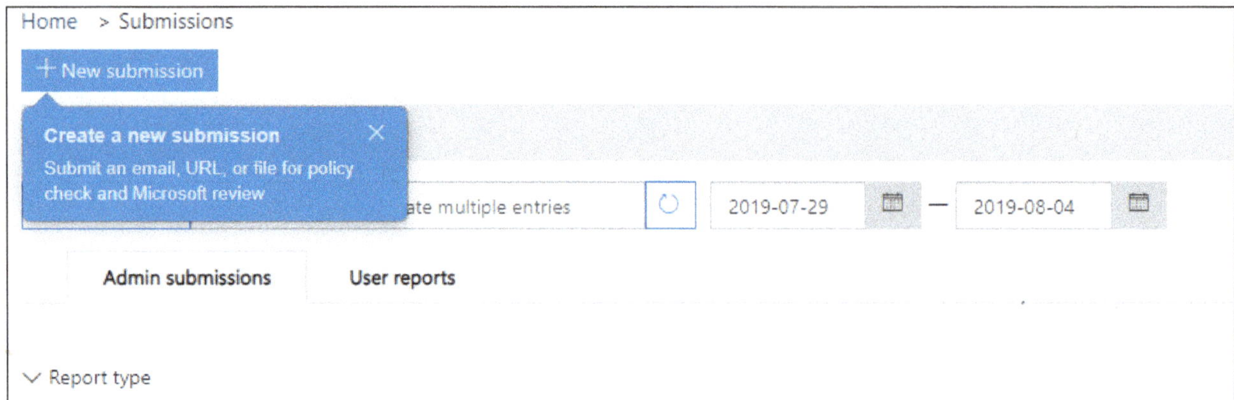

Creating a new submission here is as simple as clicking on the button, choosing the type [Email, URL or Attachment], supplying the information required for a particular submission and then click Save.

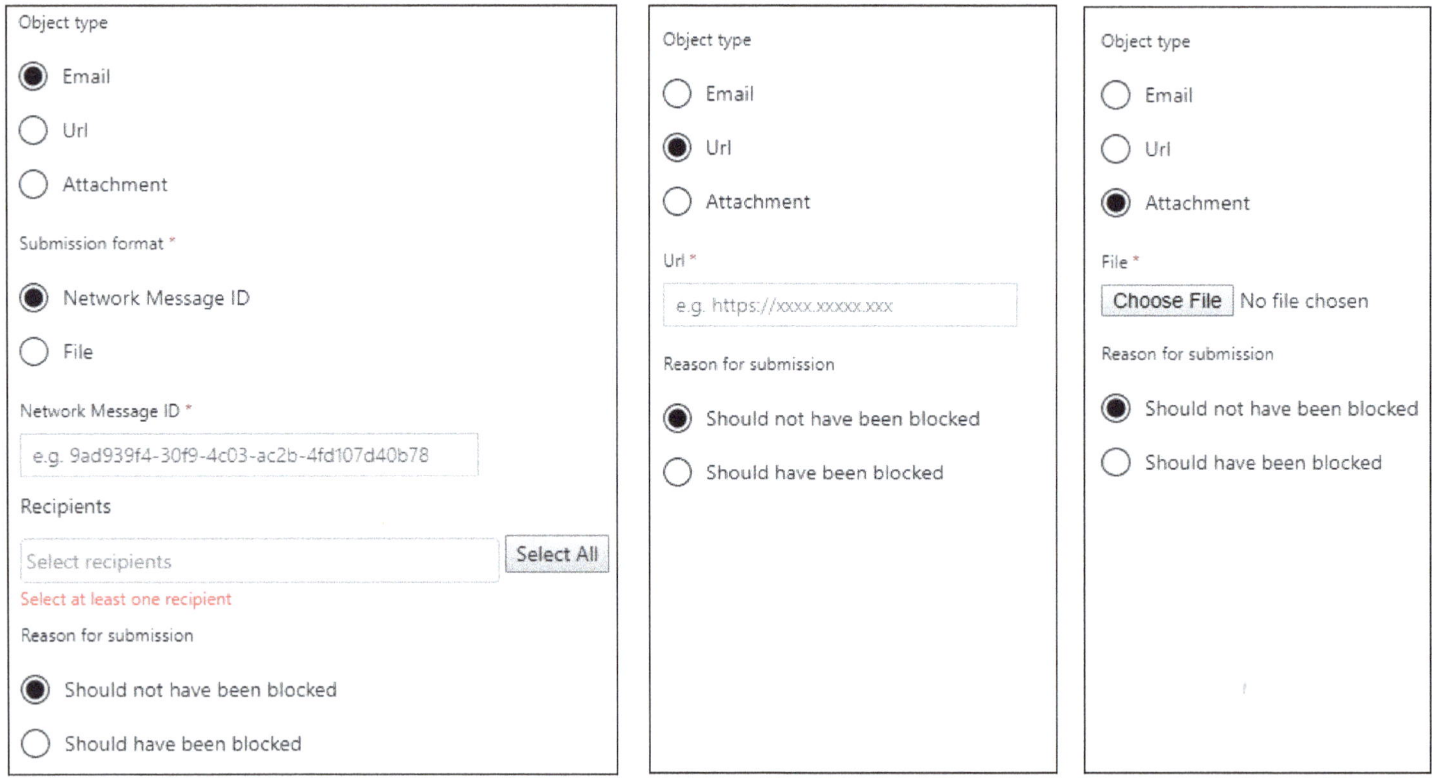

After a submissions is made, it can be tracked on this same page and they can be exported post submission.

Attack Simulator

Attack Simulator is a place where Microsoft provides a tenant with tools with which to perform some penetration tests like Phishing, Brute Force Password and Password Spray attack. These can be initiated straight from this section as seen on the next page:

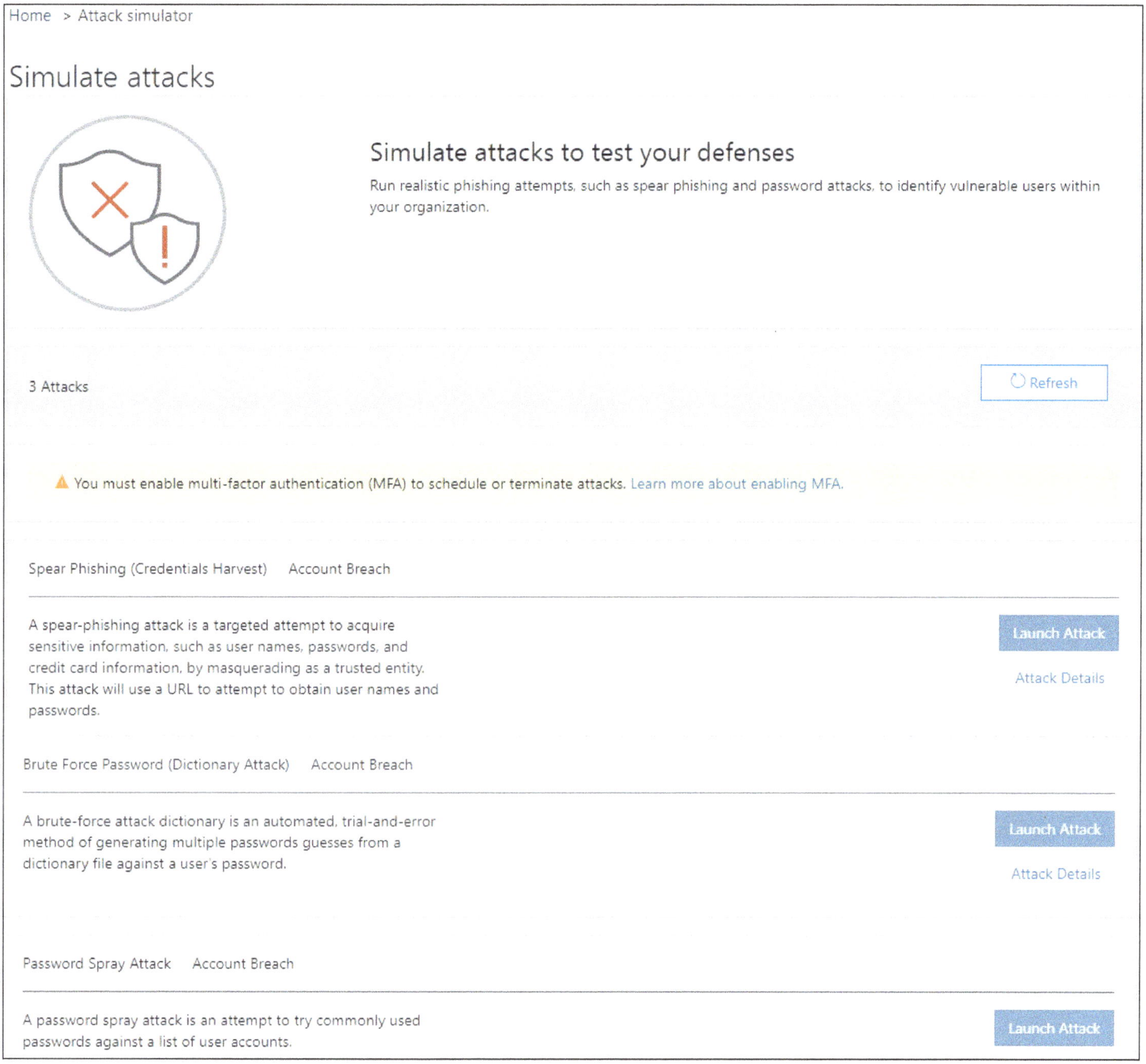

Home > Attack simulator
Simulate attacks
Simulate attacks to test your defenses
Run realistic phishing attempts, such as spear phishing and password attacks, to identify vulnerable users within your organization.
3 Attacks
Refresh
You must enable multi-factor authentication (MFA) to schedule or terminate attacks. Learn more about enabling MFA.
Spear Phishing (Credentials Harvest)
Account Breach
A spear-phishing attack is a targeted attempt to acquire sensitive information, such as user names, passwords, and credit card information, by masquerading as a trusted entity. This attack will use a URL to attempt to obtain user names and passwords.
Launch Attack
Attack Details
Brute Force Password (Dictionary Attack)
Account Breach
A brute-force attack dictionary is an automated, trial-and-error method of generating multiple passwords guesses from a dictionary file against a user's password.
Launch Attack
Attack Details
Password Spray Attack
Account Breach
A password spray attack is an attempt to try commonly used passwords against a list of user accounts.
Launch Attack

Each of the three attack simulations is well described above. Make sure to have MFA enabled as well:

You must enable multi-factor authentication (MFA) to schedule or terminate attacks. Learn more about enabling MFA.

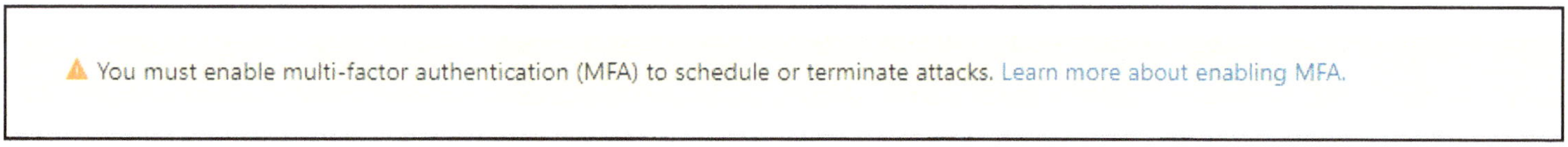

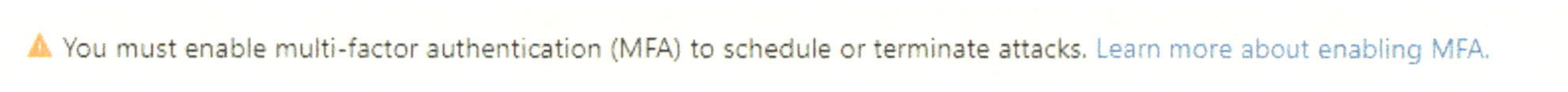

Review

This is another dashboard-like page that is focused on Incidents, Quarantine, blocked users, and some trends like Malware, your submissions and user-reported messages.

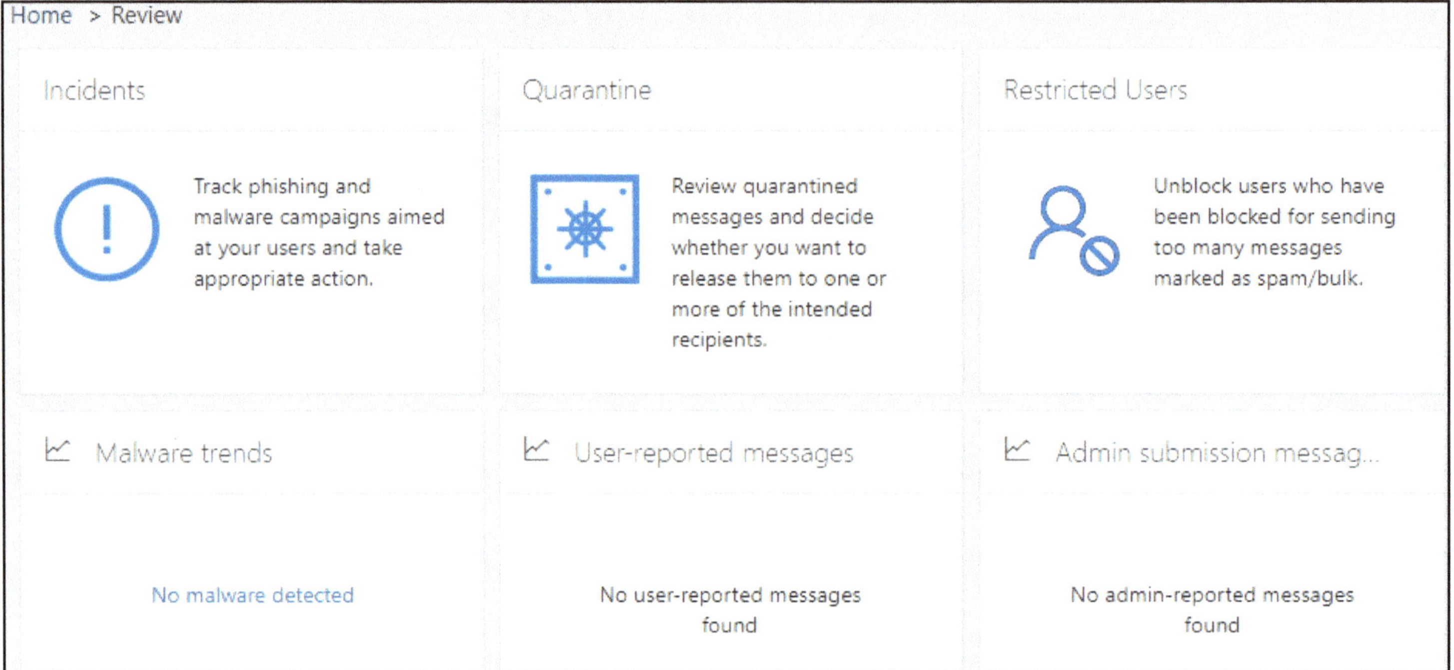

Policy

Policy is where we can configure ATP features - Anti-Phishing, Safe Attachments, SafeLinks, Ant-Spam, DKIM and Anti-Malware.

Threat Tracker

Lastly we have the Threat Tracker tab. Here is where we can see malware campaigns Microsoft is tracking and their potential impact as well as queries we perform and any trending campaigns.

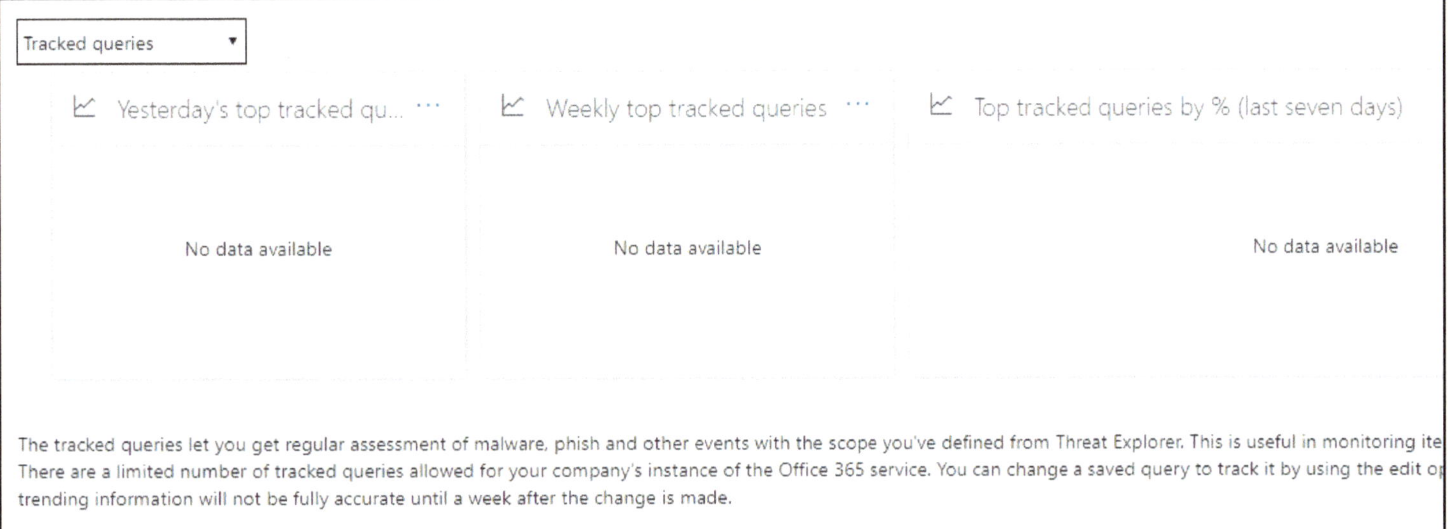

Mail Flow

Within the Security and Compliance Center, many improvements have been made to the interface for the Mail Flow section. However, there are no real cmdlets for the Mail Flow feature in the SCC. So for this section of the book we will briefly look at the Mail Flow page for the SCC. Mail Flow is essentially another dashboard for the Security and Compliance Center that highlight Mail Flow stats, top domains and even alerts for your Mail Flow:

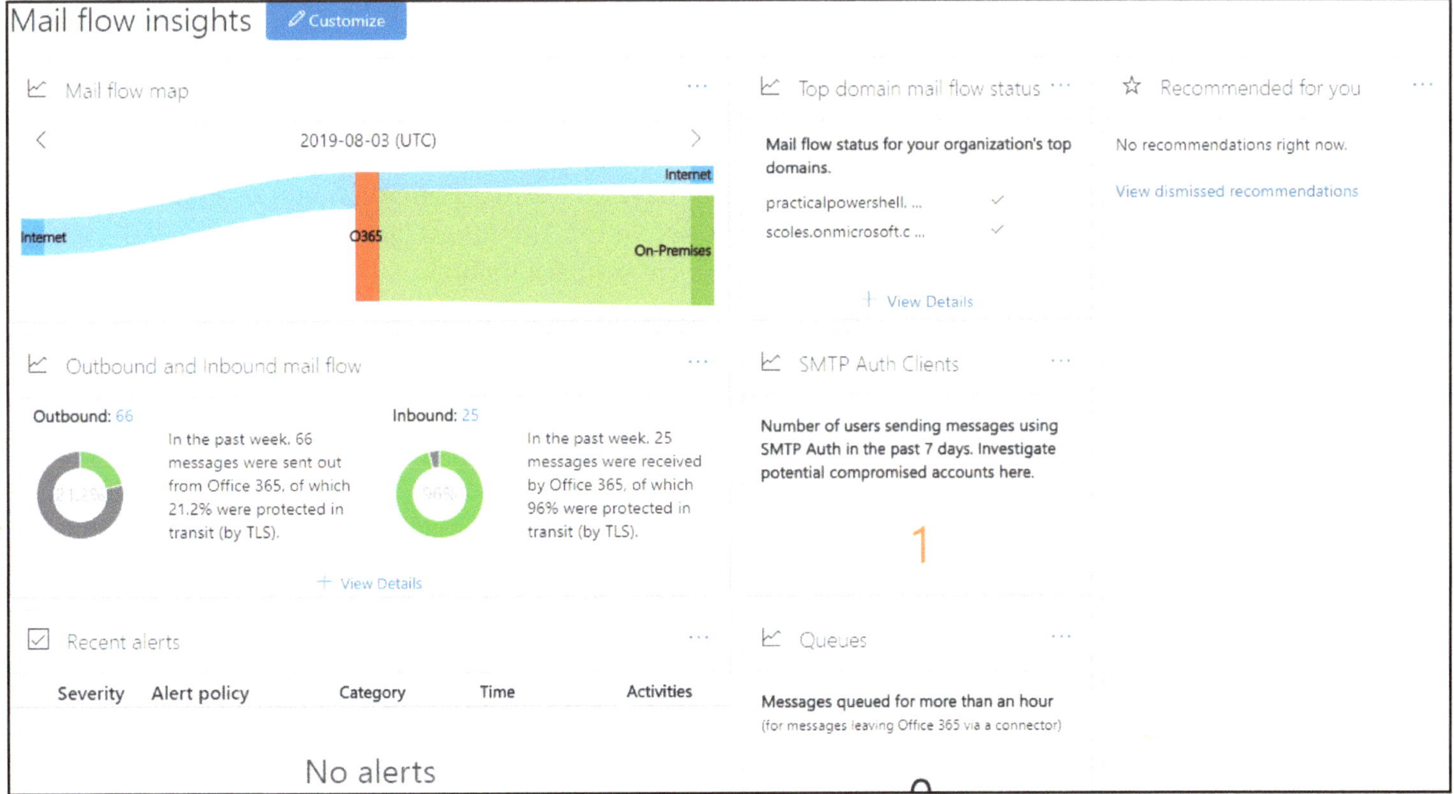

Mail Flow Map

The Mail Flow Map is interactive and we can get further details by clicking it and setting the pull-down to 'Detail':

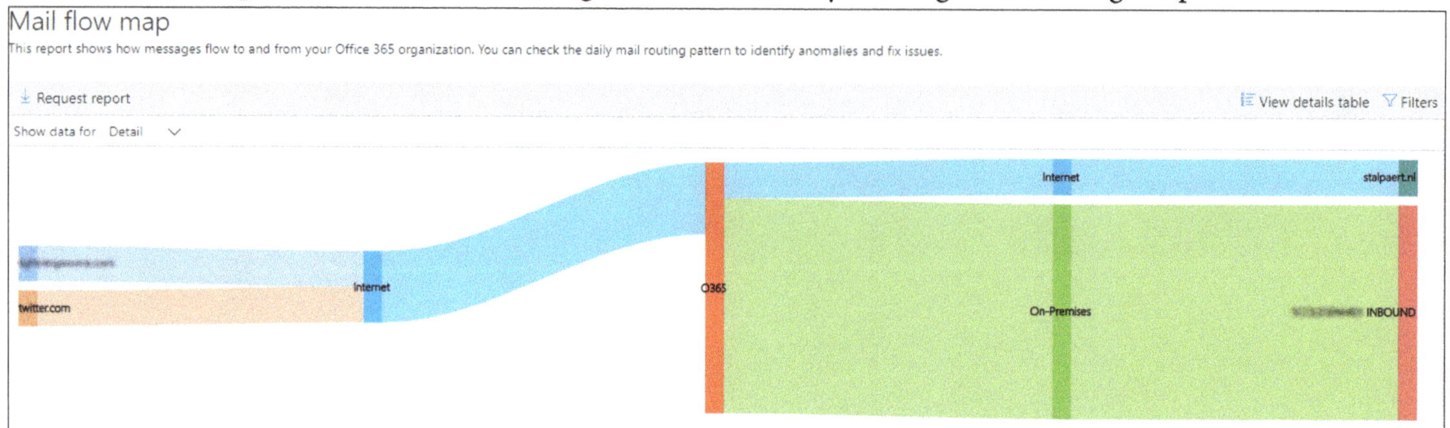

Detailed Mail Flow Map information:

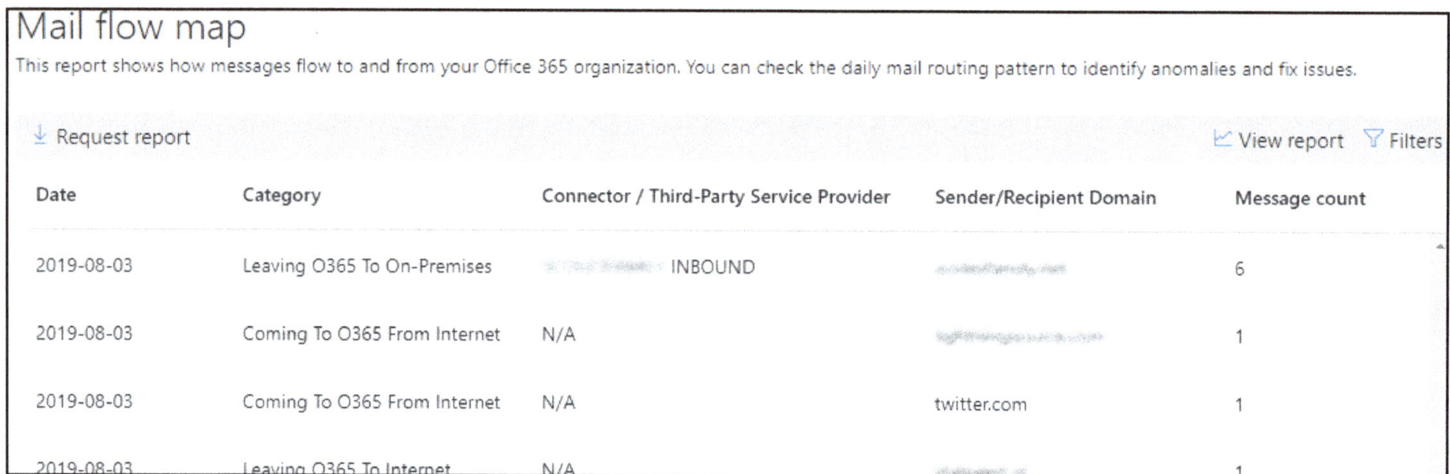

Mail flow map

This report shows how messages flow to and from your Office 365 organization. You can check the daily mail routing pattern to identify anomalies and fix issues.

Date	Category	Connector / Third-Party Service Provider	Sender/Recipient Domain	Message count
2019-08-03	Leaving O365 To On-Premises	INBOUND		6
2019-08-03	Coming To O365 From Internet	N/A		1
2019-08-03	Coming To O365 From Internet	N/A	twitter.com	1
2019-08-03	Leaving O365 To Internet	N/A		1

Message Traces

Instead of performing a message trace in Exchange, we now have access to a similar amount of functionality. We do have some default, pre-built queries that Microsoft provides for us. The advantage of this is that we do not need access to the Exchange Online Admin page, but we can perform similar functions with the Mail Flow Admin role, within the Security and Compliance Center.

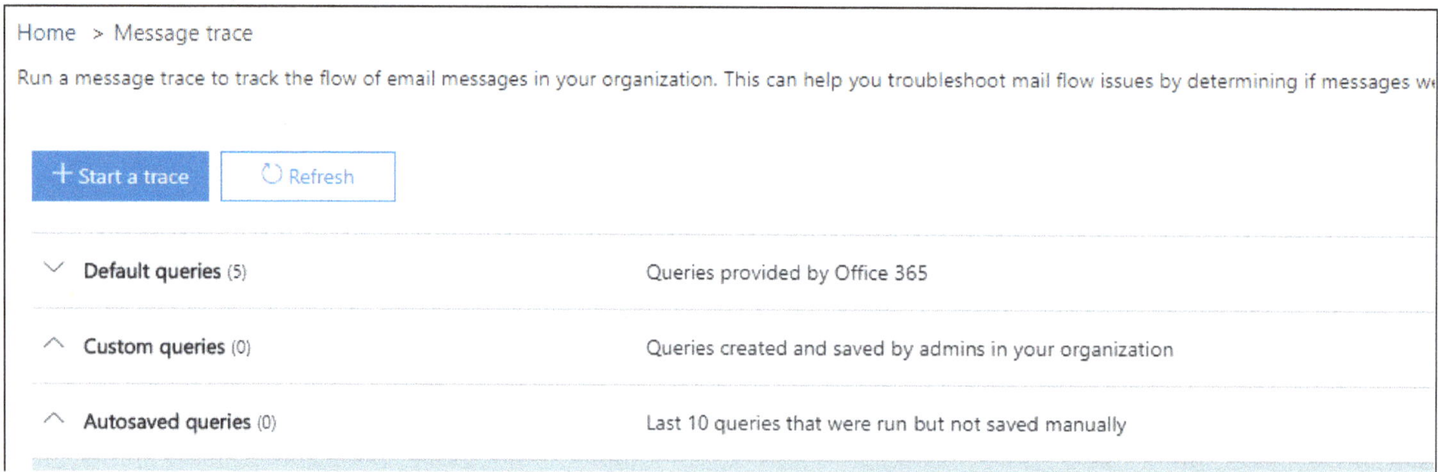

We can also create our own custom queries and save them as well as download reports for completed or pending ones. To create a new Query, we click on Start a Trace and we get this window below:

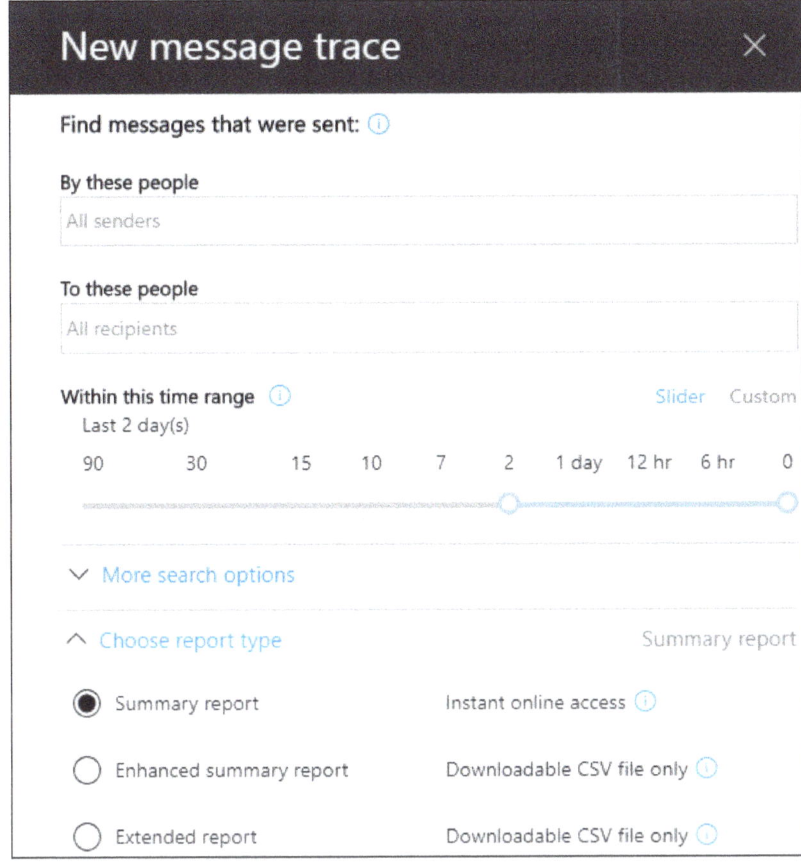

We have quite a few options to choose from - To and from, as well as what time range the messages appeared in and then we can also choose a report type for the query.

However, certain output will be restricted to reports that are not available instantly:

We can choose a few options for the reports, like delivered, quarantined and failed which could help in trouble-shooting where an email went to. If no messages are found, we get this:

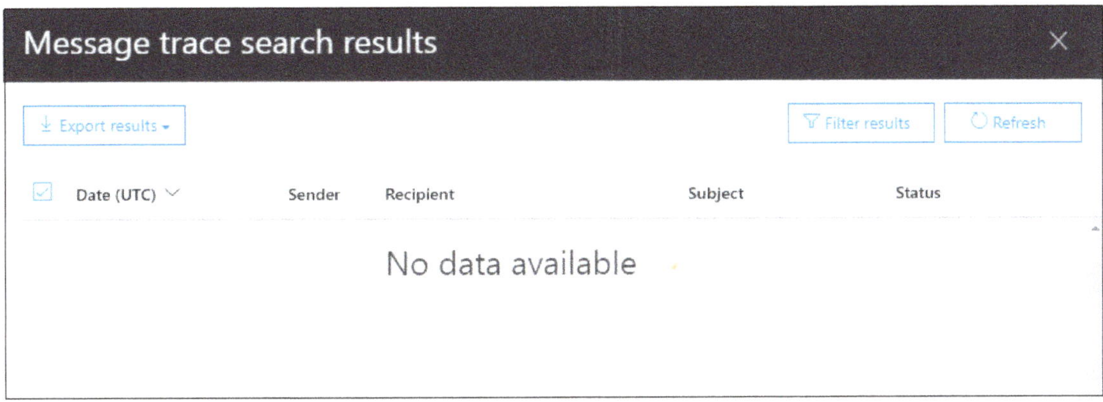

Once a query is created, it appears in your search results like so:

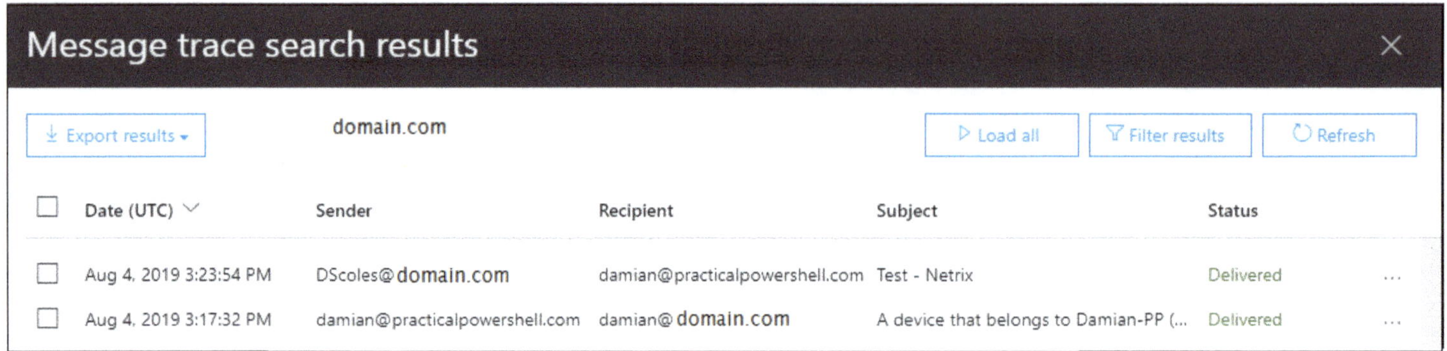

We can then export these results to a CSV file for later analysis:

```
MessageTraceSearchResult_2019-08-04T15_58_27.csv - Notepad
File   Edit   Format   View   Help
Received,SenderAddress,RecipientAddress,Subject,Status
2019-08-04T15:23:54.5135008Z,DScoles@domain.com,damian@practicalpowershell.com,Test -        Delivered
2019-08-04T15:17:32.3339979Z,damian@practicalpowershell.com,damian@domain.com,A device that belongs to
```

That's it in a nutshell for the Mail Flow portion of the Security and Compliance Center.

12 Device Management

In This Chapter

Introduction
Security and Compliance Center PowerShell
- Tenant Policy and Rule
- Device Conditional Access
- Device Configuration

Introduction

There are many options for device management and control in the world of cloud and on-premises services. Microsoft itself provides us with two different levels of this - 'free' Mobile Device Management (MDM) which is part of some licensing of Office 365 and Intune. Intune is a corporate solution for enterprise mobile device management for Office 365. Intune requires additional licensing for its increased functionality.

The PowerShell cmdlets that we will cover in this chapter are not Intune-related and are for the general MDM solution that Microsoft Provides. This is because Intune is separate from the SCC and out of scope for this book. These cmdlets are run from the Security and Compliance Center, but they work hand-in-hand to manage device access to data in Office 365.

Mobile Device Management is included in these Licenses for Office 365:

- Office 365 Business Essentials
- Office 365 Business Premium
- SharePoint 1
- SharePoint 2
- Office 365 Enterprise E1
- Office 365 Enterprise E3
- Office 365 Enterprise F1

Where can we find Device Management in the Security and Compliance Center?

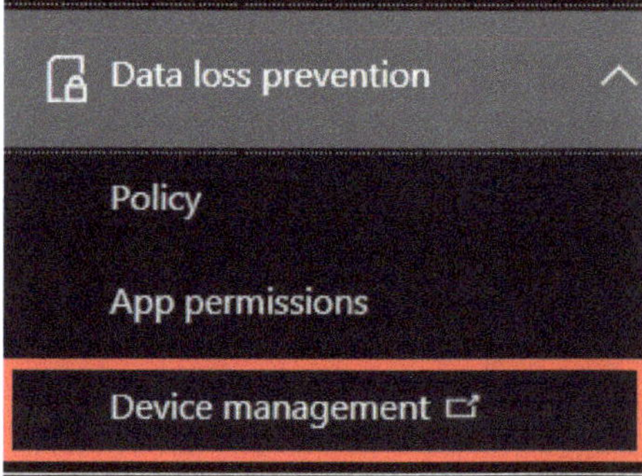

If we click on this link, it will take you to an Office 365 admin page link - https://portal.office.com/adminportal/home#/MifoDevices - which looks like this:

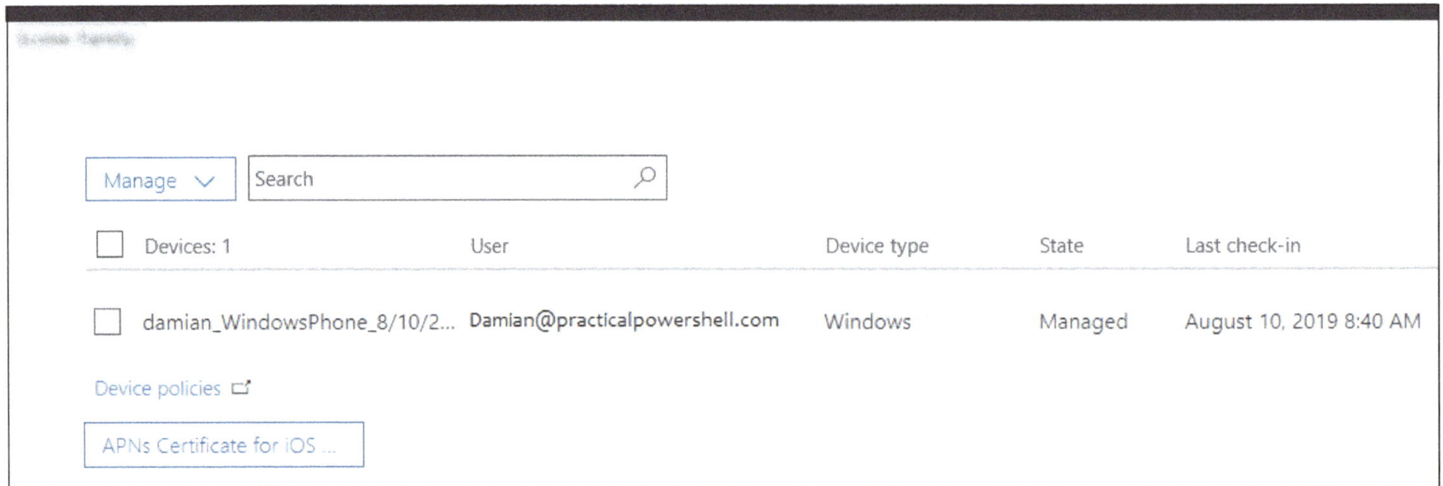

If you have any enrolled devices, they should appear here now. Because these devices are connecting to Exchange Online, some of our Device Management may need to be performed in Exchange Online.

Connecting to Exchange Online

Use the information in the link below to connect to Exchange Online:

https://docs.microsoft.com/en-us/powershell/exchange/exchange-online/connect-to-exchange-online-power-shell/connect-to-exchange-online-powershell?view=exchange-ps

Once connected, we find we have these cmdlets to manage Mobile Devices in Exchange Online:

```
Clear-MobileDevice
Get-MobileDevice
Get-MobileDeviceDashboardSummaryReport
Get-MobileDeviceMailboxPolicy
Get-MobileDeviceStatistics
New-MobileDeviceMailboxPolicy
Remove-MobileDevice
Remove-MobileDeviceMailboxPolicy
Set-MobileDeviceMailboxPolicy
```

Most of these cmdlets should prove useful for our MDM experience for devices connecting to Exchange Online. First we can list all devices in Exchange Online with 'Get-MobileDevice':

```
PS C:\> get-mobiledevice | ft FriendlyName,First*,DeviceType

FriendlyName FirstSyncTime         DeviceType
------------ -------------         ----------
Lumia 929    8/4/2019 9:04:57 PM   WP8
HTC T7575    8/4/2019 3:17:25 PM   WP
Lumia 929    11/18/2017 2:13:18 PM WP8
```

From a management perspective, only the WP8 devices will be manageable or supported from this list. The official list as of the writing of this book:

- Windows Phone 8.1+
- iOS 7.1 or later versions
- Android 4 or later versions
- Windows 8.1
- Windows 8.1 RT
- Windows 10
- Windows 10 Mobile

We can review any Mobile Device Mailbox Policies:

```
AllowNonProvisionableDevices            : True
AlphanumericPasswordRequired            : False
AttachmentsEnabled                      : True
DeviceEncryptionEnabled                 : False
RequireStorageCardEncryption            : False
PasswordEnabled                         : False
PasswordRecoveryEnabled                 : False
DevicePolicyRefreshInterval             : Unlimited
AllowSimplePassword                     : True
MaxAttachmentSize                       : Unlimited
WSSAccessEnabled                        : True
UNCAccessEnabled                        : True
MinPasswordLength                       :
MaxInactivityTimeLock                   : Unlimited
MaxPasswordFailedAttempts               : Unlimited
PasswordExpiration                      : Unlimited
PasswordHistory                         : 0
IsDefault                               : True
AllowApplePushNotifications             : True
AllowMicrosoftPushNotifications         : True
AllowGooglePushNotifications            : True
AllowStorageCard                        : True
```

Device Statistics for your phones (Get-MobileDeviceStatistics):

```
FirstSyncTime                   : 8/4/2019 9:04:57 PM
LastPolicyUpdateTime            : 8/4/2019 9:07:23 PM
LastSyncAttemptTime             : 8/10/2019 1:53:24 PM
LastSuccessSync                 : 8/10/2019 1:53:24 PM
DeviceType                      : WP8
DeviceID                        : 859D5F8274FD397B2C8D2469996464E6
DeviceUserAgent                 : MSFT-WIN-4/10.0.14393
DeviceWipeSentTime              :
DeviceWipeRequestTime           :
DeviceWipeAckTime               :
AccountOnlyDeviceWipeSentTime   :
AccountOnlyDeviceWipeRequestTime :
AccountOnlyDeviceWipeAckTime    :
LastPingHeartbeat               :
RecoveryPassword                : ********
DeviceModel                     : RM-927_nam_vzw_100
DeviceImei                      : 358331050954343
DeviceFriendlyName              : Lumia 929
```

If we want to wipe a device, we can use the Clear-MobileDevice cmdlet. A specified device will be cleared the next time it connects to Office 365. Clearing a device should be approached with caution. This is because, depending on the supported version of the device and the options you choose, a remote wipe will:

"clear all data on the mobile phone, including installed applications, photos, and personal information"

If you have a BYOD environment, this means you are wiping out personal data probably without permission of the user. Now, with the introduction of EAS 16.1 compliance devices, there is now support for an AccountOnly wipe:

"-AccountOnly
The AccountOnly switch specifies whether to perform an account-only remote device wipe where only Exchange mailbox data is removed from the device. You don't need to specify a value with this switch.
You don't need to use this switch for the DeviceType value Outlook, because an account-only remote devices wipe is the only type of wipe that's used on Outlook devices."

If your device is not an EAS 16.1 device, and this parameter is specified, an error should occur but the wipe will still succeed.

Further Reading

https://docs.microsoft.com/en-us/exchange/clients/exchange-activesync/remote-wipe?view=exchserver-2019
https://docs.microsoft.com/en-us/powershell/module/exchange/devices/clear-mobiledevice?view=exchange-ps
https://blogs.msdn.microsoft.com/exchangedev/2016/06/13/announcing-exchange-activesync-version-16-1/
https://docs.microsoft.com/en-us/openspecs/exchange_server_protocols/ms-oxprotlp/229f77ea-6518-4fe7-84fe-bd535fc6c32e

Security and Compliance Center PowerShell

Now that we've reviewed some of the background details and the interconnection to Exchange Online, let's start working with PowerShell in the Security and Compliance Center. Since the included MDM solution is pretty basic, we also find that available PowerShell cmdlets are limited as well.

What cmdlets do we have available to us in the SCC?

Get-DeviceComplianceDetailsReport	Get-DevicePolicy	Remove-DeviceConfigurationPolicy
Get-DeviceComplianceDetailsReportFilter	Get-DeviceTenantPolicy	Remove-DeviceConfigurationRule
Get-DeviceCompliancePolicyInventory	Get-DeviceTenantRule	Remove-DeviceTenantPolicy
Get-DeviceComplianceReportDate	New-DeviceConditionalAccessPolicy	Remove-DeviceTenantRule
Get-DeviceComplianceSummaryReport	New-DeviceConditionalAccessRule	Set-DeviceConditionalAccessPolicy
Get-DeviceComplianceUserInventory	New-DeviceConfigurationPolicy	Set-DeviceConditionalAccessRule
Get-DeviceComplianceUserReport	New-DeviceConfigurationRule	Set-DeviceConfigurationPolicy
Get-DeviceConditionalAccessPolicy	New-DeviceTenantPolicy	Set-DeviceConfigurationRule
Get-DeviceConditionalAccessRule	New-DeviceTenantRule	Set-DeviceTenantPolicy
Get-DeviceConfigurationPolicy	Remove-DeviceConditionalAccessPolicy	Set-DeviceTenantRule
Get-DeviceConfigurationRule	Remove-DeviceConditionalAccessRule	

Within the list above we can see cmdlet groups based on these nouns - Tenant, DeviceConfiguration, DeviceConditional, and DeviceCompliance. Let's begin by exploring Tenant settings for MDM in the SCC.

When reviewing the help for several of these cmdlets, you will notice this general guidance on all the way the cmdlets are structured:

```
DESCRIPTION
    These are the cmdlets that are used for mobile device management in the Security & Compliance Center:

    * DeviceTenantPolicy and DeviceTenantRule cmdlets: A policy that defines whether to block or allow mobile device
      access to Office 365 email by unsupported devices that use Exchange ActiveSync only. This setting applies to all
      users in your organization. Both allow and block scenarios allow reporting for unsupported devices, and you can
      specify exceptions to the policy based on security groups.
    * DeviceConditionalAccessPolicy and DeviceConditionalAccessRule cmdlets: Policies that control mobile device
      access to Office 365 for supported devices. These policies are applied to security groups. Unsupported devices
      are not allowed to enroll in mobile device management.
    * DeviceConfigurationPolicy and DeviceConfigurationRule cmdlets: Policies that control mobile device settings for
      supported devices. These policies are applied to security groups.
    * Get-DevicePolicy: Returns all mobile device management policies regardless of type (DeviceTenantPolicy,
      DeviceConditionalAccessPolicy or DeviceConfigurationPolicy).
    You need to be assigned permissions in the Office 365 Security & Compliance Center before you can use this cmdlet.
    For more information, see Permissions in Office 365 Security & Compliance Center
    (https://go.microsoft.com/fwlink/p/?LinkId=511920).
```

Tenant Policy and Rule

In your Office 365 tenant, there is an overriding Device Policy and Device Rule that is configured by default (If Device Management has been enabled). There can only be one of each of these configured in your tenant at any point in time. We can manipulate, add and remove these tenant wide rules as there is a set of cmdlets dedicated to this function:

```
Get-DeviceTenantPolicy
Get-DeviceTenantRule
New-DeviceTenantPolicy
New-DeviceTenantRule
Remove-DeviceTenantPolicy
Remove-DeviceTenantRule
Set-DeviceTenantPolicy
Set-DeviceTenantRule
```

Let's review the default Tenant Policy and Rule which we can pull with two cmdlets and

```
Get-DeviceTenantRule
```

```
ApplyPolicyTo            :
BlockUnsupportedDevices : False
ExclusionList           : {1e0ab3be-c595-46f5-82a8-f5d49f703c22}
ReadOnly                : False
ExternalIdentity        :
ImmutableId             : 00000000-0000-0000-0000-000000000000
Priority                : 0
Workload                : Intune
Policy                  : 3fb9c5bd-3c47-4f6f-834e-e052a81aaa23
Comment                 :
Disabled                : False
Mode                    : Enforce
ObjectVersion           : 25a91404-3a37-4268-8d52-08d6694cab48
CreatedBy               : Damian Scoles
LastModifiedBy          : Damian Scoles
Guid                    : f126c3ea-2d8b-44ba-9c80-a83f2580c492
Identity                : FFO.extest.microsoft.com/Microsoft Exchange Hosted
                          Organizations,█████.onmicrosoft.com/Configuration/7577c5f3-05a4-4f55-a0a3-82aab5e98c84
Id                      : FFO.extest.microsoft.com/Microsoft Exchange Hosted
```

Get-DeviceTenantPolicy

```
Type                   : DeviceTenantConditionalAccess
Workload               : Intune
Priority               : 0
ObjectVersion          : 14e5e2c3-0fe1-4599-8204-08d6694ca399
CreatedBy              : Damian Scoles
LastModifiedBy         : Damian Scoles
ReadOnly               : False
ExternalIdentity       :
Comment                :
Enabled                : True
Mode                   : Enforce
DistributionStatus     : Success
DistributionResults    : {}
LastStatusUpdateTime   : 12/24/2018 3:05:50 AM
ModificationTimeUtc    : 12/24/2018 3:05:20 AM
CreationTimeUtc        : 12/24/2018 3:05:20 AM
Identity               : FFO.extest.microsoft.com/Microsoft Exchange Hosted
                         Organizations,        onmicrosoft.com/Configuration/a6958701-c82c-4064-ac11-64e40e7f4032
Id                     : FFO.extest.microsoft.com/Microsoft Exchange Hosted
                         Organizations,        onmicrosoft.com/Configuration/a6958701-c82c-4064-ac11-64e40e7f4032
```

Now that we had a look at the configuration, what can we do with the Tenant Policy / Rule? With the Policy, we have a few options, we can change a couple of settings, remove it and then create a new one. If we remove the Policy, we will also remove the Tenant wide Device Rule as well which is something to keep in mind.

If we do not have Mobile Device Management Enabled and we try to create a new Policy or run, we will receive an error:

```
PS C:\> New-DeviceTenantPolicy
You can't run this command without activating mobile device management.
    + CategoryInfo          : NotSpecified: (:) [New-DeviceTenantPolicy], ErrorDoNotAllowWithoutMDMException
    + FullyQualifiedErrorId : [Server=BN3NAM01WS007,RequestId=56612318-eae0-4e00-bf59-d6d5f1054651,TimeStamp=8/10/2019
    3:03:40 PM] [FailureCategory=Cmdlet-ErrorDoNotAllowWithoutMDMException] F2BEA025,Microsoft.Office.CompliancePolic
   y.Tasks.NewDeviceTenantPolicy
    + PSComputerName        : nam01b.ps.compliance.protection.outlook.com
```

Now, if we have an existing Device Tenant Policy / Rule configured and we try to add a new one, we also get an error message:

```
PS C:\> New-DeviceTenantPolicy
A compliance policy with name 'a6958701-c82c-4064-ac11-64e40e7f4032' already exists.
    + CategoryInfo          : NotSpecified: (:) [New-DeviceTenantPolicy], CompliancePolicyAlreadyExistsException
    + FullyQualifiedErrorId : [Server=BY2NAM05WS007,RequestId=458161c9-41e1-4db1-a58b-9f01638b071b,TimeStamp=8/10/2019
    3:09:03 PM] [FailureCategory=Cmdlet-CompliancePolicyAlreadyExistsException] B4B86872,Microsoft.Office.ComplianceP
   olicy.Tasks.NewDeviceTenantPolicy
    + PSComputerName        : nam05b.ps.compliance.protection.outlook.com
```

If we wish to remove and recreate the Rule/Policy combination, make sure to remove the Policy first as trying to remove the rule will generate a Dr. Watson error. Removing a Policy also removes the Rule:

```
PS C:\> Remove-DeviceTenantPolicy
Confirm
Are you sure you want to perform this action?
Removing Compliance Policy 'a6958701-c82c-4064-ac11-64e40e7f4032'.
[Y] Yes  [A] Yes to All  [N] No  [L] No to All  [?] Help (default is "Y"): y

PS C:\> Get-DeviceConfigurationPolicy
PS C:\> Get-DeviceConfigurationRule
PS C:\>
```

To recreate these, we simply need to run these two cmdlets in succession - New-DeviceTenantPolicy and New-DeviceTenantRule. No need to specify any parameters, they are not required.

Now, what about changing any settings on the Policy or the Rule. What can we change if anything?

Set-DeviceTenantPolicy - we can add a comment, disable the Policy or retry distribution. Adding comment is optional, disabling the policy would be useful for troubleshooting and retrying distribution should also only be used if the DistributionStatus property of the Policy is 'Error':

```
DistributionStatus    : Error
DistributionResults   : {[Intune]Policy 'a6958701-c82c-4064-ac11-64e40e7f4032':Policy cannot be deployed to the content
                        source due to a temporary Office 365 datacenter issue. The current policy is not applied to any
                        content in the source, so there's no impact from the blocked deployment. To fix this issue,
                        please try redeploying the policy., [Intune]Rule '7577c5f3-05a4-4f55-a0a3-82aab5e98c84':Policy
                        cannot be deployed to the content source due to a temporary Office 365 datacenter issue. The
                        current policy is not applied to any content in the source, so there's no impact from the
                        blocked deployment. To fix this issue, please try redeploying the policy.}
```

To attempt a fix for this error, try this one-liner:

    Set-DeviceTenantPolicy -RetryDistribution

This will place the DistributionStatus of your Policy into a Pending state as it retries. Adding a comment is a quick option we can put into place:

    Set-DeviceTenantPolicy -Comment 'Default Device Tenant Policy (BigCompany.Com)'

Not a lot to it. For a Device Tenant Rule, we can adjust a couple of settings:

BlockUnsupportedDevices: We can block certain devices from accessing the tenant.

ApplyPolicyTo: We can choose from three options on this parameter - ExchangeOnline, SharepointOnline and ExchangeAndSharepoint. This will scope your Device Tenant Rule to the specified workloads.

ExclusionList: Determines who will be excluded from the unsupported device blocking rule.

Device Conditional Access

Conditional Access is a concept used in Office 365 that basically means that certain conditions will need to be met before a device can connect. We will need to build Device Conditional Access Policy and Rule pairs. PowerShell cmdlets available for this configuration are as follows:

    Get-DeviceConditionalAccessPolicy
    Get-DeviceConditionalAccessRule
    New-DeviceConditionalAccessPolicy
    New-DeviceConditionalAccessRule
    Remove-DeviceConditionalAccessPolicy
    Remove-DeviceConditionalAccessRule
    Set-DeviceConditionalAccessPolicy
    Set-DeviceConditionalAccessRule

Let's see if we have any Policies or Rules to begin with. The answer is no:

```
PS C:\> Get-DeviceConditionalAccessPolicy
PS C:\> Get-DeviceConditionalAccessRule
PS C:\> _
```

Since we don't have any to start with, we can review the Get-Help for each cmdlet to see what is available:

Get-Help New-DeviceConditionalAccessPolicy -Examples

```
----------------------- Example 1 -----------------------

New-DeviceConditionalAccessPolicy -Identity "Human Resources"

This example creates a new mobile device conditional access policy named Human Resources
```

Get-Help New-DeviceConditionalAccessRule -Examples

```
----------------------- Example 1 -----------------------

New-DeviceConditionalAccessRule -Policy "Secure Email" -TargetGroups 5bff73eb-0ba7-461b-b7c9-9b4c173cc266

This example creates a new mobile device conditional access rule with the following settings:


Policy: Secure Email
TargetGroups:5bff73eb-0ba7-461b-b7c9-9b4c173cc266
```

For our first example, we will create a Policy and Rule that will target users in the Legal Department. Due to requirements in their department, they're not allowed to use Bluetooth due to security concerns and the App store will also be blocked due to the corporate software installation policy. How can we do this?

First, we need a Policy for our Device Conditional Access Rule to Reference:

New-DeviceConditionalAccessPolicy 'Legal Department Mobile Policy'

```
PS C:\> New-DeviceConditionalAccessPolicy 'Legal Department Mobile Policy'

RunspaceId              : 6b33566c-9fe1-461f-b698-47089aa4bef0
Type                    : DeviceConditionalAccess
Workload                : Intune
Priority                : 0
ObjectVersion           : 82dca5cd-96a7-4bcb-61b1-08d73d0b4be7
CreatedBy               : Damian Scoles
LastModifiedBy          : Damian Scoles
ReadOnly                : False
ExternalIdentity        :
```

Next, since we need to target the Legal Department, we need the GUID from the Azure AD group:

Get-Group Legal | Ft Name,GUID

```
Name    Guid
----    ----
Legal   8503291d-cf21-4de5-8719-17fb58e95285
```

Now that we have our group and its GUID, we can create the Rule:

New-DeviceConditionalAccessRule -Policy 'Legal Department Mobile Policy' -BluetoothEnabled $False
-AllowAppStore $False -TargetGroups 8503291d-cf21-4de5-8719-17fb58e95285

```
ParentPolicyId       : 1b2b427f-5d18-41d3-82ee-055c437772b7
Mode                 : Enforce
RuleBlob             : <rule name="Legal Department Mobile Policy{394b}" enabled="false"
                       id="bb45af2b-5562-4de2-913f-dddfe5dfb237"><version
                       requiredMinVersion="1.0.1.0"><condition><and><is property="isMemberOf" type="System.Guid"><value>
                       8503291d-cf21-4de5-8719-17fb58e95285</value></is><NameValuesPairConfiguration property="Device_Se
                       curity_CameraEnabled"><value>True</value></NameValuesPairConfiguration><NameValuesPairConfigurati
                       on property="Device_Security_BluetoothEnabled"><value>False</value></NameValuesPairConfiguration>
                       <NameValuesPairConfiguration property="Device_Restrictions_AllowVoiceDialing"><value>True</value>
                       </NameValuesPairConfiguration><NameValuesPairConfiguration property="Device_Restrictions_AllowVoi
                       ceAssistant"><value>True</value></NameValuesPairConfiguration><NameValuesPairConfiguration proper
                       ty="Device_Restrictions_AllowAssistantWhileLocked"><value>True</value></NameValuesPairConfigurati
                       on><NameValuesPairConfiguration property="Device_Restrictions_AllowPassbookWhileLocked"><value>Tr
                       ue</value></NameValuesPairConfiguration><NameValuesPairConfiguration property="Device_Password_Al
```

In the future if the requirements for our Device Conditional Access Rule change, we can use the Set cmdlet to handle any changes. For example, if we now need to set a value for the 'MaxPasswordAttemptsBeforeWipe' property to 20. This way if someone is trying to break into a device, they can only enter so many codes before it wipes the device. First, the name of the Rule:

Get-DeviceConditionalAccessRule | Ft Name,GUID, TargetGroups

```
Name                               Guid                                    TargetGroups
----                               ----                                    ------------
Legal Department Mobile Policy{394b} f8c8bb1f-2e22-4eac-a437-1d749041a74e  {8503291d-cf21-4de5-8719-17fb58e95285}
```

** **Note** ** When using the SET cmdlet, we also need to reiterate the TargetGroups parameter again, hence the cmdlet above. Also note the '{394b}' in the name, this is added by the Microsoft.

Set-DeviceConditionalAccessRule 'Legal Department Mobile Policy{394b}'
-MaxPasswordAttemptsBeforeWipe 20 -TargetGroups 8503291d-cf21-4de5-8719-17fb58e95285

```
PS C:\> Get-DeviceConditionalAccessRule | Ft Name,Max*

Name                               MaxPasswordAttemptsBeforeWipe MaxPasswordGracePeriod
----                               ----------------------------- ----------------------
Legal Department Mobile Policy{394b}                          20
```

At some future date, we can also lift the restrictions entirely with the Remove cmdlets:

Get-DeviceConditionalAccessRule | Ft name,GUID

```
Name                               Guid
----                               ----
Legal Department Mobile Policy{394b}  f8c8bb1f-2e22-4eac-a437-1d749041a74e
```

Once we have the GUID of the Rule we can then delete it.

Remove-DeviceConditionalAccessRule -Identity f8c8bb1f-2e22-4eac-a437-1d749041a74e

```
Confirm
Are you sure you want to perform this action?
Removing Device Conditional Access Rule 'f8c8bb1f-2e22-4eac-a437-1d749041a74e'.
[Y] Yes  [A] Yes to All  [N] No  [L] No to All  [?] Help (default is "Y"): y
```

Next, we need the GUID of the Policy to remove:

    Get-DeviceConditionalAccessPolicy | Ft Name,GUID

```
Name                             Guid
----                             ----
Legal Department Mobile Policy·  1b2b427f-5d18-41d3-82ee-055c437772b7
```

    Remove-DeviceConditionalAccessPolicy -Identity 1b2b427f-5d18-41d3-82ee-055c437772b7

```
Confirm
Are you sure you want to perform this action?
Removing Compliance Policy '1b2b427f-5d18-41d3-82ee-055c437772b7'.
[Y] Yes  [A] Yes to All  [N] No  [L] No to All  [?] Help (default is "Y"): y
```

Device Configuration

Next we have Device Configuration Policies and Rules. Device Configuration Policies and Rules are used to configure Mobile Devices to fit a particular configuration or Corporate policy. The settings here are not meant to control device access to Office 365 like the Conditional Access ones from the previous section. We can use Device Configuration cmdlets to configure devices to a standard spec and we can target these to groups in Office 365 which allows for a more customizable configuration for your users. This way if the IT department wants to lock down devices more with a certain configuration, they can do so while opening up the configuration to users hat are at the C-Level in a corporate environment. What PowerShell cmdlets do we have access to?

PowerShell

Get-DeviceConfigurationPolicy	Remove-DeviceConfigurationPolicy
Get-DeviceConfigurationRule	Remove-DeviceConfigurationRule
New-DeviceConfigurationPolicy	Set-DeviceConfigurationPolicy
New-DeviceConfigurationRule	Set-DeviceConfigurationRule

Just like Conditional Access Policies and Rules, we have no existing or default ones to work with in a new and untouched tenant:

    Get-DeviceConfigurationPolicy
    Get-DeviceConfigurationRule

```
PS C:\> Get-DeviceConfigurationPolicy
PS C:\> Get-DeviceConfigurationRule
PS C:\>
```

Let's start off by looking at examples from each cmdlet to see what we can do with these cmdlets:

    Get-Help New-DeviceConfigurationPolicy -Examples

```
-------------------------- Example 1 --------------------------

New-DeviceConfigurationPolicy -Name "Engineering Group"

This example creates a new mobile device configuration policy named Engineering Group.
```

Get-Help New-DeviceConfigurationRule -Examples

```
------------------------- Example 1 -------------------------

New-DeviceConfigurationRule -Policy "Engineering Group" -TargetGroups 5bff73eb-0ba7-461b-b7c9-9b4c173cc266

This example creates a new mobile device configuration rule with the following settings:


Policy: Engineering Group
TargetGroups:5bff73eb-0ba7-461b-b7c9-9b4c173cc266
```

We can see from the above examples that the Device Configuration cmdlets are structured similarly to the Device Conditional Access. As such, we will start with the Policy cmdlet and then associate the Policy with a Rule.

New-DeviceConfigurationPolicy and New-DeviceConfigurationRule

For our first example the IT group has mandated some settings that must apply to all of their users. First we will create the base policy for the IT Group:

New-DeviceConfigurationPolicy -Name 'IT Mobile Device Configuration'

Then get the GUID of the IT Group:

Get-Group IT | Ft Name,GUID

```
PS C:\> Get-Group IT | Ft Name,GUID


Name Guid
---- ----
IT   7ffbd4b4-ad91-44eb-a735-86ee5809f311
```

Lastly, we will apply a restrictive policy with these settings:

New-DeviceConfigurationRule -Policy 'IT Mobile Device Configuration' -MaxPasswordGracePeriod 00.01:00:00 -PasswordMinimumLength 8 -PasswordHistoryCount 6 -MaxPasswordAttemptsBeforeWipe 20 -PasswordExpirationDays 182 -PasswordMinComplexChars 4 -PasswordRequired $True -AutoUpdateStatus NeverCheckUpdates -PasswordQuality 2 -TargetGroups 7ffbd4b4-ad91-44eb-a735-86ee5809f311

For the next example, we will create a slightly less restrictive Policy for our company's executives in order for them to use other features. However, we will change a couple of settings to be even more restrictive due to the nature of their job titles. First we will create the base policy for the Executives:

New-DeviceConfigurationPolicy -Name 'Executive Mobile Device Configuration'

Then get the GUID of the IT Group (located in Azure AD):

Get-Group Executives | Ft Name,GUID

```
PS C:\> Get-Group Executives | Ft Name,GUID


Name        Guid
----        ----
Executives  71da8431-38a1-4c44-9798-3deb0c555d41
```

Lastly, we will apply a more restrictive policy with these settings:

```
New-DeviceConfigurationRule -Policy 'Executive Mobile Device Configuration' -MaxPasswordGracePeriod
00.00:15:00 -AllowSimplePassword $True -PasswordMinimumLength 8  -PasswordHistoryCount 2
-MaxPasswordAttemptsBeforeWipe 10 -PasswordExpirationDays 365 -PasswordMinComplexChars 2
-PasswordRequired $True -AutoUpdateStatus NeverCheckUpdates -TargetGroups 71da8431-38a1-4c44-
9798-3deb0c555d41
```

We can now verify our two new Rules:

```
Get-DeviceConfigurationRule
```

PasswordRequired	PhoneMemoryEncrypted	PasswordTimeout	PasswordMinimumLength	PasswordHistoryCount	PasswordExpirationDays
True	False		8	2	365
True	False		8	6	182

If we need to modify these Rules or Policies later, we can handle that with SET cmdlets like the Conditional Access cmdlets mentioned previously. For our Device Configuration Policies, we can add a comment, we can RetryDistribution and enable/disable the Policy. In fact, if our Policies did not deploy and an error occurred, we can use the RetryDistribution switch to try and process them:

```
PS C:\> Get-DeviceConfigurationPolicy|  Set-DeviceConfigurationPolicy -RetryDistribution
PS C:\> Get-DeviceConfigurationPolicy | Ft Name,Distribution*


Name                                    DistributionStatus DistributionResults
----                                    ------------------ -------------------
IT Mobile Device Configuration          Pending                {}
Executive Mobile Device Configuration   Pending                {}
```

Just like the Device Conditional Access Policies, we can remove them with a simple one-liner:

```
Remove-DeviceConfigurationPolicy 'IT Mobile Device Configuration'
```

Lastly, if we want to modify an existing Device Configuration Rule we have a lot of options to choose from:

CameraEnabled	AntiVirusStatus	MaxPasswordAttemptsBeforeWipe
AllowVideoConferencing	TVShowsRating	MoviesRating
AntiVirusSignatureStatus	ForceAppStorePassword	WorkFoldersSyncUrl
FirewallStatus	AllowDiagnosticSubmission	PasswordExpirationDays
AllowAppStore	AutoUpdateStatus	UserAccountControlStatus
AllowAssistantWhileLocked	WLANEnabled	RequireEmailProfile
AppsRating	AllowVoiceDialing	ForceEncryptedBackup
PasswordHistoryCount	AccountName	AccountUserName
PasswordQuality	PasswordComplexity	AllowScreenshot
PhoneMemoryEncrypted	PasswordTimeout	AllowiCloudBackup
EmailAddress	SmartScreenEnabled	TargetGroups
BluetoothEnabled	AllowiCloudPhotoSync	ExchangeActiveSyncHost
AllowConvenienceLogon	AllowSimplePassword	PasswordMinComplexChars
MaxPasswordGracePeriod	AllowPassbookWhileLocked	SystemSecurityTLS
AllowVoiceAssistant	PasswordMinimumLength	RegionRatings
AllowiCloudDocSync	PasswordRequired	EnableRemovableStorage

Make sure to verify that the option you chose from the above list will work for your device. Some of the configuration items only work with a particular version or higher of a Phone OS.

** **Note** ** If more additional / more complex options are needed, Intune may be a better solution. The only caveat is that Intune may be an additional license depending on what you have already licensed.

13   Labels and File Plans

In This Chapter

Introduction
Labels
- Creating Labels
- Conditions
- Encryption
- Content Marking
- EndPoint Protection
- Additional Cmdlets

Label Policies
File Plans

Introduction

Labels are tags that applied to content that help identify certain characteristics about the content. These labels can be passive and informative while other can be restrictive and protective. As such they serve a purpose in data governance, protection and retention for your Office 365 content. Labels need planning before applying them due to their inherent nature.

Labels are now also linked between the Azure Information Protection (AIP) Labels and the Security and Compliance Center Labels using a concept called Unified Labels. This feature can be enabled in the AIP blade in your Azure AD portal. It is recommended that this be done so that you have one source of labels instead of two places with which to create these. Make sure to follow the instructions here and check for any caveats or potential issues to be cognizant of:

https://techcommunity.microsoft.com/t5/Enterprise-Mobility-Security/Announcing-availability-of-information-protection-capabilities/ba-p/261967

Label Policies are an automatic way to publish labels for use or automatic application to content in your tenant. The intent is to help with the overall management process with labels and make management easier.

In this chapter we will cover Labels and File Plans and show you how to use Powershell to manage these features in your tenant. Note that currently this feature is a work in progress.

Recently Microsoft introduced a new feature called File Plans. PowerShell for this feature is still in development and there are somethings we cannot accomplish yet in PowerShell. However, with the combination of PowerShell and the Security and Compliance Center, we can effectively create, manage and apply File Plans for an Office 365 tenant. File Plans are a way to add more context to your content in Office 365. We can tag items with Categories, Citations, Subcategories, and ReferenceID. These descriptors are intended to help with your management of Labels and content in your environment.

Labels

When it comes to PowerShell and Labels, we find that while it is possible to use PowerShell to create them, it is a rather intensive process. The reason for this is that the properties of a label that are used to control what they are used for and how they interact in your tenant, are not easily assembled. We do not have individual parameters that we can use to build for each scenario. In fact, we must essentially assemble our own criteria for the properties and apply them as one big string rather than as individual items. So we can create scripts that will allow us to 'automate' Label creation or write question-based scripts that when filled out properly will create these properties as expected. The process is harder due to a lot of double-quotes which are involved.

Now we will explore the basics of PowerShell for Labels then dive into the usage of the cmdlets.

PowerShell

```
Get-Command *label*
```

This provides us with a concise list of Label commands.

```
Get-Label
Get-LabelPolicy
Get-LabelPolicyRule
New-Label
New-LabelPolicy
Remove-Label
Remove-LabelPolicy
Remove-RecordLabel
Set-Label
Set-LabelPolicy
```

Get Cmdlets

Let's start by working with two cmdlets - 'Get-Label' and 'Get-LabelPolicy'. In a new tenant there will be no Labels to query or to review. For the purposes of this section we have some pre-created Labels we can look at.

Each of your Labels contains numerous fields and we can decide to pull just some or all of them. Perhaps the easiest way to handle this data is to export all of the Labels and Label Policies to CSV files. This would make rebuilding and referencing configuration setups much easier. To do so, we need the Export-CSV cmdlet as well as using the '-NoTypeInformation' parameter which cleans up the head output of the CSV file. Each would be documented like so:

```
Get-Label | Export-Csv c:\Labels.csv -NoTypeInformation
Get-LabelPolicy | Export-Csv c:\LabelPolicies.csv -NoTypeInformation
```

Now we have CSV files that look like this:

```
label.csv - Notepad
File  Edit  Format  View  Help
"PSComputerName","RunspaceId","PSShowComputerName","Settings","LabelActions","Conditions","LocaleSettings","DisplayName","Parent
"nam05b.ps.compliance.protection.outlook.com","4712a0b1-f897-467a-a37a-005726293596","False","[tooltip, Confidential informatio
```

Creating Labels

New Labels and Policies

When it comes to creating Labels in the Security and Compliance Center, we have two methods available to us - wizard based construction on the Protection.Office.Com website or with PowerShell. As this book is PowerShell oriented we will attempt to do so with PowerShell. When we review the cmdlets in PowerShell for new Labels, we see we have New-Label and New-LabelPolicy. What is sorely lacking for these PowerShell cmdlets is any sort of help for them. Neither the Get-Help -Examples nor Get-Help -Online is useful. In fact, there are no online pages for either New-Label OR New-LabelPolicy in Microsoft Docs:

New-Label
https://technet.microsoft.com/EN-US/library/f9591cfd-c6dc-4f1f-9884-019ce12191d1(EXCHG.160).aspx
New-LabelPolicy
https://technet.microsoft.com/EN-US/library/e6e23082-0c8f-4349-9cf2-056af3fb9e50(EXCHG.160).aspx

For a new label, we have a few available options:

LocalSettings, LabelActions, Conditions, Comment, Identity, DisplayName, Settings, Advanced Settings

However, we have no real direction on how to set these up via PowerShell, so we will create a new Label and see what we have and if we can recreate this with PowerShell. Below is a sample from a Label created in the SCC:

```
RunspaceId        : 44dca66f-6673-4d0c-8d44-013b27d985cf
Settings          : {[tooltip, You are seeing a new label for the SCC book!], [displayname, Book Test Label]}
LabelActions      : {}
Conditions        : {{"And":[{"Or":[{"Key":"CCSI","Value":"1d71e6fe-5280-4906-a951-d91c5f32b888","Properties":null,"Set
                    tings":[{"Key":"minconfidence","Value":"85"},{"Key":"maxconfidence","Value":"100"},{"Key":"rulepack
                    age","Value":"4b0182f6-058a-4fc0-8a62-d2f64c58b805"},{"Key":"mincount","Value":"1"},{"Key":"maxcoun
                    t","Value":"2147483647"},{"Key":"policytip","Value":"Please apply this label as the content
                    contains Confidential Information."},{"Key":"name","Value":"TestRegEx"},{"Key":"groupname","Value":
                    "Default"},{"Key":"autoapplytype","Value":"Recommend"}]}]}]}}
LocaleSettings    : {{"LocaleKey":"displayName","Settings":[{"Key":"default","Value":"Book Test Label"}]},
                    {"LocaleKey":"tooltip","Settings":[{"Key":"default","Value":"You are seeing a new label for the
                    SCC book!"}]}}
DisplayName       : Book Test Label
ParentId          :
Tooltip           : You are seeing a new label for the SCC book!
ReadOnly          : False
ExternalIdentity  :
ImmutableId       : 483e54e2-5258-4127-853d-71e2d263c2ab
Priority          : 3
Workload          : Exchange, SharePoint
Policy            : ea408334-44a8-4f21-ad91-552554a651af
Comment           : This is a test label for the new book.
Disabled          : False
Mode              : Enforce
ObjectVersion     : 36602ea8-b64c-450e-4a7b-08d71af7e8d1
CreatedBy         : Damian Scoles
LastModifiedBy    : Damian Scoles
Guid              : 483e54e2-5258-4127-853d-71e2d263c2ab
Identity          : FFO.extest.microsoft.com/Microsoft Exchange Hosted
                    Organizations/______.onmicrosoft.com/Configuration/Book Test Label
Id                : FFO.extest.microsoft.com/Microsoft Exchange Hosted
                    Organizations/______.onmicrosoft.com/Configuration/Book Test Label
IsValid           : True
ExchangeVersion   : 0.20 (15.0.0.0)
Name              : Book Test Label
```

From this example, let's see how we can break that down and make a production script. I initially was going to attempt a one-liner and while yes, you can indeed create a Label with a one-liner, there isn't much to it:

New-Label -DisplayName 'Confidential' -Name 'Confidential' -ToolTip 'Contains confidential info' -Comment 'Confidential 2019'

```
RunspaceId        : 0d81f0fb-c7e3-4983-90f3-e9f95e4534dc
Settings          : {[tooltip, Contains confidential info], [displayname, Confidential]}
LabelActions      : {}
Conditions        : {}
LocaleSettings    : {{"LocaleKey":"displayName","Settings":[{"Key":"default","Value":"Confidential"}]},
                    {"LocaleKey":"tooltip","Settings":[{"Key":"default","Value":"Contains confidential info"}]}}
DisplayName       : Confidential
ParentId          :
Tooltip           : Contains confidential info
ReadOnly          : False
ExternalIdentity  :
ImmutableId       : 570ea5fd-4682-4820-af11-a9cd87455b99
Priority          : 7
Workload          : Exchange, SharePoint
Policy            : ea408334-44a8-4f21-ad91-552554a651af
Comment           : Confidential 2019
Disabled          : False
Mode              : Enforce
```

Conditions

Again, while this is a Label, we don't have any Sensitive Information Types or conditions that will help make the Label even more useful. If we look at the example from the previous page, we see that the Conditions property is populated with a lot of information. When using the web interface for the SCC (Classification > Sensitivity Labels), this is easy to control with various options and information to fill out:

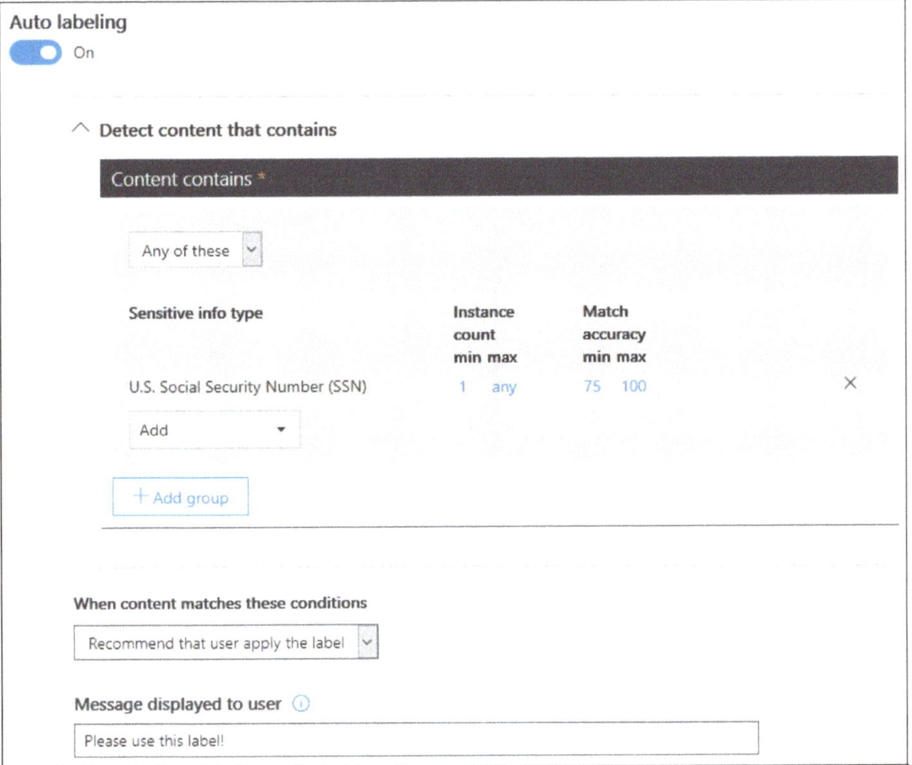

However, translating this to PowerShell is a bit of a an escape (')... Because of the amount of double quotes around everything! This means making a string that much harder to do. On the next page we will break down what it takes to do this and how to create a script to make sure it works. First, our example and the resulting Conditions property for the Label (take note of the complexity):

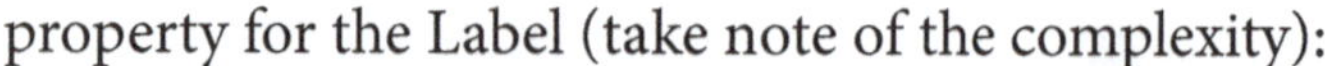

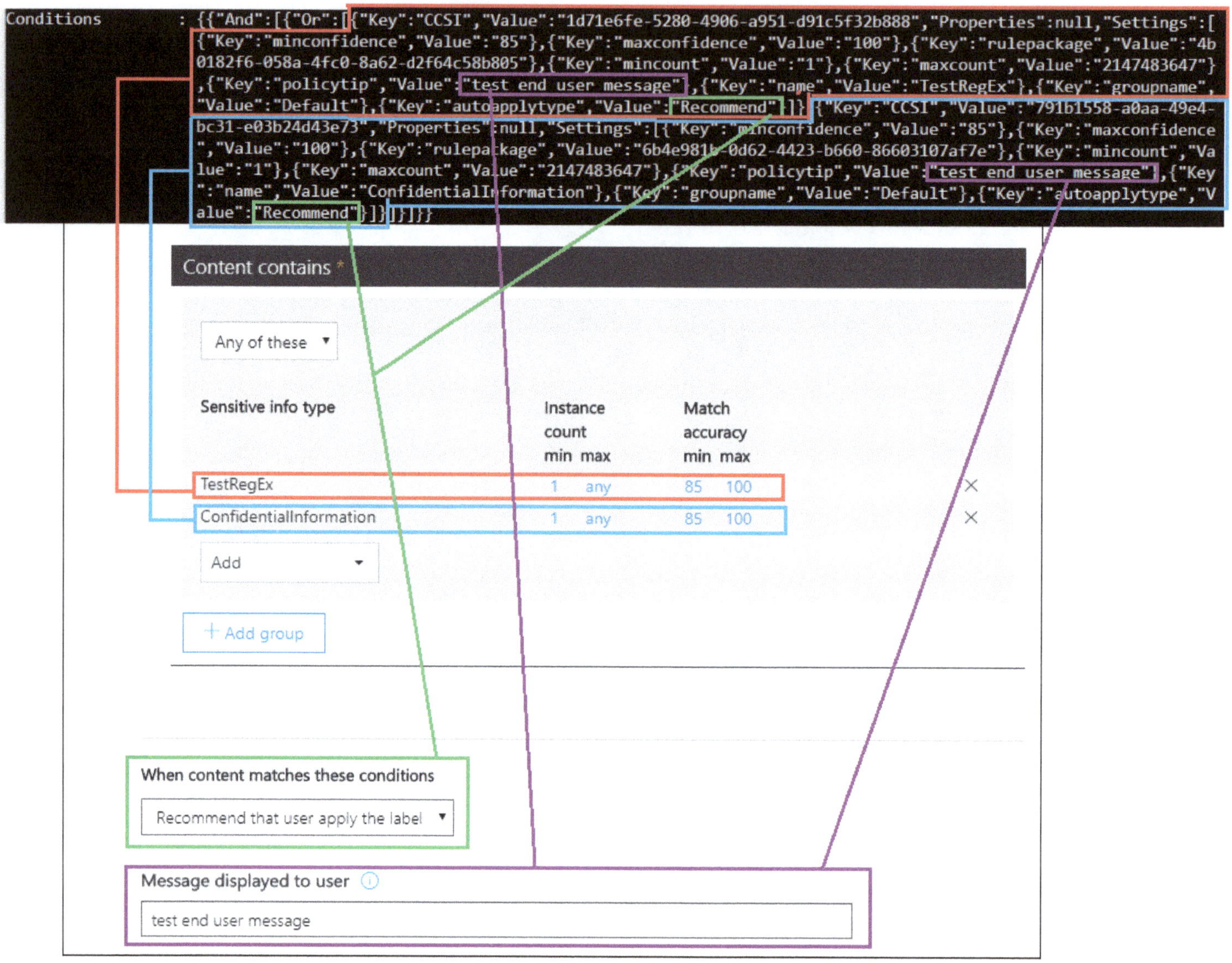

In order to approach this and be able to code PowerShell for this, we would need to analyze the fields that are required and not required to make this work as well as the actual text. First, we note that there are two bracket types used '[ ]' and '{ }'. We can use those as a guide on where to break up the strings in the Conditions field. Using those brackets and other clues, we can break down the appropriate values to their own lines and reconstruct them with PowerShell:

{{"And":[{"Or":[
{"Key":"CCSI","Value":"1d71e6fe-5280-4906-a951-d91c5f32b888","Properties":null,"Settings":[
{"Key":"minconfidence","Value":"85"},
{"Key":"maxconfidence","Value":"100"},
{"Key":"rulepackage","Value":"4b0182f6-058a-4fc0-8a62-d2f64c58b805"},
{"Key":"mincount","Value":"1"},
{"Key":"maxcount","Value":"2147483647"},
{"Key":"policytip","Value":"test end user message"},
{"Key":"name","Value":"TestRegEx"},
{"Key":"groupname","Value":"Default"},
{"Key":"autoapplytype","Value":"Recommend"}

]},
{"Key":"CCSI","Value":"791b1558-a0aa-49e4-bc31-e03b24d43e73","Properties":null,"Settings":[
{"Key":"minconfidence","Value":"85"},
{"Key":"maxconfidence","Value":"100"},
{"Key":"rulepackage","Value":"6b4e981b-0d62-4423-b660-86603107af7e"},
{"Key":"mincount","Value":"1"},
{"Key":"maxcount","Value":"2147483647"},
{"Key":"policytip","Value":"test end user message"},
{"Key":"name","Value":"ConfidentialInformation"},
{"Key":"groupname","Value":"Default"},
{"Key":"autoapplytype","Value":"Recommend"}
]}
]}]}}

Let's break down these lines to get a better understanding of what we are looking at - remember that these values are NOT stored in separate lines, but as one line of comma separated values.

Line 1: A common header that exists as the first few characters of the Conditions property when there are multiple conditions.

{{"And":[{Or":[

Line 2: Contains the ID of the Sensitive Information Type we are applying - *1d71e6fe-5280-4906-a951-d91c5f32b888*

{"Key":"CCSI","Value":"1d71e6fe-5280-4906-a951-d91c5f32b888","Properties":null,"Settings":[

Line 3: The Minimum Confident Level we choose for the Sensitive Information Type:

{"Key":"minconfidence","Value":"85"},

Line 4: The Maximum Confident Level we choose for the Sensitive Information Type.

{"Key":"maxconfidence","Value":"100"},

Line 5: The Rules Package ID # of the Sensitive Information Type specified.

{"Key":"rulepackage","Value":"4b0182f6-058a-4fc0-8a62-d2f64c58b805"},

Line 6: Minimum count of the Sensitive Information Type to be detected and triggers the Label.

{"Key":"mincount","Value":"1"},

Line 7: Maximum count of the Sensitive Information Type to be detected and triggers the Label.

{"Key":"maxcount","Value":"2147483647"},

Line 8: Policy tip show to users.

{"Key":"policytip","Value":"test end user message"},

Line 9: Name of the Sensitive Information Type.

{"Key":"name","Value":"TestRegEx"},

Line 10: Group selected as a condition of the Label.

{"Key":"groupname","Value":"Default"},

Line 11: This is the value for AutoApply or Recommend choice we make for the label.

{"Key":"autoapplytype","Value":"Recommend"}

Line 12: Caps the Sensitive Information Type and either leads to the end of the Conditions property or another Sensitive Information Type.

]},

While there are a lot of lines to sort through and understand, we can see from the above explanations that they all tie back to the decisions that we made in the GUI. The above section repeats in the same order for EACH Sensitive Information Type that is added. If we are going to add more than one, then we just need to make sure we do a loop and repeat all of these lines. One the next pages we are going to explore how we are going to convert them to lines we can write and then put them all together in a script that we can use to build custom Labels without using the SCC web interface.

To use PowerShell to write these strings, we need to work with single quotes which will allow us to encapsulate one double quotes at a time:

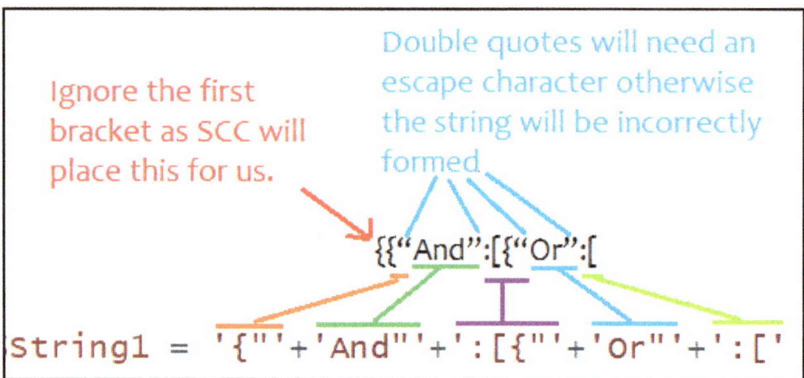

Line 1: This is the new iteration, which allows us to store the characters correctly in a string variable:

$String1 = '{"'+'And"'+':[{"'+'Or"'+':['

All other lines that have double quotes, will need to be re-written like Line 1 above.

For the next part of building conditions based on Sensitive Information Types we will need to consider some important factors. One, we need to know which Sensitive Information Types that will be used with this label. Once we have that we can then ask about some parameters for each Sensitive Information Types - Name of the Sensitive Information Type, Minimum Confidence Level, Maximum Confidence Level, Minimum Count and Maximum Count. Then we have some shared values (which you can see in the New Label creation wizard of the SCC) that apply to all Sensitive Information Types - Policy Tip, Group Name and AutoApplyType. In order to acquire these values we can then work on each Sensitive Information Type.

First, ask if we want to add a Group to associate. If we do not want to add a group, hit Enter. This sets the $GroupName variable to 'Default' which is no group defined.

```
Write-Host "Associate a group with the Label? [Hit 'Enter to leave empty]: " -NoNewline
$GroupName = Read-Host
If ($Null -eq $GroupName) {$GroupName = 'Default'}
```

Now we ask if the label should be AutoApply or Recommend.

```
Write-Host "AutoApply or Recommend to AutoAppply? ['AutoApply' OR 'Recommend']:  " -NoNewline
$AutoApply =  Read-Host
```

Lastly, we ask if we want a policy tip added:

```
Write-Host "Policy Tip for the new Label? [Hit 'Enter' to leave empty]:  " -NoNewline
$PolicyTip =  Read-Host
```

After that, we need to know how many to add:

```
Write-Host 'How many Sensitive Information Types to add? ' -NoNewline
$SensitiveNum = Read-Host
```

Once we know how many we are going to apply to the Label, we can create a Do…While loop that will allow us to ask for information on each of the Sensitive Information Types we want to add. Loop code, including a counter, called $Loop:

```
$Loop = 0
 Do {
   $Loop+
   <Code to Execute>
 } While ($Loop -ne $SensitiveNum)
```

If, for example, we choose one Sensitive Information Type, then $SensitiveNum would equal one and then in the first loop, $Loop would increment ($Loop++) from zero to one and then after the code in the Do…While loop is run, the loop would exit as $Loop (value = 1) would equal $SensitiveNum (value = 1). In another example, if we chose to do three Sensitive Information Types, then the $Loop variable would increment as follows:

```
Loop One: $Loop (1) / $SecureNumer (3)
Loop One: $Loop (2) / $SecureNumer (3)
Loop One: $Loop (3) / $SecureNumer (3)
```

Then the script would exit the loop. Inside each loop pass, we would execute these lines:

First, get the name of the Sensitive Information Type:

```
Write-Host 'Which Sensitive Information Type do you want to add?' -NoNewline
$CCSIName =  Read-Host
```

Ask for minimum confidence level: (Set to 85 if no number entered):

```
Write-Host 'Please provide a minimum confidence level [85 is default] ' -NoNewline
$MinConfidence = Read-Host
If ($MinConfidence -eq '') {$MinConfidence = 85}
```

Ask for maximum confidence level: (Set to 100 if no number entered):

```
Write-Host 'Please provide a maximum confidence level [100 is default] ' -NoNewline
$MaxConfidence = Read-Host
If ($MaxConfidence -eq '') {$MaxConfidence = 100}
```

** Note ** Confidence level values relate to the accuracy of the match results:
https://docs.microsoft.com/en-us/office365/securitycompliance/data-loss-prevention-policies#match-accuracy

Ask for minimum occurrence: (Set to 1 if no number entered):

```
Write-Host 'Please provide a minimum count [1 is default] ' -NoNewline
$MinCount =  Read-Host
If ($MinCount -eq '') {$MinCount = 1}
```

Ask for maximum occurrence: (Set to 2147483647 if no number entered):

```
Write-Host 'Please provide a maximum count [Unlimited is default] ' -NoNewline
$MaxCount =  Read-Host
If ($MaxCount -eq 'Unlimited') { $MaxCount = 2147483647 }
If ($MaxCount -eq '') { $MaxCount = 2147483647 }
```

We need to pull some properties from the Sensitive Information Type to be put into the conditions property:

```
$CCSI = Get-DlpSensitiveInformationType $CCSIName
$CCSIID = $CCSI.ID
$CCSIRulePackID = $CCSI.RulePackID
```

Next, we need to insert our variable values into each line. Now each line is in the same order as we'll need for final assembly:

```
$CCSIHeader = '{"' + 'Key"' + ':"' + 'CCSI"' + ',"' + 'Value"' + ':"' + "$CCSIID" + '"' + ',"' + 'Properties"' +
':null,"' + 'Settings"' + ':['
$RulesPackageValue = '{"'+'Key"'+':"'+'rulepackage"'+',"'+'Value"'+':"'+"$CCSIRulePackID"+'"'+'}'
$MinConfidenceValue = '{"'+'Key"'+':"'+'minconfidence"'+',"'+'Value"'+':"'+"$MinConfidence"+'"'+'}'
$MaxConfidenceValue='{"'+'Key"'+':"'+'maxconfidence"'+',"'+'Value"'+':"'+"$MaxConfidence"+'"'+'}'
$MinCountValue = '{"'+'Key"'+':"'+'mincount"'+',"'+'Value"'+':"'+"$MinCount"+'"'+'}'
$MaxCountValue = '{"'+'Key"'+':"'+'maxcount"'+',"'+'Value"'+':"'+"$MaxCount"+'"'+'}'
$PolicyTipValue = '{"'+'Key"'+':"'+'policytip"'+',"'+'Value"'+':"'+"$PolicyTip"+'"'+'}'
If ($Null -ne $GroupName) {
   $GroupValue = '{"'+'Key"'+':"'+'groupname"'+',"'+'Value"'+':"'+"$GroupName"+'"'+'}'
} Else {
   $GroupValue = '{"'+'Key"'+':"'+'groupname"'+',"'+'Value"'+':"'+"Default"+'"'+'}'
}
$AutoApplyValue = '{"'+'Key"'+':"'+'autoapplytype"'+',"'+'Value"'+':"'+"$AutoApply"+'"'+'}'
```

Now that we have all the values populated, we can assemble them all into one variable:

```
$CurrentLine  =  $CCSIHeader+$MinConfidenceValue+','+$MaxConfidenceValue+','+$RulesPackageVal-
ue+','+$MinCountValue+','+$MaxCountValue+','+$PolicyTipValue+','+$GroupValue+','+$AutoApplyVal-
ue+']}'
```

We'll also need to store all of these Sensitive Information Types in case we handle more than one:

```
$SensitiveInfoTypeContent += $CurrentLine
```

After we store all the information for each Sensitive Information Type the variable values we added are stored in a series (logical representation below):

```
Line1
Line2
Line3
```

We need to reassemble this into this format: Line1,Line2,Line3. We can do that with a -Join parameter and store it in a new variable:

```
$AllTypes = $SensitiveInfoTypeContent -Join ','
```

We also saw, from the test Condition, that we need to close all of the brackets and that looks like this:

```
$End = "]}]}"
```

Now, assembling it all in one variable ($Condition), we take the first variable ($String1) add all the Sensitive Information Types ($AllTypes) and finally the end brackets ($End):

```
$Condition = "$String1" + "$AllTypes"+"$End"
```

Now that we have all of that, we have some final informational bits that we can then use for the new label:

```
Write-Host 'Enter a name for the new Label: ' -NoNewline
$LabelName = Read-Host
Write-Host 'Enter a Tooltip for your users: ' -NoNewline
$UserTooltip = Read-Host
Write-Host 'Enter a Comment for the new Label:  ' -NoNewline
$LabelComment = Read-Host
```

With all of this we can now run a one line to create the new label:

```
New-Label -Name $LabelName -DisplayName $LabelName -Conditions $Condition -ToolTip $UserToolTip -Comment $LabelComment
```

Sample Scenario (Using our script)

For this scenario, we have to create a Label. The Label has two conditions with one being a Regex query and another is a keyword query. Each of these will use the defaults for all settings (count and confidence) for one and custom settings for the second one. The Label will be name Research Material. When we run the script, we see this:

```
---------------------
Create a New SCC Label
---------------------


Enter a name for the new Label: Research Material
Enter a Tooltip for your users: Be careful with this content, DO NOT FORWARD externally!
Enter a Comment for the new Label:  This content contains Research and Development material.
---------------------
New Label Conditions
---------------------


Add a Sensitive Information Type to the Label? [y/n] y
Associate a group with the Label?  [Hit 'Enter to leave empty]:
AutoApply or Recommend to AutoAppply? ['AutoApply' OR 'Recommend']:   Recommend
Policy Tip for the new Label? [Hit 'Enter' to leave empty]:   RESEARCH MATERIAL
How many Sensitive Information Types to add? 2

-- Available DLP Sensitive Information Type Rule Packages --


RuleCollectionName
------------------
Microsoft Rule Package
RegEx
KeywordSearch-CI
Document Fingerprint Rule Package
Microsoft.SCCManaged.CustomRulePack
ConfidentialInformation
```

```
Which Sensitive Information Type do you want to add (1 of 1)?  TestRegEx
Policy Tip for the new Label? [Hit 'Enter' to leave empty]:  Test
Associate a group with the Label?  [Hot 'Enter to leave empty]:
AutoApply or Recommend to AutoAppply? ['AutoApply' OR 'Recommend']:  Recommend
Complete String:
{"And":[{"Or":[{"Key":"CCSI","Value":"1d71e6fe-5280-4906-a951-d91c5f32b888","Properties":null,"Settings":[{"Key":"minconfidence"
,"Value":"85"},{"Key":"maxconfidence","Value":"100"},{"Key":"rulepackage","Value":"4B0182F6-058A-4FC0-8A62-D2F64C58B805"},{"Key"
:"mincount","Value":"1"},{"Key":"maxcount","Value":"2147483647"},{"Key":"policytip","Value":"Test"},{"Key":"groupname","Value":"
"},{"Key":"autoapplytype","Value":"Recommend"}]}]}]}

Name            Disabled
----            --------
SensitiveTesting False
```

Now we have a Label with Sensitive Information Types we chose to apply.

Encryption

Now what about adding Encryption and Watermarks? How can we do these with PowerShell? Similar to the Conditions section above, Encryption inserts information into a field called 'LabelActions'. Similarly it requires some parsing:

```
LabelActions        : {{"Type":"encrypt","SubType":null,"Settings":[{"Key":"protectiontype","Value":"template"},{"Key":"d
                      isabled","Value":"false"},{"Key":"templateid","Value":"b59adb38-4c1c-4c9f-8da1-cda3d8ab9c98"},{"Key
                      ":"templatearchived","Value":"True"},{"Key":"linkedtemplateid","Value":"b59adb38-4c1c-4c9f-8da1-cda
                      3d8ab9c98"},{"Key":"contentexpiredondateindaysornever","Value":"Never"},{"Key":"offlineaccessdays",
                      "Value":"-1"},{"Key":"rightsdefinitions","Value":"[{\"Identity\":\"███████.onmicrosoft.com\",\"Right
                      s\":\"VIEW,VIEWRIGHTSDATA,DOCEDIT,EDIT,PRINT,EXTRACT,REPLY,REPLYALL,FORWARD,OBJMODEL\"}]"}]}}
```

We can break down the function of each of the above keys, like so:

The Encryption setting is a global setting, which means the code can be after our Conditions loop, but before the actual creation of the Label. We could also potentially modify any code we write to also modify an existing Label as well. Let's go ahead and write code to ask questions about the Encryption feature, then create each line above, assemble the code and finally put them all together to be placed in the LabelActions property of the Label. First, we will store sets of rights to make it easier to build that portion later:

```
$CoOwner = 'VIEW,VIEWRIGHTSDATA,DOCEDIT,EDIT,PRINT,EXTRACT,REPLY,REPLYALL,FOR-
WARD,EDITRIGHTSDATA,EXPORT,OBJMODEL,OWNER\'
$Coauthor = 'VIEW, VIEWRIGHTSDATA, DOCEDIT, EDIT, PRINT, EXTRACT, REPLY, REPLYALL,
FORWARD, OBJMODEL\'
$Reviewer = 'VIEW,VIEWRIGHTSDATA,DOCEDIT,EDIT,REPLY,REPLYALL,FORWARD,OBJMODEL\'
$Viewer = 'VIEW,VIEWRIGHTSDATA,OBJMODEL\'
```

The above lines are based on what is revealed in the Encryption wizard for the Label:

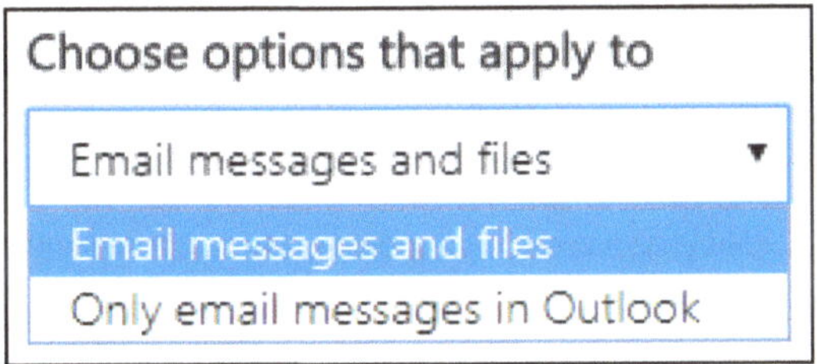

Next we can process a series of questions. The first question, at least when it comes to creating the Label, should be obvious:

```
Write-Host 'Do you want to add Encryption to this Label? [y/n] ' -NoNewline
$Encryption = Read-Host
```

Note that Encryption is not a required element of a Label, so we can ask this and skip all Encryption questions:

```
If ($Encryption -eq 'y') {
```

Next we need to decide which Encryption type we want:

Code for this question:

```
Write-Host 'Do you want to protect (1) Emails and Files or (2) Emails in Outlook [1 or 2]? ' -NoNewline
$Protection = Read-Host
```

For this section, we assume Option 1 is selected.

```
Write-Host 'User access expiration of encryption (1) Never (2) Specific Date (3) Number of days: '
-NoNewline
$Expiration = Read-Host
```

Option 1 requires no extra code. For Option 2 we will need a date entered (in this format MM/DD/YYYY):

```
If ($Expiration -eq '2') {
    Write-Host 'Please Enter a date for encryption expiration: ' -NoNewline
    $ExpirationDate = Read-Host
}
```

** **Note** ** Localized date formats can be used.

If Option 3 is chosen, then we will need a number of days between 1 and 100. We don't want an invalid number, as it will cause the New-Label command to fail. To deal with this, we can use a Do...While loop that will check to make sure the number entered is between 1 and 100. If it is not, then a $Test variable is set to $False. The While part of the Do...While statement checks the $Test variable. As long as the $Test variable is $False, the loop keeps asking for a number:

```
If ($Expiration -eq '3') {
   Do {
      Write-Host 'Enter a number between 1 and 100: ' -NoNewline
      $ExpirationNumOfDays = Read-Host
      $Test = (1 -lt $ExpirationNumOfDays) -and (100 -gt $ExpirationNumOfDays)
      If (!$Test) {Write-host 'Invalid number...' -ForegroundColor Red}
   } While ($Test -eq $False)
}
```

Next we have an option to allow for Offline Access to encrypted data. We can use a similarly crafted loop to handle this option:

```
Write-Host 'Offline Access (1) Never (2) Always (3) Number of days: ' -NoNewline
$OfflineAccess = Read-Host
If ($OfflineAccess -eq '3') {
   Do {
      Write-Host 'Enter a number between 1 and 100: ' -NoNewline
      $OfflineNumOfDays = Read-Host
      $Test = (1 -lt $OfflineNumOfDays) -and (100 -gt $OfflineNumOfDays)
      If (!$Test) {Write-host 'Invalid number...' -ForegroundColor Red}
   } While ($Test -eq $False)
}
```

From here we move on to the a harder option to code for and that is permissions. We can grant permissions to everyone in a tenant, specific users/groups and/or add email addresses. We will need a Do...While loop in order to handle:

```
 Write-Host 'What permissions to assign for Encryption? (1) All tenant members (2) add users or groups
(3) Add these email addresses or (x) Exit? ' -NoNewline
$PermissionValue = Read-Host
Do {
If ($PermissionValue -eq '1') {
Write-Host 'Enter your tenant name [tenant.onmicrosoft.com] ' -NoNewline
$Tenant = Read-host
$Identity = '\'''+'Identity\'''+':\'''+$Tenant+'\'''
}
If ($PermissionValue -eq '2') {
}
If ($PermissionValue -eq '3') {
}
```

Now that we've picked who to assign rights to, we need to pick which rights we wish to assign to them. We have five choices. Four of these choices are pre-defined roles whereas the fifth is a custom role.

```
Write-Host 'Permissions to assign? (1) Co-Owner (2) Co-Author (3) Reviewer (4) Viewer (5) Custom'
-NoNewline
$PermissionsToAssign = Read-Host
```

This is where our pre-defined roles come into play. Once we pick a pre-defined role, we can store their permissions in a variable called $AssignedPermissions which we can use

```
If ($PermissionsToAssign -eq '1') { $AssignedPermissions = $CoOwner }
If ($PermissionsToAssign -eq '2') { $AssignedPermissions = $CoAuthor }
If ($PermissionsToAssign -eq '3') { $AssignedPermissions = $Reviewer }
If ($PermissionsToAssign -eq '4') { $AssignedPermissions = $Viewer }
```

Now, if we chose Option 5, this will then allow us to pick a list of custom rights. One caveat is listed in the code is that DOCEDIT is required with other rights.

```
If ($PermissionsToAssign -eq '5') {
    Write-Host "Enter a list of rights separated by commas [i.e. ,EDIT,REPLY,REPLYALL]"
    Write-Host 'Available options - VIEW,VIEWRIGHTSDATA,DOCEDIT,EDIT,PRINT,EXTRACT,REPLY,RE-
    PLYALL,FORWARD,EDITRIGHTSDATA,EXPORT,OBJMODEL,OWNER'
    Write-Host '  ** Note - DOCEDIT is required if these rights are entered - REPLY, REPLYALL and/or
    FORWARD' -ForegroundColor Yellow
    $Answer = Read-Host
    $AssignedPermissions = $Answer+'\'
}
```

Once we have our $AssignedPermissions variable populated, we can add the components together:

```
$FullIdentity = '{'+$Identity+','+$AssignedPermissions+'}'
```

To handle multiple identities, we can compile them in an $AllIdentities variable:

```
$AllIdentities += $FullIdentity
```

And to exit our Do...While loop, Powershell looks for the $PermissionsValue to be 'x' (as referenced on the previous page):

```
} While ($PermissionValue -ne 'x')
```

Now we the permissions set for the Label.

At the end of the script, we need to assemble all of the strings into one string that we can use for the 'LabelActions' property of a Label. One note is in the Header, there is an encryption template ID. It looks like this is not a discoverable value. In order to get it, create one Label, with encryption, and then note this value. With that we can assemble the header:

```
# Overall Header (part , part 2 and the final $Header variable):

$HeaderPart1 = '{"'+'Type'"'+':"'+'encrypt'"'+','"'+'SubType'"'+':null,'"'+'Set-
tings'"'+':[{"'+'Key'"'+':"'+'protectiontype'"'+','"'+'Value'"'+':"'+'template'"'+'},{"'+'Key'"'+':"'+'dis-
abled'"'+','"'+'Value'"'+':"'+'false'"'+'},'

$HeaderPart2 = '{"'+'Key'"'+':"'+'templateid'"'+','"'+'Value'"'+':"'+'b59adb38-4c1c-4c9f-8da1-cda3d8ab-
9c98'"'+'},{"'+'Key'"'+':"'+'templatearchived'"'+','"'+'Value'"'+':"'+'True'"'+'},{"'+'Key'"'+':"'+'linkedtem-
plateid'"'+','"'+'Value'"'+':"'+'b59adb38-4c1c-4c9f-8da1-cda3d8ab9c98'"'+'},'
$Header = $HeaderPart1+$HeaderPart2
```

```
# Expiration
$ExpirationString = '{'''+'Key'''+':'''+'contentexpiredondateindaysornever'''+','''+'Value'''+':'''+$Expira-
tionData+''''+'}'

# Offline Access
$OfflineString = '{'''+'Key'''+':'''+'offlineaccessdays'''+','''+'Value'''+':'''+$OfflineNumOfDays+''''+'}'

# Permissions
$PermissionsHeader = '{'''+'Key'''+':'''+'rightsdefinitions'''+','''+'Value'''+':'''+'['
$PermissionsFooter = ']'''+'}'
$JoinedIdentities = $AllIdentities -Join ','
$PermissionsAssembled = $PermissionsHeader+$JoinedIdentities+$PermissionsFooter

# Overall Footer
$Footer = ']}}'

# Complete Assembly
$LabelAction = $Header+$ExpirationString+','+$OfflineString+','+$PermissionsAssembled+$Footer
```

We can now apply this action to a Label:

```
New-Label  -Name  $LabelName  -DisplayName  $LabelNam  -ToolTip  $UserToolTip  -Comment
$LabelComment -LabelActions $LabelAction
```

Outlook Only

Lastly, we need a code section for Outlook (email) only:

```
$OutlookOnlyPart1 = '{'''+'Type'''+':'''+'encrypt'''+','''+'SubType'''+':null,'''+'Set-
tings'''+':[{'''+'Key'''+':'''+'protectiontype'''+','''+'Value'''+':'''+'userdefined'''+'},{'''+'Key'''+':'''+'dis-
abled'''+','''+'Value'''+':'''+'false'''+'},{'''+'Key'''+':'''+'linkedtemplateid'''+','''+'Value'''+':'''+'b59adb38-4
c1c-4c9f-8da1-cda3d8ab9c98'''+'},{'''+'Key'''+':'''+'templatearchived'''+','''+'Value'''+':'''+'True'''+'},{'''+'
Key'''+':'''+'promptuser'''+','''+'Value'''+':'''+'false'''+'},'
```

One question to ask and that question is Do you want to use 'Enable Do Not Forward'?

```
Write-Host 'Enable Do Not Forward? [y/n] ' -NoNewLine
$DoNotForward = Read-Host
If ($DoNotForward -eq 'y') {
   $DNF = 'True'
} Else {
   $DNF = 'False'
}
```

Process the above choice and create the second part of the Action Label:

```
$OutlookOnlyPart2 = '{'''+'Key'''+':'''+'donotforward'''+','''+'Value'''+':'''+$DNF+''''+'}]}'
```

Add both parts together:

```
$OutlookOnly = $OutlookOnlyPart1+$OutlookOnlyPart2
```

'Outlook Only' run of the script:


```
Do you want to add Encryption to this Label? [y/n] y

Do you want to protect (1) Emails and Files or (2) Emails in Outlook [1 or 2]? 2
Enable Do Not Forward? [y/n] y
{"Type":"encrypt","SubType":null,"Settings":[{"Key":"protectiontype","Value":"userdefined"},{"Key":"disabled","Value":"f
alse"},{"Key":"linkedtemplateid","Value":"b59adb38-4c1c-4c9f-8da1-cda3d8ab9c98"},{"Key":"templatearchived","Value":"True
"},{"Key":"promptuser","Value":"false"},{"Key":"donotforward","Value":"True"}]]
```


Once we have the script code all assembled, we should get results like this (bottom of the screenshot is the Label Action value):


```
Do you want to add Encryption to this Label? [y/n] y

Do you want to protect (1) Emails and Files or (2) Emails in Outlook [1 or 2]? 1
------- EXPIRATION SETTINGS -------
User access expiration of encryption (1) Never (2) Specific Date (3) Number of days: 1
------- OFFLINE ACCESS SETTINGS -------
Offline Access (1) Never (2) Always (3) Number of days: 1
------- CONFIGURE PERMISSIONS -------
What permissions to assign for Encryption? (1) All tenant members (2) add users or groups (3) Add these email addresses
or (x) Exit? 1
Enter your tenant name [tenant.onmicrosoft.com] scoles.onmicrosoft.com
Permissions to assign? (1) Co-Owner (2) Co-Author (3) Reviewer (4) Viewer (5) Custom? 2

Add more permissions to assign for Encryption?:
 (1) All tenant members (2) add users or groups (3) Add these email addresses or (x) Exit? 3
Enter a user's email address to add [damian@practicalpowershell.com] damian@practicalpowershell.com
Permissions to assign? (1) Co-Owner (2) Co-Author (3) Reviewer (4) Viewer (5) Custom? 4

Add more permissions to assign for Encryption?:
 (1) All tenant members (2) add users or groups (3) Add these email addresses or (x) Exit? x

{"Type":"encrypt","SubType":null,"Settings":[{"Key":"protectiontype","Value":"template"},{"Key":"disabled","Value":"fals
e"},{"Key":"templateid","Value":"b59adb38-4c1c-4c9f-8da1-cda3d8ab9c98"},{"Key":"templatearchived","Value":"True"},{"Key"
:"linkedtemplateid","Value":"b59adb38-4c1c-4c9f-8da1-cda3d8ab9c98"},{"Key":"contentexpiredondateindaysornever","Value":"
Never"},{"Key":"offlineaccessdays","Value":""},{"Key":"rightsdefinitions","Value":"[{\"Identity\":\"scoles.onmicrosoft.c
om\",\"Rights\":\"VIEW,VIEWRIGHTSDATA,DOCEDIT,EDIT,PRINT,EXTRACT,REPLY,REPLYALL,FORWARD,OBJMODEL\"},{\"Identity\":\"dami
an@practicalpowershell.com\",\"Rights\":\"VIEW,VIEWRIGHTSDATA,OBJMODEL\"}]"}]}}
```


Content Marking

In addition to Encryption and Conditions, we can also add Content Markings to items.   Content Markings are stamps added to a document to fulfill a certain function. This is also done with the LabelActions property of a Label. We will follow a similar process to the above sections.

First are we adding a Watermark, Header and/or a Footer? Let's ask:

```
Write-Host ' ---- Content Marking ---- ' -ForegroundColor Green
Write-Host 'Do you want to apply a Watermark? [y/n] ' -NoNewLine
$WatermarkAnswer = Read-Host
Write-Host 'Do you want to apply a Header? [y/n] ' -NoNewLine
$HeaderAnswer = Read-Host
Write-Host 'Do you want to apply a Footer? [y/n] ' -NoNewLine
$FooterAnswer = Read-Host
```

Now, we have our answers we can now process each type of information.

For this section, we first check if a Watermark is requested:

```
If ($WatermarkAnswer -eq 'y') {
```

If yes, then we can ask a series of questions about the watermark - text, font size, direction and color:

```
Write-Host 'Enter text for the Watermark: ' -NoNewLine
$WatermarkText = Read-Host
Write-Host 'Enter a font size [1..30]: ' -NoNewLine
$WatermarkFont = Read-Host
Write-Host 'Text direction [horizontal or diagonal]: ' -NoNewLine
$WatermarkDirection = Read-Host
Write-Host 'Font color (HEX values) [#000000]: ' -NoNewLine
$WatermarkColor = Read-Host
```

Then we take those answers and create the Watermark content to go into the Action Labels:

```
$Watermark = '{"'+'Type"'+':"'+'applywatermarking"'+','+'"'+'SubType"'+':null,"'+'Set-
tings"'+':[{"'+'Key"'+':"'+'fontsize"'+','+'"'+'Value"'+':"'+$WatermarkFont+'"'+'},{"'+'Key"'+':"'+'lay-
out"'+','+'"'+'Value"'+':"'+$WatermarkDirection+'"'+'},{"'+'Key"'+':"'+'fontcolor"'+','+'"'+'Val-
ue"'+':"'+$WatermarkColor+'"'+'},{"'+'Key"'+':"'+'disabled"'+','+'"'+'Value"'+':"'+'false"'+'},{"'+'Key"'+':
"'+'text"'+','+'"'+'Value"'+':"'+$WatermarkText+'"'+'}'
```

With that we add the Watermark to a Content Marking variable for later:

```
$MiddleContentMarking += $Watermark
```

For this next section, we first check if a Header is requested:

```
If ($HeaderAnswer -eq 'y') {
```

If yes, then we can ask a series of questions about the Header - text, font size, alignment and color:

```
Write-Host 'Enter text for the Header: ' -NoNewLine
$HeaderText = Read-Host
Write-Host 'Enter a font size [1..30]: ' -NoNewLine
$HeaderFont = Read-Host
Write-Host 'Text alignment[left, center, right]: ' -NoNewLine
$HeaderAlignment = Read-Host
Write-Host 'Font color (HEX values) [#000000]: ' -NoNewLine
$HeaderColor = Read-Host
```

Then we take those answers and create the Header content to go into the ActionLabels:

```
$Header = '{"'+'Type"'+':"'+'applycontentmarking"'+','+'"'+'SubType"'+':"'+'header"'+','+'"'+'Set-
tings"'+':[{"'+'Key"'+':"'+'fontsize"'+','+'"'+'Value"'+':"'+$HeaderFont+'"'+'},{"'+'Key"'+':"'+'pl
acement"'+','+'"'+'Value"'+':"'+'Header"'+'},{"'+'Key"'+':"'+'text"'+','+'"'+'Value"'+':"'+$HeaderTex-
t+'"'+'},{"'+'Key"'+':"'+'fontcolor"'+','+'"'+'Value"'+':"'+$HeaderColor+'"'+'},{"'+'Key"'+':"'+'mar-
gin"'+','+'"'+'Value"'+':"'+'5"'+'},{"'+'Key"'+':"'+'alignment"'+','+'"'+'Value"'+':"'+$HeaderAlign-
ment+'"'+'},{"'+'Key"'+':"'+'disabled"'+','+'"'+'Value"'+':"'+'false"'+'}'
```

With that we add the Header to a Content Marking variable for later:

```
    $MiddleContentMarking += $Header
```

For this next section, we first check if a Footer is requested:

```
    If ($FooterAnswer -eq 'y') {
```

If yes, then we can ask a series of questions about the Footer - text, font size, alignment and color:

```
    Write-Host 'Enter text for the Footer: ' -NoNewLine
    $FooterText = Read-Host
    Write-Host 'Enter a font size [1..30]: ' -NoNewLine
    $FooterFont = Read-Host
    Write-Host 'Text alignment[left, center, right]: ' -NoNewLine
    $FooterAlignment = Read-Host
    Write-Host 'Font color (HEX values) [#000000]: ' -NoNewLine
    $FooterColor = Read-Host
```

Then we take those answers and create the Footer content to go into the Action Labels:

```
    $Footer1 = '{"'+'Type"'+':"'+'applycontentmarking"'+','"'+'SubType"'+':"'+'header"'+','"'+'Set-
    tings"'+':[{"'+'Key"'+':"'+'fontsize"'+','"'+'Value"'+':"'+$FooterFont+'"'+'},{"'+'Key"'+':"'+'pl
    acement"'+','"'+'Value"'+':"'+'Header"'+'},{"'+'Key"'+':"'+'text"'+','"'+'Value"'+':"'+$FooterTex-
    t+'"'+'},{"'+'Key"'+':"'+'fontcolor"'+','"'+'Value"'+':"'+$FooterColor+'"'+'},{"'+'Key"'+':"'+'mar-
    gin"'+','"'+'Value"'+':"'+'5"'+'},{"'+'Key"'+':"'+'alignment"'+','"'+'Value"'+':"'+$FooterAlign-
    ment+'"'+'},{"'+'Key"'+':"'+'disabled"'+','"'+'Value"'+':"'+'false"'+'}'
```

With that we add the Header to a Content Marking variable for later:

```
    $MiddleContentMarking += $Footer
```

Here we join all filled sections (Watermark, Header, Footer) with commas:

```
    # Join each section with a comma:
    $JoinedMiddleContentMarking = $MiddleContentMarking -Join ','
```

Last we add the Footer for Content Marking to the rest of the string:

```
    $ContentMarkingFooter = ']}}'
    $FullContentMarking = $JoinedMiddleContentMarking+$ContentMarkingFooter
    $FullContentMarking
```

When we run this code we see that the Label Actions field is generated correctly at the end:

```
    ---- Content Marking ----
Do you want to apply a Watermark? [y/n] y
Do you want to apply a Header? [y/n] y
Do you want to apply a Footer? [y/n] y
    ---- WATERMARK ----
Enter text for the Watermark: CONFIDENTIAL
Enter a font size [1..30]: 25
Text direction [horizontal or diagonal]: Diagonal
Font color (HEX values) [#000000]: #CCCCCC
    ---- HEADER ----
Enter text for the Header: Confidential Information
Enter a font size [1..30]: 12
Text alignment[left, center, right]: Left
Font color (HEX values) [#000000]: #000000
```

```
---- FOOTER ----
Enter text for the Footer: Internal Use Only
Enter a font size [1..30]: 12
Text alignment[left, center, right]: Right
Font color (HEX values) [#000000]: #000000
{"Type":"applywatermarking","SubType":null,"Settings":[{"Key":"fontsize","Value":"25"},{"Key":"layout","Value":"Diagonal
"},{"Key":"fontcolor","Value":"#CCCCCC"},{"Key":"disabled","Value":"false"},{"Key":"text","Value":"CONFIDENTIAL"}{"Type"
:"applycontentmarking","SubType":"header","Settings":[{"Key":"fontsize","Value":"12"},{"Key":"placement","Value":"Header
"},{"Key":"text","Value":"Confidential Information"},{"Key":"fontcolor","Value":"#000000"},{"Key":"margin","Value":"5"},
{"Key":"alignment","Value":"Left"},{"Key":"disabled","Value":"false"}{"Type":"applycontentmarking","SubType":"header","S
ettings":[{"Key":"fontsize","Value":"12"},{"Key":"placement","Value":"Header"},{"Key":"text","Value":"Internal Use Only"
},{"Key":"fontcolor","Value":"#000000"},{"Key":"margin","Value":"5"},{"Key":"alignment","Value":"Right"},{"Key":"disable
d","Value":"false"}]}}
```

Endpoint Protection

The last section or option we can configure on a Label is Endpoint Protection. Endpoint Protection is intended to help prevent data breaches and to protect data based on content. This has only two options - enabling it and choosing to apply endpoint DLP labels if enabled. First we ask if this is what we want to do:

```
Write-Host 'Do you want to apply Endpoint Protection? [y/n] ' -NoNewLine
$EndpointAnswer = Read-Host
If ($EndpointAnswer -eq 'y') {
```

Then once we are sure we want Endpoint Protection, we see if we want to apply DLP to files:

```
Write-Host "Apply endpoint DLP to files with this label applied? [true or false] " -NoNewline
$EndpointDLPAnswer = Read-Host
```

Then we take those two answers and create an Action Label:

```
$EndPointFinal = '{"'+'Type'"+'":"'+'endpoint'"+'","'+'SubType'"+'":null,"'+'Set-
tings'"+'":[{"'+'Key'"+'":"'+'endpointprotection'"+'","'+'Value'"+'":"'+'work'"+'},{"'+'Key'"+'":"'+'dis-
abled'"+'","'+'Value'"+'":"'+$EndpointDLPAnswer+'"'+'}]}'
$EndPointFinal
```

```
---- ENDPOINT PROTECTION ----
Do you want to apply Endoint Protection? [y/n] y
Apply endpoint DLP to files with this label applied ? [true or false] true
{"Type":"endpoint","SubType":null,"Settings":[{"Key":"endpointprotection","Value":"work"},{"Key":"disabled","Value":"tru
e"}]}
```

Additional Cmdlets

In addition to creating new Labels we can also remove and change settings on these Labels.

Remove-Label

```
Remove-Label 'Research Label'
```

```
PS C:\> Remove-Label 'Research Label'

Confirm
Are you sure you want to perform this action?
Removing Compliance Rule 'Research Label'.
[Y] Yes  [A] Yes to All  [N] No  [L] No to All  [?] Help (default is "Y"): y
```

Set-Label

With Set-Label, we can modify the conditions, display names, settings, etc. Some of these options, like conditions, require specific formatting. Be aware, that some settings will be wiped out for the new value and that may cause an issue.

Example

    Set-Label 'Research Label' -Comment 'Updated Label - 2019-08-08'

No feedback is given, but we can verify the comment is changed:

```
PS C:\> (Get-Label 'Research Label').Comment
Updated Label - 2019-08-08
```

Label Policies

Label Policies are used to help make Labels visible and usable for your end users. This is done by publishing existing labels in the SCC. If you have a set of Labels that you wish your users to use, then we need Label Policies to enable users to see and apply these Labels. Labels Policies are located in the same Classifications Tab in the Security and Compliance Center:

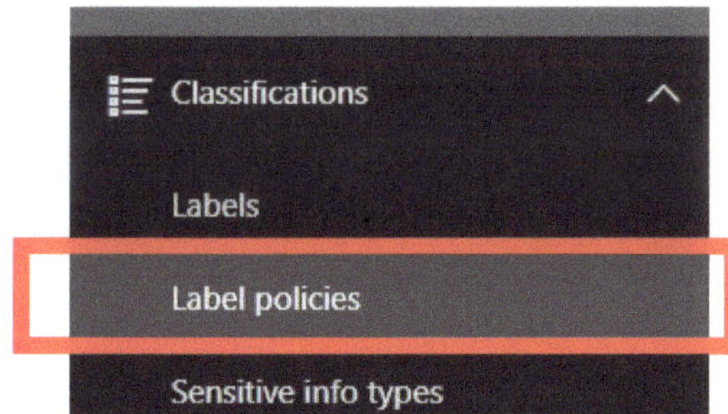

When creating a new Label Policy, we need a few bits of information. We need a name, comments and Labels to be published and we need to answer a few optional settings. Once we have that we can create the Label Policy with PowerShell.

Script to Create New Label Policy

First we need to get the name of the new Label Policy as well as any Comment we want to attach to it:

```
Write-Host 'Provide a name for the Label Policy: ' -NoNewLine
$LabelName = Read-Host
Write-Host 'Provide a comment for the Label Policy: ' -NoNewLine
$Comment = Read-Host
```

Next we generate a list of available Labels to be used on the Label Policy:

```
Write-Host '---- Available Labels ---' -ForegroundColor Yellow
Get-Label | ft
```

Now that we have a label list we can ask which ones we need to publish with the Label Policy:

```
Write-Host 'Which Labels to publish? [See provided list - can add more than one (use commas!)]: '
-NoNewLine
$Labels = Read-Host
```

All of the below settings will be stored in an array variable called '$Settings':

```
$Settings = @()
```

Next is a series of optional questions to ask and populate in the Settings property of a Label. First we can chose to have a default Label applied or no Label at all:

```
Write-Host 'Apply this label by default to documents and email [None or Label]: ' -NoNewline
$ApplyDefaultLabel = Read-Host
```

If 'None' is chosen, then the $DefaultAnswer variable needs to be blank as we won't add it to the Settings property:

```
If ($ApplyDefaultLabel -eq 'None') {
    $DefaultLabelAnswer = $Null
}
```

However, if we choose 'Label' we will ask which Label will be the default and store that in $DefaultLabelAnswer:

```
If ($ApplyDefaultLabel -eq 'Label') {
    Write-Host 'Enter default label name:' -NoNewLine
    Write-Host " [Choices - $Labels] " -NoNewLine -ForegroundColor Yellow
    $DefaultLabel = Read-Host
    Try {
            $GUID = Get-Label $DefaultLabel -ErrorAction STOP
    } Catch {
            $GUID = $Null
    }
    If ($Null -eq $GUID) {
            $DefaultLabelAnswer = $Null
    } Else {
            $ID = $GUID.guid
            $DefaultLabelAnswer = "[defaultlabelid,$ID]"
    }
}
$Settings += $DefaultLabelAnswer
```

Then we ask if we need the user to provide justification to remove a Label/lower classification Label stored in $Justification:

```
Write-Host 'Users must provide justification to remove a Label or lower classification label [y/n]: '
-NoNewline
$Justify = Read-Host
If ($Justify -eq 'y') {
    $Justification = '[requiredowngradejustification, true]'
} Else {
    $Justification = '[requiredowngradejustification, false]'
```

```powershell
}
$Settings += $Justification
```

For the next question we will see if we want to require users to use a Label and store this in $RequireLabels variable:

```powershell
Write-Host 'Requires users to apply a label to their email or documents [y/n]: ' -NoNewline
$RequireLabel = Read-Host
If ($RequireLabel -eq 'y') {
   $RequireLabels = '[Mandatory, True]'
} Else {
   $RequireLabels = '[Mandatory, False]'
}
$Settings += $RequireLabels
```

For the next question we will see if we want to provide a custom help link for end users to click on for assistance:

```powershell
Write-Host 'Provide users with a link to a custom help page [y/n]: ' -NoNewline
$Justify = Read-Host
If ($Justify -eq 'y') {
   Write-Host 'Enter custom URL address [www.test.com]: ' -NoNewLine
   $URL = Read-Host
   $URL = "[customurl,$URL]"
} Else {
   $URL = $NULL
}
$Settings += $URL
```

After that, we take the array and join all lines with a comma to produce a list format for the LabelPolicy Settings property:

```powershell
# All together now:
$AllSettings = $Settings -Join ','
```

Final step, create the Label Policy:

```powershell
# New Label Policy
New-LabelPolicy -Name $LabelName -Comment $Comment -Labels $Labels -Settings $AllSettings
```

Sample run for creating a new Label Policy:

```
---- NEW LABEL POLICY CREATOR ----

Provide a name for the Label Policy: Test Label Creator Label
Provide a comment for the Label Policy: This is just a test!

---- Available Labels ---

Name                              Disabled
----                              --------
Confidential Information          False
Confidential Information - New!   False
Research Label                    False
Book Test Label 2                 False
SensitiveTesting                  False
Research Material                 False
Confidential                      False
```

```
Which Labels to publish? [See provided list - can add more than one (use commas!)]: Confidential,Research Label
Apply this label by default to documents and email [None or Label]: Label
Enter default label name: [Choices - Confidential,Research Label] Confidential
Users must provide justification to remove a label or lower classification label [y/n]:  y
Requires users to apply a label to their email or documents [y/n]: y
Provide users with a link to a custom help page [y/n]: y
Enter custom URL address [www.test.com]: www.cnn.com
```

We can also validate the Settings property for the new Label Policy:

```
[defaultlabelid,570ea5fd-4682-4820-af11-a9cd87455b99],[requiredowngradejustification, true],[Mandatory, True],[customurl
,www.cnn.com]
```

As well as the cmdlet used to create it:

```
New-LabelPolicy -Name  -Comment This is just a test! -Labels Confidential,Research Label -Settings [defaultlabelid,570ea
5fd-4682-4820-af11-a9cd87455b99],[requiredowngradejustification, true],[Mandatory, True],[customurl,www.cnn.com]
```

File Plans

File Plan Manager is a new feature that Microsoft introduced in 2019 to the Security and Compliance Center. The intended purpose is to help apply tags to data in your tenant to help search for and discover. The feature appears to tie in multiple features of the SCC together like Labels and tags for labels as well as some compliance aspects with Citations.

In the Security and Compliance Center we are provided a new menu item as well as a new dashboard with which to manage the new feature:

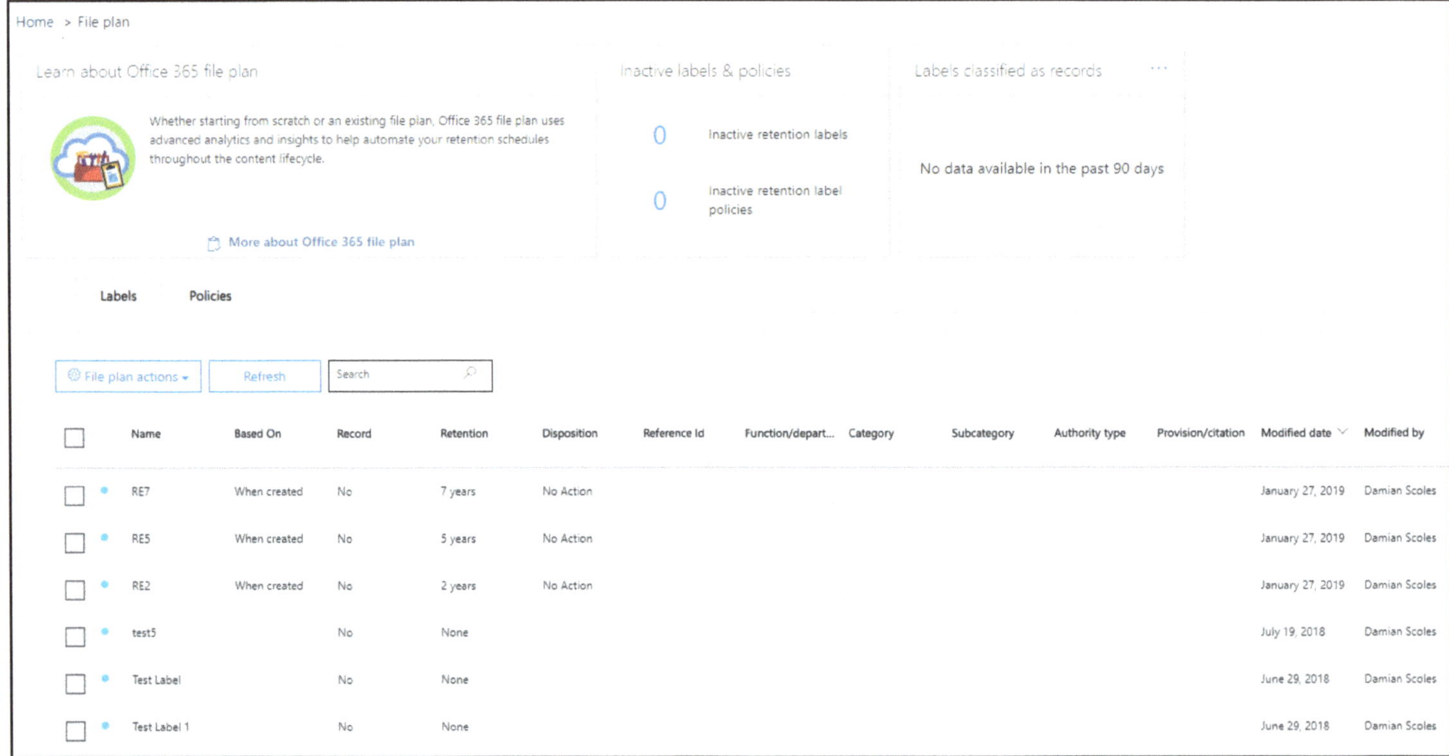

		Name	Based On	Record	Retention	Disposition	Reference Id	Function/depart...	Category	Subcategory	Authority type	Provision/citation	Modified date	Modified by
☐	•	RE7	When created	No	7 years	No Action							January 27, 2019	Damian Scoles
☐	•	RE5	When created	No	5 years	No Action							January 27, 2019	Damian Scoles
☐	•	RE2	When created	No	2 years	No Action							January 27, 2019	Damian Scoles
☐	•	test5		No	None								July 19, 2018	Damian Scoles
☐	•	Test Label		No	None								June 29, 2018	Damian Scoles
☐	•	Test Label 1		No	None								June 29, 2018	Damian Scoles

PowerShell

So what PowerShell cmdlets do we have available in the Security and Compliance Center for this:

```
Get-Command *fileplan*
```

And we get a rather long list of commands.

```
Export-FilePlanProperty
Get-FilePlanPropertyAuthority
Get-FilePlanPropertyCategory
Get-FilePlanPropertyCitation
Get-FilePlanPropertyDepartment
Get-FilePlanPropertyReferenceId
Get-FilePlanPropertyStructure
Get-FilePlanPropertySubCategory
Import-FilePlanProperty
New-FilePlanPropertyAuthority
New-FilePlanPropertyCategory
New-FilePlanPropertyCitation
New-FilePlanPropertyDepartment
New-FilePlanPropertyReferenceId
New-FilePlanPropertySubCategory
Remove-FilePlanPropertyAuthority
Remove-FilePlanPropertyCategory
Remove-FilePlanPropertyCitation
Remove-FilePlanPropertyDepartment
Remove-FilePlanPropertyReferenceId
Remove-FilePlanPropertySubCategory
Set-FilePlanPropertyAuthority
Set-FilePlanPropertyCategory
Set-FilePlanPropertyCitation
Set-FilePlanPropertyDepartment
Set-FilePlanPropertyReferenceId
Set-FilePlanPropertySubCategory
```

Creating a Label for a File Plan requires at least one of the following to be set - Reference ID, Business function or Department, Category, Authority Type and Provision/Citation. Now what exactly are these? Each of these items are freeform values intended to make it easier to filter, sort and find items with a particular tag type and value:

```
Reference ID
Business function or Department
Category
Authority Type
Provision/Citation
```

As we can see, there are quite a few cmdlets that are relevant to File Plans. Let's take a spin with these new cmdlets to see what we can use them for in our tenant.

As we know there are a few categories we can use for these File Plan related Labels, there appear to be matching cmdlets for each of the category types:

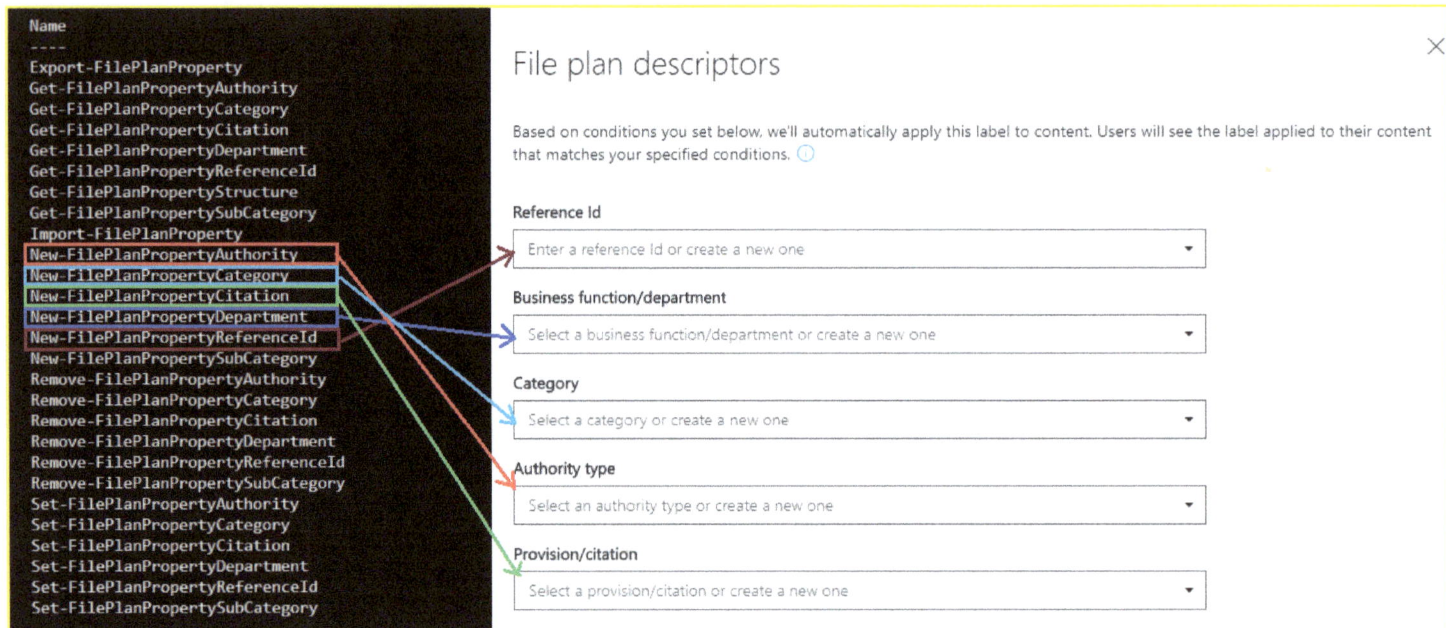

Unlike other objects types in the SCC, File Plans have some default Properties to work with. Let's see what is present by default for File Plans:

Get-FilePlanPropertyAuthority | Ft -Auto

```
PS C:\> Get-FilePlanPropertyAuthority | Ft -Auto
Creating a new session for implicit remoting of "Get-FilePlanPropertyAuthority" command...

RunspaceId                           DisplayName FilePlanPropertyType ReadOnly ExternalIdentity                     ImmutableId
----------                           ----------- -------------------- -------- ----------------                     -----------
44bc046d-22eb-444a-867c-9927cda30938 Business    Authority                     False 72e26dec-0a19-4bcb-94d2-c90855ae590b 00000000-0000-0000-0000
44bc046d-22eb-444a-867c-9927cda30938 Legal       Authority                     False 83121b5c-a9a0-4fe7-9d30-63df67e16991 00000000-0000-0000-0000
44bc046d-22eb-444a-867c-9927cda30938 Regulatory  Authority                     False 038702e1-93b6-43e3-8ef3-8c1702e896b1 00000000-0000-0000-0000
```

Get-FilePlanPropertyCategory | ft -Auto

```
PS C:\> Get-FilePlanPropertyCategory | ft -auto

RunspaceId                           DisplayName               FilePlanPropertyType ReadOnly ExternalIdentity                     Immutab
----------                           -----------               -------------------- -------- ----------------                     -------
44bc046d-22eb-444a-867c-9927cda30938 Accounts payable          Category                      False 382a38c0-bddb-49d9-96c3-c880e631118f 0000000
44bc046d-22eb-444a-867c-9927cda30938 Accounts receivable       Category                      False 5164f239-cefa-494b-8be2-0ce1433b73a7 0000000
44bc046d-22eb-444a-867c-9927cda30938 Administration            Category                      False 82d00422-1f60-46cd-9809-33ca0b4d2286 0000000
44bc046d-22eb-444a-867c-9927cda30938 Compliance                Category                      False 2c34b667-93f7-42c3-9198-e99ef32194cb 0000000
44bc046d-22eb-444a-867c-9927cda30938 Contracting               Category                      False b8a0ba75-36e5-4a0f-9571-9f4353cb20ef 0000000
44bc046d-22eb-444a-867c-9927cda30938 Financial statements      Category                      False d6e9feb5-5a39-4fca-8574-c3c782d3c50b 0000000
44bc046d-22eb-444a-867c-9927cda30938 Learning and development  Category                      False 99ab0102-9f93-4d74-8f04-e1839688c7ef 0000000
44bc046d-22eb-444a-867c-9927cda30938 Planning                  Category                      False 8d94f652-cba1-420e-bd66-5c7aeff9c1ae 0000000
44bc046d-22eb-444a-867c-9927cda30938 Payroll                   Category                      False 0813f438-00fb-4ced-837d-1b7ea33376ec 0000000
44bc046d-22eb-444a-867c-9927cda30938 Policies and procedures   Category                      False 82be75b8-25cc-405b-9afc-2d6a7cee81ea 0000000
44bc046d-22eb-444a-867c-9927cda30938 Procurement               Category                      False f40f35f8-972e-4683-b6f7-5b25d9cec0d1 0000000
44bc046d-22eb-444a-867c-9927cda30938 Recruiting and hiring     Category                      False 2ccf9199-ef59-486d-aae0-cf25dc19a4fb 0000000
44bc046d-22eb-444a-867c-9927cda30938 Research and development  Category                      False 73293e6a-5612-459e-9b74-fc9022d9e2aa 0000000
```

Get-FilePlanPropertyCitation | Ft -Auto

```
CitationUrl                                                              CitationJurisdiction                                  Displa
-----------                                                              ---------------------                                 ------
https://www.cftc.gov/LawRegulation/CommodityExchangeAct/index.htm        U.S. Futures Commodity Trading Commission (UCFTC) Commod
https://www.sec.gov/answers/about-lawsshtml.html#sox2002                 U.S. Securities and Exchange Commission (SEC)         Sarban
https://www.ftc.gov/enforcement/statutes/truth-lending-act              Federal Trade Commission (FTC)                        Truth
https://aspe.hhs.gov/report/health-insurance-portability-and-accountability-act-1996 U.S. Department of Health & Human Services (HHS) Health
https://www.osha.gov/recordkeeping/index.html                           U.S. Department of Labor (DOL)                        OSHA I
```

Get-FilePlanPropertyDepartment | Ft -Auto

```
DisplayName             FilePlanPropertyType ReadOnly ExternalIdentity                     ImmutableId                              Prior
-----------             -------------------- -------- ----------------                     -----------                              -----
Finance                 Department              False 5ff13e11-12ad-466d-bf6e-a2c9966fb36e 00000000-0000-0000-0000-000000000000
Human resources         Department              False a083b0e7-47fa-4150-8bdf-b1ed9cf5a3b7 00000000-0000-0000-0000-000000000000
Information technology  Department              False 9e984188-6b58-4277-bd77-604b0ea51f3f 00000000-0000-0000-0000-000000000000
Legal                   Department              False 89782331-5bea-4f14-be18-ed91e89ed151 00000000-0000-0000-0000-000000000000
Marketing               Department              False 525c8f55-c99e-4d21-9574-a5b4dc210089 00000000-0000-0000-0000-000000000000
Operations              Department              False 9a7592f3-4228-4267-9fd3-4df4a4f3c24d 00000000-0000-0000-0000-000000000000
Procurement             Department              False 511b5a31-237e-432d-831c-d65e231760b2 00000000-0000-0000-0000-000000000000
Products                Department              False df64c8eb-cbf7-4a17-be60-261b9f3eae04 00000000-0000-0000-0000-000000000000
Sales                   Department              False 6036318a-1709-4726-bbc0-40e01948fa0f 00000000-0000-0000-0000-000000000000
Services                Department              False 37578ad2-788f-4bc4-bec8-97e4deb8a373 00000000-0000-0000-0000-000000000000
```

The one exception is the Reference ID as there are no default ones.

Help in creating new Authorities, Categories, Citations, Departments and ReferenceIDs, all of which have no examples:

New-FilePlanPropertyAuthority
- No Microsoft Docs page
- No Help file examples

At the time of this book's release, creating these will take some effort. What we can do is see what parameters we can choose from and compare these to an existing object.

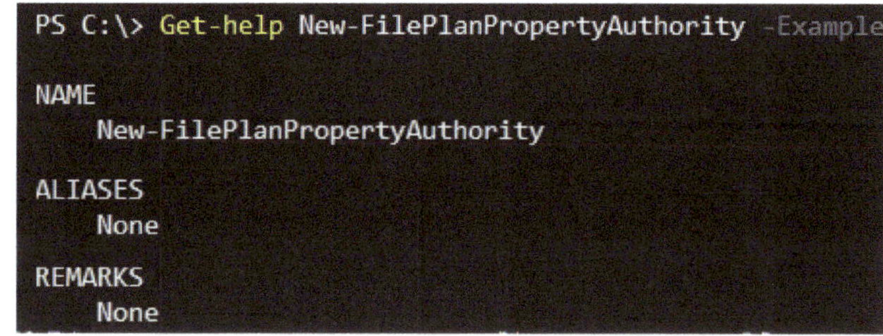

New Authority

Only real option is 'Name'. All other options are common parameters and switches for PowerShell cmdlets.

New-FilePlanPropertyAuthority -Name 'HR'

New Category

Only real option is 'Name'. All other options are common parameters and switches for PowerShell cmdlets.

New-FilePlanPropertyCategory -Name 'Information Technology'

```
RunspaceId          : 8d851f22-4514-4fc3-b53b-07a3f888e32d
DisplayName         : Information Technology
FilePlanPropertyType : Category
ReadOnly            : False
ExternalIdentity    :
ImmutableId         : 00000000-0000-0000-0000-000000000000
Priority            : 2
Workload            : Exchange, SharePoint
Policy              : 2feadfdf-fad6-4eb3-bb2a-ca92846e8892
Comment             :
Disabled            : False
Mode                : Enforce
ObjectVersion       : 9fb3634e-26cb-4cfb-2e8b-08d71789f062
CreatedBy           : Damian Scoles
LastModifiedBy      : Damian Scoles
```

New Citation

For this example we can create a new File Plan Property Citation based on the FTC's Truth in Advertising protection for consumers. We need to populate the Name, CitationURL and Citation Jurisdiction.

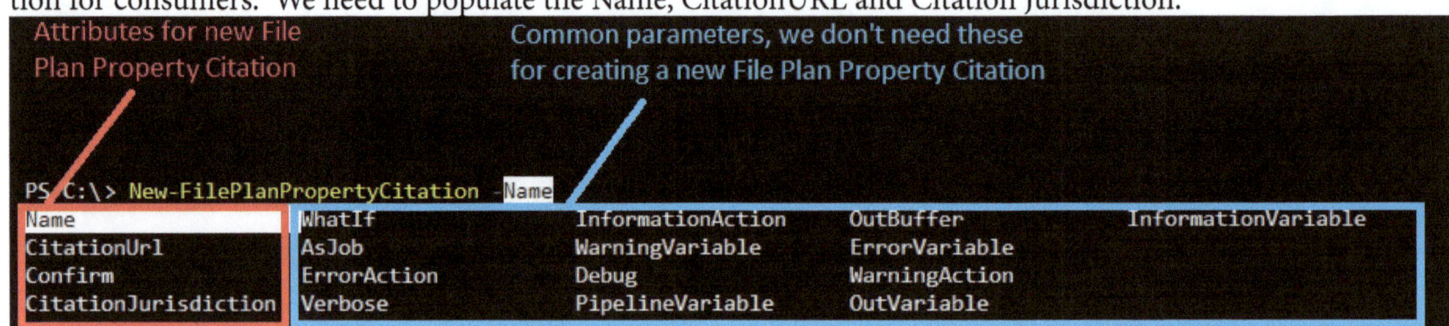

** Note ** Citations allow us to add external links to resources that pertain to the information in our tenant. Think of a citation as a reference used in a book for an extern source of further information.

$CitationURL = 'https://www.ftc.gov/news-events/media-resources/truth-advertising'
$Name = 'Truth in Advertising'
$CitationJurisdiction = 'Federal Trade Commission (FTC)'
New-FilePlanPropertyCitation -Name $Name -CitationURL $CitationURL -CitationJurisdiction
$CitationJurisdiction

```
RunspaceId           : 8d851f22-4514-4fc3-b53b-07a3f888e32d
CitationUrl          : https://www.ftc.gov/news-events/media-resources/truth-advertising
CitationJurisdiction : Federal Trade Commission (FTC)
DisplayName          : Truth in Advertising
FilePlanPropertyType : Citation
ReadOnly             : False
ExternalIdentity     :
ImmutableId          : 00000000-0000-0000-0000-000000000000
Priority             : 0
Workload             : Exchange, SharePoint
Policy               : 2feadfdf-fad6-4eb3-bb2a-ca92846e8892
Comment              :
Disabled             : False
```

Another example would be based on the Clayton Act which is focused on 'preventing and eliminating unlawful tying contracts, corporate mergers and acquisitions, and interlocking directorates.' We can build a similar set of criteria and create the new File Plan Property Citation:

$CitationURL = 'https://www.ftc.gov/enforcement/statutes/clayton-act'
$Name = 'Clayton Act'
$CitationJurisdiction = 'Federal Trade Commission (FTC)'
New-FilePlanPropertyCitation   -Name $Name   -CitationURL $CitationURL   -CitationJurisdiction
$CitationJurisdiction

```
RunspaceId           : 8d851f22-4514-4fc3-b53b-07a3f888e32d
CitationUrl          : https://www.ftc.gov/enforcement/statutes/clayton-act
CitationJurisdiction : Federal Trade Commission (FTC)
DisplayName          : Clayton Act
FilePlanPropertyType : Citation
ReadOnly             : False
ExternalIdentity     :
```

Both new objects can now be found in the SCC:

```
Get-FilePlanPropertyCitation |Where {$_.CitationJurisdiction -like 'Federal*'} |ft DisplayName,Citation*
```

```
DisplayName            CitationUrl                                                       CitationJurisdiction
-----------            -----------                                                       --------------------
Clayton Act            https://www.ftc.gov/enforcement/statutes/clayton-act              Federal Trade Commission (FTC)
Truth in Advertising   https://www.ftc.gov/news-events/media-resources/truth-advertising Federal Trade Commission (FTC)
Truth in lending Act   https://www.ftc.gov/enforcement/statutes/truth-lending-act         Federal Trade Commission (FTC)
```

New Department

```
New-FilePlanPropertyDepartment -Name 'Research'
```

```
DisplayName          : Research
FilePlanPropertyType : Department
ReadOnly             : False
ExternalIdentity     :
ImmutableId          : 00000000-0000-0000-0000-000000000000
Priority             : 4
Workload             : Exchange, SharePoint
Policy               : 2feadfdf-fad6-4eb3-bb2a-ca92846e8892
```

New Subcategory

None of these exist either and you would require an existing Category before creating a SubCategory:

```
New-FilePlanPropertySubCategory -Name 'Litigant - Employee 4569' -ParentId '73293e6a-5612-459e-9b74-fc9022d9e2aa'
```

The ParentID value of '73293e6a-5612-459e-9b74-fc9022d9e2aa' is the GUID of an existing File Plan Category:

```
ParentCategory       : 73293e6a-5612-459e-9b74-fc9022d9e2aa
ParentId             : 73293e6a-5612-459e-9b74-fc9022d9e2aa
DisplayName          : Litigant - Empoyee 4569
FilePlanPropertyType : SubCategory
ReadOnly             : False
ExternalIdentity     :
ImmutableId          : 00000000-0000-0000-0000-000000000000
Priority             : 7
Workload             : Exchange, SharePoint
Policy               : 2feadfdf-fad6-4eb3-bb2a-ca92846e8892
```

New ReferenceID

A ReferenceID is another File Plan tag we can create for our Labels. None exist by default either. The Reference ID does not have a defined format and can be any string you need for the ReferenceID.

```
New-FilePlanPropertyReferenceID -Name 'ID 821'
```

```
DisplayName          : ID 821
FilePlanPropertyType : ReferenceId
ReadOnly             : False
ExternalIdentity     :
ImmutableId          : 00000000-0000-0000-0000-000000000000
Priority             : 6
Workload             : Exchange, SharePoint
Policy               : 2feadfdf-fad6-4eb3-bb2a-ca92846e8892
```

How To Use File Plan Properties?

If we remember from the beginning of the File Plan Manager section we had a series of Labels. These Labels had some empty columns and match these five properties exactly. Basically the File Plan Properties can be applied to Labels we have in the Security and Compliance Center. Adding the properties to a Label is not an obvious process. For example, one of the Labels is called 'RE7' which is a seven year retention policy. If we review the settings/ properties we do not see any of those File Plan Properties exposed:

```
RunspaceId           : 8d851f22-4514-4fc3-b53b-07a3f888e32d
Settings             :
LabelActions         : {{"Type":"Retention","SubType":null,"Settings":[{"Key":"retentionComplianceAction","Value":"Delete"},
                       {"Key":"RetentionType","Value":"TaggedAgeInDays"},{"Key":"IsRecordLabel","Value":"False"},{"Key":
                       "RetentionDuration","Value":"Unlimited"}]}}
Conditions           : {}
LocaleSettings       :
DisplayName          :
ParentId             :
Tooltip              :
ReadOnly             : False
ExternalIdentity     :
ImmutableId          : 430feeb5-48a4-4f36-9f41-68a64555627f
Priority             : 2
Workload             : Exchange, SharePoint, OneDriveForBusiness
Policy               : ba2e4701-3c19-4825-992c-aea485226ad7
Comment              :
Disabled             : False
Mode                 : Enforce
```

How can we add the properties then? Well, let's modify this one Label in the File Plan Manager, adding some categories and see what happens. So, after changing the properties, we see this in File Plan Manager:

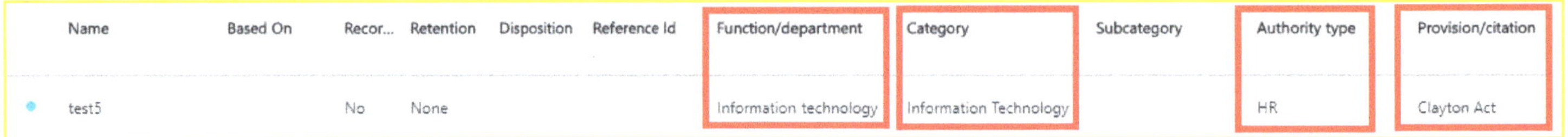

Name	Based On	Recor...	Retention	Disposition	Reference Id	Function/department	Category	Subcategory	Authority type	Provision/citation
test5		No	None			Information technology	Information Technology		HR	Clayton Act

So we see there are four new values applied to this Label. But what does this change in the actual Label that can be seen with PowerShell?

> Get-Label Test5

From the properties of this Label, we now see the changes in the LabelActions property:

```
RunspaceId           : 8d851f22-4514-4fc3-b53b-07a3f888e32d
Settings             :
LabelActions         : {{"Type":"Retention","SubType":null,"Settings":[{"Key":"retentionComplianceAction","Value":"Delete"
                       },{"Key":"RetentionType","Value":"TaggedAgeInDays"},{"Key":"IsRecordLabel","Value":"False"},{"Key":
                       "RetentionDuration","Value":"Unlimited"},{"Key":"FilePlanPropertyDepartment","Value":"Information
                       technology"},{"Key":"FilePlanPropertyCategory","Value":"Information
                       Technology"},{"Key":"FilePlanPropertyCitation","Value":"Clayton
                       Act"},{"Key":"FilePlanPropertyAuthority","Value":"HR"}]}}
Conditions           : {}
LocaleSettings       :
DisplayName          :
ParentId             :
Tooltip              :
ReadOnly             : False
ExternalIdentity     :
```

Attempting to modify the Label Actions field simply isn't possible when this book was being published:

```
PS C> Set-Label Test5 -LabelActions $NewVar
WARNING: Encountered exception: Microsoft.Exchange.Management.Transport.InvalidLabelActionException: The label action 'Retention;' is invalid,
RetentionType; IsRecordLabel; FilePlanPropertyDepartment; FilePlanPropertyCategory; FilePlanPropertyCitation; FilePlanPropertyAuthority is immu
    at Microsoft.Office.CompliancePolicy.Tasks.SetLabel.<CopyExplicitParameters>b__53_0(LabelAction labelAction)
    at System.Collections.Generic.List`1.ForEach(Action`1 action)
    at Microsoft.Office.CompliancePolicy.Tasks.SetLabel.CopyExplicitParameters()
    at Microsoft.Office.CompliancePolicy.Tasks.SetLabel.StampChangesOn(IConfigurable dataObject)
WARNING: Encountered exception: Microsoft.Exchange.Management.Transport.InvalidLabelActionException: The label action 'Retention;' is invalid,
RetentionType; IsRecordLabel; FilePlanPropertyDepartment; FilePlanPropertyCategory; FilePlanPropertyCitation; FilePlanPropertyAuthority is immu
    at Microsoft.Office.CompliancePolicy.Tasks.SetLabel.<CopyExplicitParameters>b__53_0(LabelAction labelAction)
    at System.Collections.Generic.List`1.ForEach(Action`1 action)
    at Microsoft.Office.CompliancePolicy.Tasks.SetLabel.CopyExplicitParameters()
    at Microsoft.Office.CompliancePolicy.Tasks.SetLabel.StampChangesOn(IConfigurable dataObject)
    at Microsoft.Exchange.Configuration.Tasks.SetObjectTaskBase`2.PrepareDataObject()
    at Microsoft.Exchange.Configuration.Tasks.SetTaskBase`1.InternalValidate()
    at Microsoft.Exchange.Configuration.Tasks.SetSystemConfigurationObjectTask`3.InternalValidate()
    at Microsoft.Office.CompliancePolicy.Tasks.SetComplianceRuleBase.InternalValidate()
```

So it appears that for the meantime, we can create Authorities, Categories, Citations, Departments, ReferenceIDs and SubCategories with PowerShell. We cannot change Label Actions in PowerShell. However, we are able to document all Labels with PowerShell which is good for creating an auditing report on File Plans, Labels and other FilePlan data.

Building Scripts

In This Chapter

How To Begin
Documentation of SCC
PowerShell and Change
Script Building Summary

In the previous two chapters quite a few topics concerning PowerShell were covered, with some Exchange Server topics sprinkled into the mix. Now that some basic topics have been covered let's see how these can be used in a PowerShell script and begin building your own scripts. This chapter will cover what to start with, how to add to the script, how to enhance the script, perform detailed testing and finally how to transition and use this in production with your SCC tenant.

How to Begin

When script building, having a clear goal of what is to be accomplished is advisable. In the past programmers used various methods to build scripts. The key to our method is that we need a beginning and we need an end. This method requires a seed or first cmdlet to start with and from that we need to aim for the end goal, what could be called the purpose of the script. Let's start with a real life example.

To build a complete script, to keep the process ordered and to complete the task at hand there are a series of steps that can provide a useful guide to the process. Provided below is a series of suggested steps for creating a Power-Shell script.

- Seed to start the script - usually a core concept with a corresponding PowerShell cmdlet
- Look for samples on the Internet to save time – code blocks, one-liners, routines and usage
- Loops if needed to perform iterations (Foreach, Do...While, etc.) over objects in the SCC
- Define arrays if needed for the loops or other parts of the scripts
- Functions if a process is repeatable or needs to be called on from multiple parts of a script
- Export the results
- Build in some error checking or fail safes
- Commenting - top of the script - detailed description
- Commenting - document the script

> **TIP**
>
> On the first run of any new script, either the script needs to be run in a test tenant or all PowerShell cmdlets that make changes should be commented to prevent their execution. Alternatively, you can leverage the WhatIf switch to see what the cmdlet would do. However, trailing code can react as if the cmdlet failed, as the cmdlet did not actually run.

Documentation of SCC

This book is built on practical ways to use PowerShell and building scripts in a practical manner is considered part of that overall goal. Imagine for this scenario you are the administrator of a parent company that is working to document an Office 365 environment for a recently acquired company. You want a script that will produce a report of settings, compliance related items and more that will be used to assess next steps with this acquisition. Important items to consider are Labels in use, any custom Sensitive Information Types and more. Reports will be used by the IT department as well as company executives.

Some information is confidential or at least compliance-related, so remember to store exported data on a secure drive. Additionally, not every setting or report is exportable via PowerShell or solely through the SCC PowerShell module. Secure Score reports are either accessed at https://protection.office.com or via the Microsoft Graph PowerShell module - https://blogs.technet.microsoft.com/cloudlojik/2017/09/05/using-powershell-to-connect-to-microsoft-graph-api/.

Coding the Script

In the Security and Compliance Center, we have a lot of items that can be configured and set up for an Office 365 tenant. From Labels, to Policies, to Keyword Dictionaries and Assigned Role Groups we will have quite some territory to cover with a documentation script. In order to accomplish this, we will need a few things in order to be successful. First we will need to connect to the Security and Compliance Center with an account that has the appropriate access to various features. At the minimum we want a Global Admin for the tenant, but we may also want the eDiscovery Administrator for access to Compliance Cases.

Where to Start

First, we need a log file and a directory where to export files and more as part of this process. First, to help with automation, we'll use the current path as the location for all files and store this in a $Path variable. For our general log file, a variable called $File will store the filename

```
$Path = (Get-Item -Path ".\" -Verbose).FullName
$File = 'SecurityComplianceCenter-Documentation.txt'
$Destination = $Path+'\'+$File
```

In addition to general log files, we will create exports of configuration data as needed, so the $Path variable will be valuable later in the script for specifying a destination for files exported by the script. After we have the variable set, we will move on to documenting actual configuration data in the SCC. First, we can start with a security export that shows who has been assigned to what roles. How do we do this? If we remember from the Security chapter, we need to look at Role Groups. Each Role Group could have members assigned to it in the SCC. One exception is the eDiscovery Case Administrator as this role has it's own dedicated PowerShell cmdlets. We will gather that in an additional code section.

```
$RoleGroups = (Get-RoleGroup).Name
Foreach ($RoleGroup in $RoleGroups){
    $Members = Get-RoleGroupMember -Identity $RoleGroup
```

```
    $Line = $RoleGroup | Out-File $Destination -Append
    $Line = '----------------------------'| Out-File $Destination -Append
    $Members| Out-File $Destination -Append
    $Line = '' | Out-File $Destination -Append
}
```

Sample output from this section:

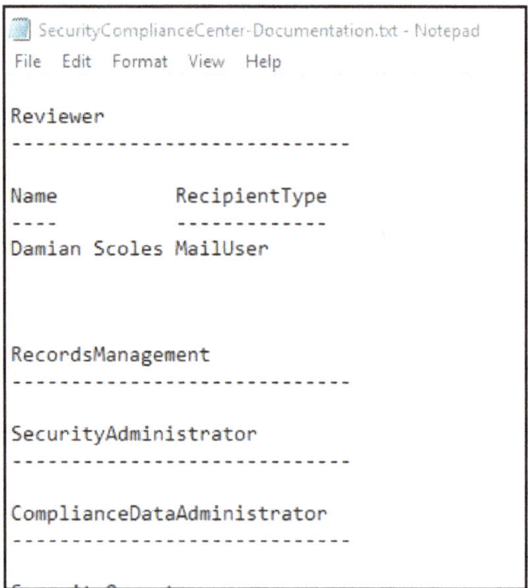

We need to add the eDiscovery Case Admin (these lines are added after the above loop):

```
$Line = ' ' | Out-File $Destination -Append
$Line = 'eDiscovery Case Admin' | Out-File $Destination -Append
$Line = '--------------------------' | Out-File $Destination -Append
Get-eDiscoveryCaseAdmin
$Line = ' ' | Out-File $Destination -Append
```

Note that all lines of PowerShell that export to the $Destination file use '-Append' at the end. We do this so we do not overwrite any existing content in that file. Also note that there are extra lines, literally, that are used for formatting as we want to make the destination log file one that someone can read.

Next we can tackle Labels, Label Policies and Sensitive Information Types. As we get into output that could be wider than a single screen, we should consider a way to widen the output placed in the $Destination file. We can do this by adjusting our buffers for the PowerShell window like so:

```
$Host.UI.RawUI.BufferSize = New-Object Management.Automation.Host.Size (500, 9999)
```

This now widens our buffer to 500 and the window size to 9999. Now we can go back to exporting Labels and Label Policies:

```
$Line = 'Labels on the Security and Compliance Center' | Out-File $Destination -Append
$Labels = Get-Label | Ft Name,Workload,Settings,LocalSettings,ToolTip,Comment -Auto | Out-File $Destination -Append
$Line = ' ' | Out-File $Destination -Append
```

We will take a similar approach to Label Policies:

$Line = 'Label Policies in the Security and Compliance Center' | Out-File $Destination -Append
$LabelPolicies = Get-LabelPolicy | Ft Name,Type,Settings,Labels,WorkLoad,Comment-Auto | Out-File $Destination -Append
$Line = ' ' | Out-File $Destination -Append

Next, for Sensitive Data Types, we have a few things that will need to be processed

Get-DlpSensitiveInformationType | Where {$_.Publisher -ne 'Microsoft Corporation'} | Ft Name, Publisher, ID, Description, RecommendedConfidence, RulePackID | Out-File $Destination -Append

We can also export the Rules Packages that are associated with these Sensitive Information Types:

$DLPRulePackIDs = (Get-DlpSensitiveInformationType | where {$_.Publisher -ne 'Microsoft Corporation'}).RulePackID

Foreach ($DLPRulePackID in $DLPRulePackIDs) {

    # Define Output File:
    $File = 'DlpSensitiveInformationTypeRulePackage-'+$DLPRulePackID+'.xml'
    $XMLDestination = $Path+'\'+$File

    # Pull current Rules Package:
    $RulesPackage = Get-DlpSensitiveInformationTypeRulePackage $DLPRulePackID

    # Export Rules Collections to XML Files:
    Set-Content -path $XMLDestination -Encoding Byte -Value $RulesPackage.SerializedClassification-RuleCollection
}

Sample XML File Result:

```xml
<?xml version="1.0" encoding="UTF-16"?>
- <RulePackage xmlns="http://schemas.microsoft.com/office/2011/mce">
    - <RulePack id="6b4e981b-0d62-4423-b660-86603107af7e">
        <Version major="1" minor="0" build="0" revision="0"/>
        <Publisher id="970da45c-b7dd-4ca3-9e2d-52340e28b2c4"/>
        - <Details defaultLangCode="en-us">
            - <LocalizedDetails langcode="en-us">
                <PublisherName>Damian Scoles</PublisherName>
                <Name>ConfidentialInformation</Name>
                <Description>Confidetial Information Keyword Check</Description>
            </LocalizedDetails>
        </Details>
    </RulePack>
    - <Rules>
        - <Entity id="791b1558-a0aa-49e4-bc31-e03b24d43e73" patternsProximity="300" recommendedConfidence="85">
            - <Pattern confidenceLevel="85">
                <IdMatch idRef="ConfInfo"/>
            </Pattern>
        </Entity>
        <Regex id="ConfInfo">Confidential Information</Regex>
        - <LocalizedStrings>
            - <Resource idRef="791b1558-a0aa-49e4-bc31-e03b24d43e73">
                <Name langcode="en-us" default="true">ConfidentialInformation</Name>
                <Description langcode="en-us" default="true">Confidetial Information Keyword Check</Description>
            </Resource>
        </LocalizedStrings>
    </Rules>
</RulePackage>
```

In addition to the normal Sensitive Information Types, we also need to gather information on Exact Data Match (EDM) information, Keyword Dictionaries. In each section we export our findings to a destination file for examination or documentation:

```
$Line = 'DLP EDM Schemas' | Out-File $Destination -Append
$Line = '---------------'| Out-File $Destination -Append
$DLPEDMSchemas = Get-DlpEdmSchema
$DLPEDMSchemas | Select Name, DataStoreName, Description, GUID, IsValid | Out-File $Destination
-Append
Foreach ($DLPEdmSchema in $DLPEdmSchemas) {
   # Variables
   $EdmSchemaXML = $DLPEdmSchema.EdmSchemaXML
   $Name = $DLPEdmSchema.Name

   # Define Output File:
   $File = "DlpEDMSchema-$Name.xml"
   $XMLDestination = $Path+'\'+$File

   # Output to XML File:
   $EdmSchemaXML | Out-File $XMLDestination
}
```

Next, documenting Keyword Dictionaries:

```
$Line = 'DLP Keyword Dictionaries' | Out-File $Destination -Append
$Line = '------------------------' | Out-File $Destination -Append
$Line = Get-DlpKeywordDictionary | Select Name, IsValid, Description, Identity, KeywordDictionary |
Out-File $Destination -Append
```

Next we will cover Information barriers as they are only accessible in PowerShell. First we need to document the general status of the Information Barrier Application in the Security and Compliance Center:

```
$Line = 'Information Barrier Policy Application Status' | Out-File $Destination -Append
$Line = '-------------------------------------------------' | Out-File $Destination -Append
$Line = Get-InformationBarrierPoliciesApplicationStatus | Out-File $Destination -Append

$Line = 'Information Barrier Policies' | Out-File $Destination -Append
$Line = '---------------------------' | Out-File $Destination -Append
$Line = Get-InformationBarrierPolicy | ft Name,Type,AssignedSegment,SegmentsAllowed,Segments-
Blocked,SegmentsAllowedFilter,BlockVisibility,BlockCommunication,State,CreatedBy,CreationTimeUT-
C -AutoSize | Out-File $Destination -Append
$Line = ' ' | Out-File $Destination -Append
```

Lastly, we will also document the Organization Segments in use:

```
$Line = 'Organization Segment(s)' | Out-File $Destination -Append
$Line = '---------------------------' | Out-File $Destination -Append
$Line = Get-OrganizationSegment | Ft Name, Type, UserGroupFilter, ObjectClass, CreatedBy | Out-File
$Destination -Append
```

Next we can move on to Data Loss Prevention (DLP) items in the Security and Compliance Center:

```
$Line = 'DLP Compliance Policies' | Out-File $Destination -Append
$Line = '-----------------------' | Out-File $Destination -Append
$DLPCompliancePolicies = Get-DlpCompliancePolicy | Select Name, Type, Mode, Enabled,
Comment, Workload, ExchangeLocation, SharePointLocation, SharePointLocationException,
OneDriveLocation, OneDriveLocationException, ExchangeOnPremisesLocation,
SharePointOnPremisesLocation, SharePointOnPremisesLocationException, TeamsLocation,
TeamsLocationException, ExchangeSender, ExchangeSenderMemberOf, ExchangeSenderException,
ExchangeSenderMemberOfException

Foreach ($DLPCompliancePolicy in $DLPCompliancePolicies) {
    $DLPCompliancePolicy | Ft Name,Type,Mode,Enabled,Comment,Workload | Out-File $Destination
    -Append
    $DLPCompliancePolicy | Fl ExchangeLocation, SharePointLocation, SharePointLocationException,
    OneDriveLocation, OneDriveLocationException, ExchangeOnPremisesLocation,
    SharePointOnPremisesLocation, SharePointOnPremisesLocationException,
    TeamsLocation, TeamsLocationException, ExchangeSender, ExchangeSenderMemberOf,
    ExchangeSenderException, ExchangeSenderMemberOfException | Out-File $Destination -Append
}
```

For DLP Compliance Rules, we will create a summary table as well as a full details export to the same file:

```
$Line = 'DLP Compliance Rules' | Out-File $Destination -Append
$Line = '--------------------' | Out-File $Destination -Append
$DLPComplianceRules = Get-DLPComplianceRule
Foreach ($DLPComplianceRule in $DLPComplianceRules) {
    $DLPComplianceRule | Ft Name, Mode,Disabled,Workload,Policy,AccessScope  -Auto |Out-File
    $Destination -Append
    $DLPComplianceRule | Fl | Out-File $Destination -Append
}
```

For the last part of the script we will pull some more Compliance information like cases, holds and more.

Compliance Cases:

```
$Line = 'Compliance Cases' | Out-File $Destination -Append
$Line = '----------------' | Out-File $Destination -Append
$ComplianceCases = Get-ComplianceCase
$ComplianceCases | Ft Name,Identity,CaseType,Status,Description -Auto | Out-File $Destination -Append
$Line = '' | Out-File $Destination -Append
Foreach ($ComplianceCase in $ComplianceCases){
    $Name = $ComplianceCase.Name
    $Line = "Compliance Case Members [ $Name ]" | Out-File $Destination -Append
    $Line = Get-ComplianceCaseMember -Case $Name | Out-File $Destination -Append
    $Line = '' | Out-File $Destination -Append
}
```

Compliance Searches:

```
$Line = 'Compliance Searches' | Out-File $Destination -Append
$Line = '-------------------' | Out-File $Destination -Append
```

```
$ComplianceSearches = Get-ComplianceSearch
$ComplianceSearches | Ft Name, SearchType, Description, ContentMatchQuery -Auto | Out-File
$Destination -Append
$Line = '' | Out-File $Destination -Append
$Line = 'Detailed Compliance Search Info' | Out-File $Destination -Append
$ComplianceSearches | Fl | Out-File $Destination -Append
```

Compliance Search Actions:

```
$Line = 'Compliance Search Action' | Out-File $Destination -Append
$Line = '------------------------' | Out-File $Destination -Append
$ComplianceSearchActions = Get-ComplianceSearchAction
$ComplianceSearchActions | Ft Name,Status,Action,SearchName,Results -Auto | Out-File $Destination
-Append
$Line = '' | Out-File $Destination -Append
$Line = 'Detailed Compliance Search Action Info' | Out-File $Destination -Append
$ComplianceSearchActions | Fl | Out-File $Destination -Append
```

Retention Compliance Policies:

```
$Line = 'Retention Compliance Policies' | Out-File $Destination -Append
$Line = '-----------------------------' | Out-File $Destination -Append
$RetentionCompliancePolicies = Get-RetentionCompliancePolicy
$RetentionCompliancePolicies | Ft Name,Enabled,DistributionStatus,TeamsPolicy,Comment -Auto |
Out-File $Destination -Append
$Line = '' | Out-File $Destination -Append
$Line = 'Detailed Retention Compliance Policies' | Out-File $Destination -Append
$RetentionCompliancePolicies | Fl | Out-File $Destination -Append
```

Retention Compliance Rules:

```
$Line = 'Retention Compliance Rules' | Out-File $Destination -Append
$Line = '--------------------------' | Out-File $Destination -Append
$RetentionComplianceRules = Get-RetentionComplianceRule
$RetentionComplianceRules |Ft Name, Mode, Disabled, ContentMatchQuery,
RetentionComplianceAction, Workload -Auto | Out-File $Destination -Append
$Line = '' | Out-File $Destination -Append
$Line = 'Detailed Retention Compliance rules' | Out-File $Destination -Append
$RetentionComplianceRules | Fl | Out-File $Destination -Append
```

Last:

```
$Line = 'Detailed Teams Retention Compliance Policies' | Out-File $Destination -Append
$Line = '--------------------------------------------' | Out-File $Destination -Append
$TeamsRetentionCompliancePolicies = Get-TeamsRetentionCompliancePolicy | Fl | Out-File $Destination
-Append
$Line = 'Detailed Teams Retention Compliance Rules' | Out-File $Destination -Append
$Line = '-----------------------------------------' | Out-File $Destination -Append
$TeamsRetentionComplianceRules = Get-TeamsRetentionComplianceRule | Fl | Out-File $Destination
-Append
```

PowerShell and Change

Before ending this chapter on the basics of building a script, a thought should be given to the longevity of your script…. PowerShell cmdlets change with features added, removed, deprecated and more….

Change is a constant at Microsoft. By the time you read this, Microsoft will probably have already added some new cmdlets to the Security and Compliance Center. Other workloads in Office 365 change every month, week and day. PowerShell change is less often, but the results are no different. New editions are made, old commands deprecated and eventually removed.

Microsoft also has enhanced new options like Cloud Shell to include ways to work with objects in Azure and Exchange Online. It is within the realm of possibility that Cloud Shell will be enhanced to work with all workloads in Office 365 at some time. This would provide an Administrator a single avenue with which to manage their Office 365 tenant. As scripts are built, effort may be required to make sure the cmdlets being used are not being deprecated. Cmdlets that are being deprecated can be found in a few ways. Simply run a cmdlet in PowerShell and if the cmdlet is being deprecated a message in yellow will reveal itself.

In any workload for Office 365 the change comes quickly. PowerShell cmdlets are added. PowerShell cmdlets are removed. Often there is no notification at all. This usually comes with features being added or removed. How do we know that the cmdlets changed? One way to keep track of the changes is to connect to the Security and Compliance Center, log the number of available cmdlets and export a list of the cmdlets to a text file. This script could be run each day or scheduled to run.

Example: Historical charts that map out the number of PowerShell cmdlets available for SCC and Skype Online. Notice the change for the SCC which increased from 125 cmdlets in 2017 to almost 250 in 2019:

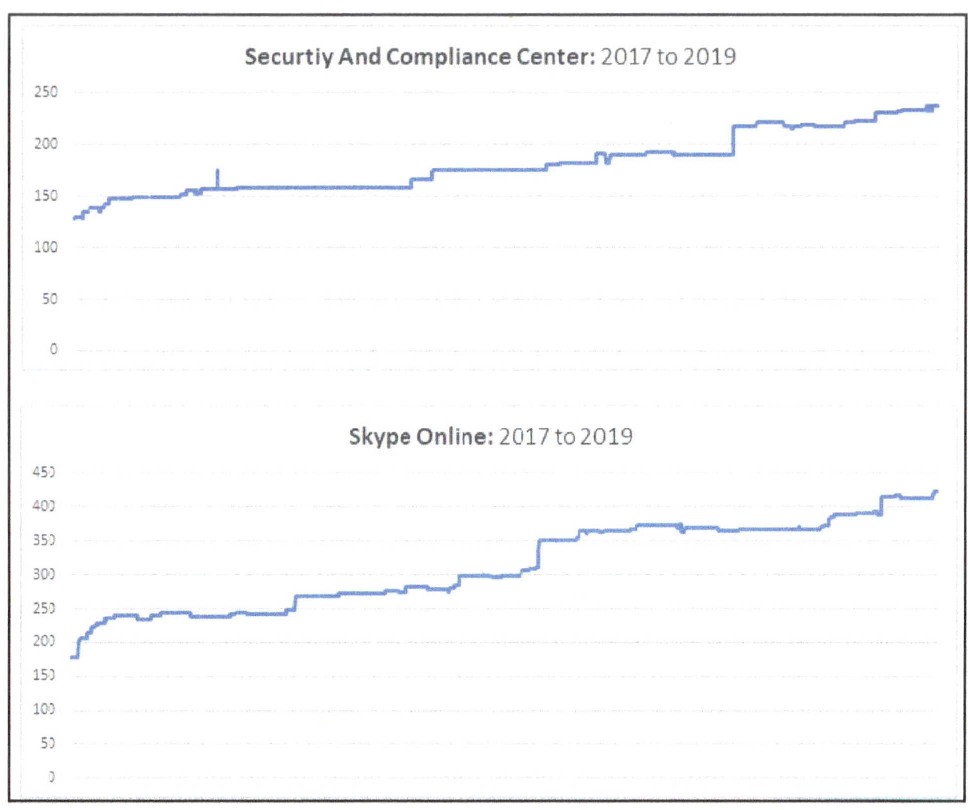

Coding the Script

Just like the first script in this chapter we will need to initiate a connection to the Security and Compliance Center. Again, we create the credentials (stored in a secure password file) to be used in the connection:

```
$Username = "GlobalAdmin@MyTenant.OnMicrosoft.Com"
$Password = Cat C:\SecureString-MyTenant.txt | ConvertTo-SecureString
$LiveCred = New-Object -TypeName System.Management.Automation.PSCredential -Argumentlist
$Username, $Password
```

Since we want to keep track of the cmdlets over time we need a place to drop the results file into. For the sake of this exercise we create a file structure like so (to keep the results organized):

```
C:\CmdletCheck - Root directory to store lists of cmdlets
C:\CmdletCheck\Historical - Store historical data
```

First step is to read in the existing CSV file that has results in it. If this is the first time a script executed, we can populate the data with a current date and a '0' to simulate the fact that there are 0 known cmdlets at this time.

```
# Read in CSV file for comparison
$CSV = Import-CSV 'C:\CmdletCheck\Historical\CurrentChart.csv'
```

Next, we can store the number of cmdlets in a variable called $SCCNum and it will be populated with the number found in the column SecurityAndCompliance in the CSV file. The $CSV variable can be read and the current number of Exchange Online cmdlets will be stored in a variable called '$SCCNum':

```
Foreach ($Line in $CSV) {
    $SCCNum = $Line.SecurityAndCompliance
}
```

The CSV being utilized for the step above has the following format:

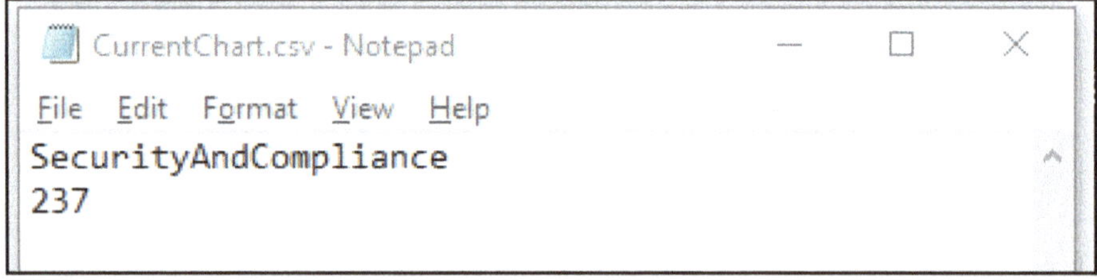

Now that we have that out of the way, it's time to connect to Office 365 and the SCC specifically. To do so, we need to use the New-PSSession cmdlet. What can we do with this cmdlet? Let's review the Get-Help:

```
Get-Help New-PsSession -Examples
```

```
Example 11: Create a session option

PS C:\>$so = New-PSSessionOption  -SkipCACheck
PS C:\>New-PSSession -ConnectionUri https://management.exchangelabs.com/Management -SessionOption $so -Credential
Server01\Admin01
```

Now the above is the closest of the examples included. In fact, we need a couple of other options:

Authentication - Specifies the mechanism that is used to authenticate the user's credentials - Office 365 uses 'Basic' for its default authentication

AllowRedirection - Allows redirection of this connection to an alternate Uniform Resource Identifier (URI)

- This is a required option for connecting to Office 365 because it needs to be able to redirect the session to the appropriate resource in the cloud

We will store the PowerShell session connection in a variable called $Session. This way we can use the 'Import-PS-Session' cmdlet to initiate the connection:

```
Example 1: Import all commands from a PSSession

PS C:\>$S = New-PSSession -ComputerName Server01
PS C:\>Import-PSSession -Session $S
```

Putting this together we get these two cmdlets to initiate the session:

```
$Session = New-PSSession -ConfigurationName Microsoft.Exchange -ConnectionUri https://
ps.compliance.protection.outlook.com/powershell-liveid/ -Credential $LiveCred -Authentication Basic
-AllowRedirection
Import-PSSession $Session
```

After the session is connected we need to query for cmdlets that are related to the Security and Compliance Center. How can we filter for these cmdlets? Well, let's see what cmdlets are available once we make our connection:

Get-Command

When that is typed in a seemingly endless stream of cmdlets is displayed. At the time of this writing, the total was around 5,338 cmdlets. How do we get an accurate count:

```
(Get-Command).Count
```

The parentheses and the '.Count' allows PowerShell to count the number of items that would be displayed if the entire list was shown. This same method could be used again, almost any variable or cmdlet that lists results. Now, looking at the list of cmdlets, we see there are a number of modules listed.

```
Get-Command | Select-Object ModuleName -Unique
```

Well, that's great, but that provides 148 module names. None of them include Security Compliance Center in the names. We need to take another approach. We know that a cmdlet like 'Get-DLP*' is an SCC cmdlet. Maybe we can get the module name from that cmdlet:

```
Get-Command Get-DLPCompliancePolicy
```

```
CommandType     Name                      Version     Source
-----------     ----                      -------     ------
Function        Get-DlpCompliancePolicy   1.0         tmp_aiujrsqt.syu
```

Nice. As can be seen by the name of the module that the cmdlet is in, it appears to be a temporary module name (Source) assigned to the cmdlet. What this means is that every time we connect a PowerShell session to Exchange Online, the Module Name for Exchange Online PowerShell cmdlets will be different. What we then have to do is first query all Modules:

```
$ModuleName = (Get-Module).Name
```

Populate a couple of variables needed for the file name:

```
$Date = Get-Date -Format "MM.dd.yyyy-hh.mm-tt"
$Service = 'SecurityCompliance'
$EmailDate = Get-Date -Format "MM.dd.yyyy"
```

```
$SMTPServer = <mail server ip address>
```

To pinpoint the module for the Security and Compliance Center Cmdlets we will check each Module until we find the Module beginning with 'tmp':

```
Foreach ($Name in $ModuleName) {
If ($Name -Like "tmp*") {
```

If the Module matches, then we can get the number of cmdlets found in the Security and Compliance Center now - notice the '.Count' at the end:

```
$NewSCCNum = (Get-Command | Where {$_.ModuleName -eq $Name}).Count
```

Lastly, we will create a txt file that will contain all of the cmdlets from this Module. The file will be named 'SecurityCompliance-< date >.txt:

```
$Service = "SecurityAndCompliance"
Get-command | Where {$_.ModuleName -eq $Name} | Select-ObjectName > "C:\
CmdletCheck\$Service-$Date.txt"
```

Now that we've gathered up the cmdlet names and a count of the cmdlets, we should clean up our PowerShell session to the Security and Compliance Center. Why should we clear our sessions? First, it closes the remote connection and allows us to run cmdlets on our local server. Second, it closes a potential security hole because of the direct connection to Exchange Online using a connection with administrative permissions to the tenant.

** **Note** ** Maximum number of PowerShell connections per user is three.

How can we close the session? Remove-PSSession:

```
Example 2: Remove all the sessions in the current session

PS C:\>Get-PSSession | Remove-PSSession

- or -

PS C:\> Remove-PSSession -Session (Get-PSSession)

- or -

PS C:\> $s = Get-PSSession
PS C:\> Remove-PSSession -Session $s
```

Using the example above we can add this code:

```
# Cleanup - Main Connection
Get-PsSession | Remove-PSSession
```

Note that the above will close ALL active sessions. For a scheduled script, this condition is acceptable as the sessions closed by this cmdlet are only the ones opened in the current script execution. It does not affect sessions outside of the PowerShell window used by the script. Next we need to begin constructing our CSV file for storing results. We start with the first row of the chart:

```
# ReWrite the CSV File
$HeaderRow = "SecurityAndCompliance"
$HeaderRow > 'C:\CmdletCheck\Historical\CurrentChart.csv'
```

Add additional row to the CurrentChart.Csv spreadsheet:

```
# New numbers
$NewRow = "$NewSCCNum"
Add-Content 'C:\CmdletCheck\Historical\CurrentChart.csv' $NewRow
```

Add additional row to the FullChart.Csv spreadsheet - Note we tag the row with the current date as well:

```
# Add row to historical data
$NewRow = "$Date,"+"$NewSCCNum"
Add-Content 'C:\CmdletCheck\Historical\FullChart.csv' $NewRow
```

Once the CSV files are updated, we need to notify someone of the changes. First, we check to see if the new number of cmdlets ($NewSCCNum) has changed from the previous number of cmdlets ($SCCNum):

```
If ($NewSCCNum -ne $SCCNum) {
```

If the changes have occurred, then:

```
$Change = "Security and Compliance Center cmdlets changed from $SCCNum to $NewSCCNum."
Add-Content 'C:\CmdletCheck\Historical\CurrentChanges.csv' $Change
```

This next variable is set because we want to send an email out:

```
$MailRequired = 1
```

Now, if the cmdlet numbers have not changed, we use the '} Else {' code section to do so. In this section we will record no change to the new CSV file:

```
} Else {
   $NoChange = "Security and Compliance Center Cmdlets did not change in number."
   Add-Content 'C:\CmdletCheck\Historical\CurrentChanges.csv' $NoChange
}
```

Once those checks complete, we can check to see if the $MailRequired variable is set to '1'.

```
If ($MailRequired -eq 1) {
```

We then set the '$Body' and '$Subject' variable for the email:

```
$Subject = "Some Office 365 PowerShell Cmdlets Changed on $EmailDate"
$Body = (Get-Content 'C:\CmdletCheck\Historical\CurrentChanges.csv') -join '<BR>'
```

Then we can send the email out with the changes that occurred.

```
Send-MailMessage -To $To -From $From -Subject $Subject -BodyAsHtml -Body $Body -SmtpServer
$SMTPServer
```

If there were no changes, and the $MailRequired is not set to 1, then we can use an '} Else {' section of code:

```
} Else {
```

We then set the '$Body' and '$Subject' variable for the email, differently then the successful email:

```
$Subject = "No Office 365 PowerShell Cmdlets Changed on $EmailDate"
$Body = "No Office 365 PowerShell Cmdlets Changed on $EmailDate."
```

Then we can send the email out with the fact no changes happened:

```
Send-MailMessage -To $To -From $From -Subject $Subject -BodyAsHtml -Body $Body -SmtpServer
$SmtpServer
}
```

Once that's complete, we can close the PS Session....

```
Get-PSSession | Remove-PSSession
```

... and remove the CSV file we no longer need:

```
Remove-Item "C:\CmdletCheck\Historical\CurrentChanges.csv"
```

Script Summary

In this sample, we used Send-MailMessage, If..Else, PSSession cmdlets, and more to make this happen. The key thing to remember is to add comments later once the script works. This will enable sharing of the script as well as help in troubleshooting it if there are any issues.

Script Building Summary

Building a script in PowerShell can take some planning and certainly takes some experimentation. An idea method would be to have some sort of test environment in order to prove out the scripts and then put it into production once the script has been vetted. Ideally the script will start with some sort of seed like mailbox information, or groups information and then expanding out to culling data points and then performing some sort of action in response to the data found. The scripts might be scheduled or run manually depending on the end purpose.

When building your scripts, make sure to take advantage of all the tools that are out there:

- PowerShell Get-Help
- Microsoft TechNet - https://technet.microsoft.com/en-us/ms376608.aspx
- Search engine - Google or Bing
- TechNet Gallery - https://gallery.technet.microsoft.com/
- GitHub - https://github.com/powershell
- MVP blog script samples

Don't ignore any help you can get from these sources. Experience will teach you that until you understand the underlying way that PowerShell operates, as well as how data could be stored in Exchange and Active Directory, it will take experimentation to get the most out of it.

A   # Best Practices

In This Chapter

- What is a Best Practice?
- Summary of Best Practices
- PowerShell Best Practices
- Conclusion and Further Help

What is a Best Practice?

The use of PowerShell, like any other code in the IT world, requires guidance and best practices to make sure the experience of the coder and end-user are conducive to its use in the real world. As such, a series of best practices has been identified. Now, some of the best practices have already been covered, and will be noted as such. Others have been developed over the years that PowerShell has been in use and lastly, some are matters of opinion. For this chapter, the bulk of our time will be spent on the middle topic of the developed best practices. At the end of the chapter we'll also explore some third party options that will help us code better with code analysis.

Summary of Best Practices

- Comment block at the top of the script
- Comments in script for documenting operation
- Useful comments
- Variable naming
- Variable block
- Matching variables to parameters
- Preference variables
- Verb-Noun-Functions and scripts
- Single task function
- Signing your code
- Filter vs. Where
- Error handling
- Write-Output / Write-Verbose
- # Requires
- Set-StrictMode
- Capitalization
- Using full command names
- Cmdlet binding
- Script structure
- Quotes
- Running applications

PowerShell Best Practices

Commenting

When it comes to PowerShell scripting, comments can be extremely useful when documenting a script, but also for troubleshooting a script's performance. Commenting is especially important for scripts that are meant for public disbursement. If someone else using your script runs into a problem, it would be ideal to either have copious commenting or to have some sort of documentation for them to reference. Below are samples we have used in the real world.

Example 1

Notice that the comment below lets us know that we are loading more modules:

```
# Load PowerShell Modules
Import-Module MSOnline
Import-Module ADSync
```

Example 2

Get Label Policies

```
# Export Label Policies

Get-LabelPolicy | Export-Csv $LabelsPolicyDestination -NoTypeInformation
```

Example 3

```
##########################################
# Variables (Labels)
$Path = (Get-Item -Path ".\" -Verbose).FullName
$LabelFile = 'Labels.csv'
$LabelsDestination = $Path+"\"+$LabelFile
```

** **Note** ** A more detailed description of PowerShell commenting is available on page 27 of this book.

Useful Comments

Another Best Practice for comments is simply to make sure to put useful information into the comment sections. Use comments to denote breaks. Use them to describe what a section does. Use them to describe variables purposes or maybe helpful troubleshooting information.

Variable Naming

Most of us are guilty of this one. Have you ever needed to create a quick script and in that script, for example, you needed a numerical counter so you could keep track of something for later? Well, I can almost guess that you used '$A++' or '$N++' to make your counters. This is a best practice that most of us need to break. The best way to handle such variables is to provide a meaningful name. If, for example, you need a list of all Labels, make the variable name '$Labels. If you need all users, make the variable $Users and so on.

Examples – Following the best practice

```
$GivenNames = (Get-User -Filter *).FirstName
$Counter++
$Labels = Get-Label
```

Examples – Not following best practice

```
$N = (Get-User  -Filter *).FirstName
$I++
$Lbl= Get-Label
```

Variable Block

In the spirit of previous best practices, another best practice concerning variables is creating a variable block. A variable block is an area of the script (at the top) that defines all the variables. It's usually started with a comment like so:

```
# Variable definition
```

Or

```
############### VARIABLES ###############
```

Then the variables to be used in the script are defined below that.

Example – from a working script

```
#############################
#     Global Variable Definitions     #
#############################
$Date = Get-Date
$Path = (Get-Item -Path ".\" -Verbose).FullName
$CaseHoldRules = Get-CaseHoldRule
$ComplianceCasesNames = (Get-ComplianceCase).Name
```

Matching Variables to Parameters

Another naming convention that should be followed, is to name variables that match a parameter or value from a query. An example of this would be:

```
$DisplayName = (Get-User).DisplayName
```

The reason for this is less confusion. This isn't necessarily a hard and fast rule. A variation of this is to name the variable after the content you intend to store. Using the above cmdlet as an example, we can construct this:

```
$Workloads = (Get-RetentionCompliancePolicy).Workload
```

The intent is to keep the name of the variable as close as possible to the name of the parameter or value. This gives PowerShell variable names a purpose.

** **Note** ** One caveat to variable names, there are a set of predefined or 'Automatic Variables' that PowerShell has and you need to be aware of. These variables names are documented by Microsoft here:

https://docs.microsoft.com/en-us/powershell/module/microsoft.powershell.core/about/about_automatic_variables?view=powershell-6

Preference Variables

What is a Preference Variable in PowerShell? Preference Variables determine certain behaviors in PowerShell for how cmdlets should process certain conditions. These conditions include Errors, Debugging, WhatIf, Warnings, etc. To see which of these variables are available in PowerShell we can run this:

```
Get-Variable *preference
```

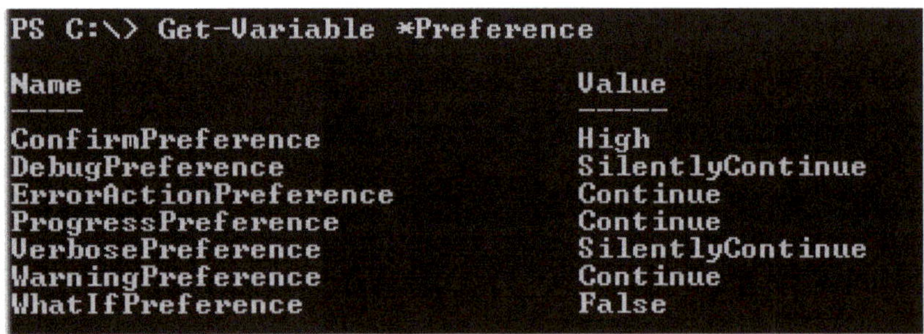

These are your default values for each Preference Variable in PowerShell. The best practice is not to change these settings globally because this configuration is what would be called expected behavior. If settings need to be changed, these should be changed on a case by case basis:

```
New-DlpSensitiveInformationTypeRulePackage -FileData (Get-Content -Path "$Name" -Encoding Byte) -ErrorAction STOP
```

Not

```
$ErrorActionPreference = "STOP"
```

If we were to run this line we would change how all cmdlets would respond to errors when run. This makes troubleshooting more difficult and changes the expected behavior in PowerShell. Also, not all PowerShell sessions and shells are configured the same. Shell/environment customizations could cause troubleshooting issues.

Naming Conventions, this time for Functions and Scripts

This is one thing we did not cover in the book in-depth or even at all. Earlier in the book we talked about naming conventions for variables in terms of capitalization and in this chapter we talked about using normal language instead of abbreviations for variables. This same concept can be extended to include functions and scripts. For these the best practice is to follow a similar naming convention as cmdlets in PowerShell. This would mean that function and script names should follow a 'Verb-Noun' naming format. Some examples are listed below:

Functions
```
Function Add-Licenses {}
Function Change-Quotas {}
Function ComplianceSearch {}
```

Script Names
```
Add-DLPSensitiveInfoTypes.ps1
Get-DLPReport.ps1
Set-RoleGroups.ps1
```

As you can see from the above examples, we tried to be descriptive of what the function or script does. The same was done with scripts.

Singular Task Functions

This is an easy one. Functions can run all sorts of PowerShell cmdlets inside of them. However, the simpler more focused they are the better. As a best practice, functions should perform a single task like looking up a hotfix or installing a particular program or maybe making a registry change. The reason for this is to keep things simple and repeatable. That is the very definition of a function. Functions should be stackable in the sense that they can be called and used to build tasks (like LEGO bricks to build a house). We want to make sure the functions we construct are not overly complex or perform too many actions. This could complicate troubleshooting.

An example of this would be:

Example
This function will get a list of users affected by Information Barriers:

```
Function GetNames ($Attribute,$Operator,$Value ) {
   # Variables
   If ($Operator -eq '-eq') {
     $Names = (Get-User -ErrorAction STOP | Where {$_.($Attribute) -eq $Value}).DisplayName
   }
   If ($Operator -eq '-ne') {
     $Names = (Get-User -ErrorAction STOP | Where {$_.($Attribute) -ne $Value}).DisplayName
   }
    Foreach ($Name in $Names) {
     $RecipientStatus = Get-InformationBarrierRecipientStatus $Name | select Alias, $Attribute,
     DisplayName, ExoPolicyID, IsValid
     $ExOPolicyIDTemp = ($RecipientStatus).ExoPolicyID
```

```
        $ExOPolicyID = $ExOPolicyIDTemp.split('\')[1]
        $Segment = (Get-InformationBarrierPolicy -ExoPolicyId $ExOPolicyID).AssignedSegment
        $Alias = $RecipientStatus.Alias
        $Department = $RecipientStatus.Department
        $DisplayName = $RecipientStatus.DisplayName
        $IsValid = $RecipientStatus.IsValid
        $Line    =    "$Segment,$Alias,$Department,$DisplayName,$ExOPolicyID,$IsValid"    |    Out-File
        $Destination -Append
    }
}
```

Signing Your Code

Signing your code will help with two things. If downloaded by someone else, it ensures that the code has not been modified by anyone after it was signed, and if there is a strict PowerShell policy in place (which there is by default) the script can be run without changing this security feature.

As this is already covered, you can find more information on Code Signing on page 41 of this book.

Filter vs. Where

When it comes to manipulating data results, the Filter parameter and the Where operation are two different approaches to narrowing data to search from. With Filter, the results are pre-filtered by a Domain Controller or other system outside of PowerShell. With Where, the results are all returned to PowerShell and then filtered. Because of this, the speed performance of the two results can vary greatly.

   ** **Note** ** If the -Filter parameter is available for a cmdlet, it should be used as it is more efficient.

This is covered on page 279 of this book.

Error Handling

When first starting to script, it isn't uncommon for there to be a reliance on '-ErrorAction SilentlyContinue' for pseudo error handling in a script. This allows for a one-liner or cmdlet to continue even if errors crop up that would otherwise end its operation. The problem with using this technique is that it can hide all errors. Errors that could be different from the original one that broke a script from running will now be hidden. A better way to handle this is to use Try and Catch. These two together can perform effective error handling where a cmdlet succeeds in the 'Try' part of the code block.

Try and Catch was covered earlier in the book and you can read more about this on page 279 of this book.

Write-Output / Write-Verbose

There are a few ways to output information while a script is running – Write-Host, Write-Verbose and Write-Output. Write-Host will immediately display the information to the PowerShell window as the script or line is run.

For example, if we were to get a list of all Role Group Members in the SCC and then display them in a certain way, we can use Write-Host to visually represent data:

```
$RoleGroupNames = (Get-RoleGroup).Name
Foreach ($RoleGroupName in $RoleGroupNames) {
    Write-host "$RoleGroupName" -ForegroundColor Green
    Get-RoleGroupMember -Identity $RoleGroupName
}
```

Using Write-Host is not recommended because a lot of scripts are run for automation and thus any output to a PowerShell window may be useless. A better option is to use Write-Verbose or Write-Output. Both of these provide a completely different option for your PowerShell script.

> ** **Note** ** Good reading on Write-Host can be found here -https://blogs.technet.microsoft.com/heyscriptingguy/2014/03/30/understanding-streams-redirection-and-write-host-in-powershell/

Write-Verbose

Write-Verbose is an additional tool for troubleshooting the operation of a script. This cmdlet can be placed throughout the script at key points to help document.

Example
In this example, we use Write-Verbose to display information being gathered by a script:

```
Write-Verbose "The $DisplayName mailbox has Case Hold policy applied."
Write-Verbose "A connection to the Security and Compliance Center could not be made."
Write-Verbose "No Compliance Tags were found."
```

If the script is run without the –Verbose switch, no output is displayed. However, if it experiences issues, we can use the –Verbose switch to trigger the Write-Verbose:

```
VERBOSE: The  mailbox has Case Hold policy applied.
VERBOSE: A connection to the Security and Compliance Center could not be made.
VERBOSE: No Compliance Tags were found.
```

Write-Output

This cmdlet can be used in two instances, it can be used to display the contents found from the running of a cmdlet/one-liner like so:

```
Get-DeviceTenantRule | Write-Output
```

This is a bit redundant as the same output can be produced with:

```
Get-DeviceTenantRule
```

It can also be used to produce the output in a variable:

```
$DeviceTenantRules = Get-DeviceTenantRule
Write-Output $DeviceTenantRules
```

However, the same process can be done without the Write-Output cmdlet:

```
$DeviceTenantRules = Get-DeviceTenantRule
$DeviceTenantRules
```

Stick with Write-Verbose for most scripts and only use Write-Host if a visual answer / question or menu is needed.

'#Requires'

PowerShell scripts can be written to be standalone or they can be written to utilize other modules or components. If the latter is the case, then the use of '#Requires' should be in the script. Adding this to a script will prevent a script from running if the requirement is missing. This is important because without this a script that references to a module or particular component that is not available will fail. The PowerShell window will be covered with red text as the script fails to run. The most common usage that we've seen is when a certain level of PowerShell is needed. PowerShell's version level could determine important items like what cmdlets are available or what switch / parameters would be available to be run by the script.

What can we require? How do we figure that out? The easiest way is to fire up your favorite browser / search engine and look for the following:

PowerShell #Requires

These search terms provide us with these results:

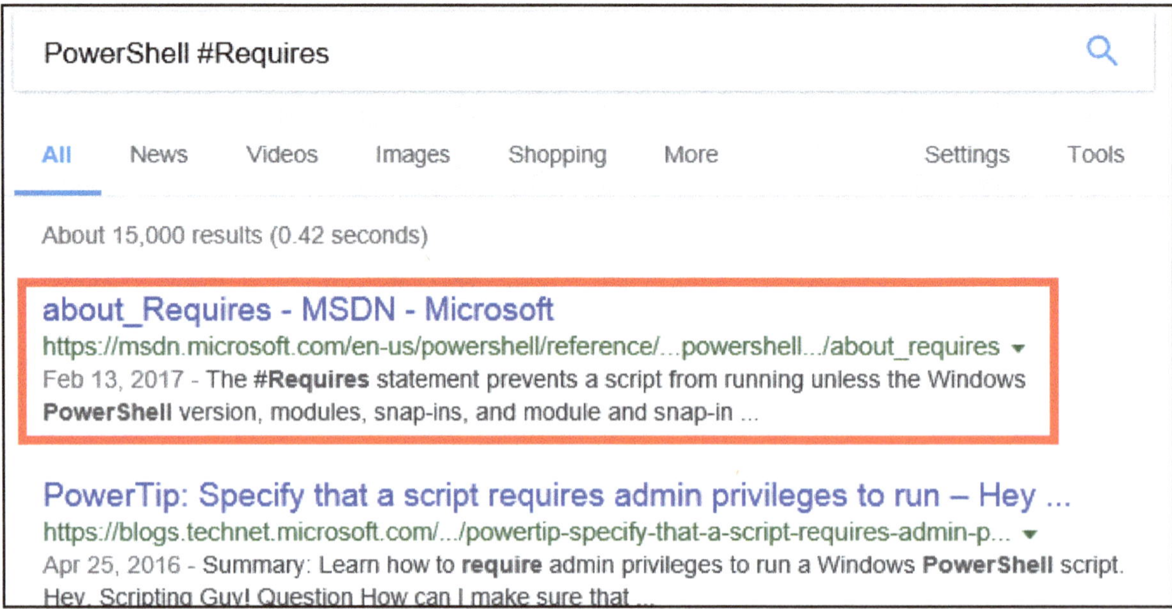

If we explore the resultant page, we find some more information on how to use the '#Requires' feature:

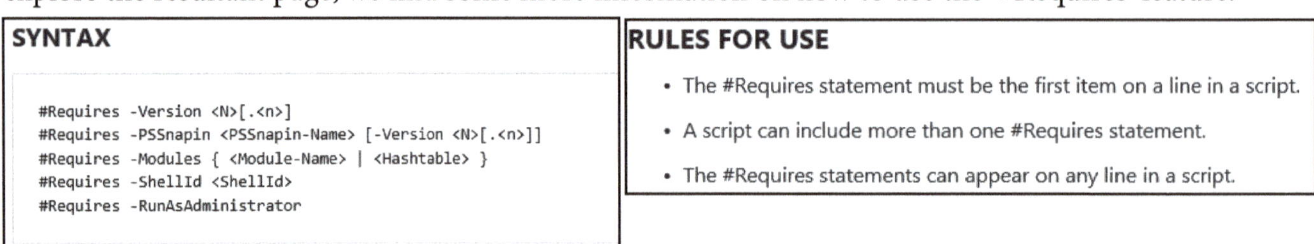

** **Note** ** It is a best practice for '#Requires' to be places at the top of the script.

Example 1

For our first example, we'll test requiring a certain version of PowerShell. The test will be run on a Windows 2008 R2 server. What version of PowerShell runs on Windows 2008 R2 by default?

$PSVersionTable reveals the following:

The PowerShell version is 3.0. As such, if we set the Requires for version for 4.0 like this:

```
#Requires –Version 4.0
```

Then when the script is run, it will fail:

```
[PS] C:\downloads>.\Test-Requires.ps1
.\Test-Requires.ps1 : The script 'Test-Requires.ps1' cannot be run because it contained a "#requires" statement for Wind
version required by the script does not match the currently running version of Windows PowerShell version 3.0.
At line:1 char:1
+ .\Test-Requires.ps1
+ ~~~~~~~~~~~~~~~~~~~~
    + CategoryInfo          : ResourceUnavailable: (Test-Requires.ps1:String) [], ScriptRequiresException
    + FullyQualifiedErrorId : ScriptRequiresUnmatchedPSVersion
```

The same script run on a Windows 2012 R2 server would not have any issue at all. It runs because if we check the $PSVersionTable, we see that Windows 2012 R2 is at version 4.0:

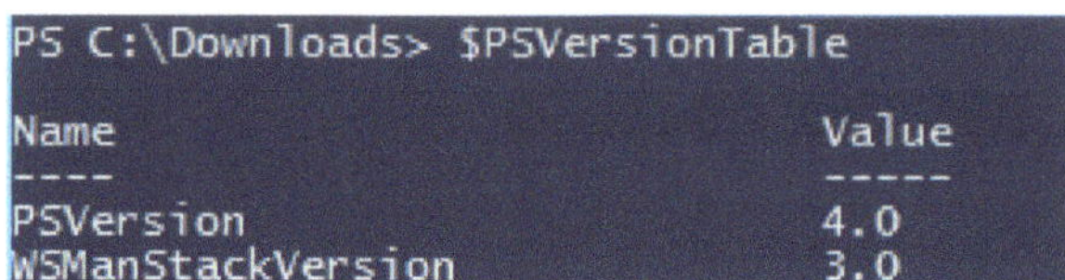

Example 2

From the Syntax provided from the MSDN page, we see that we can also require certain modules before running like this:

```
#Requires –Modules MSOnline
```

If the MS Online module is not loaded, the 'Requires' will force a module load. If the module cannot be loaded, a terminating error occurs and the script will exit.

PowerShell also provides a Get-Help for the #Requires feature. 'Get-Help Requires' will provide more detail on how to use '#Requires'.

```
[PS] C:\downloads>Get-Help Requires
TOPIC
    about_Requires

SHORT DESCRIPTION
    Prevents a script from running without the required elements.

LONG DESCRIPTION
    The #Requires statement prevents a script from running unless the Windows
    PowerShell version, modules, snap-ins, and module and snap-in version
    prerequisites are met. If the prerequisites are not met, Windows PowerShell
    does not run the script.

    You can use #Requires statements in any script. You cannot use them in
    functions, cmdlets, or snap-ins.

    SYNTAX
        #Requires -Version <N>[.<n>]
        #Requires -PSSnapin <PSSnapin-Name> [-Version <N>[.<n>]]
        #Requires -Modules { <Module-Name> | <Hashtable> }
        #Requires -ShellId <ShellId>

    RULES FOR USE

      - The #Requires statement must be the first item on a line in a script.
      - A script can include more than one #Requires statement.
      - The #Requires statements can appear on any line in a script.

    PARAMETERS
    -Version <N>[.<n>]
        Specifies the minimum version of Windows PowerShell that the script
        requires. Enter a major version number and optional minor version number.

        For example:
          #Requires -Version 3.0
```

Set-StrictMode -Version Latest

This is one that we've started adding to our scripts now. What this does is it enforces certain best practices in your PowerShell coding and forces the code to be 'Correct'. Think of this as a code check prior to execution of the script. One item that is checked is variable definition. Variables that are used in a script will need to be defined at the top of the script.

How can we configure this PowerShell cmdlet, let's review the Get-Help for the cmdlet to see:

Get-Help Set-StrictMode –Full

The valid values are "1.0", "2.0", and "Latest". The following list shows the effect of each value.

1.0
-- Prohibits references to uninitialized variables, except for uninitialized variables in strings.

2.0
-- Prohibits references to uninitialized variables (including uninitialized variables in strings).
-- Prohibits references to non-existent properties of an object.
-- Prohibits function calls that use the syntax for calling methods.
-- Prohibits a variable without a name (${}).

Latest:
--Selects the latest (most strict) version available. Use this value to assure that scripts use the strictest available version, even when new versions are added to Windows PowerShell.

Version 1 - Example:

In this example we'll use an undefined variable (one without a value):

```
Set-StrictMode -Version 1.0
If($A > 2) {
   Write-Host "Large Number"
}
```

```
The variable '$a' cannot be retrieved because it has not been set.
At C:\Downloads\TestStrict.ps1:2 char:4
+ if($a > 2) {
+    ~~
    + CategoryInfo          : InvalidOperation: (a:String) [], RuntimeException
    + FullyQualifiedErrorId : VariableIsUndefined
```

Now if we define a variable correctly and still use the strict mode, no error will occur:

```
Set-StrictMode -Version 1.0
$Count = (Get-Command *tenant*).Count
If ($Count -gt 2) {
   Write-Host "Large Number"
}
```

```
PS C:\> .\test-strict.ps1
Large Number
```

Version 2 - Example

In this example we review one of the Version 2 best practices. Let's try out the restriction on calling nonexistent properties. No sub-properties to call and no version defined:

```
$CaseHoldRule = 'test'
$CaseHoldRule.DisplayName
```

No results or errors will show with that code.

Now we try the same code with StrictMode Version 2:

```
Set-StrictMode -Version 2.0
$CaseHoldRule = 'test'
$CaseHoldRule.DisplayName
```

```
The property 'DisplayName' cannot be found on this object. Verify that the property exists.
At line:1 char:1
+ $CaseHoldRule.DisplayName
+ ~~~~~~~~~~~~~~~~~~~~~~~~~~
    + CategoryInfo          : NotSpecified: (:) [], PropertyNotFoundException
    + FullyQualifiedErrorId : PropertyNotFoundStrict
```

Best practice followed:

```
Set-StrictMode -Version 2.0
$CaseHoldRule = Get-CaseHoldRule
$CaseHoldRule.Name
```

This last example worked because the variable $CaseHoldRule has a sub-property called Name and when called it displays its value.

The last value for –Version is a bit deceptive. 'Latest' is the same as '2.0' for now. As such the best practice is to use 'Latest' so that if something is added later on, you are not stuck with old code looking for '2.0' restrictions and not something newer that was added.

Capitalization

Capitalization is just another best practice that has more to do with readability and formatting than a strictly PowerShell best practice.

   ** **Note** ** This is already covered in the book on page 27. See that section for more detail on this best practice.

Using full command names

PowerShell contains quite a few aliases (or shortcuts) that are basically shortcuts to common cmdlets like 'Foreach-Object', 'Where-Object' and 'Write-Output'. Aliases are typically used for a couple reasons:

- It's quicker to type the shortened version:

   Example

   '%' rather than typing the equivalent 'Foreach-Object'

- Simplifies the coding, can point aliases towards commands and functions.

Why not use aliases? Aliases should not be used when coding a script for the public consumption or trying to explain PowerShell coding to another person. Make sure to put full commands in so that there will be no confusion as to why something was used. For learning purposes, using the Verb-Noun format of PowerShell is more conducive then trying to get someone to learn the multitude of aliases that are present in PowerShell. For example, Security and Compliance Center has 158 aliases.

How do we find that out?

(Get-Alias).Count

```
PS C:\> (Get-Alias ).count
158
```

In addition to this, when building a new script, it would be better to have the correct syntax / commands so that if you need help troubleshooting something there won't be any head-scratching on trying to decipher aliases. Thus having the full commands is better for you and someone helping you.

Details of PowerShell aliases are covered on page 295 of this book.

Cmdlet Binding

Cmdlet Binding is used to add additional functionality to functions within a PowerShell script. Using Cmdlet Binding also allows for the use of Write-Verbose. Write-Verbose can be useful for troubleshooting a script or providing more information on a particular section of a script.

How do we use this? In this example we'll see if we can get the Write-Verbose cmdlet to work:

```
Function Test-AdvancedFeatures {
   [CmdletBinding()]Param()
   Try {
      Import-Module MSOnline -ErrorAction STOP
   } Catch {
      $Failed = $True
      Write-Verbose "Cannot load the MSOnline module."
   }
}

Test-AdvancedFeatures -Verbose
```

Without the verbose switch, no feedback is given:

```
PS C:\> .\TestVerbose.ps1
PS C:\>
```

However, with the verbose switch:

```
PS C:\> .\TestVerbose.ps1
VERBOSE: Cannot load the MSOnline module.
PS C:\>
```

In addition to this, Cmdlet Binding can also add functionality like –WhatIf or –Confirm, or even ErrorVariable and ErrorAction to a script or function. The use of this option expands options that are available for use with PowerShell functions to the point of them operating like cmdlets specifically with the switch options.

Further reading on Cmdlet Binding - https://msdn.microsoft.com/en-us/powershell/reference/5.1/microsoft.powershell.core/about/about_functions_cmdletbindingattribute

Script Structure

For ease of use, readability, and general flow, a good script structure is generally recommended. In general a script should follow something like this:

Comment block – script description, parameter definitions, versioning and more

Global variable definitions – define arrays and other variables that may need to be pre-populated like dates

Functions – there should be a section of the script near the top that defines the functions that will be used in the script (not required and also not depicted below)

Script body – where the script starts to run and use the variables and functions that were predefined in order to accomplish some task

Example Script - Structure

Comment Block

```
################################################################################
#
# .DESCRIPTION
#    Document Information Barrier settings for auditing purposes
#
# Script Version History
#     Version              : 1.1
#     Change Log           : 1.1 - Add logic for multiple recipient filters and operators
#                          : 1.0 - Initial script - document segments, users, etc.
#
################################################################################
```

Variables for Script

```
################################################################################
#   VARIABLES

# Output destination
$Path = (Get-Item -Path ".\" -Verbose).FullName
$File = "InformationBarriersDump.Txt"
$Destination = $Path+"\"+$File
$InfoBarrier = $True

# Sets Buffer Size to allow for wide output
$Host.UI.RawUI.BufferSize = New-Object Management.Automation.Host.Size (500, 9999)

# Date
$Date = Get-Date -Format "MM.dd.yyyy-hh.mm-tt"

#
################################################################################
```

Script Body

```
################################################################################
# DOCUMENTATION PROCESS

If ($InfoBarrier) {

    $Line = 'Information Barrier Policy Application Status' | Out-File $Destination
    $Line = '---------------------------------------------' | Out-File $Destination -Append
    $Line = Get-InformationBarrierPoliciesApplicationStatus | Out-File $Destination -Append
    $Line = ' ' | Out-File $Destination -Append
    $Line = 'Information Barrier Policies' | Out-File $Destination -Append
    $Line = '---------------------------' | Out-File $Destination -Append
    $Line = Get-InformationBarrierPolicy | ft Name,Type,AssignedSegment,SegmentsAllowed,Segme
    $Line = ' ' | Out-File $Destination -Append

    # Organization Sege
    $Line = 'Organization Segment(s)' | Out-File $Destination -Append
    $Line = '-----------------------' | Out-File $Destination -Append
    $Line = Get-OrganizationSegment |ft Name,Type,UserGroupFilter,ObjectClass,CreatedBy | Out

    # Users in a Segment (based on filter) and then get their status
    $Line = ' ' | Out-File $Destination -Append
    $Line = 'Information Barrier Recipient Status' | Out-File $Destination -Append
    $Line = '-----------------------------------' | Out-File $Destination -Append

    $OrgSegments =  Get-OrganizationSegment
    $AllOrgFilters = @()
    $AllRecipients = @()

    Foreach ($OrgSegment in $OrgSegments){
        $OrgFilter = $OrgSegment.UserGroupFilter
        $AllOrgFilters += $OrgFilter
    }

    $Line = "Segment,Alias,Department,DisplayName,ExOPolicyID,IsValid" | Out-File $Destinatio

    Foreach ($OrgFilter in $AllOrgFilters) {

        $OrgFilterValues = $Orgfilter -split ' -and '
        $CriteriaTotalCount = ($OrgFilterValues).count

        Function GetNames ($Attribute,$Operator,$Value ) {
```

Quotes

Quoting in a PowerShell script may not seem important, but it can determine if a script runs correctly. The use of single quotes (') versus double quotes (") makes a vast difference in scenarios with variables that may need to be called from inside the quotes. This topic was covered earlier on page 288 of this book.

Running Applications

This is the easiest of the best practices in PowerShell. When calling an executable from PowerShell, make sure to use the '.exe' file extension. If you were to call an application without the extension and the application name happens to match a PowerShell alias, then the alias is called and not the executable. One example of this would be 'sc'.

```
Get-Alias sc
```

Whereas the sc.exe executable file would need to be called directly with 'sc.exe' instead.

Conclusion and Further Help

When it comes to PowerShell, best practices are defined in order to guide us into producing better code for ourselves and others that we are coding for. Whether it means more consistent capitalization, easy to remember variables or signing the script code, the purpose is the same. The list in this chapter is in no way a comprehensive list of all best practices for PowerShell. Make sure to follow the rules suggested, but also use external information to validate. In addition to the list provided, there are vendors besides Microsoft that produces PowerShell tools to help keep your script quality. One of these products is called 'PsScriptAnalyzer'. This tool is available on Github:

https://github.com/PowerShell/PSScriptAnalyzer

The ISE from Microsoft, the newest versions, come with the Script Analyzer built in.

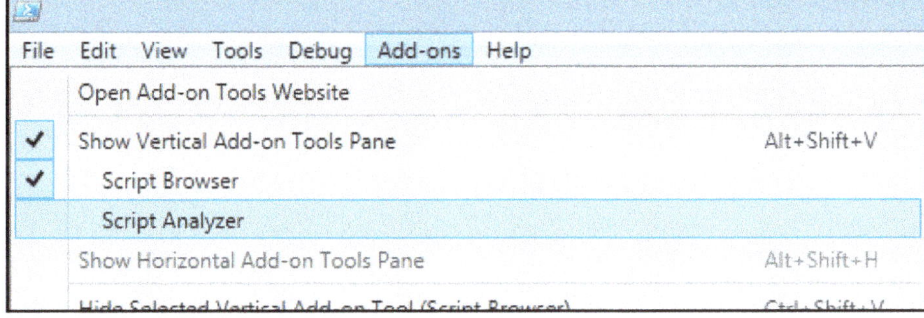

Once you have a script opened, you can run the tool with this:

On the right will be a list of suggested fixes:

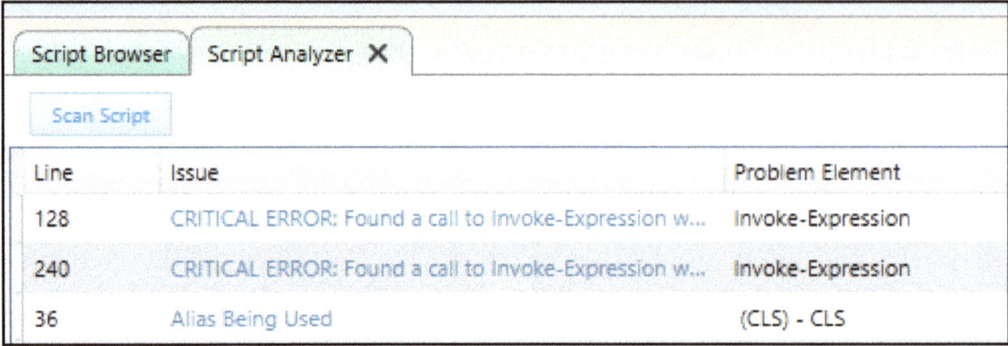

You might find the analysis to be a bit picky, but if you would like your script to be more stream-lined and accurate, then this is the way to go.

B # Miscellaneous

In This Chapter
- Introduction
- Menus
- Aliases
- Foreach-Object (%)
- PowerShell Interface Customization

Introduction

Up to this point, we've covered numerous topics from how to start out scripting to customizing Exchange Online topics in PowerShell. The topics covered in this chapter, as with the rest of the book, are based on practical experience and are ones that should prove useful in a production environment.

For this chapter, we'll cover menus, aliases, Foreach-Object filtering, and special permission cmdlets. Each of these provide some added benefit to managing the Security and Compliance Center with PowerShell. Aliases provide a way to customize PowerShell for easier coding. These shortcuts simply make coding easier. In addition to this, the shell can also be customized in terms of path, colors and window sizing.

Menus: How to create and add a menu of options in order to run functions in a script.
Alias: Creating new or using existing shortcuts for cmdlets in PowerShell.
Foreach-Object: Advanced filtering of results found from one-liners.
PowerShell Interface Customization: Going beyond the default and making adjustments for your own style.

Menus

Building menus is not a task that is necessary for one-off scripts. Menus should be used on scripts that will be run on multiple occasions, for example documenting settings in the Security and Compliance Center or for occasions where occasional input may be necessary. Another reason to use it is for a reusable script, which is especially useful for consultants who run their scripts in dozens of environments a year. The menu simply makes running the script quicker and more flexible.

In a PowerShell script, the menu can consist of two parts. The first part is the text for the menu which is the visual part of the script. The menu can be simple and singular in color or very colorful like the example given in Chapter 2. The second part is the infrastructure or back-end of the menu itself. This is where the executable code is stored and where coding needs to be performed in the form of functions that will complete the tasks the menu has called.

Sample Menu Code

```
$Menu = {
    Write-Host "************************************************************************"
    Write-Host "Compliance Cases"
    Write-Host "************************************************************************"
    Write-Host "1) Document existing cases"
    Write-Host "2) Close cases"
    Write-Host "3) Open a new case"
    Write-Host "99) Exit"
    Write-Host ""
    Write-Host "Select an option.. [1-99]?"
}
```

The above menu has been snipped from a script that is used to manage Compliance Cases that are/were created in the Security and Compliance Center. We can open, close, document and manage rights using a menu and code that goes behind it. This is where PowerShell will make calls to functions in the rest of the script to perform the functions you code for.

To start this section, construct a 'Do { } While' code block. The reason for this is that script will keep running options and displaying the menu until an exit code is chosen. So the 'Do { } While' block would look something like this:

```
Do {
    Invoke-Command -ScriptBlock $Menu
    $Choice = Read-Host
} While ($Choice -ne 99)
```

Notice that with this code, the loop will keep displaying the menu after each option is chosen until the value of 99 is selected. At that point the script will stop and exit to a PowerShell prompt. The Read-Host will store the value type in $Choice to be used for selecting which code block to run. Next, there needs to be a way to decide which option will run. What PowerShell cmdlet will allow for this?

```
Switch ($Choice)
```

However, a review of the help on 'Switch' does not reveal a lot of clues for its usefulness/functionality. However with a little bit of help from your favorite search engine, one can find this MSDN link for PowerShell functionality:

https://technet.microsoft.com/en-us/library/hh847750.aspx

We find that Switch will act like a condition tester, if a condition is fed to it, it will select that option within the Switch code section. For example:

```
$Choice = 3
   Switch ($Choice) {
   1 {Write-Host "1"}
   2 {Write-Host "2"}
   3 {Write-Host "3"}
}
```

The result of this will display the number 3:

```
3
```

Let's incorporate this into our menu infrastructure. Using the above as an example, we'll need to build code blocks for each function and we'll need to call from our example on the previous page. To make this process simpler (in terms of the scope of the menu) functions are pre-created:

Document existing cases: Produces output with a list of cases and information on the cases
Close cases: Allows us to close existing cases
Open a new case: Code for opening new cases
Grant/Remove Rights: Change rights, add rights, remove rights, etc.

With these functions created they can be referred to in each option code block. Note that it is assumed that a connection to the Security and Compliance Center has already been made prior to running any of the options.

Option 1 - This option calls the function:

```
Function DocumentComplianceCases {
   $Path = (Get-Item -Path ".\" -Verbose).FullName
   $File = 'ComplianceCases.txt'
   $Destination = $Path+'\'+$File
   $ComplianceCasesNames = (Get-ComplianceCase).Name
   Foreach ($ComplianceCasesName in $ComplianceCasesNames) {
      Write-Host "Examining Compliance Case $ComplianceCasesName" -ForegroundColor Cyan
      Write-Host "-------------------------------------------" -ForegroundColor Cyan
      Get-ComplianceCase $ComplianceCasesName | Export-CSV -Notype $Destination
   }
}
# Run function:
DocumentComplianceCases
```

```
PS C:\> DocumentComplianceCases
Examining Compliance Case Hold for some mailboxes
-------------------------------------------------
Examining Compliance Case SmartPhone Patent Dispute
-------------------------------------------------
Examining Compliance Case Merger Dispute
```

Option 2

This option calls the function:

```
Function CloseCases {
   Write-Host 'Specify the case you wish to close:  ' -NoNewLine
   $Name = Read-Host
   $Case = $True
   Try {
      Get-ComplianceCase $Name -ErrorAction STOP
   } Catch {
      $Case = $False
      Write-Host 'case not found'
   }
   If ($Case) {
      Try {
         Set-ComplianceCase $Name -Close -ErrorAction STOP
         Write-Host "Able to close the $Name Compliance Case." -ForegroundColor Green
      } Catch {
         Write-Host "Unable to close the $Name Compliance Case." -ForegroundColor Yellow
      }
   }
} # End of Close Cases Function
CloseCases
```

```
Specify the case you wish to close:  test

Able to close the test Compliance Case.
Name Status CreatedDateTime
---- ------ ---------------
test Active 5/15/2017 8:16:50 PM
```

Option 3

```
Function OpenCases {
   Write-Host 'Specify a name of the new case you wish to create: ' -NoNewline
   $Name = Read-Host
   Write-Host 'Specify a description for the new case: ' -NoNewline
   $Description = Read-Host
   Try {
      New-ComplianceCase $Name -Description $Description -ErrorAction STOP
   } Catch {
      Write-Host 'Failed to create a new Compliance Case' -ForegroundColor Red
   }
} # End of Open Cases Function

OpenCases
```

```
Specify a name of the new case you wish to create: SalesPersonnelCase
Specify a description for the new case: Holding for Sales lawsuit of 2019

Name                     Status CreatedDateTime
----                     ------ ---------------
SalesPersonnelCase Active 8/1/2019 8:59:06 PM
```

Option 99

```
99 {# Exit
   Write-Host "Exiting..."
}
```

When option 99 is selected, the script exits because of the Do {} While code block.

Pulling all of the previous code together into one script:

```
$Menu = {
   Write-Host "****************************************************************"
   Write-Host "Compliance Cases"
   Write-Host "****************************************************************"
   Write-Host "1) Document existing cases"
   Write-Host "2) Close cases"
   Write-Host "3) Open a new case"
   Write-Host "99) Exit"
   Write-Host ""
   Write-Host "Select an option.. [1-99]?"
}
Do {
   Invoke-Command $Menu
   $Choice = Read-Host $Menu
   Switch ($Choice)  {
      1 { # DocumentComplianceCases
         DocumentComplianceCases
      }
      2 { # Close Compliance Cases
         CloseCases
      }
      3 { # Open Compliance Cases
         OpenCases
      }
      99 {# Exit
         Write-Host "Exiting..."
      }
      Default {
         Write-Host "You haven't selected any of the available options."
      }
   }
} While ($Choice -ne 99)
```

Running the script provides a menu as displayed below:

```
******************************************
Compliance Cases
******************************************

1) Document existing cases
2) Close cases
3) Open a new case
99) Exit

Select an option.. [1-99]?
```

Option 99 allows for the script to exit:

```
Select an option.. [1-99]  99
Exiting...
```

If an option is typed in wrong, say 77, an error message is provided:

```
Select an option.. [1-99]  77
You haven't selected any of the available options.
```

Aliases

PowerShell aliases are shortened versions of PowerShell cmdlets. Consider aliases to be a convenience in reducing the amount of text in a script. Aliases are not necessary for writing a script but they do provide shortcuts to coding. Without aliases, each command in PowerShell just takes longer to type. The downside of aliases is that normally PowerShell is a very readable scripting language and using aliases can obscure the ability to read PowerShell in plain English. Another downside is that there is no guarantee that the alias will exist in a different environment. If the script is meant to be portable, it is advisable to not use them or at least limit their usage. If a script will be read by someone other than you, using aliases might make the script unreadable to others.

```
Get-Alias -Definition Foreach-Object

CommandType     Name
-----------     ----
Alias           % -> ForEach-Object
Alias           foreach -> ForEach-Object
```

However, what if you don't know the command that the alias is for? The above can be reverse engineered to show all aliases. To look up all aliases, simply type in 'Get-Alias':

```
CommandType     Name
-----------     ----
Alias           % -> ForEach-Object
Alias           ? -> Where-Object
Alias           ac -> Add-Content
Alias           asnp -> Add-PSSnapin
Alias           cat -> Get-Content
Alias           cd -> Set-Location
Alias           chdir -> Set-Location
Alias           clc -> Clear-Content
Alias           clear -> Clear-Host
```

Without listing them all here, there are 148 aliases defined. What may be more interesting is that aliases can be created and modified. This certainly provides for some flexibility or customization of PowerShell.

New-Alias

If there is a desire to make custom aliases for PowerShell, New-Alias is the cmdlet to use.

** **Note** ** The aliases are only good for the current session. If you close the current session, the alias is lost and when you reconnect to PowerShell the alias will not be there.

Get-Help New-Alias -Examples

```
Example 1: Create an alias for a cmdlet

PS C:\>New-Alias -Name "List" Get-ChildItem

This command creates an alias named List to represent the Get-ChildItem cmdlet.
Example 2: Create a read-only alias for a cmdlet

PS C:\>New-Alias -Name "W" -Value Get-WmiObject -Description "quick wmi alias" -Option ReadOnly
PS C:\>Get-Alias -Name "W" | Format-List *

This command creates an alias named W to represent the Get-WmiObject cmdlet. It creates a description, quick wmi
alias, for the alias and makes it read-only. The last line of the command uses Get-Alias to get the new alias and
pipes it to Format-List to display all of the information about it.
```

Sample Usage

We can create an alias for just about anything in PowerShell that we want. For this example we can create aliases for any of the *-ComplianceCase cmdlets if we wanted to.

To create these aliases, we'll use a series of New-Alias one-liners:

```
New-Alias gcc Get-ComplianceCase -Description 'Get Compliance Case'
New-Alias ncc New-ComplianceCase -Description 'New Compliance Case'
New-Alias scc Set-ComplianceCase -Description 'Set Compliance Case'
New-Alias rcc Remove-ComplianceCase -Description 'Remove Compliance Case'
```

Example result of a new alias creation:

```
PS C:\> New-Alias ncc New-ComplianceCase -Description 'NewComplianceCase'
PS C:\> get-alias ncc


CommandType     Name                                                Version    Source
-----------     ----                                                -------    ------
Alias           ncc -> New-ComplianceCase
```

There are a few parameters that can be used to customize this new alias during creation. One of the parameters is 'Option' which provides for a way to limit when the alias can be used – Global, Local, Script or Private. An alias could be enabled for only when a script runs or only while in a local session. The purpose of this option is to possibly isolate the usage of a cmdlet as to prevent unwarranted changes using the aliases. A description should be added so that the purpose of the alias is known by others.

Set-Alias

This cmdlet is used to modify any of the existing aliases to the specifics that you may want to configure for a particular alias. One of the exceptions is if the alias is set to ReadOnly. To modify one of those aliases, a '-Force' switch must be used. Here are some sample uses of the cmdlet:

Get-Help New-Alias -Examples

```
Example 1: Create an alias for a Get-ChildItem

PS C:\>Set-Alias -Name list -Value get-childitem

This command creates the alias list for the Get-ChildItem cmdlet. After you create the alias, you can use list in
place of Get-ChildItem at the command line and in scripts.
Example 2: Create an alias and omit parameter names

PS C:\>Set-Alias list get-location

This command associates the alias list with the Get-Location cmdlet. If list is an alias for another cmdlet, this
command changes its association so that it now is the alias only for Get-Location .
```

Sample Usage

In practical terms, this cmdlet would likely only be used to modify existing aliases that you've created yourself. Taking some of the aliases created in the previous section, let's make sure that the aliases are ReadOnly:

```
Set-Alias gcc Get-ComplianceCase -Option ReadOnly
Set-Alias ncc New-ComplianceCase -Option ReadOnly
Set-Alias rcc Remove-ComplianceCase -Option ReadOnly
Set-Alias scc Set-ComplianceCase -Option ReadOnly
```

What's interesting is that this same cmdlet ('Set-Alias') can be used to create a new alias as well. For example, if a new alias were needed for creating a new mailbox on-premises. The Set-Alias could be used to create this alias as well:

```
PS C:\> Set-Alias ncc New-ComplianceCase -Option ReadOnly
PS C:\>
```

Removing an Alias

Reviewing the PowerShell cmdlets with the word 'Alias' there are no cmdlets with the word 'remove' in them. How then can an alias be removed? If the solution cannot be found in PowerShell, then searching for a solution via your favorite search engine is the next step:

Search string: remove powershell alias

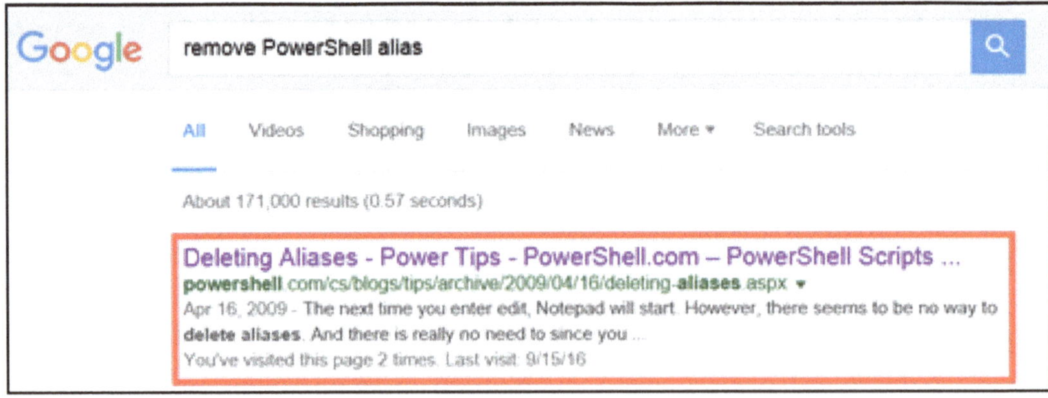

Reviewing the first link from the search, the solution to removing the alias is:

```
Remove-Item Alias:<alias to remove>
```

To remove one of the previous aliases that were created use this cmdlet:

```
Remove-Item Alias:ncc
```

However, there is an error:

```
PS C:\> Remove-Item Alias:ncc
Remove-Item : Alias was not removed because alias ncc is constant or read-only.
At line:1 char:1
+ Remove-Item Alias:ncc
+ ~~~~~~~~~~~~~~~~~~~~~~
    + CategoryInfo          : WriteError: (ncc:String) [Remove-Item], SessionStateUnauthorizedAccessException
    + FullyQualifiedErrorId : AliasNotRemovable,Microsoft.PowerShell.Commands.RemoveItemCommand
```

That means the 'ReadOnly' setting that was applied worked as expected. To remove the ReadOnly option, run this:

```
Set-Alias ncc New-ComplianceCase –Force –Option None
Remove-Item Alias:ncc
```

```
PS C:\> Set-Alias ncc New-ComplianceCase -Force -Option None
PS C:\> Remove-Item Alias:ncc
PS C:\>
```

Now if the alias is tried once more, PowerShell fails as the references have been removed:

```
PS C:\> ncc
ncc : The term 'ncc' is not recognized as the name of a cmdlet, function, script file, or operable program. Check the
spelling of the name, or if a path was included, verify that the path is correct and try again.
At line:1 char:1
+ ncc
+ ~~~
    + CategoryInfo          : ObjectNotFound: (ncc:String) [], CommandNotFoundException
    + FullyQualifiedErrorId : CommandNotFoundException
```

In the end, creating your own aliases are not necessary when using PowerShell, but creating custom aliases may be a more efficient way to write code in PowerShell.

Foreach-Object (%)

While on the topic of PowerShell aliases, there are indeed some useful aliases that point to some rather useful cmdlets. One useful alias is '%'. What does the '%' symbol stand for or abbreviate in PowerShell? We can still use the Get-Alias cmdlet, but we need some criteria for finding just the '%' character in the results. If you recall from the Filtering section earlier in the book, the 'where' filter can help find the '%' symbol. From the screenshot, we also know that the field called 'Name' will contain the value:

```
Get-Alias | Where {$_.Name -eq "%"}
```

```
CommandType     Name
-----------     ----
Alias           % -> ForEach-Object
```

By using that cmdlet we now know that the alias % refers to Foreach-Object. Some other examples of other aliases:

Get-Alias | Where {$_.Name -eq "ft"}

```
CommandType              Name
-----------              ----
Alias                    ft -> Format-Table
```

Get-Alias | Where {$_.Name -eq "fl"}

```
CommandType              Name
-----------              ----
Alias                    fl -> Format-List
```

Circling back to the '%' symbol or Foreach-Object. This particular alias provides for some interesting processing of data. Take for example a scenario where we need to get the SIP address for a user's account in Exchange Online. The address exists in the EmailAddresses property for a mailbox. It is one of a number of addresses that exist there. We can write a one-liner that can pull the entire EmailAddresses property and pull out just the SIP address. In the end, a report that shows this criteria needs to be created and the PowerShell one-liner looks like this:

Get-Mailbox | Select-Object DisplayName, @{Expression ={$_.EmailAddresses};Label='SIPAddress'} | % {$Mail = $_.SIPAddress ; $Email =$Null; Foreach ($Line in $Mail) {$Address = $Line -split ':'; $Prefix = $Address[0]; if ($Prefix -cmatch 'SIP') {$Email = $Address[1]}};if ($Email -eq $Null) {$Email = 'No SIP Address'};$_.SIPAddress = $Email;Return $_} | FT -Auto

Okay. Maybe that was a bit too much at once. Think of the above as what IT Management is looking for. To learn how the Foreach-Object or '%' alias fit into this, start with the results of just the 'Get-Mailbox' that we need for the replication information.

Get-Mailbox

```
Name                      Alias                  ServerName         ProhibitSendQuota
----                      -----                  ----------         -----------------
damian                    damian                 mwhpr1301mb2078    11 GB (11,811,160,064 bytes)
DiscoverySearchMailbox... DiscoverySearchMa...   mwhpr1301mb2205    50 GB (53,687,091,200 bytes)
john.doe                  john.doe               by2pr13mb0391      99 GB (106,300,440,576 bytes)
```

Notice that we get Name, Alias, ServerName and ProhibitSendQuota. This isn't what we need for our report. Yes, we can use Name and if we want an alias, but we really need to SIP address. We can start by using the Get-Mailbox cmdlet to reveal these mailbox properties in table format:

Get-Mailbox | where {$_.name -notlike 'Disc*'} | ft Name,Alias,EmailAddresses

```
Name       Alias      EmailAddresses
----       -----      --------------
damian     damian     {SPO:SPO_de374a39-6500-4a91-b3e7-dc0b95f8a6b5@SPO_29368d28-0dc7-46c2-80f4-0ccb8ae2c65f, SIP:
john.doe   john.doe   {SIP:john.doe@OnlineExchangeBook.onmicrosoft.com, SMTP:john.doe@OnlineExchangeBook.onmicroso
```

** **Note** ** I also filtered out the Discovery Mailbox as this is not a user mailbox.

The table looks alright, however the EmailAddresses field is a mess. We also see the SIP address in the field, but we also see every other email address as well. We need to parse that field for that address. For readability sake we will also rename the field to 'SIPAddress'.

From the field data, we can determine that there are several address types stored in the EmailAddresses field - SMTP, smtp, SIP and SPO. SPO is for SharePoint Online, SMTP and smtp are our email addresses and SIP is used for Skype Online.

Let's start with the renaming of the column for the EmailAddresses property. This can be done instead of using

'Format-Table' we can use 'Select-Object' in conjunction with 'Expression' and 'Label' formatting method, like so:

```
Get-Mailbox | Where {$_.Name -NotLike 'Disc*'} | Select-Object DisplayName, @{Expression ={$_.
EmailAddresses};Label='SIP Address'
```

This will then change the column heading to show as 'SIP Address' instead of 'Email Addresses':

```
DisplayName       SIP Address
-----------       -----------
Damian Scoles     {SPO:SPO_de374a39-6500-4a91-b3e7-dc0b95f8a6b5@SPO_29368d28-0d
John Doe          {SIP:john.doe@OnlineExchangeBook.onmicrosoft.com, SMTP:john.d
```

Now that this is in place, we can now work with the data in the field and pull out just the SIP Address. How do we go about doing this? Well, we already have the data with which we will use the 'Select-Object' cmdlet. We can now manipulate this data with a Foreach-Object, or it's alias of '%'. With this we can manipulate the data using what amounts to a PowerShell code block. In this code block we need to pull out the SIP value from the series of values in the EmailAddresses field. One of the best ways is a Foreach loop to examine each one. We only store the one value that has the key letters 'SIP' in front of it. We can also register a 'No SIP value' phrase if we do not match these letters. First is the 'Foreach-Object' to kick it off:

```
| %
```

We store all of the Email Addresses in a new variable called $Mail. Notice the EmailAddresses value can be from the current object's EmailAddresses property by putting '$_.' in front of it. We can do this with any property if we wish to do so:

```
{$Mail = $_.EmailAddresses
```

Next we configure the $SIP variable as $Null. This variable will be used to store a SIP value if found or be left empty and used to trigger the phrase about no SIP address ($Null):

```
$SIP =$Null
```

The next code section is a Foreach loop that will process each entry stored in $Email in a loop:

```
Foreach ($Line in $Mail) {
```

Each entry in the field has a Prefix (SIP, SMTP, etc) that precedes the data we need. We can split that up the values in the $Line variable using a parameter called '-Split'. With this parameter we can then decide which character to separate out with. See these sample values we need to split:

```
Prefix
     Separator Value

  SPO:SPO_de374a39-6500-4a91-b3e7-dc0b95f8a6b5@SPO_29368d28-0dc7-46c2-xxx-0ccb8ae2c65f
  SIP:damian@OnlineExchangeBook.onmicrosoft.com
  SMTP:damian@OnlineExchangeBook.onmicrosoft.com
```

We can store this separated value with the $Address like so:

```
$Address = $Line -split ':'
```

Now the $Address variable stores each part of the original field as a separate column and is numbered starting with the number '0':

```
$Prefix = $Address[0]
```

Once we store the Prefix value in the $Prefix variable we can check it to see if it contains our three special characters of 'SIP' and we also make sure that these letters are capitalized as well:

```
If ($Prefix -cmatch 'SIP') {
```

If there is a match, we can then process it by storing the address value ($Address - field 1) in a variable called SIP, like so:

```
$SIP= $Address[1]}}
```

Once this is done and all the addresses are processed, we can then check to see if the $SIP variable is empty. If it is empty, then the $SIP value is populated with 'No SIP Address' to indicate that no SIP address was found.

```
If ($SIP -eq $Null) {$SIP = 'No SIP Address'}
```

At the very end of the line, we need to then return this information back to be displayed, This requires we first use the original variable from the beginning ($EmailAddresses) as well as a 'Return' cmdlet:

```
$_.EmailAddresses = $SIP
Return $_}
```

Once all of these pieces are in place we now have a one-liner that will give us a mailbox's DisplayName and SIP address in a nicely formatted and labeled table:

```
Get-Mailbox | Select-Object DisplayName, @{Expression ={$_.EmailAddresses};Label='SIP Address'} |
% {$Mail = $_.EmailAddresses ; $SIP =$Null; Foreach ($Line in $Mail) {$Address = $Line -split ':'; $Prefix =
$Address[0]; If ($Prefix -cmatch 'SIP') {$SIP = $Address[1]}};If ($SIP -eq $Null) {$SIP = 'No SIP Address'};$_.
EmailAddresses = $SIP ; Return $_} | FT -Auto
```

However, when we run this code, we get LOTS of red. What went wrong?

```
% : Exception setting "EmailAddresses": "The property 'EmailAddresses' cannot be found on this object. Verify that the
property exists and can be set."
At line:1 char:99
+ ... Address') | % ($Mail = $_.EmailAddresses ; $Email =$Null; Foreach ($L ...
+
    + CategoryInfo          : NotSpecified: (:) [ForEach-Object], SetValueInvocationException
    + FullyQualifiedErrorId : ExceptionWhenSetting,Microsoft.PowerShell.Commands.ForEachObjectCommand
```

Well, the error message doesn't make sense, does it? The error states that the property 'EmailAddress'cannot be found on the object. It appears that the error message is related to the Mailbox object and its EmailAddresses object. However, this is not the case. The error relates to the label of the column, which is 'SIP Address' and the variable used in the Foreach-Object which is '$EmailAddresses'. These values are different, which causes the error message to occur. Instead, these values need to match like so:

```
PS C:\> Get-Mailbox | Select-Object DisplayName, @{Expression =($_.EmailAddresses};Label='SIPAddress'} | % ($Mail =
$_.SIPAddress ; $Email =$Null; Foreach ($Line in $Mail) ($Address = $Line -split ':'; $Prefix = $Address[0]; if ($Pre
-cmatch 'SIP') ($Email = $Address[1]});if ($Email -eq $Null) ($Email = 'No SIP Address'};$_.SIPAddress = $Email;Ret
$_) | FT -Auto

DisplayName                       SIPAddress
-----------                       ----------
Damian Scoles                     damian@OnlineExchangeBook.onmicrosoft.com
Discovery Search Mailbox No SIP Address
John Doe                          john.doe@OnlineExchangeBook.onmicrosoft.com
```

Code Summary

Taking all of the above information and synthesizing it, we get this long one-liner to handle the heavy lifting for us. What is nice is that we can substitute the 'SIP' phrase for 'SMTP' or even 'smtp' if we want to customize it for a different search.

```
Get-Mailbox | Select-Object DisplayName, @{Expression ={$_.EmailAddresses};Label='SIPAddress'} | %
{$Mail = $_.SIPAddress ; $Email =$Null; Foreach ($Line in $Mail) {$Address = $Line -split ':'; $Prefix =
$Address[o]; If ($Prefix -cmatch 'SIP') {$Email = $Address[1]}};If ($Email -eq $Null) {$Email = 'No SIP
Address'};$_.SIPAddress = $Email;Return $_} | FT -Auto
```

```
DisplayName                    SIPAddress
-----------                    ----------
Damian Scoles                  damian@OnlineExchangeBook.onmicrosoft.com
Discovery Search Mailbox       No SIP Address
John Doe                       john.doe@OnlineExchangeBook.onmicrosoft.com
```

PowerShell Interface Customization

Working space is important in PowerShell and this means screen buffering. Why is this important? The default line buffer limit is 300 which can be too small depending on what script output of cmdlet output is being run. For example, just running 'Get-Help New-RetentionCompliancePolicy' can overrun that buffer. This makes it hard to use PowerShell to its fullest. So, just changing the buffer size will make PowerShell that much easier to work with.

** **Note** ** These changes are local to the machine where the changes are made.

Before - 300 Character Buffer:

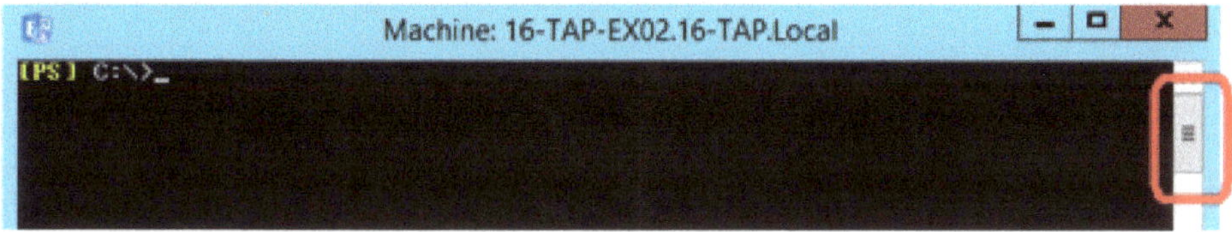

To make the change, click on the icon in the upper left and select Properties (see below):

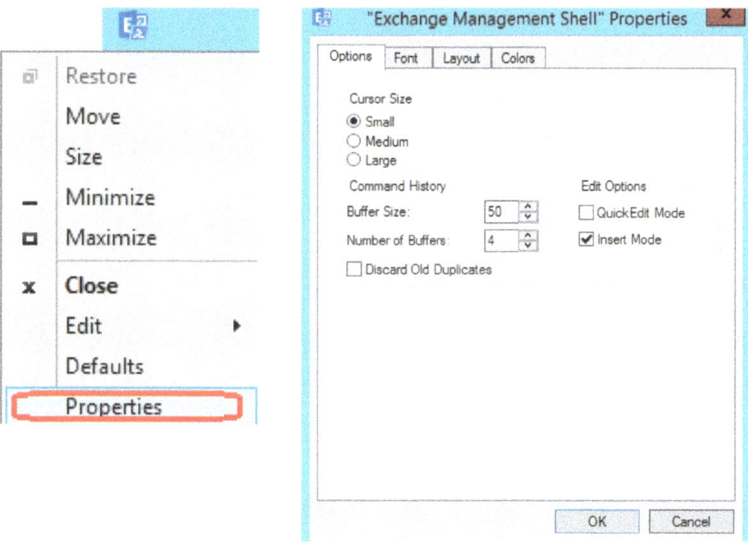

Adjust the 300 to 9999:

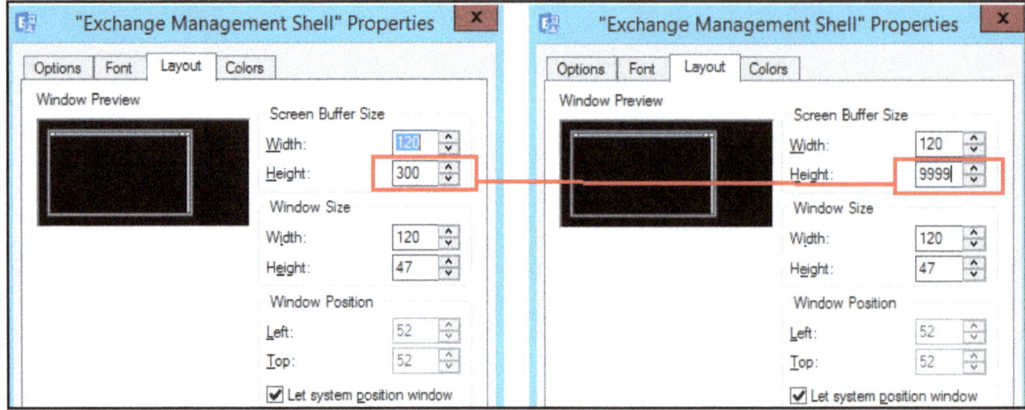

After - 9999 Character Buffer:

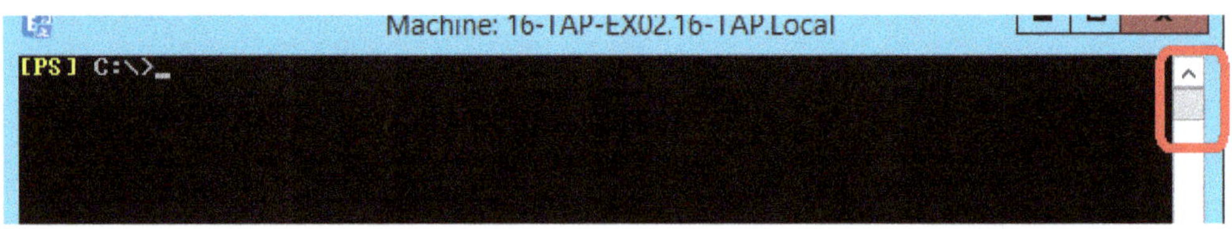

Notice the smaller size of the slider on the right. Now output from most, if not all cmdlets, will not exceed the window buffer size. If the output is in excess of 9999 lines, it may be better to export the results to a TXT, CSV or some other sort of file. Make sure to save these settings so we won't have to keep making this change.

In addition to the above, startup options can be created for the PowerShell window to customize it more. There are several locations for customization files for PowerShell and they vary in their functionality. The two we will work with for this chapter are:

For all users - PowerShell

%windir%\system32\Windows¬PowerShell\v1.0\Microsoft.Powershell_profile.ps1

Current user - PowerShell

%UserProfile%\Documents\WindowsPowerShell\Microsoft.Powershell_profile.ps1

Before creating a new one, verify that one has not yet been created. Backup the old profile if needed for later. First verify the current PowerShell profile:

$Profile

```
PS C:\> $Profile
C:\Users\administrator.16-TAP\Documents\WindowsPowerShell\Microsoft.PowerShell_profile.ps1
PS C:\>
```

To see if the file was already created and in use (if $True, then the file exists, otherwise it does not):

Test-Path $Profile

```
PS C:\> Test-Path $Profile
False
PS C:\>
```

In the above case, the profile has not been created and if we wish to add customizations we'll need to create our own file.

New-Item -Path $Profile –ItemType File –Force

```
PS C:\> New-Item -Path $Profile -ItemType File -Force


    Directory: C:\Users\administrator.16-TAP\Documents\WindowsPowerShell


Mode                LastWriteTime     Length Name
----                -------------     ------ ----
-a---         2/26/2017   6:49 PM          0 Microsoft.PowerShell_profile.ps1
```

Once the file has been created you can open this in your favorite editor.

What Can Be Added to This File

The following is a list of some of the customizations that can be performed with the profile file:

- Window sizing (height and width)
- Load custom scripts
- Windows colors

Window Sizing and Coloring

The size of the console is stored in this variable $Host which is a known variable in PowerShell.

$Host

```
Name             : ConsoleHost
Version          : 4.0
InstanceId       : 6d3a530c-8f0f-48cd-b4c1-0f5d73a3eb78
UI               : System.Management.Automation.Internal.Host.InternalHostUserInterface
CurrentCulture   : en-US
CurrentUICulture : en-US
PrivateData      : Microsoft.PowerShell.ConsoleHost+ConsoleColorProxy
IsRunspacePushed : False
Runspace         : System.Management.Automation.Runspaces.LocalRunspace
```

Notice the UI parameter is for the User Interface. To find out what is stored in it, run this:

$Host.UI

```
PS C:\> $Host.UI

RawUI
-----
System.Management.Automation.Internal.Host.InternalHostRawUserInterface
```

That was rather unhelpful, how do we see the values stored for the UI so that changes can be made?

$Host.UI.RawUI

```
PS C:\> $Host.UI.RawUI

ForegroundColor       : DarkYellow
BackgroundColor       : DarkMagenta
CursorPosition        : 0,43
WindowPosition        : 0,0
CursorSize            : 25
BufferSize            : 120,3000
WindowSize            : 120,50
MaxWindowSize         : 120,72
MaxPhysicalWindowSize : 242,72
KeyAvailable          : False
WindowTitle           : Administrator: Windows PowerShell
```

We now see the buffer size and Window Size as well as colors for the window. For this sample, the window will have a background of gray and a foreground of black. The buffer will be widened to 160 and lengthened to 6000. Next the Window Size will increase to 160 and then length to 85.

```
$Shell = $Host.UI.RawUI
$Shell.ForegroundColor = "Black"
$Shell.BackgroundColor = "Gray"
$Buffer = $Shell.BufferSize
$Buffer.Width = 160
$Buffer.Height = 6000
$Shell.BufferSize = $Buffer
$Window=$Shell.WindowSize
$Window.Width = 160
$Window.Height = 50
$Shell.WindowSize = $Window
```

The custom colors change the PowerShell window like this:

```
PS] C:\Windows\system32>cd \
PS] C:\>
PS] C:\>_
```

In the end, when the new customized PowerShell window is opened, there may be an error message displayed. The reason is that in order to load a script with the PowerShell window, the permissions for Script Execution need to be something above Restricted, which is the default permission. For example, the 'RemoteSigned' permission will allow the script to be loaded.

```
Set-ExecutionPolicy RemoteSigned
```

That will ensure the customizations will work. Loading scripts when opening a PowerShell window requires a couple of items. First changing the location of the PowerShell window to a directory where the scripts are stored:

```
Set-Location C:\Psscripts
```

As a final step of configuring the profile script, we could run another script (below) stored in the above folder:

```
.\CheckMailboxConfig.PS1
```

The example script above, would return various settings for our mailboxes - retention policies, quotas, OWA Mailbox Policy Mobile Device policies and more. Combining all of these steps together would result in this profile script:

```
# Load all shell parameters
$Shell = $host.UI.RawUI
$Shell.ForegroundColor = "Black"
$Shell.BackgroundColor = "Gray"
$Buffer = $Shell.BufferSize
$Buffer.Width = 160
$Buffer.Height = 6000
$Shell.BufferSize = $buffer
$Window=$Shell.WindowSize
$Window.Width = 160
```

```
$Window.Height = 50
$Shell.WindowSize = $Window
# Run Exchange Services check script
Set-Location C:\Psscripts
.\ExchangeServices.PS1
```

There are plenty of other options and additions that can be made to your PowerShell profile, but we will not cover all of those here.

Introduction

If you have an Office 365 tenant and you have explored the Security and Compliance Center, or your dashboard, or home screen, you may have noticed an item called 'Microsoft Secure Score'.

Now, your score will be different (higher or lower) depending on the features you have enabled in Office 365 (due to licensing) or items that you may have already configured yourself. For this chapter we are going to take a peek at this feature in the Security and Compliance Center starting with an introduction and then diving deep into each of the tasks later in the chapter.

When you first bring up the secure score, Microsoft provides a set of introductory slides at the top of the screen (which you can close once you've read them). These slides are intended to provide a quick preview of the features of Secure Score for those who have not read into the feature:

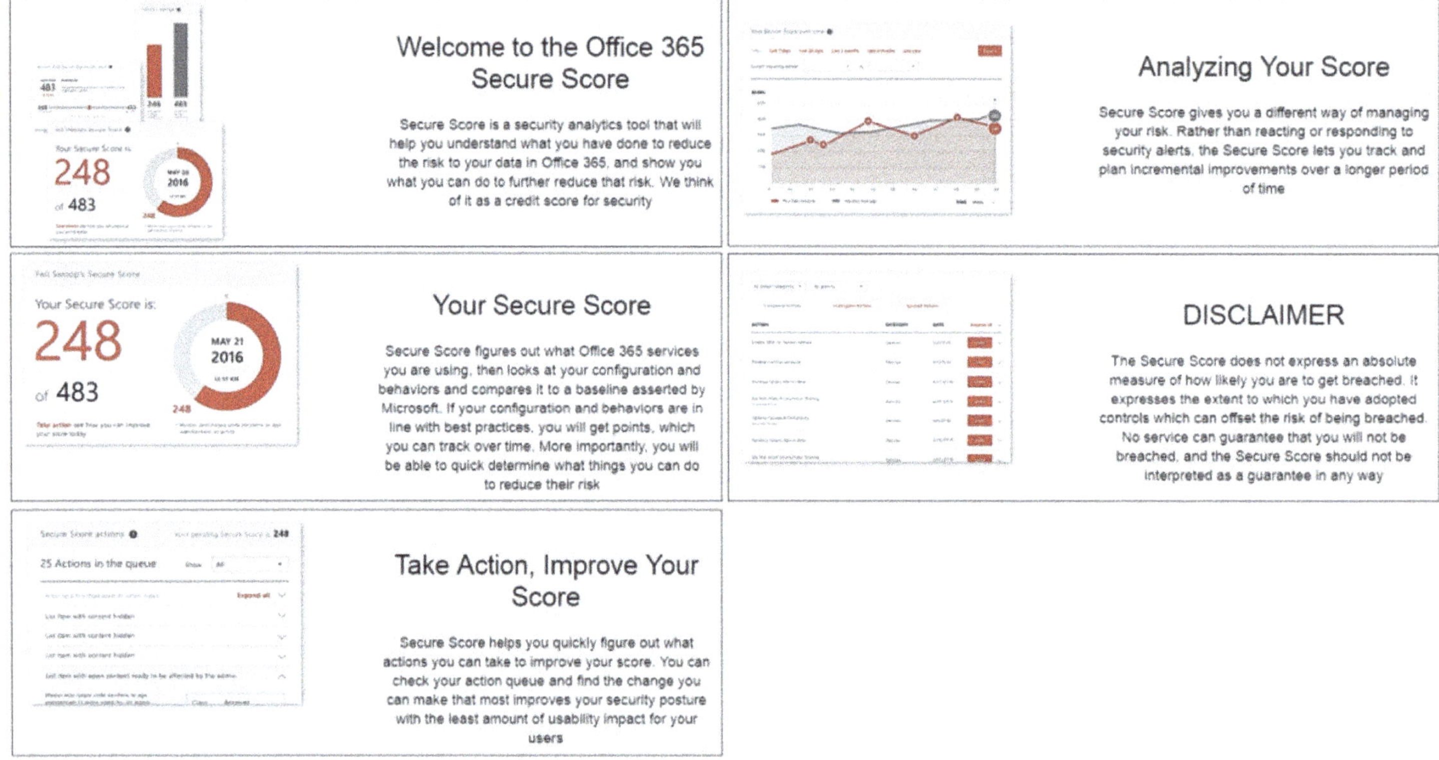

Just below these slides is your tenant's 'Secure Score Summary'. The graphic provides a visual representation of your score but also provides it relative to the maximum that your tenant's maximum score could be. Note that this again will be different tenant to tenant due to the feature set or licensing that is enabled. The current maximum with all features available is over 800 now. However, in the tenant I am using, mine is 547 as of this week:

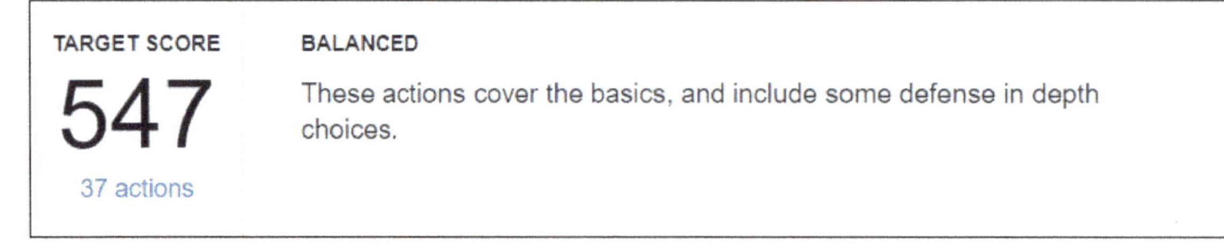

Next to this we also see a 'What's New' and a 'Risk Assessment'.

- **What's New:** Provides a quick view of the new features that are now available in the Secure Score feature of Office 365

- **Risk Assessment:** A series of shortcuts to vulnerability assessments that Microsoft thinks you should review

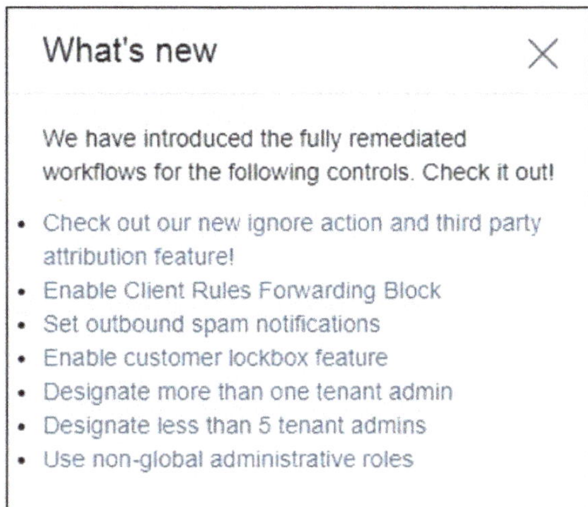

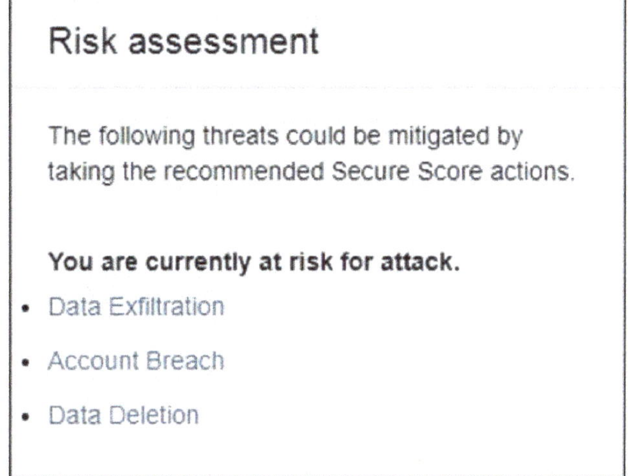

Next up we have a slider called 'Take Action, Improve Your Score':

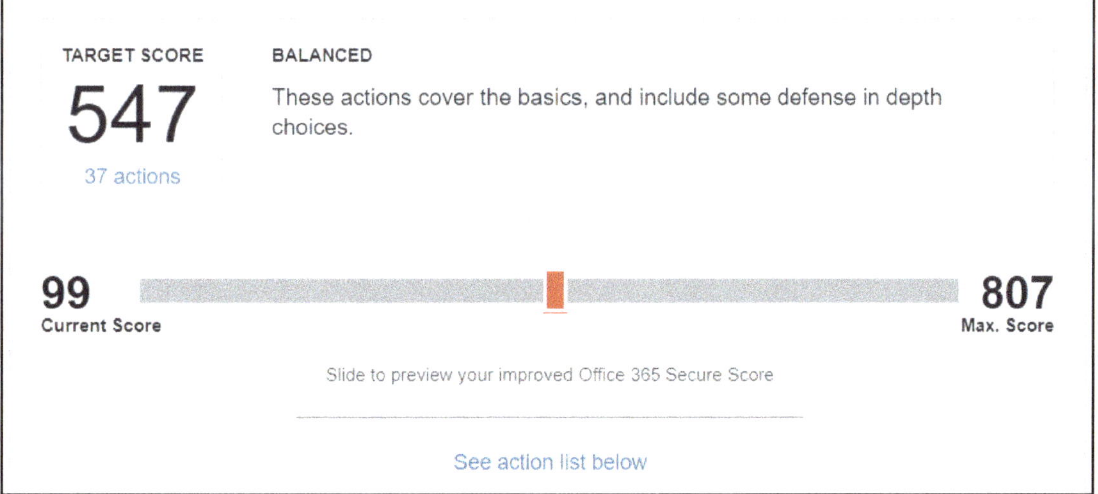

This nifty little feature allows you to essentially make a target score of where you would like to be and then displays a series of actions below to help you attain that score. These tasks range from securing email to enabling auditing to just reviewing reports on a timely basis for your tenant. With my tenant, my current target score of 547 means there are 37 actions in my queue. When the target is increased or decreased, my task list changes as well:

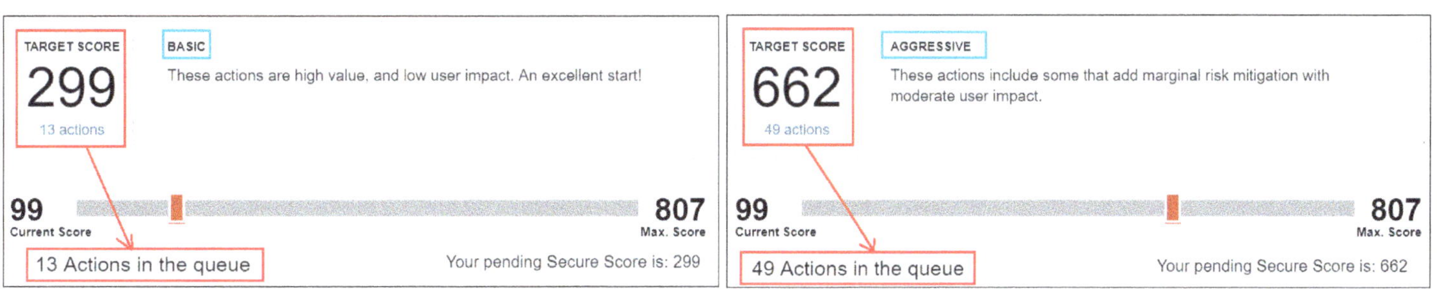

As previously mentioned, the score slider provides you with a list of recommended tasks to be completed in order to attain your score. This list can be long or short depending on where you are in your task to secure your tenant. Some possible actions items are listed below:

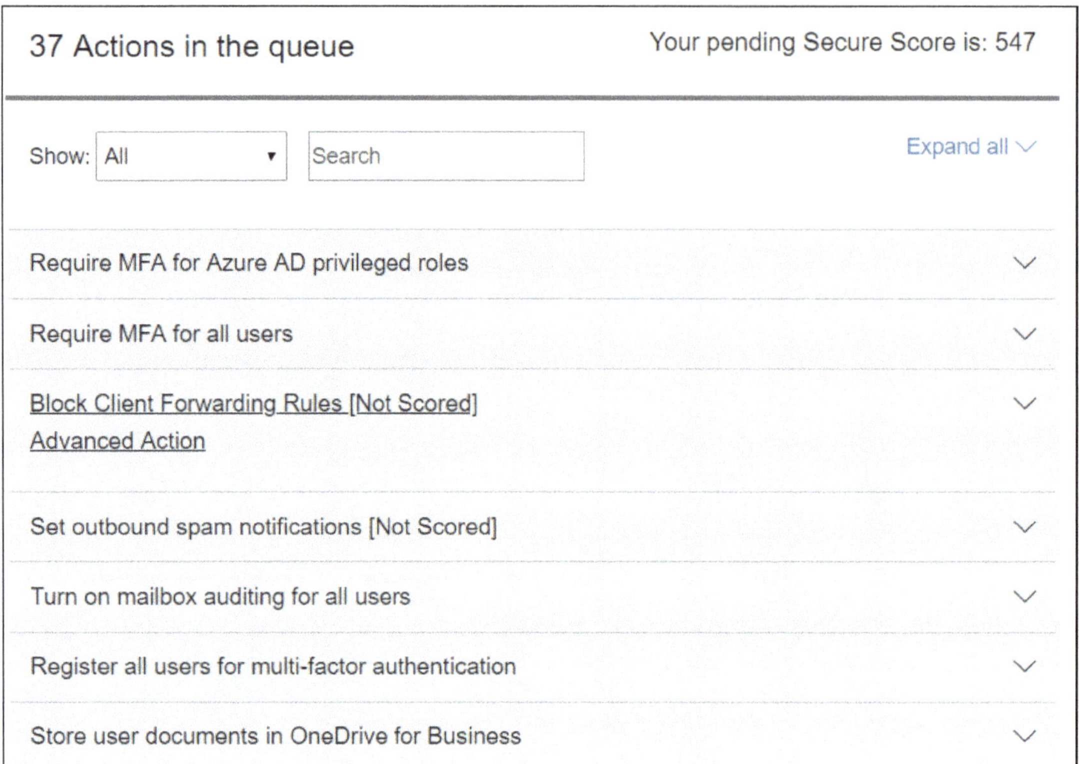

Additionally, at the very bottom of this page is link for getting advice on these changes.

The link goes to a Tech Community page, a place where you can ask questions about a particular subject and get answers to those questions from experts in the field.

Score Analyzer

Last, but not least, is the Score Analyzer tab at the top. This tab provides a bird's eye view of the changes over the past month or so for a tenant. This chart provides you with a quick view of your security score over time.

A summary table of score vs. actions is also provided:

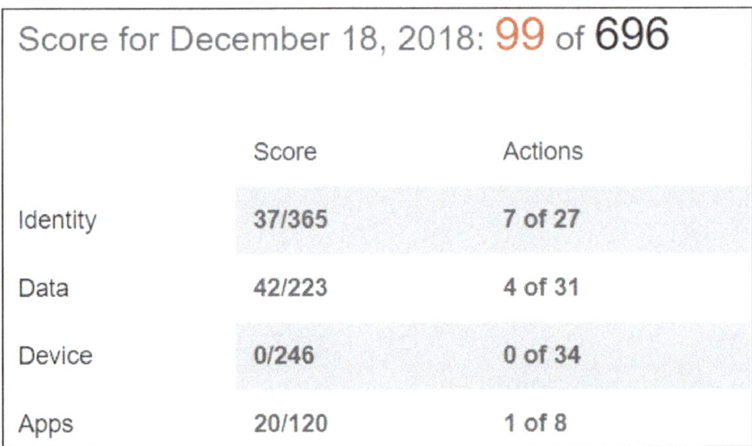

Score for December 18, 2018: **99** of **696**

	Score	Actions
Identity	37/365	7 of 27
Data	42/223	4 of 31
Device	0/246	0 of 34
Apps	20/120	1 of 8

Finally a list of actions completed with its resulting points/score awarded is at the bottom:

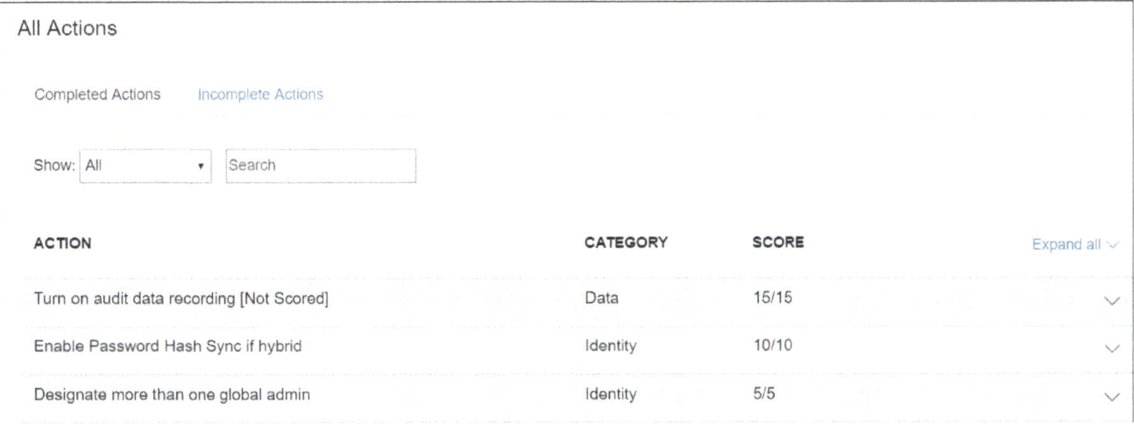

ACTION	CATEGORY	SCORE	
Turn on audit data recording [Not Scored]	Data	15/15	∨
Enable Password Hash Sync if hybrid	Identity	10/10	∨
Designate more than one global admin	Identity	5/5	∨

** **Note** ** The task list seems a bit disorganized at best and the ordering leaves much to be desired. While there are some sorting actions, I would much prefer a default sort either alphabetic or with color codes for the various levels (based on points) for these tasks, starting with the highest and ending with the lowest.

Secure Score has recently had some significant additions and removals to reflect an evolution in what Microsoft considers important to the security of your Office 365 tenant. What I noticed immediately is that the max score is over 800 now, when at one time it was between 300-450 within the past year. Also, the number of tasks has increased to 73. Microsoft has made a lot of changes to what is counted towards the Secure Score Report and has even renamed it to the 'Microsoft Secure Score'. Additionally there is a new 'Windows' score that has been added to the Secure Score report page:

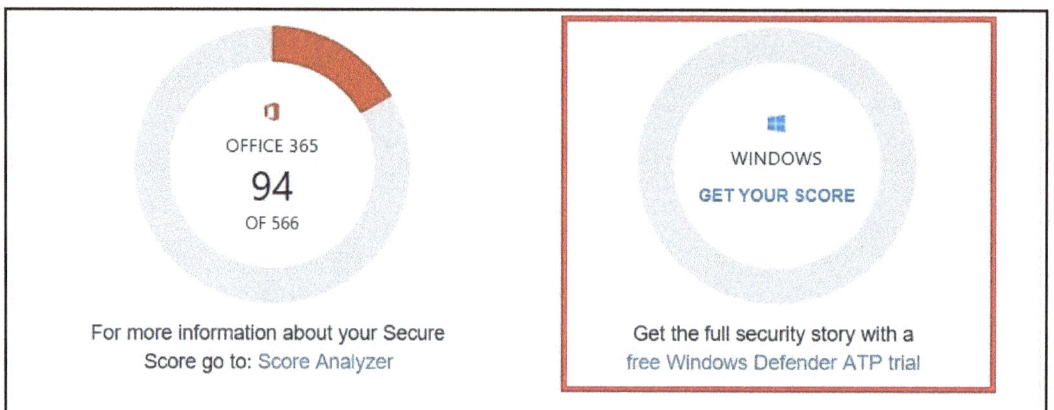

There is now a greater emphasis on using Intune to help secure your Office 365 tenant. Lockbox checking was removed, which is interesting. There is more emphasis on Risk when it comes to clients and devices (sign-in, jailbreak, etc.). Most of these changes and additions appear to be a good thing on first review.

Removed Tasks in 2018

- Review sign-in devices report weekly

- Review account provisioning activity report weekly

- Review non-global administrators weekly

- Review list of external users you have invited to documents monthly

PowerShell and Microsoft Secure Score

As of the printing of this book, there was no real good interface into the Secure Score. No direct reporting or ways to automate processes in order to raise your Secure Score. Thus, for this purpose of this book, this chapter is purely for reference. Hence the fact that it is in the very last Appendix for the book.

Detailed Analysis

For this next section we are going to review each and every task as of the printing of this book. The intent is to provide the reader a guide to the tasks listed in the Microsoft Secure Score Report. Remember this is a guide and not an absolute final answer as which tasks your tenant should apply.

——

Designate less than five global admins

According to Microsoft

"You should designate less than five global tenant administrators because the more global admin users you have, the more likely it is that one of those accounts will be successfully breached by an external attacker. We found that you have 'X' admins designated."

Threats – Password Cracking, Account Breach, Elevation of Privilege

Recommendation & Thoughts

Even for a large organization, more than five global admins can be a bit excessive. Remember these are individuals that have full control over EVERYTHING in your tenant. Do you need more than five?

So the recommendation is a definite yes, as the lower this number is the better. I feel this is on the same level as your Enterprise Admin group in AD. It is almost always too large no matter how large your environment is. Reduce it, keep it small. Even better, tie in something like Privileged Identity Management (PIM) in Azure to make the environment dynamic and manageable without exposing yourself to the risks of too many full control admins in Office 365.

——

Do not expire passwords

According to Microsoft

"While this is not the most intuitive recommendation, research has found that when periodic password resets are enforced, passwords become weaker as users tend to pick something weaker and then use a pattern of it for rotation. If a user creates a strong password: long, complex and without any pragmatic words present, it should remain just as strong in 60 days as it is today. It is Microsoft's official security position to not expire passwords periodically without a specific reason. We found that your current policy is set to require a password reset every 999 days."

Threats – Password Cracking and Account Breach

Recommendation & Thoughts

This idea has gained more traction with Microsoft over the years for many reasons. The first is that it removed some of the challenge that a regular user has trying to come up with an original password every 60 to 90 days. No need to use sticky notes or other reminders of a constantly changing password. A consistent, secure password is much better in the long run.

This one is a maybe, if only because now Microsoft is pushing for password-less access with tokens and other MFA controls. Take a look here for this option – https://docs.microsoft.com/en-us/azure/active-directory/authentication/howto-authentication-phone-sign-in.

** Note ** NIST 800-63 (co-authored by Microsoft) is a NIST recommendation to not expire passwords on a regular basis.

Do not allow users to grant consent to unmanaged applications

According to Microsoft

"You should not allow third party integrated applications to connect to your services unless there is a very clear value and you have robust security controls in place. While there are legitimate uses, attackers can grant access from breached accounts to third party applications to exfiltrate data from your tenancy without having to maintain the breached account. We found that your policy to allow third party integrated applications to access your service is currently configured to False."

Threats – Data Exfiltration & Data Spillage

Recommendation & Thoughts

Any strengthening of security for your tenant is a good idea in general. Adding third party app integration should require a security analysis to make sure that you are not providing an attack vector. To lessen an attack vector, work with your app provider to ensure appropriate security and controls.

This is a definite yes and a no-brainer. Any third party app that is integrated with your tenant then their security needs to be in place as well. If you don't have any apps, then make sure the setting is False.

Enable versioning on all SharePoint online document libraries

According to Microsoft

"You should enable versioning on all of your SharePoint online site collection document libraries. This will ensure that accidental or malicious changes to document content can be recovered. We found that you do not have versioning enabled on 'X' out of 'Y' of your site document libraries."

Threats – Data Deletion

Recommendation & Thoughts

Unless there is a business case for not enabling versioning in SharePoint, I agree that this is a good recommendation from Microsoft. Just like using versioning on documents and files that your end users edit, this would enable a similar function for your SharePoint sites in Office 365.

This is a yes and a definite option I would enable on any SharePoint sites you have in your Office 365 tenant.

Use non-global administrative roles

According to Microsoft

"You should leverage non-global administrator roles to perform required administrative work with the least privileges necessary to complete the task. Using roles like Password Administrator or Exchange Online Administrator will reduce the number of high value, high impact global admin role holders you have, which will in turn reduce the likelihood of a breach of an account with global administrative privileges. We found that you have 'X' users in global admin roles."

Threats – Account Breach, Elevation of Privilege & Malicious Insider

Recommendations & Thoughts

The least privilege model is one that should be used in any security situation, whether this is with your Office 365 tenant or on-premises. The only exception that could present itself in this model is the single administrator or small IT department where duties are not segregated due to lack of personnel.

Even with the caveats spelled out above, I would still recommend this being implemented if at all possible. Larger organizations should absolutely be using this and hopefully follow their model from on-premises AD security configuration. PIM is also another viable option.

——

Ensure all users are registered for multi-factor authentication

According to Microsoft

"You should register all users for MFA because MFA allows end users to prove their identity during risky sign-ins. We found that you had users out of 'X' that did not have MFA registered. If you register those users, your score will go up points."

Threats – Password Cracking & Account Breach

Recommendations & Thoughts

Currently this is more of an ideal scenario. This setting will require end user education, training and possibly even a cultural shift for this to work properly. Many organizations are certainly asking for this to be put in place and it is a goal to strive for.

Yes. This should be done. This increases security and adds a rather small amount of complexity for the end user.

——

Review permissions & block risky OAuth applications connected to your corporate environment

According to Microsoft

"Cloud App Security app permissions enables you to see which user-installed applications have access to Office 365 data, what permissions the apps have, and which users granted these apps access. We found you haven't investigated and banned OAuth apps connected in your tenant. We found that your enablement of this feature is set to false. If you block access to a risky OAuth App, your score will go up by 15 points. "

Threats – Data Exfiltration & Data Spillage

Recommendations & Thoughts

A consideration for this is if you have the licensing to use the Cloud App Security feature from the Security and Compliance Center. This feature requires an EMS E5 or as a separate add-on in order to make it available. Otherwise it does appear to be a good recommendation. It certainly needs to be evaluated on a case by case basis depending on what apps you are using in your tenant and if there is any need to analyze the authentication used.

Maybe – only because this is an instance where apps and the consequences of the change need to be analyzed.

——

Detect Insider Threat, Compromised account, and Brute force attempts in cloud applications

According to Microsoft

"Cloud App Security anomaly detection policies provide UEBA and advanced threat detection across your cloud environment. We found you haven't reviewed anomaly detection alerts in your tenant. We found the enablement of this feature is set to False. If you remediate an alert, your score will go up by 15 points. "

Threats – Account Breach, Elevation of Privilege & Malicious Insider

Recommendations & Thoughts

Another feature that requires the Cloud App Security feature and thus an EMS E5 license in order to use. If you have the right licensing, then this is a worthy feature to enable in your tenant.

Yes. Do this. There are enough attacks out there that this should be monitored in Office 365.

Enable self-service password reset

According to Microsoft

"You should enable self-service password because this allows banned password checking every time a user resets password. You have 'X' users out of 'Y' without self-service password reset. If you enable this, your score will go up 5 points."

Threats – Password Cracking & Account Breach

Recommendations & Thoughts

Self-service password resetting is a good feature for your tenant as it will alleviate some of the pressure and effort of any companies help desk team.

** Note that this requires it to be configured in Azure AD and P1 licensing in order to get the full effect.

Yes. Put this in place. Pilot it first as there are many options to enable to get this just right for your user base.

Do not allow mailbox delegation

According to Microsoft

"You should ensure that your users do not use mailbox delegation. While there are many legitimate uses of mailbox delegation, it also makes it much easier for an attacker to move laterally from one account to another to steal data. We found that you had 'X' active accounts out of 'Y' with mailbox delegation. If you remove delegate permissions from all of your mailboxes, your score will go up 1 points."

Threats – Account Breach, Elevation of Privilege, & Malicious Insider

Recommendations & Thoughts

There are way too many legitimate uses of this feature for me to recommend not using mailbox delegation. Understand like a lot of other features in Exchange Online that are convenient that there is always a risk that the resource will be used as an attack vector.

Maybe – Only because you may be in an environment where this is possible. Maybe you've never used delegation or permissions or anything like this. In that case, this should be pretty easy. However, the vast majority of my clients use mailbox delegation is some form or fashion and would have a hard time not using this feature.

Discover risky and non-compliant Shadow IT applications used in your organization

According to Microsoft

"Cloud discovery analyzes firewall traffic logs to provide visibility into cloud application usage and security posture of each. Log collectors enable you to easily automate log upload from firewall appliances in your network. We found your tenant doesn't have continuous discovery report configured. We found that your enablement of this feature is set to False. If you add a data source, your score will go up by 20 points."

Threats – Data Exfiltration

Recommendations & Thoughts

This features comes as part of the previously mentioned Cloud App Security, thus it requires EMS E3 or an add-on to use. It can provide some worthwhile reports if you need help with this part of your infrastructure.

If you have the licenses, then I would certainly enable the feature, if you don't but have other items in Office 365 that require an E5, this may be worth getting the E5 for those features and then utilizing all the features therein.

____

Set automated notification for new OAuth applications connected to your corporate environment

According to Microsoft

"App permission policies enable you to discover OAuth abuse in the org by identifying trending applications based on usage & permissions granted. We found that your enablement of this feature is set to False. If you enable this feature, your score will go up by 20 points. "

Threats – Account Breach, Elevation of Privilege & Malicious Insider

Recommendations & Thoughts

This does seem like a good, no-brainer to enable. If there is a way to monitor these types of connections, I am sure the security people/department at your organization would like to hear or see what is being used when connecting.

Yes. This is a security enhancement with little to no downsides. So definitely do it!

____

Enable sign-in risk policy

According to Microsoft

"You should enable sign-in risk policy. This will ensure that suspicious sign-ins are challenged for MFA. We found that you had 'X' users out of 'Y' that did not have sign-in risky policy enabled. If you enable sign-in risk policy for those 'Y' users, you score will go up 30 points."

Threats – Password Cracking & Account Breach

Recommendations & Thoughts

Another good security recommendation from Microsoft for maintaining the integrity of your logins to your Office 365 tenant. I would be hard pressed to find a good reason to not enable this feature. Yes. This is a definite one to implement. May require additional licensing.

Enable user risk policy

According to Microsoft

"You should enable user risk policy. This will ensure that potentially compromised users are automatically remediated. We found that you had 'X' users out of 'Y' that did not have user risk policy enabled. If you enable user risk policy for those 'Y' users, you score will go up 30 points."

Threats – Password Cracking & Account Breach

Recommendations & Thoughts

This is a feature that should be investigated before implementing it for any users in Office 365. However, it does sound like a good idea in order to again ensure account login integrity for your Office 365 tenant.

Yes. This is a feature that should be enabled. Just like any change of this nature, test as much as possible before rolling it out to all of the users that will be targeted by this policy.

Enable policy to block legacy authentication

According to Microsoft

"Blocking legacy authentication makes it harder for attackers to gain access. Office 2013 client apps support legacy authentication by default. Legacy means that they support either Microsoft Online Sign-in Assistant or basic authentication. In order for these clients to use modern authentication features, the Windows client have registry keys set. You have 'X' of 'Y' users that don't have legacy authentication blocked. ."

Threats – Password Cracking & Account Breach

Recommendations & Thoughts

This is an easy yet hard one to give a good recommendation for. The reason for that is simply put you would have to know what legacy auth apps are out there. If this cannot be validated, then it will be hard to turn this off tenant wide.

Yes. With a caveat. If you have no apps using legacy authentication, then it is a definite yes. Otherwise, there should be an effort made to eliminate these connections.

Enable Office 365 Cloud App Security Console

According to Microsoft

"You should adopt the Office 365 Cloud App Security Console. This console will allow you to set up policies to alert you about anomalous and suspicious activity. We found that your enablement of this feature is set to False. If you enable this feature, your score will go up by 20 points. "

Threats -Account Breach, Elevation of Privilege, Malicious Insider, Data Exfiltration & Data Spillage

Recommendations & Thoughts

If you have the licensing for the Cloud App Security Console, then there is no reason not to do this.

Yes. Like a lot of other recommendations, this is seemingly a no-brainer as it will help the admin get better visibility into their own tenant.

____

Set automated notifications for new and trending cloud applications in your organization

According to Microsoft

"Discovery policies enable you to set alerts that notify you when new apps are detected within your organization. We found your tenant doesn't have any app discovery policies configured. We found the enablement of this feature is set to False. If you enable this feature, your score will go up by 15 points. "

Threats – Data Exfiltration

Recommendations & Thoughts

Since this is all about discovery and notification of the admin of changes, I am all for this. As IT should have visibility into what is installed in their environment, this would be good step in that direction.

Yes. Turn it on. No other comment needs to be made.

____

Enable Advanced Threat Protection safe attachments policy

According to Microsoft

"You should enable the Office 365 Advanced Threat Protection Safe Attachments feature. This will extend the malware protections in the service to include routing all messages and attachments that don't have a known virus/malware signature to a special hypervisor environment where a behavior analysis is performed using a variety of machine learning and analysis techniques to detect malicious intent. We found that your enablement is set to False. If you enable Safe Attachments, your score will go up 15 points."

Threats – Phishing/Whaling & Spoofing

Recommendations & Thoughts

This task should only appear if you have an ATP license or E5 in your tenant. If you have that, then yes, this should be enabled.

Yes. Protect your users from bad attachments now!

____

Enable Advanced Threat Protection safe links policy

According to Microsoft

"You should enable the Office 365 Advanced Threat Protection Safe Links feature. This will extend the phishing protection in the service to include redirecting all email hyperlinks through a forwarding service which will block malicious ones even after it has been delivered to the end user. We found that your enablement is set to False. If you enable Safe Links, your score will go up 15 points."

Threats – Phishing/Whaling & Spoofing

Recommendations & Thoughts

Same as the previous ATP feature. Same comment on licensing and visibility.

Yes. Have the license? Enable it.

Set custom activity policy for your organization to discover suspicious usage patterns in cloud apps

According to Microsoft

"Activity policies enable you to detect risky behavior, violations, or suspicious data points in your cloud environment, and if necessary, to integrate remediation work flows. We found your tenant didn't have any activity policies configured. We found the enablement of this feature is set to False. If you enable this policy, your score will go up by 10 points. "

Threats – Account Breach, Elevation of Privilege & Malicious Insider

Recommendations & Thoughts

Another automated security monitoring feature for your tenant. Implement it.

Yes. If you have the required licenses, enable it.

Identify Shadow IT application usage in your organization by automating log upload from firewalls

According to Microsoft

"Cloud Discovery analyzes firewall traffic logs to provide visibility into cloud application usage and security posture of each. We found your tenant didn't have Cloud Discovery configured. We found that your enablement of this feature is set to False. If you create a new Cloud Discovery snapshot report, your score will go up by 5 points."

Threats – Data Exfiltration

Recommendations & Thoughts

Requires Cloud App Discovery licenses, so if you have the license, then yes, do this.

Yes, implement this.

Create a Microsoft Intune Compliance Policy for iOS

According to Microsoft

"Microsoft Intune Compliance Policies compare a devices security configuration and health against an admin defined baseline. Corporate data and resources can be restricted based on this security compliance of a managed devices. We found that an enablement of iOS Compliance Policy is False. If you create and assign an iOS Compliance Policy, your score will go up 10 points."

Threats – Data Exfiltration

Recommendations & Thoughts

On this one it will be a depends only because it depends on your licensing and if you have a third party MDM solution already in place. So if you have licensing for Intune and are not using another MDM solution, then this is something that should be implemented. I would recommend that your legal and security teams be looped in so they can help decide how to implement policies.

Yes, if you are going to use Intune. If not, a third-party application could be used and marked as such.

Create a Microsoft Intune Compliance Policy for Android

According to Microsoft

"Microsoft Intune Compliance Policies compare a devices security configuration and health against an admin defined baseline. Corporate data and resources can be restricted based on this security compliance of a managed devices. We found that an enablement of Android compliance policy is False. If you create and assign an Android Compliance Policy, your score will go up 10 points."

Threats – Data Exfiltration

Recommendations & Thoughts

On this one it will be a depends only because it depends on your licensing and if you have a third party MDM solution already in place. So if you have licensing for Intune and are not using another MDM solution, then this is something that should be implemented. I would recommend that your legal and security teams be looped in so they can help decide how to implement policies.

Yes, if you are going to use Intune. If not, a third-party application could be used and marked as such.

Create a Microsoft Intune Compliance Policy for Android for Work

According to Microsoft

"Microsoft Intune Compliance Policies compare a devices security configuration and health against an admin defined baseline. Corporate data and resources can be restricted based on this security compliance of a managed devices. We found that an enablement of Android for Work compliance policy is False. If you create and assign an Android for Work Compliance Policy, your score will go up 10 points."

Threats – Data Exfiltration

Recommendations & Thoughts

On this one it will be a depends only because it depends on your licensing and if you have a third party MDM solution already in place. So if you have licensing for Intune and are not using another MDM solution, then this is something that should be implemented. I would recommend that your legal and security teams be looped in so they can help decide how to implement policies.

Yes, if you are going to use Intune. If not, a third-party application could be used and marked as such.

Create a Microsoft Intune Compliance Policy for Windows

According to Microsoft

"Microsoft Intune Compliance Policies compare a devices security configuration and health against an admin defined baseline. Corporate data and resources can be restricted based on this security compliance of a managed devices. We found that an enablement of Compliance Policy for Windows is False. If you create and assign an Windows Compliance Policy, your score will go up 10 points."

Threats – Data Exfiltration

Recommendations & Thoughts

On this one it will be a depends only because it depends on your licensing and if you have a third party MDM solution already in place. So if you have licensing for Intune and are not using another MDM solution, then this is something that should be implemented. I would recommend that your legal and security teams help decide how to implement these policies.

Yes, if you are going to use Intune. If not, a third-party application could be used and marked as such.

Create a Microsoft Intune Compliance Policy for macOS

According to Microsoft

"Microsoft Intune Compliance Policies compare a devices security configuration and health against an admin defined baseline. Corporate data and resources can be restricted based on this security compliance of a managed devices. We found that an enablement of compliance policy for macOS is False. If you create and assign an macOS Compliance Policy, your score will go up 10 points."

Threats – Data Exfiltration

Recommendations & Thoughts

On this one it will be a depends only because it depends on your licensing and if you have a third party MDM solution already in place. So if you have licensing for Intune and are not using another MDM solution, then this is something that should be implemented. I would recommend that your legal and security teams help decide how to implement these policies.

Yes, if you are going to use Intune. If not, a third-party application could be used and marked as such.

Create a Microsoft Intune App Protection Policy for iOS

According to Microsoft

"Microsoft Intune App Protection Policies provide data security and data loss prevention for iOS and Android apps. We found that an enablement of Intune App Protection Policies is False. If you create and assign an iOS App Protection Policy, your score will go up by 10 points."

Threats – Data Exfiltration

Recommendations & Thoughts

On this one it will be a depends only because it depends on your licensing and if you have a third party MDM solution already in place. So if you have licensing for Intune and are not using another MDM solution, then this is something that should be implemented. I would recommend that your legal and security teams be looped in so they can help decide how to implement policies.

Yes, if you are going to use Intune. If not, a third-party application could be used and marked as such.

———

Create a Microsoft Intune App Protection Policy for Android

According to Microsoft

"Microsoft Intune App Protection Policies provide data security and data loss prevention for iOS and Android apps. We found that you have no Intune App Protection Policies for Android configured. We found that an enablement of Intune App Protection Policies for Android is False. If you create and assign an Android App Protection Policy, your score will go up by 10 points."

Threats – Data Exfiltration

Recommendations & Thoughts

On this one it will be a depends only because it depends on your licensing and if you have a third party MDM solution already in place. So if you have licensing for Intune and are not using another MDM solution, then this is something that should be implemented. I would recommend that your legal and security teams be looped in so they can help decide how to implement policies.

Yes, if you are going to use Intune. If not, a third-party application could be used and marked as such.

———

Create a Microsoft Intune Windows Information Protection Policy

According to Microsoft

"Windows Information Protection provides data security and data loss prevention for Windows 10. We found that an enablement of Windows Information Protection policies is False. If you create and assign a Windows Information Protection Policy, your score will go up by 10 points."

Threats – Data Exfiltration

Recommendations & Thoughts

This can be done with Intune, SCCM and some other third-party apps as well (https://docs.microsoft.com/en-us/windows/security/information-protection/windows-information-protection/protect-enterprise-data-using-wip). This is a form of DLP and worth investigating.

Yes. Protect your workstations.

———

Create a Microsoft Intune Configuration Profile for iOS

According to Microsoft

"Microsoft Intune Configuration Profiles configure device security options for mobile devices We found that an enablement of Intune Configuration Profiles for iOS is False."

Threats – Data Exfiltration

Recommendations & Thoughts

On this one it will be a depends only because it depends on your licensing and if you have a third party MDM solution already in place. So if you have licensing for Intune and are not using another MDM solution, then this is something that should be implemented. I would recommend that your legal and security teams be looped in so they can help decide how to implement policies.

Yes, if you are going to use Intune. If not, a third-party application could be used and marked as such.

Create a Microsoft Intune Configuration Profile for Android

According to Microsoft

"Microsoft Intune Configuration Profiles configure device security options for mobile devices. We found that an enablement of Intune Configuration Profiles for Android is False. If you create and assign an Android Configuration Profile, your score will go up by 10 points."

Threats – Data Exfiltration

Recommendations & Thoughts

On this one it will be a depends only because it depends on your licensing and if you have a third party MDM solution already in place. So if you have licensing for Intune and are not using another MDM solution, then this is something that should be implemented. I would recommend that your legal and security teams be looped in so they can help decide how to implement policies.

Yes, if you are going to use Intune. If not, a third-party application could be used and marked as such.

Create a Microsoft Intune Configuration Profile for Android for Work

According to Microsoft

"Microsoft Intune Configuration Profiles configure device security options for mobile devices. We found that an enablement of Intune Configuration Profiles for Android for Work is False. If you create and assign an Android for Work Configuration Profile, your score will go up by 10 points."

Threats – Data Exfiltration

Recommendations & Thoughts

On this one it will be a depends only because it depends on your licensing and if you have a third party MDM solution already in place. So if you have licensing for Intune and are not using another MDM solution, then this is something that should be implemented. I would recommend that your legal and security teams be looped in so they can help decide how to implement policies.

Yes, if you are going to use Intune. If not, a third-party application could be used and marked as such.

Create a Microsoft Intune Configuration Profile for Windows

According to Microsoft

"Microsoft Intune Configuration Profiles configure device security options for mobile devices We found that an enablement of Intune Configuration Profiles for Windows is False. If you create and assign an Windows Configuration Profile, your score will go up by 10 points."

Threats – Data Exfiltration

Recommendations & Thoughts

On this one it will be a depends only because it depends on your licensing and if you have a third party MDM solution already in place. So if you have licensing for Intune and are not using another MDM solution, then this is something that should be implemented. I would recommend that your legal and security teams be looped in so they can help decide how to implement policies.

Yes, if you are going to use Intune. Otherwise no.

——

Create a Microsoft Intune Configuration Profile for macOS

According to Microsoft

"Microsoft Intune Configuration Profiles configure device security options for mobile devices. We found that an enablement of Intune Configuration Profiles for macOS is False. If you create and assign an macOS Configuration Profile, your score will go up by 10 points."

Threats – Data Exfiltration

Recommendations & Thoughts

On this one it will be a depends only because it depends on your licensing and if you have a third party MDM solution already in place. So if you have licensing for Intune and are not using another MDM solution, then this is something that should be implemented. I would recommend that your legal and security teams be looped in so they can help decide how to implement policies.

Yes, if you are going to use Intune. Otherwise no.

——

Mark devices with no Microsoft Intune Compliance Policy assigned as Non-Compliant

According to Microsoft

"If users are not targeted by Microsoft Intune Compliance Policies, they may be accessing corporate data on unmanaged/ insecure devices. By configuring this setting, you're marking devices Not Compliant by default if the user has no Compliance Policy assigned. We found that your enablement of this feature is set to False. If you set this to Not Compliant, your score will go up by 10 points."

Threats – Data Exfiltration

Recommendations & Thoughts

This is only really valid if you are using no MDM solution at all. However there are plenty of organizations that are not using Intune and already have an app to handle this management.

This is an automatic check and while it can be ignored, you won't get any points for it's ignored.

Enable Enhanced Jailbreak Detection in Microsoft Intune

According to Microsoft

"Enhanced Jailbreak detection uses Location Services to trigger Jailbreak evaluation more frequently. By enabling Enhanced Jailbreak detection, your score will go up by 10 points. We found that your enablement of this feature is set to false. By enabling Enhanced Jailbreak detection, your score will go up by 10 point."

Threats – Data Exfiltration

Recommendations & Thoughts

If using Intune, this is a good feature. Being able to handle Jailbroken phones in a BYOD corporate environment is key.

Yes, if using Intune, otherwise no because it would not make any sense.

Enable Windows Defender ATP integration into Microsoft Intune

According to Microsoft

"Windows Defender ATP provides visibility into your organizations security posture and provides recommendations to improve it. We found that your enablement of this feature is set to False. Connect Windows Defender ATP with Microsoft Intune to up your score 10 points."

Threats – Data Exfiltration

Recommendations & Thoughts

Have Intune licensing? Then this make sense to utilize.

Yes, if licensed, otherwise no.

Enable mobile device management services

According to Microsoft

"You should use a mobile device management service such as Office 365 Mobile Device Management or Microsoft Intune. Devices, especially mobile devices, are vulnerable to attacks such as malware that can lead to account and data breaches. We found that your enablement of mobile device management services is False. If you enable a mobile device management service, your score will go up 20 points."

Threats – Account Breach, Data Exfiltration & Data Spillage

Recommendations & Thoughts

If you are not using a third-party product, then this should be used. The basic MDM can be used with certain license levels. An additional license would be required is using the higher end MDM.

Yes, implement.

____

Review blocked devices report weekly

According to Microsoft

"You should review your blocked devices report weekly. You should do this to look for devices and users that violated your mobile device management policies so you can determine if those violations were malicious or non-malicious. If you review this report, your score will go up 5 points."

Threats – Account Breach, Data Exfiltration & Data Spillage

Recommendations & Thoughts

It's a report, read it.

Yes. No further response needed.

____

Require PC and Mobile devices to be patched, have anti-virus, and firewalls enabled

According to Microsoft

"You should configure your mobile device management policies to require the PC and mobile device to be patched, have anti-virus, and have a firewall enabled. If you do not require this, users will be able to connect from devices that are vulnerable to basic Internet attacks, leading to potential breaches of accounts and data. We found that your policy is configured to [Not Measured]. If you enable this policy, your score will increase by 10 points."

Threats – Account Breach, Data Exfiltration & Data Spillage

Recommendations & Thoughts

In an ideal world, yes. If this can be enabled in your environment and be successful then it's a yes.

Yes. Anything that can be done to keep managed devices up to date on patches is a good thing.

____

Enable MFA for all global admins

According to Microsoft

"You should enable MFA for all of your admin accounts because a breach of any of those accounts can lead to a breach of any of your data."

Microsoft considers this to be of high importance and has assigned 50 points to this task alone.

Threats – Account Breach and Elevation of Privilege

Recommendations & Thoughts

This change will only affect your Global Admins for your Office 365 tenant and no end-users will be affected by the change. The second factor is typically a code that is sent via txt to a cell phone registered to that user and then entered when prompted. This change is worth it, however it may cause issues with those using PowerShell programmatically with no way to enter the second authentication information. Possible scenarios for this are Quest migration tools and running scheduled PowerShell scripts against Office 365 workloads.

Clicking on 'Launch Now' for this feature takes you right to the MFA configuration in Azure AD – MFA Page. Quite convenient and no need to dig into Azure AD to find this to enable it.

Although it will not work for 100% of your Office 365 scenarios, I would enable MFA for as many Global Admins as you can, if not all of them. ** **Note** ** An AADP P1 license is not required for Administrator MFA.

––

Enable MFA for all users

According to Microsoft

"You should enable MFA for all of your user accounts because a breach of any of those accounts can lead to a breach of any data that user has access to."

Microsoft considers this to be of high importance and has assigned 30 points to this task.

Threats – Account Breach and Elevation of privilege

Recommendations & Thoughts

This is one of those features that can turn into a double-edged sword. Adding a layer of security to protect end-users from a data breach is generally considered a good idea. However, this change will disrupt an end-user's normal flow when logging into apps for Office 365. They will have to use a second factor of authentication. While some organizations can require this for auditing or compliance reasons, most organizations may see this change as overkill for regular user accounts.

Clicking on 'Launch Now' for this feature takes you right to the MFA configuration in Azure AD – MFA Page. Quite convenient and no need to dig into Azure AD to find this to enable it.

If your users can be trained and adjust to the extra login step, then setting this feature up would be worth it as Microsoft has stated that MFA will prevent 99+% of attacks.

––

Enable audit data recording

According to Microsoft

"You should enable audit data recording for your Office 365 service to ensure that you have a record of every user and administrator's interaction with the service, including Azure AD, Exchange Online, and SharePoint Online/OneDrive for Business. This data will make it possible to investigate and scope a security breach, should it ever occur. "

Microsoft has assigned this one at 15 total points, making it a lower importance than previously reviewed tasks.

Threats – Account Breach, Data Exfiltration, Data Deletion, Elevation of Privilege, Malicious Insider

Recommendations & Thoughts

As this turns on auditing of all User and Admin activity and is enabled in the service (i.e. no extra load or end user impact), it's hard to argue against enabling this feature. The auditing is useful for determining what your admins are doing in your tenant as well as what the end users are doing. You can even review end user activity and check security information relating to password changes.

Yes, enable this feature because of its added benefits in your tenant.

———

Review signs-ins after multiple failures report weekly

According to Microsoft

"You should review the Azure AD Sign-ins after multiple failures report at least every week. This report contains records of accounts that have successfully signed-in after multiple failures, which is an indication that the account has a cracked password. "

Microsoft has assigned this one at 15 total points, making it a lower importance than some other tasks.

Threats – Account Breach, Password Cracking

Recommendations & Thoughts

Certainly an easy requirement to meet. The key thing is that this requirement needs to be met on a weekly basis. One can assume that if the information is not reviewed in that week time frame, the Secure Score report would drop 15 points.

Put this on a weekly reminder or bi-weekly reminder so that you get the points and so that your environment is monitored that much closer. So, this is a recommended action to take.

———

Set outbound spam notifications

According to Microsoft

"You should set your Exchange Online Outbound Spam notifications to copy and notify someone when a sender in your tenant has been blocked for sending excessive or spam emails. A blocked account is a good indication that the account in question has been breached and that an attacker is using it to send spam emails to other people."

Microsoft has assigned this one at 15 total points, making it a lower importance than some other tasks.

Threats – Account Breach, Phishing/Whaling, Spoofing

Recommendations & Thoughts

Any feature or automatic function that helps with outgoing or incoming Spam is welcome. In this case a notification for excessive outbound SPAM is key to alerting an admin to a possible issue with a user's account.

Turn this feature on for sure, it's an easy 15 points.

Review sign-ins from unknown sources report weekly

According to Microsoft

"You should review the Azure AD Sign-Ins from Unknown Sources Report at least every week. This report contains records of accounts that have signed-in to your tenancy from a client IP address that has been recognized by Microsoft as an anonymous proxy IP address (such as a TOR network). This isn't necessarily bad, but it is relatively rare, and could be an indication of a breached account."

Microsoft has assigned this one at 10 total points, making it a low importance.

Threats – Account Breach

Recommendations & Thoughts

Another no-brainer. It's a report. Read it.

Again, it's a serious no-brainer. Ten easy points for your Secure Score.

——

Review signs-ins from multiple geographies report weekly

According to Microsoft

"You should review the Azure AD Signs-ins from Multiple Geographies Report at least every week. This report contains records of successful sign-ins from users where two sign-ins appeared to originate from different regions and the time between sign-ins makes it impossible for the user to have traveled between those regions. This isn't necessarily bad, and there are several potential causes including sharing passwords, using VPNs, or using devices with unusual IP addresses. You should still be aware of the sources of these as it can be a very clear indication of a breached account. "

Microsoft has assigned this one at 10 total points, making it a low importance.

Threats – Account Breach

Recommendations & Thoughts

Even if you are a small company, this report should be reviewed for any suspicious activity.

Again, it's a serious no-brainer. Ten easy points for your Secure Score.

——

Review role changes weekly

According to Microsoft

"You should review user role group changes at least every week. There are several ways you can do this, including simply reviewing the list of users in different administrative role groups in the Office 365 Admin Portal, or by reviewing role administration activity in the last week from the Audit Log Search. You should do this because you should watch for illicit role group changes, which could give an attacker elevated privileges to perform more dangerous and impactful things in your tenancy. "

Microsoft has assigned this one at 10 total points, making it a low importance.

Threats – Account Breach, Elevation of Privilege

Recommendations & Thoughts

This one will take a bit more work than the past couple of tasks. It will require you to do one of two things: (1) Have a previous list of Global Admins / other admins and compare that to what is currently configured or (2) Run an Admin Audit log report looking for these changes. Perhaps the easiest ways to do this is to run a scheduled task that exports this to a weekly report for review. The included 'Review' for this feature only takes you to the lists of users in your organization. So the trigger for this task is not obvious and it is possible that the PowerShell script may not be enough.

This is worth the effort and should be put on your task list.

———

Store user documents in OneDrive for Business

According to Microsoft

"You should store user documents in OneDrive for Business because it safeguards this content against data loss."

Microsoft has assigned this one at 10 total points, making it a low importance.

Threats – Data Exfiltration, Data Deletion

Recommendations & Thoughts

With recent improvements in the product, OneDrive is a good opportunity for customers to leverage a sharing platform, especially if all of their users are in Office 365. Automatic file rollback, files on demand, and file versioning as well as protection from ransomware all make for a good use case scenario. Sharing possibilities as well as integration with Office, Exchange and more also provide benefits to end users in Office 365.

While not all organizations will be convinces to use this feature, due to either limitations of storage, compliance or security requirements, Microsoft has a compelling product at this time. Using One Drive for your organization is a decision that needs to be planned for and then executed properly while realizing the caveats of moving to a cloud storage platform.

———

Enable Information Rights Management (IRM) services

According to Microsoft

"You should enable IRM services so that your users can implement encryption and data leakage policies on specific documents and emails. This will make it more difficult for an attacker to steal valuable data."

Threats – Data Spillage, Data Exfiltration

Recommendations & Thoughts

If you have the proper licensing for this and have data that needs to be protected, then this is an option that should be pursued. With regulations that are either in process or in place today, having a way to control and protect your data and corporate information is paramount and may save you fines down the road.

** **Note** ** The 'Launch Now' button takes you to Rights Management from the main Admin page in your Office 365 tenant.

If you have the licensing for this feature and have sensitive data to protect in One Drive, SharePoint or email, enabling this is a must.

Use audit data

According to Microsoft

"You should consume your audit data either through the audit log search or through the Activity API to a third party security information system at least every week. This data enables a wide range of illicit activity detection and security breach scoping and investigation capabilities. Consuming and reviewing it regularly makes it less likely that an attacker will operate in your tenancy undetected for long periods of time."

Microsoft has assigned this one at five total points, making it a low importance.

Threats – Account Breach, Data Exfiltration, Data Deletion, Elevation of Privilege, Malicious Insider

Recommendations & Thoughts

Office 365 provides this for free and is a valuable resource for monitory activity in your Office 365 tenant. Any responsible admin should use logging on-premises or in Office 365. The fact that it takes so little to setup (just enable it) and costs your internal resources '0' to maintain it would seem to be a smart task to add to your list of management / monitoring tasks.

** **Note** ** Clicking on review takes you to the same Audit Log Search page as we used to enable auditing to begin with. Integrating this with your SEIM product may add additional cost if they charge on Events per minute.

Absolutely this should be monitored for your tenant.

––

Do not use transport rule to external domains

According to Microsoft

"You should set your Exchange Online mail transport rules to not forward mail to domains not registered in your tenancy. Attackers will often create these rules to exfiltrate data from your tenancy."

Microsoft has assigned this one at five total points, making it a low importance.

Threats – Account Breach, Data Exfiltration, Data Spillage, Malicious Insider

Recommendations & Thoughts

I can see the benefits of not having transport rules forwarding emails to external email addresses. It would take some effort for an external attacker to find the rule that would allow for this, but it could happen. That being said, I don't think this is a big deal necessarily and to be honest, I haven't run into any clients that have this sort of rule set up.

I would recommend removing any of these transport rules. If a rule is needed for business reasons, it should be reviewed to see if there are other options available.

––

Do not use transport white lists

According to Microsoft

"You should set your Exchange Online mail transport rules to not whitelist specific domains. Doing so bypasses regular malware and phish scanning, which can enable an attacker to launch attacks against your users from a safe haven domain"

Microsoft has assigned this one at five total points, making it a low importance.

Threats – Phishing/Whaling, Spoofing

Recommendations & Thoughts

I am of a mixed opinion on this one as whitelisting is a fact of life. The one caveat to this is I think Microsoft wants to restrict the whitelisting to individual email address versus a carte blanche whitelisting of an entire domain. While I can understand Microsoft's point, the flip side is if a lot of email addresses from one domain need whitelisting, then whitelisting a domain might be the best solution.

The recommendation here is a maybe simply because of the two choices that need to be made. If you can use the restrictive single email address whitelisting, that would be ideal. However, if an entire domain needs to be whitelisted, do so understanding the caveats Microsoft's expresses.

———

Review mailbox forwarding rules weekly

According to Microsoft

"You should review mailbox forwarding rules to external domains at least every week. There are several ways you can do this, including simply reviewing the list of mail forwarding rules to external domains on all of your mailboxes using a PowerShell script, or by reviewing mail forwarding rule creation activity in the last week from the Audit Log Search. While there are lots of legitimate uses of mail forwarding rules to other locations, it is also a very popular data exfiltration tactic for attackers. You should review them regularly to ensure your users' email is not being exfiltrated."

Microsoft has assigned this one at five total points, making it a low importance.

Threats – Account Breach, Data Exfiltration, Malicious Insider

Recommendations & Thoughts

Add this one to your weekly task list. This way you won't be surprised to find what mailboxes are forwarding to where.

Do this one for sure. Make it one of your tasks. No question.

———

Review mailbox access by non-owners report bi-weekly

According to Microsoft

"You should review the Mailbox Access by Non-Owners report at least every other week. This report shows which mailboxes have been accessed by someone other than the mailbox owner. While there are many legitimate uses of delegate permissions, regularly reviewing that access can help prevent an external attacker from maintaining access for a long time, and can help discover malicious insider activity sooner. "

Threats – Account Breach, Data Exfiltration, Malicious Insider

Recommendations & Thoughts

Typically this sort of action is performed by a security team or security person, depending on your company. However, for a smaller IT shop, this would just be another weekly task for the Office 365 Administrator. Having been a part of a few forensic investigations, the more information you have to uncover things, the better it is for yourself and for your employer.

Do it. Add it to your weekly lists.

Review malware detections report weekly

According to Microsoft

"You should review the Malware Detections report at least weekly. This report shows specific instances of Microsoft blocking a malware attachment from reaching your users. While this report isn't strictly actionable, reviewing it will give you a sense of the overall volume of malware being targeted at your users, which may prompt you to adopt more aggressive malware mitigations."

Microsoft has assigned this one at five total points, making it a low importance.

Threats – Phishing/Whaling

Recommendations & Thoughts

Like your antivirus reporting PCs and Servers, having a malware report for your messaging environment is ideal. There should be no doubt that an Office 365 admin should review these reports on a constant basis.

Do it. Add it to your weekly lists.

Designate more than one global admin

According to Microsoft

"You should designate more than one global tenant administrator because that one admin can perform malicious activity without the possibility of being discovered by another admin. We found that you have 'X' admins designated. If you designate at least two admins (but not more than five), your score will go up points."

Microsoft has assigned this one at two total points, making it a low importance.

Threats – Malicious Insider

Recommendations & Thoughts

While in most security cases we would want to limit admins as with all rights to an environment, having a single account with all the rights is a bad idea as well. So the recommendation for more than one account with Global Admin rights is a valid task to perform.

Highly recommended. If you have this task, do it now.

Do not use mail forwarding rules to external domains

According to Microsoft

"You should not use mail forwarding rules to forward user mail to external domains. While there are some legitimate uses, attackers will often create these rules to exfiltrate data from your tenancy."

Microsoft has assigned this one at one total point, making it a low importance.

Threats – Account Breach, Data Exfiltration, Malicious Insider

Recommendations & Thoughts

This is similar to the task for no transport rules forwarding to external domains, this task is defined for forwarding on mailboxes to external domains. However, as Microsoft expresses in the task description above, there are some legitimate reasons for these. These business cases should be evaluated on a case by case basis to see if there are other solutions.

I rate this a maybe as it will depend on what your needs are as a company. As Microsoft has rated this one point, I would certainly put this lower on your priority list.

____

SPO Sites have classification policies

According to Microsoft

"You should setup and use SharePoint Online data classification policies on data stored in your SharePoint Online sites. This will help categorize your most important data so that you can effectively protect it from illicit access, and will help make it easier to investigate discovered breaches.

Microsoft has assigned this one at 10 total points, making it a medium importance.

Threats – Data Exfiltration, Data Spillage, Malicious Insider

Recommendations & Thoughts

If you have someone that can work to classify data (internally or a consultant), then this is a task worth pursuing. If only for the benefit of knowing the importance of data stored in SharePoint, that effort is alone worth it. Combined with DLP or other rights management policies, the classifications become a powerful tool for data control against leakage and loss.

If you are able to, this should be on your list of tasks to complete.

____

Review devices sign-in report weekly

According to Microsoft

"You should review your device sign-in report weekly. You should do this to look for anomalous or new device sign-ins from potentially breached user accounts."

Microsoft has assigned this one at 10 total points, making it a medium importance.

Threats – Account Breach, Data Exfiltration, Data Spillage

Recommendations & Thoughts

Depending on what is deployed for device management, this could be a valuable task to perform. If you are using MDM or Intune, then you may already be restricting new devices or device sign-ins.

If you are not using an MDM solution then perhaps this report will help you spot something that is new and may not be one of your user's devices. If you have MDM, obviously use it to control access and use the reports for validation of your efforts to control access.

Do not allow anonymous calendar sharing

According to Microsoft

"You should not allow anonymous calendar sharing. This feature allows your users to share the full details of their calendars with external, unauthenticated users. Attackers will very commonly spend time learning about your organization (performing reconnaissance) before launching an attack. Publicly available calendars can help attackers understand organizational relationships, and determine when specific users may be more vulnerable to an attack, such as when they are traveling."

Microsoft has assigned this one at 10 total points, making it a medium importance.

Threats – Data Spillage

Recommendations & Thoughts

I find this feature useful for sharing a calendar with an external entity or person. While I understand Microsoft's contention that this information could be used for reconnaissance or nefarious activities. It's my opinion that there can be some legitimate usages for anonymous calendar sharing. Should everyone be able to do this, probably not, but it should be available for true business cases.

If you can, don't use this feature based on Microsoft's real world recommendations. Setting this could block this could block a potentially useful feature down the road.

Do not allow external domain skype / teams communications

According to Microsoft

"You should not allow your users to communicate with Skype users outside your organization. While there are legitimate, productivity-improving scenarios for this, it also represents a potential security threat in that those external users will now be able to interact with your users over Skype for Business. Attackers may be able to pretend to be someone your user knows, and then send malicious links or attachments, resulting in an account breach, or leaked information."

Microsoft has assigned this one at five total points, making it a low importance.

Threats – Data Exfiltration, Data Spillage

Recommendations & Thoughts

I find this recommendation a bit odd. As a consultant, I find that being able to communicate with my clients who use a variety of domains to be a great resource to have at my disposal. In fact, almost every company I've used Skype or Lync with has enabled external sharing.

I rate this one as a no. While I understand the trade-off involved in the anonymous sharing, I also see real world use of allowing anonymous sharing.

Review account provisioning activity report weekly

According to Microsoft

"You should review your account provisioning activity report at least weekly. This report includes a history of attempts to provision accounts to external applications. If you don't usually use a third party provider to manage accounts, any entry on the list is likely illicit. But, if you do, this is a great way to monitor transaction volumes, and look for new or unusual third party applications that are managing users. If you see something unusual, contact the provider to determine if the action is legitimate."

Microsoft has assigned this one at five total points, making it a low importance.

Threats – Account Breach, Elevation of Privilege, Malicious Insider

Recommendations & Thoughts

Going to keep this one simple. It's a report and one that should be checked. Add this to your weekly checklist.

Add it to your to do's!

––

Review non-global administrators weekly

According to Microsoft

"You should review non-global administrator role group assignments at least every week. While these roles are less powerful than a global admin, they do grant special privileges that can be used illicitly. If you see something unusual contact the user to confirm it is a legitimate need.

Microsoft has assigned this one at five total points, making it a low importance.

Threats – Account Breach, Elevation of Privilege, Malicious Insider

Recommendations & Thoughts

Same as the previous one. Any sort of report, even for slightly elevated granted permissions, should be reviewed.

Add it to your to do's!

––

Do not allow calendar details sharing

According to Microsoft

"You should not allow your users to share calendar details with external users. This feature allows your users to share the full details of their calendars with external users. Attackers will very commonly spend time learning about your organization (performing reconnaissance) before launching an attack. Publicly available calendars can help attackers understand organizational relationships, and determine when specific users may be more vulnerable to an attack, such as when they are traveling."

Threats – Data Spillage

Recommendations & Thoughts

For most scenarios, sharing all of your calendar's Free/Busy is a bad idea. In select scenarios where you are sharing information with a sister company, subsidiary, partner or other trusted entity, this option makes sense. There is a middle ground where the setting can be changed to simply Free/Busy with no details shared beyond that.

This recommendation ends up in the 'Maybe' pile. Most cases this should be off or if necessary change sharing to Free/Busy only.

IRM protections applied to documents

According to Microsoft

"You should enable and use Information Rights Management protections on email and document data. This will help prevent accidental or malicious exposure of your data outside of your organizational boundaries. Attackers targeting specific, high value data assets will be prevented from opening them without a user credential in your tenancy. "

Microsoft has assigned this one at five total points, making it a low importance.

Threats – Data Exfiltration, Data Spillage

Recommendations & Thoughts

If your Office 365 tenant has any confidential data, documents or intellectual property stored in it, enabling IRM is THE way to go. The same applies to securing emails. Enable the Encryption or making use of IRM for certain emails is a good thing in Office 365.

This one is a definite if you have emails, documents, etc that need to be protected from being copied or leaked outside your company.

IRM protections applied to email

According to Microsoft

"You should enable and use Information Rights Management protections on email and document data. This will help prevent accidental or malicious exposure of your data outside of your organizational boundaries. Attackers targeting specific, high value data assets will be prevented from opening them without a user credential in your tenancy."

Microsoft has assigned this one at five total points, making it a low importance.

Threats – Data Exfiltration, Data Spillage

Recommendations & Thoughts

Like the previous recommendation for using IRM for documents and files in Office 365, securing your emails can be just as important. Maybe you have emails that need to remain internal or perhaps they need to be blocked from printing, forwarding and more. IRM is the solution for this. If you have the licensing for these features, investing time in applying this functionality is worth it.

Again, if you have licensing for this, do it. Secure your emails and prevent potential data leakage.

Configure expiration time for external sharing links

According to Microsoft

"You should restrict the length of time that anonymous access links are valid. An attacker can compromise a user account for a short period of time, send anonymous sharing links to an external account and then take their time accessing the data. They can also compromise external accounts and steal the anonymous sharing links sent to those external entities well after the data has been shared.

Microsoft has assigned this one at two total points, making it a very low importance.

Threats – Data Exfiltration, Data Spillage

Recommendations & Thoughts

This setting is for your SharePoint links that are being shared out anonymously. The links could be shared with internal personnel, but are more likely to be shared with people that are outside of your organization. Tweaking the default expiration from infinite (no expiration of days) to something more realistic like 30, 90 or 120 days would be a good practice.

This is a must. Any anonymous links should have some sort of expiration.

———

Tag documents in SharePoint

According to Microsoft

"You should apply labels to documents in SharePoint Online. If you use document classification tags, you can author rules that leverage the label to implement specific retention/deletion policies using data loss protection (DLP) in the Security and Compliance Center. In the future there will be more DLP actions possible when labels are detected on documents."

Microsoft has assigned this one at two total points, making it a very low importance.

Threats – Data Exfiltration, Data Spillage

Recommendations & Thoughts

If you plan to use DLP to control content in your tenant, then having a categorization system or a plan on how documents should be labeled, applying controls later will be much easier. Labeling your content will also make it easier to manage later even without DLP. Take some time to plan out these labels with content owners.

Worth the time if you have content that needs to be managed online.

———

Review list of external users you have invited to documents monthly

According to Microsoft

"You should review the list of external users that you have invited to sensitive documents on a weekly basis. Attackers that have compromised accounts with sharing privileges will be able to expose sensitive data to external users for long periods of time without regular review of who has access."

Microsoft has assigned this one at two total points, making it a very low importance.

Threats – Data Exfiltration, Data Spillage

Recommendations & Thoughts

External sharing, similar to the anonymous links, is something that should be monitored because the access is granted to people outside of your organization. The method to check the access however, as directed by Secure Score, is far from ideal. Depending on your experience level, using PowerShell to automatically generate these reports might be a better option. There are existing scripts created by SharePoint experts on how to do this already.

Just do it. This is a no-brainer.

Disable accounts not used in last 30 days

According to Microsoft

"You should disable any accounts that have not been used in the last 30 days. While there may be legitimate circumstances where an account is unused for 30 days, these accounts can also be targets for attackers who are looking to find ways to access your data without being noticed."

Microsoft has assigned this one at one total point, making it a very low importance.

Threats – Account Breach, Elevation of Privilege, Malicious Insider

Recommendations & Thoughts

For this task, I think 30 days is a bit aggressive. A slightly less aggressive approach of 90 days may be better. Either way it does point out a weak area that is sometimes overlooked and that accounts for people that have left or are on leave. In some cases there are legitimate reasons to leave the accounts and sometimes these are accounts that are forgotten about. The biggest issue I see with this task is that the User management in the Office 365 Admin center does not expose last logon times. You cannot event create a 'Custom View' for this. To find this, PowerShell might be your best bet.

I put this at a yes, with caveats, because of the 30 days. This isn't to say you shouldn't review these accounts and the recommend interface from Microsoft is lacking. You should have a process in place for off-boarding users.

———

Allow anonymous guest sharing links for sites and docs

According to Microsoft

"You should allow your users to use anonymous guest sharing links for SharePoint Online sites and documents. While there are inherent risks in sharing documents anonymously, Microsoft has found that when anonymous sharing is disabled, users often use more risky methods of sharing sites and documents, email for example. A proactive approach would be to enable anonymous sharing links for customers while also educating users on the pitfalls with sharing anonymously and monitoring links shared for signs of exfiltration by an attacker."

Microsoft has assigned this one at one total point, making it a very low importance.

Threats – Data Exfiltration, Data Spillage

Recommendations & Thoughts

The irony is thick with this one, but as Microsoft points out, it makes sense. Allowing users to send out anonymous links to external users is better than alternative methods like email or even another file service like Drop Box. If the users are sending out anonymous links, you have control over how long they are active and can create reports on what is shared as well.

This is a good one to implement IF you follow the previous recommendation of restricting how long the links are active for.

———

Enable Data Loss Prevention policies

According to Microsoft

"You should enable Data Loss Prevention (DLP) policies to help protect your data from accidental or malicious exposure. DLP allows Exchange Online and SharePoint Online content to be scanned for specific types of data like social security numbers, credit card numbers, or passwords, and will alert users and administrators that this data should not be exposed."

Microsoft has assigned this one at 20 total points, making it a higher importance.

Threats – Data Exfiltration, Data Spillage

Recommendations & Thoughts

If you deal with PII like credit cards, Social Security Numbers, bank account numbers and more, then implementing DLP is a must. Microsoft has provided quite a few default templates of this type of data and covers more than just the US data types as well. If there isn't a data type present, then you can create a custom classification to be used against emails or documents in your tenant.

If you have the license to use DLP and have PII in the cloud, this is an absolute must to enable.

——

Enable Advanced Security Management Console

According to Microsoft

"You should adopt the Office 365 Advanced Security Management Console. This console will allow you to set up policies to alert you about anomalous and suspicious activity. We found that your subscription to Advanced Security Management Console is set to False."

Microsoft has assigned this one at 20 total points, making it a higher importance.

Threats – Account Breach, Elevation of Privilege, Data Exfiltration, Malicious Insider, Data Spillage

Recommendations & Thoughts

This is a feature Microsoft added back in 2016 to give admins a deeper look into suspicious activity. The only caveat to it being on this list is the requirements for its usage – "Advanced Security Management is available in Office 365 Enterprise E5 or as an add-on subscription to Office 365". For those with E3 licensing, you will not be able to complete this task.

My take is if you have E5 and can access this then you absolutely must. Dig deeper into your tenant.

——

Require mobile devices to use a password

According to Microsoft

"You should require your users to use a password to unlock their mobile devices. Devices without this protection are vulnerable to being accessed physically by attackers who can then steal account credentials, data, or install malware on the device."

Microsoft has assigned this one at five total points, making it a low importance.

Threats – Account Breach, Data Exfiltration, Data Spillage

Recommendations & Thoughts

When creating a policy for securing mobile devices, having some sort of PIN or password should be one of the first settings configured. The setting will at least prevent easy device access if the device is lost or stolen.

Definitely one to configure. This should be a basic mobile device security setting.

Require mobile devices to block access and report policy violations

According to Microsoft

"You should configure your mobile device management policies to block access to devices that violate your policy and to report those violations to an administrator. Users will be able to connect with non-compliant devices unless you block access, leading to vulnerable devices connecting to your data."

Microsoft has assigned this one at five total points, making it a low importance.

Threats – Account Breach, Data Exfiltration, Data Spillage

Recommendations & Thoughts

If you don't have a third party MDM solution in place now, then this is a valid policy setting to put in place to keep mobile devices secure.

If using the built in MDM or Intune, then this setting should be put in place.

——

Require mobile devices to manage email profile

According to Microsoft

"You should configure your mobile device management policies to require the policy to manage the email profile of the user. If you do not require this, users will be able to setup and configure email accounts without the protections of the mobile device management policy, leading to potential breaches of accounts and data."

Microsoft has assigned this one at five total points, making it a low importance.

Threats – Account Breach, Data Exfiltration, Data Spillage

Recommendations & Thoughts

Similar to the previous two – this is a function of a good Mobile Device Management (MDM) solution. Even with Bring Your Own Device (BYOD) in today's Office 365 environment, being able to control corporate data is a good thing.

If using the built in MDM or Intune, then this setting should be put in place. Outlook App profiles cannot be managed.

——

Do not allow simple passwords on mobile devices

According to Microsoft

"You should require your users to use a complex password to unlock their mobile devices. Devices without this protection are vulnerable to being accessed physically by attackers who can then steal account credentials, data, or install malware on the device."

Microsoft has assigned this one at two total points, making it a very low importance.

Threats – Account Breach, Data Exfiltration, Data Spillage

Recommendations & Thoughts

This goes hand in hand with requiring a password and is an enhancement of the password policy once it's in place.

If using the built in MDM or Intune, then this setting should be put in place. Otherwise use Exchange ActiveSync policies.

____

Require mobile devices to use alphanumeric password

According to Microsoft

"You should require your users to use a complex password with a at least two character sets (letters and numbers, for example) to unlock their mobile devices. Devices without this protection are vulnerable to being accessed physically by attackers who can then steal account credentials, data, or install malware on the device.

Microsoft has assigned this one at one total point, making it a very low importance.

Threats – Account Breach, Data Exfiltration, Data Spillage

Recommendations & Thoughts

More complex passwords should be put in place.

If using the built in MDM or Intune, then this setting should be put in place. Otherwise use Exchange ActiveSync policies.

____

Require mobile devices to use encryption

According to Microsoft

"You should require your users to use encryption on their mobile devices. Unencrypted devices can be stolen and their data extracted by an attacker very easily."

Microsoft has assigned this one at one total point, making it a very low importance.

Threats – Account Breach, Data Exfiltration, Data Spillage

Recommendations & Thoughts

Encrypting mobile devices is one way to protect any sensitive data that may be on your mobile devices. This feature provides another layer to your other configuration settings.

If using the built in MDM or Intune, then this setting should be put in place. Otherwise use Exchange ActiveSync policies.

____

Require mobile devices to lock on inactivity

According to Microsoft

"You should require your users to configure their mobile devices to lock on inactivity. Attackers can steal unlocked devices and access data and account information."

Microsoft has assigned this one at one total point, making it a very low importance.

Threats – Account Breach, Data Exfiltration, Data Spillage

Recommendations & Thoughts

Like your desktop or laptop, having an idle lockout is a good policy. This way if you accidentally misplace the device or set it down for a period of time, it will automatically lock out other people from accessing the device.

If using the built in MDM or Intune, then this setting should be put in place. Otherwise use Exchange ActiveSync policies.

———

Require mobile devices to have minimum password length

According to Microsoft

"You should require your users to use a complex password with a minimum password length of at least six characters to unlock their mobile devices. Devices without this protection are vulnerable to being accessed physically by attackers who can then steal account credentials, data, or install malware on the device."

Microsoft has assigned this one at one total point, making it a very low importance.

Threats – Account Breach, Data Exfiltration, Data Spillage

Recommendations & Thoughts

Continuing on the line of password protection for mobile devices, this simply requires a minimum length of password similar to how you configure this for your Active Directory login. While the minimum length should not be something like one or two characters and should probably be at a minimum six or eight characters.

If using the built in MDM or Intune, then this setting should be put in place. Otherwise use Exchange ActiveSync policies.

———

Require mobile devices to wipe on multiple sign-in failures

According to Microsoft

"You should require your users to wipe the contents of the mobile device after no more than 10 sign-in failures. Devices without this protection are vulnerable to being accessed physically by attackers who can then steal account credentials, data, or install malware on the device. We found that your mobile device policy requiring wipe after multiple failed sign-ins is set to wipe after infinite failures."

Microsoft has assigned this one at one total point, making it a very low importance.

Threats – Account Breach, Data Exfiltration, Data Leakage

Recommendations & Thoughts

In today's world of BYOD a lot of organizations are hesitant to implement such a policy. There are some that are prepared for complete device wipes by educating their users on the ramifications of this policy. Others will issue their own devices. However, in some cases simply using App security instead of device security eliminates the need for this policy altogether.

This is a solid maybe because it depends on if you have BYOD, issued devices or are using app security to handle mobile devices. Make a decision based on your device and user base for this one.

Do not allow Jail-Broken or rooted mobile devices to connect

According to Microsoft

"You should not allow your users to use to connect with mobile devices that have been jail-broken or rooted. These devices have had basic protections disabled to run software that is often malicious and could very easily lead to an account or data breach."

Microsoft has assigned this one at one total point, making it a very low importance.

Threats – Account Breach, Data Exfiltration, Data Spillage

Recommendations & Thoughts

For corporate devices or mobile devices accessing corporate date, a jail-broken or rooted device should be blocked. If a user wants to have this device, it would be best left to keep it a personal device and not connected to any internal systems.

Apply this setting.

——

Require mobile devices to never expire password

According to Microsoft

"While this is not the most intuitive recommendation, research has found that when periodic password resets are enforced, passwords become weaker as users tend to pick something weaker and then use a pattern of it for rotation. If a user creates a strong password: long, complex and without any pragmatic words present, it should remain just as strong is 60 days as it is today. It is Microsoft's official security position to not expire passwords periodically without a specific reason."

Microsoft has assigned this one at one total point, making it a very low importance.

Threats – Account Breach, Data Exfiltration, Data Spillage

Recommendations & Thoughts

Mixed feelings on this one. If this policy would be put in place, I would recommend a longer, more complex password for securing devices. The problem here becomes the end user and the way they handle passwords. If they can choose a good, secure password, this is a good policy. If however, they do not, then obviously the reverse becomes try.

Enable long complex passwords if enabling this.

——

Do not allow mobile device password re-use

According to Microsoft

"You should not allow your users to re-use the same password on their mobile devices. Devices without this protection are vulnerable to being accessed by attackers who can then steal account credentials, data, or install malware on the device."

Microsoft has assigned this one at one total point, making it a very low importance.

Threats – Account Breach, Data Exfiltration, Data Spillage

Recommendations & Thoughts

If passwords change over time, then not re-using passwords makes sense. That way if a password were compromised and a user re-uses that compromised password, then this could lead to a security breach.

Not repeating passwords is a good policy to put in place.

Enable customer lockbox feature

According to Microsoft

"You should enable the customer lockbox feature. This will require Microsoft to get your approval for any datacenter operation that grants a Microsoft employee direct access to any of your content."

Microsoft has assigned this one at five total points, making it a low importance.

Threats – Data Exfiltration, Data Deletion, Data Spillage

Recommendations & Thoughts

This is another feature on the list that requires an E5 licenses, so if you don't have one, then this one won't apply to you. I personally do not like this option. If you want true security or control, then providing this access would go against that philosophy. While you can limit access to your data and set an expiration on it, I believe a more interactive approach is called for when there is an issue.

This one recommendation is a no for me. If you need Microsoft's help, they are more than happy to use their screenshare technology and while this does grant them a view in to the environment, it can be limited and controlled by you. I would rather grant the access and watch. A controlled over the shoulder setup is ideal for the administrator to provide input while learning how to resolve an issue.

Index

A

Add-ADGroupMember   77
Add-ComplianceCaseMember   142, 144
Add-Content   120-122, 269
Add-DLPSensitiveInfoTypes   275
Add-Licenses   275
Add-MailboxPermission   174
Add-RoleGroupMember   2, 88

C

Clear-MobileDevice   216, 218
Connect-AzureAD   6
Connect-IPPSSession   47
Connect-MSOLService   78, 80
Connect-PSSession   48
ConvertFrom-SecureString   78
ConvertTo-SecureString   63, 78, 266

D

Disconnect-PSSession 48

E

Enter-PSSession   48
Exit-PSSession 48
Export-FilePlanProperty   251
Export-PSSession   48

F

Foreach-Object   ix, xiv, 14, 282, 287, 292, 295-298
Format-List   29, 185, 199
Format-Table   29, 185, 297

G

Get-ActivityAlert   3, 177, 180-181

Get-ADDomain   20
Get-ADGroup 78
Get-AdGroupMember   78
Get-AdminAuditLogConfig   109
Get-ADSyncConnector   69-70
Get-ADSyncRule   70-71
Get-ADSyncScheduler   66-67
Get-ADSyncServerConfiguration   70
Get-ADUser   20, 55, 64-65
Get-Alias   283, 285, 292, 295-296
Get-AuditConfig   3
Get-AzureRmADServicePrincipal   191
Get-CaseGoldRule   3
Get-CaseHold xii, 151
Get-CaseHoldPolicy   151, 154-155
Get-CaseHoldRule   30, 151-152, 154-155, 273, 282
Get-ChildItem 35-36
Get-Command   3, 5-6, 45, 48, 66, 69, 72, 83, 89-90, 107, 109, 114, 123, 126, 130, 145, 151-152, 157, 167, 177, 182, 192, 229, 251, 267-268, 281
Get-ComplianceCase v, 4, 26, 142, 148, 155, 263, 273, 289-290, 293-294
Get-ComplianceCaseMember 142, 144, 263
Get-ComplianceCaseStatistics   142
Get-ComplianceSearch   145, 148, 152-153, 156, 264
Get-ComplianceSearchAction   145, 152, 264
Get-ComplianceTag   27, 31-32
Get-Content   35-36, 122, 124-125, 128-129, 131, 133, 269, 274
Get-Credential   44
Get-DataRetentionReport   91
Get-Date   53-54, 267, 273
Get-DeviceConditionalAccessPolicy 221, 224
Get-DeviceConditionalAccessRule   221, 223
Get-DeviceConfigurationPolicy   224
Get-DeviceConfigurationRule   224, 226
Get-DevicePolicy   3
Get-DeviceTenantPolicy   219-220
Get-DeviceTenantRule   219, 277-278
Get-DLP   267
Get-DLPCompliancePolicy   263, 267
Get-DLPComplianceRule   263
Get-DlpDetectionsReport   140
Get-DlpEdmSchema   130-131, 262
Get-DlpKeywordDictionary   3, 126-127, 129, 262
Get-DLPReport   275

Get-DlpSensitiveInformationType   13-14, 27, 114-115, 117-118, 236, 261
Get-DlpSensitiveInformationTypeRulePackage   114, 117-118, 122, 126, 261
Get-DlpSiDetectionsReport   140
Get-eDiscoveryCaseAdmin   260
Get-FilePlanPropertyAuthority   251-252
Get-FilePlanPropertyCategory   251-252
Get-FilePlanPropertyCitation 251-252, 255
Get-FilePlanPropertyDepartment   251, 253
Get-FilePlanPropertyReferenceId   251
Get-FilePlanPropertyStructure   251
Get-FilePlanPropertySubCategory   251
Get-Group   3, 222, 225
Get-Help   xvi, 1-2, 6-7, 10, 63-64, 67, 110, 117, 123, 125, 130, 146, 149-151, 159-160, 163, 171, 173, 177, 182, 193-194, 222, 224-225, 230, 266, 270, 280, 293-294, 299
Get-HoldCompliancePolicy   151
Get-HoldComplianceRule   2, 151
Get-InformationBarrier   195
Get-InformationBarrierPoliciesApplicationStatus   192, 196, 198-199, 262
Get-InformationBarrierPolicy   192, 195, 200, 204, 262, 276
Get-InformationBarrierRecipientStatus   192, 204, 275
Get-InformationBarrierReportDetails   xviii, 192
Get-InformationBarrierReportSummary   xviii, 192
Get-Item   118, 155, 199, 259, 272-273, 289
Get-Label   2-4, 11, 17, 229, 247-248, 256, 260, 273
Get-LabelPolicy   229, 261, 272
Get-LabelPolicyRule   229
Get-LicenseVsUsageSummaryReport 72
Get-Mailbox   53, 55, 296-299
Get-ManagementRole 3, 107-108
Get-MessageTrackingLog   110
Get-MobileDevice   216
Get-MobileDeviceDashboardSummaryReport   216
Get-MobileDeviceMailboxPolicy   216
Get-MobileDeviceStatistics   216-217
Get-Module   66, 267
Get-MsolAccountSku 72
Get-MsolUser 72-75, 78-81
Get-Name   203
Get-OrganizationSegment   192, 200-201, 262

Get-Protection   185
Get-ProtectionAlert   182, 185-186
Get-PSSession 48-49, 268, 270
Get-RecycleBin   79
Get-RetentionCompliancePolicy   157-158, 164, 264, 274
Get-RetentionComplianceRule   157-158, 264
Get-RetentionPolicy   7
Get-RoleGroup   3, 30, 83-84, 87, 93, 102, 104, 259, 277
Get-RoleGroupMember   26, 101-104, 259, 277
Get-SupervisoryReviewActivity   xix, 167, 172
Get-SupervisoryReviewOverallProgressReport   167, 172
Get-SupervisoryReviewPolicyReport 167, 172
Get-SupervisoryReviewPolicyV   167-168, 170
Get-SupervisoryReviewReport   167, 172
Get-SupervisoryReviewRule   167, 170, 172
Get-SupervisoryReviewTopCasesReport   167, 173
Get-TeamsRetentionCompliancePolicy   157, 162, 264
Get-TeamsRetentionComplianceRule157, 162, 264
Get-User   32, 98, 203, 273-275
Get-Variable   274

I

Import-CSV   13, 15, 53-54, 63, 65, 73, 77, 106, 147, 266
Import-FilePlanProperty   251
Import-Module   66, 272, 283
Import-PSSession   45, 48, 78, 267

M

Migrate-DlpFingerprint   123

N

New-ActivityAlert   177-180, 183
New-AdminAuditLogSearch xvii, 110-112
New-ADUser 63
New-Alias   xiv, 293-294
New-AzureRmADServicePrincipal   191

New-ClassificationRuleCollection   117
New-CompilanceSearchAction   149
New-ComplianceCase 142, 144, 147, 290, 293-295
New-ComplianceSearch   145-147, 149
New-ComplianceSearchAction   145, 149-150
New-DeviceConditionalAccessPolicy 221-222
New-DeviceConditionalAccessRule   221-223
New-DeviceConfigurationPolicy   224-225
New-DeviceConfigurationRule   225-226
New-DeviceTenantPolicy   219, 221
New-DeviceTenantRule   219, 221
New-DLPCompliancePolicy   136-137
New-DLPComplianceRule   137, 139
New-DlpEdmSchema 130-131
New-DLPFingerprint 123-125
New-DlpKeywordDictionary xix, 126-128
New-DlpSensitiveInformationType   114, 124, 126
New-DlpSensitiveInformationTypeRulePackage
35-36, 114, 117, 122, 133, 274
New-FilePlanPropertyAuthority   251, 253
New-FilePlanPropertyCategory   251, 253
New-FilePlanPropertyCitation   251, 254
New-FilePlanPropertyDepartment   251, 255
New-FilePlanPropertyReferenceID   251, 255
New-FilePlanPropertySubCategory   251, 255
New-Fingerprint   124-125
New-Guid   120
New-InformationBarrier   194
New-InformationBarrierPolicy   192, 194-195
New-Item   301
New-Label   229-231, 237, 239, 242
New-LabelPolicy   229-230, 249
New-MobileDeviceMailboxPolicy   216
New-MsolLicenseOptions   74, 79
New-Object   78, 260, 266
New-OrganizationSegment   193-194
New-ProtectionAlert 182-185
New-PSSession   45, 48, 78, 266-267
New-RetentionCompliancePolicy   6-7, 157, 159-161, 299
New-RetentionComplianceRule   157, 159-161
New-SupervisoryReviewPolicy   xviii
New-SupervisoryReviewPolicyV   24-25, 167-168
New-SupervisoryReviewRule 167, 170
New-TeamsRetentionCompliancePolicy   158, 162-164
New-TeamsRetentionComplianceRule   158, 162-

165

O

Out-File   53-55, 78, 118, 199-201, 204, 260-264, 276

R

Read-Host   78, 120-122, 234-237, 239-249, 288, 290-291
Receive-PSSession   48
Remove-ActivityAlert 177, 180
Remove-ADUser   65
Remove-ComplianceCase   4, 142, 144, 293-294
Remove-ComplianceCaseMember   142, 144
Remove-ComplianceSearch   145
Remove-ComplianceSearchAction   145
Remove-DeviceConditionalAccessPolicy   221, 224
Remove-DeviceConditionalAccessRule   221, 223
Remove-DeviceConfigurationPolicy 226
Remove-DeviceTenantPolicy 219
Remove-DeviceTenantRule   219
Remove-DlpEdmSchema   130
Remove-DlpKeywordDictionary   126, 129
Remove-DlpSensitiveInformationType   114
Remove-DlpSensitiveInformationTypeRulePackage
114, 117
Remove-FilePlanPropertyAuthority   251
Remove-FilePlanPropertyCategory   251
Remove-FilePlanPropertyCitation   251
Remove-FilePlanPropertyDepartment   251
Remove-FilePlanPropertyReferenceId   251
Remove-FilePlanPropertySubCategory   251
Remove-InformationBarrierPolicy   192
Remove-Item 270, 295
Remove-Label 3-4, 229, 246
Remove-LabelPolicy 229
Remove-MobileDevice   216
Remove-MobileDeviceMailboxPolicy 216
Remove-MsolUser   80-81
Remove-MSOLUsers 80
Remove-OrganizationSegment   100, 193
Remove-ProtectionAlert   182, 186
Remove-PSSession   48-49, 268, 270

Remove-RecordLabel 229
Remove-RetentionCompliancePolicy 158, 161
Remove-RetentionComplianceRule 158, 161
Remove-RoleGroupMember 101-106
Remove-SupervisoryReviewPolicyV 167, 171
Remove-TeamsRetentionCompliancePolicy 158, 163
Remove-TeamsRetentionComplianceRule 158, 163

S

Search-AdminAuditLog 110-111
SecureString-MyTenant 266
Select-Object 267, 296-299
Select-ObjectName 268
Send-MailMessage 269-270
Set-ActivityAlert 177, 180-181
Set-ADSyncScheduler 67
Set-ADUser 53, 55, 63-64
Set-Alias xiv, 294-295
Set-AuthenticodeSignature 41-42
Set-ComplianceCase 142, 144, 290, 293-294
Set-ComplianceSearch xii, 145, 150
Set-ComplianceSearchAction xii, 145, 151
Set-Content 118, 261
Set-DataClassification 126
Set-DeviceConditionalAccessPolicy 221
Set-DeviceConditionalAccessRule 221, 223
Set-DeviceTenantPolicy 219, 221
Set-DeviceTenantRule 219
Set-DlpEdmSchema 100, 130
Set-DlpKeywordDictionary 127, 129
Set-DlpSensitiveInformationType 114
Set-DlpSensitiveInformationTypeRulePackage 114, 117
Set-ExecutionPolicy 40, 302
Set-FilePlanPropertyAuthority 251
Set-FilePlanPropertyCategory 251
Set-FilePlanPropertyCitation 251
Set-FilePlanPropertyDepartment 251
Set-FilePlanPropertyReferenceId 251
Set-FilePlanPropertySubCategory 251
Set-InformationBarrier 195
Set-InformationBarrierPolicy 111, 192, 195
Set-Label 229, 247
Set-LabelPolicy 229
Set-Location 302-303

Set-Mailbox 55, 174
Set-MobileDeviceMailboxPolicy 216
Set-MsolUser 74, 79
Set-MsolUserLicense 74-75, 79
Set-OrganizationSegment 100, 193
Set-ProtectionAlert xviii, 182, 184, 186
Set-PSRepository 6
Set-RetentionCompliancePolicy 158, 162
Set-RetentionComplianceRule 158, 162
Set-RoleGroups 275
Set-StrictMode xiv, 271, 280-282
Set-SupervisoryReviewPolicyV 167, 171
Set-SupervisoryReviewRule 167, 171-172
Set-TeamsRetentionCompliancePolicy 158, 163
Set-TeamsRetentionComplianceRule 158, 163
Start-ADSyncSyncCycle 67-68
Start-ComplianceSearch 145, 148-149
Start-InformationBarrierPoliciesApplication 192, 196, 198
Start-Process 191
Stop-ComplianceSearch 145
Stop-InformationBarrierPoliciesApplication 192

T

Test-AdvancedFeatures 283
Test-InformationBarrierPolicy 192

W

Write-Host 14-16, 27, 36-39, 65, 77-78, 87, 102-105, 115, 155-156, 234-237, 239-249, 276-278, 281, 288-291
Write-Output xiv, 271, 276-278, 282
Write-Verbose xiv, 271, 276-278, 283